D1600600

Gloria Swanson

HOLLYWOOD LEGENDS SERIES
CARL ROLLYSON, GENERAL EDITOR

Gloria Swanson

READY FOR HER CLOSE-UP

TRICIA WELSCH

2013

University Press of Mississippi • Jackson

www.upress.state.ms.us

The University Press of Mississippi is a member of the Association of American
University Presses.

Copyright © 2013 by Tricia Welsch
All rights reserved
Manufactured in the United States of America

First printing 2013
∞
Library of Congress Cataloging-in-Publication Data

Welsch, Tricia.
Gloria Swanson : ready for her close-up / Tricia Welsch.
pages cm — (Hollywood legends series)
Includes bibliographical references and index.
ISBN 978-1-61703-749-8 (hardback) — ISBN 978-1-61703-750-4 (ebook)
1. Swanson, Gloria. 2. Motion picture actors and actresses—United States—
Biography. I. Title.
PN2287.S9W45 2013
791.4302′8092—dc23
[B]   2013012739

British Library Cataloging-in-Publication Data available

"Her career is so unique, so extraordinary, that trying to condense it would be like trying to write *War and Peace* on the head of a pin."

KEVIN BROWNLOW, *THE PARADE'S GONE BY*

"I never believe *any*thing I read about *any*body."

GLORIA SWANSON TO JOHN KOBAL, 1964

CONTENTS

Gloria Swanson

CHAPTER 1

Glory

GLORIA SWANSON ALWAYS BELIEVED SHE HAD PICKED HER PARENTS. "This time," she said, she wanted "a long, exciting life," so she set her sights on a newlywed couple making love in the summer of 1898 and "willed" herself into existence, arriving "from infinity" on March 27, 1899.[1]

Joseph and Adelaide Klanowsky Swanson had begun their marriage a year earlier in a modest second-floor apartment behind Lincoln Park on Chicago's North Side. Joseph was a twenty-eight-year-old army supply clerk whose livelihood depended on his following the regiment, and he was often away from his bride. Adelaide—called Addie—was barely nineteen when the midwife placed Gloria May Josephine in her mother's arms that spring. Swanson's notion of choosing her own life—even to selecting her parents—suited her to a T. However, the self-made woman would always have trouble judging people and protecting her own best interests. For her parents she picked two young people who were not especially well suited to married life—at least not with each other. In turn, she would continually surprise and challenge them.

The child known as "Glory" was part of a large extended family where Polish, Swedish, French, and German were spoken. She resembled her father's side, with Joseph's Nordic blue eyes and his moody, mysterious temperament. His parents James (or Jöns) and Johanna had been born in Småland, Sweden, in 1840, where James worked as a shoemaker. The Swansons (or Svenssons, according to some sources) had recently arrived in Sweden by way of northern France when Jean Bernadotte, a French marshal serving under Napoleon, became king of Sweden and Norway in 1818. James Swanson's father, a farmer, struggled with an unpromising plot of land called Clayfield, and the young man felt inclined to try his luck in the New World. Lured by the abundant opportunities in America's fastest-growing city, James and Johanna came to Chicago with their four children in 1870.

Barely a year after the Swansons arrived, the Great Chicago Fire devastated the city. Fueled by strong winds and dry weather, it burned unchecked for two days, leaving almost a third of the area's residents homeless. Undaunted, the resilient Midwesterners rebuilt their city on a grander scale: Chicago would be the hub of American prosperity during much of the twentieth century. Its population doubled between 1880 and 1890, and had almost doubled again by 1900. The Swansons were part of this growth: Gloria's father Joseph was the seventh of their ten children born in the US.

Adelaide's family was also relatively new to America. Her father's parents hailed from Alsace. Despite their arrival in the States almost fifty years before Glory was born, her great-grandfather May and his wife still spoke German and French in preference to English. The old man had a long, thick white beard which the tiny girl found alarming, but the marzipan treats he offered Glory were welcome. So were the stories he told of his globe-trotting childhood. Great-Grandfather May had lived in Holland, Switzerland, and Baden-Baden, where he worked as chef to the family of the Grand Duke before coming to the US when he was twenty-six. He also riveted his young listener with tales of the Great Fire, which destroyed the family home on La Salle Street. He and his thirteen children escaped with only the clothes on their backs and had rebuilt their lives from nothing. Her great-grandfather's stories of gumption and determination would echo in Gloria's mind during her many reversals of fortune.

Great-Grandfather May's eldest child Bertha was independent and feisty. She left home at an early age to marry Horniak Klanowsky from Poland. Her domestic life was not happy, however, and after bearing three children, including Glory's mother Adelaide, Bertha left her husband. Grandfather Klanowsky was as dark and inscrutable as Great-Grandfather May was gentle. In him, Glory saw the results of heartbreak: after his wife's desertion, he could not stand to be around women and lived a hermit's life right in the center of Chicago. He employed a man as his housekeeper and kept a tight watch on his considerable bank account. "Perhaps he worried over the fact that he was known as a skinflint," Gloria recalled. "One time he started to give me a dime, but then, after studying the expression on my face most carefully, gave me a quarter instead."[2] His granddaughter would never be known for her caution with money.

Grandfather Klanowsky's eccentricity intrigued the young girl. He had helped construct the Relic House, a building fashioned entirely from objects that had survived the Great Fire. He liked new inventions and owned one of the first gramophones. His Swiss watch, the exact size in diameter and thickness of an American dollar, had been made to his precise specifications. "This was in the days when men were wearing watches that were almost an inch thick," Swanson explained. "He always liked the unusual."[3]

Glory adored her father's freethinking, artistic brothers, Charles and John, who had gone prospecting in the Klondike. Charles claimed that he could see the future, thrilling Glory with his predictions. As strict Lutherans, none of the Swanson boys was allowed to dance, play cards, or take a drink in their parents' home; nonetheless, several brothers were afflicted by alcoholism. A beloved and cosseted only child, Gloria—whom her parents often called "Baby"—longed for siblings and the busy, noisy chaos of a large family. She admired her Aunt May, who had adopted a child when she was unable to bear one of her own. Gloria was eager to grow up so she could have lots of babies.

As a child Gloria was a whiz on roller skates: "the best on the block," she recalled proudly.[4] She had a lemonade stand and helped her mother make doughnuts, picking the ones dusted with the most sugar for herself. She dressed her black cat in her doll's clothes and took him for a ride in her baby carriage, getting scratched for her trouble. She sneaked a look at her Christmas present (a huge doll) and wrestled with her conscience about whether she should tell her parents that she had peeked. (She did not.) She caught her hand in the clothes wringer and remembered screaming in pain, blood everywhere, and Adelaide so distressed that one of Gloria's aunts had to take her to the doctor.

On a visit to her Aunt Clara's in Detroit, she got trapped in the restroom on the train and had to be rescued. Again, Adelaide was prostrate. The incident made an impression on the five-year-old; even as an adult Swanson would suffer from claustrophobia. Being locked in a dark clothes closet as punishment was in fact Gloria's first memory. "Tears and fear gripping my heart," she promised over and over that she would never be naughty again.[5] She remembered her parents quarreling and her mother's tears. Once she ran away from home, packing her doll's trunk and dragging it half a block away. There she sat, hoping her parents would beg her to return before dark. They were "too wise" to do so: she had to make the decision herself.[6] As one childhood friend remembered, "Everybody adored her, but she was just a little devil and full of the dickens."[7]

What Glory enjoyed most was being dressed up in clothes her mother made for her. Before she could play with the other children at parties, she recalled being "plunked on a table or chair for all the other mothers to examine my hand-sewn dress, petticoats, and of course, my little panties."[8] Adelaide refused to dress her daughter like the other girls: "If [they] were wearing teensy ribbon bows in their hair, I had giant poofs."[9] This created some tension, as Addie's mother-in-law thought being singled out would spoil the child.

The disapproval of her fierce Grandma Swanson shamed Glory: she tried valiantly to stop sucking her thumb because her grandmother deplored it. Not much could be done about her large teeth, though the dentist assured Addie they would eventually fit Glory's face. Addie tried to draw attention away from her daughter's big ears with oversized hats, earmuffs, and wide hair ribbons. The other kids teased Glory about her long uptilted nose, telling her to stay out of the rain so she would not drown. There was altogether a lot of attention paid to Glory's appearance. The fuss over her "horse teeth" in particular made the child feel "like a freak . . . so I thought I might as well dress like one."[10]

Addie poured her creative energy into her daughter's wardrobe. When black patent leather was in fashion, Glory wore white kid or hand-dyed shoes instead. She was the first girl to have her hair cut in a Buster Brown bob, the first to wear socks. Even as a child she instinctively guarded her fashion secrets. When asked where her mother had gotten the tailored (boys') wool coat with brass buttons, she dodged the question: "If all the girls suddenly broke out in boys' overcoats, I wouldn't want to wear mine."[11]

Being one-of-a-kind was important to Swanson from an early age. School, however, made little impression on the dreamy child, who doodled away her days in class, waiting for the bell to ring and imagining her life as an adult. Her most potent fantasy was of being a mother, with six children lined up on either side of a long dining table, though she was fuzzy on the "Mr." who would make her a "Mrs." He seemed incidental to her dreams of babies, adult clothes, and—thanks to her father's and great-grandfather's stories—travel.

When her father told Gloria that he was being transferred to Key West, she was thrilled. Now she would see the world, which was the beginning of being a grownup. Though she loved her mother's fussing over her clothes, Gloria was at heart Daddy's girl. No one seemed as intelligent or as remarkable as her father. She had no idea why she had to be bored in school when Joseph could explain everything in such a mesmerizing way. He knew everything in the encyclopedia.

Key West, as yet unconnected to the mainland, proved just as exotic to the eight-year-old as any foreign port. She loved the train ride south and was photographed roller-skating in front of the Capitol in Washington, DC. In Tampa, she smelled tangerines and had her first thrilling sight of an alligator. Gloria acquired an eighteen-inch baby alligator as a pet, but when she leaped out from behind a door waving the creature, the family housekeeper soon found him another home back in nature. On the voyage out to Key West, a storm blew up, and Gloria had her first bout of seasickness, as the boat plunged up and down in the waves.

They had a lovely house near the ocean with verandas on three sides, a banyan tree in the yard, and a banister perfect for sliding down. It was an idyllic spot, and the child loved the soft air and all the new smells of flowers and fruit. Her parents seemed more relaxed on island time, too. Gloria remembered fussing over new hairstyles for her mother and picking up shells on the pebble beach.

Gloria was enthralled by the pomp and circumstance on the post. There were parades, bugles signaling the hour, and a big cannon fired off at sunset, which delighted the small girl. There were always baseball games to watch, and her father taught her how to fish. The soldier who ran the commissary even kept lemon drops for her. Gloria was tickled when a raccoon, trained by the soldier in charge of the uniforms, got into some red ink and made a big mess everywhere. She thought Key West was paradise.

However, when Gloria was taken by buckboard to a convent school with several other children from the post, she cried and protested so much that her parents were distressed. She didn't want to be a nun, Gloria wailed: she didn't like the way nuns dressed. Her friend Jessie Porter had a tutor, and Adelaide gratefully accepted the Porters' invitation to let Gloria study alongside their daughter. Classes were held outside in the Porters' garden, which made lessons tolerable and daydreaming easier.

At Sunday school, her teacher noticed that Gloria had a fine voice and asked if she would like to do a solo in church. Her favorite song was "Listen to the Mockingbird," but she chose "The Rosary," a love song favored by turn-of-the-century opera singers. It was beyond Gloria's years, but after her performance, Venice Hayes, an actress visiting from New York, introduced herself and asked Gloria if she had taken voice lessons. No, Gloria replied, but her mother had: she had imitated Addie's singing style. Miss Hayes invited Gloria and her parents home for dinner. She wanted Gloria to sing for her father, an actor wintering in Key West. Frank Hayes was putting on a show for the locals, and he asked the child to perform a song.

Gloria began practicing a popular tune, "As Long as the World Rolls On," which appeared in four hit recordings in 1908. Though she was eager to show off her pretty new white dress and polka-dotted hair ribbon, the child still had to be pushed out onto the stage when the time came. Once her mouth was open, however, Gloria sang effortlessly and artlessly, charming the audience and winning round after round of applause. It was a sound she liked.

Major hurricanes hit Key West in 1909 and 1910, destroying government buildings, tobacco factories, and homes. The October 1909 storm smashed 95 out of 100 boats in the harbor, and martial law was imposed to prevent looting. Gloria always remembered the howling of the wind and the sound of the water rushing under their house, which had been built on stilts. She and Addie were holding each other, trembling and praying, when Joseph burst through the door, soaked to the skin. He had narrowly escaped being hit by roof slates, which were "flying around like feathers."[12] They heard one of the house's chimneys crash down.

Frightened but unharmed, Addie and Gloria agreed that summer—storm season—in Key West was the ideal time for an extended visit to Chicago. In any case, "ladies with white skins were considered too delicate for the tropical summers," Swanson explained.[13] The women began spending five months each year in Chicago, a routine migration that moved Gloria in and out of different schools, with little chance to catch up or get her bearings. She would attend sixteen different grammar schools.

Addie signed Gloria up for drawing lessons at Chicago's Art Institute, and the girl was captivated by what she glimpsed beyond the children's classroom. She wanted to be an artist or a singer when she grew up—and a mother, too, naturally. Gloria missed her father, but she knew without being told that Addie preferred their life in Chicago—or more precisely, their life without her father.

Joseph Swanson was a heavy drinker who was charming but feckless. The family should have been comfortable, given his military salary and the perks of his job, plus the sum Addie inherited when her well-to-do father died. Yet money seemed to slip through Joseph's fingers; he liked gambling but did not have especially good luck. "He was always in love with my mother," Gloria recalled, "but had been a sort of Peck's bad boy. He had worried her a great deal."[14]

In Chicago, the female Swansons lived with Addie's mother Bertha, the strong-willed woman whose flight had broken Grandfather Klanowsky's heart. Bertha offered her daughter free and plentiful advice on how to raise her child and how to mend marital fences (a subject in which she had dubious expertise). Bertha and Addie disagreed frequently, a sour mix of frustration and competition mingling with their affection. Yet when her marriage became strained, Adelaide retreated with her daughter to her mother's house, and eventually in turn provided a home for the aging Bertha. Swanson remembered Bertha as the only member of her family who truly enjoyed and celebrated her fame.

Caught between her demanding mother and her judgmental in-laws, Addie agreed to go along when Joseph was once again transferred, this time to Puerto Rico. Gloria was unperturbed by the change in friends and schools; she preferred being with adults anyway. It was part of her plan to skip as much of childhood as possible. Her other great wish was expressed in her nightly prayer for an exciting life. That prayer precluded any squeamishness about moving on, though Gloria never got used to the sea voyages that took the family to the island. Just the mention of a boat made her green around the gills.

Puerto Rico was even more enchantingly beautiful than Key West. The eleven-year-old wrote her grandmother about seeing pineapples grow and riding her first horse: the spirited creature ran off with Gloria barely holding on. Her indulgent parents bought her a (more tractable) pony of her own, whom she named Mr. Gibbs. She and Addie rode on the beach most days, Gloria wearing a proper riding habit, never breeches. With her creamy olive skin and striking blue eyes, she made a convincing Spanish lady for Carnival. Dressed in a mantilla and long black gloves, Gloria promenaded on the plaza with the other young ladies. Her friend Harriet remembered her as a tastemaker: "Even then you had a flair for fashion," she wrote Gloria when they were in their eighties. "Bena and I cut out our paper dolls from *Ladies Home Journal* . . . and you cut yours from *Vogue*."[15]

Gloria couldn't wait to grow up and wanted to dress the part, pestering her mother until Addie finally gave her one of her castoff gowns. One day Gloria and another friend dressed up and called on an officer's wife. Wearing long skirts with starched high collars and hats with veils, they pretended to be married ladies new to the post. They handed calling cards to the maid to make themselves look more authentic, then gave themselves away by giggling madly. Gloria kept trying to pin her skirts and blouses so that they looked like adult styles: "I would try to get out of the house that way but usually I'd get caught and sent upstairs to put my skirt up where it belonged and my hair down where it belonged."[16]

The idea of playing a role took hold. When a school musical called *The American Girl* was announced, her friends went out for the chorus, and Gloria landed the starring role. The production was held in the Opera House, with a real dressing room, a proper stage, and tiers and tiers of boxes. In case there was any doubt about who had the lead, Joseph painted a gold star with Gloria's name on it on her dressing room mirror. He helped his daughter apply her makeup, and Gloria thought her father could have been an artist like his brothers.

Joseph's pride in his daughter's talent was not shared by Addie, a homebody who could not fathom Gloria's willingness to display herself on stage. Addie had a habit of looking at her daughter "as if she were looking at a three-headed monster," Gloria said. "She [didn't] understand at all how she gave birth to me."[17] That night, however, the rest of San Juan society was looking at her with pleasure and approval. The officers were there in their army whites, the ladies in fine dresses. There were even flowers from her first beau, another military brat named Peter Stewart. Gloria Swanson's theatrical debut was a resounding success.

Peter was more playmate than boyfriend. His family also lived in Artillery Park, and the two children ran across the roof connecting the wings of their building to play. One night, they planned to camp out there. They pitched a tent made of rugs and hung a room divider before getting spooked by the nighttime noises and creeping back home to safety. They acquired a goat and built a cart to ride around the island. Whenever they started down a hill, however, both children jumped in; they ended up dragging the goat behind them. They traded the goat for a pair of chickens; when one escaped and got eaten, Peter decided they should barbecue Gloria's chicken as well. A shy, handsome boy a bit younger than his pal, Peter had no truck with other girls; he liked Gloria because she liked adventures.

Her father did not approve of the attention she received from another boy. Manolo Martinez wanted to carry Gloria's books home from school, but he "wasn't a member of the Army Post set," Gloria recalled, "so my father soon put a stop to that." She retaliated by carrying her books on her head, "aping all the natives."[18] The mildly rebellious act helped her posture and made her petite frame—she was just over five feet as an adult—seem taller.

"My father is probably the person that I was in love with," she claimed. "I can remember when I was quite young—thirteen, fourteen—the awakening of sex . . . [My father] smelled good to me. I have a nose like a rabbit—I always associate this sense of smell with people that I like." She valued Joseph's opinion over anyone else's. "I was forever asking my father about [the] stars above our heads. Down in the tropics where you see the Southern Cross, the stars seem so close to you. You have roof gardens, and the evenings are so balmy, and they caress you. There's something about the tropics that lends itself to the . . . mystic side of life. When he'd explain what the star was, I wasn't satisfied with that. I wanted to know what was beyond the star. . . . I was very close to [my father] as a youngster," Swanson said. "I got a great education from him—much more than I ever got out of school."[19]

Joseph counseled his daughter not to hurry her awakening: life was 95 percent anticipation and 5 percent satisfaction. "Savor every moment," he said. "The 5 percent doesn't last very long." At thirteen, Gloria recalled, "I had just become a woman, and didn't quite understand."[20] Yet she always remembered her father's words, sensing the wisdom behind them.

The first moving pictures Swanson saw, Danish imports playing in Puerto Rico, did not impress her. Yet by 1911 her visits to Chicago included trips to the movies, and she wrote in her school workbook, "Francis X. Bushman is my favorite."[21] Many other schoolgirls felt as she did. In an era when magazine contests helped popularize film stars, Bushman notched up title after title: he was the "Most Handsome Man" in America and the "King of the Movies." His wavy hair and expressive eyes cemented his reputation as the leading man of the moment. Better yet, this paragon of manhood was close to home, at the Essanay Film Manufacturing Company on Argyle Street in Chicago.

In 1914, Gloria paid a visit to the studio, a trip for which she dressed carefully, in her most chic outfit: a big checked skirt—a long one, finally—and a cutaway jacket over a blouse with a peplum. She was riveted by what she saw in the busy, loud, apparently chaotic former warehouse. Multiple pictures were being made at the same time; there was no need for quiet on the set because the movies themselves would be silent. In fact, the noise, as Frank Bushman said, "was like a boiler factory."[22] Carpenters built sets as directors shouted orders to actors, instructing them to feel sorrow or show mirth. The actresses had gorgeous dresses, which the teenager observed closely. When she remarked that it looked like fun to make a movie, her tour guide pounced. Could he have her address and telephone number?

Swanson always insisted she had accompanied her Aunt Inga to Essanay as a lark, but others claimed that she engineered her first movie role. Whether Gloria was "a movie-struck Chicago teenager . . . hanging around outside the Essanay studio" hoping to be spotted by Francis Bushman (who was known to like a pretty face) or a protected young girl plucked by chance from anonymity can never be known.[23] A budding beauty of almost fifteen with a saucy lift to her chin, Swanson was unusually fetching, yet she believed her looks mattered less than her willingness. "In those days there were no casting bureaus. They couldn't call up and say, 'Send 300 extras over,' or 3,000 or even 10. They had to ask their relatives and friends off the street to come in . . . so they were only too happy to get one [who] might do."[24]

She was instantly offered a walk-on part. Gloria Swanson's first appearance on camera shows her handing a bunch of flowers to Gerda Holmes, who was playing a bride. The pay was $3.25, "an absolute fortune" for ridiculously easy work.[25] She treated herself to a dill pickle on her way home.

The next day, Gloria went off happily to spend her windfall. Later, Addie complained that movie people had been calling all day: they expected Gloria back at work. No one had told the extra girl that they would have to reshoot the movie if she did not finish her scene. Gloria agreed to return to Essanay for another day, then another, but she felt rather cool about the experience. Acting seemed neither difficult nor especially rewarding, and she disliked the crude comedies she saw being made at Essanay. Cross-eyed Ben Turpin was funny? A mad crush of bodies falling every which way was funny? People throwing pies and being hit by flying objects was funny?

The movie people seemed crazy, too. "Lightning" Hopper, one of Essanay's most successful directors, directed by screaming at everyone to go faster and faster. When Gloria innocently wore a different suit to work on her third day, the head of production screamed at *her*. A prop man had painted a portrait of Swanson in the first outfit for use in a scene, and she had ruined the effect by changing her clothes. She hurried away from the irate producer, convinced—and satisfied—that her career in the flickers was over.

Gloria had been invited to spend a month in New York with a new friend she made while the girl's wealthy family was cruising in the

Caribbean. Joseph, now stationed on Governors Island, would meet his daughter's train and escort her to Staten Island. In the summer of 1914, Gloria was more excited about her first solo venture into the world than her first appearance in moving pictures. The movies had made her richer by $9.75; that would have to be enough.

Medora Grimes moved in a sophisticated whirl of country club parties, tennis matches, and tea dances; she was the first girl Gloria had ever seen smoking. The Grimes' home seemed palatial, and Gloria admired the way Medora's rooms were decorated according to her own taste. Medora taught her visitor the latest dance steps in preparation for her first evening dance. They wondered if they would be permitted to tango, which many considered daring, even wicked.

At the club that Saturday evening, a boy named Livingston Parmalee asked if he could dance with the girl everyone was calling "the Cuban Princess." He led Gloria smoothly around the dance floor, and he smelled wonderful. When he kissed her on the lips, Gloria felt dizzy. She became convinced that the kiss had made her pregnant; something that intense and perfect had to be what made babies. "The earth had shaken under me," she recalled, "and I felt I would never be the same."[26] She talked it over with Medora, telling her friend that she had "suddenly felt weak and noticed perspiration [down] there."[27] Medora's mother had to do some explaining before Gloria calmed down.

Back in Chicago Gloria found a letter from Essanay, offering her work as a guaranteed extra. She would be paid for four days every week, whether they used her or not, and more if she was needed more often. She would get a staggering $13.25 per week—more than enough to pay for singing lessons to prepare her for a career in opera. War in Europe had just been declared, and her father would probably be transferred again soon. She and her mother would join Joseph once he was settled somewhere, and Gloria figured one more slowdown in her education would make little difference. Though she knew Joseph would disapprove, she talked Addie into letting her quit school—temporarily, of course. When she signed on with Essanay, Gloria was barely fifteen years old, and had finished only a few months of high school, but her formal education was over.

She took the trolley to work each morning at the prosperous, bustling movie studio. The company was named after its two founders, and Gloria liked Mr. Spoor (a former film distributor and the "S" of Essanay), though she saw little of Mr. Anderson (the "A"). Anderson was professionally known as "Broncho Billy," and he wrote, directed, and acted in a western adventure film every week of the year, mostly made in the company's California branch outside San Francisco. The first western star, Anderson was as famous as Mary Pickford, the Girl with the Golden Curls.

Gloria's new Essanay colleagues included Francis Bushman, Beverly Bayne, Ruth Stonehouse, Bryant Washburn, and Edmund Lowe. Louella Parsons worked in the scenario department, devising stories for dozens of one- and two-reel pictures; she remembered Swanson as an "ambitious youngster who used to park her belongings outside my office door."[28] One of the earliest movie companies, Essanay was deeply unadventurous, its founders committed to making profitable short pictures rather than expanding into feature production as other companies were doing. The company's slogan was "the first to standardize photoplays," and—one historian sniffed—"their releases showed it."[29]

With her petite figure and pretty ways, Swanson seemed a natural for the studio's society dramas. She observed the other actresses closely. Estelle Scott "looked as though she'd always come out of a bandbox." Beverly Bayne, the biggest female star at Essanay, was "simply magnificent," with "the loveliest face you ever saw." Bayne was the subject of speculation among the extra girls because she was always closeting herself with Francis Bushman. When the glamorous leading man—who wore a big amethyst ring, smoked cigarettes wrapped in lavender paper, and had a lavender limousine—visited Bayne in her dressing room, the girls eagerly spied on the couple: "Our ears were waggling and we were climbing up on our dressing tables and trying to peek through holes . . . We assumed they were in love."[30] In fact, Bushman was married with five children, which he was contractually obliged to keep secret so he would seem accessible to his fans. He was more than accessible to Bayne: they married a few years later and established a home called Bushmanor.

Like everyone else at Essanay, Bushman punched the clock; in 1914, he made more than forty pictures. In 1915, Swanson had a small part in one, *The Ambition of the Baron*, a story of political intrigue. Bushman remembered her as "a pert little girl who stuck out her tongue" at him.[31] She remembered slapping his face when he dared touch her knee. (She then went into her dressing room and wept.) Swanson had her first credited role in *The Fable of Elvira, Farina and the Meal Ticket*, based on a story by popular humorist George Ade. Billed as "Gloria Mae," she played the daughter of a socially ambitious mother and a newly rich father (the meal ticket). Tutored in elegant ways on a trip to Europe, mother and daughter come back to America and lord it over everyone at home.

"Most of the time there wasn't even a script to work on," Bayne re-called. "In the silent movies we didn't learn lines. We learned a story's continuity and how to put ideas across with expressions and gestures."[32]

As Gloria got more substantial parts, she thought less about singing. She preferred playing women of the world—like the temptress hired to break up a duke's marriage to an heiress in *The Romance of an American Duchess*. Costumed and coiffed to look thirty, Swanson relished her big emotional scenes.

After one onscreen crying jag, she received a compliment she trea-sured: Helen Dunbar, an experienced stage performer, told Gloria that she would be a good actress one day. The young girl responded immedi-ately, "Yes, I know I shall be very famous. I shall be great." Then she was embarrassed by her own arrogance. She had responded without think-ing, "Just like I'd say, 'Yes, I know I have red pajamas on,' or 'I'll have a cup of tea.'"[33] Yet she had no doubt that it was true.[34]

It was not all drama on the Essanay lot. Since exhibitors considered comedies a fundamental part of an evening's entertainment, the con-tract players were expected to play funny roles, too—and silent comedy by and large meant slapstick. Decades later, artists and scholars would celebrate slapstick's surrealistic satire and burlesque, but in 1915 many people simply considered it "vulgar, amoral, and antiestablishment."[35] So when Gloria was assigned to work with an English comedian Essanay had hired away from Mack Sennett for the astronomical price of $1,250 a week, she was not pleased.

Although Essanay had called itself "The House of Comedy Hits" since 1907, the studio had "never developed a major comedian of its own."[36] Now the management was determined to get its money's worth by publicizing Charlie Chaplin's arrival in Chicago. Essanay ads hailed him as "the most wonderful comedian ever seen on the screen . . . in himself a guarantee of ESSANAY QUALITY."[37] Everyone at the studio wanted to get a look at Chaplin when he reported for work in January 1915—whereupon the comedian did an impromptu jig for his new audi-ence. Edward Arnold, then an extra at Essanay, described the fascina-tion: "Chaplin's acting . . . was so dynamic, yet subtle. Whenever he was doing a scene, the other members of the cast would behave as though they were hypnotized. Everybody stood still, and watched him. Even the stage hands would leave their work and gather around."[38] He was given the best of everything at Essanay: the newest stage, a skilled cameraman, and his pick of actors.

As a leading lady for his first picture, Chaplin selected Gloria Swanson—and then spent all of one long morning trying to make her funny.[39] "Oh, God!" he exclaimed. "I could not get a reaction out of her. She was so unsatisfactory that I gave up and dismissed her." Chaplin said Swanson later told him she had been "deliberately uncooperative" because she hated the whole idea of appearing in comedy.[40] Swanson seconded Chaplin's story: "All morning I felt like a cow trying to dance with a toy poodle." Charlie did his best: "He kept laughing and making his eyes twinkle and talking in a light, gentle voice and encouraging me to let myself go and be silly. He reminded me of a pixie from some other world altogether." Yet Swanson couldn't get the feel of his "frisky little skits." She also claimed she had made "very little effort": "I would have been mortified if anybody I knew had ever seen me get kicked in the pants or hit with a revolving plank by an odd sprite in a hobo outfit."[41]

Another theory about the failed collaboration between Chaplin and Swanson holds that Gloria "resembled Chaplin too much in stature, coloring, and certain aspects of personality to be a perfect foil."[42] Swanson did skillful impressions of Chaplin in later years, and—especially in 1924's *Manhandled*—looked something like the diminutive comedian. She claimed that Chaplin, seeing a picture of her in that role, even mistook her for himself. In those days, she said, "I looked more like Chaplin, my face was rounder and . . . I had puppy fat."[43] Perhaps Chaplin would have rejected Swanson as a leading lady even if she had tickled his funny bone.

Chaplin spent two weeks on *His New Job*, a satire of moviemaking in which he portrayed an incompetent worker who screws up every job on the Lodestone Studio lot. Gloria ended up with a small part; she can be seen in the background of the first scene in the studio office, typing away. Utterly absorbed in her clerical duties, she never once looks up, never cracks a smile. The solemn young actress could scarcely have dissociated herself more completely from the proceedings. Fifty years later, when Swanson visited Chaplin on the set of *A Countess from Hong Kong*, they laughed together about the experience. "'Do you remember when you kicked me twelve times in the *derrière*, and then threw me out?' she asked. . . . 'Ah, yes,' replied Chaplin. 'Well, I always thought you'd make a better *dramatic* actress.'"[44]

Chaplin too was serious—about being funny. Unfortunately, he found Essanay more like a factory than the free, creative environment he had enjoyed at Keystone under Mack Sennett's leadership. "The studio personnel were stuffy and went around like bank clerks . . . the business end of it was very impressive, but not their films. . . . It was anything but conducive to creative work." He complained that they "deal[t] out scenarios like playing cards every Monday morning" and closed up shop promptly at 6:00 every evening, regardless of what was happening with a scene. "Their last consideration was the making of good pictures."[45] After *His New Job*, Chaplin left Chicago, finishing his Essanay commitment in California. His first Essanay films "would make him world famous, hyped and interviewed endlessly, merchandized and sung about in the street."[46] By the summer of 1915, Charlie Chaplin was a name on everyone's lips, and Gloria Swanson had passed up whatever chance she might have had to be his leading lady.

Soon she had been at Essanay for a year, bringing in more money all the time—money that helped finance Addie's independence from Gloria's father. The army had sent Joseph to the Philippines, but there was only intermittent talk about the family joining him there. It seemed impossibly far from the life the women were living in Chicago. Gloria's work was distancing her from Addie as well. "In a way, it was good," Gloria said. "She pushed me out of the nest, and I had to fly on my own wings . . . She didn't think for me. I had to think for myself."[47] Addie was the opposite of a stage mother, yet for the rest of her life, Gloria lamented the fact that she had no one in her corner, no family member to cheer her on, advise her, and look after her interests in the cutthroat motion picture business. It was as though once she stopped costuming her only child, Addie lost interest in Gloria.

Gloria's friend June Walker lived with them for a time. When Gloria learned that June had no family and no place to stay, she picked June up "just like you pick up a little kitten," and brought her home. June was like the sister for whom Gloria longed. The two played the piano and danced around the apartment together, sharing clothes and laughing about everything. "She was a little minx," Gloria said. "If some beau came to call on me, she'd get out of his sight, and she'd give an imitation of him . . . I could see it, but he couldn't, and I was supposed to keep a straight face."[48] June sang and danced and had an effervescent personality; Gloria thought she would be a natural in the movies. Her efforts to get her friend a job at Essanay fell flat, however. June eventually headed east and made a career on Broadway: she was the original Lorelei Lee in *Gentleman Prefer Blondes*.

The studio was full of young people starting out in movies. Colleen Moore began at Essanay. So did Rod LaRocque and Agnes Ayres. Gloria made a lifelong friend in Virginia Bowker, another young actress moving between comic and dramatic parts. One comedy series made in Chicago featured a klutzy immigrant maid, "Sweedie," who got into rough-and-tumble comic scrapes in dozens of popular shorts. The series had little logic and less character development, so being cast as a coed in *Sweedie Goes to College* would not normally have pleased Gloria. But this time she was fascinated by the star of the series, a brash, burly man named Wallace Beery.

It is hard to imagine Beery, who made a career of playing ruffians in the 1930s, as a maid in drag. Yet audiences loved his "Sweedie" pictures, rocking with laughter at the large man's oversized antics as a maid trying—and failing—to be dainty. It is even harder to imagine Beery as Gloria Swanson's beau. Fourteen years older than Gloria, he had already had his share of adventures when he joined Essanay in 1913. He had worked in a train yard and as an elephant wrangler for the Ringling Brothers; he had acted in musical comedies and sang in comic operas in New York, often to acclaim.

Beery would always have his detractors. He was known for upstaging other actors and for playing pranks that were more cruel than funny. "Beery's relaxed and extroverted joviality put people at ease," says one historian. "He appeared to be nothing more than a friendly, straightforward kind of guy, but underneath he calculated with a single-minded determination to get exactly what he wanted."[49] One colleague called him "a bull of a man, crude, impatient, unable to understand weakness of any kind."[50] Another concurred: Beery was "one of the least liked big actors at MGM."[51] Even his friends conceded that he was a difficult man. As the free-spirited Louise Brooks said, "Away from work a honey bear, Beery was the meanest bear alive on the set."[52]

He showed Gloria his honey bear side. She found his strength attractive and liked his deep singing voice and the way he played piano for her on the set. When he offered to drive her home in his Stutz Bearcat, she accepted—and took the ride of her life. Beery was a fast driver with quick reflexes who handled his car with finesse. He could easily outrace the traffic cops and loved to show off his speed and control. He managed to persuade Gloria that he was only marking time with Sweedie, that he, too, desired more serious roles. She began confiding in him. Wallace Beery soon became "the one person I could talk to about everything."[53]

In later years, Swanson would be defensive about her romance with Beery. Other women "made fools of themselves about him," she explained. "He was always a woman's man and . . . a very entertaining person. He was not . . . a very handsome man, but he was a very attractive, strong person. When he became really famous, of course, he was ever so much heavier than he was when I first knew him." Photos of Beery at this time show a well-dressed, just-shy-of-handsome man. He made a credible love interest in Gloria's 1915 picture *The Broken Pledge*, a light-hearted story of three college girls who vow to remain single, until they meet Beery and his two pals on a camping trip. As Gloria said, "I was in love with him in a schoolgirl way."[54]

Beery had a taste for younger women and a reputation to go with it. Rumors circulated about Gloria after she got in Beery's car, though she dismissed them: "All the girls wanted to go [riding with him], and I was the one that somehow made it."[55] In October 1915, however, when the angry parents of another underage actress threatened to prosecute Beery, the randy actor was packed off to the California branch of Essanay to get him out of the way.

Everyone was talking about going to California, though there were mixed reports about moviemaking there. Francis Bushman had been to the coast in 1914 and pronounced it "appalling." The westerners had a lousy work ethic: "The minute we turned our backs they were out in the sun or playing billiards. It'll never work."[56] Yet D. W. Griffith's 1915 epic *The Birth of a Nation* was a more ambitious picture than anyone had ever seen. It made Essanay's short, formulaic films seem old hat. It made everything seem old hat. California was where the opportunities were.

Soon after Beery's departure, Swanson lost her job at Essanay when another actress complained about her behavior with Beery. Gloria thought Edna Mayo was really steamed because Gloria was cast as Mayo's daughter, though there was only a small age difference between them. Yet she didn't really mind; she had learned what Essanay could teach her. Underneath her elaborate costumes Gloria had been "as much a female impersonator as Mr. Beery" when she began at Essanay.[57] Now the shy child who worked hard at appearing adult was gone. Though she was only sixteen, Swanson had grown up quite a bit by the time Wallace Beery left town. She, too, would soon be drawn west, to be part of what was happening out in California.

CHAPTER 2

Funny Girl

IN FEBRUARY 1916, GLORIA AND HER MOTHER ARRIVED IN LOS ANGE-
les, looking for a new beginning. Packed deep in Gloria's trunk was a
letter of introduction to Mack Sennett, an acquaintance she wasn't sure
she wanted. Her experience at Essanay had not made her any more impressed with funny movies or the people who made them. Now, however, she had another role to consider: breadwinner for her shrinking
family. Adelaide had left her husband, a choice which pulled Gloria away
from her father as well.

Wallace Beery met the train when Gloria and her mother disem-
barked. He had made the eight-hour drive from the Essanay studios at
Niles to welcome Gloria and Addie to California. Escorting them to their
new apartment on Cahuenga Boulevard, he told Addie that he hoped to
be working in Hollywood soon himself. His brother, Noah, was making a
good living playing heavies for Jesse Lasky. When Wally came south, they
would bring their parents from Kansas to share the good life. Conditions
at the Niles facility were primitive; the mostly male companies were
roughing it, making western adventures and comedies. As far as Beery
was concerned, it was the Klondike, and he couldn't wait to get out.

Beery chauffeured the two newcomers around Los Angeles. He was
gentlemanly and attentive, a good guide, though Gloria did not think
much of her new home: "The city seemed to be composed entirely of
factories, empty lots, gas stations, telephone wires, drugstores, open markets, and barns. Here and there cows ate weeds beside rickety houses."[1]
They chuckled at the strange costumes of people on the street. People
dressed funny here, Beery explained, to attract the attention of movie
producers and talent scouts. Everyone was hoping to be spotted, and
a crazy outfit—an oversized hat or a checkered suit—might get you a
second look. Beery assured Gloria that she would not need to parade

around in funny clothes to attract the attention of a film producer: her introduction to the head of the Keystone studio was the most valuable thing in her luggage. They would "crash" Hollywood together.[2]

Beery seemed more mature, more polished and serious than he had in Chicago. Gloria concluded that the trouble there had scared him. As Wally advised her to hurry over to meet Mack Sennett, he was "firm as a father."[3] Shortly after her arrival in Los Angeles, the young actress hopped on the streetcar to Edendale and presented herself at the front offices of the Keystone Film Company.

If Swanson thought she was ill-suited to Essanay's brand of comic hijinks, Keystone meant moving from the frying pan straight into the fire. Company founder Mack Sennett had worked in vaudeville and burlesque before deciding that a film studio specializing in comedy could be a lucrative proposition. He made no bones about his ambitions for the cinema: "We made funny pictures as fast as we could for money." Keystone churned out fast-paced one-reelers at a very fast pace, about two per week. The pictures were sold "like gingham for girls' dresses—at so much per yard." To meet the apparently insatiable demand, Sennett craved a steady supply of "roaring extroverts devoted to turmoil."[4] He put together a crack company of comic players who exceeded his requirements for speed and crazy inventiveness.

Sennett's pictures were wild affairs based on raucous physical antics. The company took advantage of public assemblies, feeding off the energy of crowds and treating the spectators as free extras. When a fire truck careened down the street, the Keystone players followed close behind, ready to turn any situation to hilarious effect. The crazy chases and bruising romps of the Keystone Kops, egged on by the Bathing Beauties, were perennially popular. At home on the lot, Sennett supervised filming while soaking in an oversized bathtub in his office high above the outdoor sets. He hollered instructions and corrections from the tub.

Given the improvisational genius of the players, Keystone comedies could be built around situations rather than highly planned sequences. The comic repercussions of putting funny lady Mabel Normand, her screen lover, his wife, and Mabel's pet dog together in a hotel appears in one film script simply as "Consternation, etc."[5] Regular pairings, like the creative partnership of Normand and Fatty Arbuckle, allowed players to rely on each other's talents while enhancing the company's overall efficiency. Keystone also turned out madcap parodies of popular movies made at other studios, titles like *Uncle Tom Without the Cabin* or *The Shriek of Araby*.

Sennett was a shrewd judge of talent, and he recognized in the young transplant from Chicago someone he could use. He wasn't too impressed by the wrapping, however; he gruffly pronounced Swanson's makeup "a joke" and her clothes "terrible."[6] Swanson was put off by Sennett's unfriendliness and disgusted when he spat cigar juice near her feet. Yet when he offered her a job, she said yes.

He delivered her into rough, capable hands. Charley Chase, an experienced and clever comedian, directed Swanson's first two Keystone pictures. They were zany affairs, long on action and indifferent to decorum. A studio synopsis of *A Dash of Courage* describes a chase scene: a car goes down a flight of steps, hits a wall, and explodes. The passengers, including Gloria, are "blown up in the air and go flying through the clouds." The young male lead, riding along on his bicycle, calls to Gloria, who "falls from [the] clouds and lights on Bob's handle bars."[7] It was rowdy, undignified stuff.

Bobby Vernon was Gloria's new, physically compatible movie partner: "a little runt of a thing, just my size," Gloria remembered.[8] *A Dash of Courage* was wilder than the pictures she and Vernon would soon be making, and probably gave Gloria pause about her new job. However, Wally Beery had begun work at Keystone, too; he was playing the Chief of Police, and his presence steadied her.

The older actor enjoyed the camaraderie and unpretentious atmosphere at Keystone, and Gloria found herself looking to him for direction. Since the films were short, an actor needed to create a character quickly and memorably. Simply staying afloat with all the scene-stealers at Keystone was a challenge as well. Nothing seemed to scare Wally, and his big personality and unshakeable sense of fun helped Gloria feel more at home in Hollywood.

Even at fast speeds she felt safe with him. After work and on weekends the pair took off in Wally's car, exploring southern California's empty roads and wild terrain. One glorious day they went to the San Bernardino Mountains to fish. The last time she'd been fishing, Gloria remembered, had been with her father in Florida. They stopped at roadhouses, and Beery, a talented musician, commandeered the piano, everyone singing along with him. He told jokes and made a point of including Gloria in his impromptu acts. He did hilarious imitations of everyone at the studio, including Mack Sennett himself. She was smitten, and later remembered these outings—and Beery's invariable performances—with pleasure, recalling how people responded to him: "I'd never seen an audience love a performer so much."[9]

Behind the wheel of a car, Wally was "like a great dancer," Louise Brooks recalled; his responses and his timing were perfect.[10] Beery's calm, daring, and expertise excited Gloria. When he taught her to drive, she was nearly delirious with pleasure: "I'd never had such a thrill. . . . There was roaring in my ears. My hands were wet." The teenager "loved the feeling of all that power, frightening though it was."[11] To be chosen—to be taught—by a man who could handle such equipment masterfully, and who was at once avuncular, tender, and knowing was a heady experience.

Sennett soon assigned the team of Vernon and Swanson to a new director who was eager to show what he could do. Gloria charmed Clarence Badger: "Her figure was petite and shapely. Her face and eyes were unusually beautiful, a kind of winsome, appealing beauty. She radiated personality." She was also nervous. Sennett was a critical boss who expressed his frustrations out loud, sparing no one. Badger, however, set a different tone. He was ready and willing to help his players and wanted them to rely on one another. The reward would be worth it, he pledged: "If by our joint efforts a knockout job did result, not only myself, but all, would be well set in pictures." Badger's approach helped Gloria relax; soon she was contributing to the story confidently, as the other Keystone players did. Badger claimed that she "sparkled with ideas." After seeing their first picture, Sennett shouted, "It's a bear, Badger! A bear!"—by which he meant a sure-fire success.[12]

Sennett was right. In nine popular two-reelers, Gloria (often called "Gloria Dawn") and Bobby attracted a wide audience while playing at teenage courtship. They literally played: games of tennis, musical numbers at the piano, fetch and chase with their frequent costar, Keystone Teddy, an enormous Great Dane. Gloria and Bobby encountered obstacles like greedy guardians and disapproving parents seeking socially advantageous matches for their children, and he was often fickle or flighty. Yet true love—aided by a little ingenuity—always won out. Surviving stills show a sweet-faced young couple, obviously very young, dwarfed by the grown-ups around them.

Their small stature presented comic possibilities. In *Teddy at the Throttle*, Bobby flirts with a woman easily a foot taller than he is. Gloria steams from the sidelines, waiting to tweak him by the ear and pull him away. She can't even reach the other woman's ear, but Bobby is her own size: they are a pair of pipsqueaks. Swanson's glamorous persona got the boot, too. Her Essanay roles made Gloria seem older than her age, but Sennett intended to take advantage of her youth and freshness. In fact, Gloria's

Keystone days, and the romantic mayhem she made with Bobby Vernon, were a welcome second childhood.

At Keystone anything could spice up or inspire a film. When Gloria's enthusiasm for driving became known, they made *The Danger Girl*, in which she plays a speed demon. Country roads were primitive in 1916, but after a few quick lessons in how to execute tight turns and handle the bumps and rough curves, Gloria was ready. They filmed her scenes behind the Beverly Hills Hotel, then some distance outside town and patronized by rich old people who gawked at the film company. For part of the picture Gloria was dressed as a man, and she practiced by mimicking her male colleagues' gestures. Yet she took every opportunity to look good: a child actor at Keystone remembered Gloria ducking into his family's house to iron her wrinkled skirt before the cameras turned.[13]

The Danger Girl fits the pattern of her Keystone shorts. Bobby gets distracted by an older, more sophisticated woman, and Gloria has to regain his attention, but without compromising her girlish virtue. She first tries pouting, which is adorable but doesn't work. Then she gets angry and comes up with a plan to get even, which is even more adorable. With a striking economy of gesture, Gloria communicates a feisty determination to recapture her beau's wandering attention. Whether she is whacking Bobby over the head with the flowers he gives her or hauling off and punching a villain, she flirts with but never quite crosses the line to vulgarity. She may dress like a man and drive like a demon, but it's all in the service of love. Gloria always needs the near-oblivious Bobby to save her from the trouble she's found—and he always races to her rescue, thoughts of any other woman vanished.

The films Swanson made under Mack Sennett's supervision were milder and more restrained than the classic Keystone comedies. There was little in the way of punishing acrobatics to injure the young actress's dignity, and she never—not once—took a pie in the kisser. Swanson called them "light" comedies: "There were no big fat people or cross-eyed people or skinny people . . . and there were no bathing girls in the picture."[14] No fat people (like Roscoe Arbuckle, her oversized Keystone colleague, who was lighter on his feet than people half his size). No cross-eyed people (like Ben Turpin, who was busily stealing scenes from Chaplin at Essanay while Gloria couldn't be bothered to be funny). And definitely, absolutely no bathing girls: Swanson disavowed a connection to the Sennett Bathing Beauties more vehemently than she challenged any other story about her professional life. She insisted she could not swim and was terrified of the water—as if their swimming prowess was the main qualification the

Beauties possessed. This amused Sennett, who loved to needle Gloria by pretending he remembered her as a Bathing Beauty.

Why was Swanson so insistent on this apparently small point? The answer has to do with what it meant to be a film comedienne in early Hollywood. "All those girls who did comedy were tough," Miriam Cooper remembered.[15] When they played as hard as their male colleagues (as Mabel Normand did), they were seen as unwomanly. Further, the sheer physical exertion of their labors provoked speculation about their sexual appetites. Alan Dale explains: "Pratfalls . . . imply that the heroine is altogether too physically available." Then, too, actresses associated with slapstick were unlikely to be offered romantic or dramatic leads; it was already easy to be typecast. Last but not least, funny women were unimportant. They were in pictures, but the pictures were seldom about them. Even Mabel Normand was seldom "the motive spirit" in her pictures: "Her function . . . [was] to be peppy, more of a morsel than average, and to suffer outrage."[16] Buster Keaton, who cast his own wife in his films, said he used "three principals—the villain, myself, and the girl, and she was never important."[17] A stint with the Bathing Beauties was a credential not all Sennett's graduates were eager to publicize.

After a very short courtship, Beery proposed marriage to Swanson. After a very short hesitation, she accepted. Even as she agreed to marry Beery, however, she was feeling hurried out of the nest. Her mother, happily liberated from Gloria's father, had decided she wanted a divorce. Addie seemed finished with motherhood, too. She and Gloria had taken a new, larger apartment, one where Addie could entertain her friends— and her new beau. She was making herself a lot of new clothes, but had largely stopped sewing for her daughter. Gloria believed her mother was trying to tell her something: "If I was old enough to leave school and command a large salary, then I was old enough to stay home alone nights and give her a chance to have some life of her own."[18]

Addie was unimpressed by her daughter's movie career. She enjoyed the money Gloria was earning but found the whole enterprise of movie-making short of respectable. It did not make her proud the way a singing career would. The hard-working young actress couldn't help feeling a bit resentful, a bit lost: "I could see less and less place in her life for me."[19] Yet Addie had begun relinquishing responsibility back in Chicago, when her teenage daughter was dressing up as a much older woman to play the sophisticate at Essanay.

Gloria felt strained with her father, too. Despite her success, she was painfully alone: "I couldn't tell [my father] that Mother was looking ten

years younger and having the time of her life." Nor could she tell Joseph
that at sixteen she was earning more money than he was—and for making silly comedies. Gloria was being pushed to grow up even faster by
a mother who couldn't be pleased by her daughter's achievement, and
trying to keep her mother's secrets from her father, while her own success shamed her and kept apart her from him. She kept it all to herself:
"I wound up writing him as few letters as possible, about nothing that
mattered."[20]

Swanson wasn't sure she loved Wally Beery, but her parents' divorce
had shaken her ideas about love. She knew she found him attractive.
More importantly, she felt safe with the older man. Since she was bringing home the family paycheck, Gloria considered herself emancipated.
She didn't believe she needed her mother's permission to marry. So
Gloria and her fiancé—who was still working part-time in northern
California—each arranged to take her seventeenth birthday off from
work. Without telling anyone their plans, they headed off in his roadster
to get married.

What followed was a story out of a Keystone comedy, one that could
be titled *Her Disastrous Wedding*. Gloria was ready and waiting, her small
satchel packed, when Beery arrived early in the morning, having made
the long drive down from Niles. They told Addie they were taking a
day trip to Santa Barbara two hours away to celebrate Gloria's birthday.
After a glorious drive at the then-hasty speed of 30 mph, the couple
arrived in front of the registry clerk. The clerk, however, didn't believe
that Gloria (who had lied about her age) was nineteen. She demanded
a birth certificate. To Swanson's humiliation, Beery tried to argue with
the woman. When that inevitably failed, they decided to return to Los
Angeles, pick up Addie, and get married—with full parental consent—in
Pasadena. Gloria saw "the perfect honeymoon retreat" Beery had promised her receding in their taillights as her angry fiancé turned the car
around.[21] They flew back to Los Angeles, racing against time before the
city offices closed, their precious day off was lost, and Wally had to head
north once again.

At home, Gloria lost no time persuading her mother to accompany
the couple to the altar. Addie, she explained, "was preoccupied with romance at the time, and I must have been a walking advertisement for it
that afternoon, flushed with the wind and sun after four hours in the car
and childishly animated in the expression of my feelings for Wally and
the urgency of getting to the license bureau. She didn't have to ask me
if I was sure . . . she could see I was sure." The threesome headed out

again, crammed into the open car. Addie was fearful whenever Beery hit the gas, but her daughter kept pleading with her fiancé to go faster. It felt to Gloria like a marvelous "race into marriage."[22] They ended up interrupting a minister and his wife as they sat to their dinner, but at the end of Gloria's long and hectic birthday the couple was legally married.

Beery was ready to treat his new mother-in-law to dinner, but Addie insisted on leaving the newlyweds alone, if they would drop her at the train station. However, the last train to LA had departed, so they went in search of a hotel with two rooms instead of one. Mama would be coming on the honeymoon after all. They had a fancy dinner with wine, joking about what Beery would tell his friends about his wedding night.

Years later, it was the bride who had the story to tell, and she skipped few details. Her new husband had a drink in the hotel bar while Gloria made herself ready. Then Wally entered their room, pulled her to him, and pushed her backward onto the bed. In his excitement Beery was rough with the inexperienced girl, and decades later Swanson was as unsparing about his performance as he was of her virginity:

"His beard was scraping my skin and his breath smelled. He kept repeating obscene things and making advances with his hand and tongue while he turned his body this way and that and awkwardly undid his buttons and squirmed out of his clothes. Then he forced my body into position and began hurting me, hurting me terribly. I couldn't stand it. I begged him to stop, to listen to me, and finally, when I couldn't stand it any longer, I screamed. He told me to be quiet, not to wake the whole hotel, and he said it in a voice of quiet, filthy conspiracy. The pain became so great that I thought I must be dying. I couldn't move for the pain. When he finally rolled away I could feel blood everywhere. I lay there absolutely terrified and repulsed until I heard him snoring."[23]

Gloria spent the remainder of the night, like many sheltered girls before her, in a state of shock and dismay. She waited for the pain to go away. She wondered where her ardent, funny, gentle beau had gone. She understood the enormity of her own ignorance about the rest of married life: what else might be expected of her? She hoped her mother in the next room had not heard her screaming. Finally, she realized she could do nothing to escape from her new husband, whom she had taken for better and, most definitely, for worse: "I had spent the whole day racing around California, even lying, to get a marriage license as if it were a ticket to heaven, and I had only managed to be brutalized in pitch-blackness by a man who whispered filth in my ear while he ripped me almost in two."[24]

Beery headed north in the morning and the chastened young bride and her mother rode quietly back to Los Angeles on the train. A day after becoming a married woman, Gloria was going home with Addie as though nothing had happened. Yet the distance between mother and daughter had widened exponentially: "I suddenly realized . . . that although my mother and I were looking out of the same window, we were not seeing the same things on the other side, and we never would."[25] More alone than ever, Gloria waited for Beery to find a new home for the couple to share.

We have only Swanson's account of her first months as Wallace Beery's wife, but the picture she painted was bleak. The rickety house on Alvarado Street into which she moved with Beery, his brother Noah, and their parents was small and airless. Her new in-laws were as quiet and hard to know as her husband was loud and rambunctious. (Mama Beery, however, offended by persistently making food Gloria found hard to stomach; she remembered with loathing the lingering smell of boiled cabbage in the house.) Wally's parents seemed downright elderly to the teenage bride. On the other hand, her new husband was like an overgrown child or a puppy. He thought little about the consequences of his actions. He had hardly any self-control. He was messy; he was a nonstop performer and a show-off. A closer acquaintance with Beery revealed not one trait that the dissatisfied young wife felt she could love. Any feelings of safety he had engendered had evaporated on their wedding night.

She also quickly learned of his improvidence with money. Always short of cash, Beery was used to working with little thought of tomorrow. Swanson, on the other hand, came from a more settled middle-class background and was proud of her Keystone earnings, an impressive $65 weekly.[26] If her father struggled to keep money in his pocket, her mother had taught her to value a well-kept home and nice possessions. So when Beery began cashing her weekly checks she was dismayed: "I never saw one penny of my money while I was married to him."[27] Then Beery explained that her salary was going to back payments on his car, which would otherwise have been beyond his salary. He had been supplementing his pay with work as a studio manager up at Niles, earning more in the electricians' union than as an actor.

This was all strange to Gloria. Her own pay packets seemed ample, but she had no experience with cars and budgeting and running a household. Beery reassured her with a rare gift—a lovely dark brown hat—and she tried not to dwell on the fact that her wages had paid for the extravagant present. The young bride was especially eager to accept her husband's comfort because she had just made a momentous discovery: she was pregnant.

In Swanson's colorful memoir, events occur hard on one another's heels, with impeccable, practically comic timing. As she tells it, no sooner did she realize that she was expecting than she learned Beery had been fired, personally chewed out by Mack Sennett and sent from the lot. With a steely determination to protect the father of her unborn child, the young wife marched in to confront the studio chief and insist that Beery be rehired, threatening to leave Keystone herself if Sennett refused. She saved Beery's job, though she never learned why he had been dismissed.

On her way home, Gloria spied Beery with another woman in his roadster—a woman wearing a hat identical to the special one he had given her. He must have bought two hats, one for his wife and another for this mystery woman. Hurt and puzzled, she pored over the possibilities: "Was it a coincidence? . . . [H]ad he bought two, so that people we knew would think he was out with me if they saw him? That he was a joker, a gypsy, and a womanizer I knew, but was he also a cad, an operator, a monster? Was he trying to protect me at the studio while he fooled around?"[28] According to Swanson, the couple had so little contact, given the long, busy days both were putting in at the studio and their own estrangement, that she never learned the truth. Yet it is typical of Swanson's mythmaking that Beery's hat trick occurred just as she left Sennett's office, having championed her errant spouse.

Excited about her pregnancy in spite of her doubts about her partner, and eager to begin what she hoped would be a large family, the actress looked for an opportunity to share her news. Beery greeted the announcement of her pregnancy with enthusiasm but was adamant that Swanson keep working as long as she was up to it. He had big ideas about publicizing them as a married team at the studio. Despite her hesitation about the physicality of her work at Keystone, the actress agreed. However, not long into her pregnancy she had a bout of morning sickness so severe that Beery, after conferring with his mother, went out looking for something to soothe it. She took five of the pills he handed her as his mother watched silently from the doorway and immediately began to feel sicker. Swanson came to in a hospital bed, a nurse gently reassuring her that she was young and strong enough to bear many more babies. First, Swanson said, she cried. Then she resolved to get out of bed before Beery came to pick her up. She slipped quietly back into the house on Alvarado Street, packed her bag, and went home to Mother.

Swanson claimed she took the medicine bottle to a nearby pharmacy. She asked the druggist for a refill, explaining that a friend had suggested the pills as a remedy for morning sickness. "He looked me straight in the eye," she said, before saying that whoever had given her the pills "couldn't be much of a friend." The man continued, "What I usually recommend when folks come in here and ask for this stuff is that they think it over. If I were you, I wouldn't take a chance on killing myself. I'd just go ahead and have the baby."[29] Swanson's disillusionment with Beery was complete. Her marriage was over.

Through a long career and a long, active life, Gloria Swanson lost few friends. She married many times and took many lovers, remaining on cordial terms with almost all her exes. Yet she had nothing good to say about Wallace Beery after the first flush of their hasty courtship, and over the years that followed, she told the story of their brief marriage in a way that was consistently unflattering to him. The memoir she published at the end of her life differs little in this respect from the versions she prepared decades earlier. Swanson always had a hard time talking about her first marriage, and there is less within her voluminous archives about Beery than about anyone else in her life. She kept no souvenirs of their time together. If she had a tendency to airbrush the story of their courtship, the picture of the older man she painted for publication was full of ugly details almost too villainous to be believed. Beery is boorish and brutal: after raping his bride on their wedding night, he tricks her into miscarrying their baby.

The carefully crafted starkness with which this portrait is limned reflects the woman who produced it. The tale is told with a steely flair which Swanson undoubtedly possessed. It is a story about innocence lost and disappointment suffered, but it is also about picking oneself up and getting on with things. It is about survival. It is not hard to see why Swanson's assessment of her first husband remained coolly unforgiving: he was her first serious romance and her first big heartbreak, the man who careened through her youth before betraying her at a particularly vulnerable moment. A move to a new and strange city far from her childhood home coincided with the breakup of her family, a sense of strain and distance between her parents and herself, and her assumption of the adult responsibility of earning a living. Beery was a confident, larger-than-life older man who pursued her avidly and onto whom she projected her fantasy of being at once an adult and a protected child.

The challenges of marriage were probably beyond this particular couple. Beery's long bachelorhood and rugged independence didn't help much; neither did his lack of finesse with his terrified teenage bride on their brief honeymoon. Many newlyweds of the era shared quarters with their parents or in-laws and survived the experience—but once Swanson saw (or imagined) Beery's mother as a brooding presence eager to help her son abort his new wife's baby, there literally was no going back. Whether Beery actually supplied the pills or simply failed to protect and support his young wife emotionally remains unknown. Yet Swanson, who made a habit of marrying in haste, did not here begin a habit of repenting at leisure. She simply moved on.

Moving on, of course, meant going back to work. Swanson kept her distance from Beery on the lot, offering him chilly collegiality but little more. Nonetheless, pretending to be happy in order to perform convincingly had a tonic effect on the young comedienne. She threw herself into her work, enjoying the respect her opinion commanded when the cast tossed around ideas for stories or situations. Judging from the films themselves, the more ideas in a picture, the merrier.

The featherlight *Teddy at the Throttle*, made a year into Gloria's Keystone period, was typical. Gloria Dawn is an orphan; Wallace Beery plays her rascally guardian who, the titles explain, is "secretly feathering his nest" with her money, aided by his villainous sister. The scheming guardian tries to force Gloria to marry him; when she refuses, he hauls her onto the train tracks, ties her down, and waits, mustache twirling, for a locomotive to make her into mincemeat.

By this time, the train tracks were a hoary film cliché, good only for a laugh. Gloria whistles for Teddy the wonder dog, who alerts Bobby to the girl's plight before jumping aboard the train to alert the engineer. Teddy saves the day, and Gloria, Bobby, and the Great Dane hug as the lights come up. All these intrigues, as well as a scene in which Gloria plays the ukulele for the dog and another in which party guests fly comically through the air—just for the fun of it—take less than twenty minutes.

Teddy at the Throttle combines young romance, adult machinations about money and social standing, and great dog tricks in one package. By the time it appeared, Gloria and Bobby had fans across the country, as did Teddy, who appeared in more than three dozen Sennett films and got his own fan mail. He was even interviewed by *Photoplay*: "'Who's your friend, Teddy?' 'Woof, waff, wuff!' (Translation: 'Gloria Swanson.')"[30]

The girlish romantic scrapes Swanson got into onscreen, however, were a far cry from her adult troubles. She had been separated from

Beery for several months when they filmed *Teddy at the Throttle*, their last film together, and Swanson described the production in melodramatic terms. She had to steel herself to perform alongside Beery, and her evident aversion angered him. As they prepared the final scene, she said, "I could feel a tremendous nervous tension building up between us." Then art imitated life: "Wally, in full villain's make-up, let out a roar and grabbed me." He carried her, kicking and screaming with real fear, to the train tracks, where he used brute force to tie her down with a piece of chain, leering and laughing as she pummeled him in terror. When the scene ended, Clarence Badger was elated with the footage. Swanson claimed the director untied her himself: "He could see the red marks on my wrists and feel me shaking like a leaf."[31] She and Beery had not been performing.

This made a terrific story and was probably an accurate description of Swanson's emotional state; Beery played a frightening villain. However, Swanson's hands weren't even tied for the scene: they had to be free for her to retrieve the dog whistle that summoned Teddy to her rescue. At Keystone, moreover, the players were expected to take their tumbles and nurse their bruises without complaint. Yet—to hear Swanson tell it—her ordeal was not yet over: the shot of the train bearing down on her remained. Swanson had been afraid to perform the dangerous stunt herself, so the stunt man, clothed in a white dress to look like Gloria, was waiting for his cue. The players around them began to laugh at how ludicrous the burly man in drag looked next to tiny Gloria. When she heard Beery laughing louder than everyone else she felt he was challenging her, and she spoke up. She would do the stunt after all.

She lowered herself into position. She heard the cameras grind and the train engine rumble. The sky above her darkened as she went down into the hole. Finally the train stopped, inches from her body. The crew members clapped, and the director kissed her. "I felt wonderful," Swanson said. "I knew that Wally must be looking at me, but I didn't look back. I had just said good-bye to him forever."[32] Gloria's tale of escaping the villain's clutches and then—despite his mockery—bravely performing the demanding stunt shows her flair for the dramatic. It would be another two years, however, before the couple would be divorced and she was beyond Wallace Beery's reach forever.

In the meantime, she was seeking new professional challenges. According to contemporary reports with which she no doubt cooperated, Swanson yearned to be a dramatic actress, to play sultry, romantic roles: "Probably Mack Sennett knows what he is doing when he keeps

Gloria in parts in which she has scored such huge successes. But. . . . Miss Swanson will never be satisfied until she has, for once at least, been a screen vampire and wrung some hero's heart." At Sennett's insistence, Gloria would appear in *The Nick-of-Time Baby* looking her girlish self, her hair "loose and curly, her eyes a-sparkle with merriment, and her frock girlish and dainty." But the photo accompanying this story showed Gloria "as she best likes to be—a full-fledged vampire with hot, glowing eyes that stir your soul."[33]

The 1917 image shows Swanson with chin up, hair slicked back, deep décolletage, and bare shoulders. Her lips are a dusky color, her brows thin and dark against her very pale face. She looks anything but girlish. Albert Witzel photographed many screen stars; he also did portfolio shots for aspiring actors. It seems likely that Gloria invested in a session with Witzel to show her adult appeal, and unlikely that Sennett would have been happy to see his little comedienne doing so.

On the contrary: Sennett's in-house newsletter publicized the release of *The Nick-of-Time Baby* with a picture of Keystone Teddy carrying Gloria and Bobby's baby to lunch at the studio cafeteria, hardly the stuff of which glamour legends are made. When the newsletter ran a picture of Swanson looking a bit more soulful than usual, the writer (often Sennett himself) poked gentle fun at her dramatic persona: "Gloria isn't always tragic but she can be on occasion. The Director has just given [her] a 7:30 call."[34] Soon, however, Swanson would be done playing second fiddle to a dog.

Despite the bustle and activity around the Keystone lot, Sennett was in trouble. Keystone was only one leg of the Triangle Film Corporation, and Sennett's partners, D. W. Griffith and Thomas Ince, were struggling to keep their parts of the business afloat. Although Sennett's short films remained popular, they could not fill theater seats unless combined with features. In the late spring of 1917, a year after Gloria arrived at Keystone, Griffith left Triangle, taking Douglas Fairbanks with him. By June, Ince would be gone, too. Mack Sennett was alone.

He responded by trying to cut costs wherever possible. He dropped players from his roster and issued instructions to monitor the productivity of his remaining staff closely. In June, he cabled the studio's general manager to "prepare all companies for immediate production of cheap and speedy stories regardless of quality." Any players who balked at being downgraded were to be let go. A few days later things were even worse. "Remove my name entirely from all pictures," Sennett wrote. "Try to stretch all single reelers possible into two reelers regardless of quality."[35] The atmosphere at Keystone, never tranquil, now became fraught. One of the performers terminated was Gloria's partner Bobby Vernon; her director Clarence Badger was on his way out, too.

Swanson knew what it meant when she was rushed into a new film opposite two established players. She was a close observer of her environment, a quick study, and—despite her youth—a seasoned actress who had been featured at two different studios.[36] She was one of the survivors, yet she could hardly have imagined herself in a more disagreeable situation.

In *A Pullman Bride*, Swanson was literally yanked back and forth between two suitors more occupied with their comic rivalry than enamored of her. By 1917, Mack Swain and Chester Conklin were venerable institutions in the slapstick world. At 6 feet, 2 inches and close to 300 pounds, Swain used his bulk effectively, often playing against much smaller partners. He sported a painted mustache and stagy makeup designed to emphasize his theatrical villainy. Conklin, by contrast, was a former circus clown, a small fellow whose signature mustache—a huge, droopy affair—threatened to overwhelm him. Two inveterate scene-stealers, they were up to their oldest tricks in *A Pullman Bride*. The young actress had all she could do to keep up with them—but keep up she did.

Swanson plays a girl rushed into marriage with Swain by her mother, who is convinced that the big man is a successful capitalist. Her rejected suitor Conklin refuses to take no for an answer and accompanies the pair (and Mama) on the honeymoon, which takes place aboard a train. They race through the train, falling in and out of compartments, and staging a food fight in the dining car. A shortage of berths means that Mama has to share a bed with her daughter, while both men try to get in. Desperado Oklahoma Pete is also on board, and his effort to rob the passengers leads to mayhem. The action zips right along, moving at a quicker pace and featuring much rougher stuff than Swanson's Badger-Vernon pictures. Gloria even takes a pratfall, which she executes perfectly. Looking directly ahead, her mouth a small O, she falls straight backward, her technique and self-control exquisite.

Swanson was suited for slapstick. She was little enough to be hauled around and hoisted up with ease, and her timing was good. But she put her finger squarely on what made her Keystone performances successful: "I played [my comedy] like Duse."[37] She claimed she didn't get all the jokes in her pictures: "The fact that I was so serious made it twice as funny."[38] Without the size and middle-aged stodginess that Margaret Dumont brought to her Marx Brothers pictures, Swanson had something

of Dumont's straight-man sensibility. She was—however inadvertently—a hoot.

She was also wretched. *A Pullman Bride* played havoc with Gloria's
idea of herself as a budding romantic lead, and the chaos off-screen at
Keystone made it clear that there would be more where Conklin and
Swain came from. She groused, "I never worked with people like this and
they started throwing soup and pies around. I didn't like it at all. . . . You
could kill yourself, get [a] concussion. I wasn't a tumbler. I'd never practiced any of this sort of nonsense."[39] Swanson thought she had an understanding with Sennett that she was to be featured in more refined
comedies. She evidently believed she could be part of Keystone without
being defined by the studio's anarchic sensibility. Now she feared that at
any moment, a pie would have her name on it.

As a rule, Sennett preferred not to handle sweet young things roughly
onscreen. "Movie fans do not like to see pretty girls smeared up with pas-
try," he said. "Shetland ponies and pretty girls are immune."[40] Yet there
were always exceptions to the rule at Keystone, and under the pressure
of his tightening belt, Sennett was likely in no mood to accommodate
Swanson's pretensions to gentility. When she went to him complaining
about her latest picture, they had a frank talk about her future.

Sennett thought Swanson could have a career in comedy if she would
come down from her high horse. She could be another Mabel Normand.
Swanson rejected the offer imperiously: "'I'm sorry, Mr. Sennett,' I said,
'but I don't want to be another anybody.'" As usual Swanson tells a good
story, of how she weighed her gratitude to Sennett against her need to
be free "to act a whole new way." As Sennett held her contract aloft, "a
silent clock counted ten for both of us. I waited until he tore the contract
in two. Then I left."[41]

Mack Sennett took it all in stride. By the time Gloria defected, he had
grown accustomed to the passing parade. He offered a list of his alumnae
with pride: "Every talented person who ever worked for me, and this
with no exceptions . . . left the Sennett menagerie to make more money elsewhere. Turpin, Arbuckle, Langdon, Keaton, Murray, Swanson,
Chaplin, and even Mabel [Normand] eventually flew my roost." He
could not resist adding, however, "Only two come to mind with enormous bank accounts today, Charlie Chaplin and Harold Lloyd."[42] Sennett
was sure he would have the last laugh.

CHAPTER 3

Triangle

IF GLORIA SWANSON EVER SERIOUSLY CONSIDERED LEAVING MOVIES, her budding fame decided the question: she liked being famous. However, she wanted to make serious pictures. Everyone told her this was unlikely: "In those days, once you were a villain with a black moustache you were branded. Once you played butlers you played butlers for the rest of your life."[1] Swanson determined that her best chance was to approach a studio with both a comedy troupe and a dramatic section; at least she would be nearer to her ambition.

Garbed in a bottle-green suit with a squirrel collar for which she had plunked down the last of her Keystone cash, Swanson took the trolley out to Culver City. Triangle had survived the departure of its three founding directors, and film production was humming along.[2] Clarence Badger had landed at Triangle, and he immediately offered Gloria a part in his current short comedy. But she was after bigger things—preferably features—and more challenging work than the one-reelers Badger was in a position to provide.

To her surprise, her background in comedy led Jack Conway, a Triangle director with ten years' experience, to offer Swanson the lead in his new feature. He had seen her in *The Danger Girl*, he said, and needed just such a spitfire for *You Can't Believe Everything*, an action-oriented drama about honor and self-sacrifice. A feisty young woman, Patria, literally fights off unwanted suitors, and is later falsely accused of spending the night with one. She cannot clear her name without betraying the confidence of her crippled friend Jim, whose long illness has left him so despondent that he attempts suicide. Patria's courageous effort to rescue Jim meant that Swanson—a non-swimmer who was terrified of the water—would have to dive into deep water one dark night to save her costar.

The stunt gave Swanson a chance to look good while she behaved heroically. Patria would see her friend go into the water, then rip off her evening dress. Under it she would be wearing only a skimpy chemise known as a "teddy bare." Determined to make a success of her first feature, Gloria was reluctant to tell Conway she was afraid. The suave director's energetic competence made her want to rise to the occasion—or at least to the surface. So Swanson visited the local YWCA for swimming lessons, then stared at the people splashing about before bolting for home.

When the time came, the oily water off the Wilmington docks in San Pedro, where the government was building warships by day, did not calm her fears. Nor did the lack of electric lighting: the scene was illuminated only by flares. A fifteen-foot jump off a dock in the black of night might make for fabulous lighting opportunities, but the young actress needed all her courage to leap off what felt like the edge of the world. Gloria "raced onto the dock as though . . . shot out of a cannon."[3] Finally, she came sputtering up from the depths. Dog paddling frenetically, she clambered into a waiting boat and was quickly bundled into a blanket against the chilly night air. She had passed her first real acting test.

She had also developed a serious crush on her director, a married man. Jack Conway, like Gloria, was a high school dropout, but she found him "refined, sensitive, intelligent, and generous . . . he was amusing and unaffected and attractive besides."[4] Though others called Conway "aggressively heterosexual," Swanson claimed he refused her overtures, unwilling to mix business with romance.[5] However, he used her attraction to him to elicit her increasingly skillful performances.

Feature films required different techniques than the shorts to which Gloria was accustomed, and since Conway had come to directing from acting, he understood the other side of the camera in a way many directors did not. With his guidance Gloria learned how to modulate her performance for closer shots and how to sustain an emotion throughout a sequence. He also taught her to time her spoken lines so the intertitles used in silent pictures would not break the flow of her performance. Many images were cut in half by the titles, she explained: "You had to convey everything in the first few words of a line and still have something left for the end. You had to know where the titles were going to be. Listening and reacting had to be delayed, controlled. What seemed unnatural on the set became natural on the screen." Then you had to forget about it, or "the camera would catch you thinking."[6] The director even coached Gloria on how to do her hair and makeup.

Conway's straightforward style appealed to Gloria, who disliked intriguers and indirection. She enjoyed working with directors who were considered men's men, so long as they appreciated her contributions and treated her squarely. Absorbed by the new skills she was learning, Swanson found taking direction from Jack Conway like dancing with a skilled partner or "going to an elegant party everyday."[7] It was far different from the rude conditions at Keystone and far more to her liking.

The pace was nonetheless streamlined at Triangle. Features ran fifty-five minutes and were allotted around ten days' production time, so the days were long and busy. The excitement generated on the lot by the Conway-Swanson picture, however, made the front office take a greater interest in the new girl. They decided not to release *You Can't Believe Everything* until they had built interest in Swanson through some strategic casting and publicity. They hurried Gloria into her second and third films opposite two of Triangle's most reliable leading men. William Desmond played her opposite number in *Society for Sale*, a melodrama about an American model who tries to buy her way into British society by paying a poor aristocrat to introduce her as his fiancée. Of course, the impoverished man falls genuinely in love with her. Before the wedding she runs off with Lord Sheldon, a divorced libertine who turns out to be her long-lost father. She is of noble birth after all, has boatloads of money, and can marry the penniless aristocrat who loves her.

William Desmond was a Triangle stalwart who made ten or eleven features a year; he was forty to Gloria's nineteen. He had to put up with the star treatment the studio was giving the young actress, and to pose or wait around endlessly for the glamour shots they needed of her. Swanson got the feeling that both Desmond and her next leading man, J. Barney Sherry, were not happy about her gobbling up so much time and attention or about being used to support the studio's new acquisition rather than vice versa. Sherry was another Triangle workhorse. In *Her Decision*, he played the husband Gloria takes in order to support her pregnant-and-abandoned sister. Because Gloria, a stenographer, loves another man, Sherry lives platonically with her (though he, too, adores her). Eventually Gloria rejects her faithless beau and realizes she loves the selfless and devoted Sherry.

With three pictures prepared, the studio began what was for Triangle a publicity blitz, releasing *Society for Sale* in April 1918 and *Her Decision* a mere three weeks later. Theaters typically played features for a few days or at most a week, and constant turnover was crucial: it kept seats full. By flooding theaters with her pictures, however, Triangle was gambling that Gloria Swanson would find—or even create—an audience. Publicity materials mentioned that Gloria was "a former comedy queen" playing her first dramatic part.[8] Yet the studio was hesitant to trumpet Swanson's Keystone past, lest audiences reject her in more serious roles. They took a middle course, identifying Gloria for the benefit of anyone who knew her name or face without belaboring the comedy connection.

By the time of her two June 1918 releases, *Station Content* and the delayed *You Can't Believe Everything*, the studio was more confident of the young star's reception. They began claiming her comic background to highlight her multiple talents: "Though Gloria Swanson was known to be a very clever comedy actress in Keystone comedies," one press release states, "very few suspected that she possessed the emotional depth and histrionic power to perform roles of a serious order. [With her last pictures] she immediately sprang into the good graces of metropolitan critics and picture lovers." Triangle encouraged exhibitors to post pictures of Swanson in their lobbies to show off her beauty, which "merits decided attention."[9]

The films were zippy melodramas. In *Station Content*, Swanson is the bored and lonely wife of a telegraph operator stationed in a remote outpost. She leaves her husband, becoming first a successful Broadway actress and then the paramour of the railway owner. She saves both her husband and her lover when she stops a train from going over a broken trestle during a storm. This leads her inevitably back to her husband's side as the lights come up. Such shifts gave Gloria a chance to develop her range as an actress, and she liked being the strong, active heroine in the railway rescue scenes rather than the damsel in distress.

Once again, Triangle advertised Swanson's beauty but found a use for her comedy past by applauding her physical courage. "Any studio actress would have quailed at the thought of [riding down the tracks] and then pitching herself over a cliff after standing in the glaring light of the locomotive to stop its headlong flight to destruction. But Miss Swanson has a record for gameness and daring . . . acquired during her connection with Keystone comedies in which death-defying feats were an ordinary occurrence. She lives up to her record most commendably in this picture."[10] The studio also prepared paper throwaways printed with the line, "Nights with Gloria Swanson, Triangle star, at the Throttle," echoing the name of her popular Keystone Teddy short.[11] "This little girl is going to make good," the head of Triangle publicity proclaimed.[12]

By the summer of 1918, however, Swanson was finding her time on the "Triangle treadmill" exhausting, and much less glamorous than she had expected.[13] She was rushed from film to film, and it was plain hard work. Huge skylights above the actors made the sets stiflingly hot. Her colleague Pauline Curley remembered workers "bringing in buckets of ice water in which the actors could cool their arms."[14] Away from work there were compensations, including a new bungalow on Court Corinne, a step up from where Gloria and Addie had been living. She had her own car, too, a Kissel Kar Silver Special Speedster. But Wallace Beery was holding up the divorce his estranged wife craved. International politics helped prolong her marriage: married men were less likely to be drafted, and Beery was in no hurry to go to war.

Moreover, Swanson could see that her studio work would not be challenging for long. It was her good fortune—better luck than she probably realized—to be teamed at Triangle with extremely competent directors, including Frank Borzage, who also had acting experience and a subtle but sure hand with his players. Gloria had gained her footing quickly. Yet the only director with whom she really enjoyed working was Conway, and he was leaving Triangle. The peripatetic Conway seldom stayed anywhere for long, preferring to freelance. Mobility was part of the motion picture game, and Gloria soon felt ready to move on herself.

Making a change seemed simple: Swanson was not under contract at Triangle but working on a week-by-week basis. They had kept her busy, quickly raising her salary from $85 to $100 a week, but she considered herself a freelancer. An attractive offer appeared in the form of a call from Cecil B. DeMille. Summoned to his office at Famous Players-Lasky, Swanson came face to face with the man she would always consider her mentor in the motion picture industry. When DeMille invited her to work for him, she agreed immediately.

Nothing could have been more tempting. The 1916 merger of Adolph Zukor's Famous Players Film Company with Jesse L. Lasky's Feature Play Company had created a mega-studio, much more than the sum of its parts. The star power Famous Players-Lasky had assembled under its banner was impressive: it had six of 1918's top ten stars under contract. To be brought—by invitation, no less—into the company that was home to Mary Pickford, Marguerite Clark, Douglas Fairbanks, William S. Hart, and Wallace Reid showed real confidence in Swanson.

Then there was the magnetism of the man himself. DeMille had directed the first feature made in Hollywood, *The Squaw Man*; he and his brother, William, practically put the town on the map. As a cofounder of Lasky's Feature Play Company, there was no director more personally powerful than DeMille. He was "Almighty God himself" in the film industry.[15]

Swanson recalled her first impression of him: "Any notions I may have had of style or elegance evaporated the moment I was ushered into Mr. DeMille's paneled office. It was vast and somber, with tall stained-glass windows and deep polar-bear rugs. Light from the windows shone on ancient firearms and other weapons on the walls, and the elevated desk and chair resembled nothing so much as a throne. I felt like a peanut poised on tottering high heels."[16]

DeMille stood to welcome her. At thirty-seven he seemed "ageless, magisterial. He wore his baldness like an expensive hat, as if it were out of the question for him to have hair like other men. A sprig of laurel maybe, but not ordinary hair. . . . He came over and took my hand, led me to a large sofa and sat down beside me, and proceeded to look clear through me."[17]

When Swanson coolly informed Triangle's front office that she would be leaving for Famous Players-Lasky, they stopped her short. Because she had accepted a raise from the company, Triangle argued that Swanson had also accepted an implied contract for an extension of her services. Gloria was over eighteen and had knowingly accepted the pay hike; therefore she was committed to them. Unused to having his way blocked, DeMille at first refused to accept Triangle's reasoning. Swanson spent a long weekend biting her nails while the case went into arbitration. When the decision came, she was crushed: despite her high hopes of entering DeMille's high-powered sphere, she would be reporting to work at Triangle for the foreseeable future.

It was her first big professional disappointment, and Swanson liked having her will thwarted no better than DeMille. She felt like "a whipped puppy" when she was brought back into the Triangle office to sign her formal contract; signing the paper with a flourish and flinging herself out of the office did little to ease her wounded pride.[18] She felt keenly her difference from the established stars, who had others—usually family members—to help them manage their business affairs. Mary Pickford's mother had handled her career since Mary was a child. Adolph Zukor told Pickford he did not need to diet: "Every time I talk over a new contract with you and your mother I lose ten pounds."[19] Douglas Fairbanks and Charlie Chaplin relied on their brothers. Lillian and Dorothy Gish leaned on each other, their mother, and (Swanson suspected) D. W. Griffith. The Talmadge girls had each other; Joe Schenck, Norma's husband and a powerful film producer, also looked after his wife and her two sisters. Everyone else had a father or brother or uncle protecting his interests—everyone except Swanson, whose father was far away in the service and whose mother couldn't be bothered. The Triangle dispute hurt Gloria in part because it underscored her isolation. Forced to acknowledge that she knew little about business, she was nonetheless thrown back on her own resources.

Back at Triangle everything aggravated her. The pace was exhausting: Swanson had the lead in eight features in 1918, which amounted to a tenth of the studio's output. After the company's initial reluctance to put her under contract (which would have committed Triangle to carrying her salary whether she was in production or not), Swanson began to wonder if her paycheck accurately reflected her value. Pictures had a much higher chance of succeeding if a star's name appeared on the marquee. Top figures in the industry—except Pickford and Chaplin, who commanded astronomical sums—took home between $300 and $3,000 a week. One thousand dollars a week was no longer uncommon. The $100 Swanson had been proud to pocket now looked like a bargain rate for her talents.

Triangle enabled Swanson to make the unlikely leap from comedy shorts to dramatic features, and she continued to polish her craft there. Yet even someone with little formal education and no business advisor could see that the studio's efficiency worked against a performer's individual interests. In fact, the higher you rose at Triangle, the harder you were expected to work to push films out quickly. Before he left, Jack Conway had ridiculed the new studio motto "Clean Pictures for Clean People," criticizing the way Triangle lumped its productions together, the wheat mixing with the chaff in the promotional process.[20] In the second half of 1918, while she ran out her Triangle clock, Swanson quietly absorbed more professional lessons than how to shape her appearances before the camera.

Triangle's "Clean Pictures" campaign was part of Hollywood's belated response to the conflict in Europe. By the summer of 1918 the US had been at war with Germany for a year, but—aside from some early "preparedness" films—few pictures had dealt with the clash. As news of the bloody battles fought in France reached America and families started mourning their casualties, the studios finally began producing war pictures for the domestic market, encouraged by the government's recent decision to declare the film industry a vital enterprise.

Few pictures made during the war included combat scenes; however, many featured spies and secret agents. They were seldom subtle; the most rabid had names like *The Claws of the Hun*, *The Kaiser's Shadow*, or *The Prussian Cur*. Many of these films suggested that average citizens could play a role in the conflict. As Kevin Brownlow explained, "Audiences preferred propaganda about themselves. The films they went to see suggested that individuals determine the course of history."[21] Swanson portrayed one of those courageous citizens in a trio of melodramatic propaganda pieces.

Reporting for her next assignment somewhat dispiritedly, Swanson was surprised to find in Albert Parker another like-minded colleague. A transplanted New Yorker who began as a stage actor, Parker directed Swanson in two tales of self-sacrifice, blackmail, and personal redemption through patriotism. In each she was a young wife whose domestic problems have large, international implications. In *Shifting Sands*, her character has a secret she cannot reveal to her wealthy diplomat husband: that she is an ex-convict, wrongly imprisoned for—as studio publicity had it—"the crime of the shameless woman."[22] (Actually, she was framed for robbery by a rejected suitor, but "shameless" played better on advertising posters.) When the man whose lie sent her away reappears, he is no longer simply a lustful German—now he is a lustful German spy. He tries to blackmail Swanson to get state documents in her husband's possession. Gloria can only unmask him by coming clean about her own past.

Triangle thought it had a winner with *Shifting Sands*, which combined matrimonial and patriotic causes and allowed Swanson to wear both prison garb and a society matron's beautiful gowns. Sexual blackmail was a popular motif in the 1910s, and studio publicity expected women to recognize the young wife's dilemma: "How many homes are standing on SHIFTING SANDS because the husband and wife fail to tell ALL when they are wedded?" Publicists cautioned, however, that *Shifting Sands* was "not a war picture," but "a vital story of a woman's soul, crucified by the villainous bestiality of a pitiless persecutor who sank so low as to be treacherous to the country that harbored him, and who finally paid the penalty for his treachery."[23] The melodrama was paramount: nothing should disrupt movie patrons' enjoyment of the revelation of a young wife's sexual past.

The studio continued to bill Swanson as a "Triangle discovery" with *The Secret Code*, where she played a senator's wife who navigates the choppy waters of wartime diplomacy. Her husband's jealous female advisor—a German spy—almost persuades the senator that his wife is passing state secrets to the Kaiser via encoded messages in her crocheting. The ludicrous plot unravels when Swanson turns out to be nest-building: she is expecting a baby. The German threat had even infiltrated an American marriage.

Part German herself, Swanson was by turns entertained and disgusted by such cinematic fare, though thanks to her congenial director she was having "a perfectly marvelous time" at work once again.[24] Al Parker poked delightful fun at their patriotic scripts and paid Gloria solicitous attention, amusing her by adopting a British accent when he wanted to be stylish. He was another married man who was always promising to leave his wife (they remained married for thirty-five years).

One evening, he and Gloria were parked in a secluded spot near the Beverly Hills Hotel, when Wallace Beery suddenly appeared. He hauled off and punched Parker, knocking him flat and departing before Parker could splutter out a word. Swanson was aghast, worried that Beery would cite Parker as a co-respondent in their divorce suit. However, Parker quickly proposed a chivalrous solution: he would drive his car into a tree in order to explain his black eye.

Despite her dalliances with older married men, Swanson insisted everything was aboveboard: "I was a very strait-laced young lady. There was nothing promiscuous in my background. Marriage was the important thing and the moral thing and anything beyond that was bad. It was not in my code."[25] Life in Hollywood, however, was Gossip Central, and her neighbors at Court Corinne—including Gloria's underemployed Keystone colleagues Alice Lake, Maude Wayne, and Teddy Sampson—speculated endlessly about the romantic lives and extracurricular affairs of anybody the least bit famous. Gloria disliked the group's idle chatter, observing that the most spectacular stories were fueled by inaction and alcohol. "I would not have made a good nun or sorority sister," she observed ruefully.[26] Gloria gave her neighbors a wide berth; by day's end she was usually too exhausted to accept many invitations anyway.

She became friends with Sylvia Joslin, a divorced artist, and with actress Beatrice LaPlante, who left her native Toronto for Hollywood but had trouble parlaying her few movie roles into a career. She and Gloria had more fun away from the studio, anyway. They went out with Jack Conway and John Gilbert (whom Gloria found dull company, though she later said she "had come within an ace" of marrying Conway).[27] Bea was a sympathetic companion, Gloria's first real friend in California. They remained close for years.

While Swanson waited for her own divorce to become final, her mother's came through, and Addie quickly remarried. Gloria was unimpressed by Matthew Burns, "a small man with ginger hair and a ginger mustache. He had a funny voice and smelled of cough drops. . . . I could see no reason in the world why my mother should blush at the mention of this man's name."[28] Though she could not accept Burns as a replacement for her father, Gloria recognized that Addie, not yet forty herself, had a right to another chance at happiness, even if it was with this odd little man. With her mother's departure, however, she was lonely. Gloria begged Bea LaPlante to move in with her. Better yet, why didn't they spend some of Gloria's Triangle money and get a big house? She was aching to get away from Court Corinne.

The two friends rented a large, furnished house from Tyrone Power Sr. Displaying some of the careless grandiosity about money that characterized her star persona, Swanson also hired a maid and began giving parties, including several large gatherings for soldiers stationed in Los Angeles. She served hot dogs, sandwiches, and beer; they played gramophone records and danced. There were high-spirited, goofy games: they hauled a child's slide in from the yard, coated it with talcum powder, then slid down, shooting across the floor and into the empty dining room. Swanson laughed in later years at the memory of the soldiers' bottoms covered in powder. The house on Harper Avenue became her refuge: six days a week she played sophisticated older women, but on Sundays, she became a teenager again. She didn't miss running the Court Corinne gauntlet of half-buzzed, out-of-work actresses whose jealousy simmered beneath the surface.

As the war drew to a close, the film industry had a backlog of war movies to hustle into theaters, and Gloria had a sense of *déjà vu*: when Keystone got in trouble, it started pumping out shorter, cheaper pictures, with little concern for quality. Now Triangle, never on very firm financial footing, was wobbling. "Lightning" Hopper, known since Essanay for his speedy economy, was her new director, and he led the cast as he had back in Chicago, by "scream[ing] himself hoarse."[29] The excessively convoluted plot of *Wife or Country* featured Swanson as a stenographer who exposes a female-led spy ring. Eventually—but not soon enough— the German agent swallows poison and dies, freeing Gloria to marry the man she loves. Chalk up another patriotic triumph for the average working woman. In her memoirs, Swanson wrongly remembered herself as the character who took poison; by this point in her Triangle career she may well have felt like it. She had only disdain for the film's "overacted, overdirected, overpatriotic nonsense."[30] The company barely bothered to advertise its last, tired war pictures.

Swanson made one more feature at Triangle before she jumped ship. *Everywoman's Husband* was practically a dress rehearsal for the six sophisticated films she would make with Cecil DeMille. A young wife follows her mother's advice and keeps her new husband on a short leash, nagging and correcting him constantly. As a result he soon finds a lovely model to keep him company. When the wife learns that her own father took a mistress to escape her mother's "policy of domestic repression," she is horrified and sets out to regain her husband's love.[31] Decked out in the latest, most luxurious gowns, she recaptures her spouse. The picture presented an up-to-the-moment consumerist perspective on what keeps a partner attracted and attractive: fashionable clothes and current hairstyles. Yet even Triangle's in-house publicist commented, "Gloria Swanson's work is excellent, as usual, but she has not the opportunities in this production she should have." He felt she was the one "being held in leash."[32]

Triangle was foundering. Yet when the company manager told Swanson the studio would not be able to exercise its option on her contract, offering her the chance to end her work a few months ahead of schedule, the actress balked. Triangle had thwarted her opportunity with DeMille, and she was not inclined to release the studio from its obligation to her: she had several months' salary coming. Then the manager explained that DeMille had repeatedly tried to borrow Swanson and offered to let Famous Players-Lasky know she was now available. Her hopes reviving, Swanson agreed to move on.

She eventually realized that being forced to stay at Triangle was the best thing that could have happened: "It gave me another year and a half of experience. I grew up . . . in leaps and bounds."[33] At Triangle, she successfully made the transition from rough-and-tumble comedienne to elegant leading lady, a move the studio endorsed and plotted. Her first few Triangle pictures had shown Swanson as capable of stopping a runaway train and diving off a darkened pier into deep water, physical feats that recalled her Keystone knockabout days. By the time she left, however, she was cocooned in increasingly fabulous dresses but moving less and less. For the rest of her long and restless career, Swanson would do her best work in films that allowed her to wear gorgeous clothes *and* to caper like a Keystone comic. Whenever she managed both to parade and to romp, she would be in her element.

CHAPTER 4

The Lions' Den

SWANSON ALWAYS REMEMBERED HER FIRST SCENE FOR CECIL B. DEMILLE. She was in costume, packing a trunk, with lights and cameras trained on her. Suddenly a noise of whistles and car horns erupted, and people started dancing, hugging, and shouting for joy: the war was over. The euphoria on the lot seemed like a good omen to Gloria, who was also feeling jubilant.[1] For the second time she had landed, not only on her feet, but another rung up the professional ladder. However, she was too busy to take much notice of the world outside the studio gates: working for Mr. DeMille was a full-time job.

The new featured player found everything about working at Famous Players-Lasky impressive. The director was fully in charge, his control apparent even before the cameras began cranking on *Don't Change Your Husband*. DeMille called his cast and crew together to review the scenario, and Gloria felt she was part of a carefully designed project, not something flung together as quickly as possible. She also observed that no one volunteered any criticism of the director's plans.

She had already undergone another DeMille ritual. "No leading player was hired without benefit of a ceremony in the boss's office," said one longtime employee.[2] The director apologized to Gloria for trying to lure her from Triangle, fearing he had done her a disservice with her employers. Swanson, however, was not sorry at all. She had learned that when she suddenly became available, DeMille dismissed his leading lady. Though they were already two weeks into production and it meant starting over, he wanted Gloria for the part. This would have been unthinkable at Triangle.

DeMille encouraged Swanson to wander through the sets, familiarizing herself with the furniture and props furnishing her screen home. How wonderfully sensitive, she thought, to know that a woman would want to fuss with the décor: "I would walk around, open the magazines, make it look as if it had been lived in. [I would] try to work out some pieces of business that might denote the mood I was in."[3] The flowers in the vases were real; so were the furs and jewels. There was even violin music to set the mood.

DeMille had a plan for the young actress. He had been making lavish, expensive period pictures; now he wanted to capture something of the modern temper. Gloria could help him satisfy the public hunger for "modern stuff with plenty of clothes, rich sets, and action." He would not give up what Jesse Lasky called "spectacle stuff" but incorporate it into his tales of contemporary marriage.[4] DeMille's most recent picture, *Old Wives for New*, had dared to suggest that a mismatched couple would be better served by divorce than staying together. Adolph Zukor found this shocking and insisted on testing the picture with preview audiences, who were less shocked. *Old Wives* did brisk business.

DeMille's approach with Swanson and Elliott Dexter was simple. *Don't Change Your Husband* concentrates on the destructive impact of an average married woman's dissatisfaction with her husband. DeMille and scenarist Jeanie Macpherson devised an elegant premise: a modern marriage is in trouble, and divorce and a new, more desirable spouse seem the answer. But rather than embracing divorce, *Don't Change* presents it as a wrong move that will itself be corrected. After finding a new mate, the wife leaves him, too, reconciling happily with her first husband. Screwball comedies like *The Awful Truth* and *The Philadelphia Story* would have fun with this premise twenty years later.

The film's curious title came amid a barrage of marriage-oriented problem pictures, movies with names like *Should a Wife Forgive?* (and its opposite number, *Should a Husband Forgive?*). Other films asked *Should a Woman Divorce?*, *Should a Wife Work?*, *Should a Woman Tell?*, *Should She Obey?*, and—perhaps not surprisingly, given all the confusion—*Should a Girl Marry?* By 1920, one film advised a complete withdrawal from the field: *Don't Ever Marry*. If audiences were ready to patronize pictures on these topical questions, DeMille was happy to provide them.

DeMille's innovation was his exploration of a woman's fantasy life. In lavishly imagined scenes, Swanson's Leila sees three "priceless gifts" her silver-tongued seducer offers: pleasure, wealth, and love. Her wildly idealized vision of pleasure includes nymphs, doves, and diaphanous gowns—every romantic cliché in the book. For love we see a nearly naked Leila reclining in a sylvan scene, being fed grapes by a muscular, nearly naked faun.

The fantasy of wealth, however, is where DeMille goes overboard. Leila pictures herself in an opulent palace with marble pillars and tapestries. She wears a glittering, beaded, tightly fitted gown and elaborate headdress. Muscular men bear gifts, draping ropes of pearls around her neck. The throne on which she sits is, unbelievably, made of three huge black men in shimmering loincloths. The spectacular, excessive pageantry makes clear just how disappointed Leila will be with any one real man. A dissolve brings us back to the present and Leila back to herself; she can no longer tolerate her husband's "corned beef and cabbage existence." Is it any wonder?

Swanson's character was "a pagan little creature," clucked one reviewer.[5] Yet DeMille had done something clever with *Don't Change Your Husband*: he delivered a realistic portrait of life (as one title says) after "several dull gray years of matrimony"—a topic few movies have treated. The picture indulged the wife's complaints and her desires, inviting viewers to sympathize with Leila's disappointments. Then, after lowering the boom on her, DeMille provided a fairy-tale ending, reinstating Leila in her marriage to a good man who had cleaned up his own act. Audiences ate it up and clamored for more.

DeMille's new leading lady was impressed. The picture's budget was a good deal higher than what she was accustomed to, the money visible in the extravagant costumes, sets, and props. The young woman whose mother had dressed her to perfection, offering her for the appreciative scrutiny of family and friends, was now at the center of Cecil DeMille's fantasy, surrounded by what she saw as the best of everything, and being paid handsomely for it.

DeMille's direction impressed Swanson, too. He spoke privately to her about the action she was to perform in a scene, allowing her to work out the specifics of gestures and timing for herself. He was capable of terrifying rages when questioned too closely: "One day shortly after I started work on the film, a young actor asked Mr. DeMille if he would explain to him how he wanted him to play such and such a scene. 'Certainly not!' Mr. DeMille bellowed. 'This is not an acting school. I hired you because I trust you to be professional. *Professional!*' he thundered. 'When you do something wrong, *that* is when I will talk to you!'"[6]

This approach suited Swanson. Many early film directors pantomimed actions, expecting performers to mimic their gestures. Swanson disliked being shown what to do and was proud that DeMille never had occasion to thunder at her. To be safe, however, she spent her lunch breaks huddled in the projection room, watching the previous day's rushes with the director and crew. She rapidly observed a difference between her own skilled but intuitive performances and her colleagues' more controlled, expert acting. Eager to expand her repertoire, she began paying closer attention to her costars' performances and practicing her craft more consciously.

Her leading man, Elliott Dexter, had a wealth of acting experience; he also had the best scene in the film, when he realizes his wife has left him. Gloria watched the scene again and again, examining Dexter's performance and realizing how powerful film acting could be: "Here was what every woman who had ever left a husband wanted to see—how he looked when he first understood that she was gone. Motion pictures allowed her to be a fly on the wall at the most secret moment of her husband's life. No wonder people sat enthralled in darkened theatres all over the world in the presence of those big close-ups. Their effect was indelible."[7]

Swanson started her next picture after a brief break for the Christmas holidays. *For Better, For Worse* was less lavishly staged, but it too contained an elaborate fantasy sequence. Sylvia Norcross declares her beau (the reliable Elliott Dexter) a coward, agreeing to marry his rival in uniform directly after she has imagined herself in three different historical periods, sending three different soldier beaux off to war. First she is a Viking maiden, then a fair lady sending a warrior to the Crusades, and finally a Revolutionary lass waving farewell to her independence-minded young man. Again, the film explores contemporary marriage mores and the power of fantasy to motivate behavior; Sylvia makes a romantic choice she quickly regrets but gets a second chance because divorce is available.

These fantasy sequences could be inserted anywhere the director had a mind to put them. They stretched the boundaries of DeMille's home front narrative and created the prestigious look of a period film while holding the budget down. They became a trademark of his pictures with Swanson, making her seem a woman for all ages. Gloria loved playing the capricious Sylvia, whose fuller acquaintance with war matures her; she also loved the fantasy inserts, believing they deepened her contemporary character. She felt more at home on the set, thanks to Elliott Dexter's kindness: "I was clearly not used to making pictures with real jewels and real roses any more than I was used to being treated like a duchess by a director who behaved and spoke like a sultan."[8] There was a caste system in town, and Dexter and his actress wife, Marie Doro, helped Swanson make this crucial transition.

Her December 1918 contract with DeMille paid her $150 a week. Within four months she would get $200 weekly, and as much as $350 a week within two years. Swanson could not believe her luck. Although once again she had been romanced into accepting what Robert Birchard calls "a bargain-basement salary," she felt anything but exploited.[9] The nineteen-year-old was thrilled by the warm interest DeMille showed her and loved the sense that she was part of something glamorous, intelligent, and *au courant*.

The press was beginning to pay attention to Swanson, who was not above needling the studio just a little. "Since I have been working for Mr. DeMille," she told one reporter, "I am always broke. . . . Unless someone takes me in charge and curbs my wild extravagance I shall become a State charge." Her new director had whetted her appetite for beautiful things, and after a day at Famous Players-Lasky, her own house seemed shabby, her own clothes drab: "It's mighty hard to wear a robe costing say a thousand dollars . . . and then go to the dressing room and put on my comparatively poor best."[10] Such stories—whether written entirely or helped along by FPL publicists—simultaneously exploited and cautioned against Hollywood profligacy. These stories were also darkly prophetic: Swanson really was developing new and lavish tastes. Her fame, associated with extraordinary wealth, created a standard she would struggle to maintain.

By and large, Los Angeles society turned up its nose at movie people, whom they considered *arrivistes*. Many wealthy California homeowners had seen their lawns churned up, their windows broken, and their flowerbeds demolished by camera crews shooting without authorization. FPL's workers were no different than Keystone's or Triangle's in this regard; they too snatched shots wherever they could. Cinematographer James Wong Howe remembered that the DeMille crew all wore puttees to help them make a quick getaway: "[We] could clear the picket fences and not get our cuffs caught."[11] (Howe also remembered working late: without enough money to stay in a hotel, he slept in Swanson's silk-sheeted bed on the set.) There was otherwise little interaction between residents of the new and the old Los Angeles. "We had nothing in common with them," Colleen Moore explained.[12]

One evening at the Ship Café, however, Swanson met an attractive, wealthy young man from Pasadena with an intoxicating combination of good looks and charm who challenged her ideas about almost everything. Craney Gartz came from established California money (his mother had inherited the Crane bathroom fixtures fortune) and had the exquisite

manners, clothes, and education to prove it. He disliked and disapproved
of the movies—as he was expected to do—but not because they lacked
respectability. He thought they were a waste of time and a distraction
from what really mattered: the struggles of people like Emma Goldman
and Joe Hill and the ideas of Freud, Nietzsche, and Marx. Craney's family put its money where its mouth was: his mother paid the legal fees to
defend anarchists, socialists, and others clamoring for workers' rights and
political freedom.

He was not the staid, straitlaced society man she would have predicted, given his vast wealth. While waltzing her divinely around the
dance floor, Craney insisted that Gloria admit her work in motion pictures was ridiculous, a waste of energy and talent. He knew, he claimed,
that she was simply waiting for a man to marry her and take her away
from all of it. Not, he hastened to add, that he would ever be that man—
marriage was not for him. Anyone with modern ideas could see it was
dead—hadn't Ibsen proved it? And Isadora Duncan? Swanson was
dumbfounded. This gorgeous young man, who hummed softly to her as
they danced, dropped a dozen intriguing names in five minutes, while
vehemently rejecting the sacred goal of marriage. He was irresistible, and
the battle was on: she would change his mind.

Craney took Gloria to the Pasadena Country Club, where motion picture people were generally refused admission. He lectured her about politics and gave her cartons of books to read: Shaw, Lawrence, Joyce, Wilde.
He urged Gloria to educate herself. He talked endlessly about wanting
to go to Russia, the most exciting place on earth. He had nothing but
contempt for the US government and could name all the ways America
had failed to live up to its promise. It was only a matter of time until the
people rose up and took their country back. Craney never stopped talking about his beliefs, which Swanson thought were hopelessly idealistic.
The only time he was quiet was when he was kissing her, which he did
expertly: "He was an incredibly dashing and handsome man, and in spite
of my desire to tell him he should go fly a kite, I found myself physically
content to nestle in his arms."[13] She could not get enough of his black
curly hair and chiseled features and knew she was falling in love.

Craney soon declared his love for her and asked Gloria to spend the
night with him. She was stunned by his direct approach and tried fruit-
lessly to explain her commitment to the ideal of marriage. They bickered
continually, then fell time after time into each other's arms. Gartz refused
to hold a job because he didn't need the money and wouldn't take the
salary from someone who did. Swanson couldn't take a man who didn't

work seriously; her own work ethic was too strong. ("I intend to work until I drop dead," she told an interviewer that year.)[14] She nonetheless found herself considering everything in terms of what Craney would say about it. Though he had never worked a day in his life, she had to concede that he knew a lot. When Gloria went up in an airplane for the first time, she couldn't wait to tell Craney, a flier himself, and crowed over having gotten airborne without his help. Yet she loved his soft heart; he was always picking up stray dogs and bringing them to Gloria to adopt.

Their arguments followed a pattern: "Craney couldn't understand why I wouldn't give up pictures and run away with him. I told him I wasn't going to live with anybody I wasn't married to. I wasn't even divorced. He said if I had lived with Wally for those two months *without* getting married, I would never have had all the trouble I'd had getting a divorce." When she told him she had a contract with Mr. DeMille, "he said he was worth $30 million and could buy and sell Cecil B. DeMille any day of the week. I told him he could not touch Mr. DeMille if he were standing on stilts."[15] If Craney seemed immovable, Swanson recognized her own strong stubborn streak. She too would do as she pleased, and more than anything else, it pleased her to take direction from Mr. DeMille. (Not that she did whatever DeMille demanded: when he wanted Gloria to have her nose bobbed and straightened, she flatly refused. If lighting her was a challenge, so be it.)[16]

When the cast and crew began work on her third DeMille film, Swanson sensed unusual excitement in the air. The property was prestigious, even for FPL: a well-known stage play by J. M. Barrie, the Scotsman who had created Peter Pan. Barrie's friend Arthur Conan Doyle had suggested the premise of *The Admirable Crichton*: a king and a sailor are shipwrecked together, and the natural leader replaces the one society has anointed. Barrie made the king an earl and provided him with a haughty, marriageable daughter. The sailor Conan Doyle envisioned became a butler in Lord Loam's household, and the family's near-disaster at sea occasioned its new domestic arrangements in an island paradise.

Barrie's work had the kind of cachet Hollywood understood: it was clever but not highbrow, combining fantastic escapes with upper-crust settings and characters. To assuage fears that the film's name would signal a nautical story (even Jesse Lasky had been mispronouncing "admirable" as "admiral"), and to sidestep the unpronounceable "Crichton," DeMille changed the title to *Male and Female*.[17] He also shifted the story's emphasis to the love story between the overindulged, headstrong Lady Mary and the strong, virile Crichton.

The picture was a "special production," which meant it had been allotted a hefty budget. FPL planned a major ad campaign, and Lasky insisted on procuring high-quality stills. Karl Struss, the great Pictorialist photographer, predicted correctly that the pictures he made of Swanson were worth the time and trouble they took. They would be among the most iconic images of the actress: "Had she known me better she would have put her arms about [me] and given [me] a lovely smack!"[18] (DeMille's special production also attracted the eighteen-year-old Walt Disney, who earned $12 a week sketching ads for the film.)

DeMille devoted particular effort to *Male and Female*'s big sequences. One of the most famous shows Swanson entering her morning bath. The spoiled young aristocrat lounges her way across her enormous, extravagantly appointed boudoir. Two attendants open her robe, holding it wide to make a screen as she steps down into a sunken tub. Swanson's nakedness is suggested rather than revealed: when the robe is lowered she luxuriates, partially submerged, in the bath. Then she is helped from the pool and led across the room to a shower, where she is rinsed with rosewater. Peekaboo is the game, and DeMille issued Swanson explicit directions about how to play it. One account has him shouting, "Prolong it! Relish the smell of the rosewater." Calling for "more rapture," he told Gloria to "make the fans feel like they are going down with you."[19] Swanson claimed that DeMille protected her privacy on the closed set: "I was covered—every bit of me—until I got down into the pool and you saw my arm and shoulders, which is what you'd see in an evening gown."[20]

The actress's nudity was only part of the fascination. The setting, a rarely seen area of the home, was equally compelling to audiences. After *Male and Female*, bathroom scenes became a fetish with DeMille. He repeatedly created luxurious spaces gleaming with chrome and crystal, marble and mirrors, full of products designed to beautify and perfect the body. Some of these scenes aroused consternation: the American Legion of Decency protested that they weren't, well, decent. Yet DeMille remained master of this space, and his vision of how the wealthy washed up persisted in the public imagination.

The director's affection for a well-appointed bathroom could apparently be traced to his childhood memories of a weekly dip in a dark, discolored barrel. As DeMille recalled, "The cockroaches used to come out, look at you and say, 'Hi, boy.'"[21] If cleanliness is next to godliness, Hollywood was holier thanks to C. B. DeMille. Soon stories about the stars' bathrooms appeared, tales of sunken tubs and toilet seats upholstered in sable. To the end of her days, Swanson denied having solid gold taps on her bath.

Male and Female created plenty of opportunities to show off Swanson's lovely figure. In the shipwreck scene, she is trapped in her luxury cabin as water pours in. At last she clambers out, her low-cut, soaking wet dress clinging to her curves. The ship was in fact battered against the rocky shore; leading man Tommy Meighan almost drowned, stuck between the tossing boat and the rocks. Swanson cut her legs trying to get onto dry land, and DeMille, admiring her game attitude, gave her a nickname: "Young Fellow." All this time the Young Fellow was covered in skintight, dripping satin.

The rented yacht taking the company to Santa Cruz Island for two weeks' shooting also encountered severe turbulence, turning even the experienced sailors green. No one could touch the gorgeous picnic prepared for the trip. Gloria's dog fell overboard and had to be rescued. However, the mishaps brought the company together, and they had more fun than anyone getting paid had a right to have. The merry group roughed it, living in tents like the castaway British household they played onscreen. Gloria bunked in with Lila Lee, who played a scullery maid, and the two had a marvelous time figuring out how to steal scenes back from Theodore "Daddy" Roberts, who was the displaced Earl. They spoke in mock English accents like their characters, relaxed together, and cheered each other on. "We were all strangely happy and alert and in touch with one another. We behaved as I had never known a bunch of movie people to behave. We seemed to be in a crucible of excitement and tenderness," Swanson recalled.[22] She credited DeMille with all of it.

Tommy Meighan, a tall, strapping, forty-year-old Irishman, was a sturdy, intelligent partner for Swanson. (A 1921 screen acting manual called them "a pair excellent in its screenic balance.")[23] The happily married Meighan enjoyed flirtations with his leading ladies, and his affability made everything fun: when Gloria as Lady Mary bit Meighan's arm too energetically, he laughed and offered her some salt and pepper.[24]

The story called for Meighan, dressed as Crichton in a fur loincloth, to rescue Swanson by shooting a leopard, which he then drapes across his shoulders. The grateful young woman (also clad in skimpy animal skins) then drapes herself on Meighan. However, the chloroformed leopard started reviving partway through the scene, and Meighan began swearing under his breath. Swanson recalled, "When the scene gets to a point where he's supposed to throw [the cat] aside, he's got the strength of a giant and this thing goes flying through the air and goes blunk. . . . All the men, you know, they saw one drop of blood and they had a fit."[25]

The infamous "Lion's Bride" sequence proved Swanson's mettle beyond any doubt and provided one of the indelible images of the silent era. In a fantasy insert the former butler, costumed as a king, lords it over a recalcitrant virgin slave, Swanson in a low-cut gown. The king gives her a choice: offer herself to him or be fed to the lions. The scene restaged a painting that had hung over Gloria's grandmother's piano; it had always frightened the child. Nonetheless, she gamely pulled on her elaborate costume for the scene and prepared for her biggest screen moment yet.

The slave girl was gorgeously—if improbably—swathed in a long, backless dress with ropes of pearl beading, a costume so heavy Swanson could hardly walk in it.[26] An enormous headdress of white peacock feathers, which the superstitious studio hairdressers deemed unlucky, completed the outfit. The young slave drew herself up proudly and descended, one slow step at a time, into the black lacquered swimming pool that served as the lions' den, watched by half a dozen big cats—and two trainers, positioned out of camera range. A second later, one of the lions leaped toward the top of the pool, landing a dozen feet from Swanson. "He stared at me, I stared at him," she recalled. "In another second I was whisked off my feet, thrown up to the camera stand, and from there I was thrown to somebody else and somebody else and before I knew it they had me outside this enormous set."[27]

She recovered with a glass of sherry before going back—literally—into the lion's den. Thirty years later, actress Lois Wilson vividly recalled Gloria perching atop one of DeMille's high stools, preparing for another take. "She didn't weigh one hundred pounds soaking wet," Wilson said, shuddering. "Career or no career, no one would ever have made me do that."[28] Crew members were carrying broomsticks, chairs, and washing boards to defend themselves. Though one lion watched Swanson closely, his head bobbing up and down with each step she took, on the second try she managed to get to the bottom of the pool, and they got the shot. "It was a matter of counting, one-two-three-GO and I did, pulling up as many beads over my head as I could and scrambling up the stairs and stumbling and everything else. That was a day's work."[29]

The film's biggest moment was still to come, as Swanson posed with a lion stretched out across her naked back. DeMille asked the actress discreetly whether she was menstruating: if the lion scented blood, she could be in danger. Trembling, Swanson took her place on the floor, her back covered with a piece of canvas so the lion's paws would not scratch her and draw blood. Karl Struss remembered shooting the scene through a hole in the bars of the cage; DeMille "was standing outside with a gun in his hand trained at the lion in case anything should go wrong and was more scared than [Gloria] was."[30] As Swanson looked out through the cage, she saw her father, who had arrived in California to visit his daughter, only to watch her being sacrificed.

The trainers positioned the lion—who was not tranquilized—across Swanson's back, then slowly pulled the canvas shield aside. "There is something about facing danger that is not quite so bad as having to close your eyes or turn your back to it," she recalled. "I had my back to this animal and I couldn't see him because my eyes were closed." The whip cracked, the lion roared, and the cameras turned. Swanson never forgot the feeling of the lion's breath on her back: "It was the most fantastic sensation, like hundreds of vibrators from the tips of your toes to the ends of each hair on your head. Every atom of my body vibrated when the lion roared."[31] Even recalling it in later years made her shiver. Yet she also wondered as she lay there if her demanding, excitable director might not shoot her if she failed to make good in the scene.

"My heart was doing a jig," she recalled, as she was led shaking from the set.[32] DeMille claimed to be relieved to see Gloria sniffling, at last showing some sign of emotion; she was a woman, not just his "Young Fellow." He took her to his office and brought out a tray of jewels, inviting her to choose one as a reward. She perched on his lap and considered the dazzling array before selecting a tiny mesh purse with a large square sapphire. Then she was on her way to see the first man she had ever loved.

That evening when Gloria left the studio on her father's arm, Captain Swanson and his daughter had not seen each for almost five years. He was transferred to the Philippines a year before Gloria and Addie went west; when America entered the war, he went to France. The Swansons divorced in 1918, and it was another year before Joseph, still in uniform, arrived in California. Thinner, with bloodshot eyes and a nervous manner, he seemed ten years older. He also seemed bewildered by the change in his daughter. Although he had always urged her to have "violin strings" (the family shorthand for guts), Joseph was alarmed when he learned Gloria wanted to take flying lessons.[33] He begged her to promise she would not fly again, a pledge she made reluctantly. She hardly knew the man she once thought knew everything. It was no wonder that when she introduced Joseph to her director, she made a revealing verbal slip: "Daddy," she said, gesturing from Captain Swanson to Cecil DeMille, "I want you to meet my father."[34]

Gloria hoped her father would take an active interest in her affairs. Even as she reveled in her new success and her work with DeMille, the young woman often felt alone: "Everybody had somebody to fight battles for them or stand between them and the precipice . . . I had no one."[35] Yet Joseph seemed out of his depth, and Gloria realized that the unhappy man had burdens of his own. He had not recovered from the loss of her mother (he would never remarry), and his war experiences had taken their toll as well. Her roommate, Bea, thought Captain Swanson might have "the army disease"—a dependence on narcotics—which terrified Gloria.[36]

Since Addie, now remarried, refused to see her ex-husband, Gloria felt responsible for him. She had been cruelly disappointed by Wallace Beery's failure to shelter or advise her, and now it looked like she might end up supporting her father. At a loss about how to talk to Joseph about drinking or drugs, she nonetheless determined to make him comfortable and happy for as long as he stayed in California. There was no point in expecting more than he was able to give.

As if on cue, another older man crossed her path. A tall, distinguished gentleman in his early forties sent his card to Gloria's table one night while she was dining with her father and Bea. Herbert Somborn was the sophisticated, self-confident president of Equity Pictures, the distribution company which handled the films of Clara Kimball Young. He carried Miss Young's compliments to Gloria and invited her to dine at Young's home the following week. Swanson was initially more intrigued by the prospect of meeting Young than she was by seeing Somborn again. Mostly forgotten today, Young was one of the most admired stars of the early film industry, known for her worldly roles and dignified grace. With her lover, director Harry Garson, Young had begun her own production company and controlled her career to an unprecedented degree. Now under contract to Equity, she was at the pinnacle of her profession when Gloria accepted Herbert Somborn's invitation.

Meeting Miss Young did not disappoint. She had a magnificent home and was a charming hostess. Young had worked with Gloria's former director Al Parker on her upcoming picture *Eyes of Youth*. It was a top-drawer production in every way, and Somborn predicted it would be an enormous hit. The two women compared notes on working in show business, Young advising Gloria to be generous with her fans. The young actress was happy to be guided by the experienced pro, noting with wide-open eyes the superb jewels Miss Young was wearing to dine at home.

Gloria was most impressed, however, with the older woman's ability to talk business on an equal footing with the men at the table. Young discussed "stock issues, mortgages, bylaws, injunctions, and powers of attorney with the same confidence other women might display in reciting a recipe for angel food cake." The movie business, Gloria realized, could make a woman "completely independent—turning out her own pictures, dealing with men as equals, being able to use her brain as well as her beauty, having total say as to what stories she played in, who designed her clothes, and who her director and leading man would be."[37] Swanson's words describe the path she herself would forge in the years ahead. The postwar period in Hollywood offered new opportunities for women who were strong enough—and determined enough—to seize them. The memory of her encounter with Clara Kimball Young lingered with Swanson, who was beginning to realize how lucky she had been to land right where she was.

While Swanson was observing her hostess, Herbert Somborn was observing her. He recognized that the rising star had much in common with his partner Harry Garson's leading lady. Like Young, Gloria had enormous presence, a confident bearing, and a refined quality that did not hide a spark of stubbornness. Both actresses had a rare ability to wear clothes and shine in both comedy and drama. Somborn's courtship of Swanson reflected what he had learned by watching his own business partner court and then manage Clara Kimball Young. He moved quickly yet deliberately, wooing Gloria with his attentiveness and sophistication more than his passion. He sent her a cunning basket of flowers and mosses that was subtler than the showy arrangements Craney Gartz sent daily. Somborn seemed respectful of Gloria, but underneath she sensed a powerful man used to getting his way.

She was fascinated by his knowledge of the entertainment industry; over their increasingly frequent dinners, Herbert helped Gloria see the movie business as a business. He was shocked to learn she had no agent and no manager. He knew Gloria revered Mr. DeMille but gently wondered if her contract was all it should be. Once again, Gloria began to dream of a man who could guide her through the Hollywood maze.

Somborn did not offer to become that agent or that manager; he was much too busy with Equity Pictures. He continued to date Gloria while conducting his business on both coasts.

She looked forward to her evenings with Somborn, partly as a relief from the demands Craney Gartz was making. The pair continued to fight and make up, make up and fight. "With us, a fight could start over anything," she recalled. "On long drives in his car we always got into arguments. I had to be ready to walk home in my dancing shoes." The people Gloria knew talked about the movie business avidly; Craney talked about movies only to sneer at them. The fantasy sequences Swanson found so stirring in her DeMille films Craney dismissed as trite rubbish. She defended her mentor: "Mr. DeMille with his pictures was doing more to change the world than all Craney's talk. He was encouraging people to dream dreams, to *want* to be millionaires."[38] When Craney came on the set of *Male and Female* and loudly derided the silliness of motion pictures, Gloria stomped off but couldn't stay angry with him. Although she took a perverse pleasure in arguing with Gartz and felt she more than held her own, Gloria began to tire of the pull between their strong attraction and Craney's endless demand that she give up the work she loved.

After an evening of close, slow dancing, Gartz presented Gloria with a white-gold diamond bracelet and asked her to come home with him right then and make love. She refused, unwilling to risk compromising her divorce from Beery. More importantly, she wanted marriage, and Craney scorned the idea. All the married people he knew were miserable; marriage was a corrupt, moribund institution. Just as he had mocked DeMille and the business of making movies, now he mocked Gloria as a bourgeoise who was afraid to love him without society's permission. She accused Gartz in turn of fearing that she cared only for his money; he didn't trust her enough to marry her.

The two quarreled bitterly, and she flung his gift back at him. Gartz had landed one blow, however, that Gloria could not deflect. He said she did not trust him, either: she would not risk a career-ending scandal, lest their relationship sour and she not be able to return to show business. As someone who had learned to rely on herself, Gloria thought things over, refusing his calls and slowly realizing that Craney had gotten it right. They were at a standoff.

Herbert Somborn, she felt, would never put her in such an ugly position. After a hard day's work for DeMille—work she had no intention of giving up, thanks all the same—the older man presented a pleasant, low-key diversion. She felt no passion for Herbert, but she admired his intelligence, his unruffled demeanor, and his quiet, determined pursuit of her. He had exquisite manners: he had a small gardenia tree delivered with his apology when he was late. Another time Gloria found a jade necklace tucked into a bunch of flowers he sent. After Craney's demanding, argumentative, restless fervor, Herbert's attentions were soothing; Gloria felt "totally safe" with him.[39] Before she knew it, he was proposing marriage: "I didn't know what to reply. I hardly knew the man." She stammered that she was not sure how soon her divorce would be final. Herbert was undeterred—he wanted only her pledge. He promised to call for her answer in a week, and Gloria understood from his tone that "he was much too busy ever to consider placing a second such call."[40]

She considered Somborn's romantic declaration as she might a business proposition, wanting to see in this stranger a careful, deliberate man who would care deliberately for her: "He was a restful person to be with. He did everything well. He never raised his voice, but he always seemed to get what he wanted. . . . He kissed well, without any awkwardness or detachment. He seemed to be saying that although he didn't have the time or inclination for even a few hours of flirtatious petting, I could expect him to make love passionately, seriously, and with thorough competence, for many years to come."[41]

Gloria must have been tired and strained indeed, to make Herbert Somborn's restfulness so attractive. At twenty, with a marriage and miscarriage behind her, she had been in the movie business for almost five years. Careening back and forth between the impetuous, headstrong Craney Gartz and the sober, responsible Herbert Somborn, her head alight with visions of independence, jewels, and stately homes, Gloria felt she deserved a break. Craney was outraged that she was taking Herbert's offer seriously: did she know he was a Jew? For all his radical talk, Swanson believed Craney was worried about what his country club friends in Pasadena—"where Jews, actors, and dogs were usually lumped together"—would say.[42] After a "very, very bad quarrel," she threw him out.[43]

Craney made one last offer—not the proposal of marriage for which Gloria longed, but a plan to guarantee her financial independence during her lifetime and to make her his heir. However, he absolutely refused to marry, insisting they had to be free to leave each other. If she had hoped that Somborn's proposal would push Craney to pop the question, Gloria at last acknowledged defeat. "Neither of us could ever give in," she reflected. "The strongest, perhaps best, part of our relationship had been arguing like spoiled brats about things we believed in. It was possible that neither of us could endure the idea of resolving our arguments once and for all and living maturely together. Nevertheless, until the instant he drove away, I wanted—I almost willed—him to kiss me and drag me off with him."[44]

The sexual excitement, coupled with vehement arguments about values and the conviction that there is only one way to stand in the world, sounds a lot like adolescence. When she bid farewell to Craney Gartz, Swanson relinquished the part of herself that might have struggled effectively and productively, albeit with a less determined partner, to find her own middle course. She chose instead to accept the guidance of a surrogate father, a well-tailored, confident, and cultivated man twice her age. The next weekend, when Herbert called for her, Gloria told him quietly that she would be his wife. It was the partnership of a passionate woman who was not yet sure how to channel her passions and a businessman whose business would hit a slump just as his wife hit her stride.

CHAPTER 5

In the Family Way

THE BUZZ ABOUT *MALE AND FEMALE* WAS HEADY, AND FPL WANTED Swanson right at its center. The studio sent Gloria and her grandmother Bertha to New York for the film's premiere at the palatial Rivoli Theatre on Broadway, even springing for a private drawing room on the train east. The days of Swanson having whole railcars to herself were not far off.

Hungry for self-improvement, Gloria read thirty-seven Haldeman-Julius paperbacks on the five-day train trip. The distinctive Little Blue Books were inexpensively bound paperbacks that promised "a University in Print." They offered Gloria a crash course in the classics she had missed in school and whetted her appetite for more learning. It is wonderful to picture the young actress pondering a volume of Plato as the train clicked along, or cackling over Rabelais. Using the train as her portable class-room became a lifelong habit; Swanson enlarged her perspective as she traversed the country.

Male and Female remains memorable for its humor, its modernity, its sense of luxury, its spicy sexual combativeness, even its campiness. The New York and Boston papers liked it, though *Photoplay*'s reviewer car-ried a barb in his quill of plaudits: "A truly gorgeous panorama," the picture was also "a typical DeMille production—audacious, glittering, intriguing, superlatively elegant, and quite without heart," like a flower "glowing with all the colors of the rainbow and devoid of fragrance."[1] Audiences nevertheless went mad for *Male and Female*, and it grossed a million dollars, earning back almost ten times its production costs. Benjamin Hampton observed in 1930 that the picture followed "an al-most perfect recipe for box office success, filled with comedy, romance, thrills, and sex appeal, the latter element being supplied principally by Gloria Swanson." Since the postwar audience was "fundamentally curi-ous about only money and sex," Hampton claimed, "DeMille was in no further doubt about the kind of picture he would make."[2]

Both Swanson's performance and her stunning costumes were noted approvingly; for the first time, she was getting the star treatment. Gloria herself was primarily excited about seeing her friends in New York. Medora Grimes and June Walker came up to her suite at The Plaza, yet things seemed different: "Everyone acted a little funny, as if I had changed."[3] Perhaps it was all the newspaper reporters requesting interviews, or the artists showing up to do pictures of Swanson. She was beginning to be recognized in public; even her visit to an art gallery got press coverage. Perhaps it was the modern attitudes she evinced in her interviews: the match between DeMille's racy pictures and their young star's progressive opinions seemed perfect. Journalists wanted to know Swanson's thoughts about love, marriage, and especially divorce.

She obliged them: "All marriages are not love marriages. When two people stand before the church altar, it is not always God who is joining them. More often it is expediency, or a desire for social position, or money, or even curiosity. . . . Such marriages should not last. No mistake should be irretrievable. After all, marriage is just a game. The more elastic the rules, the less temptation there is for cheating . . . divorce should be made more easy, instead of more difficult." She also liked divorce as a subject for movies: "Without it we would go back to the same milk-and-water hokum again." The availability of divorce meant that married couples would keep courting rather than taking each other for granted. The young woman who proclaimed defiantly to reporters that she "believe[d] in divorce as an institution" would take Husband #2 before the year ended.[4]

Swanson's "shocking sermons" alarmed the studio. Fearful that DeMille's pictures would be banned in Boston, FPL publicists tried to divert the conversation to sartorial topics. They assigned costumer Clare West to accompany Swanson to interviews, to keep attention focused on the actress's hair and clothing. "I was too outspoken, so they tried to tone me down," Swanson remembered.[5] Almost immediately, newspapers started carrying reports of her fabulous gowns while putting distance between the actress and her femme fatale screen persona. Swanson "wants it distinctly understood," said one article, "that she is not a vampire, either in reality or on the screen."[6] She told another reporter it wasn't the "languid, oriental type" who was the real-life home wrecker but "the little, fluffy-haired miss with the innocent eyes that makes men forget their wives."[7] The only kind of indulgence Gloria sought in New York was "a wonderful orgy of shows, clothes, and other festivities."[8]

Swanson was "Exhibit A" on a prescribed round of society visits. She went to the homes of several of New York's wealthiest and oldest families, coming away disappointed: "It wasn't nearly as interesting as Mr. DeMille had made it seem in the movies. I looked at them and they looked at me. . . . I didn't bother to go back again."[9] Motion pictures were still considered disreputable in certain circles. They subjected young women to influences their parents could not control, including modern ideas about sex equality, and to the attentions (welcome or unwelcome) of the men who loitered about the theaters. Irving Berlin even had a hit song about it: a well-dressed young woman halts in front of a movie theater, telling her date, "If That's Your Idea of a Wonderful Time, Take Me Home." In 1919, the New York establishment was reluctant to embrace a movie actress, especially one trumpeting the attractions of divorce.

Male and Female nevertheless generated bags of fan mail and was held over in city after city. Far from being banned in Boston, evidence was mounting that a star had been born. The pecking order in Hollywood during this period was "extra, bit player, leading lady or man, featured player, star," and Swanson was hurtling toward the top.[10] Before *Male and Female*, FPL publicists had tried out a sporty persona for the actress. She was photographed duck hunting (allegedly her favorite pastime), holding a rifle, and removing an egg from a bird's nest. Readers were told that Swanson's friends considered her a female Douglas Fairbanks: "When the fishing season opens it is Gloria, the glorious, who catches the first trout and who is first on the trail of the deer [during] hunting season."[11] With the success of *Male and Female*, however, FPL realized that Swanson was a horse of a different color. From now on, publicity efforts would concentrate on her glamour.

Now Swanson was pictured in her dressing room with her personal hairdresser, an African-American woman named Hattie, dreaming up the elaborate styles she wore in her films. Fan magazine readers got tips on how to reproduce the Center Marcelled Part with Low Pompadour (an informal style good for under a hat), the Gloria Swanson Band (a more formal effort), and the Beehive (suitable for evening dress, with silk ropes wound diagonally over its height). Swanson proclaimed, "There is an appropriate coiffure for every woman for every occasion. One would not think of wearing a negligee at a formal dinner. And yet many women, through carelessness, make just as grave a mistake in the matter of their hairdresses."[12] Going behind the scenes at the studio let fans believe they knew Gloria intimately (see how she creates the illusion!), even as she remained marvelously distant (in her private dressing room with her personal hair stylist).

In fact, Swanson was fast becoming a trendsetter, both in big cities and small towns: the *Los Angeles Times* called her "a sort of fad with young women all over the country, so far as her striking little mannerisms and her particular manner of dressing is concerned."[13] *Photoplay* concurred: "Gloria is the rage. She is imitated wherever films are shown! She is a la mode. We'll have Gloria perfumes and powders and Gloria hats and Gloria gowns. Somebody will write a song about her. . . . Where will it all end?"[14] Features on Swanson's costumes appeared in papers nationwide: the tightly fitted moleskin dress, the gown with the black and white pearl train (*"every* gown had a train," Swanson recalled), the fan of peacock feathers, the sables and ermines that wrapped her, the real jewels she wore, the magnificent flowers she carried.[15]

Before DeMille, there were few wardrobe departments. Actors supplied their own costumes; director Dudley Murphy got his first Hollywood job as an extra in *Male and Female* because he owned a tuxedo, the only requirement of his walk-on part.[16] No one, however, possessed the kind of outfits Swanson was wearing in her pictures. Soon feature stories began positioning the actress herself as a regular gal who wished she could take all those gowns home. FPL publicists let it be known that every evening, Gloria had to hand the jewels she had worn over to the detectives hired to keep an eye on them during filming. Back in the vault they went.

Swanson always complained that working with DeMille gave her champagne tastes: she wished she could send him her bills. She agreed with her director, however, about dressing the part: "Gloria believes in the psychology of clothes. Put her in short dresses and bob her hair and she wants to play around like a child. But swathed in an evening gown with her hair high and heavily ornamented—she immediately becomes the society woman of poise and dignity and grace."[17]

She was preparing to create a new home, again as a bride. After announcing her engagement to Herbert Somborn in November, Swanson misdirected the press—for the first time but not the last—about her actual wedding plans. Although her fiancé was "a very wonderful man," she claimed the ceremony could not take place for months because of her "deep . . . attachment" to her work.[18] Gloria and Herbert were married quietly at the Alexandria Hotel on December 20, 1919, as soon as her divorce from Wallace Beery became final. The newlyweds honeymooned at the Alexandria (having announced they were going to San

Francisco), and Gloria relished the luxury of lounging around, doing absolutely nothing. Herbert was affectionate and generous on Christmas, and Gloria pledged "my love and life just yours" on her card to him.[19]

Even as she took her vows, however, Gloria "felt like running away." She had agreed to marry Somborn in a fit of pique with Craney Gartz: "I probably just said yes because I was subconsciously trying to thwart [Craney]. He begged me not to marry Herbert Somborn, but I'd said I'd promised to and I was going to and that was that."[20] Swanson's stubbornness was not always her best trait.

She had high hopes that Herbert would manage her career, but in the short term, Equity Pictures took her new husband away. Immediately after their honeymoon Herbert left for Chicago on business. Gloria sent him letters and telegrams several times daily, proclaiming her love and saying she did not know how to fill the hours before his return. (Somehow she managed. She rode, shopped, and socialized before returning to work herself.) Gloria's letters also routinely berated Herbert: for not waking her to say goodbye, for not calling when he promised, for failing to respond immediately. She might "love and worship" the man she was now calling "Daddy," but like her first husband, he had a mind—and business woes—of his own.[21]

The Equity Pictures Corporation was locked in a battle with Lewis Selznick, former manager (and lover) of Clara Kimball Young. Harry Garson had lured Young to Equity, but Selznick was not reconciled to his loss; he was loudly, publicly disputing Equity's rights to her services. The unfavorable publicity Selznick generated put a real strain on the small company, since Young was its most important asset. Tempers were rising: Selznick's eighteen-year-old son David even took a swipe at Harry Garson one day in the dining room of the Astor Hotel. (The older man saw the blow coming and punched Selznick in the nose.)

Demand was down, yet Garson was hiring more expensive talent, even though he himself was threatening to walk out, since Equity could not provide enough funds for the pictures he was contracted to make. Somborn was having trouble delivering finished Clara Kimball Young films and was forced to go hat in hand to Equity's franchise holders, asking them to advance money for future pictures when they had not received those for which they had already paid. It was a nightmare. Without a steady supply of capital, the firm could not stay in production—and without a steady supply of films, Equity could not attract the financing required to make more pictures. It was a perennial problem for small companies, and one of the reasons the industry would soon be ruled by the five "majors"—Loews, Paramount, Fox, RKO, and Warners—who could attract financing and stay stable by producing large numbers of movies on an absolutely regular basis. On December 31, his first New Year's Eve with his new wife, Herbert Somborn was working late. "This looks like a bad beginning for a happy new year," he conceded in a telegram to his Equity partners in New York.[22]

It did not take Gloria long to sniff out that Herbert's business was in trouble. However, in early 1920 she discovered a serious problem with her own contract. Swanson had originally signed with Famous Players-Lasky for $150 per week. The studio had the option, then standard, to renew the contract at specified intervals, which would increase the actress's salary by an agreed amount. (FPL could also drop its option on her services.) Swanson's salary had been bumped up, first to $350 and then $450 a week, right on schedule. But when she was due to make the next pay grade, she realized that she was the only signer of the contract. Since the studio had neglected to formalize the agreement, Swanson was technically free to go.

Of course, she had no intention of going anywhere; she loved working with DeMille. Yet she also recognized her increasing value to the company and the bargaining power it gave her. Herbert was on the road when Gloria realized her contract was out of order, so the new bride once again took care of her own business. She negotiated a new agreement with FPL: "I asked for everything that I wanted because I knew that they wanted me."[23] What Swanson longed for was a bungalow of her own. Since her elaborate gowns and hairdos consumed hours of each working day, she wanted some privacy while she was readied for her close-ups. Her new hideaway was perfect: specially constructed from floor plans she approved, it had a small sitting room with space for a gramophone and a chaise longue, a mirror, and lovely windows on two sides. It also had a shower, bathroom, and dressing room. Her colleague May McAvoy remembered Gloria's as "a beautiful, good-sized bungalow," the best at FPL. The other featured players had to share the little house next door to Gloria's private quarters, but she, DeMille, and Wally Reid were "the big shots on the lot."[24] Gloria also negotiated a small additional raise in pay.

Swanson was more than satisfied with her horse-trading. Back at work the day after Prohibition began, she felt very pleased with herself. Herbert, however, did not congratulate Gloria. He pointed out angrily that Clara Kimball Young earned upwards of $25,000 per picture plus a portion of the box office receipts; she could make additional money by endorsing anything she chose. (Swanson's new contract prohibited her from making endorsements, a concession she had not considered.) Herbert berated Gloria for negotiating her contract without an attorney to represent her interests. He snorted with derision when Gloria told him Mr. DeMille's lawyer had looked over the papers. Somborn showed Gloria her name on movie marquees all over town. She was the draw in her pictures, he said; the studio heads should recognize that and compensate her appropriately.

As Gloria listened to her husband rant, she recognized uncomfortably that Herbert had expected her to bring a big salary into their marriage. He pointed to the new corporation four of the biggest talents in town had formed to gain control of their own pictures and profits. Charlie Chaplin, Mary Pickford, Douglas Fairbanks, and D. W. Griffith were now the United Artists, and "those Eastern European Jews," as Herbert dubbed Zukor and Lasky, would have to sit up and take notice. Then he soothed his wife, saying she had nothing to worry about: he himself would take over her business dealings as soon as the Equity crisis abated. Maybe he would even arrange for her to work with Marshall Neilan, who had directed Mary Pickford and Blanche Sweet. Unenthusiastic about the prospect of leaving DeMille, but determined to be reassured by her husband's interest, Swanson decided to wait and see what Herbert could arrange. "For years I'd dreamed of having someone I could trust and lean on," she remembered. She turned to Herbert hopefully: "Whatever you say, Daddy."[25]

DeMille always said, "The public, not I, made Gloria Swanson a star," but he gave her upcoming projects careful consideration.[26] He contemplated making *The Wanderer*, a biblical epic with Swanson as a beautiful harlot who tries to seduce the prodigal son. Lasky, however, was relieved when negotiations for rights to the expensive period piece fell apart. DeMille also considered *Susan Lenox, Her Fall and Rise* for Swanson, but Lasky worried that it would "stir up . . . censorship agitation."[27] (The role went to Garbo in 1931.) They ultimately settled on *Why Change Your Wife?*, a sparkling comedy of manners in which the young star seemed perfectly at ease. Made in September and October 1919 before their trip to New York, its release was delayed while movie patrons across the country flocked to see *Male and Female*.

The new picture cleverly reversed the premise of *Don't Change Your Husband*. This time Swanson and DeMille showed a sloppy hausfrau who refashions herself into a stunning seductress and reclaims her unhappy former husband from his shrewish new wife. *Why Change Your Wife?* pleased viewers who enjoyed Swanson's fetching gowns and elaborate hairdos and those who relished DeMille's modern notions about matrimony. It was a rousing success, like *Male and Female* returning almost ten times its cost ($129,349).[28]

Swanson and Tommy Meighan have undeniable sexual chemistry as Beth and Robert Gordon. Too bad Beth is self-righteous and dull: she spends her evenings mending while listening to classical music. She rejects her husband's invitation to spend an evening at the Follies, looking down on him through horn-rimmed spectacles. Beth refuses to show off her legs in the fashionable negligee Robert brings home as a gift. After too many nights of having his behavior corrected by his dowdy wife, Robert succumbs to the attractions of Bebe Daniels's Sally Clark, who is (the intertitles proclaim) "legally a widow and optically a pippin." The long-suffering husband gets in one lecture of his own before he decamps, telling Beth he wants "a woman, not a governess; a home, not a convent; a sweetheart, not a judge."

A series of reversals and coincidences transform new wife Sally into a nagging, demanding partner and Beth into a ravishing heartbreaker dressed in the newest, most outrageous fashions. Willing to try something new at last, Beth orders half a dozen gowns which must be "sleeveless, backless, transparent, indecent." She instructs the dressmaker, "Go the limit!" Predictably, Robert and Beth meet and rekindle their attraction; just as predictably, new wife Sally does not want to see her meal ticket go back home.

When the two women tangle, however, it is anything but predictable. They fight—literally—over which of them will care for Robert, who has slipped on a banana peel and cannot be moved from Beth's house. They kick, punch, and shove one another until both are breathless, their clothes ripped and hanging off their bare shoulders. At last, Sally exits, declaring there is only one good thing about marriage: alimony. The film ends with Robert and Beth on their second wedding night, locked in a tight clinch. Now she wears a revealing gown, tosses away her record albums for his, and welcomes his dog onto the furniture. "Ladies," the final title warns, "if you would be his sweetheart, you simply must learn when to forget that you're his wife."

In DeMille's marriage comedies, the characters get hitched readily, but marriage induces cranky bickering rather than promoting harmony and ease. Nonetheless, the reality that courtship doesn't last for most couples was cleverly linked to the notion that the familiar evil (one's present spouse) was probably better than the unfamiliar object of fantasy.

Critics liked Swanson's star turn as Beth Gordon and approved the fit between the director and his leading lady: "Gloria Swanson is certainly [DeMille's] finest bit of clay," said *Motion Picture Magazine*. "She reflects his messages better than any mirror. . . . [she] is as refined and as rich as the almost improcurable attar of roses."[29] Bebe Daniels turned in a snappy performance as Sally, and filmgoers buzzed about the catfight between her and Gloria. They had more food for thought once DeMille publicized the way he handled his own marital problems. "Women get into a habit of picking," he said, advising that "Such a habit . . . should be handled instantly."[30] (He claimed he had trained his own wife never to say "don't" to him.) DeMille told Adela Rogers St. Johns he had not spent a Saturday night at home during eighteen years of marriage. His wife had never once questioned his whereabouts: it was natural for a man to transgress.

DeMille's private life fascinated Hollywood insiders. The director was at the center of a small circle of intensely devoted women who were both his collaborators and his mistresses. DeMille had installed his lady-like, indulgent wife, Constance, and his mother, Beatrice, in a palatial home in Griffith Park, but every weekend he got away to his retreat, a secluded ranch in the Santa Monica mountains he named "Paradise." There screenwriter Jeanie Macpherson, film editor Anne Bauchens, and secretary Gladys Rosson, the core members of his so-called "harem," serviced the director and his career. It was a remarkably stable arrangement; actresses who succumbed to DeMille's charm came and went, but the harem remained intact for decades. Many marveled at the way these women shared the director's attentions, but the occasional blowups only heightened the spice and drama of life with Cecil DeMille, who likely encouraged competition among his mistresses.

The most important member of the harem was Jeanie Macpherson, who wrote or adapted more than twenty-five DeMille pictures during their thirty-year collaboration. Taken by her blend of feistiness and talent, DeMille described Macpherson as "a funny little tornado with a nose that turned up, and hair that curled up, and a disposition that turned up, too." A struggle for sexual dominance is at the heart of many of the DeMille-Swanson pictures; rumors circulated that the brawl between Swanson and Bebe Daniels in *Why Change Your Wife?* was modeled on a real-life skirmish between Macpherson and actress Julia Faye, who was also sleeping with DeMille. The director approved his screenwriter's spunk: "Jeanie had no physical strength, but she was like a tarantula—when she got her fangs into anything you could not shake her loose."[31]

Swanson was as fascinated by DeMille's entourage as anyone else but disliked the way Jeanie watched her, as though she was afraid Gloria would come too close. In fact, Gloria was infatuated with her director. Weekend invitations to Paradise were the talk of the town, and Swanson recalled hearing "perfectly magnificent stories" about DeMille's parties. One of her friends had honeymooned at Paradise. A child dressed as Cupid welcomed the newlyweds, and on the first night, everything was red: flowers, glassware, even a red kimono for the new husband. On the second night, everything was white. "He always did everything in the grand style," Gloria sighed.[32] However, some found DeMille's weekend parties labored: Sheilah Graham called them a "Big Production" with too many rules and too much stage managing.[33] Until 8:00 alcohol was withheld and the ladies had to wait on the men; then the roles reversed, and the liquor flowed. Late at night the parties got wilder. Charles Bickford said DeMille had a blonde, a brunette, and a redhead delivered to him; he described striptease games in DeMille's private cottage.[34] Cecil's niece, Agnes de Mille, said simply, "What went on there, goodness only knows. No gentleman talked; Cecil's family never asked."[35]

DeMille generally preferred not to sleep with his leading ladies and kept his distance from Gloria. He teased her, however, about the rumors that the two of them had babies hidden away: "Be sure to leave the key under the mat," he called out as Gloria left the set, a joke she did not find amusing.[36] One night while they watched the rushes for *Male and Female*, Gloria climbed onto his lap and put her arms around his neck. "I sat there, I never moved," DeMille told his granddaughter. "I never put her back in her seat or expressed any emotion. I kept my hands to myself. I think it was the hardest thing I ever did." The choice, however, was simple: "I had a star who was in love with me. I could pull more out of her in a day if we remained friends. If we became lovers I would have lost some of my control."[37] Swanson never received an invitation to Paradise. In spite of DeMille's alleged foot fetish and Gloria's lovely, tiny feet, the only parties she attended were those hosted properly by Constance at the DeMille residence in town. The fantasies in which he starred Swanson, however, would prove powerful—and lasting—enough.

Soon after her second wedding, Gloria discovered she was pregnant. She yearned to start a family, and memories of the child she had lost dimmed as she contemplated a rosier future. Even if Herbert was away more than he was home, Gloria felt confident she could manage. After her troubling experience with Wally, however, she resolved to keep her condition to herself for a bit.

Her next DeMille picture was *Something to Think About*, a confused tale that left viewers scratching their heads. Swanson plays Ruth, a blacksmith's daughter who leaves her village to be educated, thanks to her rich but crippled fiancé David. When Ruth suddenly marries another man, her father curses her, asking God to keep his daughter from his sight—whereupon a stray spark from his forge blinds him. At the same moment, Ruth's husband is killed in an accident, leaving her destitute and despondent, with a baby in her arms. David prevents Ruth's suicide, marrying her though he is bitter that she does not love him. The well-to-do family lives together joylessly until Ruth, guided by a wise old servant, has a sort of religious conversion. She exerts the power of "right thinking," and her mental effort brings David to her. He throws away his crutch and walks upright into Ruth's arms, pledging his renewed love. She is then reunited with her sightless but forgiving father.

Neither Swanson nor her costar Elliott Dexter thought much of the script. It was not subtle, but as DeMille collaborator Mitchell Leisen observed, "DeMille had no nuances. Everything was in neon lights six feet tall: LUST, REVENGE, SEX."[38] The part nonetheless offered Swanson a chance to show her range. As Robert Birchard notes, "She goes from school girl, to young woman, to social outcast, to society matron."[39] People were now watching DeMille's pictures for fashion trends: The *New York Times* reviewer overheard a woman compliment Dexter's stylish jacket at the story's dramatic climax. If *Something to Think About* went on too long, like an after-dinner speaker who didn't realize anything more would be "nothing to think about," the *Times* conceded that at least DeMille's pictures always looked good.[40]

Swanson loved working with Cecil DeMille. She knew many considered him a harsh taskmaster, but she admired his high standards: "If you didn't do the job he demanded of you, you got hell, no question about it. He stood for no nonsense." Everyone hustled to accommodate him: "He would take off his coat and hold his arm out, and his Filipino [assistant] would be there to pick it up. He'd start to sit down and wouldn't even look behind him—there'd always be a chair shoved under his derrière. There was a kind of bugle sound just when he was going to arrive. So everybody got in position, got ready to work—our hearts beat faster."[41]

Acknowledging that DeMille "was inclined to say very rude things to people," Swanson nonetheless declared that "in my whole association with him, he never said anything that was rude, that hurt my feelings, that might have a double meaning, anything that I could misunderstand." Though she was unafraid of DeMille, she was also proud never to have occasioned his anger. He even protected her: "If anyone came near me to suggest anything, he'd throw them right off the set. He did this once to [Jeanie Macpherson], said, 'Leave my actress alone. She knows what she's doing.'"[42] Others might call him "C. B." but his Young Fellow always called her director "Mr. DeMille."

Once the picture ended in late March, Gloria confronted the task she had been dreading: telling Jesse Lasky she was pregnant. She faced her employer, aware that he was unlikely to share her joy. "There goes your career," Lasky said.[43] He pleaded with Gloria not to derail her own bright prospects in the business, nor to discount the studio's investment in her. There was no chance the fickle public would remember her face in a year's time: she would lose the momentum she had built. More significantly, she would not be able to return to the screen in featured roles, since audiences would not accept a mother as a romantic lead.

For most actresses the choice was clear: "If you were in motion pictures, you could be married," explained actress Billie Dove, "but if you had a baby, you were no longer considered romantic. Therefore, a baby was out of the question for me."[44] Mary Pickford acknowledged the difficult trade-off but thought it was immutable: "Actresses should realize when they deliberately choose a public career they have no right to disappoint the public—and no right to privacy. As a toy of the public, that's part of the price."[45] This was the prevailing belief, and no actress had yet challenged it successfully.

But Swanson was stubborn: "I said, 'Now just a moment, Mr. Lasky. I'm a woman first and an actress second.' I thought he was going to have a stroke."[46] In fact, she told Lasky, she intended to have twelve children. Her baby was due in October, and her contract expired in January. Swanson insisted not only on putting off her next film until after her delivery but also that she would seek a renegotiated contract on her return to FPL after she gave birth. Her pregnancy made her unable to work before the first of the year regardless.

Lasky, displeased, tried to invoke the contract provisions for a two-year option on Gloria's services, citing FPL's ability to extend her obligation for any missed period. Swanson held firm: her husband had advised her that these provisions were not enforceable. Lasky said he would have to confer with his partner Adolph Zukor and with Mr. DeMille. But he was not optimistic: any time off screen would make her less rather than more valuable to the studio.

Prepared for this interview, Swanson now played her trump card. She hoped after the new year to star in pictures her husband would produce for her: she intended to leave Famous Players-Lasky anyway. "Now I could tell he was worried," Swanson remembered. Lasky urged her to make no hasty decisions until he consulted his colleagues, assuring Gloria that she was "family" at FPL.[47] Swanson left the interview knowing Herbert would be pleased, though she herself did not enjoy crossing the studio management. She had found a home at FPL and was a lot less sanguine about working with her husband than she wanted Lasky to see.

For the time being she was free. The studio could not shoehorn the visibly pregnant actress into her costumes, so she rested and dreamed, spending long afternoons sunbathing, driving the coast roads, and breathing the citrus-scented air. As famous as she was fast becoming, Swanson—like other stars of her generation—was still able to move about town unmolested as the 1920s began. Soon that freedom would be severely curtailed: the publicity machine that kept stars in the public eye also drew fans anxious for a glimpse of their idols, making it near-impossible for the stars to live normal lives. By the end of the 1920s, more than three quarters of a million people, hopeful young performers and eager speculators of all stripes, had moved to Los Angeles.

Herbert and Gloria had been living at the Alexandria Hotel since their marriage, and one day the manager came to the door. Their bill was long overdue, he explained apologetically; the hotel had no choice but to cut off the couple's credit. When Swanson protested that there must be a mistake, the manager said he had approached Mr. Somborn for payment several times already. A quick rummage through Herbert's desk revealed many unopened or overdue bills. Gloria was appalled: "It seemed our whole glamorous life together had been charged. Even the necklace Herbert gave me before we were married had not been paid for."[48]

When she confronted Herbert that evening, he shrugged off her concern. Things would look up soon; he felt certain of it. In the meantime, it was important to keep up a prosperous front. To betray any financial insecurity would invite attack and weaken both his and Gloria's bargaining power in Hollywood. Swanson understood that her growing fame made it harder for Herbert to keep a low profile himself: "Although he could pull in his belt and sit out slack periods as a bachelor, he could not do so with a wife at his side."[49] Even as she promised to trust him, Swanson realized this kind of uncertainty was not what she had bargained for. Being part of Herbert's changeable business felt like high stakes gambling—not the safe, secure future she wanted for their family.

Herbert's business woes showed no sign of abating. Gloria recognized uncomfortably that his hopes were concentrated on her, while she wished he would focus on his own stalled prospects. She wanted him to support her and their baby, not vice versa. In fact, she wondered if putting her career in Herbert's hands was wise. Jesse Lasky had practically snarled when she mentioned her husband's name; Gloria herself disliked Herbert's cynicism about DeMille and the studio management. The pressure on her to negotiate her own—and her child's—future became even more intense. She drew out enough money to pay their bills, then signed the lease on a modest new apartment.

Then Lasky came back with a new offer. After some fanfare he announced that FPL had great plans for Swanson: they had decided to make her a star. This was momentous news. Rather than being pitched out, she was being promoted. Lasky did not need to explain to the young actress what this meant: the company had real faith in her ability to carry a picture.

However, Swanson immediately saw the drawbacks of this scenario. Being a star meant that a movie's success or failure would be synonymous with her own. She would not be paired with another equally famous costar; it would cost the studio too much money. Nor would she work with DeMille again; since he also had a recognizable name and reputation, she would be partnered with other directors. There was no guarantee, however, that they would have any insight or special ability; she could be used to carry weak stories or second-tier talent. Gloria recalled her experience at Triangle, where she had been hurried into one inferior film after another as the studio hastened to take advantage of her success. Moreover, FPL could drop her option if her pictures did poorly. No, thank you, she told Mr. Lasky: she did not want to be a star. Not even when he mentioned a staggering figure—$2,500 a week for five years—did Gloria relent. Undeterred, Lasky sent her off to see DeMille, knowing Swanson trusted her director's advice.

DeMille was ready for her. Chuckling, he reassured Gloria that he knew all about the studio's plans and thought they were making a wise choice in starring her. DeMille reminded Swanson gently that they had already made five pictures together and that the movie business thrived on variety. He claimed a starring position would actually make Swanson more secure: from now on, the studio could not abandon Gloria without risking its even larger investment in her. She would have excellent stories and first-rate collaborators, maybe even her choice among them. Projects would be prepared with her talents in mind. He himself had handpicked her first director, Sam Wood. DeMille encouraged Gloria to trust his judgment. Sighing, Gloria agreed, though privately she felt she had been asked to trust too often lately.

She was taking instruction in the precepts of Christian Science, thanks to a new friend whose calm, intelligent way of examining situations impressed Gloria. Peggy Urson's advice to the expectant mother—to slow down and to concentrate on the present moment—was deeply attractive to Swanson. The positive thinking Peggy emphasized also seemed like a natural, easy way of keeping herself steady despite her worries. In fact, the power of mind over matter had been the subject of *Something to Think About*, and Gloria pondered the way her character in the picture used mental force to draw her distant, unloving husband toward her. Her positive thinking had even healed his lameness. The more Swanson mulled over the connection between the film's moral lesson and what Peggy was telling her, the less coincidental it seemed. She determined to pay attention and stay positive.

She spent the last few months of her pregnancy quietly, preparing for a natural delivery at home, without painkillers. Her early labor pains on the morning of October 6 seemed manageable, but Swanson was glad she had a Christian Science practitioner to coach her. As the day wore on, however, she sensed her labor was taking too long. Herbert wanted her to go to the hospital, but she refused. Finally, fearful she would harm the baby, Swanson let her husband summon a doctor; after almost twenty-four hours of fruitless labor, she was exhausted. She panicked at the thought of being injected with anything, so the doctor administered chloroform. When Gloria awoke early on October 7, they put a tiny little girl in her arms. With a diaper tied around her head, the baby resembled "a little Polish peasant."[50] She was perfect.

The besotted parents decided to name her Gloria. The new mother said, "The first thing [the baby] did was to reach for my breast, and the ecstasy overwhelmed me."[51] Swanson would become an outspoken champion of breastfeeding, describing with satisfaction the powerful early days of bonding with her child and providing everything the baby needed naturally. She was unusually forthright about the physical pleasure of nursing her child, too, even posing for some professional photographs—pictures she published in her 1980 memoir—of herself feeding baby Gloria. Swathed in a lacy shawl, the young mother looks relaxed and radiantly happy.

Although she had been forced to accept anesthesia and a doctor-assisted delivery, Swanson never relinquished the ideal of natural childbirth.

It was another fifty years before the practice was generally accepted as preferable for mothers and better for children. Of course, babies had been coming at home, with the assistance of midwives and without medication, for centuries. Modern medicine, however, promised to free women from the primitive birthing process. For Swanson to embrace natural childbirth and breastfeeding wholeheartedly and publicly put her well outside the norm for her era.

A flood of telegrams, letters, and flowers deluged the apartment. Jesse Lasky sent a magnificent basket of flowers with his and Adolph Zukor's good wishes: "May your little daughter grow up to be as famous and beautiful as her talented mother." Tommy Meighan sent hopes that the two Glorias "would Glory us forever." Showman Sid Grauman proclaimed, "The little girl that called at your home this morning is a greater treasure than all the Grauman million dollar theatres stretched from coast to coast." "Put me down for eastern rights," read a cable from one of Herbert's Equity colleagues: the baby was a sure-fire hit. Gloria even heard from her new director Sam Wood.[52]

Cecil DeMille came in person, bearing a pearl necklace with a diamond clasp for the baby. After admiring little Gloria's beauty—despite a small dent on her cheek from the doctor's forceps—he got down to business. He had a favor to ask: would Gloria consider making one last movie with him? He felt there was one more story they needed to tell. Swanson did not even try to hide her pleasure at the prospect and agreed immediately. Herbert, however, was furious when he heard the news. How dare she agree to make another movie for the studio—essentially for free—and without even consulting him? He recognized immediately what a shrewd move it was for FPL.

Swanson may have barely noticed the success of *Something to Think About*, but with this new and compelling evidence of Gloria's drawing power and versatility, the studio had no intention of letting her go. Now Lasky and DeMille proposed a picture featuring all four of DeMille's leading ladies: Bebe Daniels, Agnes Ayres, Wanda Hawley, and Swanson. An ensemble picture would be easy to produce and should have strong box office value. FPL's ultimate aim was to cut all four of these actresses loose from DeMille, so the picture would be a "sentimental farewell appearance" for the director's current company.[53]

FPL was also hedging its bets by supporting Swanson on her first venture since news of her latest production, baby Gloria, hit the press. She had the lead role in *The Affairs of Anatol* but did not have to carry the picture. The three other actresses were featured in segments in which Swanson barely appeared. If the new mother was not camera-ready, or if audiences proved fickle, FPL had limited its risk and could move on quickly. Some speculated that the studio hoped to create a stock company, moving toward "the virtual abolition of the star system."[54]

In *Anatol*, Swanson plays a young wife whose attractions finally win out over those of three other temptresses who attract her weak-willed husband. Anatol (Wallace Reid) is distracted by women who need rescuing. He meets up with a childhood sweetheart who has gone astray (Hawley), a farmer's wife who needs some quick cash (Ayres), and "the wickedest woman in New York," Satan Synne (Daniels). Each woman deceives Anatol in her own way, and each time his wife takes him back. Anatol knows he has the perfect companion at home, but until his wife stays out all night with his best friend, she cannot command her husband's attention. Swanson's part was familiar—it recapped several of her DeMille hits—but atypical of the public persona expected of a new mother.

No expense was spared to depict the characters' fabulous lives. The sets and costumes had gorgeous art nouveau styling by Paul Iribe, with stunning color sequences inspired by new techniques of multicolor lithography. Color extended the extravaganza, making the film's fantasy of consumer excess more potent; even the characters' monogrammed cigarettes were red. Critics found *Anatol* "a magnificent puppet show, legitimately and logically excessive in every way," featuring a lively "spirit of banter and satire."[55]

Somehow, it worked. The film did not excite anyone's indignation by misrepresenting motherhood. Audiences embraced *Anatol*; another hit, it earned back seven times its cost. Swanson had broken the parenthood barrier simply by refusing to take no for an answer, and it had a liberating effect on other actresses: "I had my child and it was like an epidemic," Swanson claimed.[56] The only trouble she had came from Jeanie Macpherson, who offended the tired young mother by making unkind remarks about Gloria's baby weight. When DeMille saw she was upset, he took his star aside, telling her gently that people would always be jealous of her and that she must learn to "take the cream and leave the milk."[57] As Swanson prepared to move ahead without DeMille to guide her, she vowed to remember her director's good advice.

Swanson's private life would never be fully controllable by her employers. However, her strong will, business acumen, and ambition coincided precisely with FPL's decision to begin considering longer-term commitments to its talent. Swanson negotiated for her pregnancy as she would any other movie deal: with a lively sense of her own box office value. She did not need a husband to help her figure that one out.

CHAPTER 6

The Great Moment

THE BIGGEST SPLASH IN HOLLYWOOD IN FALL 1920 WAS MADE BY A woman in her mid-'50s with flaming red hair and emerald eyes who had come to California to create a movie scenario for Gloria Swanson. British novelist Elinor Glyn was part of Adolph Zukor's plan to hire prominent authors to write for the screen. Glyn had produced the most notorious book in recent memory: *Three Weeks* chronicled a young man's erotic coming of age in Lucerne and Venice under the tutelage of a mysterious older woman. Its unashamed endorsement of sensuality made for ripe reading: it was denounced, banned, and devoured everywhere. For years, Glyn's book appeared as a prop on movie sets. "If a director wanted to show that one of the characters in his film was leading a racy life, all he had to do was show her holding a copy of *Three Weeks* in her lap," said James Card. "Just holding the book was enough to tag her as modern and independent."[1]

A sample of Glyn's racy, modern, independent work:

They were sitting on the tiger [skin rug] by now, and she undulated round and all over him . . . till at last it seemed as if she were twined about him like a serpent. And every now and then a narrow shaft of the glorious dying sunlight would strike the great emerald on her forehead, and give forth sparks of vivid green which appeared reflected again in her eyes. Paul's head swam, he felt intoxicated with bliss.

"This Venice is for you and me, my Paul," she said. "The air is full of love and dreams; we have left the slender moon behind us in Switzerland; here she is nearing her full, and the summer is upon us with all her richness and completeness—the spring of our love has passed. . . . We will drink deep of the cup of delight, my lover, and bathe in the wine of the gods. We shall feast on the tongues of

nightingales, and rest on couches of flowers. And thou shalt cede
me thy soul, beloved, and I will give thee mine—"
  But the rest was lost in the meeting of their lips.[2]

The book's purple prose elicited howls of laughter from those who did
not fall under its sway. It was (inevitably) parodied: Buster Keaton's
comic short *One Week* was named after it, and popular doggerel cracked
wise at its expense:

> *Would you like to sin*
> *With Elinor Glyn*
> *On a tiger skin?*
> *Or would you prefer*
> *To err with her*
> *On some other fur?*

  Zukor paid Glyn $10,000 to write "a slinky story" for Swanson's first
starring role, from a title FPL had already devised: *The Great Moment*.[3]
Zukor got more than he bargained for with Mrs. Glyn, who had a genius for self-promotion and promptly began appearing all over town.
She turned up at parties and dances, creating a buzz with her aristocratic
bearing and exotic looks (one observer said Glyn's face had "a charmingly enameled look").[4] Her proclamations on style, romance, and—most
famously—who had "It" in the movie capital were perfect fan magazine
fodder.
  What made Elinor Glyn an expert? Her self-confidence and panache
were unassailable: a strikingly beautiful woman who looked twenty
years younger than she was, Glyn made fashion rather than aping it. Her
talented sister, Lucy (who became Lady Duff Gordon after making a very
good marriage), supplied Elinor with exquisite gowns from her London
fashion house. Lucy created flowing, sensuous garments in luxurious
fabrics for her upscale London clientele, women interested in modern
clothing that moved with them.
  "Madame" Glyn (as she preferred to be known) also fancied herself
psychic and was fond of making occult pronouncements about the past
lives of those she met. She presented herself as otherworldly, but Glyn
was used to hard work. A single mother, she churned out at least one
novel in Britain every year to support her family, in addition to articles
in the popular press. Her grand style of living nonetheless meant that, as

Cecil Beaton said waspishly, "Mrs. Glyn's financial situation was always somewhat hazardous."[5]

Gloria was one of the first to fall under her spell. Glyn was filmed for a few insert shots in *The Affairs of Anatol*, and Swanson found her "devastating . . . like something from another world."[6] The admiration was not initially mutual. Mrs. Glyn objected to Swanson playing her heroine, calling the actress "such a marionette and so common," an opinion that rapidly circulated around town.[7]

Then again, Glyn thought everyone in Hollywood common. Since she could not pick her leading lady, she set about remodeling the one she had been given. Swanson proved amenable to guidance on how to dress, move, speak, and even what to read, while Glyn let it be known that she would not be responsible for the "vile bad taste" of sets not arranged to her liking or costumes she had not approved.[8] (Her contract gave her no such authority, and the men who hired Glyn often earned her scorn by chuckling at her pronouncements.) Swanson, who had just left one mentor behind, found in Madame Glyn a different kind of guidance, something DeMille could not give her: lessons in how to be a diva.

Once they began work on *The Great Moment*, Glyn published a new, more favorable opinion of the new star. In a column syndicated to two million readers, she proclaimed Swanson "the most vivid personality on the screen today. She is an exquisite creature, with perhaps the loveliest eyes I have ever seen. . . . I feel that she has an old soul struggling to remember its former lives. I do not think that she has had a part that has done her talent justice."[9]

The scenario Glyn prepared from an original story featured two roles for Swanson: she is both the Russian gypsy who enchants a titled British diplomat (before conveniently dying in childbirth) and the couple's daughter. Fearing that blood will tell and that the child will take after her wild mother, her father has raised Nadine in seclusion. The young woman is pledged to marry a dully appropriate suitor when she meets a dashing American engineer, played by venerable leading man Milton Sills, in her father's Nevada gold mine. The film has to get Swanson hitched to Sills with the maximum of romantic interest while capitalizing on the "wild blood" theme.

One scene became infamous even before the picture's release: Swanson and Sills are riding out in the Nevada hills when she is bitten on the breast by a rattlesnake. They are far from civilization, and (naturally) the only way Sills can save her is by sucking out the poison.

When the producers explained to Mrs. Glyn that her scene would create a furor, she insisted that nothing could be changed or the story would collapse. Glyn relented only after the controversy had generated plenty of publicity: the wound could be located on the heroine's shoulder. The fuss attracted viewers, and most accounts of the film still say Swanson was bitten on the breast. Assistant director Henry Hathaway, then starting his career at FPL, observed drily, "[The scene] where Gloria got bitten on the tit . . . was the great moment in the picture."[10]

Madame Glyn's story coyly exploited contemporary concerns about racial purity by having the happy ending turn on whether Swanson's gypsy will control—or be controlled by—her mixed blood. "Gypsy" was movie shorthand for wildness and freedom: female gypsies especially provoked audiences by suggesting that women could be sexually voracious and uncontrollable. *The Great Moment* appeared amid worries about new temptations to which young women were exposed: one sequence shows Nadine being led astray at a party that turns into an orgy. One reviewer observed that the story would "satisfy the subconscious requirements of any reasonable woman," which were "a master—and lots of love."[11] Madame Glyn's scenario pushed any number of buttons.

Elinor Glyn was a masterful self-promoter whose big secret was that she was not nearly as bold as she appeared. Charlie Chaplin, who grew very fond of her, claimed Glyn's "sensational" reputation was based on a misunderstanding of her true character: "No one was more staid. Her amorous conceptions for the movies were girlish and naïve—ladies brushing their eyelids against the cheeks of their beloveds and languishing on tiger rugs."[12]

However, Glyn's mixture of respectability and daring was perfect for FPL, and Swanson observed her closely. Despite their disparity in age— Glyn had thirty-five years on Swanson—the two women began socializing together. Movie society was beginning to coalesce around fancy dress occasions, and glittering venues like the Alexandria Hotel, with its gold-leafed lobby and Tiffany glass skylight, or the Cocoanut Grove nightclub in the new Ambassador Hotel were perfect places to see and be seen. There was dining and dancing to Paul Whiteman's jazz orchestra, with the press always invited to see what the stars were wearing. Madame Glyn gained access everywhere; Gloria marveled as the older woman simply stared down the maitre d' at the Ambassador's Patent Leather Room, the most exclusive place in town, when he dared suggest her large party could not be immediately seated. Swanson would soon patent her own equally effective brand of gorgon gaze.

For the American Society of Cinematographers Ball, Glyn wore an emerald headdress and necklace, but her young protégée's outfit of black jet beads created a sensation. *Photoplay*'s reporter claimed that "Gloria Swanson, with fewer clothes on than I have ever seen in a public place, was . . . so beautiful that she outshone her old self."[13]

FPL encouraged Swanson to dress and act the part of a star in public, as it created excellent publicity for her movies. Since she had always loved beautiful things and looking different and stylish, Gloria quickly gained a reputation for her fashion sense and her readiness to spend a fortune on her clothes. What she wore to dinner or a premiere was described in endless detail for a hungry audience of fan magazine readers.

An early disappointment of her post-DeMille partnering with director Sam Wood was *Under the Lash*, in which Swanson played a drab farmer's wife in (of all places) South Africa. Russell Simpson was Gloria's unhappy husband; once they had to stop a scene because a moth got into his long, detachable beard. The film was a flop, and Lasky told Swanson the studio understood why: her fans expected to see her in luxurious clothes. They might overlook Gloria's tiny daughter, but they would not accept the star in anything second-rate or inexpensive. FPL would act accordingly in designing Swanson's future projects.

Conspicuous by his absence was Gloria's husband. Herbert's business had not improved, even as the industry boomed, and a frosty distance grew between the couple. Because Herbert was miserable in their small apartment, Gloria agreed to relocate to the Ambassador Hotel. Yet after a month they moved again, at her insistence, to a less expensive bungalow at the Beverly Hills Hotel. Gloria found it challenging to make a home with Herbert, who was often moody and critical. She was tired of his insistent questions about her much more successful career. Her interest in her marriage faded.

Little Gloria's difficult birth had left Swanson with a small tear that needed surgical repair. She had hurried back to work, however, eight weeks after the baby arrived. Reluctant in any case to trust herself to doctors, Swanson started on a self-prescribed regimen of colon cleansing, which many at the time wrongly believed would prevent infection. Tired from nursing the baby and working all day, Swanson snapped when Herbert questioned her about these frequent internal baths. "Herbert and I had never had any fun," she recalled, "and I had never really loved him. I had merely felt secure with him, and now . . . he was the least secure person in my life. I had made the same mistake with Herbert that I had made with Wally. I had married someone I admired like a father, not someone I wanted for a husband and lover; and in both cases, once my trust vanished, so did my warm feelings."[14]

Fifteen months after her second marriage, Swanson quietly rented a small suite of rooms in nearby Silver Lake, a hilly, rural section of Los Angeles that was an easy commute to the studio. It was not a formal rupture, in part because she was reluctant to give Herbert grounds to sue her for desertion. She had made that mistake before: when she left Beery, he became the injured party, and she had to accept divorce on his terms. When Gloria stopped by their bungalow, however, Herbert had moved out, leaving behind a letter apologizing for the failure of their marriage and asking that they work out his visitation of baby Gloria. Herbert's desertion of their legal residence, combined with his letter, gave Swanson grounds for divorce.

How the studio would feel about it was another matter. FPL publicity had encouraged audiences to accept Swanson as both a mother and a leading lady, often "quoting" her on the sacred bond of matrimony and the beauty of family life. A second divorce would be hard to swallow, and Swanson by now understood that the studio had a say in her personal affairs. Without a husband to provide for her—though Herbert had never really been that—she would have to work out something with FPL to gain her release from her marriage. When Jesse Lasky gave her a firm, swift no to a quick divorce, she was prepared to wait.

A distraction arrived in the form of Marshall Neilan, a charismatic Irish director known for his heavy drinking and high living. "Mickey" loved decorating and entertaining and did both on a grand scale, hosting parties that kept him chronically broke. If Swanson wanted a playmate, she could not have done better than Neilan. Their first meeting had taken place on a dance floor a year earlier, when Mickey broke in on Gloria's partner and, waltzing Swanson across the ballroom, asked her to marry him. Amused, she said she had just agreed to marry Herbert Somborn. Mickey said that was fine—all he asked was that Gloria place him on her list of future husbands. He could wait, he said, because he loved her. And off they spun across the floor.

It was like something out of a movie. Since Neilan had been acting, writing, and directing for a decade, perhaps that is not surprising. He often directed Mary Pickford and Blanche Sweet and had an excellent reputation for understanding actors and staging scenes. (Pickford thought his suggestions saved her *Madame Butterfly* from being *Madame Snail*.)[15] In spring 1921, while Swanson's marriage to Herbert Somborn was foundering, Mickey Neilan again danced her way. After her husband's doom and gloom, Neilan's joie de vivre delighted Gloria. Even Madame Glyn was taken by Mickey's Irish charm and told Swanson to "nab him."[16] Despite Neilan's ongoing romance with Blanche Sweet, they became a couple, and Gloria once again started enjoying life.

Being romanced by Neilan meant late nights and lots of nonsense: Swanson called him the "Pied Piper," because the party was always at its height wherever Neilan was.[17] Once the film folk were out of sight of the flashing camera bulbs, they were like "a pack of circus performers getting together." The gang included Charlie Chaplin, Doug Fairbanks, Mary Pickford, Elliott Dexter, Tommy Meighan, Olive Thomas, and Jack Pickford. Gloria remembered fun and games and crazy stunts: "We were like a pack of kids. You'd look up and there would be somebody walking with an umbrella . . . [on] a beam across the center of the floor one story up."[18] Or they would hire an orchestra, and before long they would be playing all the instruments, while the hired musicians looked on. The elegant waiters dressed in sixteenth-century naval officers' uniforms at Venice Beach's Ship Café didn't tone down the antic behavior of the famous patrons: Buster Keaton was spotted jumping out the porthole-style windows.

They would head out to the Vernon Country Club, which was not a country club but an after-hours place all the way at the end of the streetcar line (reportedly also the best place to buy drugs in Los Angeles). Prohibition barely slowed the pace of the drinking when Neilan was around. Swanson remembered driving back to town at dawn, with Mickey—or his buddy Charlie Chaplin—"standing up in the back seat of an open car, and making pantomime speeches to the street sweepers and vegetable truck drivers we passed."[19] High spirits and camaraderie were the rule: loving Mickey Neilan meant being ready to switch at any moment from romance to hijinks. Mickey loved practical jokes, and Swanson, who had barely cracked a smile while working with some of the funniest people in show business at Keystone, found herself learning to laugh.

Everybody loved Mickey, who wore his talent and success lightly. He was genial and generous to a fault: though Neilan was pulling down $125,000 per picture by the late teens, money simply ran through his fingers. This was too bad, since he also had a talent for alienating his bosses. When he was on a binge, Neilan left actors and crew members waiting around, a cardinal sin in an industry that was becoming more and more businesslike. Once, when Neilan failed to show up for a complicated out-of-town shoot, Mary Pickford sent people looking through every speakeasy in San Francisco for him. Eventually, Pickford directed the scene herself—only to spot Neilan among the bystanders beyond the ropes to one side of the set. Looking perfectly satisfied, Neilan complimented her and disappeared again.

Neilan enjoyed deflating large egos, and sometimes his irreverence got the better of him. He made a powerful enemy with a famous quip: "An empty taxicab drove up and Louis B. Mayer got out."[20] Mayer did not get the joke when Neilan substituted an image of a kitten meowing for the new logo of a lion roaring at an M-G-M premiere. Diplomatic when he wanted to be, Neilan could also be his own worst enemy. Colleen Moore put her finger squarely on the problem: "Mickey Neilan preferred making a witticism that was repeated all over town to making a great motion picture."[21]

Most latter-day assessments of Neilan focus on the waste his alcoholism made of his talent. Those who knew him nonetheless remembered him fondly. "For all his wisecracks, he was a kind, warmhearted person," Moore said. "He made a million dollars and ended up without a dime. He didn't lose it on the stock market as many people did. He spent it—spent it on a great big glorious time. . . . He was a charming, crazy, obstinate Irishman who lived a full and exciting life—a complex man and a maddening one sometimes, but never a dull one."[22]

In rare quiet moments over the years, Swanson contemplated what she called her "father complex," speculating that if Joseph Swanson had been less of a drinker or more of a stable presence in her life, she might have accomplished her heart's fondest wish: to be married and have a family life. "I am not an envious person, but I do envy happily married couples—people who have married and lived together twenty-five, thirty-five years. It's been a very real and very deep desire in me." More pragmatically, she observed in herself "two separate personalities trying to go like two railroad tracks—parallel—and sometimes the train went off the track. It made for wrecks. Always my domestic life suffered more than my professional life."[23]

As the child of a charismatic, alcoholic parent, Swanson longed to be cared for. She had looked for a father in each of her two older husbands, Wally Beery and Herbert Somborn, yearning to be protected and guided by a wiser, more experienced man. Now she was finding a different part of her missing father in Mickey Neilan, a lover with a brilliant creative mind and a great sense of fun—another intelligent, irresponsible man. However, her life had taught her how to take care of her own business. Though Swanson would be drawn to older, competent men in charge and to sexy, fun-loving rascals alike, it would never be easy for her to cede control to anyone else.

Jesse Lasky was none too pleased by Swanson's public dalliance with livewire Neilan. FPL was also pressuring Swanson to allow her baby to be photographed for publicity purposes, which she adamantly refused to do. Even when executives told Swanson that many believed her child was disabled or mentally handicapped, Swanson would not relent: "Gloria signed no contract with Mr. Lasky," she said firmly.[24] She intended to raise her daughter outside the glare of photographers' bulbs.

Gloria skipped the funeral in August 1921 of her mother's husband Matthew Burns, believing her presence would draw too much attention. She was drawn, however, into an unpleasant controversy that fall when her mother was sued by her late husband's relatives, who were contesting his will. The tabloid-friendly story alleged that Adelaide had paid longtime family friends to introduce her to Burns, a wealthy man in ill health whom she had targeted. She used her daughter to draw Burns in, then tricked him into marriage, inheriting an estate worth $60,000 to $1 million. Burns, so the story ran, was really in love with Gloria, whom the newspapers began calling "Baby Vamp."

Swanson called the charges "too absurd to discuss" and prevented her mother from speaking to reporters.[25] In July 1922, a jury threw out Burns's will on grounds of mental incompetence, and Adelaide moved in with her daughter. "I don't care anything about the [money]," Swanson fumed. "What's that? I can earn [it] easily myself and I certainly can take care of my mother . . . [Burns] adored my mother and it is so silly to say that I 'vamped' him."[26] Gloria provided a home for her mother off and on for the rest of Adelaide's life.

Scandals of all kinds were rocking Hollywood. In September 1921, FPL comedian Roscoe "Fatty" Arbuckle was arrested for manslaughter after a wild party in San Francisco went horribly wrong, and a young woman ended up dead. People whispered that the 320-pound Arbuckle had raped Virginia Rappe with a bottle of champagne or a piece of ice. Others said that Rappe, who died of peritonitis from a ruptured bladder, had been accidentally injured by Arbuckle in rough horseplay at the party, her health already compromised by a botched abortion several days earlier. Every detail that emerged from the compromised, corrupt investigation was reported; many were invented. Amid claims of witness tampering and extortion, Arbuckle's first two juries deadlocked. A third trial acquitted the comedian—he even got a public apology—but FPL canceled his $3 million contract. He was finished in Hollywood.

Even if the industry had backed Arbuckle, American audiences were outraged and would likely have boycotted his pictures. Because tales of Hollywood passions and scandals sold so well, the press often fabricated stories, embroidering them from the slimmest threads. These stories showed a terrible discrepancy between the upright studio version of the film stars' lives and the imperfect—occasionally even sordid—reality.

In February 1922, FPL director William Desmond Taylor was found dead in his bungalow, shot in the back. Taylor was implicated in a complicated web of drug use and sex play and was rumored to have an extensive lingerie collection labeled with the names of his Hollywood conquests. He was having an affair with the ingénue actress Mary Miles Minter. Had Minter—or perhaps her mother—shot him? Mabel Normand and Taylor had argued shortly before his death, and stories of Normand's cocaine habit circulated, damaging her high-profile career. Or maybe the butler did it: Taylor's valets had been convicted of forgery, embezzlement, and soliciting sex from young boys. Maybe it was a robbery. Maybe it was a paid hit. Studio representatives, summoned before the police, left a hopelessly contaminated crime scene, but Taylor's household was a darker and wilder place than middle America was ready to accept.

Lovely young Olive Thomas's death in a Paris hotel, declared accidental, was also mysterious. Thomas overdosed on mercury bichloride, a drug prescribed for her husband Jack Pickford, but no one knew whether or why she had taken it. Maybe Pickford had administered the lethal dose. Rumors that Thomas was despondent over her struggling marriage appeared alongside reports of cocaine parties and orgies. Plagued by alcoholism and the long-term effects of syphilis—a legacy of his womanizing ways and the reason the mercury was in his drug cabinet that fateful night—Jack Pickford would also die young.

It was becoming common knowledge that Wallace Reid, FPL's handsome, successful romantic lead, was addicted to the morphine he was given after being injured on location. Although Reid was famous as a racecar driver, Swanson refused to let him even give her a lift to work while they were making *The Affairs of Anatol* together. The great heartthrob's odd behavior gave Swanson "the jitters," and she avoided him whenever possible.[27] After a wrenching and fairly public struggle to kick the habit, Reid died of an overdose in January 1923.

To protect American viewers from Hollywood's sordid ways, some states were setting up censorship boards, with more threatened. These boards could create any standards they felt reflected local sensibilities (including outright bans). Moviegoers in Kansas, for instance, were less likely to see Swanson's nearly-nude dip in *Male and Female* than were New Jersey viewers (though they probably knew such a scene existed).[28] Such cutting often resulted in garbled, incoherent films.

In the wake of the 1919 Black Sox scandal, a federal judge was appointed commissioner of baseball, on the theory that stringent oversight would restore the game's good name and set standards by which players would be held accountable. Hollywood hired Will Hays, former postmaster general, to do the same thing for the movies. Hays's mandate was broad: his office had authority "to handle public relations on a national scale [and] to secure the unified effort needed toward industry self-regulation."[29] He was to make sure no one else needed to regulate motion picture content or the conduct of the players. If successful, his efforts would lessen the costs to the industry of local, state, and federal censorship; eliminate the likelihood of bans and boycotts; and bring the industry onto a firmer footing with the public. It was a big job—but even at the princely salary of $100,000 a year, Hays earned less than the stars whose professional and private lives he oversaw.

Hollywood gave Hays a high-profile welcome. He appeared at a star-studded banquet for 1,500 at the Ambassador Hotel, and held an all-industry rally at the Hollywood Bowl, with attendance practically mandatory. He visited the studios, pitching his program of industry self-regulation to the workers, though no one initially knew what to make of him. While Will Hays created as much good will and publicity as possible, Swanson and her friends found themselves under uncomfortably close scrutiny. Because the headline-grabbing scandals featured the players rather than their movies, Hays's campaign would naturally focus on their personal lives. Soon "self-regulation" would be presented to stars as a fact of life in Hollywood.

Swanson of course knew all the names in the headlines. She saw Mary Miles Minter, William Desmond Taylor, and the troubled Wallace Reid at FPL daily. "Ollie" Thomas had been at Triangle with Gloria, and Roscoe Arbuckle had worked there before he moved to FPL. The group often socialized together: Jack Pickford was a drinking buddy of Mickey Neilan's, and Taylor was one of Mickey's closest friends.

In fact, after working late on the night following Taylor's murder, Swanson, Jack Pickford, Mary Minter, and Neilan met at Neilan's house to discuss the shocking news. There were few secrets within the movie community: Mary Minter's affair with Taylor was not one of them, and Neilan took Minter aside to tell her that he had tried—unsuccessfully—to

retrieve her love letters from Taylor's bungalow. According to evidence
Minter gave the police, Neilan was concerned for her privacy. He wanted
to warn her that the case was likely to be "a terrible thing," with enough
notoriety to go around.[30]

The police in turn questioned Minter about Neilan as a possible suspect, as he had also been a beau of Minter's, maybe a jealous one. They
were particularly interested in Minter's tales of how Neilan kept proposing marriage to her. Minter, however, made it clear that she had always
treated his proposals as lighthearted fun. She elaborated: "Mr. Neilan's
traits are well known. . . . He flits here and there like a swallow. We
are all charmed with his personality, but don't take him seriously. . . .
Marshall is the typification of the happy-go-lucky Irish spirit and temperament. He does perfectly terrible things to everybody, but everybody
loves him. They are always glad to see him again. As to harboring any
deep-seated malice, I don't believe he is capable of it. . . . No matter how
angry I would become with him somehow you can't bear malice against
that boy."[31]

Minter's picture of Mickey Neilan describes a lover, not a husband:
a proposal was apparently his standard seduction strategy. Swanson,
however, unlike Minter, took Neilan seriously, and in Hollywood's new
climate of fear and enforced decency, her relationship with the playboy
was "like playing cops and robbers with loaded guns."[32] She was married,
Neilan kept offering to marry every actress he fancied, and the studio
stood to lose if word of their affair leaked out. DeMille biographer Charles
Higham tells of finding a blackmail note, stuffed between the pages of a
scrapbook in the DeMille archive, which offered to hush up Swanson's
affair for a price. Higham claimed that correspondence between Lasky
and DeMille indicated that "the money was paid—at midnight at a deserted intersection in downtown Los Angeles."[33] Such cloak and dagger
escapades may be apocryphal, but for everyone in Hollywood, the stakes
were high.

On a daily basis, however, the cameras were rolling, and Swanson was
expected to appear refreshed and relaxed in front of them. Remembering
fondly her long rides on the beaches of Puerto Rico, she decided to
splurge and bought herself a horse. She frequently rode Cochette, a five-
gaited Kentucky mare, to work at the studio, tying the horse to a tree
outside her bungalow before submitting to the endless ministrations of
the costumers, makeup artists, and her brilliant hairdresser Hattie. One
morning when she arrived for work in her jodhpurs—DeMille's trademark garb—Gloria did an impromptu imitation of the director. She was

expertly mimicking his gestures for a small audience when DeMille himself appeared. He laughed at his Young Fellow's antics, though he would have crucified a lesser light for a smaller offense.

Cochette was strong and sure-footed, and Gloria often spent her one day off—Sunday—riding in the Hollywood Hills with her friend Lois Wilson, who was also under contract at FPL. Occasionally Gloria kept a riding date with a young actor she had befriended while he was doing bit parts around town. Rudolph Valentino was a shy young man who often seemed despondent about his future in Hollywood. Swanson had first seen Valentino on screen in a small role in *Eyes of Youth*, the Clara Kimball Young picture that was Herbert Somborn's calling card. Herbert liked Valentino and had hoped to use him for another film. To Swanson, Rudy spoke quietly and sympathetically about how Miss Young's career had been destroyed by her poor choices in independent production. Gloria grew to trust Rudy, confiding in him about her frustration with her marriage, her desire for a divorce, and her fear that she would not succeed as a star.

Like Gloria, Valentino was unhappily married and would soon divorce. Swanson found it hard to reconcile his "dreadful reputation" as a gigolo who was paid for dancing with women with Rudy's kindness and his good manners.[34] While they rested their mounts high in the hills, the pair looked down at Hollywood below and talked about their dreams. Swanson was touched when Rudy presented her with a lovely riding crop as a birthday present. It helped that she did not find him sexually attractive. In fact, though both Gloria and Lois liked him enormously, they privately agreed: Rudy would never make it as a leading man because he was funny looking. As Swanson recalled, "He had ears like a faun."[35] So they were pleased but surprised by the furor created after the March 1921 premiere of *The Four Horsemen of the Apocalypse*. Valentino had lobbied hard for the role of Julio Desnoyers, whose transformation from wastrel to tragic lover and valiant soldier was only enhanced by the actor's ability to dance the tango perfectly.

Suddenly, shy Rudy was being branded a Latin lover and stampeded by Hollywood phonies. Swanson hosted a small supper party after the film premiere to celebrate her friend's triumph, though she had little good to say about the people who claimed they'd recognized Valentino's talent all along. (She also pointedly ignored Wallace Beery, who appeared in the film as a vicious German officer.) However, his overnight success and his new relationship with Natacha Rambova, who had designed some of Swanson's costumes for her DeMille pictures, meant Rudy was seldom free to ride and relax. Their lazy Sundays were another casualty of Hollywood success. Being a star, Swanson reflected ruefully, seemed to mean becoming more and more isolated.

Her Gilded Cage

ONCE FPL'S MANAGEMENT TEAM REALIZED THAT SWANSON'S VIEWERS would not be satisfied seeing her in frumpy clothes or cheap settings, they looked to control costs another way. Her newest picture was a re-tread, an unused episode from *The Affairs of Anatol* featuring Wallace Reid and Elliott Dexter as friends both in love with Swanson. Sam Wood fleshed it out with a week's shooting. Then FPL gave it the enigmatic title *Don't Tell Everything* and hustled it into theaters. This was a clever way of keeping Wally Reid, who was unwell and unable to work, on screen; he made only one more film before his death in January 1922. Yet it was thin gruel fashioned from leftover DeMille stew.

Thus far, Swanson was not overly impressed by her new director. Sam Wood had little of the creative artist about him, Gloria felt, dismissing him as "a real estate dealer at heart."[1] This was too bad, since Swanson bloomed when she felt a director's confidence in her and her contributions. At least his sets functioned smoothly and efficiently. (For his part, Wood was beguiled by Swanson and named his infant daughter for her.) If Swanson was not inspired, she was too busy to worry much about it; her transition to starring parts barely gave her a moment to think. Production typically took two months per picture, with ten days between assignments—days devoted to interviews, fittings, and other more or less mandatory publicity tasks. Madame Glyn's life tutorials also kept Gloria occupied.

When Jesse Lasky called Swanson to his office, she gave herself a pep talk before she entered: if Lasky asked her something unreasonable, surely she should have nerve enough to say no. She almost laughed when she heard that Lasky wanted her permission to share star billing for her next picture, *Beyond the Rocks*, with her friend Rudolph Valentino. Rudy was working at FPL (now more frequently known as Paramount) and had made a stir in *The Sheik*. The management was puzzled by Valentino's success. As Adolph Zukor said, "We certainly did not expect him to convulse the nation."[2] However, audiences were alight for him, and Paramount wanted to cash in. Since her contract stipulated that Swanson would not share star billing with anyone, Lasky was asking her a favor.

She thought quickly about what she most wanted—a divorce—but knew Lasky was unlikely to budge. Mickey had been telling Gloria that she needed to see the world, and the prospect of getting out of Hollywood for a while was alluring. So Swanson negotiated for a European vacation at the studio's expense in return for accepting Valentino as her costar. She was very pleased with the bargain and knew Madame Glyn, who was writing the scenario, would be thrilled. Glyn had wanted Valentino for *The Great Moment*, arguing that he and Swanson would have devastating screen chemistry. So Gloria gave Lasky something she was happy to concede in exchange for a lovely, long, all-expenses-paid trip abroad. "When I came out of his office," she recalled, "I realized I wasn't a bad businesswoman."[3] Swanson would sail to Europe after finishing her first year's quota of five pictures.

Paramount pulled out all the stops for *Beyond the Rocks*, filmed during the winter of 1921. The clash between Mrs. Glyn's erratic but colorful brilliance and Sam Wood's steady craftsmanship had made for an uneasy partnering on their first film. Now, however—her ruffled feathers smoothed by *The Great Moment*'s success and her new Paramount assignment—Madame Glyn was gracious. She approved the scale of the production: the picture was set in London, Paris, Switzerland, and the Arabian desert, moving from modern-day drawing rooms to Versailles in flashback.

Fifty gowns were made for Swanson, publicized as costing a (clearly exaggerated) $1 million. Fantasy time travel, thanks to a reimagining of the "gallants of long ago," gave Gloria the chance to wear dresses Marie Antoinette would have considered overblown. For a pageant acted at a British country house, Valentino appeared as a romantic highwayman, with Swanson playing the proper young woman he abducts. These fancy-dress dream sequences created continuity for Swanson's established audience: women who loved fine clothes and imaginative romantic adventures. Valentino kidnapping a proper British woman reprised his sexy role in *The Sheik* (some of that film's unused footage appeared in *Beyond the Rocks*). Even when a studio picture was new and original, it carefully recaptured or recycled attractions associated with its star players.

Madame Glyn took credit for teaching Valentino to kiss the palm, rather than the back, of a woman's hand, also claiming she taught both Rudy and Gloria a good deal about "the art of making love before the camera."[4] Everyone was seeking inventive ways to make love, since Will Hays's new guidelines limited movie kisses to ten feet of film (around three seconds of screen time). Each kiss was now being shot twice: once for release in America, with a longer version for international audiences. "Poor Rudy could hardly get his nostrils flaring before the American version was over," recalled Swanson.[5] The friends sometimes had a hard time taking their pretend lovemaking seriously. One repeated bit of romantic business had Valentino sniffing delicately at Swanson's scented lace handkerchief, and Swanson arranged for one of her hankies to be filled with minced garlic. Rudy tended to be melancholy, and Gloria considered it both a duty and a pleasure to create fun around him.

Mrs. Glyn stayed safely behind when the cast and crew shipped out to Catalina for location shooting, and without the pressure to meet her stringent standards for sophisticated conduct, everyone relaxed. During breaks from filming there were charades and tennis and pillow fights. The troupe commandeered a hotel ballroom in Avalon, and Valentino and Swanson gave an impromptu dance exhibition, the locals lining up to watch the Latin lover and the queen of glamour strut their stuff. It wasn't all fun: for one scene, Swanson had to learn to capsize a small boat so she could fall out of it and be saved from drowning by Valentino. Swanson panicked as she was dunked repeatedly in the ocean, and Wood ordered retake after retake as the actress fought off her rescuer. Finally, she got so tired and bedraggled that she relaxed and let Rudy do his job.

Beyond the Rocks strains credulity. Valentino rescues Swanson from death not once but twice, the Alps look like they are made of cardboard, and Swanson's elderly husband essentially commits suicide so his wife can be with her lover. Credulity, however, was never one of its selling points. The electricity between the two leads was what the studio was banking on, and that was a shrewd investment. When a pristine print of the film, long considered lost, turned up unexpectedly in the Netherlands in 2003, modern viewers got a chance to see Swanson and Valentino as they had not been seen for decades. Their glamour and charisma made *Beyond the Rocks*, more than eighty years after its original release, an international success.

Swanson was moved briskly through her next two pictures: in 1922, she had new releases in theaters in March, May, September, and November. The apparently endless demand for fresh motion pictures was heightened by the studio's acquisition of movie theaters: now they had screens and seats they needed to fill. This meant changing movies twice weekly. It also meant that not every picture had to be special. Reviews of individual pictures became less important than favorable mentions of the carryover commodity, the star. Studio managers tried to shape a star's persona efficiently, anxious to tailor an actor's newest film to his or her last success. Swanson's pictures, like those of other stars, were deliberately made to seem familiar. *Her Husband's Trademark* and *Her Gilded Cage* again featured the actress in love triangles; she was either wrongly matched or wrongly accused of infidelity. She always wore expensive, elaborate outfits, even if the plot rendered them improbable. There was exotic travel, even if it too seemed unlikely: in one picture, Gloria went to Mexico, in the other to France. Sexual dynamics, however, were always at the core of the story. Everything was driven by problems of love, desire, honor, and fidelity.

Swanson's leading men, however, were generally not as charismatic or active as the characters she played. When she wasn't needed to boost the appeal of an up-and-coming performer, Swanson got experienced but lackluster male leads. The love triangle theme was no accident: she had such a strong presence that it generally took two male players of average capability to hold the screen against her. Swanson's burgeoning salary also meant that it behooved the studio to keep costs down on the other players. For *Beyond the Rocks*, Swanson earned more than twice what Valentino was paid, but he was paid a good deal more than the serviceable male leads who were her colleagues—but not her "costars"— in her next films. Whether she played a trophy wife in *Her Husband's Trademark* or a cabaret dancer in *Her Gilded Cage*, it was opposite older, undemanding, veteran leading men who were expected to set off their female counterpart. Gloria carried the picture.

By April, Swanson was eager to throw off the heavy sequined capes, climb out of the beaded gowns, and unpin the high-piled, turbaned hairdos that made up her acting life. She needed a break, and the prospect of a long European vacation thrilled her. The only pang she felt was at leaving baby Gloria for six weeks, yet her child was in excellent hands with the nanny Madame Glyn had secured. Peggy Urson accompanied Gloria as her secretary and companion; Mickey Neilan would meet her in Paris, though this was top secret.

There was one nagging bit of business: the studio wanted Swanson to renew her contract early, for an unspecified number of films per year.

Her pictures had been making boatloads of money, and Paramount was nervous that Gloria would get a more attractive offer. Filmmakers in Europe were competing with American studios to put talent under contract: in the silent era, a German production might feature a leading man from Sweden, an actress from the US, and supporting players from all over. Swanson decided to let Jesse Lasky wait.

A crowd of reporters gathered to see Swanson off when the *Homeric* sailed from New York on April 15, and Louella Parsons thought Gloria seemed as keyed up as a child going to the circus. Swanson told Parsons she did not want to waste one minute of her precious time abroad: "I shall probably travel around with a Baedecker in one hand and a sandwich in the other."[6] She and Peggy had a large, comfortable cabin, and Gloria was not seasick once during the week-long crossing. The twenty-three-year-old dismissed the movie business from her mind for the first time in eight years.

Swanson was immediately taken up by an older British gentleman, "Sir Somebody Alexander," who insisted on changing her hotel reservation to Claridge's, arranging her London itinerary, and generally smothering her with attention. She spent much of the crossing with Prince Miguel de Braganza, grandson to the king of Portugal. It was her first experience with royalty, and others were shocked by the way Gloria teased the prince—an informality he apparently found refreshing. None of the other men on board, she laughed, was "as affluent as Sir Alexander or as pretty as Prince Miguel."[7] When she at last set foot on British soil, a letter from Jesse Lasky was waiting. Paramount was taking up her option: Swanson would be earning $5,000 a week for five pictures a year.

The grandeur and elegance of Claridge's was a revelation. Footmen in powdered wigs and silk breeches answered Gloria's every request. She developed a taste for plovers' eggs and loved the sight of top-hatted men in cutaways walking down Bond Street. Prince Miguel and Sir Alexander were also in the hotel, and Swanson alternated between the two men in a lively round of dinner invitations and parties.

Swanson seldom considered herself entirely out of play romantically: since she was not married to Mickey Neilan, she felt free to see whomever she wanted. She tripped off to Paris for a few days with Prince Miguel before Mickey arrived. When Swanson learned that the prince loved music, she bought him every kind of cheap noisemaker—drums and whistles and kazoos—she could find. She bought lovebirds in a Parisian market and had them sent to the prince via American Express;

the dignified man had to collect the birds and carry their little wooden cage through the streets. It was a charming interlude, and Swanson had no regrets when Prince Miguel left for Spain. They stayed in touch for years.

Swanson had ignored her last letter from Paramount, and another was waiting for her in Paris. The terms had gotten a little bit sweeter: they were offering a three-year deal, with her salary to go to $5,000, then $6,000, and finally $7,000 a week. She would do four, not five, pictures a year. It felt like carte blanche to go shopping, and Gloria and Peggy went on a spree. "I suppose I acted like a drunken sailor in terms of money," Swanson recalled, as the pair went from Worth to Poiret to Paquin and Lanvin.[8] Hemlines were shorter in the fashion capital. Anita Loos had celebrated her arrival in Paris a few months earlier by chopping off several inches from her skirts before she even left her hotel. Though Loos and Constance and Norma Talmadge had been daunted by their icy reception at Lanvin, Swanson's reputation as a fashion trendsetter was known in Paris.[9] The designers were delighted to have her patronage, since anything she wore would get wide press coverage. Gloria and Peggy were staying across the street from Cartier's, and the temptations were almost too much to bear.

Then Mickey Neilan arrived for what the couple considered their unofficial honeymoon. They moved into the Hotel Crillon, doing Paris in grand style, and Gloria fell in love with the city. Mickey knew all the best places and was at home everywhere, as much in his element in Paris as in Hollywood. They drank champagne at elegant restaurants, then wandered through the flower markets, Mickey loading Gloria down with armloads of rare and fragrant blossoms. The evening might end with Mickey commandeering the piano to play jazz tunes with the band after hours at some little dive. They saw Versailles and the Louvre, Montmartre and Malmaison. If you wanted a Paris honeymoon, Mickey Neilan was the best partner possible. Neither of Gloria's legal marriages had generated the heat and light this forbidden pairing provided.

Yet even Paris was not all roses. Neilan had a mean streak that surfaced when he drank, and Swanson had already seen his temper. She was nonetheless surprised by her own anger when Mickey appeared late one evening drunk and disheveled, ruining the romantic evening they had planned. He had run into an old friend, he said, and they stopped for a drink. Swanson snorted: Neilan had clearly polished off the better part of a bottle. They began fighting, and as the argument escalated she declared she would not marry him—at which point Neilan wove unsteadily over to the tall windows, threw them open, and climbed out onto the balcony, declaring he would kill himself.

Gloria felt perversely indifferent, suggesting coolly that he should go up to the roof if he meant business: their suite was only on the third floor. This enraged Neilan, who staggered back into the room, murder in his eyes. He looked for something to throw and finally grabbed his bamboo walking stick, threatening to break it over Gloria's head. The stick was so pliant, however, that it jumped out of his hand and hit the ceiling before landing on his own head. While Neilan shouted and swore, Swanson, hysterical with laughter, fell over backwards in her tiny French chair. Then Neilan, indignant, stalked across the room and yanked on the door handle, a fragile bit of Limoges that came off in his hand. He finally got the door open and made his exit, Swanson still immobilized on the floor, weeping with laughter. It was like something out of a Keystone comedy.

Neilan at last saw the farcical nature of his display: a moment later he rang Gloria from the hotel lobby, laughing so hard he could barely speak. Would she put on her hat and come down and go dancing with him? She would; she did. They danced all night before coming home tipsy at dawn to make love and snuggle in their huge bed. They would live to fight and make up again another day.[10]

They moved on to Berlin, but Swanson found the architecture heavy, the food heavy, and the mood—despite a kind of enforced gaiety—heavy as well. The mark was worth almost nothing in the postwar economy. She and Neilan were staying in the luxurious Hotel Adlon, and Swanson reflected that with her new salary she could have bought a hotel or a chateau herself. She visited the UFA film studios and met Ernst Lubitsch, who would soon be directing his witty, elegant, ribald comedies in the US. But Berlin, though impressive, was "a very sad place," and Swanson was not anxious to return to Germany.[11]

On the voyage home, Swanson kept mostly to her cabin, as would become her customary practice when traveling. She needed to rest after her European "honeymoon," and she was in a thoughtful mood. She relished the memories of her trip:

We saw every tourist sight there was to see, and bought everything we could carry or have delivered. I had never tasted trifle or crois-sants or had pancakes with whipped cream for dessert. I had never heard an English actor doing Shakespeare. I had never seen the cancan with splits, as I did in Montmartre, or a cabaret act of men in women's clothes, as I did in Berlin. I had never seen real French

fashions on beautiful women strolling naturally along grand boulevards. I had never seen a Cubist painting or heard of Dada. I had
never been in anything like Westminster Abbey, or Notre Dame, or
the Charlottenburg. I had never sat at a café sipping mineral water
or a stein of beer. I had never used a bidet.[12]

Swanson felt at home in London and Paris; she would find it difficult to
be confined to Hollywood in the future.

She had also come to a decision about Neilan: "If Mickey had made
me see Paris, Paris had also made me see Mickey." Gloria loved Mickey
more than she had ever loved—or felt likely to love—any other man.
She felt he needed her, needed "saving" from his alcoholism and help
with his faltering career.[13] But her freedom was a distant prospect; even
after she received studio approval for a divorce, it would take more than
a year to finalize. In the meantime, she was becoming a major earner for
Paramount, and the studio could not countenance her scandalous relationship with Neilan. The freedom the couple enjoyed in Europe was not
possible in Hollywood, where Gloria would be under ever closer scrutiny, and where a false step could ruin her career. As a single mother, she
could not risk her daughter's security on a man who, she recognized, was
profoundly unreliable. Yet she could not simply cut her "naughty boy"
adrift.[14]

Before she sailed for home, Gloria had a strangely serious conversation with Mickey about their future. She would keep her promise to
marry him, she said, but first he needed to keep a promise he had made
long ago: to marry Blanche Sweet, the woman with whom he had been
involved, as director and lover, for almost ten years. Gloria loved Neilan
but could not marry him; Blanche Sweet could and probably would,
despite his affair with Swanson. Then later sometime, when they were
both between marriages, Mickey and she would marry. They would go
back to their original plan; the timing just wasn't right at the moment.
"I felt [Sweet] deserved his name and his support," Gloria reasoned. "I
felt he owed it to her."[15] Swanson's assumption that Neilan's union with
Sweet would not last was the least cockamamie thing about her proposal. With two failed marriages behind her at 23, Gloria was not inclined to
believe too strongly in the unbreakable bond of matrimony.

Having exacted Gloria's renewed promise to marry him "someday,"
Neilan agreed. With Swanson standing nearby, he phoned Sweet and
asked her to meet him in Chicago, where they would be married. "It
must have been quite a shock to her to hear this," Swanson recalled with

a touch of asperity, but Sweet agreed.[16] As Swanson sailed home, her lover was a few days behind her, on his way to another bride, a match she had engineered. Gloria breathed a sigh of relief along with the salt air: Mickey Neilan had always meant trouble. What Blanche Sweet was thinking was anyone's guess, but Colleen Moore spoke for Hollywood when she wrote of Neilan's "spectacular" romance with Swanson: "Like the basketball team that gets knocked out early in the tournament by the ultimate champion and takes what satisfaction it can . . . , Blanche . . . was displaced by a woman who didn't just represent glamour. She invented the word."[17]

Blanche Sweet and Mickey Neilan were married in Chicago in early June. If the new bride thought Neilan had ended his relationship with his glamour queen, she had a rude surprise ahead: by 11:00 that same morning, Swanson claimed, "he was having breakfast with me."[18] When Mickey left for New York with Sweet, he continued to send Gloria gifts, love letters, and dozens of flirtatious, teasing telegrams. Back in Los Angeles, he bought Sweet a big house but moved home to live (as before) with his mother. The press was confounded, but no one could prove that anything sinful was going on. However, the song on everyone's lips that season was "Wonderful One," a melody Neilan had written—as was widely reported—for Gloria Swanson.

Back at work, Sam Wood put Swanson through her paces in a film whose coy connections to his star's life were hardly accidental. The title character in *The Impossible Mrs. Bellew* is accused of infidelity; her reputation blackened, she agrees to give up her child for his own good. Mrs. Bellew then goes to France to devote herself to pleasure, since nothing means anything. The final reel vindicates her reputation, reunites her with her son, and validates her relation with a much nicer man than her violent, unfaithful husband. Every movie fan in America knew that Gloria Swanson was the mother of a young child, that she had a troubled marriage which almost certainly featured an extramarital dalliance or two, and that she had just come back from a lavish trip to the continent. The pleasures knowledgeable viewers gained from measuring Swanson's "real" life story against what she performed in her pictures helped create a demand for more and more information about her private life.

Paramount was not anxious to cooperate with efforts to pry into Swanson's real romantic affairs, preferring to refocus attention on the expensive costumes she wore on and off the set. The fan magazines pictured Gloria in her Paris finery, with elaborate descriptions of her outfits, speculation about how much they cost, and comments from the star herself. When Gloria was glimpsed after hours with her legs decoratively painted rather than stockinged, stockings went swiftly out of fashion. She explained that women in Paris—even stenographers and shopkeepers' wives—were fashion innovators who would not wait for others' approval: "Your Parisienne . . . is not bothered by such inhibitions. If she decides she looks better without stockings—off they go—and if others wish to follow it is all right with her."[19]

Film exhibitors cooperated with local businesses to get movie patrons excited about the stars. A Quanah, Texas, theater owner persuaded a local milliner to make "a special Gloria Swanson hat" which they would send to the star after *Her Gilded Cage* finished its run. Five hundred invitations to view the hat went out. The millinery shop offered a few duplicates for sale to the ladies of Quanah: they sold out immediately, and all the fashionable young Texans came to see the picture.[20] When *The Impossible Mrs. Bellew* showed Swanson using a perfume called Christmas Night, the manufacturer sold a million bottles of the scent almost overnight.[21] Movie fans also enjoyed reading about fashions they could not afford to purchase. When Gloria attended a production of *Carmen* at the Hollywood Bowl wearing diamonds in the heels of her slippers, fan magazines described her tiny feet approvingly.

Around this time there was a debate about whether Swanson was an actress or just a clotheshorse. The close connection between her lifestyle and her roles irked some, though it explained her continued appeal to others. Moreover, even her most favorable notices called equal attention to her costumes and her performances. One reviewer said, "It appeared for a few moments that Miss Swanson was to be permitted to act [in *Her Gilded Cage*]. . . . We are among those who believe Miss Swanson can act if she is given a chance—why waste her talent simply because she can wear clothes like a model?" The writer called for "a production that would stimulate the brain as well as tickle the aesthetic palate!"[22] Another reviewer dismissed Swanson's movies as "gown pictures": "She changes her dresses for every new emotion, or even when there is no emotion. The Queen of Sheba would have turned pale at such raiment." Yet "movie picture officials" said that women, especially in rural areas and small towns, insisted on this type of movie.[23] So the studio was content to order up dozens more costumes for Swanson featuring sophisticated, up-to-the-moment—and occasionally bizarre—looks.

The Impossible Mrs. Bellew and Swanson's next feature, *My American Wife*, had attractive leading men in Conrad Nagel and Antonio Moreno. Swanson, however, found them about as inspiring as she found her director Sam Wood. Paramount was positioning Moreno to replace Valentino, since Rudy was arguing with the studio about his contract, and Moreno's good looks and physical bearing lent credibility to his casting as an Argentinian diplomat. *My American Wife* was set in South America, with scenes of embassy balls, horse races, duels, and a spectacular Carnival of Flowers shot partly in Texas. Gloria was happier about visiting her father, who had been posted to Texas, than about the movie.

The real unexpected benefit from *My American Wife* was meeting Aileen Pringle. The two actresses were chatting on the set when Swanson asked Pringle what she thought of Tony Moreno. "Not much," Pringle replied. "Obviously he's never had an idea above the waist."[24] Swanson instantly recognized a kindred spirit; she loved Pringle's dry wit and take-no-prisoners attitude. Pringle had been raised in Europe and had wider horizons than the movie business; Gloria admired the feisty independence that often cost Pringle acting jobs. She pressed her favorite books on Gloria, including her friend H. L. Mencken's *In Defense of Women*. Aileen Pringle stood out "like a sore thumb—but a very beautiful one" in Hollywood because of her intellectual interests and her refusal to be intimidated by anyone.[25] Mickey Neilan also liked Aileen, and the three frequently spent evenings together. Pringle witnessed Gloria and Mickey's stormy, passionate relationship (Swanson said she "refereed" their fights).[26]

Although she had a few steadfast female friends, Swanson generally preferred the company of men. "I have very little admiration for females," she said. "I'm not one of these gals who can spend luncheon with three or four or five [women] who are going shopping or going to play bridge. I have nothing in common with them. I don't know what to talk to them about. I am not interested in the last price they paid for a new bonnet or their servant problems or their men problems." Her friends were professional women, who had "more to think about and more to talk about."[27]

Swanson relied on Lois Wilson, whose warmth and generosity were endearing. An Alabama schoolteacher, Wilson came to Hollywood after winning a beauty contest; she worked steadily but never quite got her big break. Lois's mother and sister lived nearby, and the Wilson home became a refuge from Gloria's increasingly complicated Hollywood life. She could turn up at Lois's at any hour and be certain of a welcome: "If I had some big emotional thing going on, I'd go over to her house and spend the night, or she'd come to mine."[28] Wilson was a staunch Catholic who loved babies, though she never married or had children of her own.

Lois was one of the first people to whom Swanson confided her secret wish: she wanted to adopt a child, a boy close in age to little Gloria. She wanted her daughter to have the companionship she herself had missed as an only child. Sooner or later she would be divorced from Herbert Somborn, but the twenty-four-year-old had decided that if she couldn't marry Mickey Neilan, she would never marry again. She planned to adopt as a single parent. This was unusual but not unheard of, except for a Hollywood star. Swanson had already surprised everyone by returning to work after giving birth. Becoming a mother had not done her career any harm; in fact, she was much more famous now than she had been then. Through the summer and fall of 1922, Swanson quietly began visiting orphanages, donating playground equipment and toys to the Lark Ellen Home for Boys.

Nothing in Los Angeles stayed secret for long, and in October the *Los Angeles Times* broke the story that Swanson was trying to adopt a little boy.[29] Without detailing her plans, Swanson gave several interviews in which she described the moment she first held her baby daughter: "Of all the thrills that the world offers that is the greatest. To have a little atom of humanity close to you and know it is the greatest gift life offers is a divine thrill indeed. . . . The thrill of being a mother lasts and lasts and lasts."[30] Finding a child to adopt, however, was a slow process. Gloria used the time to get a home ready for her growing family.

To her delight, a beautiful property she had long admired came on the market. 904 North Crescent Drive was a stunning two-story Italian Renaissance-style mansion with a red tile roof and a colonnaded entrance way. The pie-shaped property was directly across from the Beverly Hills Hotel and had large, sloping lawns and an enormous terrace planted with mature palms and acacias. The industrialist King Gillette had built the house with his earnings from the disposable razor blade: during the war, every American soldier had been issued a Gillette razor kit. The 24,000-square-foot house had twenty-two rooms, five bathrooms, and a magnificent interior staircase. It even had an elevator, though Swanson, who suffered from claustrophobia, would never use it.

With characteristic decisiveness, she immediately met the asking price of $250,000, though she had to borrow money from Mickey Neilan for the down payment. Barely a year earlier she had been embarrassed by Herbert Somborn's unpaid bills and had felt constrained to move from a hotel suite they could ill afford. Now, with an escalating salary and a longer term contract, she was living a much grander life. Swanson's enormous new home did not seem out of proportion, given the showplaces her movie colleagues were buying or building. Douglas Fairbanks and Mary Pickford had the palatial fourteen-acre Pickfair, with its own in-ground pool. Mr. DeMille had a house in Beverly Hills; so did Corinne Griffith, Charlie Ray, and Pauline Fredericks. Frances Marion and her husband, western star Fred Thomson, were also building there. Within a few years, Beverly Hills was booming: its pre-1920 population of fewer than 700 grew by 1925 to 7,500. A year later it was 12,000.[31] The community wasn't planned; "it just happened, like Topsy," Swanson said.[32]

Their enormous weekly paychecks were burning holes in many prosperous performers' pockets. It quickly became de rigueur for a star to have a luxurious home, often one built to order. Buster Keaton considered his $300,000 home both a safe investment and a reward for his hard work. "It took a lot of pratfalls . . . to build *this* dump," he told visitors as he showed them around the Italian-style villa.[33] Keaton estimated that his wife spent $1,000 a week on clothing, acknowledging that he indulged himself as well: "I bought myself everything I wanted, including the finest clothes, cars, hunting and fishing equipment. I spared no expenses on our huge swimming pool or on the patio I had built behind the house. I spent $14,000 moving to the rear of the house forty-two towering palms that had lined the drive in front."[34] Keaton's extravagances included a brook stocked with trout and an aviary full of quail. There were tennis courts, a miniature version of the villa for a playhouse, and—allegedly—gold-leafed bathroom fixtures.

Adolphe Menjou, whose own career was booming, said, "Unless a person earned $1,000 a week he was a mendicant. If he didn't have a swimming pool, three saddle horses, four servants, and an Isotta-Fraschini town car, he was a peasant."[35] Colleen Moore offered this explanation: "We splurged on homes and cars and clothes and swimming pools, partly . . . because our intensive work schedules didn't permit such luxuries as travel, partly because what started out as necessities or conveniences became status symbols, and partly because most of us had more money than sense."[36]

Swanson particularly liked the idea of going from a gorgeous, well-appointed movie set to an equally beautiful home and threw herself into refurbishing the house's interior. "To a woman there is nothing much more desirable than beauty," she said. "It satisfies an inner craving that is a vital part of her life. So I wear as pretty clothes as I can, and live in as beautiful a home as possible. Getting the best you can is not extravagance, provided you can afford it."[37] She filled the house with paintings and tapestries and covered the walls of a large ground-floor reception room in spectacular peacock-colored silk. The breakfast room was done in shades of gold and cream. The room that made the biggest splash was the master bathroom: it was made of black marble and reportedly featured a gold tub (which Swanson denied). Mickey Neilan egged her on, then surprised her with an early birthday gift: he had a construction crew build Gloria a movie theater with seating for twelve next to the billiard room in the basement.

904 was Swanson's first real home of her own. By late fall 1922, renovations were complete, and she began entertaining. In addition to dinner parties, movies, and dancing, she would hire magicians to perform, or hypnotists to make the guests do amusing things while in a trance. Running a large establishment required help: soon a cook, a gardener, as many as four butlers, a laundress, and a chauffeur were reporting for work daily, along with Swanson's secretary, her personal maid, and little Gloria's governess, who lived with the family. Ivan, a silky-coated Russian wolfhound, protected the household.

The large staff on retainer meant that Gloria's Sunday riding parties were now catered. On a ride in the woods, the actress and her friends enjoyed sumptuous spreads prepared by her cook, or servers would hand around beautifully arranged picnic food in large tents erected on the beach. The hostess was occasionally the main attraction: for one beach party Swanson appeared in a skimpy black patent leather bathing suit. Lois Wilson said Gloria never went near the water but kept everyone's attention riveted to her bare knees: her daring swimsuit did not include stockings.

Swanson loved entertaining, and most of Hollywood sampled her elegant, lively hospitality. There were always unusual guests: she hosted everyone from Admiral Byrd (who showed Gloria and Aileen his route north on Swanson's big globe) to Kahlil Gibran, Jascha Heifetz, and HRH Prince George, Duke of Kent. Gloria often wondered what King Gillette's two maiden sisters, who had lived quietly in the house before Swanson's menagerie moved in, would think if they could see the bustle and excitement there now. One night in November, Charlie Chaplin, Pola Negri, Lois, Aileen, Mickey, and Sam Wood came to dinner. Gloria's director admired the house so much that he wanted to use it in their next picture, *Prodigal Daughters*. Although Swanson would not as a rule let photographers into the house, she agreed, and in January 1923 the actress's real home substituted for the Fifth Avenue mansion her flapper character in the film abandons.

The new film was her ninth with Sam Wood. Swanson thought *Prodigal Daughters* dully repetitious, at best a variation on a theme: her character's adventures end with rescue in the form of marriage. Despite her parents' disapproval, the scandalously modern "Swiftie" strikes out for Greenwich Village. She gets caught in a raid on a speakeasy and is almost forced into marriage as a way to pay her gambling debts. The picture's ad campaign played to the generation gap opening up in America: "Parents! Aren't you aghast at the reckless pace your daughters are setting? Daughters! Do you think your parents are hopelessly old-fashioned?"[38] Dozens of flapper movies threatened—and titillated—viewers with the new freedoms young women were demanding. Advertisements for *Prodigal Daughters* represented "The Seven Deadly Whims":

> *New lips to kiss*
> *Freedom from conventions*
> *A new world for women*
> *No more chaperons*
> *Life with a kick in it*
> *The single moral standard*
> *Our own latchkeys.*[39]

Other promotional materials released under Swanson's signature, however, emphasized how "true and loveable and responsive to good impulses" modern young women actually were. Paramount promoted *Prodigal Daughters* as both an exciting story of girls gone wild and "a mirror to our girls which will benefit them in no small way, held as it is by a friendly hand."[40]

This was all routine stuff for Swanson, who was getting bored with both her director and her roles. "Retake" Wood was not visually inventive, and he broke actors down with endless reshoots yet gave little instruction about how he wanted a scene played. (Groucho Marx claimed that Wood's motivational speech was limited to "All right, gang, let's get in there and sell 'em a load of clams.")[41] Wood was amiable enough, and Swanson liked playing mah-jongg with his wife Clara between scenes. Yet she recognized with increasing frustration that her post-DeMille roles were neither inspiring nor challenging her to reach beyond her limits.

The studio seemed more interested in the glitz of big premieres—another new phenomenon—than in telling substantial stories with compelling characters. Everything had to be the biggest yet: the premiere of *My*

American Wife at Grauman's Metropolitan Theater was a case in point. The new art deco cinema was the largest ever built in Los Angeles. It seated almost 4,000 and had the longest theater balcony ever constructed. The opening night show began with the unfurling of the world's biggest flag and "The Star-Spangled Banner" sung by a chorus of 500. More than 40 violinists played Schubert's "Ave Maria," 200 dancers performed a ballet, and 100 "California beauties" appeared in a stage pageant.[42] Swanson's film was the culmination of the evening.

Paramount was thrilled with its decision to make Swanson a star. The profits from her pictures, the publicity attendant on her every move, and the huge bags of fan mail she received daily proved her success. She even showed up in the cartoons: when Felix the Cat visits Hollywood, he gets an eyeful of Gloria in her dressing room. "That's how I got like this," cross-eyed Ben Turpin tells Felix. Mervyn LeRoy, who played Gloria's brother in *Prodigal Daughters* and became a good friend, remembered leaving the studio with Gloria in the evening and being ignored while crowds surrounded her.

Swanson, however, was becoming frustrated: "[In] every picture I made . . . the train got longer, the hairdo more complicated, until I got so fed up I started screaming: I don't want to be a clotheshorse. Let me out of this thing. I want to be an actress. I want to do character parts. I want to do fun things."[43] Swanson disliked repeating herself, yet repetition could be construed as the point of stardom: the creation of box office value on which both producers and audiences could rely. Their enormous paychecks compensated the stars extravagantly, but Swanson was beginning to feel she was in a gilded cage.

Some reviewers observed an unwelcome artificiality in her performances, and they too blamed her "gorgeously bizarre and theatrical" costumes. One was "an exquisite combination of pink silk tights, silver cloth and pearl beads, set off by a headdress of clusters of many colored bird of Paradise feathers."[44] She also had a stuffed bird of paradise on her wrist. Another dress was made of 3,000 ermine tails strung on seed pearls. "Gloria Swanson wears spangles nearly all day," one reviewer said.[45] Another claimed that Swanson had "accomplished a feat" simply by standing upright in her gowns. Her headdresses offered another encumbrance: "With her head heavily encased in the most elegant what-d'ye-call-'ems, trimmed with pearls, and all sorts of jools, [Swanson] showed that she could still smile and look fascinating. These head torturers were jammed down over her brow, leaving nothing but her pool-like eyes on exhibition."[46]

Reviewers blamed "the apparent decline in her mimetic ability" on the studio, protesting that Swanson "couldn't shine through the thick wrapping of elegant duds that were put upon her."[47] However, one realist observed, "Gloria Swanson wears clothes too well to be forced into a role where clothes are a secondary consideration."[48] Her cage might be gilded, but the door was apparently locked.

All Swanson's frustrations vanished one afternoon in March 1923 when the phone rang. The orphanage was on the line: a four-and-a-half-month-old baby boy was being brought down from San Francisco. Was she still interested in adopting? Prospective parents could examine the children they were considering, and Swanson believed she would know immediately whether Sonny Smith was destined to join her family. She could scarcely contain her excitement as the car bearing the child pulled into her driveway:

> Before the car had stopped, I was in the back seat extending my arms. He was handed to me—his head was in my cupped hands. The silence stood still as each of us held our breaths. His violet-blue stare was passing judgment, I am sure. Wild thoughts were bumping into each other. Why oh why or how could your mother have given you up? What are you trying to say to me in your silent stare? And then a miracle happened—he smiled at me. *At me*! And I squeezed the breath out of him and felt like laughing and crying. I was kissing his little fingers.[49]

Gloria carried the baby into the house, calling everyone to come meet the new member of the family. Little Gloria promptly christened him "Brother," a name the boy never quite lost.

All the new mother knew of her son's past was his name—which she changed to Joseph in honor of her father—and that his parents were students, his father an Irishman from San Francisco. The baby was a bit undernourished; she was sure it was because he had not been breast-fed. She set out to fatten him up, and within a few months Brother was chubby and bow-legged. Swanson refused to acknowledge the standard six-month probationary period: that moment of mystical communication with Brother was all she needed. The baby was incorporated into the household without delay.

Once again, Swanson refused to allow the child to be photographed, even though people speculated openly that Joseph was her own child, the adoption a fiction designed to hide his illegitimacy. He was said to resemble Cecil DeMille, Sam Wood, and practically every other man Swanson knew in the movie business. This amused Gloria, since she had been making four pictures a year and could not possibly have hidden a pregnancy during that time. Lois Wilson, who was totally captivated by Joseph, was incensed by the stories, however, and defended Gloria wherever she went. "I practically wasn't invited places," Wilson recalled, "because it was like waving a red flag in front of a bull to say [untrue] things about people that I loved."[50]

After thirty years as friends, Gloria and Lois compared notes about their reputations, Lois declaring, "Gloria is the kind of personality that is always going to be talked about." Swanson concurred: "If I was in a room fully clothed for five minutes with some men, mayhem! Lois could walk out of a room with a dozen men in a black chiffon nightgown after two hours and they'd say, 'Oh, somebody must be ill in there. She's taking care of them.'" Amid peals of laughter, Wilson conceded, "I probably had a better reputation than I deserved and you had a worse one than you deserved."[51]

None of this would seem a laughing matter later that spring. One afternoon, Swanson opened her mail and was stunned to see that Herbert Somborn was suing her for divorce. Her initial feeling of satisfaction—at least she would be free, since the studio could not prevent Herbert from ending his marriage—turned suddenly to fury, when she saw that the grounds were adultery. Worse, the papers named more than a dozen men as her partners, among them many of her Paramount colleagues, including Cecil DeMille, Sam Wood, Jesse Lasky, Adolph Zukor, and a handful of Paramount executives; Mickey Neilan was also named. "He had men [on the list] whom I'd only met casually," Swanson remembered, "or only seen once. Some I didn't know at all."[52] Herbert was demanding a settlement of $150,000 to compensate him for what he claimed was his role in negotiating his wife's Paramount contract.

Since Swanson's salary had doubled in January and she was now earning $5,000 a week, Herbert's timing was exquisite. No court could deny his wife's box office value, and it would be impossible to prove that Somborn had not assisted in her negotiations with Paramount. Gloria dismissed the overblown accusations of infidelity as Herbert's attempt to accomplish his real goal: the settlement money. More than anything else, however, the claim that Herbert had gotten her the lucrative new contract made Swanson see red. She took pride in her dealings with the studio and decided on the spot to fight Somborn in court. She was damned if she'd pay him a penny.

She called Herbert and complained that his accusations were outrageous. He replied calmly that it did not matter: fighting them would take months and would ruin her career. She insisted she would never submit to his blackmail. "Love is a very strange thing," she mused. "Here was a man who was ready to ruin the mother of his child, but if he got paid, he wouldn't do it."[53]

The next day Swanson was summoned to Cecil DeMille's home. A copy of Herbert's divorce papers had been delivered to the studio as well, and DeMille ushered her into his library to discuss her husband's claims. Somborn had been hinting to the press that he expected his divorce to be hotly contested, and people would be paying close attention. DeMille expressed his sympathy but made the studio's position clear: the divorce had to be kept out of the papers. Swanson countered by saying that the sexual accusations were baseless, as DeMille well knew, since he and Gloria had never been intimate. Couldn't he see that Herbert's list was absurd? The director pointed out gently that not all the accusations were false: Mickey Neilan's name was on the list.

Swanson felt that was a low blow, since the studio had prevented her from divorcing Herbert when she could have filed on grounds of desertion and married Mickey. She would not give in to Herbert's blackmail. She would not say he had been her agent when he had done nothing to earn it. DeMille said he understood Gloria's position but asked her not to decide rashly. It would be better if her divorce remained private. Gloria agreed to sleep on it, though she knew she would not change her mind: she was going to court.

DeMille put his arm around her, and as she left the house, she ran straight into a uniformed Western Union delivery boy carrying a telegram for DeMille. The director scanned it, then handed it to Swanson without a word. The telegram offered brief but succinct instructions: the Swanson-Somborn matter was to be settled out of court, quietly and immediately, for the good of the motion picture industry. It was on no account to be allowed to create a scandal in the press. The telegram was signed by Will Hays.

"If I had gotten hit with a hammer between the eyes, I couldn't have been more taken aback," Swanson claimed. "This was not to be lightly taken. . . . When he used the words 'the entire industry is concerned,' I must say I was floored and I left there quite weakened."[54] Swanson was in "such a state of emotion—rage, embarrassment, disappointment, most of all a sense of complete despair" that she could barely drive home.[55]

Reeling, Swanson gathered her closest friends. Lois, Aileen, and Mickey sympathized with her predicament but saw no way out. She could not fight against Will Hays; she would have to settle. Her father was visiting, and he agreed. Picking up his new little grandson, he told Gloria she needed to keep her priorities straight. A scandalous divorce would not do her children any good. Moreover, the orphanage could still reclaim Joseph, whose probationary period had months to run. Gloria realized that he was right: viewed from any angle, Herbert had outfoxed her. She could not sacrifice her children's welfare for her own pride. She felt foolish for not having insisted on a divorce earlier, when the studio had balked but the terms were her own. Now the divorce was hers but the conditions galling. Her father's loving advice was her only consolation: "It was as if he had bandaged my knee with his big white handkerchief."[56]

Paramount offered to have its lawyers negotiate with Herbert's attorney, Milton Cohen, to try and reduce the settlement. They halved Herbert's asking price and advanced Gloria the money to pay him; now she literally owed Paramount for her divorce. She forced herself to read the paperwork, which included the hated claim that Herbert had procured her contract for her. DeMille told Gloria that the studio also expected her to do one more movie for them as repayment. Smarting, Swanson agreed, though she recognized that Paramount was taking advantage of her weak position: "This was what they had been after for some time. They had always wanted me to make one more picture a year which automatically would reduce the price of my salary per picture."[57] The additional film would be her fifth that year; Paramount was reclaiming the concession Gloria had wrung from the studio by dodging its offers as she toured Europe. Beyond the blow to her pride, though, she reckoned her divorce would cost "six weeks out of my life and some cash."[58] At least her family remained intact.

There was one more sting in the scorpion's tail: her new contract contained a morals clause. Such clauses were becoming the norm in Hollywood, where stars' behavior could damage studios' fortunes. Swanson's new contract stipulated, among other offenses, that if she was "charged with adulterous conduct or immoral relations with men other than her husband," Paramount could dismiss her. Even if such charges were unproven, if they were "published in the public press," she could lose her job.[59]

"The studio was putting me on a tight leash," Swanson said, "telling me that unless I toed the line, they could cut me off. I was angry and humiliated, but I signed everything. . . . And after I signed, everyone hugged me and kissed me and told me how brave I had been." Once she was divorced, she observed wryly, "Nobody seemed to care how much I saw Mickey or anybody else. I could go dancing every night. As long as Herbert couldn't sue me again, and nobody else had any reason to, we were all in clover once more."[60] At least she had DeMille as an ally to help her deal with people who were neither noble nor forthright. She was glad he was on her side.

Despite the studio's misgivings about a scandalous divorce, Swanson's next picture played with the idea of multiple marriages. A costume drama with a farcical tone, in *Bluebeard's 8th Wife* Gloria is a newlywed who learns that her husband has a secret: she is his eighth wife, not because he has murdered the first seven, but because he has divorced them. Convinced that her husband does not know the value of matrimony, Swanson's character tries to provoke him to divorce her. Because he truly loves her, he refuses. The eighth time's the charm—except that for Swanson, it wasn't. Paramount was spending less and less on her costars: Gloria's cut-rate leading man Huntley Gordon was himself pushed into nine Paramount pictures that year. Sam Wood, once again in charge, showed no more sensitivity to the comic possibilities of the story than he had to the dramas in Swanson's other films. (The more congenial Ernst Lubitsch remade *Bluebeard* with Claudette Colbert and Gary Cooper in 1938.)

One night soon after her divorce, Swanson attended an industry banquet, a chore she generally disliked, and found herself seated next to Will Hays. They had had no contact since his intervention in her divorce proceedings, and she did not look forward to an evening in his company. She was icily polite, until Hays finally asked if he had offended her in some way. Gloria responded coolly that she had not appreciated his telegram. When Hays stared at her blankly, she explained that she had seen his instructions to Mr. DeMille. Then Hays flatly denied ever having sent such a telegram. Now Swanson was the one taken aback. A moment's conversation persuaded her that Hays was not lying—which meant that someone else had been.

Cecil DeMille, the man she considered her mentor and ally in the industry, who had given Swanson her best roles and her happiest experiences on set, had betrayed her trust. "He laid for me the foundation of one of the most outstanding careers in Hollywood," Gloria said.[61] She was devastated: the man who could orchestrate such a deception while proclaiming his sympathy for her was not worthy of the faith she had placed in him. DeMille had played her expertly. Of course, she had believed in the telegram: the Western Union boy was perfectly costumed, his arrival perfectly timed. It was a scene "directed by one of the great directors of the industry," designed to bring her in line with what the studio wanted.[62] Herbert's threats to destroy her reputation hurt a lot less than this treachery.

She phoned Mickey, but he had been drinking and was no help. There was no point in talking to him about anything unless he was sober, and that was not often. Gloria acknowledged privately that Mickey too was "a great liar and cheater": he was a bad bet as a long-term partner.[63] During a sleepless night she recalled all the times she had defended DeMille against his detractors; memories of Craney Gartz's contempt for him came flooding back. She had little respect for Jesse Lasky but had felt very differently about her former director: "Mr. DeMille was my idol, on another plane altogether from the rest of Hollywood. Since the first day I walked into his office, he had been the standard by which I judged everything else in the motion picture industry. No matter who criticized him to me . . . my opinion of him had never changed. I had never been able to think of myself as even remotely his equal."[64] Now even DeMille's nickname for her, "Young Fellow," seemed less complimentary, less a testament to Swanson's buoyancy and spirit than a mark of her naivcté.

Gloria had always disliked having to figure out the movie business on her own. She flattered herself that she did pretty well with negotiations, and her thriving career seemed to bear this out. DeMille's duplicity, however, made her feel profoundly alone, and her bitter disappointment had lasting repercussions for her career.

This story remained one Swanson had a hard time telling. Her unwillingness to tell it fully may help explain why she delayed publication of her memoirs until late in her life, despite the many drafts she prepared over several decades. She never confronted DeMille, and her pain at her mentor's deception never entirely healed. Swanson's sense of betrayal gives more poignancy to the trouper's bravado she brought to her portrayal of Norma Desmond in *Sunset Boulevard*, a landmark performance in which the ruined silent film queen longs to be reunited with Cecil DeMille, who directed her twenty-five years earlier.

In the meantime, the "Young Fellow" was a survivor. She presented herself at Jesse Lasky's office, relishing his surprise when she said she knew about the charade with the telegram and thought she could have him jailed on fraud charges. Yet Lasky was unrepentant: keeping Swanson's divorce out of the papers was a matter of importance for the industry, whether Will Hays had said so or not. (Lasky frequently marveled at Gloria's fire, telling a colleague after one of her rages: "What a temperament! Isn't she magnificent?")[65] Satisfied for the moment by his admission that Paramount had deliberately tricked her, Swanson considered her next move carefully. She remembered a story Herbert told her about a man who caught a butcher cheating. The man declined to turn the butcher in to the police and ended up with free deliveries of meat for the rest of his life. She had nothing to gain from fighting publicly with the studio, and there might be something she could get from Paramount for accepting the deception quietly.

What Swanson wanted was better pictures and a more inspiring director, but the studio had no interest in changing either her clotheshorse roles or her collaborators. Then Mickey suggested she seek out his friend Allan Dwan. He felt confident that Swanson and Dwan, who had just directed Douglas Fairbanks's lively, playful *Robin Hood*, would like each other. Better yet, Dwan was working at Paramount's East Coast studio. Perhaps Gloria could negotiate a break from Hollywood.

When Dwan said he would love to work with her, Swanson was elated. She quickly came up with a good old-fashioned strategy to get what she wanted: she lied. She told Jesse Lasky that the surgery she had delayed since little Gloria's birth could no longer wait. The best physician was in New York; she wanted to go there to regain her health. Lasky graciously gave his permission, and Swanson left California in July for what was supposed to be a two-week trip east. She had no intention of coming back to Hollywood anytime soon.

CHAPTER 8

East Coaster

SWANSON WAS IN A REBELLIOUS MOOD AS SHE FLED TO NEW YORK. She felt bruised by DeMille's betrayal and angry at Paramount's unwillingness to see her as anything other than a clotheshorse. Lasky and company had manipulated her; now they would get a taste of their own medicine. Before Gloria dealt with her female trouble, she intended to take care of some movie business. She presented herself to Walter Wanger, the general manager of Paramount in New York: she was here about the role of *Zaza*.[1] Allan Dwan wanted her, and she wanted it. Her health crisis would keep.

Few people could stop Swanson when she was in steamroller mode, and there was no real reason why she should not play Zaza. She was under contract to Paramount, and *Zaza* was a Paramount property. Thus, Gloria engineered her happy and productive eight-film collaboration with Allan Dwan. It was one of the golden times in Swanson's long career, as she remade herself yet again, the glamour queen developing a comic, lighthearted persona in both her films and her private life. She took greater control of her work, developed greater faith in her own judgment, and began the journey toward producing her own films. Though Swanson postponed the operation that had been her ticket east, her time in New York healed and strengthened her in many ways.

Her new director Allan Dwan had himself gone east to seek the freewheeling autonomy he had enjoyed in Hollywood only a few years earlier. Dwan was preparing to make *Zaza* in Astoria when Mickey Neilan suggested he collaborate with Swanson. It was the substantial role she had been seeking: Zaza is a French music hall performer who becomes the mistress of a wealthy man.[2] She leaves the stage for her lover, then gives him up for the sake of his child. Zaza returns to performing, and the couple reunites years later after the wife's death. The melodramatic plot

118

also promised to be fun: vivacious Zaza is the toast of the town before being tamed by love.

Almost immediately Swanson knew she had made the right move. Working with Dwan was wonderful. He thought picture making "the doggone most fascinating game there is," and his productions combined efficiency, hard work, and fun. "Pictures must be made fast," Dwan claimed. "If you muddle around with them, you lose your clear vision. You cannot hurry art, of course, but you can hurry commercial production. Get your art in hand before you start to produce and you'll save yourself a lot of time and trouble."[3] Dwan valued collaboration and spontaneity, finding Swanson an enthusiastic contributor: "She was always just perfect . . . a wonderful worker . . . and very jolly—a clown if there ever was one."[4]

In one scene, Zaza is on a swing high above her audience, tossing flowers down on a group of eligible Parisian bachelors when a rival cuts the swing's rope. Zaza tumbles to the ground, wounding her dignity more than anything else. A catfight settles the score between the women. They had no duplicates for the prop furniture, and none for the Norman Norell costumes, so Dwan instructed his leading lady to make the fight good: they could only do it once. Swanson remembered breaking the furniture and "mopping up the place" with the other actress despite being physically smaller.[5] She acknowledged her competitive spirit: "I play to win. Otherwise I don't play." Dwan liked that edge and knew how to use it. Swanson recalled proudly that he said his new player had "the body of a woman but the brain of a man."[6]

She was also proud that she had learned to cry on demand—no glycerine for this girl. She described the physical challenge: "Crying for the screen is hard work that leaves you with aching temples and with . . . muscles along the jaw throbbing and tugging. . . . It's the most tiring thing I do."[7] She stayed in character for a big dramatic scene in *Zaza*, weeping quietly in a corner while the crew set up lights and hauled props around. Her director was thrilled with the "remarkable" results: "There seems to be no limit to the depth and variety of her emotions."[8] Dwan quickly earned Swanson's friendship and loyalty.

She took three adjacent suites at the Gladstone Hotel—one for herself, one for her children, and one for "friends and guests and parties."[9] She also rented Joe Schenck and Norma Talmadge's house on Little Neck Bay in Queens, which had plenty of room for the children to play.[10] With her family gathered around her, she prepared for the surgery she had dreaded—and delayed—for almost three years. Though it wasn't a major procedure, the operation did not go well. While Gloria was recovering, her doctor recommended drug therapy next, then another operation.

Swanson flatly refused: she would take her chances. When the doctor warned her that another infection could make her infertile, she tuned him out. The failure of this surgery had undermined what little faith Gloria had in traditional medicine. She planned to try to cure herself by natural means, by exposing herself to the light of the sun, even though her doctor said the chances of her remedy working were "one in ten thousand."[11]

Willpower was always Swanson's strong suit, and the medical establishment brought out her fiercest side. Equipping herself with a box of medicine droppers and lots of sterilized saline, she went into seclusion at the Bayside house. She propped her legs up and scissored them open, so that the sun could shine in on her private parts. It was like "being strung upside down on a clothesline," she recalled.[12] Several times an hour she applied sterile water to the spot. It was more than faintly ridiculous, but Swanson brought to her home remedy all the power of positive thinking she could muster.

After a few stiff, uncomfortable days, Gloria felt better. She presented herself to her surgeon, who confirmed her intuition. The unlikely combination of sunlight and saline had done the trick: she was healed. In fact, he said, she looked like a virgin again. The experience powerfully affirmed Swanson's commitment to natural remedies. She would never again trust doctors, she vowed, and especially not surgeons, who were too inclined to cut out what Mother Nature had put in. She pledged to take care of herself, a promise she kept. She practiced yoga, took massages, and preferred osteopathic practitioners to mainstream physicians. Her faith in alternative medicine and especially diet as a way to prevent disease grew as the years passed, becoming a central tenet of the actress's personal philosophy.

Gloria was happy to get back to work. She confided in a new friend, screenwriter Forrest Halsey, that she wanted to play Peter Pan in Paramount's upcoming production, a long shot for the glamour queen of the movies. Author J. M. Barrie had approval of casting: if he could see Swanson as Peter Pan, the studio might agree. Halsey suggested she approach Sidney Olcott about his upcoming picture *The Humming Bird*. The story of a Parisian gamine who runs a crowd of street thieves in Montmartre, the role was practically a dry run for *Peter Pan*, demanding a level of physicality and boyishness that Gloria was eager to try. Halsey called it a "britches" part, since Toinette disguises herself as a boy to fight alongside her lover in World War I.[13] Swanson finagled permission to keep working on the East Coast.

She felt "unleashed" by the company and the freshness of the New York approach to filmmaking. Astoria was "full of free spirits, defectors, refugees" from Hollywood, and Gloria relished her liberation from the excessive costumes and swanky sets that had dominated her Hollywood productions.[14] The New York pictures were not cheaply made; in fact, *The Humming Bird*'s trench scenes were so convincing that viewers thought they were actual war footage.[15] Swanson's new directors skillfully motivated actors by soliciting their input and cheering them on; Dwan especially "could push the most phlegmatic member of the cast to peaks of excitement."[16] After fifty years in the business, he described directing: "It isn't a job, it's a disease. . . . I'd do it free, I like it that well."[17]

Swanson recalled her early days with Bobby Vernon and the Sennett team; now she felt more relaxed and able to enjoy herself, and it showed in her work. Whether Toinette was picking pockets or being tossed unceremoniously into jail, Swanson turned in a sparkling performance that conveyed the character's impish pride in her criminal skills. Both *Zaza* and *The Humming Bird* were huge hits, and Paramount agreed to keep the Swanson-Dwan team together. Gloria could call New York home.

Swanson recognized that the strait-laced new secretary Paramount hired for her was a spy, expected to keep tabs on Gloria so she didn't pull any more fast moves like the "health crisis" that brought her to New York. However, Gloria soon persuaded Jane West that she needed a companion and confidante more than the studio needed a detective, and the two grew close. Swanson had a curious charisma—a mixture of imperiousness and winning charm—that made others want to help her. Even those she initially irritated typically came to find her appealing. Interviewers often seemed puzzled by Swanson's magnetism; one observed that Gloria was "always being waited upon by some one . . . She has a way of letting others share responsibilities and of assisting her in every way. Some one is always saying 'Cream, dear?' and taking care of her cup of coffee, or 'Let me carry that for you, honey?' and she's a sort of royal princess wherever she travels." This writer found her "delightfully contrary," concluding that "Gloria is not spoiled or selfish, but she's centered her mind on acting to the exclusion of all other pursuits or duties."[18]

Another interviewer complained that Swanson was nowhere to be found for their appointment. When Gloria did at length appear, she continued to carry on several other conversations, answering the interviewer's questions perfunctorily and without even glancing at her. Nonetheless, this reporter decided that "Gloria Swanson isn't so bad as she sounds." When they "really started talking," she was "extremely charming," ready to share stories about her children and to laugh merrily when Jane West told a joke at her expense.[19] Swanson's absorption in whatever she was doing was sincere: once you got her attention, you had it. But it wasn't always easy to get. As she herself observed, "When I was working, I was like a horse with blinders. They once came to me and told me that my house was on fire, and I said, well, go upstairs and ask them if it is insured. I was busy."[20] Her relentless focus sometimes made her seem cold or indifferent.

In early October 1923, Joseph Swanson suffered a massive heart attack and died at fifty-two. The burial took place in Chicago after a military funeral, and Swanson went west to meet the coffin and say goodbye to the first important man in her life. Holed up in her train compartment, Swanson felt bereft, utterly heartbroken. She knew her father had become a sad, lonely man; he had never recovered from his separation from Adelaide. Gloria saw Joseph as "the most complicated figure" in her life.[21] She recognized that she had tried to find her father in her own two failed marriages, but could not foresee that she would keep looking for him in other troubled and troubling men.

The car carrying Gloria from the funeral to the cemetery took a roundabout route, past all the places she had known as a child: her kindergarten, her grandmother's house, even the local candy store. "We went in the most extraordinary fashion, zigzagging back and forth for no good reason. . . . It's as if my father were showing me all these places which I hadn't been to for so long."[22] Swanson believed herself mildly clairvoyant: she occasionally had premonitions or felt telepathic connections with people not physically present. She took this in stride, seeing it more as intuition or guidance than as anything dramatic or frightening. Her mood on the trip back east was more peaceful; Gloria was certain that Joseph continued to watch over her.

Her mother was another story. Adelaide was receiving menacing letters which threatened to reveal details of Gloria's relationship with Mickey Neilan and to sue Adelaide for breach of promise and Gloria for alienation of affection. It turned out that Adelaide had pledged to marry a much younger man, who had a cache of love letters to prove it. When Adelaide severed the connection, he became bitter and vengeful. Once again, Gloria's mother was in the papers, and it fell to her daughter to help pick up the pieces. Ultimately, the Los Angeles Police Department declined to press charges against the man, who said Adelaide had broken his heart.

The gossip about her mother's romantic life had scarcely abated when rumors of Gloria's own death surfaced. Paramount was said to be hushing it up and had employed a double to stand in for Swanson. It turned out to be surprisingly difficult to quell the stories: exasperated, Swanson offered to let reporters touch the mole on her chin as proof of her authenticity.

New York City was thrilling in the 1920s, and Swanson's fame opened every door. She went everywhere: to see Jeanne Eagels, Fanny Brice, John Barrymore, and Walter Huston on stage; to hear jazz by Louis Armstrong and Duke Ellington and Bessie Smith; to see Bill Tilden play tennis and Babe Ruth play baseball; to dances and dinners and concerts and parties. She sat with George Gershwin's family when he performed *Rhapsody in Blue* at Carnegie Hall. (George gave Gloria a hand-drawn caricature of himself, and Ira wrote Gloria into the lyrics to "Funny Face.") She practically haunted the Metropolitan Opera, where she met her idol Rosa Ponselle.

Swanson was hardly anonymous herself: "Eddie Cantor apologized to me from the stage for a joke he had cracked about me the week before, and everyone applauded. People also stood up and applauded when I entered a box at the Metropolitan Opera House to see Eleonora Duse."[23] Being recognized in such good company was heady, and the hard-driving power of the city matched Swanson's own high energy. Her new friends were sophisticated, lively, and smart, and it was contagious: she felt sharper and brighter in their company. Swanson quickly found she preferred the stimulation and bustle of New York to the insular preoccupation of Los Angeles, with its one big industry. Everything that interested her—movies, music, literature, fashion—seemed to connect in New York.

She met the violinist Jascha Heifetz after one of his Carnegie Hall recitals, and soon they were a couple. Heifetz loved showing Swanson the city that had welcomed him as a teenage immigrant from Russia. Forrest Halsey introduced Gloria to gay New York, and she got a huge kick out of the bitchy, witty, unapologetically out company he kept. Halsey wrote five of Swanson's films; they could dream up new scenes and even new stories while they were out on the town. Work and play meshed in New York.

She looked up the brother of a California friend and was quickly taken under LeRoy Pierpoint Ward's wing. "Sport" was a handsome architect who was "unofficial master of the most fashionable midnight revels in Manhattan."[24] He and Gloria recognized each other as kindred spirits immediately, becoming lifelong friends. Sport knew absolutely everyone and presented Swanson to fashionable Manhattan society, which was no longer dominated by the stiff families of the "400" she had encountered on her 1919 trip east for FPL. Now youth, intelligence, creativity, and fun mattered most, and Swanson fit right in.

Before long Sport and Gloria were cohosting open houses. Sundays found an assortment of the brightest and best talents in the city gathered in Gloria's suites at the Gladstone.[25] Frank Crowninshield, the art collector and editor of *Vanity Fair*, became a regular. So did Condé Nast, who published *Vanity Fair* and *Vogue*. He brought Edward Steichen, the photographer whose 1924 portrait of Swanson became an American classic: her face swathed in black lace, her eyes large and luminous. (Steichen envisioned Gloria as "a leopardess lurking behind leafy shrubbery, watching her prey." She was "a dynamic and intelligent person" whose mind worked "swiftly and intuitively.")[26] Jimmy Walker, soon to be mayor of New York and one of Sport's best friends, came often, as did John Farrar, the poet who would found two publishing houses. Theatrical producer Leland Hayward and some of the Algonquin Round Table writers showed up. None of these people tolerated fools gladly. Their conversation was an education for Swanson, who gravitated toward intelligent men.

More than any other rite of passage, however, Sport and his friends valued a clever prank: "You were nobody until you had been the butt of one of Sport Ward's elaborate practical jokes."[27] Plumbers appeared at Gloria's apartment after midnight, live turkeys on set during her love scenes. Jascha Heifetz and Sport competed to see who could pull the most outrageous stunts, Gloria first playing along and then dreaming up pranks of her own. She felt a new looseness, a sense of relaxation and creativity among her freewheeling New York friends. The girl without a sense of humor was finally finding her funny bone.

It was hard for Swanson to go about the city without being recognized. When Gloria wanted Sport to take her to a burlesque show, he protested that they would be hounded by her fans. She offered to wear glasses, and Sport scoffed: her teeth were what gave her away. Then he had a brainstorm. He produced some sticky stuff and asked her to bite down, and voila! Dentures covered Swanson's prominent teeth. "I must have looked like Gargantua," she remembered.[28] They wept with laughter—until she could not get the false teeth out of her mouth. When little

Gloria came around the corner and Swanson tried to smile at her, the child ran screaming from the room.

New York was good for Gloria. As she relaxed into her new life, a different kind of healing came in the form of an unexpected apology. Attorney Milton Cohen had represented Herbert Somborn in his divorce from Swanson, masterminding the ugly strategy which won Somborn a large settlement fee. Cohen sought Gloria out in New York, explaining that he had believed Somborn's claims of her promiscuity to be true. Now he knew otherwise and was anxious to make amends. Could he perhaps perform a service for her? Cohen and Swanson became friends. He represented her off and on for years, often declining to charge the actress a fee in order to make up, Swanson conjectured, for his original misjudgment of her. She liked Cohen and appreciated his effort to right the wrong he had done. But she also believed her own new feeling of ease—her sense of humor, even—helped make this reconciliation possible.

Since she was now planning to stay in New York indefinitely, Swanson bought a comfortable, green-shingled twelve-room colonial farmhouse on twenty-five acres in the village of Croton-on-Hudson. It was an idyllic, unpretentious, private spot for the family a short drive north of the city. At the junction of two rivers, with leafy glades in summer and ice-skating in winter, the village was something of an artists' colony.

Feeling freer and more creative than she had in California, Swanson began dabbling in other arts herself. She tried her hand at writing poetry, with the encouragement of Condé Nast. She had always enjoyed drawing and was a good caricaturist. Now she began sculpting in clay, first modeling little Gloria's head. When Swanson came home from the studio at night, she often stopped to take a look at her work in progress. When little Gloria ran in to say hello, her mother picked up where she left off, studying her daughter and shaping the clay. It was completely absorbing: "Sometimes I'd find that I'd been standing there two hours without having taken my hat or coat off." Swanson became a proficient sculptor, practicing the art for the rest of her life. The artists Gloria knew typically had more abilities than the one for which they were famous: "We all have these talents, but some people have let the bars down and let [them] come through."[29]

Swanson felt pretty certain she was no good at marriage, though her next film put a temptation in her path. *A Society Scandal* told the story of a woman who falls in love with—of all people—the lawyer who ruins her character's reputation in a messy divorce case.[30] It featured not one but two handsome young leading men. Ricardo Cortez was being promoted as a Valentino-style Latin lover (though he was a butcher's son from the Lower East Side). It was Rod LaRocque, however, whom Swanson found devastating. He was tall (6 feet, 3 inches) and stunningly handsome, with "nostrils like a race horse."[31] They had a big love scene together right away: "Within three days I was in love. Within a week Rod proposed."[32]

They had a lot in common: both were from Chicago and were close in age. LaRocque had worked at Essanay and for Cecil DeMille. He was as inquisitive about the world as Gloria, and she respected his drive to educate himself: "All you had to do was bring up a subject—a word—and . . . he would spend hours, days, weeks . . . and get volumes on the subject."[33] Rod's fascinating mind matched his gorgeous physique.

Yet for once Swanson hesitated. Rod was everything she wanted: a passionate lover and someone who understood her world. However, he was fiercely possessive, and right away they began quarreling about the time she spent with other men. Swanson loved New York and adored the company of the intelligent, creative people—mostly men—she found there. She also enjoyed flirting and being pursued, flitting from one suitor to another. Yet she did not see why Rod should feel so challenged by her open houses or her nights on the town with other friends. She could not, or would not, comprehend his jealousy. "I had a lot of intellectual catching up to do," she mused. "I couldn't get enough of brainy, interesting people. And Rod could not understand that need in me, or accept it. He couldn't share a wife."[34]

Her priorities were clear: she would value and protect her independence. What Rod could not abide in a romantic relationship he easily accepted in a friend, and during his long marriage to actress Vilma Banky, he and his wife counted Swanson among their dearest friends.

A Society Scandal put Swanson back in beautiful clothes. This time, however, the gowns were streamlined and elegant rather than elaborate and restricting. Her audiences welcomed the glamour but also observed a new aura of confidence and simplicity in the actress's bearing. Now when she had a "clothes role," she dominated it instead of it dominating her. Adela Rogers St. Johns observed a "transformation" in Swanson: "When you look back on the way she has come and see what she has made of herself in the past ten years, it's utterly intriguing to think what she should be at the end of another decade."[35]

After almost ten years in the movie business, Swanson had greater confidence in her own judgment. She had learned to nurture her own talent, as her New York adventure showed. She had also learned she had to take care of herself. One way she did so was by respecting her intuition. Another was by varying her film roles rather than passively accepting whatever the studio put forward. Gloria privately formulated a plan to see that each of her pictures was "so totally different that the audience would never know what to expect from me."[36]

This meant she had to be proactive, as she had been with *Zaza* and *The Humming Bird*, thinking ahead to the next project, and even the following one. It required a kind of autonomy few actors in the industry were practicing and which the studios did not encourage. It was, although Gloria did not know it yet, a step along the road to becoming totally independent herself.

She recognized, for instance, that plum film parts depended on good stories. The prevailing wisdom in the industry, however, was that an established star did not need a strong story; his or her pictures would sell regardless. Since she liked tinkering with stories and enjoyed the company of writers, Swanson determined to be as hands-on as possible in the selection or shaping of the projects intended for her.

She found an opportunity right away. Her next picture, *Manhandled*, had a provocative title but no real story yet. Paramount distribution chief Sidney Kent had selected the name after learning that the new Hays office regulations forbade any depiction of "manhandling" in the movies. The Dwan crew's assignment was to get as close to the forbidden topic as possible, retaining the excitement and allure of that word while telling the story of a department store salesgirl. Frank Tuttle was the writer, and he, Allan Dwan, Swanson, and Jane West cooked up a scheme to work on the script while scouting locations in Miami. A working vacation in Florida would let them escape the dreary New York winter.

When Miami turned out to be dismal and rainy, Havana beckoned. Cuba was enjoying Prohibition-free prosperity; its casinos and luxury hotels were famous. Jane's brother Paul, an executive with the powerful United Fruit Company, put not one but four Rolls-Royces at their disposal. Gloria told Allan that people used to call her the "Cuban Princess": her strange light eyes always attracted attention.[37] She got lots of attention in Cuba, but Dwan said now it was because she was a movie star. Next to Chaplin's, Swanson's was possibly the best-known face in the world.

The group visited nightclubs, where the rumba was so risqué it made prim Jane blush. They were invited to ex-President Garcia Menocal's hacienda and taken to tour the sugar refineries and gamble in the casinos. One evening, Swanson inadvertently upstaged Eleonora Duse at the Opera House. The audience members were so thrilled to see Gloria that they gave her a standing ovation rather than the aging diva. She also received unwelcome attention from an admirer who sent her—daily and anonymously—several large uncut jewels, accompanied by explicitly detailed obscene letters. She was appalled but understood that some men saw her as "the *femme fatale* they wanted me to be, one who wore shimmering transparent gowns and bobbed her hair and rode with the Sheik."[38] Gloria didn't want anything to do with the jewels and donated them to a charity auction.

Another time the car Gloria was traveling in with the ex-president and his bodyguards got accidentally-on-purpose separated from the car carrying her friends. Then, the ex-president squeezed her knee. When she tried to inch away, the man on her other side put his hand on her other knee. With horror she realized they were not even going toward the yacht club, as promised. "I got really terrified," she remembered, "and started talking really fast. 'I don't know what happens in your country,' I said, 'but if anything happens to me and I don't arrive at a spot where I'm supposed to be, the marines come out. It will be in the newspapers and headlines.'"[39] After an angrily muttered conversation in Spanish, the driver turned the car around, and a few minutes later Swanson, her legs shaking, fell into a frantic Jane's arms. It was time to go home.

Two weeks had disappeared while they relaxed and enjoyed the Cuban warmth. On the way home, Swanson suggested that maybe *Manhandled* could be about a salesgirl whose foray into high society ends up with her kidnapped and almost raped "by the richest, most dignified, most distinguished man in Cuba, or perhaps even by the ex-president."[40] No, the others agreed: it was too unbelievable. Sometimes the truth was stranger than the movies.

Manhandled nonetheless turned out to be one of Swanson's happiest filmmaking experiences. It is utterly delightful, in part because she once again plays against type, bringing a determined feistiness to the role of Tessie McGuire that viewers used to Gloria's glamour roles could not have predicted. Tessie wasn't an exotic music hall performer like Zaza or a pickpocket like the Humming Bird, but a regular gum-chewing girl. Tessie's boyfriend is preoccupied with an invention he is trying to perfect. When Jimmy forgets a date with her once too often, she accepts an

invitation to a party with some ritzy characters. There she does imper-
sonations, and the party guests laugh at her for all the wrong reasons.
Nonetheless, she lands a position pretending to be a Russian aristocrat,
Countess Offernutski, for an elite fashion house. When Jimmy comes
looking for Tessie—his invention now a smash success—he turns away
in dismay; he thinks she has gotten her fancy gowns by being "manhandled." They both have a few things to learn before their happy ending.

Before the shoot, Swanson researched her role as a working girl. The
actress, who had never held a traditional job, spent two days as a sales
clerk at Gimbels. She disguised herself in a blonde wig, stuffing cotton up
her nose and chewing gum in her cheeks. Makeup changed the shape of
her lips and brows, and she applied white powder to her face. She even
padded her bra. No one was in on the secret; she was just another new
girl on the sales floor. Once on the job, however, Gloria's competitive
spirit kicked in: she wanted to prove that she could outsell the girl next
to her.

She noted the casual ways and conversational style of her co-workers,
filing away mannerisms to use later. At lunchtime, the movie star spent
fifteen cents on two doughnuts and a cup of tea, gladly resting her sore
feet. She was enjoying herself, searching for butter knives and scented
soaps in the crowded sales department, when on her second day someone spread the rumor that Gloria Swanson was in the store. When Gloria
was recognized, recalled Dwan, "There was pandemonium."[41] The movie
queen had to make a run for it.

The other research Swanson did for the role was a lot less enjoyable.
Dwan sent her to ride back and forth on the New York City subway,
shuttling between Grand Central and Times Square. She again went out
in plain clothes, "in the funniest, most awful-looking outfit that looked
no more like Gloria Swanson than my left ear—she *looked* like she'd been
working all day long at a real bargain counter," said Dwan.[42] Swanson,
who disliked enclosed spaces, gamely boarded the crowded train—and
then got shoved around until she was totally disheveled. She couldn't get
off because the passengers boarding pushed her back on. When she finally stumbled out into the light, she looked so disreputable a taxi driver refused to take her to her hotel. She insisted that she was Gloria Swanson,
whereupon the cabbie claimed that he was Rudolph Valentino! A policeman escorted her into the Gladstone and presented her to the doorman,
who (on Allan Dwan's instructions) pretended he didn't know her.

Dwan thought whatever revenge Gloria might take was worth it: her
performance was terrific. Tessie's subway ride, where her favorite hat

gets ruined in the crush, was funny, convincing, and fresh. Dwan praised Swanson's contributions: "She'd add and contribute a lot. And we practically had no scripts—we used to manufacture things as we went. But Gloria was always full of hell, always pulling things. It was always fun with her—a game."[43]

One of her contributions was an impromptu imitation of Charlie Chaplin. After work one day, Swanson was feeling relaxed and loose and started messing around with a coworker's derby hat. Before long she added a mustache, a cane, a funny walk, and some of Chaplin's grimaces. Swanson knew Chaplin socially, and everyone knew the Tramp's mannerisms. In a wink, Dwan incorporated her improvisation into the film's story. Swanson needed this kind of validation to do her best work, and her new flexibility and ease brought her accolades.

Her first comedy since her Keystone days earned Swanson rave reviews. "It is a real characterization," said the *New York Times*, repeating the point to stress the film's "real artistry" and the leading lady's credentials as a "real actress." The audience agreed, breaking into spontaneous applause during the film.[44] "We think *Manhandled* is the best thing that Gloria Swanson ever did," *Movie Weekly* crowed. "She proves herself a greater actress than even we, her staunch admirer, believed her to be. She is a comedienne of the first water . . . Her Chaplin impression is as brilliant as anything we ever saw on the screen."[45] Her earthy portrait of the little gum-chewing commuter with the plain, cropped hairdo gained Swanson what her glamour queen roles had not: respect.[46]

"Allan and New York represented some kind of rebirth for me," Swanson said.[47] She felt like a member of a real creative team in Astoria: "We did what we wanted. We read a lot of stories, and if we couldn't find a story that was already written, we made one up."[48] She didn't really mind that her next film, the forgettable *Her Love Story*, was another costume drama about a princess who secretly weds a handsome military captain against her father's wishes. Forced nonetheless to marry the ruler of her small Balkan kingdom, she shocks everyone by proclaiming that the child she has borne is not the king's. She is packed off to a convent posthaste. Eventually, her exiled young husband returns from Down Under to rescue her and their child. The picture was "far inferior" to Swanson and Dwan's recent work, though reviewers dutifully admired the elaborate wedding gown Swanson wore.[49] She herself recalled only her character's waist-length chestnut wig. *Her Love Story* was "the kind of silly . . . picture I was a bit embarrassed to make."[50]

Another source of embarrassment was the feud Swanson was supposed to be having with another Paramount star. Pola Negri had come to Hollywood from Russian-occupied Poland by way of Germany, in the first wave of talent seduced from Europe by American film companies. Pola was gorgeous and had a mysteriously exotic background; her father was said to be a Gypsy violinist.[51] By way of her brief marriage to a count, she was a countess. Pola became famous playing *femmes fatales*, and her taste for luxury was famous as well. Canny Paramount publicists decided to create additional interest by manufacturing a rivalry between Gloria Swanson, the most powerful actress on the lot, and Pola Negri, the new talent.

Stories began appearing in the press describing the two actresses' competing demands: if Gloria had something, Pola wanted it, too. On her arrival in Hollywood, Pola saw Swanson's bungalow. Proclaiming it "a nice leetle house" in her charming Polish accent, she wondered where hers was. Paramount complied, building Negri a bungalow to order. Pola understood the power of close shots, and demanded in her fractured English that her directors "Make da beeg face—Make da beeg head."[52] Between the "beeg face" and the "leetle house," Pola learned the ropes quickly.

The two women were said to be viciously competitive with one another. Pola was superstitious about cats, so (the story went) Gloria set a bunch of stray cats loose on Pola's set, disrupting the diva's concentration and creating a scene. Swanson ridiculed the idea: she barely knew Pola Negri, though she had hosted a dinner party to welcome Pola to California. Gloria felt secure in her own position at the studio; however, she resented the two actresses being portrayed as "squabbling little vulgarians."[53] The whole idea of the feud was "pure nonsense."[54]

Negri claimed that she "did not believe . . . for one moment" that Swanson was responsible for the plague of cats on set: "Gloria was too professional for that."[55] The fan magazines were nonetheless full of stories about how Pola's followers painted their lips and nails red and powdered their faces in emulation of their idol, while Gloria's fans showed their loyalty with unpowdered cheeks and a single dangling earring. (Swanson started this fad inadvertently, when she lost the mate to a favorite pair of earrings and continued to wear just the one.) Gloria, it was said, would not appear at a studio event until after Pola had entered and vice versa. Negri recalled both women pouting in their dressing rooms one evening, until (she claimed) she became bored and caved in.[56] Negri believed that if Swanson had not agreed to go along with the feud, they could have been friends, but as Charlie Chaplin (Pola's one-time fiancé and someone altogether shrewder about the movie business) said, "The twisted feline angle was manna to the publicity department."[57] Swanson and Negri were worth more to Paramount as enemies than friends.

Paramount not only played up the notion of a battle between the two actresses for screen supremacy but also kept the two snapping at each others' heels. Swanson played a Balkan princess in *Her Love Story*; a month later Negri was a Russian czarina in *Forbidden Paradise*. If Swanson costarred with Rod LaRocque, he would likely appear with Negri next. It may have been a coincidence that LaRocque and Negri had a much publicized romance soon after he and Swanson parted: "Pola without a man was like California without sunshine," smirked Miriam Cooper, whose husband Raoul Walsh directed both actresses.[58] It was less likely a coincidence that Swanson impersonated a Russian countess for *Manhandled*. All things Russian were in vogue at the time, but the Countess Offernutski was pointed right at Pola Negri.

Paramount chief Adolph Zukor stoutly maintained that the women "fought it out for queen of the studio," adding, "We had to walk the line between the two very carefully. If one was given a service or a favor that was denied the other, the studio would in all likelihood have been shaken to the ground."[59] The prevailing myth was that the US was barely big enough for both actresses: Pola commanded Hollywood, while Swanson reigned in New York.[60] Zukor's portrait of Swanson, however, was a bit more nuanced: "On the set," he said, "Queen Gloria could be temperamental, refusing to make scenes over, criticizing her wardrobe, the scenery, or her dressing quarters. But finally someone would say, 'Look, Gloria, we've got to get the work done,' and she would come down to earth. The little Chicago west side girl was never far below the glamorous surface."[61]

As the summer of 1924 began, Swanson was thinking less about Pola Negri than about *Peter Pan*. Jesse Lasky was evasive when she broached the subject, but after talking it over with Forrest Halsey, Swanson decided to do as she had when she came to New York for *Zaza*: she would present herself directly to J. M. Barrie and ask for the job. She was confident that her lively characterizations in *Zaza*, *The Humming Bird*, and *Manhandled* would persuade the author she was right for the role. After all, she reasoned, she had been part of the success of *Male and Female*, and more people had seen the screen adaptation than had ever seen Barrie's stage play. Under the circumstances, she was peeved that Paramount wasn't championing her cause.

Never mind: Swanson quietly had some photographs taken of herself as Peter Pan and told Lasky she needed a month's European vacation. Gloria and Jane sailed on the *Homeric* in early June; only Swanson's closest friends knew her intentions. On board was Ben Spock, a 6-feet, 4-inch Yale student en route to Paris for the Olympic trials. He was completely tongue-tied at meeting the famous actress, so Gloria called him "Big Ben but no alarm." He won a gold medal but gained greater fame as the child care expert Dr. Spock.[62]

On her arrival in London, however, she learned that the part had already been cast: Barrie chose Betty Bronson, a seventeen-year-old ingénue with little screen experience, for his Peter Pan. Disappointed, Swanson recognized that Paramount wanted not only a new face but a younger one. This was becoming worrisome: although she was only twenty-five, Swanson had heard people claim definitively that she was as much as ten years older. The appetite of screen audiences for fresh faces was enormous, and few movie stars remained on top for more than five years. The 1920s had a particular fetish for youth: *Peter Pan* is, after all, the story of a boy who refuses to grow up. Swanson recalled, "It seemed then we were all young. There were never any old people." Times were "plush. . . . There was not just enough, but more than enough."[63] *Peter Pan* was Swanson's first intimation that there might not always be enough.

Swanson consoled herself with a quick shopping trip to Paris before sailing home again. On board the *Leviathan* bound for New York, a man dressed as a ship's steward served dinner in Gloria's cabin, then struck a pose and began playing gypsy melodies on the violin. It was her friend Jascha Heifetz.

Heifetz cheered Swanson up immensely. Douglas Fairbanks and Mary Pickford were also on board, and Heifetz proposed to trick them as well. Swanson outfitted herself as a chambermaid, and with Heifetz once again in costume, they barged into Doug and Mary's stateroom early the next morning, banging around and stage-whispering in faux French. Mary was wearing a chin strap, Swanson recalled, and when she couldn't quiet the interlopers, she roused Doug. In careful French, he politely asked the cleaners to leave. They ignored him, for good measure dumping a flower vase onto the bedclothes. The prank made a shambles of the stateroom, but Swanson knew it would be "a wonderful crossing."[64]

It was a rare opportunity for the stars to spend time together, and they discussed business for hours. Doug and Mary were now independent producers under the mantle of their own company, United Artists; they wanted to control their own careers and keep the profits from their pictures. Swanson complained about Paramount's failure to support her for *Peter Pan*. She had even instructed Jane to tell the studio she wasn't returning to the States. They would have to come up with something big to mollify her, and she knew what she wanted: to make her next picture in France. As the big ship steamed across the Atlantic, Swanson talked over her plans with the founders of United Artists. She was determined to make this dream come true.

CHAPTER 9

French Idyll

WHEN GLORIA SWANSON WAS PASSIONATE ABOUT SOMETHING, EV-
eryone around her knew it. She was on fire for *Madame Sans-Gêne*, a
project Forrest Halsey had found with a great role for her that cried out
to be shot in Paris. The studio agreed: a high-profile period picture, made
in cooperation with the company's French office, could be a very good
idea. Paramount wanted to develop demand for its stars in Europe as a
way of strengthening its hold on business abroad.[1] Furthermore, productions could be mounted in Europe for a fraction of their cost in America,
and the prestige of adapting an internationally successful play for Swanson would be considerable.[2] More swiftly than she expected, Gloria's
French project got a green light.

She remained in New York long enough to make one more picture.
In *The Wages of Virtue*, a story of love and revenge set in Morocco, Gloria
plays Carmelita, a spirited café proprietor who kills to protect the Foreign
Legionnaire she loves. The plot strained credulity, and Algiers in Astoria
suddenly paled by comparison with location shooting in France. Like her
other collaborations with Allan Dwan, however, the picture gave Gloria
lots to do. She impressed the crew and amused herself by carrying everything on her head as she had learned in Puerto Rico: "I got so good at it
[that] I could carry a glass of wine."[3] She also carried on a flirtation with
her leading man, Ben Lyon (though he considered it an engagement).
Despite what one reviewer called a "millstone" of a title, *The Wages of
Virtue* was "thoroughly engaging," its leading lady "lithe and vivacious."[4]
Gloria "adored" the picture, but she was in a mood to adore everything:
she was going to France.[5]

Everything about Swanson's return to Paris in October 1924 was larger than life. So many people crowded into the Gare Saint-Lazare when
she arrived that the police had to intervene. She pulled up to the Hotel
Crillon in a Renault the length of a train carriage. The whole family was

there—Gloria, the children and their governess, Adelaide, Jane West and her mother, a secretary, and Gloria's maid. The Prince of Wales suite was so full of flowers you couldn't see out the windows.

Eighty reporters packed into the Crillon to hear about Swanson's plans for *Madame Sans-Gêne*.[6] The large-scale production was based on a true story spanning several decades of French history and mixing patriotism, love, and comedy. Swanson was to play the carefree washerwoman who does Napoleon's laundry while the future emperor is still a lieutenant. She becomes a duchess by marrying one of Napoleon's favorite officers, but her free-and-easy behavior causes a scandal at court ("Sans-Gêne" means "Devil-May-Care"). Napoleon orders her to divorce her beloved husband so he can marry someone more distinguished. When her actions reveal that she is a true patriot, however, Napoleon lets her keep both her husband and her place in society. Madame Sans-Gêne has the last word, boldly reminding the emperor that he still owes her money for his laundry bill.

Set against a backdrop of war and revolution, the picture offered Swanson's fans both new and familiar pleasures. While the French story and authentic setting promised an exciting showcase for her talents, she would play the kind of roistering free spirit viewers had loved in *Zaza* and *The Humming Bird*. The story's rags-to-riches premise featured Swanson in both simple, unpretentious outfits and glamorous, elaborate gowns.

They wanted to shoot in the Palace of Fontainebleau, the Chateau de Malmaison, and the Chateau de Compiègne, the tale's real-life locations. However, no film company had ever been permitted to use these historic sites, and Adolphe Osso, head of Paramount in Paris, was not sanguine about gaining access. Swanson, however, would not take no for an answer. *Madame Sans-Gêne* was the first shared production between France and America, so they had to get it right. They were making a film of a well-known French play with deep roots in French history. Aside from the screenwriter, cinematographer, and leading lady, the cast and crew were French, many from the Comédie Française. Swanson had come all the way to France to make the picture; she was determined to use the authentic locations.

Mais non, madame, shrugged Osso: those places were sacred to the French. They were off limits. Swanson was adamant, but her flashing eyes and patented pantomimes did not move the producer to action. Very well, she thought: if Osso would not help her unlock the gates of Fontainebleau, she would find someone who would.

If she was unimpressed with her producer, Swanson knew she was lucky in her director. Léonce Perret's connection to *Madame Sans-Gêne* went deep: he had been onstage with the play in the 1890s. Perret was an ace when it came to directing comedy; his "heavyset body and large open face" had made him beloved in the popular "Léonce" films—bright, witty short comedies named for their director/star.[7] Perret understood actors because he had been one himself. He was experienced and efficient—a must given the scale of the production—and everyone liked him. If she couldn't have Allan Dwan, Perret was a good replacement.[8]

Delays mounted as the company confronted French bureaucracy. "We showered gifts and flowers on [government officials'] mistresses and wives—the interior, the exterior, the minister of this, that, and the other thing," Swanson recalled.[9] Every time they secured a location, another government official showed up demanding another permit. Swanson spent so long toasting her feet by the stove near the set that she blackened her period slippers. One day, by moving swiftly and posting lookouts every few yards, the eager cameramen managed to snatch a few shots in a doorway at Fontainebleau before anyone could stop them. Mostly, they waited.

Location, location, location: keeping Swanson's entourage in the fiendishly expensive Hotel Crillon would bankrupt even Paramount, so she rented a five-story townhouse on the Place des Etats-Unis from the Marquise de Brantes. The owner's full staff was included, even a dauntingly formal butler named Alexandre. This was no bargain rental. The ground-floor reception rooms were filled with eighteenth-century paintings and furniture. A huge marble spiral staircase led to the upper floors (or you could take the wrought iron lift). The second-floor drawing room ran the width of the house, with fireplaces at either end and Gobelin tapestries on the walls. Huge windows overlooked a beautiful old garden, letting in spectacular light. There were suites for Addie, Jane, and Mrs. West, a large nursery for the children and their governess, and countless guest rooms. The fifth floor housed the servants; Swanson never even saw the kitchen on the basement level.

Orange taffeta drapes made the light in Gloria's private chambers warm and cozy. Her suite had a library full of rare books. On one wall there was even a secret door: you pushed a button on a book called *La Porte*, and the door swung open. It led into a strange small salon—an opium den?—done in purple and red chiffon, with slipper chairs and a gondola-style chaise longue. Swanson's bedroom was dramatic, with black walls and floors and a black marble fireplace; its centerpiece was an enormous red lacquered Chinese bed. (On her first night in the house, Gloria scared herself reading a story by Arthur Conan Doyle and passed a sleepless night in that bed.) The bathroom could have held thirty comfortably: "The bathtub was a fountain. Water came out of the side of the wall, and filled this huge thing made of green tile . . . three or four people could have gotten into it and taken a couple of strokes. . . . We had a wonderful time in that house."[10]

The only thing troubling her was that she could not speak French. To take a more active part in *Madame Sans-Gêne*'s production, Swanson needed help: she asked her friend André Daven to find her a translator. Daven introduced her to a pal of his who had been working in an insurance office in Paris and who "looked like an American football player." Gloria's first impression of Henri de la Falaise was that he did not sound French: "The moment he opened his mouth, you would have thought he had lived in America all his life."[11] Henri was handsome, impeccably turned out, and had beautiful manners. He came by his aristocratic bearing legitimately: though he had no money, Henri could trace his family back to the thirteenth century. He also had a title, the Marquis de la Falaise de la Coudraye.

Gloria's translator soon became indispensible. He was always at her elbow, prompting her with the correct terms of address, murmuring the right words in her ear. She came to rely on his good judgment and his calm confidence. Though people rarely suspected it, Gloria was often shy with strangers. The foreign setting for *Madame Sans-Gêne* could also be overwhelming. With Henri de la Falaise around, however, navigating the strange waters of French film production seemed a lot easier.

Finally, they received permission to film at Fontainebleau, Malmaison, and Compiègne. This was unsurprising, since Paramount was spending fourteen million francs on the picture—enough to make ten films in France in 1924.[12] Gloria, however, remained irritated with Adolphe Osso's passivity; after she gave the producer a piece of her mind, "he did not open his mouth" for the rest of the picture.[13] This suited Swanson perfectly. Her conversation with Doug and Mary on board ship had intrigued her. She was toying with the idea of becoming a producer herself and was happy to try out the part now.

With the final diplomatic knots untied, the company had the run of France's greatest historical sites. On the first official day at Fontainebleau, ten marshals of Napoleon greeted Swanson with flowers and speeches. After this the production seemed charmed, with warm welcomes wherever they went. Fontainebleau's curator, Georges d'Esparbès, became their ally, unlocking the palace's treasures and allowing them to use whatever they fancied. Workers dusted off the Empress Josephine's carriage so Swanson could be filmed riding in it. They dressed the sets with objets d'art, including a 2,000-year-old chess set made of rose quartz and jade that a Chinese emperor had presented to Louis XV. D'Esparbès gave Gloria a tiny piece of green silk brocade from the drapes in Napoleon's library, which she cherished. He even let her climb into Napoleon's bed. (Gloria was convinced that d'Esparbès slept there himself some nights, so obsessed was he with all things Napoleonic.)

Authenticity was part of the appeal of historical pictures: the details mattered. Yet the cast and crew felt they were part of something bigger than a single movie. Swanson recalled that the extras wore their costumes with pride: "They never had their wigs askew like American [actors] do." During a battle scene, a piece of the scenery fell and hit an extra, knocking him unconscious. They rushed the man into the prop room and got him some brandy. When he came to, he raised his glass and cried, "Vive la Sans-Gêne!" "Anybody else would have sued us," Swanson said, but the actor promptly went back into battle. "He wouldn't be left out of it at all."[14]

Extras were chosen for their resemblance to the people pictured on the palace walls. One man was the portrait of Richelieu come to life; Swanson figured he was probably a descendent of the cardinal. Her leading man, Emile Drain, could have doubled for Napoleon, whom he portrayed in ten films during his career. Swanson believed that using French talent eased some of the tensions the company would otherwise have faced, and the actors made the place come alive again: "It was a magnificent sight to see several hundred people dressed in period costume . . . in those beautiful, unbelievable rooms. You felt like you were back in those times."[15]

A lot of the budget went to costuming the large cast. Swiss designer René Hubert used everything from rough linen to ermine for Swanson's outfits as the laundress-turned-duchess. He created "the perfect wardrobe," Gloria declared. "In every single one of his designs, he . . . underlined Sans-Gêne's character in the most tender, captivating way."[16] Hubert became Swanson's preferred stylist; they collaborated for years on both her costumes and her personal wardrobe.

She never looked lovelier than in *Madame Sans-Gêne*, a film preserved today only through still images. There was a new softness and luminosity to the actress's face, however, that required no cinematographic tricks: she was falling in love. Throughout the complicated arrangements for the location shooting, Henri de la Falaise had been at her side, smoothing her path. During the long days of filming and the late dinners that followed, he had been there. For the first time in a long time, Gloria felt someone was taking care of her, and it was powerfully seductive. She fell under the spell of the charming, polished, but penniless Frenchman.

The gulf between the actress and the translator narrowed when the company traveled to Compiègne in northern France, the summer residence of the French monarchs. They were staying at a small inn and spirits were high. After dinner one night, they decided to put on a floor show in a local restaurant. René Hubert arranged ad hoc costumes for Henri and his brother Alain, for Jane West and Arlette Marchal, the young actress who played Napoleon's sister. "One by one," Swanson recalled, "people disappeared and came back as various characters."[17] However, Gloria seemed to vanish entirely. She had hidden among the local women, pulling a shawl over her head and using pillows to make her shoulders big and her tummy round. The women had understood her pantomimed directions and cheerfully helped the movie star dress as one of them.

Everyone screamed with laughter when Gloria was unmasked, but amid the hilarity, she was thoughtful. The company was pulling together, becoming a family, and she noticed how well Henri fit in. Despite her language difficulties and the bureaucratic struggles the production had endured, Gloria felt at home in France. She just wasn't sure yet what that meant.

Henri and Gloria were constantly together, and their bond strengthened on a short goodwill trip to Brussels for Paramount, where they called on the embassy and visited veterans' hospitals and orphanages. Screaming crowds surrounded Swanson's small party at the train station; Gloria got pushed into a doorway and couldn't get free. Finally, Henri reached her, and they ran, the mob following behind. They flung themselves into the limousine—whereupon the driver made it clear that this was not Gloria Swanson's vehicle. He wanted her and Henri out, pronto, but Gloria was too frightened to move. Then someone pulled her car up alongside the limo, and they scrambled out of one and into the other. Another door opened, and Forrest Halsey dove into their limousine face first. He was a tall man, and his legs stuck out as someone tried repeatedly to slam the door. "Why he didn't have both legs amputated I will never know," Swanson said.[18]

Back at the hotel, a reception committee was waiting: though Gloria still felt tense and weak, there were hands to shake and champagne toasts to drink. After a quick dinner sent up to their rooms, they went off to the theater—or rather, the theaters. Paramount had organized a Gloria Swanson film festival in the city, plastering her image throughout Brussels. She made the rounds of at least ten theaters in one evening: "I no sooner get in and sit down than immediately the 'Star-Spangled Banner' [plays], and I get up. Then I sit down, and then it's the National Anthem, and I get up again, and everyone applauds. The picture goes on, and I am whisked out of that theater. The same procedure goes on all over town."[19]

They never got to sit through a movie, and Henri told Gloria he had never actually seen any of her pictures. The excitement Swanson generated was not lost on him, but Henri was not especially interested in her fame or her movies. Swanson found this intoxicating. Then Henri asked how long she had been famous. "Too long," she told him.[20]

More sobering were their visits to the soldiers' convalescent hospitals. The scars from the Great War were still fresh, and the soldiers they visited were hesitant with Gloria but talked easily to Henri, who had been awarded a Croix de Guerre for bravery.[21] As a member of the Chasseurs Alpins, France's elite mountain infantry known as the "Blue Devils," he had been seriously injured and had almost lost a leg.

Now it was Henri's turn to show Gloria his world. Over dinner he opened up, telling her about his experiences in the trenches. Henri had been on the battlefield while she was acting in Keystone comedies and making silly pictures about espionage at Triangle. He had shared shell holes with dead Germans and lived off the decaying food he found there. He spoke in a matter-of-fact way, and Gloria marveled at his tales of the truces that allowed French and German soldiers to swim together in the river before going back to face each other as deadly foes. Her admiration added to her strong attraction to him.

When they returned to the hotel, Henri apologized: he had nothing to offer her but himself. Gloria gazed at him, slowly but surely taking every other suitor off her list: "There was no list now. There never would be again. There was only Henri de la Falaise de la Coudraye." They went to her room together. As she recalled, "If the presidents of France and America and the whole of the Belgian press and Will Hays himself had been there in the corridor, I would have swept past them proudly and closed the door of my suite behind us."[22]

As the holidays approached, Swanson realized she had never been happier. Henri adored her children, and they treated her enormous house as a playground, with games of dress-up and hide and seek. Once

Henri hid in a fireplace and came out covered in ash and cinders, which thrilled the children. The sound of whistling drew Gloria to her bedroom window one morning. A scruffy gardener in a blue overall waved to her, and just as she was about to turn away, he pulled off his mustache and grinned: it was Henri. "Every day we managed to play some kind of game," she recalled. "They were delightful times."[23]

Gloria was falling deeper in love with Henri and deeper in love with France. He took her to little bistros, each with its own character. One restaurant numbered each duck served; they were then in the hundreds of thousands. She loved the signs of history everywhere, the plaques in smoky bars saying that Napoleon had played chess or drank there.

For Christmas, a holiday Gloria celebrated with childish delight, she decided to create an unforgettable party and raced home every night to work on the arrangements. Thirty came for dinner, and a small, perfectly proportioned Christmas tree decorated each table. Every guest received a beautifully wrapped gift: either gold cufflinks or a gold bracelet from Cartier. André Daven said, "Gloria was always generous—that is to say, extravagant—in the way she treated her friends."[24] In Paris she spent lavishly, feeling that France had been good to her. She could afford it: her salary was going up to $7,000 a week on January 1.

This was a progressive party, with guests shifting tables between courses and ending where they began for dessert. Despite the complexity of the arrangements ("higher math," Swanson groaned), everyone would get to visit with everyone else during the sumptuous meal.[25] Several dozen more guests arrived for after-dinner festivities. There were skits, with a specially built stage and roles for everyone. Even Adelaide, who shunned the spotlights in her daughter's world, was persuaded to take part (she played a dead Russian, to Gloria's amusement). The dinner guests put on a vaudeville show for the late arrivals, and André Daven made beautiful programs on parchment paper.

The biggest effort went into the production of a short, filmed burlesque of *Madame Sans-Gêne*. The roles were reversed: men played the women's parts and vice versa. Gloria took the role of Napoleon, with makeup and padding to make her resemble Emile Drain. After midnight, the holiday decorations were shifted aside, and the dining room was transformed into a Montmartre café. There were candles in bottles on the tabletops; waiters in aprons served hot spiced wine. Painted backdrops courtesy of the studio tricked out two bars, one as American, the other French. The dancing and music went on until dawn.

André Daven remembered his hostess's energy: "She could dance until six in the morning, then take a bath, dress, and sleep in the car to arrive fresh and ready to work at the studio, never showing any sign of fatigue. . . . Léonce Perret could not believe it."[26] The evening was glorious, and at the center of it all was Gloria, radiantly in love and surrounded by the people who mattered most to her. She called the party "one of the highlights of my life."[27]

Inspired by the Christmas revelry, Gloria decided to throw a full-fledged costume ball, with everyone wearing silly or grotesque costumes. That evening the hostess appeared in a glistening, silvery gray gown that was practically backless. A long rope of pearls held with a diamond clasp trailed behind her. As her guests agreed that Gloria looked stunning, she whirled around: from the front she was a pudgy, big-bellied man with a red nose and a gray mustache. The transformation was absolute, the hit of the evening. "That fall and winter could with no exaggeration have been called the Swanson Season," she recalled. "Never had the French press treated a star more lovingly or covered one more fully. Until Josephine Baker arrived and danced the Charleston and stole half of the limelight, I was the toast of Paris."[28]

Gloria and Henri planned to marry as soon as the waiting period for her divorce from Herbert Somborn—then a year, according to California law—elapsed. She was looking joyously forward to making a life with Henri and her children. Little Gloria had turned four a few months earlier. "She knew what it meant to have a daddy," the actress explained, "but it was something new for Brother. He was overjoyed when I told him that Henri was going to live with us in America. . . . The first time he said the word 'Papa,' in the French fashion, with the accent on the last syllable, I thought I would melt."[29] The couple hoped to have several more children, and Gloria was eager to become Henri's Marquise.

They hoped to be married in France in mid-January, to take a short trip to the Riviera afterward, and to sail for the States in early February. Then French bureaucracy struck again: the papers required to prove that Gloria's divorce was final got lost in transit. She wasn't free to marry Henri without the proper documentation, and they could not travel to the US together without being married. Several nail-biting weeks passed slowly. Henri finally arranged for a representative of the American embassy to be present at the wedding to vouch that Gloria was single.

At last, on the morning of January 28, 1925, they presented themselves at the town hall of the XVIth arrondissement. The mayor, who had been sworn to secrecy, begged to be allowed to invite his wife. There were only a few other guests: Adelaide, Henri's brother Alain, Jane and Mrs. West, André Daven, René Hubert, and Madame and Léonce Perret. The mayor made a little speech, stumbling over the provocative names of some of Gloria's movies. *Why Change Your Wife?* and *Don't Change Your Husband* did not sound auspicious when read aloud at the actress's third wedding. The bride looked beautiful in a beige embroidered suit and hat. Henri once again translated for her, only now the words were shared vows of love and fidelity. A few short minutes later, Gloria was the new Marquise de la Falaise de la Coudraye. They celebrated at the Plaza Athénée, where the couple had moved for a quiet Parisian honeymoon. Gloria was ecstatic.

Adelaide was a lot less pleased. She told Gloria she "had made a terrible mistake marrying a penniless Frenchman, no matter what his name was."[30] Her cold response wounded Gloria, as did her mother's changed travel plans: Adelaide was leaving for America on a separate ship. She wanted to be on her own, away from the Swanson circus. Gloria remembered this as "an emotional time" for her mother, saying sadly, "She can just take so much of me and then she can take no more."[31]

Though dismayed by her mother's reaction, Swanson knew she had found the right partner in Henri. "For the first time in my life," she said, "I was in love with a man quite near my own age, and he happened to be a handsome, *galant* French nobleman, the kind every American woman dreams about. He had no faults that I could find: he wasn't in pictures, he didn't drink, and he didn't have a string of marriages behind him."[32] She was entirely satisfied with her choice. On her wedding day she told a reporter, "I want BABIES! I want at least six more of my own and I intend to have them. I will also adopt two or three more besides. I may be a vamp on the screen, but I am a mother at heart."[33]

Gloria may have sounded ebullient, but the new bride had a troubling secret: she was already pregnant. The problem was the morals clause in her Paramount contract, which allowed the studio to dismiss her for sleeping with a man who was not her husband. She had been counting the days until her divorce documents came through because she wanted to marry Henri as quickly as possible. Now, however, anyone who could count would know Swanson was already pregnant at her wedding.

No matter how she figured it, she was in trouble. If the press got wind of her condition, the studio would have no choice but to terminate her contract. She had handed Jesse Lasky—who had tricked and manipulated her when she wanted to divorce Herbert Somborn—the power to end her career. Even if Lasky kept Gloria on, Paramount would renegotiate her contract on terms more favorable to the studio. This pregnancy had come at the very moment when Swanson's growing star power would have allowed her to dictate the conditions under which she worked. She could expect to name her projects and her price. With a new contract due to be negotiated, she was in line to become one of the highest paid stars in movie history. And there was no telling how others in Hollywood, even the freewheeling United Artists, would react if Paramount gave her the boot. A weak offer from her current studio would damage her earning power elsewhere as well. Everything she had worked for could be lost if she had a baby a wee bit early.

Swanson felt this was a decision she had to make on her own. It was not fair to burden Henri, as she saw it, with "the price of her career." She was also becoming a realist when it came to economics and marriage. If she lost her movie contract, she thought, she might also lose Henri: "We had both gone past the stage where we could be happy in a garret."[34] Though the prospect made her heartsick, she asked André Daven to help her arrange an abortion. She resolved to tell Henri what she had done when she was once again pregnant and could bring his child to term.

In her memoir, Swanson described this episode in compelling and heart-wrenching detail. She spoke of slipping out of Henri's arms early one morning, having invented a business meeting that would occupy her several hours. She spoke of her feelings of foreboding and felt she saw the face of death, "beckoning or warning, I couldn't tell which." Even as Daven comforted her, she felt a dark sense of déjà vu. She had been told once before, when she lost Wally's baby, that she was young enough to have more children. "I had thought [Wally] had done the most monstrous thing in the world, and now I was preparing to do it myself. Furthermore, I was doing it for the same reason Wally had, probably—to save my career."[35] Nonetheless, she steeled herself and went to meet the doctor. She felt she had no other choice.

In 1925, abortion was dangerous and difficult. Beyond the illegality of the procedure, there was the serious problem of treating infection in the era before antibiotics. Since shame, fear, and silence prevailed, we will never know how many desperate women died this way. Swanson already had a serious aversion to the medical establishment, and as the doctor's assistant bound her arms to the operating table and brought out the ether, she was terrified.

André brought her home after it was over. The hotel was full of Swanson's friends and staff trying to manage the news of her marriage.

Adolph Zukor had sent the couple a check for $10,000 as a wedding present; Paramount hoped they would reenact the ceremony for the cameras. There were dozens of requests for interviews and photographs. The suite was full of flowers; their smell was overwhelming. There was an enormous amount to do before they could leave for America. Pleading exhaustion, Gloria crawled into bed for a nap.

At first, everyone thought Gloria was overtired, in need of a rest. René Hubert booked his passage to the States, taking the children with him so Gloria could regain her strength. However, after three days it became clear that Swanson was seriously ill. When her temperature reached 104, they took her by ambulance to the hospital. There Gloria hovered between life and death, lost in a mist of self-recrimination and delirium.

Her doctors feared tetanus and finally established that Swanson had blood poisoning: there was no known cure for either. At one point, her doctor loomed over her with a long hypodermic needle that to the feverish woman looked like something one would use on a horse. "The doctor was afraid to use this medicine, but on the other hand he was afraid not to because he thought I'd die anyway. He walked up and down the hall until Henri grabbed him and screamed at him, 'Do something! Make up your mind!'"[36] Later, Swanson recalled her hallucinations: "Death was in the room. Mine, this time."[37]

Whenever she woke, Henri was there, haggard with exhaustion but unwilling to leave her side. He lived at the hospital. Adelaide, however, had departed for home before anyone realized how ill her daughter was. All the way across the ocean, she heard reports of the expected death of Gloria Swanson. Reporters had gathered, as alert for news of Swanson's death as they had been for information about her marriage. Henri later told his wife about going out into the street in the early morning to get air and being violently sick from stress and fear. Workmen off to their labors "would call to him and whistle at him and make fun of him" because they thought he was ill from a long night's drinking.[38]

Only a few weeks earlier, Henri had been a carefree young bachelor about town, an habitué of the Ritz Bar who had seen many Parisian dawns. Now he was a new husband with a famous wife whom everyone expected to die. Outside the hospital windows he saw reporters stationed at a small café across the way; they seemed like "undertakers waiting there to write [Gloria's] obituary."[39] When Swanson's fever finally went down and stayed down, Henri gleefully declared that she "had fooled them all." For the newsmen, Andre Daven said, "Gloria was not an individual with human ties, but an actor in a drama whose death was demanded to make the story a good one."[40]

A long recovery was ahead for Swanson. She and Henri missed their sailing; their departure was postponed several more times before Gloria was strong enough to make the trip. Her hair had been shorn, and she was too weak to stand, but she didn't want to stand anyway. "Now that my life was saved," Swanson said, "I wanted to die. I was so tired and exhausted from fighting. They had to drag me out of bed. Then I would fold up my legs, like a naughty child between two people who are trying to make it walk. I'd cry and say I wanted to go back to bed."[41]

Henri was an excellent nurse. He and his friend the Baron d'Aiguy took Gloria to Versailles, where she managed to walk slowly between tables in the Hall of Mirrors. After a week she went the length of the corridor where the 1919 Peace Conference had been held. To amuse the convalescent, Henri took her on carriage rides around the palace grounds, telling her stories of French history. "He was a beautifully educated boy and an intellect by nature," Swanson recalled. "I admired him very much, extremely. He was a wonderful companion and a very tender person."[42]

Henri never reproached Gloria for her decision to have an abortion, but she never forgave herself. More than fifty years later she called it "the greatest regret of my life."[43] Only shortly before her death would she finally lay down her burden of guilt and shame.

CHAPTER 10

American Royalty

GLORIA AND HENRI FINALLY SAILED FOR AMERICA IN MID-MARCH. PAR-
amount was eager to have Swanson home, to show her fans she was
ready to make movies and to show her on her new husband's arm. If two
divorces was nothing to brag about, all was forgiven when the actress
acquired an attractive, titled Frenchman as Husband #3. Gloria, still delicate, was much less excited about returning to the States: she had some
idea of what Paramount expected. Her marriage and her illness had kept
her in the headlines for weeks, giving the studio "millions upon millions
of dollars' worth of free publicity."[1] Yet Lasky and Zukor were adamant:
she had to be in New York for the premiere of *Madame Sans-Gêne*.

Swanson used the peace and quiet of the crossing to rest and read the
heartfelt letters sent by fans during her convalescence: "Surely you must
know how we feel you belong to us all . . . [and] the anguish of your
countless fans when we were being told the little star was fading—so far
away there over the ocean."[2] Her fans knew only that Gloria had been
seriously ill—possibly as a result of internal injuries after falling from a
horse—and had undergone an emergency operation.[3] What happened in
Paris would not become public knowledge until Swanson herself told the
story years later.

As New York harbor came into view, Henri pointed out the famous
skyscrapers, as thrilled as a child. He clutched his wife's hand, unaware
that her heart was pounding for a different reason: Swanson had seen a
fast clipper jammed with newsmen coming to meet the boat. "It was just
a swarm of people," she recalled.[4] "They were hanging on the sides."[5]
Swanson was always news, but Henri was a public relations dream. Story
after story gushed about his ancient family and his aristocratic title. He
was handsome and athletic; he was rich (or so they said); he was a war
hero. Henri was related on his mother's side to the Hennessy cognac producers in Ireland, so when reporters wanted to tone down his patrician

qualities, they commented on his "Irish" traits: as Swanson's interpreter, Henri "literally talked his way into the heart of the cinema queen," one story proclaimed.[6] Another mused, "I am inclined to think the Irish in him is predominant, for he wins you at once with that frank, ready smile and easy manner."[7]

They were also ready to claim him as American. The editor and publisher of *Photoplay*, the country's most influential movie magazine, described Henri's arrival: "'That chap a Frenchman?' was the comment of one of Gloria's friends after meeting the marquis. 'I'll tell the world he's an American to his hip pocket! Henry's all right.' That tells the story. He rings true, this young aristocrat. . . . [He is] a regular fellow. If he had shown one sign of losing his head, got off on the wrong foot only once— *wow!* But he has come through apparently unconscious that anybody was watching him—and everybody is calling him Henry."[8] Everywhere they went, people liked Swanson's sociable, easygoing, "pleasantly democratic" husband.[9] Jesse Lasky found him a "wonderfully charming fellow" and got a kick out of calling him "Hank."[10] "France had never had a better ambassador," his wife declared proudly.[11]

The young couple faced tremendous scrutiny around the clock, in the guise of social events intended to welcome them home and celebrate their marriage. Traffic stopped for a parade to the Astoria studios, followed by a reception for the newlyweds. Paramount gave an enormous party for them at the Park Lane Hotel, with several hundred invited for dinner and several hundred more for dancing afterwards. The orchestra played "La Marseillaise" as Gloria arrived on Henri's arm, while young women in Marie Antoinette costumes handed out two-cornered Napoleon hats. The company created tableaux of each of her Paramount pictures, as a tribute to the studio's leading player and a reminder of her many triumphs. Swanson was in the last year of her contract, and everyone knew she had become much, much more valuable. Before new contract negotiations opened, the studio hoped to soften her up.

At the Ritz-Carlton, the couple had no privacy at all. They could not have the children with them—Gloria and Brother went to the Croton house with the governess—because they were practically under siege. People lurked in the hallway, some unashamedly peeking through the keyholes. Once they discovered a reporter sleeping in their closet. The maids and valets "carried a constant stream of reports to the newspaper people down the hall: what food we ordered, what color Henri's pajamas were, what I was going to wear," Swanson said.[12] Then there were the interviews, the photo sessions, and the endless jangle of the telephone.

"We never finished a sentence. We might as well not have lived under the same roof."[13]

As hard as this was for Swanson in her weakened state, it was entirely new to Henri. Everything in America was bigger, louder, done on a grander scale. Henri was good-natured but found it all bewildering. His new wife recalled, "I don't believe from the time Henri arrived here that he opened his mouth. . . . Things were happening so fast and furiously from the time we opened our eyes in the morning until we were dead tired and fell into bed at night . . . it was an incredible kind of life."[14]

For the premiere of *Madame Sans-Gêne*, Henri invited the Grand Duke and Duchess of Russia as his and Gloria's guests. When they arrived at the Rivoli Theater, however, the streets were so thronged with fans that the limousine couldn't get near the curb. (The streetcars had been taken off Broadway to make room for the premiere traffic.) The foursome got out in the middle of the street, the police immediately forming a cordon around the star and her husband. Their guests had to fend for themselves. When the Grand Duke and Duchess finally made it into the theater a half hour later, their finery was torn and bedraggled. The duchess's egret hat was tilted over her eyes, making her look tipsy. Swanson was mortified: "They were not pleased at all . . . We never saw the Duke and Duchess after that."[15]

The film received a warm welcome, and the theater looked spectacular draped in French and American flags, but Swanson was too tired and overwhelmed to take it in. In any case, the police ushered Gloria and Henri out by a side door once the picture began in order to avoid the crush of movie fans waiting for her.

When she and Henri went out on the town, they made a stir whether they wanted to or not. (Paramount often tipped off reporters about Swanson's plans, thus guaranteeing a crowd of stargazers.) When the pair tried to see *Rose Marie* on Broadway, a huge crowd prevented their entering the theater. As they took their seats quietly after the play began, "the performance on stage halted, the houselights came up, and the entire audience gave the famous couple a standing ovation."[16] It was easier to stay in the hotel and have friends come to visit them.

Gloria was determined, however, that Henri would see something of New York. She enlisted Sport Ward's help, and the men toured the Empire State Building and the Statue of Liberty together, becoming fast friends. When Henri wanted to hear Irish tenor John McCormack perform, Gloria got tickets for a small party including Sport and screenwriter

Jim Creelman. During the interval, Sport and Jim each thrust two drip-ping chocolate ice cream cones at her and Henri. Carnegie Hall was packed to the rafters for the classy, dressy event. People craned their necks to see what was going on, and a rumble of laughter went through the theater as Gloria, her hands full, tried to hold the messy treats away from her beautiful gown. Henri had never seen an ice cream cone before and wasn't sure what to do with two of them. Sport kept wisecracking: he knew Gloria when she used to like ice cream, he said, offering to get her raspberry if chocolate wasn't good enough for a marquise.

Gloria was thinking of smashing a cone into Sport's face when the lights flickered off, signaling the end of the interval. As attention turned to the stage, "I got the brilliant idea of putting this mess down on the [floor] in front of us, and so did Henri." They relaxed and were enjoying themselves when it became clear that the melting chocolate was flowing down the theater aisle: "At the next chance, we got out and stayed out." Sport "was just as pleased as Punch."[17] He would not allow Gloria to get too big for her britches. Despite her own considerable experience in the spotlight, the scale of the reception they were getting surprised even the Hollywood veteran. Her celebrity was like a third party in the new mar-riage. Swanson could not help wondering what her new husband was making of it.

Paramount hired a private railway train to take the entourage west to California, where Swanson would promote *Madame Sans-Gêne*. "We milked the transcontinental trip for all we could," Jesse Lasky recalled. "It was too good a publicity break to pass up."[18] The train was filled with Paramount sales reps, theater owners, and distributors on an all-expens-es-paid, cross-country party. If Swanson had been expecting any peace and quiet, she was mistaken: the journey was "a carnival."[19]

Along the route, as the train pulled into endless small towns, Swanson was summoned from her compartment—sometimes wearing only a robe, or wiping cold cream quickly off her face—to see her fans holding signs with "Welcome home, Gloria" blazoned in huge letters. Adela Rogers St. Johns highlighted the poignancy of the star's shorn locks: Gloria's hair-style wasn't a new trend but "a haircut just like your little brother gets."[20]

Swanson was scrutinized, her fans and detractors alike eager to see whether this marriage had changed her. Adolph Zukor claimed that early on the trip, "Gloria was royalty . . . but she thawed rapidly. Before long she was a big participator in crap games."[21] Others enjoyed stories of her new husband putting the marquise in her place. When Gloria's nose "tilted a bit in midair" as she greeted fellow passengers on her ocean crossing, *The New Yorker* gleefully chronicled Henri's gentle reproof: "Don't be a snob, Gloria."[22] Tales of Swanson's high-handed behavior persisted, if only because they made excellent copy. A young director reportedly explained to the actress that "his three principal interests were really fishing, Airedale dogs, and Staffordshire pottery. 'I have only one hobby myself,' responded Miss Swanson. 'I like to live like a queen.'"[23] Others called her "Napoleon in skirts."[24]

The most famous (apocryphal) story has her cabling Paramount about her imminent return to the US: "Am arriving with the Marquis tomorrow. Please arrange ovation."[25] Stories like these made Swanson see red. "I have never gone out and sought publicity," she insisted.[26] Yet she knew that to the studio, "I was money. Their money. That's how they saw me. They would never let me do anything to diminish my value or hurt the industry. . . . They cared only about That Woman Up There on the Screen."[27] She also knew that Paramount hoped to flatter her into signing another contract, a prospect she flatly refused to discuss.

If Henri was stunned by his wife's intense life, Gloria was happy to see him relax, especially when there was fun on offer. Henri loved the elaborate prank Paramount staffers arranged while the train was stopped in Albuquerque, New Mexico. They made a show of hiring some "scouts" and "gunfighters" to keep their small party safe from Indian raids during a tour of the area. Once they were sure the Frenchman was a bit unsettled, they headed into the wilderness—and were promptly "attacked" a mile outside the town limits. With great fanfare, the "gunfighters" held off the marauders and gave Henri a Wild West show to remember.[28]

Their arrival in Los Angeles could not have been more dramatic than if it had been staged by, well, a movie company. Two brass bands were playing at the station, where the mayor welcomed Gloria and Henri. From a platform strewn with flowers and decorated with bunting and banners, Cecil DeMille made a speech welcoming Swanson; he seemed "overcome with emotion."[29] "The faces on that platform were like the Last Judgment—everyone I'd worked with or known in Hollywood," Swanson recalled.[30]

She saw friends and colleagues from Keystone, Triangle, and Paramount: her directors Clarence Badger, Al Parker, Frank Borzage, Sam Wood, and Jack Conway. Mack Sennett was there; so were Chester Conklin and Bebe Daniels and even Francis X. Bushman from Essanay. Her leading men were there: Tommy Meighan, Elliott Dexter, Ben Lyon,

Ricardo Cortez, and Rudolph Valentino. Rod LaRocque was smiling up at her. So was Mickey Neilan, whom she had thought the love of her life. Douglas Fairbanks, Mary Pickford, Charlie Chaplin, D. W. Griffith, and Joe Schenck represented United Artists.

She and Henri walked down a long red carpet. Then a motorcycle cavalcade, sirens blaring, escorted their white Rolls-Royce to the studio. The streets were lined with fans throwing flowers. Sid Grauman's usherettes rode alongside on white, flower-bedecked ponies. When they reached the studio, all the employees—carpenters and electricians as well as writers, set designers, and hairdressers—were outside. Edith Head, then a fledgling costume designer, recalled tossing roses at Swanson as she alighted from her car, a vision of elegance and beauty.[31] Work had shut down for the morning so that everyone could greet the returning star. A huge banner hung over the studio gate. It simply said "Home."

Swanson had never considered California home, but the warmth of her welcome made it tempting. She had not been in Hollywood since her frustrated departure two years earlier, but now she broke down and wept. Her mother and the children had arrived on the coast ahead of Swanson, and she was desperate to see Gloria and Brother. Yet when they finally walked into 904 North Crescent Drive and were greeted with ecstatic shouts and hugs, she realized that her marriage faced a formidable challenge: "My house. My children. My possessions. My friends. My studio calling . . . How could it ever become 'ours?'"[32]

Everything conspired against the couple as they tried to get to the premiere that night. A traffic jam snarled the approach to Grauman's Million Dollar Theater, with fans lined up along the sidewalks cheering for Swanson "in unison like a football crowd."[33] When the car stopped, fans climbed on it, "clustering like bees," Henri said, "on honey."[34] When Gloria, Henri, and Adelaide—who had consented to come to her first-ever movie premiere—entered the theater, the spacious lobby was deserted. The ushers told Swanson that the movie had just begun. Annoyed with herself for being late to her own premiere, she quietly entered the darkened auditorium.

Suddenly lights blazed, and an orchestra began to play "Home, Sweet Home." The capacity audience rose to its feet, singing and cheering as Gloria and Henri made their way down the aisle. Colleen Moore thought they "looked like a king and queen from some mythical . . . kingdom."[35]

Adela Rogers St. Johns recalled the night as one of classic Hollywood's most glittering occasions:

Gloria Swanson stood there wrapped in cloth of silver, glittering with diamonds. Behind her, in white tie and tails, red ribbon across his shirt front, color flashing from decorations and medals, [was] the Marquis, Hollywood's first titled bridegroom. Then that audience of hard-boiled critics, every rival star, founding fathers, presidents and vice-presidents of vast film companies, social leaders and workers in every branch of picture making, began to yell like Indians, until cheers still going on outside faded before those inside. . . . I think we knew that the spectacular figure was our Movie Star of all time. . . . Hollywood paid her a tribute that night it has never equaled for anyone else.[36]

The crowd drowned out Jesse Lasky's speech; he finally gave up and the picture began. But not even on this special night would Henri see one of his wife's movies all the way through. During the first reel, the head usher told Swanson that the police could not control the fans outside and she should leave by the back door now. As they crept out of the crowded theater and were whisked away by their police escort, Adelaide clutched her daughter's hand, saying it must be the happiest night of Gloria's life.

It wasn't that simple for Gloria. She was deeply moved by her colleagues' show of love and support and grateful for the wonderful opportunities she had enjoyed. Yet she also had a restless feeling of foreboding. It was all too much. She had been working hard for years, certainly. Nonetheless, she was just twenty-six: what heights were left for her to scale? Swanson intuitively understood that her colleagues saw her as the prodigal, returned home from adventures outside the fold. They saw her as Lazarus, almost literally returned from the dead. They definitely saw her as Cinderella, who had married her handsome Prince in a fairytale happy ending.[37] So where else could her story lead? If she was so high up, where could she go but down? She was also preoccupied by sorrow at the loss of the child she had been unable to carry: "I was thinking of the price I had paid two months ago to be able to walk down that orchid-strewn aisle. . . . I had had to sneak to a French surgeon like a criminal and sacrifice a child I was carrying."[38] Swanson selected this episode to begin her autobiography, signaling its significance in her life story. She would always remember the glittering evening that should have been her sweetest triumph as "the saddest moment of my life."[39]

The full force of her predicament hit Swanson as she and Henri settled into life in Hollywood. She had a year to run on her Paramount contract, and the studio would offer her the moon to sign another agreement.

However, being back in LA reminded the actress what a stranglehold the movie business had on those working in it. She wanted to live in Paris, or maybe New York. She also remembered all too well how Lasky and company had treated her when they had the upper hand. She was determined not to find herself in that position again. If she had divorced Herbert Somborn when she wanted to, she would not have had to delay her marriage to Henri. A wedding even a few weeks earlier would have made it possible for her to carry Henri's baby to term. Although Swanson did not generally nurse grudges, she held this one tightly.

She also recognized that her Paramount pictures were only as good as the stories and collaborators she was assigned. The studio would do what was best for its long-term profitability, and she did not come first in its calculations. Since Paramount was the richest, most prestigious studio in town, there was really nowhere else for Swanson to go. The only other option was independent production—which meant going into business with United Artists. If Gloria signed with them, she could make her own decisions about what stories to film and when. She could hire writers and directors who thought as she did and whose first allegiance would be to her. Henri could get involved; it could be a family business, the kind she had envied other stars. Best of all, she would not have to make movies as though they were widgets on a production line. Paramount cared only about putting a new Gloria Swanson picture on the screen every season; exhibitors had to book "at least six other Paramounts" to get one Swanson picture.[40] She was tired of being a "mortgage lifter," tired of making lots of money for studio executives whom she had to beg or trick into allowing her any creative authority over her work.[41]

The prospect of returning to Paramount for her next movie made Swanson feel exhausted and depressed. She put off returning calls from the studio, watched piles of invitations to parties and receptions pile up, and brooded. The one ray of light came from having her family under her roof again. Henri tended her as though she were a delicate flower, and Gloria once again blessed him for being indifferent to her movie career. His love was the greatest luxury she possessed.

Her French physician had recommended a six-month rest, but the sooner Swanson went back to work, the sooner she would be a free agent. So she and Allan Dwan got together to talk about *The Coast of Folly*, in which Gloria had two roles: a rebellious woman who deserts her family for a life in high society and the woman's daughter. Mother and child do not meet again until the daughter is grown and the mother has remarried and become a countess. Mom appears just in time to save her daughter from making the same scandalous mistakes she herself made when young.

Gloria decided to play Joyce, the daughter, as an athletic, energetic type, in contrast to the languid society beauties she had often portrayed. Swanson's love of disguise got free play with the mother role: she hid herself in the costumes and mannerisms of a much older woman. In stills from the film (all that remain of the picture), the young marquise is unrecognizable: her hair is gray and she is dressed in the ornate style of a woman desperate to appear fashionable. Gloria considered it a compliment when viewers—who often entered in the middle of a picture—did not even know she was playing the countess: "I was like Lon Chaney up there. I was playing this strange old woman and I loved doing it."[42] It became one of her favorite roles.

Since Gloria was playing two parts, there were frequent costume changes and long hours in makeup. Dwan hit upon the idea of saving the convalescent's energy by wheeling her back and forth between her bungalow and the set in the caned chairs that were part of the Palm Beach movie décor. This, however, was taken as a sign that Swanson had put on airs: now she was too good to walk like other mortals. People saw not a game young woman returning to work too quickly after a life-threatening illness but a haughty, demanding movie star, a marquise being carried in a sedan chair. Dwan got a kick out of Gloria's discomfiture. He immediately instructed everyone to address Swanson by her full title: Would the Marquise de la Falaise de la Coudraye indulge them by moving a bit farther to the right? The papers lost no time in attributing this, too, to Swanson's regal conceit.

Dwan also kicked into high gear the interrupted "feud" with Pola Negri, who was working nearby. He found it comical that Negri's arrivals on the set were greeted as big events, with everyone expected to hush as the star appeared. So he staged an entrance for Swanson. She was paraded to the set in her chair, an umbrella held over her head. Then he had a small orchestra play a fanfare. When the Negri crew complained that Pola "couldn't emote" with the musical disruption, Dwan hired a high school marching band. "[There] must have been seventy people in the damn thing," he snickered, "and it pretty near shook the scenery down."[43] Some things would never change in Hollywood, but at least Allan Dwan helped Swanson laugh at them.

Soon after her return to the coast Gloria got a call from Maurice Cleary: United Artists had authorized him to open negotiations with Swanson on a producing contract. Cleary suggested a six-picture deal, with one or two movies delivered per year. Swanson would get stock options, her pictures' profits (after they had recouped their costs), and a percentage of distribution profits. Cleary stressed that the number of films was negotiable. In fact, everything was negotiable.

Swanson listened attentively. Her most rewarding film work since she became a star had been done on the periphery of the system. In New York and Paris, she had enjoyed more creative control than she was likely to get in Hollywood. But was she ready to take a giant step farther away from the studio, to go out on her own? Gloria wasn't sure she wanted to continue working at all, but to walk away from her career when she had just sacrificed her pregnancy and risked her health to keep it going seemed foolish, too. She was the breadwinner for her family, like it or not. She told Cleary she would discuss his offer with her husband.

United Artists was formed in 1919 by four members of Hollywood's elite: Mary Pickford, Douglas Fairbanks, Charlie Chaplin, and D. W. Griffith. They wanted creative and economic control over their films, and so far they seemed to be making a go of it. Studio executives had joked that putting actors and directors in charge was like letting the lunatics run the asylum, but everyone watched as pictures like *Robin Hood*, *Orphans of the Storm*, *The Three Musketeers*, *Way Down East*, *Tess of the Storm Country*, and *The Gold Rush* wowed audiences and critics alike.[44] Being invited to join this company meant that Swanson was at the absolute pinnacle of the movie business.

However, independent production was not for the faint of heart. It meant leaving the security of the studio: the weekly paycheck, the well-oiled machinery that made, distributed, and promoted motion pictures steadily and efficiently, and—most of all—access to the theaters in which to show them. The major companies were becoming more major by the minute, as they bought or built theaters across America, thus guaranteeing exhibition venues for their pictures.

Swanson had gotten involved in post-production work for the first time with *Madame Sans-Gêne*, and the experience gave her a new perspective on filmmaking. Her contract offered her no authority over the editing of any of her pictures. Such control by a star was unheard of (outside of United Artists, that is). However, Gloria was not pleased with the version of *Madame Sans-Gêne* in circulation. "The picture is not at all what it should be," she complained to an interviewer, "and much of the fault lies in the editing."[45] A motion picture production should be like a symphony, she explained, with everyone following the lead of the conductor and striving to realize his vision. Why shouldn't a star lead a production? He would be the one blamed, the one whose popularity would suffer if the picture did not succeed. Swanson's brief experience helping edit and title *Madame Sans-Gêne*, a film she knew intimately, boosted her confidence in her judgment. Her ideas about the singularity of vision at work in a great film, however, would not gain currency for almost fifty years.

Swanson was in no hurry. She considered UA's proposal, sat back and waited to hear what Paramount would offer, and prepared for her very rosy future. She told Henri they would accept whatever social invitations he wanted, and any worries she might have had about his happiness evaporated: Henri fit in beautifully, his manners so polished that he was welcome everywhere. They dined at Pickfair with Mary and Doug (though Gloria privately found Mary a stodgy hostess). They entertained at home as well, though 904 had one decided drawback. Sightseeing buses were beginning to rumble across Hollywood, filled with tourists eager for a glimpse of their favorite stars at home. Since Swanson's house was on a pie-shaped bit of land directly facing the street, her family had little privacy outside.

She had to admit, though, that making *The Coast of Folly* in Los Angeles had been a good idea. Gloria had a real home to return to each night and a chance to unwind with her family after hours. Henri had won her children's hearts, and they appeared in court as a foursome that May when Swanson finalized her adoption of Joseph.[46] Although she had been low and tired, prone to depression when she returned to California in March, as the summer of 1925 began Gloria once again felt how lucky she was.

Madame Sans-Gêne was currently in "road show" presentation across the country, with limited release and higher admission prices. Ticket buyers got commemorative programs and souvenir *Sans-Gêne* coins stamped with Swanson's face. Reviews had been mixed, praise for the film's authenticity trumping complaints about the story's incoherence (which Swanson blamed on Paramount's cuts). Nonetheless, the public's fascination with Gloria, enhanced by her marriage and illness, clearly boosted her box office appeal. When the *Times'* critic went back for a second screening of the film he called "[a] dream of delight," the enormous theater was still packed, people standing in the aisles on a bright spring afternoon.[47]

Gloria was ready for a conversation with Jesse Lasky about her future: this time she held all the best cards. Her antipathy to Lasky had, if anything, grown since her marriage, but when he made it clear that Paramount would reward her handsomely for renewing her contract,

Gloria was interested. She had come to the conclusion that it would be a mistake to leave the industry: "I would never know anything as well as I knew pictures . . . [W]hy should I leave them if I could change the things I hated about them?"[48] She invited Lasky to her house so that she and her husband could hear his offer together: Henri would be involved in any decision she made.

They had agreed to approach Lasky first about the European version of *Madame Sans-Gêne*, which would have its Paris premiere in December. Henri asked Lasky politely for assurances that the picture would be shown uncut in France, and Lasky promptly asked Henri to represent Paramount abroad—on salary, of course. He then got to the point of his visit: he wanted to double Swanson's salary. When she appeared unimpressed, he asked her point blank if she had received any other offers. She acknowledged that United Artists wanted her. With them she would enjoy complete artistic freedom. What's more, she would not be expected to make additional pictures or sign any morals clauses. Lasky understood that old business was being settled and immediately agreed: Gloria's contract would have no additional pictures and no morals clause.

Lasky then raised his offer from $14,000 to $18,000 a week—every week, whether she was working or not. Swanson inquired mildly whether that was a million dollars a year. It was not. With that the meeting was over, Swanson having announced that she would take some time to consider Paramount's offer.

Swanson had to admire Lasky's negotiating skills, even as she fought back dismay about her husband's: "Poor, dear, sweet Henri . . . Mr. Lasky had retired him from the field in a minute merely by accommodating him . . . Whatever Mr. Lasky paid him, he would get back hundredfold in free publicity if Henri and I promoted the film in Europe. Henri was too noble in every way for Hollywood." Gloria was glad she was not "salivating at the thought of making a million a year" but also knew she had outperformed her husband from start to finish. Henri had been "even more courtly and diffident" than she feared.[49] He showed little appetite for the tough negotiations that were part of Hollywood business. Once more she would have to rely on herself.

Lasky remembered this scene differently: "I suppose any woman who has the world at her feet and is treated like an empress long enough will begin to feel like one." He thought he had made Swanson an offer she could not refuse: $300,000 a picture for three pictures a year, plus her choice of directors and stories, a personal wardrobe designer, and a share of the profits. It was a handsome proposition, and Lasky left the house "disheartened."[50] Paramount nonetheless hoped Gloria was not ready to leave the negotiating table.

Swanson, however, was deeply reluctant to remain in the Paramount fold. First there was her considerable anger about the way the studio had manipulated her private life. She also had serious reservations about the way the studio had managed her career. Swanson believed that the practice of putting stars into as many pictures as possible as quickly as possible could hurt her in the long term; if she stayed at Paramount, she would have to be constantly vigilant on this score. She pictured the beautiful young girls waiting outside the studio gates, hoping for their chance at movie stardom. Paramount could decide to replace her at any time.

Swanson was also convinced she could get what Lasky was offering and more at UA. She would pick her stories, her directors, and more as a matter of course. She could work less often and make more varied and interesting pictures; there would be no more formulaic numbers churned out so fast they were practically calculated to tire and bore viewers. In fact, Swanson believed she herself had made most of the choices—often against the company's wishes—that had brought her fame. She had insisted on more varied stories, collaborating closely with the best writers and directors. She had had a hand in every part of the production of *Madame Sans-Gêne*.

Then, too, at UA Henri could have a role in her career—which, after all, had brought them together. If her gentlemanly husband was not going to become a Hollywood mover and shaker overnight, Swanson nonetheless trusted him and wanted to work alongside him. She considered the other members of UA: "If Charlie Chaplin from the London slums could produce; if Mary Pickford with no education at all could produce—why shouldn't I try?"[51] Although she did not have a burning desire to produce her own films, Gloria believed she could do the job.

In late June, she attended the gala premiere of Chaplin's new UA feature. *The Gold Rush* had been a long time in the making, and Swanson could imagine just how tense and determined Chaplin must have been to pull off such a brilliant feat. A critical and commercial success, it would earn $6 million. *The Gold Rush* was the perfect example of UA's shining success.

While she was weighing her options, Lasky came back with another offer. Paramount would pay Gloria $22,000 a week, bringing her annual salary to more than a million dollars. She would also receive half the profits from her pictures. The company wanted to rehire Swanson "at any price," Lasky explained. "Her pictures bolstered our whole program. To get them, exhibitors were compelled to give playing dates to blocks of weak features that we might otherwise have trouble selling. . . . Gloria was worth very much more to us than her pictures brought in."[52]

Swanson later confessed that her knees were "shaking" at the thought of rejecting such an offer.[53] However, what Lasky did not understand was that for Swanson a challenge was like a red flag to a bull: it was irresistible. Once she feared she couldn't do something, she pushed herself to do it. The non-swimmer had feared and dreaded jumping sixty feet into the cold nighttime waters off that high pier for her first Triangle feature, but she did it. Swanson did not simply refuse to be deterred by her fear; she used it as a spur. Her intuitions she trusted, but her fears she battled. She knew that if she went into independent production, she would have no one to blame but herself if her career stalled. It was a perversely exciting idea. So she did as she had done before: she jumped.

On July 15, 1925, she signed a contract avowing her commitment to produce six pictures for UA. Though there would be no public announcement for some time, in early 1926 Gloria Swanson would become the fifth United Artist.

Swanson's next picture promised to be something of a lark: she, Allan Dwan, and Forrest Halsey were reuniting for a comedy called *Stage Struck*, part of which would be shot on location in a small West Virginia town. Before that, the family had a month's vacation in New York. Swanson had purchased a penthouse apartment on Sixth Avenue and Fifty-Eigth Street which Sport Ward was renovating. Now Swanson had a place to call home in the US city where she felt most at home. She had also acquired a beach house in Malibu and planned to renovate the Croton house as well.

The highlight of the summer was undoubtedly the ten days Swanson and company spent on the Ohio River. The residents of New Martinsville welcomed the Paramount players, housing the cast and crew in their own homes and bringing Swanson freshly cut flowers and homemade cakes and pickles daily.[54] Having a Hollywood movie company move in right next door was the biggest thing the small town had seen in years.[55] Everyone was eager to get a glimpse of the star and her entourage. They seemed a motley crew: "[There was never] a rarer group of birds on one porch: A Hollywood movie director, a French marquis, a French dress designer (René Hubert), a Mack Sennett villain (Ford Sterling), a six-foot blonde siren (Gertrude Astor), and the Queen of the Screen herself . . . looking like a dwarf beside Gertrude."[56]

The assistant director brought in some young girls from town, dressed them as French maids, and offered Gloria her pick. "Gloria said, 'Get them out of here,'" Dwan remembered. "They dug up some plain-looking dame to come in to take care of her. She didn't want Henry fooling around with those little girls."[57] No sense in looking for trouble. Soon the local girls were copying Swanson's short haircut, and the star understood her obligation not to repay the town's hospitality with contempt for its standards. (The locals were kind, she said, but "churchy and staid.")[58] Homegrown crooners serenaded them during the long twilit evenings, and the southern summer cast its sweet spell. It was a remarkably tranquil production.

Part of the story took place on an old-fashioned riverboat, and Paramount hired a beauty called the *Water Queen*. The entire town gathered to watch Ford Sterling do his carnival barker's act down by the riverside. Twenty-five hundred volunteers turned up for a scene requiring a few hundred as extras, and town businesses closed for the day so everyone could attend "Gloria's picnic."

The production gave a boost to the local economy, as tourists arrived daily, hoping for a glimpse of Gloria Swanson. (The *Wetzel Democrat* estimated that 10,000 out-of-towners visited within five days.)[59] The newspaper published daily "Gloriagrams" for Swanson's star-struck fans, reporting what the actress wore and what local society mavens had lined up to see her and be seen that day. New Martinsville felt decidedly superior to Wheeling, which Paramount had passed over in favor of the smaller town.

The opening montage in *Stage Struck* gave movie patrons a real eyeful. In a three-minute early Technicolor sequence, Gloria's character accepts accolades for her portrayal of Salome and is hailed as "the greatest actress of all time—no role too difficult—each a triumph adding new lustre to a name already glorious." She is shown in one glamorous outfit after another, with the headdresses, feathers, and furs Swanson made famous and familiar in her clotheshorse roles. "Each new whim of attire [is] accepted by the world of elegance as fashion's decree," the title proclaims as one dazzling color follows another—gold and green, purple and scarlet.

Then the picture downshifts, back to black and white. What has clearly been a fantasy sequence ends as Jenny, a small-town girl who yearns to be an actress, comes back to earth with a jolt. In real life she is a tired waitress in a diner, leaning against a coffee urn and contemplating an endless pot of baked beans to be served and dishes to be washed. There

are no adoring fans and no fabulous clothes; there is no glamour whatsoever. Jenny is a hard-working but klutzy young woman—she can't even
turn a flapjack without flipping it onto her head—who is secretly in love
with her coworker. Orme can't see Jenny because he is blinded by the
movie stars whose pictures he pins all over his walls. So Jenny wants to
be an actress; she is struggling through a correspondence course on the
subject but getting nowhere fast.

Then the showboat comes to town, and she has a chance to perform. Unfortunately, the show manager sends tiny Jenny onstage as the
Masked Marvel, a female boxer pitted against the much larger, stronger
actress who has been amusing herself with Orme. A hilarious slapstick
mismatch ensues: what is supposed to be a fixed fight becomes a battle
over Orme. When Jenny is unmasked and humiliated, she tries to commit suicide by jumping off the riverboat—only to have her bloomers get
caught on a nail. She hangs there unceremoniously, the impresario praying, "Oh Lord, give strength to her trousers." Orme fishes her out, calling
her a fool. Did she really think he'd be crazy enough to want to marry
an *actress*? A final Technicolor scene finds the pair blissfully married and
working side by side in their own snappy little diner. A sign hangs on the
door: "No actresses allowed."

Stage Struck delightfully captured the dreams of many American girls in
Swanson's audience, some of whom had probably been her neighbors in
West Virginia. It pitted their fantasies of extravagance and luxury against
their more certain prospects of close-to-home happiness. (Mischievous
actress-in-training Thelma Todd reportedly sneaked onto the diner set
one evening and nailed or glued down everything that moved—every
cup, spoon, plate, door. The joke: now everything was stage *stuck*.)[60] *Stage
Struck* shrewdly invoked both Gloria's glamour roles and her comic characterizations of working girls. Her turn as the little waitress who could
was one of the sunniest, most confident performances of Swanson's career, the kind of part that always served her well.

Back in Gloria's real world, a process server made headlines by claiming that Swanson had slapped him hard across the face. The actress dismissed the man's defamation suit as frivolous and ridiculous—just as she
ignored the document he delivered. Swanson was being called to testify
in the divorce case of a New York couple, something she considered an
occupational hazard, saying she was cited every time an unhappy wife
found the actress's picture in her husband's wallet.[61]

Gloria was glad to revisit France with Henri that fall to finalize arrangements for *Madame Sans-Gêne*'s European premiere. Yet she felt more

fragile than her summer romp in West Virginia suggested. She was shaken, in fact, quite unexpectedly. *Her Love Story*, an assignment Swanson had dismissed as a clotheshorse picture, was playing in Paris. In the film, Gloria's character bears the child of the man she loves, rejecting the king to whom she is (bigamously) married. Gloria got an unhappy shock from a billboard advertising the picture outside a theater on the Boulevard des Italiens: it showed a huge set of scales, with a crown on one side and a baby on the other. "The message was clear," she said. "Your throne or your baby? I had such a violent reaction when I saw it towering over me that I almost fainted. Henri rushed me back to the hotel, where I wept for hours."[62] If Swanson had not terminated her pregnancy, she would have given birth that summer.

The couple cautiously proceeded on a planned trip south, and the rest did Gloria good. Accompanied by André Daven, they motored toward the Riviera, feeling the stress lift with every mile. The trio toured the fourteenth-century Palais des Papes in Avignon and visited the local vineyards. In Marseilles, Henri and André took Gloria to a legendary brothel notorious for its list of famous guests. "What a surprise!" André remembered. "Gloria tried to remain incognito, but at the very entrance the girls recognized her and tried to start a party." As they traveled on, through Cannes and Monte Carlo, Swanson was recognized more and more often. "The voyage lost its charm," André said, as they were besieged by autograph seekers.[63]

In Paris, they learned that someone had challenged the authenticity of Henri's title, calling it a movie publicity stunt: Gloria Swanson was not a real marquise. Henri treated it lightly, joking, "We are all descended from Adam," but the marquise herself was provoked.[64] After Henri produced copies of records from the state registry in Rouen documenting his pedigree, the papers were forced to print retractions, but that did not stop some from taking swipes at the star. The press had always treated Gloria kindly. Suddenly, however, it felt like Swanson's intuition was correct: she had nowhere to go but down, and some reporters seemed happy to help her.

Her next-to-last film for Paramount was *The Untamed Lady*, an uninspiring Fannie Hurst story about a spoiled, bad-tempered society girl tamed by a good man who knows how to manage her properly—that is, with a firm hand. Swanson was annoyed to learn that Allan Dwan was not directing the picture. Paramount had gone back to its "one egg per basket" policy for her last films, and she was the egg.[65] It was even worse than she expected: she thought the director was insufferable. Frank Tuttle hid his nervousness and uncertainty behind a façade of arrogance, and Swanson repeatedly went over his head to have her way, indifferent to his irritation. It is not clear that Tuttle was the insufferable one on the set.

Swanson was in any case restive and nervous herself. When the cast went to Pinehurst, North Carolina, to shoot some riding scenes, she had a sudden strong premonition of disaster. Though she had ridden since she was a child, Gloria told Tuttle they had to redesign the sequence because she refused to get on horseback: she had received "a voiceless warning" not to ride. It was "a command of terrifying force . . . I couldn't dream of ignoring it."[66] She never mounted a horse again.

Despite her frustration with her director, Swanson soon realized she had been wasting an opportunity. She decided to treat *The Untamed Lady* as her own film school, attempting to learn as much as possible about film production on the job. She began questioning everything and everyone, driven now by a sense of engaged curiosity, even urgency. She would soon be responsible for running a movie production herself.

That fall Henri opened an office in New York to begin looking after his wife's affairs and was immediately deluged with offers. No announcement had been made about the star's defection to United Artists, but speculation was rife. No one wanted to miss an opportunity to snag Gloria Swanson if she was leaving Paramount. In fact, Gloria was casting around, albeit quietly, for her first UA project. All of a sudden everything was fodder for her future screen career. She went to the theater; she went to the movies; she read everything she could get her hands on. Who knew when she would find a story to buy or someone to hire? Younger actresses were sizing her up, too: Louise Brooks at the Follies, Thelma Todd at Paramount's summer acting school. One young woman who wasn't even an actress yet sneaked out the window of her dorm room at Bryn Mawr to see Swanson in *The Untamed Lady*: Katharine Hepburn considered Gloria Swanson part of her cinematic education.[67]

Sometimes old friends tried to push you down. Tongues were wagging about Mickey Neilan's new picture. *The Skyrocket* was the story of a girl from the wrong side of the tracks whose star rises quickly in Hollywood. Sharon Kimm—possibly modeled on Gloria Swanson—lets fame go to her head. She spends money like water, turning into a superficial, self-centered brat. Many saw Neilan himself in the characters of Dvorak, the powerful director who helps ruin the star, and Mickey, the star's childhood-friend-turned-screenwriter who rescues her when her world collapses. Swanson loftily ignored the buzz; she habitually disregarded any distasteful references to herself. However, she might have done well to pay attention to Neilan's business plan: his new picture had been made with the help of a clever financier named Joseph Kennedy.

While Mickey Neilan was telling his tale of a woman's comeuppance, Swanson began work on her last Paramount picture. *Fine Manners*, however, offered a playful treatment of a similar subject. Swanson is Orchid Murphy, a girl from the wrong side of the tracks—a chorus girl, to be precise—educated in high society ways by a wealthy man (Eugene O'Brien), who then finds he liked her better before. The twist is that it suits the showgirl just fine to be her real self. No comeuppance is required, and none occurs.

Once again, Swanson got to dress up and dress down, to turn up her nose as the stuffy society woman and to turn handsprings as the vibrant chorus girl. Behind the scenes, however, things were not so happy. Swanson argued with her new director, Lewis Milestone. Paramount replaced him with another new director, Richard Rosson, the brother of Gloria's cameraman Hal.[68] Swanson found him "a delightful surprise." Both Rossons had been with Gloria in Paris, "so we knew we could have fun together." This would always be an important criteria for Swanson, something she needed to let her own creativity surface.

She also enjoyed being partnered with Helen Dunbar, the dowager aunt who teaches young Orchid to be fashionably supercilious. Dunbar was the leading lady at Essanay who told the teenaged Swanson that she would be a good actress someday: "[Helen] had been there when the egg cracked open and I emerged," Swanson recalled. Dunbar was much too gracious to remind Swanson of her youthful callowness, and Gloria kept a sense of perspective and humility in the older woman's presence. By *Fine Manners*, she realized, "We were two old pros."[69]

Then without fanfare, her Paramount contract was played out, and Swanson was once again free. It was time to see what the old pro could do on her own.

CHAPTER 11

Declaration of Independence

IN SPRING 1926, THE PAPERS WERE FULL OF THE NEWS THAT GLORIA Swanson was going independent. Reports of how much money Paramount had offered her to stay varied widely, but all the numbers were jaw-dropping. While she finished her last Paramount picture, Swanson tried to learn her new business. In addition to selecting her upcoming projects, as a one-fifth partner in United Artists she was suddenly immersed in a flood of details and decisions relating to the company's ongoing affairs. Should UA partner with Metro-Goldwyn-Mayer to gain better access to theaters? Should it buy or build theaters of its own? How should UA manage foreign rights?

Some of these debates had been going on for years. The four founding partners were independents who often disagreed vigorously yet had a policy that all decisions must be unanimous. Pickford, Chaplin, Fairbanks, and Griffith had been in the movie business a long time and had learned the hard way to protect their individual interests. They often had different ideas about how UA could best do this. Chaplin, for instance, wanted as little to do with financing others' films as possible; he did not need financing from UA and did not want to incur the risk of providing it to others. Pickford, on the other hand, wanted to expand in order to stabilize the company for the long term.

As Swanson sorted through the proposals piling up in Henri's office, she understood that being her own producer would require much more business expertise than she had imagined—or possessed. She was still working full-time for Paramount. Every day on the set she struggled to observe as much as she could of the production process, and every night she struggled to learn what she needed to know as a United Artist.

Eventually, Swanson was just struggling, her poor manners on *Fine Manners* a function of exhaustion finally catching up with her. In the past year Gloria had almost died. She had returned to Hollywood with a new husband and made three pictures. She had finalized the adoption of her son, bought a home in New York, and turned down a million-dollar contract to throw in her lot with a bunch of independents who—it turned out—barely spoke to one another. As the spring days lengthened, the weight of her responsibility—to the children, to Henri, to her large staff, to herself—felt crushing. Swanson was observed "weep[ing] copiously" at a Broadway play, and in tears at a screening of *La Bohème*, while Henri sat alongside her, "nervous and visibly embarrassed."[1] The flu sent her into quarantine, but she continued to feel ill, paralyzed by the enormity of her undertaking. Swanson's last Paramount film wrapped amid rumors that the star was having a nervous breakdown.

She spent several weeks confined to her penthouse apartment, unable to do anything except rest. Swanson's energy and self-confidence had for once failed her, and it was "a very frightening experience."[2] She regained her balance and perspective slowly. Thankfully, there was little fanfare, *Photoplay* noting blandly in midsummer that the actress had "recovered from her nervous breakdown" and was back at work.[3]

Swanson expected partnership in UA to involve "board meetings over coffee on the terrace at Pickfair and help in a jiffy if I should ever need it." Instead, it meant "long, grueling business sessions in New York with Joe Schenck and a shrewd gang of lawyers, accountants, and bankers."[4] To make the profit-sharing part of UA a reality, the company needed reliable income. That meant acquiring more talented contributors (to bump up the number of films in distribution) and running the company more efficiently. The founding partners had enlisted Joe Schenck to do both.

Schenck, a Russian immigrant, was a brilliant businessman. With his brother, Nick, he had parlayed an East Coast amusement park into a partnership with Marcus Loew, who owned an important chain of movie theaters. Schenck had guided his much younger wife, Norma Talmadge, to Hollywood stardom; he also managed her sisters' film careers. As an independent, he had produced successful pictures by Buster Keaton and Fatty Arbuckle. He knew everyone and was well-liked, though you had better watch out if you were invited to play cards with him. The only stakes Joe Schenck knew were high.

Now he was Swanson's partner, too. Determined to run her own production unit and to participate in the company she had joined, Gloria once again felt a sting of disappointment in her beloved husband. Henri was charming people all over New York, acting as unofficial French ambassador, joining committees for the stabilization of the franc, and speaking at "French Week" events. However, he was very little help to his wife. The man with whom Gloria was most involved on a daily basis was Joe Schenck, whom she called her "worthy adversary and masterly teacher."[5]

Their relationship turned stormy one Friday afternoon, when an emissary of Schenck's arrived unexpectedly at Gloria's penthouse. He needed Swanson's signature immediately on a deal involving her shares of preferred stock in UA. Swanson's hesitation—which she saw as standing up for herself—caused Schenck embarrassment. He was a quick-thinking, inventive dealmaker who knew how to move fast when he saw an opportunity, but Swanson would not—as she saw it—be railroaded into signing away options and taking on obligations until she thoroughly comprehended her choices. "Had I been a man it would have been easier for him to swallow," Swanson said. "Schenck never forgave me."[6]

Now that she was self-employed, Swanson's income was tied directly to whether she had a film in exhibition, and Schenck pressed Gloria to choose her first project. He also advised her to shoot the picture in California. Though her UA colleagues were busy with their own productions, they would be able to help and support Gloria on the coast. Gloria, however, did not want to go west: she vastly preferred working in New York. Then she had a falling out with UA business manager Maurice Cleary, who had brought her into the company and on whom she had hoped to lean. She had to rely on Joe Schenck.

Figuring out how her first picture was to be financed and sold was particularly challenging. UA had recently created a subsidiary to offer financing to partners who needed it, but understanding the ins and outs of the Art Cinema Corporation was daunting. Swanson dragged her heels, holding out for financing on terms she preferred, but this brand of negotiation was anathema to Schenck. Didn't Gloria understand that he was looking out for *her* company's long-term interests? He was her ally, not an adversary. Schenck called the finance contract she wanted "unreasonable and ridiculous," but Swanson was unbowed.[7] For a woman recovering from a nervous breakdown, she showed steely resolve. She notified the company's sales manager that no one—by whom she meant Joe Schenck—had the right to speak on her behalf. When the time came, she and she alone would authorize the sale of her picture.[8]

Over the summer, Cecil DeMille contacted Gloria: he was preparing *The King of Kings* and thought she would make a splendid Mary Magdalene. Swanson considered this gesture from her old mentor a real kindness and was unhappy to refuse him. "Five weeks ago I fell ill with a nervous breakdown," she wrote, "and it is all I can do to pull through this last picture." She signed off with "fondest love."[9]

Gloria's illness and indecision delayed a planned August beginning for her picture; the story itself had not even been selected. After her contretemps with Schenck, Swanson cabled DeMille, saying confidentially that she might be free to be his Mary Magdalene after all, and asking for definite terms and dates.[10] If she took a job with DeMille, she could possibly finance her UA picture herself. It was tempting, but it was also the kind of trap that starved UA of product. D. W. Griffith, for instance, kept signing on to work for others to improve his cash flow; his outside commitments then repeatedly precluded his making his own films. Griffith had more or less stepped down from UA, the company he had founded, and Joe Schenck, a different style of filmmaker entirely, had stepped into his place. For Swanson, going back to DeMille was a kind of defeat, one it would be hard to admit so quickly.

By mid-July, Swanson and Schenck had come to terms. Swanson agreed to guarantee personally any production overage beyond a healthy budget of $550,000 for her first picture, with her $150,000 salary for picture #2 held against any sum she could not finance herself. Schenck felt he had made "drastic concessions," but he was anxious to get Gloria's show on the road. He insisted on story approval, however, worried that she would select pricey projects.[11] Only when Milton Cohen had double- and triple-checked the new contract did Swanson write to DeMille to refuse the "magnificent part" he had offered her: "Time and money are tying me up and preventing me from doing my heart's desire."[12] DeMille's offer had arrived when she felt particularly low; it went some way toward repairing the hurt of his earlier betrayal. Swanson was also learning that as a businesswoman she could not afford to burn any bridges: diplomacy mattered.

A top contender for Gloria's first picture was a World War I tale of valiant female soldiers fighting the German army in Russia, though its gruesome title—*The Women's Battalion of Death*—put everyone off. At last, though, Swanson decided on a remake of Clara Kimball Young's 1919 hit *Eyes of Youth*. It was not an adventurous choice, but she was feeling less courageous by the minute: "I settled for the kind of film I was sure I could make well and that audiences had never failed to respond to: a romantic story with several handsome leading men and a variety of love scenes and a wardrobe of dazzling creations. Just the kind of picture I blamed Mr. Lasky for making, I realized; but I was scared."[13]

She acquired the rights, found a writer to provide a fresh adaptation, and then made another safe choice by hiring Albert Parker, who had directed the original screen version of the story. They were old friends: Parker had directed two of Gloria's Triangle pictures and had taken a punch on the kisser from a jealous Wallace Beery without flinching. Even better, he was already a UA director; his new Technicolor feature with Douglas Fairbanks, *The Black Pirate*, was a big success. Parker knew *Eyes of Youth* inside out and, Swanson fancied, would want to surpass his earlier effort. When his manager insisted on a two-film contract, she accepted the terms, glad to see some continuity ahead.

Once the Swanson Producing Corporation was set up in the summer of 1926, Gloria could make contracts, rent facilities, and pay bills. She acquired a board of directors, with a vice-president and treasurer, a production manager, an auditor, and her first-ever public relations professional. (When Adelaide visited New York, Gloria had her mother named secretary of the board.) She rented William Randolph Hearst's Cosmopolitan studio on 127th Street in Harlem and started casting her picture.

Gloria's leading man was a good-looking young Southerner she had seen onstage that spring. John Boles had a sophisticated, courtly air but funny ears, "like little flaps which didn't belong to his head."[14] When Swanson suggested he have them fixed, she suddenly remembered DeMille telling her to get a nose job: being a producer meant that everything was your business. She hired a bona fide star of the Metropolitan Opera to play a stage impresario: Andres de Segurola had an impressively grand, commanding presence. Douglas Fairbanks's young, pretty niece Flobelle would play Swanson's sister.

The new producer also had to arrange for every other part of the production: what the audience would see (wardrobe, sets, and props) and everything it wouldn't (catering, construction, and equipment). She had to hire the people who would make it all happen: the electricians, musicians, cameramen, and prop men. Arrangements were needed for developing the rushes, doing the editing, taking still photographs, making prints, and on and on. Luckily, her collaborators quickly became friends. Swanson had a facility for making others want to help her, even though she disliked delegating responsibility and often struggled to relinquish control. People responded to her energy, her curiosity, and her valiant determination to get everything right. It didn't hurt that Gloria was beautiful, but it was her enthusiasm that made her charismatic, that drew people to her. Her (mostly male) staff members became like family, loyal and indispensible. It went both ways: when Gloria's production manager Pierre Bedard married, she and Henri were matron of honor and best man, and the ceremony was held in Swanson's penthouse.

While Gloria spent long days preparing the picture, Henri returned to France to renew his visa. He was away most of the summer. When one interviewer asked Gloria about her $2 million insurance policy (a requirement of production financing), Swanson said, "Everything is insured but Henry's affections."[15] She couldn't have been too worried, though, judging by the passionate letters he sent: "I love you so—I love you so—that I don't know what to do! If I could only be close to you right now—I would take you in my arms and squeeze you so tight—so tight that you'd be breathless—and my lips close to yours. . . . I would smother you with kisses, long ones deep ones ferocious ones I would bite your ears chew your cheeks mess you up, but here I am far out at sea alone in my little cabin as sad as can be and what are you doing? Miles miles water and each twist of the screw is taking me away away I love you." Henri's many letters always included loving greetings to Gloria and Brother, his "two angels."[16]

Swanson was asked constantly about her marriage. She told one interviewer that her two previous "matrimonial experiences" were not mistakes, since they helped her to value Henri: "Five years ago I wouldn't have been able to recognize, much less appreciate, such traits as kindness and sincerity and loyalty and truthfulness and dependability as I have found in Henry." His virtues were genuine, "not assumed like a pretty mask to be cast aside later."[17]

Though she missed Henri, Gloria was far too busy to dwell on it. By summer she was at least free of her paralyzing self-doubt and could focus on the tasks ahead. She had little time for socializing; when she could, she relaxed with the children at the Croton house. Swanson protected Gloria and Brother from media attention, although notice of them tended to be approving: "The nicest thing about Gloria," one magazine said, "is her unaffected love for her children. And the children reward her with a spontaneous and informal affection that is a pleasure to see. . . . Gloria dresses the children in plain clothes, designed for rough wear. I wonder if passersby in Central Park ever suspect that the two healthily disheveled youngsters are Gloria Swanson's."[18] Most of the time, however, Gloria and Joseph were in the care of Miss Simonson, the governess who raised them. Most of the time, their mother was at work.

Then came the news that Rudolph Valentino was in the hospital, gravely ill with peritonitis. Swanson had not seen much of Rudy since *Beyond the Rocks*, and their relations had cooled considerably. She disliked his wife and producing partner, Natacha Rambova, and was likely irritated that Rudy's last contract with Paramount was on better terms than she herself got. The competitive Swanson was no doubt pleased that her French picture had been made in France, while Rudy's *Monsieur Beaucaire* was shot in Queens. Yet they had much in common: like Swanson, Valentino had fought with Paramount for independence. He too had wanted to broaden his acting roles and challenge himself.

Gloria had run into Rudy briefly that summer when Henri was embarking for Europe. Now she waited and worried with the rest of the world as Rudy's condition worsened. Only a year ago Gloria herself had been dangerously ill; now she could see what the media furor must have been like. Henri returned in time for the bad news of Valentino's death, and they attended his funeral together. Swanson found the spectacle distasteful, and everyone was stunned by the display his "fiancée" Pola Negri made when she collapsed over the coffin. Yet even as Rudy's death transformed him once and for all into the iconic, ideal lover, Gloria grieved the loss of the unassuming young man she had known. "He haunted me for weeks," Swanson said, as she prepared to remake *Eyes of Youth*, the film that had first brought Rudolph Valentino to Hollywood's attention.[19]

Just before filming began in September, Swanson made a deal with Samuel Rothafel: her first UA film would open the grand new theater "Roxy" was building near Times Square. The showman pledged that his 6,000-seat picture palace—to be named the Roxy, naturally—would outshine every other theater then in existence. Would Swanson do him the honor? Now they had a home—and a deadline.[20]

The Love of Sunya (as the picture was now called) was built around the story of a wandering swami who offers a young woman a look into his crystal ball. Sunya has the chance to see her future with each of four suitors. Creating a unified storyline from the four disparate episodes was a challenge, and Swanson wanted to make the crystal ball sequences visually stunning. It was not enough that René Hubert was creating dazzling gowns for the star; now it was Gloria's job to make sure the entire picture was worth watching.

The decision to hire avant-garde filmmaker Dudley Murphy to provide special effects seemed like an inspiration. Murphy had worked on *Ballet mécanique*, an experimental short that was the talk of the art world in 1924. Its whirling, abstract, mechanized shapes and mesmerizing moving camera created a strange, hypnotic world. Swanson imagined—hoped—that Murphy would dream up something original for the scenes in which Sunya sees her mystical visions. Cecil DeMille and Allan Dwan often employed cutting-edge designers and innovative technologies to give their pictures a fresh look. Since several of Swanson's best-known films had elaborate dream or fantasy sequences, she felt a special pressure to make *Sunya*'s visions look good.

Gloria liked Murphy and the link he provided to the modern art scene. One autumn night, he came up to her penthouse with several other New York filmmakers. They had a smuggled print of the newest cinema sensation from the Soviet Union, and wanted to use Swanson's projector to watch it. The unofficial New York premiere of Sergei Eisenstein's revolutionary film *The Battleship Potemkin* took place in her apartment, on a screen made from Gloria Swanson's bed sheets.[21]

If she hoped to capture the excitement of the avant garde by bringing Dudley Murphy onto her team, however, Swanson was vexed and disappointed by his indecisiveness on the set. He was neither as technically adept nor as efficient as she needed him to be. As Murphy slogged along, the film fell behind schedule.[22]

The untrained actors Swanson hired also struggled more than she expected. Neither Flobelle Fairbanks nor Andres de Segurola had appeared on camera before, and it took awhile before they were comfortable. Swanson was also frustrated by her "discovery" John Boles's inexperience.[23] Maybe he was distracted by his infatuation with the boss: Swanson said Boles followed her around "like a puppy." She griped, "I had to be like the schoolmarm [who] says to Johnny who has a crush on her, 'It's time to go home.'"[24] Nonetheless, Swanson exercised her option on his services in December, bumping Boles's salary from $250 to $500 a week to keep him under personal contract. He was her first acquisition, and she thought she could find another role for him soon.

She was much less satisfied with Al Parker. During a long and complex shoot the director offered less leadership and less inspiration than Swanson felt owed, given his $60,000 paycheck. Bringing Parker back to a project he had done successfully seven years earlier had looked like a good idea, but once on the job, he seemed tapped out. Though Joe Schenck had eliminated a contract provision naming Swanson codirector, in the event of a conflict Gloria's judgment would prevail. She often wanted to take the reins herself.

As the weeks wore on, the expensive, slow picture seemed to be slipping out of control. Swanson recognized ruefully that she had gambled on Parker as an experienced director and gotten someone tired and stale. She had gambled on actors new to the screen and then battled their inexperience. She had hired an avant-garde filmmaker for a commercial film and gotten an artist willing to tinker forever rather than a craftsman used to turning out a product on a schedule. Even working in New York was harder without Paramount's resources. Now that Swanson was a competitor, the studio had no interest in making anything easy for her. She had an inkling that some of her trouble getting and retaining a crew originated at Paramount's directive.

Swanson knew that other actors who tried to go it alone had not fared well. "Motion picture companies chastised any star that wanted to produce pictures," she reflected. "When the actors—Mary, Douglas, Chaplin—banded together, they had more strength."[25] But her UA colleagues were 3,000 miles away. Even Joe Schenck had more or less disappeared, once the organizational i's had been dotted and t's crossed.

It was a mess, and she was responsible. Swanson later acknowledged that she had "bruises everywhere to show for [her] stubbornness."[26] She resolved to take a hard look at her business plan before she moved on to her next picture. At the moment, though, there was no time. In fact, she had to make sure her own frustration and fatigue did not show in her performance. She needed to be fresh, responsive, and glowing on screen, but after endless retakes and many sixteen- and eighteen-hour days, that required real acting. Had Mary Pickford been around, she might have commiserated: "I have to worry so much about distribution," Pickford claimed, "that my ability as an actress is impaired."[27] One of Sunya's futures showed her as a worn, tired schoolteacher scrubbing her classroom floor after hours. Swanson felt she had something in common with that character.

On December 9, the last day of shooting, Swanson breathed a sigh of relief. She had been forced to borrow money to keep going, as a planned six-week shoot mushroomed into twelve weeks. All told, she would spend nine months on *Sunya*. However, she took real pride in the solution she had found to her special effects problem. She had hired Russian-born engineer George de Bothezat, whose inexperience proved beneficial: since he did not know what film cameras could and could not do, he invented fearlessly, using creative, unconventional tactics. Soon the issues that stymied Dudley Murphy were happily resolved.

Bothezat also bucked up the flagging producer considerably. "From the day he arrived, I lost the smell of fear and defeat," Swanson said.[28] Bothezat was an eccentric, quirky fellow who had pioneered the invention of the helicopter. When he wasn't trying to perfect his Flying Octopus, he was publishing essays on topics from aerodynamics to economics. Swanson enjoyed the company of scientists and inventors, and with Bothezat's arrival, her own sense of pleasure in making things returned. (Swanson and Murphy parted amicably. She would hire him again in the future, preferring when possible to work with people whose company she enjoyed.)

She had been forced to settle with Maurice Cleary, however, who claimed Gloria owed him for helping negotiate her UA contract. Ironically, Cleary threatened to sue her at a time when Swanson was kicking herself, wondering why she had declined more than a million dollars to go out on her own. Her vice president and treasurer, Tom Moore, advised Gloria to settle quietly, and she paid Cleary $10,000 with a pledge of $15,000 more in a year's time, when profits from *Sunya* should be available. If her movies made more money, she would owe him more. If she sold her UA stock, he would get a cut. The arrangement galled Swanson, but she paid up and tried to put it out of her mind. She knew that everyone wanted a piece of her success. She just hoped there would be a success at the end of the day.

After a brief Christmas break in Croton with Henri and the children, she returned to work with renewed purpose. Thankfully, the Roxy's elaborate construction had delayed their joint opening until spring: Swanson needed the time to finish *The Love of Sunya*. She had never been so involved in the post-production process before. Through January and February, they worked on editing, titling, and the picture's promotional campaign. Henri contributed French titles for the European release, while Russell Ball and Ernest Bachrach took dozens of glamour shots of Swanson in every pose. She contracted with composer Harold Flammer for a theme song called "The Love Waltz," which exhibitors would cue "at least eight times during the run of the photoplay."[29] Gloria got a share of every copy of the sheet music—then a thriving industry—sold internationally for five years.

During the course of editing, Swanson decided to cut the sequence in which she appeared as the dowdy schoolteacher; it didn't fit the successful image she deliberately sought in her first release.[30] She remembered that some moviegoers had not even recognized her dressed as the middle-aged countess in *The Coast of Folly*. This time, she needed everyone to know who she was.

In late February, Swanson screened the picture for a group of her friends. Predictably, they came up with "a million suggestions for small changes I knew there was no time to make."[31] She herself could see all the film's flaws. However, if *The Love of Sunya* wasn't everything it might have been, it was nothing to be ashamed of. It represented a lot of hard work and a lot of experience gained.

One afternoon shortly before the opening, Swanson was alone at home. While she fiddled with her radio dial, she decided to have a cup of tea. She rang the bell for a servant, but the maid was on an errand, and everyone else was out of earshot. Suddenly she had an idea. The radio sent wireless signals: couldn't a device be developed which would transmit a unique signal to each person in the household? Each servant could have his own device, and she wouldn't need to ring a bell or call out. Such an invention would be a boon to busy people intent on communicating more rapidly and efficiently. All of a sudden, the applications of the device seemed both clear and far-ranging: "I started fantasizing," she said. "It could be used in all kinds of buildings—factories, police stations, skyscrapers."[32]

She couldn't wait to talk it over with George de Bothezat, who offered to put her ideas on paper and begin a patent application. Swanson was over the moon: she had an insatiable curiosity about scientific things and was thrilled by the possibility that she could become an inventor. It was every bit as good as being a film star—maybe better.

While Swanson and company invented *The Love of Sunya*, Roxy had kept up his end of the deal. No one in New York would miss the opening of the theater he called "The Cathedral of the Motion Picture." Not that anyone could get tickets: the 6,000 seats were available by invitation only (at $11.00 a head), with requests for more than 2,000 seats unfilled. In the weeks before the opening, reporters toured the sumptuous theater, filing awed descriptions. "Roxy's new home is brilliant, exuberant, palatial," said *The New Yorker*, "a truly fine expression of what a place of entertainment should be." The theater, done in shades of rose and gold, had "beauty and dignity without being pompous." The sight lines were perfect, the seats commodious, and there was—for once—enough leg room: "One may get in or out without being passed along like a box of chocolates."[33] Real care had been taken with acoustics, lighting, and stage mechanics, and the backstage facilities resembled those of a small city. As the *New York Times* said, "Everything in the Roxy Theatre seems to be the largest in the world."[34]

Roxy had clearly gotten his $12 million worth, and being part of the opening gave *Sunya* a great deal of free publicity. Gloria gladly posed for her picture while adding a slick of paint way up on the theater's top balcony.

For the opening on March 11, the streets were so full that 125 policemen were deployed to keep order. It was a happy crowd, shouting greetings to celebrities entering the theater: Charlie Chaplin, Harold Lloyd, Irving Berlin, the mayor, the governor, the New York senators. Roving spotlights mounted on trucks illuminated each new arrival. When Gloria and Henri arrived, fans lifted the tiny star off her feet and swept her toward the theater.

Ticket holders enjoyed an elaborate stage show. A man dressed as a monk opened the festivities by intoning solemnly, "Let there be light," and there was light—everywhere. It shone on the orchestra accompanying the corps de ballet, on the chorus singing Southern songs, and on the vocalist premiering Irving Berlin's "Russian Lullaby." The lights went down for the big-screen presentation of congratulatory letters and telegrams; even President Coolidge sent good wishes. A Vitaphone short offered selections from *Carmen*, impressing the audience with the newest film magic: synchronous sound.

The main event of the evening began with smoke swirling magically around the edges of the movie screen. Without any introductory titles, viewers were carried into a fantasy of the distant past in Egypt, to Swanson's first encounter with the far-seeing swami. It was an unusual opening, but the audience soon settled into the picture, applauding both the beautiful gowns and the striking special effects. By the final sequence, when Sunya tells the oracle that each person must "look into the crystal" of his own soul, Swanson knew there was no reason to fear. At least in New York, her picture was a hit.

The reviews were mostly positive, though some faulted Swanson for choosing shallow "claptrap" for her debut. The choice of *Sunya* was "not nearly so important as [Swanson's] independence warrants," carped *Picture Play*, before acknowledging that *Sunya* had "beautiful settings, fine direction, [and] a capable cast."[35] The *New York Times* was more complimentary, calling *Sunya* "an infectious production which holds the attention from the minute it decorates the screen."[36] The scenario was "well-constructed" and the material "far more suitable . . . than any in which [Swanson] has appeared for some time," with Gloria offering "sharply different characterizations" for each of her roles.[37] The *New York Herald Tribune* gave *Sunya* a solid rave, calling it "engrossing" and "superb" throughout: "Miss Swanson does more whole-souled and convincing acting than ever we have seen her do in all the years we have admired her."[38]

The combination of Gloria Swanson and the Roxy was a triumph: 51,000 patrons saw *The Love of Sunya* during the theater's first two days in business. Swanson was pleased and relieved, though in later years she was hard on *Sunya*, claiming, "It was a turkey then and it's still a turkey."[39] She was rightly proud of what she had accomplished as a fledgling producer, but her aversion to risk also nagged at her. Perhaps she should have chosen a new story—or commissioned one. She might have selected a more inspiring director. Swanson determined to move more boldly and confidently in her next venture.

One thing she knew was that she couldn't make her second picture in New York. Joe Schenck had been right: East Coast production was too hard without the full support of the industry. Six days after her big opening, while *The Love of Sunya* was still packing audiences into the Roxy for its exclusive engagement, Swanson packed up her household and herded everyone onto the train. They were going to California.

CHAPTER 12

Let It Rain

FOR HER TWENTY-EIGHTH BIRTHDAY, THE GIFT SWANSON WANTED most was a juicy part in a great story. She hoped to show her fans and detractors alike the kind of picture she was capable of making. If *The Love of Sunya* had not been an adventurous choice, now she would err in the opposite direction.

Swanson's salary for her first UA picture was a hefty $150,000: if she had stayed with Paramount, however, she would have made twice that amount during the nine months she spent on *Sunya*, even at her former rate of $7,000 a week. Never mind how much more she would have pulled in at the tripled weekly salary the studio had offered. Paramount had also routinely paid for many of Swanson's additional expenses: cars, travel, hotels, assistants, and so forth, costs she now had to shoulder herself. As an independent, Swanson could keep whatever profits her films made. In practical terms, however, her revenues depended in part on how long she spent on each picture. With her income now tied directly to her productivity, she needed to have her next project ready to go.

Yet she vacillated over her second film. She considered—and rejected—*Cash Customers, June Brides, The Spendthrift, The Big Chance, Widow's Intentions*, and *Rich Relatives*, as well as a Greenwich Village-themed picture along the lines of *The Humming Bird. The Women's Battalion of Death* was still kicking around, too. She bought an original story by Ouida Bergère: *Desert Love* was a female version of *The Sheik*, complete with kidnappings, desert hideaways, and villainous suitors challenging the maiden's one true love for her hand. (A vendor immediately offered to supply Gloria with exotic animals: camels, tigers, even the world's smallest elephant.)[1] As title followed title, a frustrated publicist requested a name to use as a placeholder—something, anything that could stand in for the next Gloria Swanson picture so that the papers could talk about it.

Joe Schenck liked *The Last of Mrs. Cheyney* and thought he could get Allan Dwan to direct. After she went with Doug and Mary to see it staged, however, Gloria wasn't sure it was right for her. She asked Schenck to buy *The Woman and the Puppet*, in which a femme fatale works her erotic magic during Carnival in Seville.[2] In early May, Swanson's office announced her next three pictures: first she would play the "fascinating, emotional, impulsive senorita" in *The Woman and the Puppet*. Then there would be a lavish version of Cleopatra, "the most fascinating charmer of all ages." Third up would be *Battalion of Death*. Publicist Lance Heath proclaimed by wire that these would be "three strikingly different characterizations . . . first story being beautiful romance second flaming love third heroic drama."[3]

None of the announced productions reflected Swanson's real plans. She was secretly pursuing a much more radical course: to purchase the rights to *Rain*, the controversial Broadway play the major Hollywood studios had agreed to keep off the screen. *Rain* dramatized the battle between Sadie Thompson, a jazz-loving young prostitute, and the self-righteous Christian missionary determined to save her soul. Set in sultry Pago Pago after Sadie arrives to conquer the local enlisted men, the contest between the young woman and the married Reverend Davidson heats up after Davidson gets the governor to order Sadie off the island. Sadie is willing to repent her sins but not to take the boat back to San Francisco, where she faces jail. Davidson, however, is unrelenting: Sadie must show her penitence by accepting her punishment. They struggle and pray together, Davidson committing suicide when he realizes he is as lustful as any other man. Sadie's gramophone starts up again, louder than ever, and she goes back to her old ways. It was dynamite, a story full of sex and religion set to the ceaseless drumming of the tropical rain. The only problem was the ban.

By 1927 the studios had been working with Will Hays for five years toward shared goals: preventing federal film censorship and keeping state, local, and church groups from cutting or banning their films. They had recently hammered out a list of "Don'ts and Be Carefuls" to guide the selection and treatment of movie material. The "Don'ts" were subjects to be avoided entirely by motion pictures, such as profanity, nudity, "sex perversion," childbirth, and ridicule of the clergy. The "Be Carefuls" were topics to be handled prudently. This much broader list cautioned against creating sympathy for criminals, showing methods of crime (such as safecracking and robbery), "excessive or lustful kissing," or women "selling [their] virtue."[4]

Rain, which violated the taboo against disrespect for the clergy and whose protagonist was a woman who sold her virtue as often as possible, was too hot to handle. The studio heads had explicitly declared it off limits: if self-censorship was to work, they reasoned, they would have to forego such tasty fare for the greater good. As yet, however, there was no policy for enforcing this pact. The ban on *Rain* was very much a gentleman's agreement.

Gloria Swanson was no gentleman. Nor had she been invited to join the Association of Motion Picture Producers and Distributors of America, whose members pledged to abide by the Hays Office self-censorship "formula." So she didn't see why she should consider herself restricted by it: "Filming *Rain* in 1927 was the maddest idea in the world, but every other idea suddenly seemed dull."[5] It had all the hallmarks of a successful picture. It was a recognizable, even notorious, property with a challenging part for the leading lady and a great role for an older man. It had an exotic setting, a small cast, and no costly period costumes. Since the studios had agreed not to film *Rain,* the rights should be inexpensive. Swanson needed some guarantee, however, that she would not run afoul of Will Hays herself.

The agreement made by the studios governed the adaptation of novels and plays; it said nothing about short stories. *Rain* had begun life as "Miss Thompson," a Somerset Maugham story, before John Colton turned it into the prohibited stage play. Swanson's brilliant idea was to bring the Maugham story to the screen, thus exploiting a technicality in her favor.

She planned her approach to Will Hays carefully. Over lunch at her home, Swanson told Hays she had found a short story she wanted to film but hoped to clear it with him first. It was "a powerful story about tolerance and reconstruction" featuring a fanatical clergyman who needs correction himself—though the minister could become a reformer on-screen.[6] Hays encouraged filmmakers to confer with him before they proceeded rather than asking for approval after the fact. When Gloria told him the author was Somerset Maugham, Hays expressed his admiration for the writer. Then Swanson named the story—which of course was different from the name of the forbidden play.

No doubt feeling expansive after his fine meal, Hays failed to recognize the tale he himself had declared unfit for the screen. He told Swanson he could see no problem with her choice of material. The story would be told again and again: "'Will you make your permission official in the morning?' asked Miss Swanson. 'Nonsense,' Mr. Hays [responded], 'it is official now.'"[7]

With the all-clear from Hays, Swanson authorized Maurice Revnes to buy the story rights and—just to be safe—rights to the play, too. *Rain's* price had fallen considerably since the ban. Under no circumstances, however, was Revnes to identify the buyer: Gloria's name would drive the price right back up again.

Swanson confided her plan to Joe Schenck with some trepidation, but he crowed with delight: he wished he had thought of it himself. He hoped, however, that Hays would not cave in to the pressure the Motion Picture Association would bring once Swanson's intention became public knowledge. Jesse Lasky had been stuck with the expensive rights to *An American Tragedy* after association members complained to Hays about the provocative novel. It was important to get *Rain* cheaply, in case something went wrong and they had to drop it.

Swanson's search for a new project also meant lining up new talent. Although Al Parker had traveled west with her entourage, Swanson wanted another director for her second picture. *What Price Glory?* had impressed her and Henri, though the director was said to be a man's man who did not know how to work with women. Impressed by Raoul Walsh's confident style and the deft way he inserted comedy into a war drama, Swanson called him anyway. They had instant rapport, and she decided on the spot that—whatever picture came next—she would make it with Raoul Walsh. He was a big, unpretentious Irishman with a sense of humor, a love of gambling, a habit of drinking, and a reputation as a fine craftsman. Walsh had assisted Griffith on *The Birth of a Nation*, also playing John Wilkes Booth in the picture. He was a friend of Allan Dwan's and had directed Doug Fairbanks in *The Thief of Bagdad*. Walsh liked the notion of trying to make *Rain* and thought that Fox, where he was under contract, would probably lend him to Swanson.

A confirmation came—in code—announcing that Gloria Swanson was the proud owner of "The Two Molehills of Nebraska," for which she had paid the bargain price of $60,000.[8] Lindbergh had just landed in Paris, and all America was rejoicing. A festival atmosphere prevailed as Swanson and company gleefully started exploring travel options for location shooting in Tahiti. They ordered costume sketches for a "cheap snappy outfit" which could be worn by a modern San Francisco street-walker.[9] They borrowed a first-rate cameraman, George Barnes, from Samuel Goldwyn, started casting, and nailed down a loan contract with Fox for Raoul Walsh to write and direct. The announcement that Swanson's next UA release would be *Sadie Thompson* coincided with the gala Los Angeles premiere of *The Love of Sunya* in late May. They were careful not to identify the new picture with *Rain* but indicated that it would be shot in San Francisco and the South Sea islands, the "actual locale" of the story.[10]

The fancy footwork fooled no one. Unlike Will Hays, all of Hollywood immediately recognized what Swanson had done. Attorneys for John Colton and Somerset Maugham accused her of misrepresenting her interests in the story purchase; they sought to enjoin Gloria Swanson Productions from making the picture.[11] Joe Schenck received a telegram signed by all the association members—whom Walsh called "the pinochle club" for their after-hours chumminess.[12] It registered an angry protest against Swanson making *Rain* under any title whatsoever and appealed to Schenck "to stop the production of this picture at all costs," continuing, "We do not believe that any individual member has the right to jeopardize the interests of all the members." The "refusal to produce salacious books and plays" had been a "cornerstone" of the association. To destroy the good will built up would be "unforgiveable and unwarranted and a direct violation of promises we have made the public."[13]

The telegram was bad news, since the signers represented the major studios and several theater chains: together they had the power to prevent *Sadie Thompson* from appearing on screens. They could also stop Swanson from getting or keeping a cast and crew, since many of her workers would come on loan from these studios. VP and Treasurer Tom Moore imposed an immediate news blackout. No one was to say anything to the press about *Sadie Thompson* until the situation was resolved.

Swanson was unmoved: the members' own pictures routinely challenged standards of good taste and morality. She thought they were annoyed because they wanted to make *Rain* themselves but were "too dishonest" to say so: "I had reached up and picked the biggest plum of all."[14] The telegram signed by fifteen Hollywood men reminded Swanson of the list of her sexual partners Herbert Somborn produced when he wanted a good divorce settlement. In fact, some of the same people were on this list. (One unfamiliar name, Joe Kennedy, belonged to a distributor new to the business.) Gloria was also peeved that the telegram had gone to Joe Schenck rather than being addressed to her.

Then Schenck got a letter from Will Hays—another missive that bypassed Swanson. It contained a copy of the telegram the association members had sent Hays protesting Swanson's "subterfuge" and claiming that if *Rain* was allowed, there would be no reason to avoid other controversial properties. "No action is too strong for us to take," they avowed, "to protect our individual and collective interests."[15]

The more she thought about it, the angrier Swanson became. These men didn't even have the decency to approach her directly. The company wasn't "Joe Schenck Productions" but "Gloria Swanson Productions." Her name, her reputation, and her money were on the line. She would reply to their charges herself.

Swanson wrote to the association members declaring herself "in sympathy" with their purposes. She believed *Sadie Thompson* could be produced "in a clean manner without offending the clergy" and said she had pledged as much to Will Hays when he granted her permission to produce the film. Swanson promised she would not in the future make any picture which the association banned. Since she was not a member of the group, she emphasized, this was the "first commitment" she had made. However, with more than $200,000 tied up in the project and "a great deal of time and thought" invested, she could not easily let *Sadie* go. She hoped the association members would "be generous and broadminded" and withdraw their complaint. As everyone knew, the story of *Sadie Thompson* was itself "a great lesson in tolerance."[16]

Only Marcus Loew bothered to reply; he said he had been pressured into attaching his name and offered to help if he could. Gloria reached out to Hays, promising again to make a picture that would offend no one. Although the actress had played him expertly, Hays saved his fighting mettle for times when it counted. He gallantly kept his word to her and went to New York to placate the angry association members. With Marcus Loew also on Gloria's side, it looked like there would be no real battle over *Sadie*.

Nonetheless, the sales staff was under strict instructions. No one was to make even the faintest reference to *Rain*: the production was always to be called *Sadie Thompson*. None of the film's title cards would allude to the forbidden play, and no screen character would utter the word "rain," despite the constant downpour the plot required. The publicity blackout continued.

To assuage Somerset Maugham's ire at having sold his story so cheaply, Swanson hired him to write a sequel, an original tale to serve as the basis of a second picture chronicling Sadie's adventures after she leaves Pago Pago. When Maugham said he had lost out on a similar proposal from Fox after the ban on adapting *Rain* came down, Swanson snorted with laughter: Fox had denounced her efforts to produce *Rain* but had hoped to cash in, too. She had little choice but to match Fox's offer of $25,000 for "a scenario full of colour and action."[17] The price of *Sadie* was rising, but at least Maugham would not sue her.

There were other worries, unfortunately, and they all revolved around money. Al Parker had advanced Swanson $20,000 to help her make *The Love of Sunya*, volunteering the cash when she was feeling strained and harassed during production. He had also willingly agreed to defer his salary for the second picture in his two-film contract while he expected to continue directing Swanson. After she hired Raoul Walsh, however, Parker felt angry and insulted and tried to call the debt in. He could not force Swanson to pay him more quickly, but a bitter ex-director telling his story around town did not help Gloria's public relations. Her cash flow was tight, and the story made things awkward.

Swanson knew that her plans for *Sadie Thompson*, which combined a famous story, an expensive star, and a world-class director, went against accepted industry practice: she was "filling the basket with eggs."[18] Only at United Artists was such ambition possible. Her staff combed through the company's expenses, trying to streamline operations, yet they dared not cut back too obviously. They downsized rather than closed Gloria's New York and Paris offices. They loaned John Boles to Fox, then quietly dropped Swanson's option on his services.

It didn't help that *Sunya*, now in release, was performing sluggishly at the box office and running into problems with local censor boards. In Springfield, Massachusetts, it was prohibited for Sunday viewing. In Denver, San Antonio, and Milwaukee, revenues were so disappointing that the UA sales rep wanted to offer the theaters partial refunds against the high guarantees they had paid. It wasn't fair—or good for long-term business—to let exhibitors take the loss unassisted. Despite a few high-profile openings, *Sunya* was not the hit Gloria wanted.

Swanson also needed help getting her personal finances in line. It cost a lot to keep the home and staff a star of her magnitude was expected to maintain. Henri did not have any real income, though he was considering a Peugeot dealership in Los Angeles. His periodic trips to Europe, required by his visa status, cost the couple $1,000 a week that spring. They had been trying without success to rent Gloria's New York apartment; the Croton house, which Tom Moore had persuaded Swanson to sell, languished on the market. There were debts to Cartier's for jewels and Jaeckel's for furs—totaling $36,000 in unpaid bills.

In fact, the more closely he looked into Gloria's finances, the more dismayed Moore became. "The situation here is really serious," he reported in midsummer. "Substantial payments" were needed to prevent any number of petty lawsuits.[19] Moore would spend more time than he liked fending off creditors to whom Swanson owed as little as fifty dollars. "Bluffing" Cartier's extremely persistent bill collectors occupied months.[20] Swanson seemed not to understand: she wondered why there was no money to help Adelaide with her expenses, or why so much fuss should be made over the premium on the disfigurement insurance she was now required to carry. When Paramount had been picking up many of her personal and incidental expenses, her salary had stretched a lot farther.

Worse, the IRS had questioned her tax returns, which claimed the cost of Swanson's expensive wardrobe. She argued that the public expected her to dress like a star on and offscreen. The government argued that only apparel used in "the actual making of pictures" was deductible; she owed the IRS $15,000, payable immediately.[21] (After Jesse Lasky backed Gloria up, the tax man dropped his investigation of a frightening charge called "fraudulent evasion.")[22] Yet even as Swanson's team encouraged her to scale back her personal expenses, the papers criticized her for twice appearing publicly in the same clothes.[23]

Now she was in the uncomfortable position Herbert Somborn had occupied during the early days of their marriage. Then he had begged Gloria to help him keep his profile high, and she had insisted on cost cutting. She now understood in a pointed way how Hollywood quickly sniffed out any sign of strain or failure.

Then Maurice Revnes, who had masterminded the purchase of *Sadie*, resigned in a huff after Swanson refused to give him "complete supervision" over the picture.[24] He wanted her to relax and concentrate on acting, a luxury she no longer felt she had. However, no one expected Revnes to go to the press with tales of the injustices he had suffered at Swanson's hands. "He is full of resentment," production manager Pierre Bedard noted with dismay.[25] The company did not need anyone blackening Gloria's reputation as a businesswoman.

Swanson's secret fear was that the stomachaches plaguing her would make her too ill to play the role of Sadie. She imagined having to offer the plum part—her part—to another actress. She also resented the remarks "Uncle" Carl Laemmle, head of Universal, had recently made about female producers: "It costs from fifty thousand dollars to a million or two to make a picture, and I can't afford to bet that much money on uncertain physical strength . . . I would rather risk my money on a man."[26]

Swanson needed to be well to lead the production; she also knew the cameras would pitilessly reveal any physical weakness. However, since she loathed and detested doctors, she didn't know where to turn for help. She was convinced that Valentino's death had been hastened, if not actually caused, by the negligence of his "greedy, careless" physicians, an opinion she expressed freely.[27] Finally, a friend suggested a doctor with a small practice up in Pasadena.

When Swanson met Dr. Henry Bieler, she was not impressed. His office was nothing special, and the "no smoking" signs led her to expect a lecture on her nicotine habit. When she told Bieler she had stomach pains, however, he asked Swanson to name all the foods—and all the ingredients in all the foods—she had eaten the previous evening, carefully noting them down in a list. The actress's cook had prepared a lavish, multi-course meal for a small dinner party Gloria had hosted. She had proudly served her guests cocktails and hors d'oeuvres, then chicken and fish, peas and asparagus with hollandaise sauce, raspberry trifle, and champagne. There were different wines with each course. No one had complained. Everyone had enjoyed the meal.

Then Bieler explained to Swanson that so many foods, taken in such mixtures, acted like poisons in the body. No animals, not even pigs, he said, ate such combinations. He asked her to visualize each ingredient from her meal being piled onto a plate. As he read her list aloud to her, she felt strangely nauseated. Then he asked the question that would resonate with Swanson for the rest of her life: "Why do you treat your stomach like a garbage pail?"[28]

She was rattled and powerfully moved by the simplicity of Dr. Bieler's idea: simple, plain foods were better for you. In fact, Bieler believed that diet was the cure for pretty much everything. You couldn't afford to ignore pain, he said: it was a God-given warning to change your ways. There was no better or more reliable way to do that than to change your diet. Bieler did not believe in drugs of any kind—not even aspirin. Given a chance, he said, the body would heal itself.

He prescribed a cleansing diet, telling Gloria to eat a puree of zucchini, string beans, and celery. After a week on this modified fast, her body would be purged of toxins. Bieler warned Swanson that she might feel worse before she felt better, but she felt better already. "His words made perfect sense to me," she said.[29] The visit cost $3.00.

Swanson liked the idea that she was responsible for taking care of her body, and that it would respond to her directly as a result of how she cared for it. It was simple, like the saline-and-sunshine home remedy she had used for her internal abscess. She had a strongly positive feeling as she began her new regimen. There were "a few rough days as my body gradually eliminated the poisons built up in it." However, Swanson soon felt "like a different woman . . . [B]y the time we went into the studio to start shooting *Sadie*, my skin was glowing, my eyes were clear and sparkling, and my nerves were calm."[30] She was a convert. The mixture known as "Bieler's broth" was a staple of Swanson's diet for the next sixty years.

Swanson's renewed vigor—her sparkle and snap—were evident in her portrayal of Sadie Thompson, a fierce, smart, unbreakable woman who comes close to breaking. Gloria set herself to offering a fresh perspective on the character, welcoming the chance to play a tough cookie after all the hoopla about her being a marquise with her nose in the air. She instructed Raoul Walsh to make Sadie as spicy as the censors would allow and to turn up the heat during the love scenes.

They were delighted to borrow Walsh's friend Lionel Barrymore from M-G-M for the pivotal role of Davidson, the controversial minister-who-couldn't-be-a-minister. Barrymore was delighted to accept the $1,875 a week he would be paid. He made no bones about his motivation for working, happily recounting how his agent had warned him away from a two-reel comedy "in which my chief function was to let comedians bop me on the head with a rubber hose. Easiest work I ever did. [But my agent] almost perished of apoplexy, [saying] 'This will kill you in pictures. Even a Barrymore can't survive this.' 'You don't know Barrymores,' I said. 'We survive anything that pays.'"[31]

All the roles were filled—including four native Samoans who would furnish their own costumes and props—except for the small but important part of Sergeant Timothy O'Hara. "Handsome" is a tough but kind soldier who is unfazed by Sadie's sordid past and wants to marry her. The character had been added to *Rain* on stage, giving Sadie a happier ending than in Maugham's darker vision. Swanson and Walsh knew they needed O'Hara in the picture as well, yet Swanson had a devil of a time finding her "Handsome." She saw "at least forty men" for the part, including Victor McLaglen and Douglas Fairbanks Jr., who was not yet eighteen.[32] "Swanson turned them all down," Walsh recalled.[33]

They had begun shooting the picture without him when Swanson realized that the ideal O'Hara was right in front of her: she wanted Walsh to play the part. Though it had been years since the director had done any acting, he could not resist Gloria's entreaties.

"I cannot tell you how happy I am, for he is exactly Sergeant O'Hara," Swanson wrote Moore in July. She acknowledged the slow production start but said, "We are now getting along splendidly. I am most enthusiastic and the rushes justify my hopes."[34] Bedard was more guarded:

"[Casting himself] is a risky business and [Walsh] more than anybody else realizes it."[35] At least he had a reputation as a fast worker.

Everyone agreed it was out of the question to spend $30,000 taking the company to the South Seas: Catalina was much handier. Forty-seven workman went off to build sets for production designer William Cameron Menzies. If anyone could make the California coast look like Pago Pago, Menzies was the man. Despite their shaky beginnings, Bedard soon felt all was well. "Our relations with Mr. Schenck are most amicable and harmonious," he wrote Moore. "Deducting accumulating charges, story, and Gloria's salary, the picture is being made for a song."[36]

The company went to Catalina in late July, and Swanson felt her excitement building: *Sadie* was going to be box office dynamite. Lionel Barrymore was giving a first-class performance: though beset by family troubles and often in pain, when he was working, nothing distracted him. As his brother John said, "Playing with [Lionel] is like riding a bicycle behind a Rolls Royce—you make better time."[37]

The only problem Swanson had with Lionel Barrymore was that, after a week in the same clothes as Davidson, he smelled bad. He was beginning to be too strong to stomach during their long, intense scenes together. So she did what producers do: she delegated, assigning two assistants to remove the offending costume from Barrymore's dressing room, where he invariably napped after lunch. He would have to appear in fresh clothes. Not a word was said, but afterwards, the odor was gone for good. "Bathing, of course, didn't alter his performance. Clean or dirty, deodorized or pestiferous, Lionel Barrymore had nothing to learn about acting."[38]

Walsh's script described Sadie as "a young frivolous creature . . . who bears all the indications of having lived a life in search of pleasure. . . . She is always affable, fond of a good time and has a great desire to make a friend of everyone she meets. She is at all times making an effort to tolerate and be tolerated. But she can fight, very much as any inoffensive animal will do, when cornered by some relentless adversary."[39] Walsh believed Gloria's characterization of Sadie was right on target: "Her feeling for the part . . . gave her acting a hint of feral grace. Her complete lack of self-consciousness was another asset that turned her into a very believable prostitute." Swanson's Sadie was "a typical fancy girl of any waterfront from San Francisco to Yokohama."[40]

The sexual chemistry between Handsome and Sadie was also convincing. Walsh avoided "like poison ivy" the alluring women he directed, fearful of losing his authority on the set. Swanson, however, already was the boss. Soon their kisses were longer than the Hays Office allowed. Away from the outside world on Catalina, things heated up, and by the end of filming, Walsh was in love with his leading lady. What drew him to "this radiant girl" was her naturalness: "I never thought of her as the Marquise de la Falaise. To me she was just Gloria, as genuine as sunshine, a warm, unpretentious human being."[41]

Walsh's marriage to actress Miriam Cooper was ending, and their divorce was celebrated on the same night in two different Hollywood houses. Swanson hosted a party for Raoul, while Norman Kerry and Erich von Stroheim threw one for his wife. Cooper described her party: "The first thing I saw was a big photograph of Raoul on the grand piano—framed in a toilet seat. There was a lot of liquor floating around and after a while people began jumping in the swimming pool with all their clothes on. It was a hell of a party."[42]

If actual divorce parties were infrequent, matrimonial life in Hollywood was in near-constant flux. Hollywood marriages were often unconventional, too. Joe Schenck had recently separated from Norma Talmadge, who had fallen in love with Gilbert Roland during the filming of *Camille*. Schenck gallantly moved aside, but made sure the next three Talmadge films he produced partnered his estranged wife with her lover: they made good box office. Marriage was one thing, business another.

At twenty-eight, Swanson was on her third marriage. Practically since the day she and Henri arrived in the States, the press had been asking, "How Will Gloria's Marriage End?"[43] Their union had borne more scrutiny than many with stronger foundations could have endured. Now, however, Gloria was so busy with *Sadie* that she had almost no time for her husband. She told Henri the picture would "collapse" if she did not stay focused, and that he "would have to be daddy and mommy both with the children . . . Everything I had ever worked for was riding on *Sadie Thompson*, and I was not going to let anything or anyone defeat me."[44]

Swanson's penchant for growing attached to her leading men and directors was not exactly a secret in movie circles, and her new director thought little of Gloria's husband. Walsh called Henri a "parlor cat" for his refined manners, sneering that "the playboy marquis" didn't have too much power at home: "What Gloria wanted, Gloria got." Just the same, he thought Gloria was disappointed in her marriage. Barrymore poked sly fun at Henri, too. "[Lionel] had a habit of muttering asides," Walsh explained. "When the script called for him to say, 'At any hour, day or night, when you need me I will come,' he looked over a shoulder and added, 'I hope Falaise didn't hear that.'"[45]

Rumors began circulating that the couple had separated and that Henri was living at the Garden of Allah, actress Alla Nazimova's former home. Swanson denied the stories, but she had clearly become a bit less infatuated with her charming, sophisticated husband. If *Madame Sans-Gêne* had been a comfortable setting for Henri, showing his smooth and relaxed manners to perfection, the rough-and-tumble world of *Sadie Thompson*, and of Hollywood commerce in general, was less so. In France, he had a useful role to play; in California, however, he was superfluous. Gloria was overwhelmed by work and money cares; producing movies took far more effort and fierce concentration than she had expected, with no end in sight. On the other hand, Henri dabbled: running Gloria's nominal office in New York; writing short stories as possible movie subjects; and now this car business.[46] Whatever help her husband provided she could easily have gotten elsewhere, less expensively and with less fuss.

Then, too, Swanson was an actress, and her current role—a pleasure-loving streetwalker who endures a conversion attempt before shaking herself free—was not the kind of role in which her marriage to Henri had cast her. Raoul Walsh was drawn to tough, sassy women who weren't too particular about their virtue, and that was who Swanson would be for the duration of *Sadie Thompson*. Henri, on the other hand, had fallen in love with a vivacious patriot who survives the Revolution to become a duchess. His love had made Gloria a real–life marquise. Swanson contained all these women, but it was not clear that the men she chose could partner her in all her guises.

In *The Love of Sunya*, Swanson's character looked into a crystal ball and saw that the penniless man who truly loved her would make her happiest. The magic of the movies showed Sunya the future, and she chose accordingly. Unfortunately, in the summer of 1927 Gloria Swanson did not have a crystal ball; if she had, she might have made a different choice.

Henri left Los Angeles for France on business in August, and the papers described the film-worthy farewell his wife gave him: "As the train began to move the Marquis leaned out the window and Gloria catching at his hand rained kisses all over it as she raced along with the train."[47] He pooh-poohed the rumors of marital problems before he sailed: "We are as happy as the birds in the May, and why the public should wish us to be unhappy is more than I can understand."[48]

Nonetheless, the tenor of his letters home from this trip was different. He sent his wife daily—occasionally more frequent—missives describing his trip and his loving feelings for her ("Good morning angel excellent trip so far but miss you love you terribly"). Yet he was often clearly perplexed by her lack of response. One letter sent to Catalina spoke of the two women in his life: "By now you are . . . all made up as Sadie Thompson but under the makeup the real sweet you that I love is hidden. It is to that Gloria that I am writing."

Whether that Gloria was listening was another story. Henri continued, "Darling, when I say I love you it does not represent one millionth part of what I feel. You are so sweet so nice to me so indulgent and kind that my heart breaks at times when I realize that I am unable to repay you of it all otherwise than by loving you. . . . You see, Dear, I suppose that all through my life I have been rather starved [of] affection, and I am of the stupid kind that can't live without it. . . . I know we could be happier, but the things that worry us now are material. . . . I know that the future is ours. . . . I love you with all my soul and body."[49]

As he traveled on, Henri continued to put his thoughts on paper for his wife far away: "The trouble with me is that I am too much centered in you. You are my axle. If I leave you I am helpless, which of course is nice but wrong. It would be all right if you had the same feeling about me but you can't."[50] The fear Henri expressed in France as their courtship began—that he had nothing to give Gloria but love—now seemed his reality. He felt he was in his wife's debt for everything, a debt he could only repay by loving her. But Swanson was a woman who vacillated between wanting deep, steady romantic love (with a dose of playfulness thrown in) and being in thrall to strong but unreliable men who offered to take care of her and her complex affairs. It was Henri's deep misfortune that he considered Gloria his "axle." As he was beginning to see, he would not be hers.

In any case, Swanson was preoccupied by a crisis on set: Sam Goldwyn had recalled their borrowed cameraman, the brilliant George Barnes. They were at a crucial point in filming and had to decide whether to start again with a new cameraman or try to match Barnes's work. The latter was the least expensive solution, provided they could find a compatible cameraman. This was a serious problem. Movies were not shot in sequence, and top-notch camera operators had their own unique styles. Incompatible approaches to the cinematography would be distracting and disruptive. They tried out five cameramen before Oliver Marsh came on board, a last-minute loan from Marcus Loew. After a lot of delay and confusion, the picture got back on track.

Swanson was miffed at Joe Schenck, who "could have rectified this with one telephone call."[51] Better yet, they could have avoided it by choosing another cameraman from the start: Schenck had wrongly

believed he could talk Goldwyn out of reclaiming Barnes. It was "a costly mistake" that set the production back $50,000–$85,000.[52] Swanson
found Schenck unsympathetic, even dismissive of her concerns during
this calamity; she privately thought he was trying to "spank" her for the
embarrassment she had caused over his UA stock deal.[53] The only consolation was that reshooting allowed for improvements to the story.[54]

Shortly after the fiasco with the cameramen got sorted out, Gloria realized she needed to borrow at least another $100,000 to finish the picture:
Sadie's $550,000 budget was almost depleted. No matter what economies
they made on set, there were still costs associated with editing, titling,
making film prints, advertising, and the like. Swanson knew Schenck
could get the money she needed from Art Cinema, UA's finance company, but "had a feeling he would make me stoop to pick it up."[55] She
was adamant that he would not tie provisions she did not like to the new
finance contract. She knew Schenck held UA's interests closer to his heart
than her own individual needs and was already annoyed that what she
considered his mistake with the cameraman had cost her so much money.

Quite aside from *Sadie Thompson*, UA was looking for more from
Swanson than she wanted to give. Schenck had instituted new fees (for
checking contracts and to cover distribution costs) and a new policy of
selling films in advance of their production. Swanson balked at these
changes, mostly because she didn't really trust Schenck. She couldn't
help feeling her life had gotten harder, not easier, since she joined UA,
and Joe Schenck was the face of the company to her.

She was also afraid that UA wasn't asking enough money for her important new film and insisted that *Sadie* be sold for a higher price than
that commanded by "any other woman star in UA."[56] She complained to
Moore that she was "absolutely in the dark" about these crucial figures.[57]
A new note of tension and mistrust crept into her communication with
even her closest advisors. Both Moore and Schenck reassured Swanson
that *Sadie* was being treated like the big success everyone expected it to
be: the UA sales force was anxious to show her "what a big gross really
looks like."[58]

Yet the real bone of contention was the finance contracts—the one
to finish *Sadie* and the one for her next picture. Swanson was refusing to sign, despite both Moore and Schenck's importuning. Schenck
repeatedly claimed that the Art Cinema contracts were "absolutely fair"
and that Gloria was "stopping the wheels of progress."[59] When Moore
learned that Swanson was trying to use several lots she owned on
Wilshire Boulevard as collateral for a privately financed loan to finish

Sadie, he hastily explained that she could neither sell nor mortgage the property to get money for the picture. "To do so would amount to fraud," he cabled urgently; her previous creditors had to be repaid first.[60] Moore sent Swanson "a very serious warning": unless she signed a viable contract soon, he said, "Your whole status in UA will be in serious condition. . . . Any delay will cost more than best contract obtainable."[61] However, Swanson remained obdurate, her distrust stronger than her instinct for self-preservation. She would wait until the last possible minute to sign the contract for funds to finish *Sadie*, and she would not budge regarding a finance contract for her next picture.

Ignoring Al Parker had not made him go away, either. Now he was seeking 25 percent of the profits from *Sunya*, and behaving (in Moore's words) "more like a jilted woman than like a business man. He seems to be vindictive and a little unbalanced and by brooding over the situation, has convinced himself that he has been treated badly and his reputation seriously injured."[62] Yet Swanson had not made much effort to smooth Parker's ruffled feathers. Perhaps she felt too beset by other cares; perhaps she was indifferent.

Swanson was unwilling to give Parker a share in *Sunya*, since she had pinned her hopes as an independent on the money she would make from her films' box office returns. She needed the profits from *Sunya* to go forward with her next picture, but she was also suspicious about how much money she would be signing away were she to consent. She repeatedly asked Moore to get UA to account for *Sunya*'s revenues, then seemed unwilling to accept what he told her: that the picture was not making the kind of money for which they had all hoped.

Sunya was also having trouble with the censors abroad. It had been banned in Tokyo. Irish censors said *Sunya* promoted "an acceptance of the doctrine of re-incarnation," which went against Christian principles.[63] An offer to cut the offending "Egyptian" scene (part of the film's prologue) was unsuccessful: the Irish declared the picture "100 percent unfit for exhibition."[64] The same scene caused a stir in Paris, and—local cultures being what they were—UA thought it might actually help the picture on the continent.[65]

Sunya was a disappointment, which raised the stakes even higher on *Sadie*. Then Parker indicated he would settle for 25 percent of the profits from *Sadie Thompson* instead: no one wanted to give him that. Parker cast a shadow over *Sadie* for months before Swanson was induced to accept the inevitable and repay her debt to Parker with a portion of *Sunya*'s takings.

The bad press his mutterings created was new to Swanson, who had apparently exhausted the supply of sympathy and praise which accompanied her return to the States with Henri a mere two years earlier. One of the most vitriolic columns anatomized her every fault, characterizing her as critical and capricious: "She is too prone to listen to advice from people who gush and yes around her for what they can get out of her. Furthermore she lacks the vision and the depth of versatility. . . . Gloria Swanson . . . stands pretty much alone at this writing. She has burned bridges and dealt too carelessly with people to get an SOS answer should *Sadie Thompson* go the way of her last few offerings."[66]

The producer-star would have done well to ponder some of these criticisms. Most of Swanson's problems had been brewing for some time, and most were worsened by her inability to trust associates who told her hard truths. She could not do everything herself but had a difficult time relinquishing control. She knew little about business yet insisted on learning on the job. Even as she tried to get the experience and information to make good decisions, another wave swamped her. There were simply not enough hours in the day for all the jobs she was trying to do.

For example, Swanson's absorption in *Sadie* meant she was not giving as much attention as she needed to her next picture, which ought to be ready to go once *Sadie* was completed. By the time she agreed to proceed with *The Last of Mrs. Cheyney*, they were too late: Allan Dwan had just signed with First National. Then Schenck had a brilliant idea. How about the dapper German import Ernst Lubitsch? *Cheyney* was exactly the kind of stylish comedy at which he excelled. Swanson and Lubitsch would have made a dazzling pair; his continental sophistication and sly sexual innuendo would doubtless have created a brilliant, brittle world in which Swanson would have shone. He was also quick, efficient, and had a deservedly big name. As Schenck said, "He knows what he is doing all the time."[67] Yet after a conversation with Mary Pickford, Swanson told Schenck that she wasn't interested.

Swanson turned to Doug and Mary occasionally for advice on her UA-related decisions and always found them helpful. Bedard considered the pair "her closest and staunchest supporters," and was thrilled that Gloria was "no longer isolated" as she had been in New York.[68] Doug especially had been generous to Gloria, even making her a personal loan of $10,000 when she was worried about money earlier that spring. (He was not pressing Swanson for repayment, but Moore nearly hit the ceiling when he learned there were even more debts outstanding.) Despite his happy-go-lucky persona, Doug was a capable businessman whose pictures always returned profits. Mary's business acumen was legendary: Mack Sennett said she was a woman who "found charm in finance."[69]

Mary had firsthand knowledge of Lubitsch. He had directed *Rosita*, her first effort to play a grown-up part. They clashed over who was in charge, and Pickford emerged victorious but unsatisfied: she thought *Rosita* was "the worst picture, bar none, that I ever made."[70] Schenck warned Gloria that if she decided on Lubitsch, she would have to leave the entire production in his hands, as "he will not brook interference."[71] Suddenly Swanson was convinced that Lubitsch was "perhaps a trifle too subtle for average public."[72]

Despite her distrust of the others advising her, it didn't occur to Swanson that Pickford was possibly the worst person to help her assess a director. The two women were cordial rivals rather than friends. Mary had begun United Artists, but Gloria was currently demanding that her pictures be sold at higher prices than Pickford's, which could scarcely have pleased the company founder. Moreover, Pickford's appeal was based on her girlish sweetness and the golden curls she called "that blonde chain around my neck."[73] Swanson claimed that Mary was jealous of her freedom: "Mary'd come over to my bungalow with her little bee-stung lips and pout 'I want to do Sadie Thompson' . . . She affected being a child, with her little Mary Janes and those damned curls, and I'd wear these enormous high heels and act like I towered over her. I'd say very imperiously, 'Get out of here, you little shrimp, I'm Sadie Thompson.'"[74]

Swanson's public was looking for something very different than Pickford's. Mary had already steered Gloria away from *The Last of Mrs. Cheyney* once; now Swanson left this conversation with Pickford dead set against Lubitsch, a director who would probably have gotten her best from her. Pickford later admitted that "Lubitsch could understand Pola Negri or Gloria Swanson, but he didn't understand me."[75] She evidently did not make that distinction apparent to Gloria. Looking back on this period with some bitterness, Pickford said, "In the early days United Artists was a private golf club for the four of us. Then we let too many other stars in and it began to change."[76] Gloria Swanson was part of that change.

Schenck must have fumed when Swanson rejected Lubitsch and opened discussions with Sam Taylor, who was unenthusiastic about *Cheyney* and tried to interest Gloria in remaking a 1916 Norma Talmadge picture, *The Social Secretary*. Swanson would be a beautiful stenographer who, weary of being harassed at work, disguises herself as a plain Jane, with comic and romantic results. Taylor wanted Ronald Colman and

Marie Dressler for the other big parts. Yet a month later Swanson was still uncertain.

Her *Humming Bird* director Sidney Olcott contacted Gloria about re-uniting, and Elinor Glyn wrote to say that the heroine of her new novel would be an "ideal" part for Swanson: "It would be such fun if we could make [a] marvelous picture together again like *The Great Moment*. No one knows your qualities or genius as I do or could help to demonstrate them more strongly."[77] Swanson replied politely but knew she needed to go forward, not look back. It could not have helped that Mrs. Glyn had recently listed Swanson among the screen idols who "once had IT," but no longer did.[78] Thank God for Billy Haines: the devastatingly handsome actor reportedly bowed to Glyn before assuring the older woman, "You, of course, certainly do have It. But, madam, you left the 'sh' off of it."[79]

Then Swanson again reversed course and told Schenck that Lubitsch "would be excellent director for *Last of Mrs. Cheyney*," which was back on the table as her next picture.[80] Unfortunately, Lubitsch was no longer available. Even if he had been free, Swanson had not yet accepted a finance contract so she could not have offered him a deal.

Swanson was relying less on Moore—whom Schenck thought was "an excellent man" and "the only real good man" Swanson had on her board—than on Bedard, who was in California and supported her on a daily basis.[81] Both Schenck and Moore thought Bedard gave Gloria poor advice. Schenck put it as strongly as possible: "You spent $200,000 more than should have been spent on Sadie and that would have been additional profit for you. If I may say it you listen to people who yes you to draw a salary and you suspect your friends who are really interested in seeing you make good."[82] Swanson wasn't listening.

She was frustrated with both her financial advisors: she thought Schenck too partial to UA's needs and Moore too polite to fight hard for her. Finally, after months of negotiating, Swanson knew what she was looking for. Her new contract should fold in money to pay Al Parker and Doug Fairbanks; those should always have been Gloria Swanson Productions' obligations rather than her private bills. A new contract should provide money to pay for Swanson's car and driver, her travel expenses, and at least some part of her wardrobe. These were business expenses, since the public expected her to uphold a certain standard of luxury. A new contract should also have provisions for when a picture went over budget, so that the busy star and producer was not forced to go out looking for loans in the middle of production. The Art Cinema Corporation had been founded to help the United Artists with production financing, not to wring concessions out of its members while they were over a barrel.

These were more or less reasonable expectations for a star of Swanson's magnitude, but it took her an awfully long time to figure them out. She had not trusted her advisors sufficiently to put her financial affairs in their hands, and so she spent a lot of money learning her new business. It would be hard for her to catch up, no matter how successful *Sadie* was: too much of Swanson's expensive learning curve was tied up in it. She had her completion contract, but no financing for her third picture and no advisors in whom she felt real confidence.

Once a rough cut of *Sadie* was assembled, Swanson threw a big cast party to celebrate. Henri was back from France, and Raoul Walsh had moved on to Mexico, content to leave his happy diversion with Swanson an on-set romance. With money to finish editing and titling the film in hand and her creditors momentarily satisfied, Swanson moved quickly, and in early November the film was ready for a sneak preview.

The response of the sample audience augured well for her second independent venture. Most preview cards were enthusiastic, praising the picture and calling Gloria "wonderful," "superb," "positively beautiful" in "a very human performance." To be sure, *Sadie* rubbed some viewers the wrong way: "There is nothing educational or uplifting in the whole picture." "I think it was rotten. It sure was immoral. I don't think such pictures should be allowed to be shown. It certainly was a slam on our Christian nation." "This picture is the rottenest most immoral production I have ever seen."[83] *Sadie Thompson* left no one indifferent: viewers loved it or hated it. If they loved the picture, it was because of Swanson. If they hated it, it was because they saw a holy man corrupted by his desire for a beautiful woman. Swanson knew she had a hit, possibly a big one.

She headed to New York for a few days, ostensibly on business for *Sadie*. In fact, she was intent on getting a fresh perspective on financing for her next film, and had asked Robert Kane, who had been in charge of production for Paramount at Astoria, to put her in touch with an advisor. She left Henri in California, relying on him once again to be mother and father to Gloria and Brother while she took care of business.

Swanson's brief trip east inexplicably turned into a month's absence. Her staff, anxious to finalize *Sadie Thompson* for a December premiere, peppered Swanson with questions and pressed her for decisions. Was she satisfied with the cutting? What about the titling? Did Davidson still seem like a religious figure, or had their changes resolved that problem? What about music? She left most of the telegrams unanswered.

Then the routine queries became urgent. They needed to get one hundred prints made. They were in danger of losing even their guaranteed bookings if they did not produce a print for the Hays Office to approve (a requirement now that they had joined the association themselves). An early December premiere date came and went. Then they had to cancel a December 26 opening. Swanson's absence and her silence meant that the million final decisions coordinating *Sadie*'s distribution and exhibition stopped dead.

No one seemed to know what Swanson was doing, though she was exchanging cryptic messages with Bedard: "Everything great," she wired him, and "I am terribly happy about everything."[84] He was "busting with curiosity to hear the good news."[85] Her secretary reported that the actress's funds were "very low," but that Swanson was "very happy."[86] She had taken a box at the opera, was organizing a party in her suite at the Barclay Hotel, and had begun buying new gowns. Henri, normally a patient man, became peevish: "Dearest can't understand what is keeping you away so long since Milton [Cohen, her attorney] claims it is not business . . . Really darling am very distressed . . . I do not believe in these separations and you did not use to either. Love you but am very sad."[87] He was puzzled by his wife's sudden decision to rent their house to Hollywood newlyweds Norma Shearer and Irving Thalberg. It meant moving her family into a rental property for the holidays—but what Gloria wanted, Gloria got.

Then, just as suddenly as she had disappeared, Swanson checked back in. She returned to California and began signing off on decisions and accepting options she had dismissed earlier. She did everything to get *Sadie* ready, but nothing to finalize her next project. She offered no explanations. At least, thought Moore with resignation, they would have a picture in theaters soon. *Sadie* was once again moving forward.

At the end of the month, Swanson received an invitation from Jack Warner to see a new picture his company was opening. *The Jazz Singer* would change almost everything for Swanson and her contemporaries, but on the night of December 28, 1927, there was a party atmosphere at the Criterion Theater. The silent stars of Hollywood sat back and marveled—as drawn in by the picture, by Al Jolson's performance, and by the sounds coming from the screen as any other movie fans.

As the year drew to a close, Gloria Swanson Productions' vice president and treasurer Tom Moore was hard at work on a new plan for his boss's financial future. He doggedly outlined a series of cutbacks designed to get Swanson out of the debt she had amassed ever since *Sunya* started going overboard. She had followed one nine-month production peri-od—on a picture that had barely broken even—with another film that took longer still, and that picture was not yet in release. Moore declared that Swanson had to stick to "a careful budget" for her household and personal expenditures, and it must be overseen by an auditor to make sure there were "no items omitted or concealed."[88] There could no more private loans, no more clothes or jewelry, until things stabilized.

Moore understood that his plan was likely to be unpopular. Nonetheless, he wanted to help Gloria get back on top and knew an austerity program was necessary: "This plan or some similar one must be followed if Miss Swanson is to survive as an independent producer."[89]

Moore did not know that Swanson had quite another plan in mind. Within a few days she would make a clean sweep of things. Almost ev-eryone on her board—including Moore—would be dismissed, and a new group appointed, courtesy of a white knight from Boston named Joe Kennedy. Gloria Swanson had exactly $65.00 in the bank.[90]

CHAPTER 13

The Swamp

JOSEPH KENNEDY LOOKED NOTHING LIKE ANY BANKER SWANSON had ever met. The boyish, freckled, blue-eyed Irishman wore an ill-fitting suit, and his thick Boston accent made him seem more like "any average working-class person's uncle" than the man who had been the youngest bank president in America.[1] Paramount's Robert Kane had suggested that Swanson discuss financing for her next picture with Kennedy, but at first she could not understand why. They met at the Savoy Plaza, and Kennedy said his whole family was impressed that he was lunching with Gloria Swanson.

He watched her pick at her braised vegetables, while she eyed the hearty meal set before him. To break the ice, they talked about their children. Kennedy's wife, Rose, was carrying the couple's eighth child, and he expressed alarm that Gloria's son had not yet been baptized. Then they turned to business, Swanson laying before him the two finance proposals she had gotten, one from Joe Schenck, the other from the Bank of America.

Kennedy examined the proposals briefly, then peppered Swanson with questions. He wanted to know whether her accountant had been trained in up-to-date business methods, the kind taught at his alma mater, Harvard. He asked about her European grosses, and Swanson explained her fear that her pictures were being undersold abroad; she had not gotten figures she trusted from the company. Kennedy broke into raucous laughter when she described how Mary Pickford's mother used to stand in the back of the theater counting heads—anything to prevent Mary from being cheated. Gloria couldn't be in all her theaters herself and despaired of knowing what was really happening with her pictures' profits.

Then Kennedy suggested a solution—the first of many. She should ask Paramount for some figures for pictures distributed in Europe in the last year; any worthwhile accountant could project Swanson's revenues from there. Kennedy elaborated: the motion picture industry needed to be run like any other business. He suspected Gloria had been seeing too much red ink and too little accounting that really accounted for the normal ebb and flow of business.

About six months earlier, Kennedy said, he had organized a graduate seminar on the movie business at Harvard. More than a dozen representatives of the industry, including Will Hays, Marcus Loew, Jesse Lasky, Adolph Zukor, and Cecil B. DeMille, had lectured on the art and commerce of the motion picture; he had published a book preserving the lectures. Swanson chuckled, picturing Hungarian immigrant Zukor instructing the blue bloods at Harvard, but Kennedy said they had turned hundreds away at the door. Everyone wanted to learn how the movie business worked.

Swanson found his enthusiasm infectious—until Kennedy suddenly asked how she had slipped *Sadie Thompson* past Will Hays. When she said she had simply asked for permission to film the story, Kennedy guffawed. Bristling at the insinuation that she had "vamped" Hays rather than outsmarting him and the other producers, Swanson turned icy.[2] Kennedy told her he had signed the producers' protest as a favor to the men who participated in his Harvard seminar. It was nothing personal.

Swanson knew her lunch companion was a movie producer but did not know what pictures he had made. The brash, confident man wilted a bit as he admitted that his movies to date had been successful but unexceptional westerns and action stories. The biggest star in his stable at FBO was literally a horse: Silver King, ridden by western actor Fred Thomson. "After all his grand opening talk," Swanson recalled, "he was going down in total defeat."[3] Finally, Kennedy recommended she accept Joe Schenck's offer; he proposed no alternative plan of his own. Swanson figured the lunch had been a waste of time and doubted she would ever see Joseph Kennedy again. He had not even paid for his meal.

Robert Kane had told Kennedy he thought Gloria "needed handling."[4] Maybe they should propose to handle her together, Kennedy offering financing and Kane managing her UA productions. Shortly after meeting with Swanson, however, Kennedy told Kane he didn't think he could do anything. Swanson was "not in any position to trade" and should take what UA was offering: "I think the trouble is that she got herself all spread out with debts . . . and told too many people about it."[5] Nonetheless, Kennedy called Swanson, saying he had asked Sidney Kent from Paramount to pull some European numbers together. The evidence of Kennedy's initiative pleased Gloria; maybe there was more to him than she had seen. There was only one small catch, Kennedy said: Sidney Kent needed a favor in return.

Kent and his wife were divorcing, and Kent wanted a delay his wife was not inclined to grant. Her attorney was Swanson's friend Milton Cohen. Would Swanson call Cohen and ask him to persuade Mrs. Kent to agree? Swanson was willing to consider it, but Kennedy pushed her to act promptly, to make the call while he waited. "Ordinarily I disliked being pushed or coerced, but his urging had an almost playful tone to it, as if . . . it was fun to get things done quickly and efficiently."[6] Not knowing quite why she was agreeing but intrigued by the charismatic Irishman, Swanson placed the call.

Then Kennedy asked to take Swanson to dinner to discuss her business plans. He called for her early, looking more polished than he had at lunch and carrying an orchid corsage. Swanson hated orchids. On the ride out to Long Island, Kennedy presented her with a book of lectures from his Harvard symposium on film with her name stamped in gold. She would find her name inside, too: Kennedy had cited *The Love of Sunya* in his lecture as an example of the need for quick sales in the film business. *Sunya's* distributors could charge $50,000 for the picture's initial ten-day run at the Roxy, but nine months later in Oshkosh, they would only get $7.50 for the film: pictures were perishable goods.[7] "He was like a schoolboy," Gloria said, calling the book "the most expensive doorstop I ever owned."[8]

At the restaurant, Swanson realized her host was not used to dining alone with a lady. The large menu with no prices "startled him." This meat-and-potatoes man "was ill at ease, not knowing what to do next."[9] When she again ordered a plate of steamed vegetables, he asked if she was on a special diet. Gloria told him how Dr. Bieler had converted her to simple food, and Kennedy confided that he sometimes feared he was developing an ulcer. However, he dismissed her suggestion that he see Dr. Bieler himself, saying he had the best doctors in Boston on the job. When Swanson teased him by imitating his broad Boston A's, Kennedy relaxed. When he was really amused, he whacked his thigh with delight. Swanson found herself trying to elicit his hearty laugh, his groan of pleasure at one of her jokes.

They spent the evening absorbed in talk about the movies, something Swanson usually abhorred. Kennedy's curiosity was boundless: he wanted to know about making pictures in France, about publicity and budgeting at Paramount, and even—especially—why Swanson had refused to renew her contract. Stars wanted a voice in decisions that affected them, she said; performers often had a very good understanding of both their talents and their limitations. Besides, Swanson said impishly, she would only have been the third or fourth star to be offered a million dollar contract—but she was the first to turn one down. Caught unaware, Kennedy bellowed his approval with one of his great big laughs.

He asked what Gloria thought about giving an annual prize for the best picture and the best performance in a movie, an idea Swanson dismissed. How could you determine that Doug Fairbanks was better than Charlie Chaplin? It was like saying one color was prettier than another. Besides, she disliked the idea of actors competing. Kennedy thought she was missing the point: annual awards would generate untold amounts of publicity—and money—for the movie business, and maybe raise the prestige of the industry as a whole. He lectured her about the potential of movies to spread American values and sell American goods throughout the world. Kennedy's passion for his subject and his unabashed enjoyment of their conversation made him a fascinating companion. To her surprise, Gloria felt herself drawn toward him.

At the end of the evening, Kennedy told Gloria he wanted to finance her next picture. More than that, he wanted to work closely with her to make it a major success. He was only interested in making an important picture, so the property she had mentioned in passing simply wouldn't do. Even its name—*Rockabye*—sounded insufficiently grand. That was the problem with Hollywood: everybody thought smaller than they should. It was a crime not to make a fortune in the movie business, but you needed a great story and a great director. His great star was sitting across the table from him.

"I felt in my bones that I had just passed a significant evening," Swanson recalled. "I had no doubt in my mind that I had stumbled on the right business partner to straighten out my career." When Swanson felt intuitively that she was on the right track, she seldom hesitated. In Kennedy she met her match: a business partner known for his rapid and decisive action. Over the next few weeks, while her husband and her colleagues out west wondered what she was doing, Gloria conferred with Joe Kennedy, relishing his gimlet-eyed assessments of the movie business and the people in it. She determined to throw in her lot with the man she called "a strange hybrid of banker, film distributor, and university intellectual."[10]

Since Kennedy needed a full picture of her affairs, Gloria authorized his team to examine her books. Almost immediately her secretary Grace

Crossman was on the phone: men in fedoras had arrived and were asking to see the marquise's papers. They looked like gangsters. There was
nothing to worry about, Swanson explained: they were Harvard men.

Though Joe Kennedy's Hollywood experience was of recent vintage, it
was impressive. Called in to help reorganize the troubled FBO studio in
1926, he had bought the company. He then quickly acquired the Keith-
Albee-Orpheum vaudeville chain, with its 700 theaters, and became
associated with Pathé, an American studio with deep roots in France.
Kennedy also had strong connections with David Sarnoff of RCA, who
had developed the Photophone sound system for talking pictures. There
was no telling where he would go next.

Kennedy told Swanson that her financial picture was even worse
than she suspected. Her affairs were rife with irregularities, problems
she would never have had with a proper staff looking after her interests.
He called her board members "deadwood" and said he needed to reorganize her finances from top to bottom.[11] Kennedy told Milton Cohen
much the same thing: Gloria "ha[d] mortgaged her future" and needed
to consider "some method of cleaning up the slate without a serious
loss to her present picture prestige." Though her overhead was too high,
Swanson's "earning power [was] great."[12] He wanted to perform "emergency surgery."[13]

Kennedy told Gloria not to worry: he would take care of everything
when he came out to California in a few weeks. She should relax, enjoy
the holidays, and leave it all to him. He cautioned Swanson to say nothing to anyone about their plans.

Despite her independence, when a powerful man offered Gloria support, she found it—and him—intensely desirable. "This man wanted me
to lean on him—something I had never done in my life," she said. "I had
worked since I was [a teenager]. I was tired and frightened. It was good
to have someone say I'll take care of whatever worriment [you] have.
Henri wanted so much to help, but he was bewildered—and why not,
having been transplanted from a sane, normal life to one of complete
unreality and madness."[14] So with her hopes high and her mouth zipped,
Swanson went back to California to iron out the last details for the premiere of *Sadie Thompson*.

When he arrived in Los Angeles, Kennedy was not alone: he never traveled far without the assistants he called his "four horsemen."[15]
They did make him look a bit like "a movie gangster traveling with
his hoods—only these were hoods with Irish faces and names."[16] The
Boss, as they called Kennedy, relied on their unconditional loyalty and

discretion: Betty Lasky called the horsemen "working-class replicas of the boss" who were "willing to carry his secrets to the grave if necessary."[17] Eddie Moore was closest to the Boss: Teddy Kennedy would be named after him. Moore was "the sweetest of the four scouts," Swanson believed, "and the most sensitive. Everybody loved him."[18] E. B. Derr was a math whiz who could work out complicated problems with the accuracy and speed of a calculating machine. Heavyset Ted O'Leary looked like a bouncer, and quiet Pat Sullivan could have been a New York policeman.

Yet the burly men were happy to get down on the floor and play with Gloria's children. They couldn't do enough for Swanson, who was impressed with their smooth efficiency. When she hurt her knee playing with Gloria and Brother, the horsemen took care of the children, had the cook hold dinner, and got her to the hospital with a minimum of fuss.

They promised the same efficiency in arranging her affairs. Derr began the paperwork to reorganize and rename her company: Gloria Productions would be headquartered in Delaware. Kennedy explained that a dummy corporation made it easier to settle Gloria's bills and put the financing for her next picture in place. Swanson was one of the corporation's presidents and also one of its directors. Her new officers were longtime Kennedy staffers and affiliates, all experienced businessmen.

Kennedy wanted to move forward quickly, not tie up her time and money. This appealed to Swanson: it had taken the better part of a year— and many tiresome meetings—to set up Gloria Swanson Productions. Kennedy chuckled over a telegram that Derr, filing papers in Delaware, sent: "There was never a corporation formed with the speed that this one was formed . . . I have been the busiest cup of tea in New York City . . . If I don't go to jail on this deal, I never will. The rest of the organization are wondering what in hell I am running around for all the time, but what they don't know will never bother them."[19] Derr was proud that not even Joe Schenck knew about their plans until after the corporation had been formed. Secrecy was Kennedy's norm: he preferred that no one outside his circle know his—and now Swanson's—business. He communicated with his staff indirectly, often in code; the horsemen referred to Swanson in writing as "the client." (After Pat Sullivan took Swanson to the train station, he wired Derr, "Bundle left on Florida special tonight.")[20]

Kennedy wanted Gloria to let her staff go since it would reduce her expensive overhead. Besides, he claimed, they had got her into this mess. In early January, Tom Moore's contract was abruptly terminated; Pierre Bedard was fired a few weeks later. Only Gloria's publicist and her personal accountant survived the purge. Kennedy said his large staff would take care of anything she needed: his employees were always looking for ways to curry favor with him. Besides, Gloria could call on the horsemen anytime. Once she decided to trust her business concerns to Kennedy, Swanson did so fully. She was nonetheless dismayed to receive a telegram from Milton Cohen, who had fallen under Kennedy's axe. "Regret your attitude exceedingly," Cohen wrote. "Wish always to be your friend but never your lawyer[.] Please arrange immediately for other counsel."[21] Swanson said, "I felt as though I'd been slapped," but quickly rationalized the lawyer's dismissal, reminding herself that Cohen had helped Herbert Somborn accuse her of promiscuous adultery. He was upset because he had been "kicked off the gravy grain," just as Kennedy's men said her staffers would be.[22]

Pierre Bedard also felt unjustly treated. He particularly resented being given no warning: "After your assurances that my position with you was secure . . . this comes as a distinct surprise. [I] cannot believe that after our close association and friendship you would treat me with less consideration than the most menial employee."[23] If Swanson had the queasy feeling that she had behaved badly, she ignored it.

Kennedy wasted precious little time on those he determined were out. When he took over the KAO theater chain, he flattened Edward Albee, company founder and elder statesman of vaudeville, when Albee dared make a suggestion. Kennedy's words went beyond brusque: "Didn't you know, Ed? You're washed up. You're through."[24] A performer who worked with Kennedy remembered him as "the toughest kind of businessman, the kind that scares me. . . . Sam Goldwyn, Louis B. Mayer, Jack Warner and Harry Cohn were pussycats compared to Joe Kennedy."[25]

Kennedy had a bitter pill for Gloria as well: he wanted to settle all her outstanding debts by selling rights to both *The Love of Sunya* and *Sadie Thompson* to Art Cinema. Given the high expectations for *Sadie*, Joe Schenck was likely to find this offer attractive. Kennedy proposed to suggest it after *Sadie*'s New York opening but before the picture faced the censors in the smaller markets. Since Kennedy calculated that *Sadie* needed to make over a million dollars' profit for Swanson to break even, this could be a good deal for her. Gloria had resisted giving up a share in *Sunya* to repay her debts earlier, but relinquishing *Sadie* was even harder: more of her heart and spirit was in it. However, no one could predict how much money the picture would make, and Swanson was tired of gambling. With one stroke of the pen she relinquished all rights to her first two independent films. She would put her trust in Joe Kennedy.

Even more significant was Swanson's signature on a power of attorney for Derr giving him authority to make decisions for the corporation. Yet as soon as Swanson signed, she felt a terrific sense of relief. There would be no more complicated, nitpicking negotiations about distribution percentages or deferred salaries; how well her picture was doing in Sweden or Czechoslovakia or Argentina would no longer be her daily concern. Kennedy and his horsemen would streamline her company and run it as it ought to be run. She was free to concentrate on what she knew best: making pictures.

Then Kennedy offered what Gloria had wanted when she joined UA: a job for Henri. As European director of Pathé, he would commute between California and Paris on company business. Swanson was thrilled: "It would make him distinctly his own man. . . . Henri would no longer be on salary with me in some vague position with no real authority." For Kennedy it undoubtedly had another attraction: he had fallen hard for Swanson and was happy to send her dashing war-hero husband far away. "In a few brief sessions," Swanson claimed, "we had rearranged the world."[26]

To celebrate their collaboration and inaugurate their partnership, Kennedy invited Gloria and Henri to join him on vacation in Palm Beach. En route to Florida in January 1928, Swanson recognized her mounting excitement about seeing Joe again. She knew he had "a schoolboy crush" on her, yet she had also learned that Kennedy had an "overpowering personality" and disliked anything obstructing his desires.[27] He had Craney Gartz's passion and volatility and Cecil DeMille's authority and ambition. Both were strong, charismatic men who knew what they wanted and tolerated little interference; both had been powerfully attractive to Swanson.

On their arrival, Henri was claiming their baggage when Kennedy came barreling into Swanson's compartment—"like a cyclone," she said. "He pushed me back into the drawing room, said a few excited words, and kissed me twice. Just as quickly he released me."[28] When Kennedy straightened up, he bumped into an overhead bin, smacking his head. His glasses fell to the floor, and he knelt to grope for them. When he came up, the knees of his white trousers were stained, and Swanson's lipstick was smeared all over his face. Swanson cracked up, and Kennedy laughed, too. This Keystone moment was anything but funny, however: Henri was a few feet away while Joe Kennedy was telling Gloria he had missed her. Brought face to face with her desire for him, she said she had missed him, too. Then Kennedy wiped the lipstick off his collar. When he greeted her husband, he seemed perfectly serene.

Kennedy filled Gloria's hotel suite with orchids. He sent endless corsages until she finally told him that she always—and only—carried a single fresh carnation. (He immediately began wearing one in his boutonniere.) Eager to show his guests off to Palm Beach society, Joe arranged parties and dinners and excursions. This was old hat for Gloria and Henri, but she got a new kick out of it whenever she saw her partner's face: "Joe Kennedy beamed as if he were P. T. Barnum presenting Lavinia and Tom Thumb or a pair of unicorns." Swanson found Joe's pride in his ability to crack the upper echelons of privilege endearing; he clearly took pleasure in being part of a social scene from which his Irish ancestors would have been barred. "About his background and his religion he made no apologies whatsoever, and I admired him tremendously for that."[29]

In Palm Beach, Swanson's flirtation with Joe Kennedy became serious. The four horsemen invited Henri and Gloria to go deep-sea fishing, and Gloria begged off to go shopping. She was relaxing in her suite when Kennedy appeared at the door: "He just stood there, in his white flannels and his argyle sweater and his two-toned shoes, staring at me for a full minute or more, before he entered the room and closed the door behind him. He moved so quickly that his mouth was on mine before either of us could speak. With one hand he held the back of my head, with the other he stroked my body and pulled at my kimono. He kept insisting in a drawn-out moan, 'No longer, no longer. Now.' He was like a roped horse, rough, arduous, racing to be free. After a hasty climax he lay beside me, stroking my hair. Apart from his guilty, passionate mutterings, he had still said nothing cogent. I had said nothing at all. Since his kiss on the train, I had known this would happen. And I knew, as we lay there, that it would go on."[30]

Kennedy's four shadows now began shadowing Henri, who learned more about deep-sea fishing than he ever wanted to know. Swanson felt confused, guilty, and anxious not to hurt her husband; she also felt "completely wrapped up in this wild man's passion and the world he represented."[31] Thus began a classic bedroom farce. When the husband was onstage, the lover moved off—and vice versa. In late February, Henri left for France to begin his duties at Pathé; Kennedy came out to Hollywood on business. When Henri was due back in California, Kennedy arranged to be in New York or Boston. This dance went on for months.

With each of Henri's voyages, stories of trouble in Swanson's marriage surfaced. Henri told reporters he stayed away just long enough to get the divorce rumors started, so he could have the pleasure of denying them.[32] Now, however, there was a disturbing undercurrent to the stories: they were true. In late March, Joe gave Gloria a birthday party. Sport Ward made a funny Mount Rushmore-style composite picture of her first three husbands to mark the occasion. Wally, Herbert, and Henri made an odd trio, but another monumental figure in Swanson's life was not pictured.

By March, Kennedy had rejected all the properties Swanson was considering for her next picture. He was intrigued, however, by the prospect of working with a director many considered an authentic genius. An Austrian immigrant who had been in Hollywood since 1914, Erich von Stroheim made expensive, ambitious pictures. He often acted in them, his portrayals of villains so finely drawn that he was billed as "The Man You Love to Hate." Stroheim's unstinting perfectionism routinely made trouble for him. He was famous for going over budget in the name of getting every detail right and was always having his films yanked away because they were too long. When Stroheim was screening a long cut of *The Merry Widow* for Irving Thalberg at M-G-M, he told the producer that one character had a foot fetish. "And you have a footage fetish!" Thalberg replied.[33]

No one today can say whether Stroheim's masterpiece *Greed* was originally eight-and-a-half or nine hours, but even the cut version preserves Stroheim's unflinching, relentless examination of the grotesque and depraved. One critic explained, "He has one simple rule for direction. Take a close look at the world, keep on doing so, and in the end it will lay bare for you all its cruelty and its ugliness."[34]

If this sounds as far from a Gloria Swanson production as might be imagined, consider that Stroheim was equally famous for devising erotic, exotic plots performed on expensively dressed sets. His stories of seduction and betrayal featured aristocrats at play; for *Foolish Wives*, he reproduced Monte Carlo's main square in minute, loving detail. Stroheim's pictures reliably drew public attention, even if they did not always make pots of money. Universal decided to make his excesses work for the company, advertising *Foolish Wives* by declaring, "He's going to make you hate him! Even if it takes a million dollars of our money to do it!" As one colleague said, "Genius flows [from Stroheim] like water from a well. Perhaps charged water, fizzing and hissing out of a siphon bottle, would be a better description."[35]

Such was Stroheim, the director on whom Kennedy set his sights. The trio met on Catalina in March, and Swanson found Stroheim a paradox: he was "gracious and charming but at the same time aloof and conceited."[36] He held court magisterially but also praised *Madame Sans-Gêne*, sympathizing when Swanson told him Paramount had ruined the American cut of the film: Paramount was even now doing the same thing to *The Wedding March*. Then he spun a tale for Gloria and Joe that made them decide on the spot that Stroheim should direct Swanson's next picture.

The Swamp told the story of an orphaned convent girl, Patricia Kelly, and her dramatic changes of fortune. After a chance meeting, a prince romances the feisty Kelly, kidnapping her for a midnight supper before he reluctantly accepts an arranged marriage with the (mad) queen. When his enraged fiancée discovers them, she whips Kelly from the palace and throws the prince in jail. Then Kelly is unexpectedly summoned to the deathbed of her aunt, who runs a dance hall in German East Africa. The aunt promises Kelly's hand in marriage to a rich old man; the wedding ceremony is performed as the aunt receives last rites. Kelly becomes an infamous saloonkeeper but holds herself aloof from her husband. At last her prince finds her and marries her.

Stroheim, who wrote his own screenplays, had a reputation as an orator who "could argue a bone out of a bulldog's mouth."[37] The bone he sought from Kennedy and Swanson was full control over a film that would be expensive and complex to shoot. The picture would have two equal halves: the scenes of Kelly's innocent romance with the prince to be echoed by the African scenes, in which she comes of age in the rough-and-tumble dance hall. The happy ending would make her Queen Kelly.

There was no doubt that the picture would be important; everything Stroheim did was important. Swanson recalled, "The strange story reminded me of nothing I had ever heard before, and . . . it was richly cinematic from beginning to end. Moreover, it was flattering and intriguing to sit and listen to a story imagined especially for you by a major artist."[38] She had a few reservations: she wondered whether audiences would accept her—a woman heading for thirty—as a schoolgirl. She also knew Stroheim's reputation as a spendthrift and perfectionist. Nonetheless, she had a feeling that working with Stroheim would change her life. Gloria looked at her partner: Kennedy was beaming, ready to jump in with both feet.[39] There was champagne all around.

When they were in private, Swanson voiced her concerns to Kennedy. He waved them aside; he intended to hire two producers to keep Stroheim in line. Bill Le Baron and Ben Glazer would be his watchdogs when Kennedy's other business kept him away. She shouldn't worry about a thing, he said. She should "just come on the set looking pretty."[40]

Gloria felt disinclined to worry. It was luxurious to rely on another's judgment, even though—she was happy to see—her own had been correct about *Sadie Thompson*. The film opened to exceptional reviews, singling Swanson out for praise. The *New York Times* called her performance "an outstanding achievement."[41] The *Washington Post* agreed: "She etches in bold and fiery strokes a character that will rank among the most skillfully limned ever created for the camera."[42] "It isn't so often we're treated to a swell star in a picture worthy of her," *Screenland* declared.[43]

Joe Schenck accepted Kennedy's offer, and Art Cinema acquired both *Sadie* and *Sunya*. Swanson was relieved at not having to follow the box office figures, not having to fret about whether UA was publicizing her pictures adequately or selling them at high enough rates. She had enjoyed refusing Joe Schenck's finance offer, though UA was pressing her about her next project. (Her schedule had called for two pictures per year.) She was happy to turn those headaches over to Joe Kennedy.

Kennedy was pressuring Gloria to have her son Joseph baptized, and Lois Wilson, another Catholic, backed him. Swanson had confided in Lois about her affair, telling Lois that Kennedy wanted to stand godfather to the boy. Henri was a Catholic, though not an observant one, and he approved, too. Swanson's own religious convictions were rather vague and abstract, but she consented and Brother was baptized, adopting his godfather's middle name as well. Joseph Patrick Swanson would be persistently but wrongly identified as the son of Joseph Patrick Kennedy. For her sins, Lois Wilson spent years defending Gloria from the charge that she had borne Kennedy's illegitimate child.

One immediate benefit of Swanson's hiatus from producing was time with her children. Gloria was now almost eight and loved to read; Joseph was a happy little fellow of six. They were in the capable hands of "Sammy," their beloved governess, but Swanson knew she had missed most of their infancy. They were back in residence at 904, and Gloria remembered these months as a precious family time. Henri, however, was away for long stretches in France, learning his new job.

Joe Kennedy had taken a house with a tennis court a few blocks away on Rodeo Drive—a clubhouse, really, with his assistants in residence and business conducted at all hours. In May, they finally signed a contract with Stroheim, who would earn $25,000 for writing *The Swamp* and $50,000 for directing. He could be terminated immediately if he fell behind schedule or went over budget.

Swanson celebrated with a trip to New York. At Brentano's bookstore she picked up *Psychoanalysis and Love*, *Sex and the Love Light*, and Ovid's classic manual on seduction, *The Art of Love.*[44] It seems unlikely she was planning new ways to seduce her husband, who was on his way back from Paris. Gloria's feelings toward Henri now seemed more prosaic than passionate: he was "a thoroughly unexceptional man whom I had no wish to divorce."[45]

Perhaps she was considering the sexual instruction of her current lover: Kennedy was not known as a man who took the art of love seriously. Though Doris Kearns Goodwin calls this relationship Kennedy's "first fully sustained affair," Laurence Leamer claims that "Joe approached sex like fast food, bolting it down and then getting on with the rest of the day."[46] However, Swanson was not a run-of-the-mill conquest. Moreover, she was a woman with a strong sex drive and an unembarrassed approach to satisfying her appetites.

A certain amount of decorum was necessary, since neither Kennedy nor Swanson wanted to disrupt their households. George Cukor claimed that all Hollywood knew of the affair: "That doesn't mean they went around walking openly on the boulevards holding hands or linking arms . . . but if anyone saw the look on Joe's face when he was with Gloria, it was clear that he was infatuated."[47] "Unlike Rose," says Goodwin, "[Gloria] was fascinated by the smallest details of his business dealings, and . . . she was able to ask questions that engaged his mind and activated his talent. At the same time, the warmth of their affair was kindled by Gloria's keen sense of humor, merry wit and sharp tongue."[48]

How and when Rose Kennedy learned of her husband's infidelity has prompted a great deal of speculation. In any case, she pointedly ignored her husband's liaison, a posture made simpler because she and Swanson were thousands of miles apart. In February, however, a few weeks after Gloria and Joe began their affair in Florida, Swanson sent a large bouquet of flowers to Rose in Boston, offering congratulations on the birth of baby Jean. Partly because Joe insisted on bringing his wife and his mistress together, Rose's deliberate blindness became her practiced routine.

When Henri returned from France in May, he seemed like another man—happier, more invigorated, more purposeful. At first Swanson thought his new job was responsible for the change. Then one night Henri was with Charlie Chaplin at a Hollywood nightspot when an explosion injured several people, one critically. It was a deliberate act of sabotage: the police arrested a Russian expatriate for placing incendiary devices around the club.

Then another bombshell hit. News reports revealed that the gorgeous young actress Lili Damita was the guest of honor in Henri's party that night. A few months earlier, Kennedy had urged Henri to see if he could tempt Damita into taking up a Hollywood career.[49] The rumors flew that Henri had tempted Damita right into his bed. Swanson could hardly reproach her husband, given her own infidelity. Henri had said nothing to her about Joe Kennedy "out of a cultivated European good sense to let such affairs run their course." However, they were both "relieved" when Henri left again almost immediately for Paris. They parted "in the spirit of a couple who had been married thirty-five years instead of three and a half."[50]

Through the summer of 1928 Kennedy's house was "buzzing" with casting and design plans for *The Swamp*.[51] Will Hays had approved the story idea, the script was progressing, and sets were going up on the rented FBO lot. A British newcomer to Hollywood became their leading man. Though Walter Byron did not have much of a public profile, Stroheim often saved the spark for his villains—or in this case, Swanson hoped, for his heroine. (She thought matinee idol Jack Gilbert was dull before Stroheim took him in hand for *The Merry Widow*; now Gilbert was a firebrand.)

The Swamp was not a clotheshorse role for Swanson. Her costume for the first half of the picture consisted of a school uniform and a long white nightgown with the prince's jacket worn over it. At least Stroheim's infamous obsession with the number of buttons on every military uniform would not affect her production, though she did have to manage a wig with two long braids. If the costumes were simple, the sets were anything but: the queen's palace was full of marble, tile, crystal chandeliers, polished wood, paintings, and statuary.

Stroheim was committed to a tight sixteen-week shooting schedule and was agreeable about the few changes the producers requested. (First up was renaming the picture: *The Swamp* became *Queen Kelly*.) He told reporters that he had "changed his attitude" about filmmaking: "I am more philosophical . . . I am, so to speak, aged in wood, mellower."[52] Not everyone was so sanguine. When Kennedy told Louis B. Mayer that he had engaged Stroheim to direct, Mayer replied cautiously, "At least, if you weather the storm, you will have something worth talking about."[53] Swanson's staff members were excited: "We should have a picture as good, if not better, than *Sadie Thompson*. The combination of Miss Swanson and von Stroheim is an ACE."[54]

Though preparations for *Queen Kelly* were moving slowly, Gloria remained unworried. She had taken $65,000 in advances on her salary by July but wasn't looking too closely at the papers she was occasionally asked to sign: "I was so happy to be free of responsibility that I never questioned anything resembling money." She assumed the financing Kennedy arranged for *Queen Kelly* was "close to or better than the deal he thought I should accept from Schenck. . . . I find it impossible to discuss money matters with someone [when] you are emotionally involved—I trusted him completely and . . . I didn't want to come out of this most comfortable dream state."[55]

Hollywood loved movies showing how fame went to actors' heads, and that summer filmgoers were laughing at the story of Peggy Pepper, a slapstick comedienne who renames herself "Patricia Pepoire" once she becomes a movie star. King Vidor's picture took a playful swipe at Gloria Swanson, the comic-turned-marquise—and as she had done with Mickey Neilan's similar film, Swanson averted her majestic gaze and waited until *Show People* went away.

In September, Gloria attended a very exclusive party at Pickfair for Prince George of Kent, the youngest son of King George V. Mary and Doug hosted a formal dinner for fifteen with dancing for one hundred afterwards. According to Robert Windeler, "Nobody could compete with Mary . . . . [She] had a solid gold dinner service, a footman behind every chair and crystal placecard holders." The only problem was that Mary's parties were, to Gloria's thinking, "deadly."[56] The prince agreed: he loved the high life and couldn't even get a drink at Pickfair. He asked Gloria if they could slip away so he could see more of the famous movie colony. He pinched Gloria's shoulder every time they danced past someone he wanted to invite along—Chaplin, Aileen Pringle, and half a dozen others received the royal nod. Swanson fibbed to Mary that she was expecting a call from Henri in France. One by one they sneaked away from the most important party of the summer.

They filled the car with champagne from Gloria's private stash and drove out to the Plantation Club, where they danced and drank until 3:00 a.m. Then Swanson brought the group, plus several musicians, back to her house. They roused her English butler and her English cook so they could meet the prince, woke Gloria's friends Virginia Bowker and Lois Wilson, and partied until dawn. The band played, everyone sang, Chaplin performed, and Gloria's staff served an impromptu breakfast as the sun rose. When the papers carried reports of their late-night shenanigans, Kennedy told Gloria how much he regretted being out of town.

However, poaching her royal guest probably did nothing to soften Mary Pickford's antipathy toward her UA partner.

The big surprise of the summer came from an unexpected source: Gloria's mother. Adelaide wrote in August, explaining that after "a sweet romance," she had accepted a proposal of marriage from Charles Woodruff, a Chicago musician. The couple had been secretly married since May. "I hope darling you will forgive me for not telling you sooner and understand my position. I know the thing that will concern you most is my happiness and *truly* Gloria I am extremely happy. . . . Remember you are still my little girl."[57] Everyone else in the family already knew about the marriage.

Why Adelaide kept this news from her daughter is a mystery. Perhaps she thought Gloria would disapprove; maybe she wanted some independence from the "little girl" who paid her bills. Swanson had supported her mother for years, supplementing Addie's investment income and paying her bills when she traveled. She had defended her mother when Matthew Burns's family challenged his will and when Addie's disastrous liaison with her young blackmailer soured. Since she could not bear Gloria's "three-ring circus" for long, Swanson had rented a separate house for her mother near Crescent Drive.[58] Addie had not stayed long, however, before departing for Chicago, where she met and married Mr. Woodruff. She clearly preferred to have her own home, far from the spotlight Gloria commanded but could seldom escape. Her globe-trotting daughter was always in the headlines, always being mobbed and pursued. Adelaide would remain a distant, elusive figure, someone for whom Gloria yearned but whose love she never seemed certain of possessing. Addie quickly tired of Gloria and did not seem to mind that her daughter knew it.

In late September, Stroheim had his massive script for *Queen Kelly* delivered to Kennedy on a silver platter held high by Hollywood extras dressed as Nubian slaves in lion skins.[59] To be on the safe side, Kennedy asked Robert E. Sherwood, movie critic for *Life* magazine, to assess the script, then told Gloria Sherwood had pronounced it "the best film story ever written."[60] (Sherwood's imprimatur was not easy to come by: he called Stroheim "a genius . . . badly in need of a stopwatch" in his review of *Greed*.)[61] Swanson simply declared it "the biggest script I'd ever seen."[62] With Stroheim's cooperation, the producers Kennedy had hired reduced it from 735 scenes to a still-lengthy 510. So far it seemed like Kennedy's men could handle Stroheim. Work continued on the elaborate sets, with publicity capitalizing on Stroheim's reputation for both opulence and accuracy. Von was said to be importing African animals for several scenes: they had a more authentically wild spirit.

The merger of FBO with RKO gave Joe Kennedy access to the newest sound recording technology. Despite the expense, he was beginning to wonder whether *Queen Kelly* should not be a talkie. It would mean preparing two different versions, since many theaters were not yet equipped to show sound pictures. There would be all kinds of unexpected adjustments. Paramount had recently performed a sound test using a gown from one of Swanson's old pictures. The dress was hung with garlands of pearls, and their rustling sounded like "a terrific Indiana hailstorm."[63] Sets would have to be doctored or duplicated, and Swanson would need a dialogue coach, as was now de rigueur for any star speaking on camera.

They prepared, then held back, publicity releases announcing that *Queen Kelly* would be "the first complete UA talkie."[64] Then they considered making a part-sound film and asked Stroheim to place sound cues in the script so that synthetic sound (a kind of dubbing) could be added after shooting. Stroheim had planned for a silent picture and was justifiably skeptical about sound. He remembered Kennedy predicting, however, that audiences would flock to sound pictures, preferring them over silent films, however artfully made: "His exact words to me were: 'Von, the lousiest sound film will be better than the best silent film.'"[65] Despite his misgivings, Stroheim obligingly signed a new contract pledging to direct sound sequences should the producer determine they were necessary.[66] Though sound would add appreciably to *Queen Kelly*'s budget, they were starting to think in terms of how and when—rather than whether—to add it to the picture.

With preparations for shooting nearing completion, Kennedy prevailed upon Swanson to come east for a visit. The cross-country trip was a delightful family vacation; the children "had grown up into enjoyable company at last."[67] Joseph was enchanted by the train, pretending to be the conductor and the engineer by turns. Gloria, who had been sick with mumps over the summer, pored over her favorite books, as blissfully unconscious of time passing as her mother was when she was reading. Swanson blessed Joe Kennedy once again for the respite that allowed her time with her children. She was unwilling, however, to visit the Kennedys' home in Riverdale, though she let Gloria and Brother attend the children's Halloween party without her. When they returned, they were excited about their new friends. Gloria said Jack Kennedy wanted to know about her father Herbert Somborn, who owned the Brown Derby, "because Tom Mix goes to his restaurant for lunch."[68]

Swanson was not sure what to make of Kennedy's willingness to mix their two families. He also seemed unconcerned about their being seen out on the town together: they were "business associates." She explained carefully that "business is done in the daytime if both associates are married," though Sport Ward served as their unofficial chaperon. According to Swanson, Kennedy claimed he had been "faithful" to her: "There had been no Kennedy baby that year." Joe told Gloria that "what he wanted more than anything . . . was for us to have a child." Stunned, Swanson threatened to leave for California on the spot if Joe mentioned the idea again: such an escapade would end her career. "After that he was a lamb," she said.[69]

Another strange thing about this affair was that Gloria's husband worked for her lover, which was managed with a naturalness that seemed positively European. Henri and Joe were regular correspondents, and their exchanges have a surprisingly confidential flavor. When Henri was away in France, Kennedy advised him about Gloria's state of mind. At the end of October, Joe asked Henri not to disturb his wife as she prepared to go before the cameras at last: "Everything here perfectly okey [sic] far as you concerned have no anxiety and don't upset her because we now almost three months late."[70]

"Three months" was putting it mildly: *Sadie Thompson* had been finished for almost a year when the cameras began turning on *Queen Kelly*. The trade press had noted Swanson's absence from the screen: "Her 1928 record rests upon *Sadie Thompson*, a good effort and a much talked-about one. But Miss Swanson can not afford to let the months roll by without pictures."[71] (During her time off, on a dare, she had visited several studios disguised as a Hollywood hopeful looking for work. No one recognized her.) Now Swanson was rested, eager to work with Stroheim, and determined to stay out of the producer's job.

Shooting began November 1, and they quickly captured three important sequences. It was an auspicious start: "Those first rushes were breath-taking," Swanson recalled. "Every scene was alive with glowing light play and palpable texture. You could almost smell the thin Havana cigars and taste the Viennese coffee and feel the dew on the grass. Each image seemed richer and more dazzling than the one before."[72]

This was not hyperbole: *Queen Kelly* was absolutely gorgeous, one of the high-water marks of the silent era. Swanson had never appeared more radiant, and cameraman Paul Ivano's proficiency with lighting immediately put to rest any question of her being too old for the part. (Gloria said Stroheim "stripped a dozen years off" her.) Von was an

inspiring director, and on his lips "Madame la Marquise" sounded natural, not the jokey title Allan Dwan had made it. He might ask Swanson
to repeat an action so many times she lost count, but the dailies "looked
like paintings created by a master of a girl I didn't quite know."[73]

However, Stroheim ridiculed and belittled those who did not meet
his exacting standards. "Poor Seena Owen," as she became known on
set, had the unenviable part of the mad queen. Her first appearance was
daring: stretched out naked on a bed, she was covered only by a large
white cat. Stroheim made Owen repeat a few simple actions again and
again. "After a couple of hours," assistant cameraman William Margulies
recalled, "the cat started scratching her."[74] By this time they had been
working almost twenty-four hours.

Stroheim had no qualms about breaking an actress down to reach
the truth in a performance: "I must undermine this surface of acquired
false technique and bring out the real feeling that is like a kernel beneath a girl's superficial charm. . . . I crush them, beat them down with
satire, with harsh words, with scorn. They are ready to quit. Then I get
at the real soul and guide its natural unfoldment."[75] Since Swanson was
Stroheim's boss, however, he could not employ his usual methods.

In fact, she often intervened in Stroheim's temper tantrums. Von fired
Paul Ivano repeatedly ("four times a day," Ivano said), and Swanson rehired him just as often. Once, Margulies said, Swanson berated Stroheim
the same way he lit into others: "'So, you sonofabitch, I wait ten years to
find a cameraman to photograph me and you fire him.' She says, 'You're
fired.' And [Stroheim] walked off the set. About a half hour later they all
come back with love and kisses."[76] None of this drama was new to Ivano,
who had collapsed of heat exhaustion during the brutal Death Valley
shoot for *Greed*. Yet when he wasn't being the man you loved to hate,
Stroheim was "one of Hollywood's most genial souls."[77]

A true obsessive, Von had to be reminded to eat and sleep. After an
all-night session, when he called for one more set-up, Margulies told
the director off: "I said, 'You go to hell. It's seven o'clock Sunday morning. I'm going home.' So he said, 'Okay, let's go home.'" ("Home" for
Stroheim during the shoot was Madame Frances', a nearby brothel.)[78]
The cast and crew snatched what rest they could. The flu flattened a
good number of them, its spread exacerbated by exhaustion. Swanson
moved into her dressing room on the lot for the duration. Nonetheless,
the film began to fall farther and farther behind schedule.

They went into overtime most days, with long periods devoted to relatively insignificant goals—not that Stroheim saw them that way. "About

two weeks ago," he complained to a coworker, "when we went over the plans of the lower palace hallway I told you that I did not like the crest center landing in a molding, because it looked to me wrong. I just discovered that the frame is still there for the crest. Please change it. I want the crest as relief against wall without any frame. Have this changed before it is too late."[79] No doubt because he had run into schedule problems on other films, Stroheim kept detailed records chronicling factors beyond his control or work not done to his specifications. He often stopped the production until things were put right. Many of these delays were for background details which would scarcely be glimpsed on screen.

As the weeks wore on, Swanson wondered where Kennedy's watchdog producers were. They were occupied elsewhere: Le Baron had new duties at RKO, and Kennedy himself had appointed Glazer head of production at Pathé. Both gave only intermittent attention to *Queen Kelly*. "As producers," says Richard Koszarski, "they were the least intrusive pair von Stroheim ever had to deal with."[80]

Despite her growing unease, Swanson felt she was in the hands of a real artist: "He was so painstaking and slow that I would lose all sense of time, hypnotized by the man's relentless perfectionism. A scene that Allan Dwan or Raoul Walsh would have wrapped up in an hour might take Von Stroheim all day, fondling and dawdling over the tiniest minutiae . . . But his exactitude always paid off in the rushes, and it was a course in the art of filmmaking to hear him defend his choices and explain his reasons—rare occasions, to be sure, for in general he considered himself to be his own best audience and only critic."[81] Swanson's words echo those of many of Stroheim's colleagues: he demanded and got the best they had to offer.

When Kennedy arrived from New York several weeks into production, he was surprised at the cast and crew's exhaustion. He put a stop to the overtime but overlooked the enormous amount of film being shot and the emphasis on small details. Confident that Stroheim was making their important picture, he told Gloria not to worry and left again for the East Coast.

They tried to condense the script, scrapping some scenes and locations and dismantling partly constructed sets. By mid-December, Swanson estimated it would take another three or four months of shooting—at $5,000 a day—to finish the picture. This was way in excess of the original budget, even without the addition of sound, which was still expected as an extra cost. Worse, she realized that Stroheim was quietly adding back scenes they had eliminated earlier. Kennedy's assistant, E. B. Derr, came on board, wiring the Boss that *Queen Kelly* was "a picture and a half and Von knows it. He must cut four or five reels . . . and every [cut] suggested he calls milestones. I wish he had one around his neck."[82] Though Stroheim seemed tractable enough early in the production, he was returning to his old habits.

Worse, when Derr and Glazer looked at Stroheim's plans for the African scenes, they came to an alarming conclusion: the picture was "highly censorable." The scene of Kelly's arrival at her aunt's African nightclub—aptly named The Swamp—was full of "bawdy details of drinking, gambling, dancing, and fighting." Stroheim had shown white women dancing with black men, white and black solders fighting over prostitutes, and men dancing cheek to cheek, all of which was prohibited. Glazer wanted Stroheim to "confine himself to the minimum of footage and the minimum of ribaldry."[83] They had a dangerously long picture that was likely to go over budget—and if *Queen Kelly* couldn't get past the Hays Office, they had no picture at all.

The European scenes were lovely, but Gloria wondered if there had not been a worm in the apple from the beginning. On practically the first day of filming, they had shot a scene she thought was "typical light Von Stroheim decadence, of the sweet, harmless, titillating sort."[84] Kelly, walking in the park with her classmates, meets the prince out riding with his men. When the elastic in her pantaloons gives out and they slide to the ground, everyone laughs, and the spirited Kelly picks up her bloomers and throws them at the prince. He pretends to pocket them, before ordering the soldiers to turn about face and tossing the panties back to Kelly.

Swanson had learned that after she left the set, Stroheim directed Walter Byron to pick up Kelly's pantaloons and sniff them before putting them in his pocket. She was appalled: "The idea of putting such an act into a film was . . . unthinkable."[85] At the time she said nothing, under the injunction to worry only about her own part. Now she knew she had been right to be concerned. The questionable scenes had been in the script, but she had relied on Stroheim to exercise good judgment—to do voluntarily what a full-time producer would have forced him to do. In Stroheim's hands, The Swamp had unquestionably become a brothel, and the playfulness of the exchange with Kelly's panties had gone beyond suggestive.

Since it was in her best interests to hide the production's dirty linen, Swanson issued a publicity statement describing the "excellent progress" they were making: "He truly is the great Von Stroheim and I am thankful it has been made possible for him to direct this picture."[86] Stroheim returned the compliment: the star was doing "magnificent work" and was "absolutely marvelous."[87]

Production halted for a week over Christmas, and Gloria was determined to get back some of her depleted strength. Henri was home, and with Joe Kennedy on the East Coast, they had "a happy, loving time."[88] Swanson said, "I can understand how someone can develop a split personality. When I was involved in my work . . . I wanted [Joe's] broad shoulder by my side. I couldn't possibly seek Henry's advice or exchange ideas with him—I felt protected by Joseph." Yet she could also say truthfully, "I loved Henry. I wanted to be in his arms."[89]

There was a surprise waiting for her when work resumed on January 2. During the break the company had moved to the Pathé lot, where Kennedy had a lavish, well-appointed bungalow built as a Christmas present for Gloria. It had a large living room with a grand piano. (The latest plan was for her to sing near the end of the picture, and Kennedy had hired Irving Berlin to compose two songs. Swanson was rehearsing with Mario Marafioti, Caruso's vocal coach.) Her bungalow also had a full kitchen, a large bedroom "with a black and silver bed on a mezzanine floor," a bathroom with a black tub, a dressing room, and a fitting room.[90] It was as big as Marion Davies's—the one nicknamed "The Trianon" after Marie Antoinette's palatial playhouse—with a secluded entrance that bypassed the main studio gate. (Unbeknownst to Swanson, it also had a bugging device pinned up in the ceiling.)[91]

With a $19,000 price tag, the bungalow was an expensive gift. Gloria was delighted and didn't ask any questions: "I could only surmise that Joe Kennedy was starting to do very well for himself in the movie business. And that he loved me."[92]

When they began shooting the African scenes, however, Swanson's remaining confidence in Stroheim vanished. The director intended the second half of the picture to be the reverse of the first: where the European scenes were glamorous and polished, those set in Africa were bestial and rough. Stroheim later claimed the European scenes were only "the prologue to the actual story which was laid in Africa."[93] What seemed alarming in the script was even worse on screen: the Africa of Stroheim's imagination was a place of teeming, heaving, poisonous decay. Swanson could not imagine how it would get past the censors, nor how her audience would receive her in the role of a convent girl who—it was now clear—became the de facto madam of a low-class brothel.

They had moved far away from the initial conception with which Stroheim had wooed her and Kennedy. Then he had described Kelly as "a beautiful young creature of Irish extraction, gorgeous and graceful as a peacock, but cold, calm, calculating and mercenary. Most of the time she has all the grace, charm, haughtiness and deportment of a born aristocrat, but on provocation she flies into the most unreasonable rage."[94] That Kelly was a character Swanson understood, but the one Stroheim intended to put onscreen was a different matter entirely. Feeling out of control and trapped by the way the film—her film—was going, she complained to Kennedy. Joe sent Gloria to see Cecil DeMille, who managed to make her feel calm and capable. Afterwards she wired Kennedy in New York: "DeMille inspired confidence and courage. Watch my smoke."[95]

The peace would be short-lived, although stories of what actually happened on the set differ. Swanson's version put her squarely at the center of the drama. She claimed her breaking point came during the filming of Kelly's wedding sequence. The young girl was being married, against her will, to an old man. As Swanson described it, Stroheim "had turned [Tully Marshall's character] into a leering, slobbering, repulsive cripple. Mr. Marshall was playing the part to the hilt, as a sort of demented, twitchy lecher in a greasy suit . . . Mr. von Stroheim began instructing Mr. Marshall, in his usual painstaking fashion, how to dribble tobacco juice onto my hand while he was putting on the wedding ring. It was early morning, I had just eaten breakfast, and my stomach turned. I became nauseated and furious at the same time."[96]

Swanson walked off the set and did not return. She called Joe Kennedy in New York and asked him to come out to California, pronto. *Queen Kelly* ground to a halt while Swanson waited for her white knight to rescue her once again.

CHAPTER 14

People Will Talk

WHEN SWANSON WALKED OFF THE SET OF *QUEEN KELLY* IN JANUARY 1929, she had already spent more than $600,000 on Stroheim's vertiginous vision of a convent girl's coming of age. Swanson, however, was not a schoolgirl but a veteran performer and producer with almost fifteen years' experience in the business. She shut down an expensive picture because, finally, she trusted her own judgment. She knew the film would be unacceptable to the censors and her fans, and she was unwilling to spend more time and money on a project she herself found objectionable. *Queen Kelly* would ultimately be an important chapter in the real-world education of its star.

After Gloria's distress call, Joe Kennedy engaged a consultant to review the footage. Eugene Walter's assessment was lengthy and scalding: "In an attempt to be bizarre and unusual . . . the director has been vulgar, gross, and fantastically impossible . . . He has utterly lost every element of human, natural characterizations." There were serious problems with story construction throughout: the plot was clumsy, implausible, and "deadly monotonous." Walter found nothing to like in any of the main characters, and as a star vehicle it was unacceptable. Swanson's character was "negative, retreating, passive and at no time does one single, solitary thing which would show any evidence of strength, or individuality, of charm . . . Any third class leading woman could play the part." Stroheim had made Kelly "either the most exasperating sap or a potential prostitute." Then, too, "the ethics of a convent girl . . . living off the earnings of prostitutes and running a house of ill fame, are at least questionable."[1]

Then Walter saw the African scenes:

Here language fails me. Outside of the clumsiest and most unbelievable expedients for telling the story, we have this revolting spectacle of the Madam of [the] whore-house on her deathbed . . . being given the last rites by a shiny, sweating nigger priest. . . . [It] is revolting and smacks of sacrilege. When this ceremony is over . . . a mouthing, tobacco-spitting, indescribably repulsive character . . . induce[s] the colored priest to marry the unwilling [Kelly] to him. I am a non-Catholic, but I have never been so shocked, so revolted at anything I have seen in years. . . . It was in execrable taste. Following this the picture shows the repulsive, repugnant man entering the bride's chamber for his first liaison, while he beckons to a crowd of thirty or forty prostitutes of the bawdy-house to take a peek while he accomplishes his end.[2]

It might be possible to "disinfect" the African scenes, Walter concluded, but "the picture as it is now is not coherent, believable, in good taste, human, or acceptable from any possible angle." For Stroheim's gorgeous sets and lighting effects he spared one sentence: "The production is magnificent [but it is] gilding the manure pile."[3]

How had *Queen Kelly* gotten so far out of hand? Not surprisingly, accounts differ. Some blame Swanson and Kennedy, who should have kept a closer eye on Stroheim. The director needed one strong producer, not several absentee associates. Furthermore, the script should have been cut to size before production began. Stroheim reliably presented certain challenges: as Swanson noted, "It could cost $2,000 just to get a close-up of an ashtray."[4] These challenges could—at least in theory—have been managed more adroitly. Yet Stroheim's determination to put his own vision on screen led to what Richard Koszarski calls "truly flagrant abuses" of the understanding he had with his leading lady and producer.[5] Combine this with Kennedy's longing for a prestige production to raise his own profile in the industry and Swanson's desire to rely utterly on her lover's judgment. Add the uncertainty attendant on the coming of sound, and in *Queen Kelly* you have the makings of a perfect storm.

Swanson worried and waited for Kennedy to arrive: "My brain twirled. I walked floors, I tossed in bed. How do we save it? Does one cut the first third of the picture and still save the story? My imagination went wild—it had full rein."[6] Derr advised Kennedy that Stroheim was in "flagrant violation" of his contract and urged him to stop the director's paycheck immediately. Kennedy proposed instead that Stroheim finish the silent picture for European distribution. Another director could prepare a sound version for the American market.[7]

Early reports of the shutdown of the picture blamed Stroheim: "He was a sure way of losing money," said one journalist. "Gloria is far too good-hearted ever to make a business woman. She is surrounded by worthless hangers-on, to whose advice she is always ready to listen, although it has consistently led her in the wrong direction. There ought to be a law against artists of her caliber getting involved in business matters."[8] Poor Gloria had to deal with the "hundred . . . emergencies" of film production "while she is wearing the grease-paint and should have her mind free for her work," said another.[9]

Over the next weeks and then months, many in Hollywood took a stab at the troubled picture, including screenwriter Eddie Goulding, DeMille writer Clara Beranger, playwright Laurence Eyre, screenwriter (and future director) Delmer Daves, Swanson's old director Sam Wood, *Queen Kelly*'s production manager Harry Poppe, and stage actress Laura Hope Crews, who had been hired as Gloria's dialogue coach. According to Swanson, "They'd come out [of the projection room] blaspheming, saying, 'What has [Stroheim] been doing? This is censorable.'"[10] The dance hall sequence "would never pass . . . even if you had Bronco Billy riding though it in full western regalia . . . *Sadie* was mild compared to this."[11] Yet no one could see a way to fix *Queen Kelly*'s problems.

When Kennedy finally arrived in California, he approved Stroheim's dismissal but declared the script doctors Swanson brought in "hopeless."[12] She said it was Kennedy who felt hopeless: "He slumped into a deep chair, put his hand in his hands, and grunted and groaned like a hurt animal. His first words were in a quiet voice: 'I've never had a failure in my life.'" Then he rose, shouting and cursing the director and "those martini-drinking bastards," Le Baron and Glazer. "He put his arms around me," Swanson said, "and presently I felt my face was wet."[13] Joe Kennedy was crying. "For weeks," she recalled, he was like "a beached whale, all his tremendous energy drained, all his lust for ambition mortified."[14] Joe was particularly troubled by the idea that the picture (in Rose Kennedy's words) "would offend millions of Catholics."[15] The mood at his Rodeo Drive headquarters was dark. Swanson claimed that she suggested they roll up their sleeves and get to work; there was plenty of help available in Hollywood.

Kennedy described their encounter differently. He wrote to Henri, who had visited Joe in Palm Beach before sailing to Europe in January: "I went out there and found Gloria in very bad shape in the hospital, as the result of practically a nervous collapse. She was down to 108 in weight and her attitude towards the picture, and everybody connected with it, was quite hostile." She was murderously angry at Glazer—whom she "hates, loathes, and despises," Kennedy said—for neglecting her picture; she would not accept him as a replacement for Stroheim.[16]

Kennedy put a Norwegian masseuse on 24-hour call for his distraught star. Madame Sylvia massaged the "picture girls" in Hollywood for several years before publishing a tell-all memoir.[17] She remembered her first visit to the marquise's establishment: "The house staff gave [me] the works . . . [I] passed through about ten pairs of hands." At last, Gloria appeared in her nightie. Hers was "a clear case of overwrought nerves," and it took "two hours of gentle, soothing rubbing to get the overexcited star to sleep."[18]

She was overexcited from her conversation with Kennedy, who had set Gloria straight on her obligations to the production: *Queen Kelly*'s debt was her debt. "There is no need to go into the personal reaction of Gloria toward owing me considerable money on the picture," Kennedy wrote Henri, "but it was far from a pleasant one." Gloria had gone to see Jesse Lasky, hoping to get some work at Paramount. This astonished Kennedy: "We had a very drastic showdown . . . and I insisted that some sort of a finish must be made because there was too much money at stake and too much loss of prestige if the picture was not finished."[19]

It must have been a rude awakening. Swanson suddenly understood that she was responsible for a picture no one knew how to finish, and her lover had no intention of footing the bill. Although she claimed in her autobiography that she had signed only a power of attorney, this was a convenient fiction. Swanson's signature was on quite a few documents detailing her agreement to Kennedy's financial plan—a plan that was now in serious jeopardy if *Queen Kelly* failed. Privately, the actress acknowledged that she had neglected to read much of what was put before her: "All his boys came running to me for my signature on this and on that. If I had wanted to read [the papers], I would have had the time."[20]

Unfortunately for her, the contracts Swanson signed "less often detail the actress's and her advisor's legal or financial obligations to each other than they delineate her obligations to him and to entities connected to him."[21] The papers linked her financial future to Joe Kennedy. Since her United Artists contract prohibited Swanson from working for any other studio until she delivered three "specials" to UA, she could not have worked for Paramount in any case.[22] Gloria often sought advice (and even jobs) from former associates when she was in a spot, though it must have galled Kennedy to have his leading lady run to Lasky. Swanson's emotional outbursts, her breakdown, her inability to keep her business to herself: these were anathema to a man whose principles were self-control, stoicism, and privacy.

However, Kennedy seemed surprised by how rapidly Swanson regrouped. By early March, she had regained her lost weight and was in "rather a cheerful mood."[23] Some of this was due to the support of her friends, who tried to keep Gloria's sinking ship afloat and her spirits high. Eddie Goulding prepared a comic decree from "the Board of Directors of the Salvage Association" pledging "their best efforts in the salvaging of the tidbits of *Queen Kelly* (to-wit: those bits not depicting the insanity of the director)" and assuring Swanson of their "unswerving loyalty in this stupendous, gigantic, colossal, and jumboaic adventure."[24] It was signed by almost everyone associated with the picture. Yet there were precious few laughs to be had amid this wreckage.

That spring Kennedy hired Austrian director Paul Ludwig Stein to shoot an all-talking conclusion to the picture. Publicity memos carefully worded to obscure any breath of trouble explained that "the audible version of *Queen Kelly* has been in preparation ever since completion of camera work on [the] silent picture more than one month ago."[25] They hoped for a late summer release. Stein began shooting sound tests on April Fool's Day, not an auspicious date; ten days later, *Queen Kelly* closed down once again. Kennedy now thought they needed more than a simple infusion of sound; he ordered the preparation of an entirely revised sound script.

They aimed to go back into production in the autumn, a prospect about which Kennedy was uncharacteristically diffident. "Whether it will ever get started, whether it will ever see a finish, whether (when it is finished) it will be any good, I can give you no information whatsoever," he told Henri.[26] They would tinker with *Queen Kelly* for the rest of 1929 and into 1930, as the stock market soared and then collapsed, as Gloria and Joe's love affair flared out and then fizzled, as Gloria and Henri grew farther apart. The important picture's costs were now spiraling toward $800,000.[27]

Kennedy and his horsemen had insulated Gloria from money worries while she worked on *Kelly*, and no one pushed her to see too many details now. If Swanson had insisted, she may have had a hard time getting a comprehensive picture of her affairs. The editor of his papers characterizes Kennedy as "stubbornly unyielding to examination. . . . He guarded his privacy zealously and covered his tracks impeccably, and there are conspicuous gaps in his papers."[28]

Swanson's financial obligations were nonetheless real and ongoing. Her tax bill for 1921–1926 was monumental: the IRS determined that she had deducted over $250,000 in disallowed personal expenses. Yet the message Swanson got—or at least the message she heard—when Kennedy took over her affairs was that better accounting would reverse her misfortunes. "Anything I wanted I could have," she remembered wryly.[29]

Despite the economies Kennedy's reorganization of her office had created, Swanson's household was still expensive to maintain. She was paying for her teenage cousin to attend military school and regularly sending her mother substantial checks (she was also being asked to find employment for Adelaide's new husband). Gloria's friends often came and stayed for weeks: Virginia Bowker had cared for Gloria during the difficult period after *Queen Kelly* shut down. "Every star had a little court of old friends and relatives," Swanson explained. "You became their hostess and protectorate."[30] She tried to repress a full awareness of her financial woes. Since the only way to fix them was to make another picture, Swanson was wide open to a suggestion from one of her "salvage team" members.

Eddie Goulding thought Gloria should just scrap *Queen Kelly* and move on. Stroheim's picture was old-fashioned; she should join the talkie revolution. Swanson was amused by Goulding, a fun-loving Englishman with an idea a minute. One of his ideas had been to send her twenty telegrams on her thirtieth birthday in late March. Hour after hour the Western Union delivery boy appeared at Swanson's door, bearing happy-go-lucky messages: at 10:10, "HURRAH HURRAH WOOF GOULDING" arrived. One minute later, another appeared: "MANY HAPPY RETURNS OF THE DAY EDMUND GOULDING." Then came: "ISN'T IT NICE TO HAVE A LOT OF WIRES ON ONE'S BIRTHDAY EDDIE GOULDING." On and on it went: "ISN'T SHE POPULAR WHAT A LOT OF TELEGRAMS SIR EDMUND." "I THINK THE CONFUSION OF A LOT OF TELEGRAMS ARRIVING HELPS A BIRTHDAY EDDIE GOULDING." At last they stopped: "ONCE MORE I REPEAT HAPPY BIRTHDAY EDDIE."[31]

A versatile writer and director who spent six months on Paramount's payroll experimenting with sound technology, Goulding believed current pictures had not yet revealed the possibilities of sound: "They are old-style movies with a little sound superimposed upon them."[32] He had written one all-talkie which would become an enormous hit for M-G-M. *The Broadway Melody* cost $280,000 and grossed $4 million, even before every theater was equipped to run sound pictures.[33] Formerly silent star

Bessie Love talked and sang in the film: "In the middle of the micro-phone panic," *Photoplay* declared, "Bessie Love is one of the few stars who know where their next Rolls-Royce is coming from."[34]

Joe Schenck had arranged a live radio broadcast in March 1928, so the UA members could demonstrate that their voices were suitable for talkies. Chaplin, Fairbanks, Swanson, John Barrymore, and several other stars gathered in Mary Pickford's bungalow, each speaking briefly about the movies (Swanson warned young girls not to try to crash Hollywood). After the press was barred from witnessing these first encounters with the microphone, however, rumors circulated that the stars had covered for one another. Seeing was believing.

Swanson had actually made a talking picture three years earlier, as a lark. New York City's all-male Lambs' Club had a long-established tradi-tion: no women allowed—not no how, not no way. Gloria "crashed" the annual Lambs' Gambol at the Metropolitan Opera House in a short film made by Allan Dwan and Lee DeForest, one of the inventors of motion picture sound. Gloria, Henri, and Tommy Meighan were shown (and heard) in conversation on screen, Swanson offering a comic denuncia-tion of the Lambs' refusal to allow women. Henri "enlivened the scene with volcanic and explosive French."[35] After Swanson "started to sing the club song," Dwan recalled, "two or three people threw her out."[36] A telegram from the real Gloria Swanson at home in Beverly Hills was read after the film.

Eddie Goulding made an all-dialogue picture seem like a walk in the park, not a frightening feat of technical wizardry. When he pitched Gloria an idea for a talkie about the unselfish love of a working mother for her child, she felt her confidence returning. The high-spirited director might be just what she needed.

Swanson determined to approach Kennedy carefully. She instructed her chauffeur to take them to the studio by the most circuitous route; she had important business with the Boss and wanted no interruptions. "I may have to flirt with him to get my way," she thought. As they drove down the coast, Swanson pitched Goulding's idea. Why shouldn't she be the first major female star to make an all-talking picture? *Queen Kelly* was getting nowhere. It would do her good to stop worrying about it and make another film quickly. She had never liked the idea of her sound debut tak-ing place in an African brothel, anyway. "Maybe we should not be afraid to be pioneers," she pleaded. "That's what built this crazy business."[37]

Kennedy, preoccupied by his prestige film and unimpressed by Goulding, made what he probably thought was a meaningless concession.

He was going east for a month; Gloria and Goulding could take a few weeks to come up with a script. After that, he wanted her attention back on *Queen Kelly*.

If Kennedy thought Swanson was indulging in a fantasy about making a sound picture quickly, he was dead wrong. Freed to work with a more compatible director than Stroheim, Swanson brought her best energies to play. Where Stroheim was undoubtedly an artist, maybe even the genius his publicity proclaimed him, his highly personal vision left little room for the kind of creative partnership Swanson enjoyed most. Goulding was far more flexible than Stroheim and liked the give-and-take of collaboration. A craftsman with a strong sense of narrative construction, he also had a strong sense of fun. (Louise Brooks called him "the most joyful being I would ever meet.")[38]

There was only one problem with the way Goulding worked: he was like a butterfly, flitting from one flower to the next. He had ideas galore, but people who worked with him quickly learned that it was a struggle to get Goulding to remember what he had dreamed up, let alone record it on paper. Jesse Lasky Jr. remembered his father offering Goulding $25,000 for a marvelous story he made up one afternoon by the pool: "[Eddie] began to weave a tapestry of words, a story pouring from him like spirit speech through a psychic medium." The mirage vanished when it became clear that the storyteller had forgotten his story as quickly as he told it. "[Its] wonderful effect . . . was the magic of Eddie Goulding himself, a magic which he could not solidify and put into form."[39] Budd Schulberg recalled the same thing happening when the "inspired ad-libber" told his father, producer B. P. Schulberg, stories. He called Goulding "half artist, half charlatan (the ideal Hollywood mix)."[40]

Now it was Swanson's job to get Goulding to focus and concentrate on turning out a tight script within the four weeks Kennedy had agreed to finance. She enlisted two helpers: Laura Hope Crews, the actress who was Gloria's dialogue coach, and a court stenographer, so that none of Goulding's evanescent brilliance could escape. The trio settled into Swanson's breakfast room, which they dubbed "The Sanctuary," to write *The Trespasser*. Their witness took down every word that passed during the "wild, tragic, hilarious," often farcical month.[41]

They encouraged, cajoled, and argued with each other by turns as the story took shape. Eddie came up with the situations and characterizations; Laura, who had a terrific ear for the spoken word, helped craft the dialogue. Gloria played clean-up, making sure Eddie did not change her character too much from his original conception or make her sound

Ingénue.

Age eight, with her signature hair bows.

Promotional picture for *A Pullman Bride*, in the detested "Bathing Beauty" costume.

The Sultan's Wife, 1917. Gloria is whispering in the Sultan's ear.

With Bobby Vernon, Keystone Teddy, and Wallace Beery in *Teddy at the Throttle*, 1917.

The young bride with Wallace Beery, 1917.

...eery in drag as "Sweedie."

As an improbably glamorous Christian slave in Karl Struss's publicity still for *Male and Female*, 1919.

The Lion's Bride, *Male and Female*, 1919. Publicity still by Karl Struss.

Marooned on a desert island with Thomas Meighan in *Male and Female*, 1919.

Captain Joseph Swanson.

Don't Change Your Husband, 1919.

ndraped for Alfred Cheney Johnston, c. 1919.

Second husband Herbert Somborn.

With baby Gloria, 1920.

Mickey Neilan, the man Swanson called the "Pied Piper."

Waiting for the moth to fly out of Russell Simpson's beard in *Under the Lash*, 1921.

mping for Nickolas Muray, 1922.

With Rudolph Valentino on the set of *Beyond the Rocks* (1922). Elinor Glyn and director Sam Wood stand on the platform.

Kissing the open palm, a Valentino signature gesture.

A "britches" part, 1924's *The Humming Bird*.

Zaza, 1923. The hand-painted designs on her legs substituted for stockings.

Seen by Edward Steichen in 1924 as "a leopardess watching her prey." Courtesy of Steichen/*Vanity Fair*
© Condé Nast.

COVARRUBIAS

Caricatured by Miguel Covarrubias,
c. 1924. Courtesy of Covarrubias/
Vanity Fair; © Condé Nast.

Riding the NYC subway as Tessie in *Manhandled*, 1924.

Posing as Peter Pan, 1924.

With her translator Henri de la Falaise on the French set of *Madame Sans-Gêne*, 1924.

With Gloria and Joseph (aka Brother), 1924.

As Madame Sans-Gêne, the laundress . . .

. . . who becomes a duchess.

Returning to America as the Marquise de la Falaise with her new husband. Her cropped hair is hidden under a large hat.

Incognito as the Countess in
The Coast of Folly, 1925 . . .

. . . and in a second
role as the Countess's
athletic daughter.

As the little waitress confiding her daydreams in *Stage Struck*, 1925.

Imagining herself as Salome in *Stage Struck*, 1925

With director and costar Raoul Walsh in *Sadie Thompson*, 1928.

With John Boles in *The Love of Sunya*, her first feature for United Artists, 1927.

adie Thompson, 1928.

With Lionel Barrymore.

At home in Beverly Hills.

Not afraid of the microphone.

Joseph P. Kennedy and Henri
de la Falaise in Biarritz, 1928.

In trouble with Seena Owen in *Queen Kelly*, 1928.

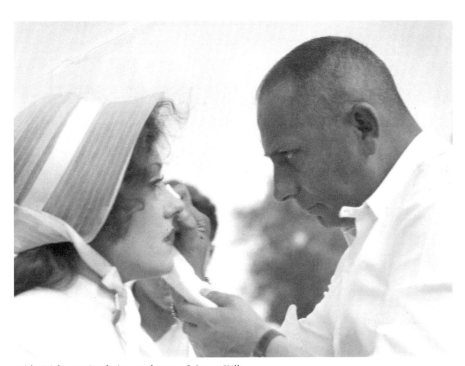

With Erich von Stroheim on the set of *Queen Kelly*.

Contemplating her rosy future in sound pictures, 1928.

With Eddie Goulding, Noel Coward, and Laura Hope Crews in 1929.

...reamlined in *The Trespasser*, 1929.

With Melvyn Douglas in *Tonight or Never*, 1931.

With fourth husband,
Michael Farmer, c. 1932.

Amusing Laurence Olivier in *Perfect Understanding,* 1933.

On a tiger skin for M-G-M's planned remake of *Three Weeks.*

With Herbert Marshall, 1934.

Family portrait, mid-1930s.

With Adolph Menjou, her political ally, in *Father Takes a Wife*, 1941.

With Billy Wilder.

Fifth husband William Davey, 1945.

On the set of *Sunset Boulevard*, 1949.

Ready for her close-up as Norma Desmond in *Sunset Boulevard*, 1950.

On tour for *Sunset Boulevard*, 1950.

En route to London with Michelle, 1950.

In London for the Command Performance of *Sunset Boulevard*, 1950.

Oscar night, 1951. In the foreground left is Judy Holliday, winner of the award for Best Actress.

In *Nina* on Broadway with a stunned-looking David Niven, 1951.

With her mother in 1961.

In the ruins of the
Roxy Theatre, New
York City, 1960.

As Charlie Chaplin with
Carol Burnett, 1973.

As the murderous matriarch in *Killer Bees*, 1973.

Her sculpted self-portrait.

ith sixth husband William Dufty, 1976.

What becomes a Legend most?
Blackglama fur ad, 1981.

Gloria Swanson, New York, September 4, 1980. Photograph by Richard Avedon.

too British. They stopped to eat only when Goulding visibly wilted and took him for walks around the property when he insisted on a break: "He didn't have a leash on, but truly we were afraid to let him out of our sight."[42] After a few nights Laura moved into Swanson's guest room. They worked night and day, pushing themselves to meet Kennedy's deadline.

Swanson always remembered this interlude with pleasure, though they alternated between laughing until they cried and battling like tigers. When Eddie and Laura fought, Gloria refereed, and vice versa all around. When he had had enough of his collaborators (for whom he had some choice names), Goulding locked himself in the bathroom, refusing to come out.

After ten days of writing and fighting, Laura broke down in tears: she had to get out of the house. Eddie and Gloria urged her to go home and relax—but before the evening had ended, Laura was back: the Swanson and Goulding show was the best entertainment in town. After almost four weeks, Gloria was happy with the script. There was "not a single extra word—nor extraneous scenes."[43] They were ready for Kennedy's verdict.

"My dining room looked like a board of directors' room," Swanson said, with "nothing but stern faces sitting around a massive table." Yet as she, Eddie, and Laura prepared to do a table reading of the script, only the Boss's four horsemen were present: Joe Kennedy had not even come. "Because it was such a tight script, we whizzed through it in no time," Swanson recalled. Then there was "a long sigh of relief, and smiles, smiles, smiles" all around.[44] The group went for a celebratory lunch at the Rodeo Drive house, where Kennedy was waiting. Fearing another failure, he had been too anxious to come himself.

They had to go back to the drawing board one more time: Goulding thought *The Trespasser* needed a song. The coming of sound had made musicals enormously popular. Since Gloria had a lovely voice and had been preparing to sing for *Queen Kelly*, a musical number or two seemed like a good idea. Eddie, Gloria, and Laura returned to the Sanctuary to try out songs. Melodies by Ivor Novello and George Gershwin were top contenders, until one morning Swanson received "a frantic intercom call" from Laura summoning her to the guestroom. There she found Laura "sitting upright in her bed, curlers in her hair, a tray on her tummy, and Eddie Goulding at the foot of the bed whistling." Laura motioned to Swanson to be quiet and listen, then whispered, "Remember the notes."[45]

By the time Goulding was through, Laura and Gloria knew they had
found the melody they needed: their scriptwriter and director was also a
songwriter. However, when Gloria asked him to sing it again, he claimed
he had forgotten it already. They jogged Eddie's memory until he reproduced the tune, in snatches, from start to finish. Swanson knew it
would be a hit song. Now they needed to commit it to paper, but none of
them knew how to write music. The stenographer had a record of their
entire collaboration—"script dialogue, gossip, arguments, and sandwich
orders"—but she could not take musical dictation.[46]

So they went in hasty pursuit of someone who could. Gloria and Laura
tried to keep Goulding singing, humming, whistling—anything—while
they located a musician. He complained that he was getting dry and awfully bored. At last, Gloria got Eddie to sing his song over the phone to
someone who could transcribe it. Eddie's friend Elsie Janis wrote some
lyrics and coached Swanson on how to put the song over. "Love, Your
Magic Spell is Everywhere" became Gloria's first hit gramophone recording and her signature tune, struck up by orchestras wherever Swanson
appeared for years.

The inaugural Academy Awards ceremony, honoring pictures made in
1927 and 1928, was held in May 1929. Swanson had received a nomination as Best Actress for her role in *Sadie Thompson*, along with Louise
Dresser and Janet Gaynor, who won for three performances.[47] As she
declined her invitation to the awards dinner, Gloria recalled how Joe
Kennedy had championed a movie competition at their first meeting.
She was not impressed with the so-called Academy: "It was the same
bunch that . . . ganged up on me and tried to scare me out of making
Sadie Thompson." Swanson found it ironic to be recognized for the film
the pinochle club had rejected. "The studio as usual told its chattels who
to vote for. But it was a secret ballot. I guess there had to be a lot of rebellious prostitutes for me to get enough votes to rate an honorable mention as an also-ran."[48]

Her trials as an independent producer made her suspicious about the
accolades being handed out. She had enjoyed little cooperation when
making *Sadie Thompson*, the picture her financial troubles had forced her
to relinquish. Now others were profiting from its success. Come to think
of it, all she had to show for *Sadie* was a small speedboat named after her
character in the film. Swanson did not even like boats.

There was little time to feel moody or resentful, however, as arrangements for *The Trespasser* moved forward with unusual swiftness.
Preparations for shooting a sound film often uncovered obstacles and

created delays. Since it was impossible to cut and re-dub sound, record-ing conditions had to be perfect. Cameras were housed in soundproof blimps the size of refrigerators so the noise they made would not inter-fere with the sound being recorded. (Swanson remembered seeing cam-eras muffled in blankets, looking "as if they were dressed for a storm.")[49] This meant that cameras could not move much. The electrical current employed for sound was so finicky that it was a challenge even to switch cameras: turning one camera's power off could create a dip in the record-ing power of another.

Eddie Goulding's study of sound technology came in handy as they prepared Swanson's new picture. Gloria got another big break: Sam Goldwyn let them borrow George Barnes, who brought a young camera-man with him. Gregg Toland, the inventive, quick-witted cinematogra-pher who later made film history shooting *Citizen Kane*, claimed his first feature credit on *The Trespasser*. The creative team rapidly decided that in order to protect the sound, they would waste film. If they ran a dozen cameras at once, they could view the action from every possible angle. They would cover both their sound and image needs; the result should always be a useable take. It should even be possible to move the camera, mounted on a dolly.

Their technical rehearsals were unusually detailed and precise. Barnes and Toland spent up to nine hours setting up a day's work, but after only two hours of shooting, they had fifteen minutes of useable footage in the can—a good result by any standard, and a relief after Stroheim's deliber-ation. The expense of the running film was easily offset by the economy of getting it all right the first time. They virtually flew along, thanks also to the bulletproof script. Goulding's craftsmanlike work, his impeccable preparation, and his unassailable confidence made sound film produc-tion seem easily manageable.

The can-do spirit on the set was contagious. Gloria said Laura Hope Crews was like "a wise and firm mother [who] tolerated no nonsense [and] made me work hard." (Laura, however, disliked Joe Kennedy: he "contributed nothing creative, just threw his weight around.")[50] Swanson became as involved in the plans for *The Trespasser* as she had been detached from those for *Queen Kelly*. Inspired by her "prolific, tal-ented, and amazing" director, she remembered "having a ball" on the set: "There was such happy excitement surrounding this picture, and it was all so easy. Laughter and fun had come back into our lives."[51]

Worried that she would forget her lines, Swanson made some unusual cue cards: "I wrote the dialogue on somebody's shirt-front so that I could look down at his chest, and it would give me confidence."[52] Tales were told of every major star's fear of sound, but the rapid, efficient pace of production on *The Trespasser* indicates that Swanson quickly overcame any uncertainty about being recorded.[53] "The whole picture was made in twenty-one shooting days [and] cost less than any picture I ever made."[54] She felt fully present, fully invested.

The Trespasser was a classic melodrama made powerful by Swanson's strong performance. A wealthy young man marries beneath him, and his snobbish family separates the newlyweds. The marriage is annulled; the son marries someone more suitable. A year later the abandoned wife and her infant son are living in a tenement when her former employer, a powerful lawyer, rescues them. He loves Marion and sets her and her son up in a luxury apartment; on his death, he leaves his mistress a fortune. When her former father-in-law learns there is a male heir to his line, he tries to take her child from Marion. For his own good, Marion relinquishes her son to his father's family. She eventually reconciles with her first husband and is reunited with her child.

Swanson's performance was easy and unforced. As one intimate explained, "[Goulding] realized that the key to her transition in sound was to go back to her roots. So he wrote her character as a little secretary from Chicago because that's where she came from. . . . The character and Gloria's personality [came] together. Eddie was brilliant that way."[55]

The Trespasser was a marvelous showcase for Swanson. It had few of the flaws of the early talkies, and her voice—low, well-modulated, and thrilling—was a revelation. The serviceable Broadway actor Robert Ames partnered her, though at forty he was a decade older than Clark Gable, who had tested but was thought too rough for the role. The settings and costumes convey a streamlined glamour, and the cinematography is spectacular. Even the now-hoary cinematic cliché of the fallen woman giving up her child was fresher when Swanson brought it to the screen. The worthy mother she played in *The Trespasser* would become a staple of films in the next decade, drawing stars like Marlene Dietrich, Barbara Stanwyck, and Bette Davis.[56]

Shooting on *The Trespasser* wrapped at the end of June. The picture had been so carefully planned that cutting was a snap, and a silent version was prepared and titled by late summer. The world premiere was planned for September in London. Confident she had a hit on her hands, and not yet ready to face *Queen Kelly*, Swanson headed to New York in July for a well-deserved vacation.

Her affair with Joe Kennedy had been strained by the Stroheim de-
bacle, but Gloria and Joe were by no means ready to call it quits. With
their new film almost ready for release, the lovers wanted to relax and
play together. Since Joe was bringing Rose to Europe for the premiere,
Swanson took the plunge and accepted his invitation to Hyannis Port
before she sailed: she and Rose may as well get their meeting out of the
way. In a flashy assertion of her presence, Swanson arrived by seaplane.
If Joe thought Gloria was going "to throw a shawl over [her] scarlet letter," he was mistaken.[57]

Mrs. Kennedy rose to the occasion by declining to reveal any sense of
strain whatsoever. She welcomed her guest graciously, showing Swanson
around the house (which boasted a theater equipped for sound pictures),
taking her to the beach club, and refusing to give even the slightest hint
that she knew of Swanson's relation with her husband. "Rose was living in a world where social hypocrisy had been elevated to a high social
form," says Laurence Leamer.[58] She seems not to have seen Swanson as
a serious threat to the stability of her marriage—rightly, as history would
demonstrate. The Kennedy children, however, made their feelings
known. That summer there were two fan clubs in the neighborhood,
one devoted to Gloria Swanson and one to Constance Bennett. None of
the Kennedy girls wanted to be in the Swanson fan club, recalled a childhood friend—even though Gloria herself came to their clubhouse to sign
autographs.[59]

During Gloria's visit, twelve-year-old Jack Kennedy, anxious to impress his father, stowed away on the *Rose Elizabeth* when Joe took Gloria
out on the boat. Jack was apparently planning to help out if his father,
an indifferent sailor, got in any trouble. He was hiding below when the
sounds on deck made it painfully evident that his father and the actress
were not conferring about business. Embarrassed, the boy jumped off
the boat and swam for shore. His father dove in after him and managed
to get Jack, who was already wearying, back on board. Then he and his
mistress coached the youngster on what he was—and was not—to say
about the adventure. The lessons Jack Kennedy learned from his father
stayed with him, influencing his relations with the women in his life.[60]

Joe had gone west to California on "movie business" as his own father lay dying that spring, hoping he would make it home before P. J.
Kennedy's passing. In the end, he had not even made it back for his father's funeral. Yet Rose held her head high and admitted no vulnerability
in her marriage.

This stance would be put to the test on their European trip. Gloria and Virginia Bowker sailed to Paris in August, where Rose and Joe's sister, Margaret, joined them.[61] The odd little group did Paris and Deauville together, escorted by Gloria's husband. Virginia knew all about her friend's relationship with the Boss, of course, but she and Gloria never figured out how much—or even whether—Rose knew about the liaison, which had been going on for more than a year and a half.

Swanson was willing to play along: if Rose didn't acknowledge anything amiss with her husband, that was fine by Gloria. "The curious part of the whole situation," she recalled, "was that I felt no guilt about Rose. She was an enigma to me. She didn't show any signs of caring if Joe was possessive of me. She treated me as if I were one of the family. I wanted to say, little do you know, but I couldn't, because there were times when I was sure she didn't know and times when I was sure she didn't care." Kennedy's "brazen" behavior seemed to leave little doubt about his feelings for the star: "He never left me out of his sight, and if his wife wanted to find him, all she had to do was find me."[62] Kennedy even acted the part of the jealous lover, confronting another man for staring at Gloria.

If she was unconcerned about betraying Rose, however, Gloria claimed she was "tortured with guilt" about Henri, who certainly understood the attention Joe Kennedy was paying her: "If only I could put into words the kind of love I felt for him. It was a mixture of so many categories of love. Maybe the guilt was compounded by not having borne his child."[63] Yet Gloria's attitude was finally not that different from Rose's: neither woman believed the Swanson-Kennedy affair would destroy her marriage. Henri too was playing along. His part was the old-world sophisticate who overlooks his wife's adultery, takes a job with her lover, and squires the Boss's wife and sister around foreign capitals in the name of European refinement.

Several times Henri seemed close to broaching the subject. "I almost wanted him to," Gloria recalled. She half-hoped he would order her to give up the motion picture business and move to France with him: "But he didn't. He couldn't. Joe Kennedy had compromised us both with his promises of enduring security, which Henri wanted as least as much as I did."[64] Gloria hoped Henri would wait until her fascination with Kennedy had run its course. She hoped her husband knew she would return to him.

Rose Kennedy claimed she had "special personal memories" of this European trip. Rose's Paris memories included being eclipsed in the couturier's salons by Swanson: "She was the great celebrity. I, by comparison, was a nobody, just the wife of the producer." The wife of the producer said gamely, "It was fun being with [Gloria] and sharing in the excitement she generated."[65]

It was considerably more exciting in London, where Swanson was practically stampeded outside *The Trespasser*'s West End theater. "London Women Fight to See Miss Swanson," the headlines trumpeted. "Eight burly London policemen were swept off their feet tonight by a mad rush of women bent on catching a glimpse of Miss Gloria Swanson . . . 'I will see her if I am killed for it,' cried one young woman who led the attack."[66] Swanson never liked facing a mob, but it was nothing new for her. (At the New York premiere in November, the crowds were so dense that four handlers had to lift Swanson overhead: they carried her into the theater horizontally.)

For the producer's wife, such chaos was something else again. Rose's special personal memories of *The Trespasser*'s London premiere included being shoved to the front of the car they were traveling in. That way, if the windshield got broken in the melee, Swanson's fabulous face would not be cut. "I realized her face was more valuable than mine," Rose recalled, "but I got rather nervous myself."[67]

The Trespasser was the first major American talkie to have its world premiere in London. (Another sound picture was playing to lively interest: Norma Shearer had a hit with *The Last of Mrs. Cheyney*.) Since it was also its star's sound debut, there was an extraordinary amount of publicity. They held the boat train, which was full of dignitaries in striped trousers and cutaways ready to welcome Swanson to England, while she shopped for perfume. Everywhere she went they fended off reporters as well as fans: "I thought this kind of thing only happened in America," Swanson commented after one crush.[68]

A few special appearances created even more excitement about Gloria's presence in London. She sang at a concert broadcast by the BBC: "I was so nervous . . . I didn't even know what key I was singing in," she recalled.[69] Happily, her performance was well-received and her voice pronounced an authentic match for the one heard on screen. Swanson also hosted a tea party for several hundred "Nippies," as the waitresses at the Lyon's Corner House restaurant chain were called. London was unused to such publicity stunts, and the papers were divided about whether they wanted more. "Laboriously contrived tricks of publicity" would never appeal to the average Londoner, sniffed one reporter.[70] However, with mobs greeting Gloria wherever she went, this was anything but obvious.

The star, however, was not entirely enjoying her return to the spot-light: she had received a severe shock. Shortly before the *Trespasser* premiere, Swanson opened an envelope addressed to the Marquise de la Falaise. Inside was a love letter intended for Henri from Constance Bennett. Its contents left no doubt whatsoever: the pair was having a serious affair. Swanson was devastated; her own infidelity had not pre-pared her for the possibility that her husband might make a significant new commitment of his own.

Constance Bennett was an unforgettable combination of the blasé and the combative. She was spectacularly unimpressed with the movie business and had walked away from it once already. However, Bennett never shied away from a fight and often sought one, as much for her own entertainment as anything else. She was a gorgeous lanky blonde who was whip-smart, with a sophisticated sense of style and an intense love of having her own way. She was, in short, a lot like her rival Gloria Swanson. Bennett left the movies in 1925 to marry a rich American playboy. They partied their way through Europe until Bennett tired of both her husband and expatriate life. Joe Kennedy had dispatched Henri to hire her for Pathé.

Swanson had ignored the gossip about her husband and Lili Damita. However, she could not tell herself that Constance Bennett was harm-less. The business of the misaddressed letter she found contemptible, the oldest trick in the book. Bennett's French was excellent; there was no way she would have made such an elementary grammatical error. She meant for Swanson to read the letter.

Gloria was both hurt and angry. She announced to Joe and Rose that she was divorcing Henri; she refused to allow him to escort her to the premiere. She retired to her suite, banishing her husband to the other end of the hotel. Rose described the actress's mood as "cold, regal rage."[71] Her attitude, however, created a dilemma: for Swanson to appear at the premiere without the marquis would upstage *The Trespasser*'s opening. Henri was publicity gold. Everyone loved him, and the frisson of glamour her husband's title and debonair good looks created for Swanson could not be bought.

Rose Kennedy recalled lengthy discussions as Joe's team tried to man-age the rift between Gloria and Henri: "Some of the sessions at the Ritz [were like] negotiat[ing] a complex international treaty among friendly and unfriendly powers." Kennedy eventually rendered his verdict: he would not allow "a disagreement between a husband and wife" to in-terfere with the picture.[72] The marquis and marquise would walk down

the red carpet together at the premiere. They could make any arrangements they wanted in private, but that night they would act the part of a
happy, loving couple. Gloria's private heartbreak could not compromise
The Trespasser's success.

Rose seconded her husband's decision. "Joe was right in forcing her
to go on with the show," she told Doris Kearns Goodwin, "and to pretend at least for the moment that everything was fine. It was not easy to
calm Gloria down but since Joe had a bit of control over the situation, as
Gloria and the Marquis *and* Connie Bennett all worked for him, his will
prevailed."[73] As Goodwin notes, the news of Henri's affair must have put
an extra strain on Rose; Gloria offered a more potent threat now that her
marriage was breaking up. Characteristically, Rose thought Gloria should
adopt her own approach: circumspection and a stiff upper lip.

Swanson may have acted her way through the premiere, but she appeared radiant and glamorous in chinchilla trimmed with blue. After *The
Trespasser*'s London triumph, Gloria and Virginia sailed back to the States.
Rose and Joe were on the same boat, and Gloria took advantage of the
travel time as usual to rest and recuperate. In Rose's version, however,
Swanson was despondent during the crossing, and Joe had to prevail
upon her to greet reporters when they arrived in New York. As Rose saw
it, "From that moment on all sorts of rumors began to fly" about Joe's
association with Gloria: "Because she and Joe were together on deck and
I was nowhere to be seen, reporters mistakenly decided that something
was going on between the two of them . . . But I knew I never had a
thing to worry about and I only felt sorry for poor little Gloria."[74]

Rose and Gloria gave different accounts of their European trip, each
version demonstrating the teller's desire to control her own narrative.
Rose stoutly maintained that she felt only pity for Gloria; Joe had helped
save the actress from professional disaster. Rose painted a picture of
Swanson as a troubled diva who lived in an environment of "excitement, fun, and crises."[75] By contrast, Rose presented herself as calmer
and steadier. She resolutely refused to acknowledge any close relation
between her husband and the star or to register any distress about the
rift in her own marriage.

For her part, Swanson was puzzled by Rose: "Was she a fool. . . . or a
saint? Or just a better actress than I was?"[76] In Swanson's version, Rose
and Joe had sailed to Paris with her and Virginia (rather than returning
home together), Joe paying Gloria obvious attentions and ignoring his
wife. From the beginning of the trip, Swanson hinted, it should have
been apparent to Rose that her husband was straying. Swanson also

conveniently omitted the troubling discovery of her own husband's infidelity from her memoirs, rearranging events to save face.

In her account, Henri's betrayal did not tarnish her London premiere because Henri did not yet know Constance Bennett. (Swanson claimed to have introduced the couple, adding that Henri did not even remember meeting Bennett. However, they had run in the same European social circles for several years by this time.) According to Swanson, she herself suggested to Kennedy that he hire Bennett, who then took to hanging around the Rodeo Drive house. Bennett's charms, however, left Kennedy cold; Gloria said he commented that Bennett "couldn't hook the boss."[77]

Yet by the time Swanson sailed for home in fall 1929, Bennett had been keeping company with Henri for several months and had not one but two pictures for Kennedy's Pathé awaiting release.[78] Gloria remembered the unwelcome revelations of her European trip in a way that salved her pride. As she told it, Henri only became involved with Bennett once she herself had more or less finished with him. She would not present herself as the "poor Gloria" of Rose Kennedy's story.[79]

On her return to New York, Swanson took a suite at The Plaza, where according to Joe Kennedy, she was "not at all well."[80] He wrote Henri that Gloria was in bed and was expected to stay there for the remainder of the week. Swanson's staff was keeping things from her, like the news that both her children had tonsillitis, for fear of upsetting her. Kennedy made it sound as though Gloria, reclusive on the crossing, was again on the verge of a breakdown.

It seems possible, however, that Kennedy was still simply unable to understand the emotional temperament of a star like Swanson. Where he repeatedly portrayed her as overwhelmed by the pressures of her work or prostrate with grief over her marriage, other sources showed Gloria up and functioning smoothly. During the week when Kennedy declared the actress "not at all well," the *New York Times* found her lively and engaging, running Gloria Productions from her hotel suite. She managed "a battery of baritone interviewers" one afternoon, pledging to continue singing on screen and even to make a widescreen musical in color. The phone rang incessantly; she was sketched and photographed while answering questions. The actress "returned thrust for thrust," said the reporter, "quickly, dutifully, courteously, correctly." She "conduct[ed] the afternoon as a [symphony] leader might his music."[81]

Maybe Swanson acted the part of the damsel in distress for Kennedy, exaggerating her emotions to elicit his sympathy and support. Perhaps she revealed more of her true self to her lover: she later claimed she had trusted Joe more than she had ever trusted anyone. Or maybe an occasional "breakdown" simply relieved the pressure inside: as a *New Yorker* profile stated matter-of-factly, "When things grow too thick, Gloria has a fit of good old-fashioned feminine hysterics and feels better."[82]

Whatever her personal distress, she could be happy about one thing: *The Trespasser* was a huge success. An astonishing 88,000 people saw the picture during its opening week in London. Practically every show— with seven screenings a day—sold out that week.[83] The New York fans and critics were every bit as enthusiastic as the British had been: even though technical difficulties played havoc with the sound at the Rialto, its star's performance came in for lavish praise. *The Trespasser* showed Gloria Swanson to be "more of an actress than ever." She had turned in a "sensitive interpretation" of her character and was "natural," "restrained," "charming," and "tremendously effective." Swanson's singing was "most pleasing," her speaking voice "clear as a bell."[84] The film was held over for more than six weeks; its earnings broke UA records.

Now that Swanson had turned in three pictures to United Artists, she was free at least to consider other options. She sang on the radio in New York, and her teacher Signor Marafioti wanted her to train her voice seriously; he thought she could make a good living as a singer. She was also contemplating a stage play. Kennedy asked Henri to look for a good French or German production they might acquire cheaply. If Joe Kennedy was disappointed that the project Swanson and Eddie Goulding had dreamed up had been the one to make a great success, rather than his own prestige picture *Queen Kelly*, he wasn't saying.

CHAPTER 15

The Crash

WITH *THE TRESPASSER*, SWANSON SUCCESSFULLY MADE THE TRANSI-
tion to sound. She had a host of new opportunities to explore, including theater and the singing career that had been her childhood dream.
However, the end of her thirtieth year also found her separated from her
third husband and humiliated by a romantic rival. Swanson's affair with
Joe Kennedy was finally losing steam; the financial problems he had
pledged to solve had not been improved by their association. *Queen Kelly*,
the film they had made together, was still a shambles, and *The Trespasser*,
a critical and popular hit, was more her baby than theirs. Once again,
Gloria took stock as she headed from New York to California, away from
Henri and Joe and toward a promising but uncertain future.

On the way, she and Virginia Bowker attended the Chicago premiere of *The Trespasser*. Aside from her father's funeral six years earlier,
Swanson had spent no time in her hometown since becoming a star. She
visited her childhood home and got a chuckle when she learned that the
current occupants were using the room where she was born for smoking hams. Gloria visited her mother and saw for herself that Adelaide
was happily married. She put aside her hurt feelings, rejoicing in Addie's
good fortune. She and Virginia made a sentimental trip to Essanay, remembering when they had shared a tiny dressing room and pretended
to be older than they were. They screened a print of *The Fable of Elvira,
Farina and the Meal Ticket*, the short that was Swanson's first screen credit, and Gloria collapsed into uncontrollable laughter. Fifteen years had
passed; she was now a world-famous movie actress, on top of the heap
and wondering how long she could balance there.

The Chicago opening of *The Trespasser* was another success, as were
the Los Angeles and San Francisco premieres. The film filled theaters
wherever it played, and Gloria received dozens of congratulatory letters from friends and colleagues. Condé Nast wrote; so did Elinor Glyn

and Jane West, who said her mother had cried hearing Gloria sing on the BBC. Even Swanson's *Queen Kelly* nemesis Barney Glazer offered his "sincerest compliments and congratulations": "I always knew you were good, Gloria, but [had] not expected to find a speaking actress of such exquisite poise and finish."[1]

All too soon it was time to return to *Queen Kelly*, to see what could be done to salvage the film for exhibition. Eddie Goulding hoped that he, Kennedy, and Swanson might form a small unit and continue making pictures together; he had another script almost ready for Gloria. However, Goulding, who read his contracts quickly when he read them at all, had carelessly agreed to work on *The Trespasser* on a straight salary, week-by-week basis. Now he was the writer-director of a hit movie and the composer of a hit song and had nothing much to show for it. At least Kennedy had promised him a $10,000 bonus as well as a share in the royalties for "Love, Your Magic Spell is Everywhere." Yet when Eddie's lawyer approached Joe about these payments, Kennedy flatly rejected the claim, calling Goulding a "bum" whom he had rescued from unemployment.[2]

Only when Kennedy turned back to the neglected *Queen Kelly* did he make Goulding an offer: if Eddie would direct a sound version of the picture, he could have his bonus and the share in *The Trespasser*'s song profits. Goulding took one look at the new script and turned Joe down as decisively as Kennedy had refused him.[3] "Kennedy felt a little number like *The Trespasser* was not worthy of his consideration," said Bill Dufty.[4] Now the shoe was on the other foot, as Goulding once again declared Joe Kennedy's "important picture" unsalvageable.

Nonetheless, in early December Kennedy assembled as many members of the original cast as possible. They planned to spend nineteen days filming a restructured script by Lawrence Eyre and Laura Hope Crews under the direction of Richard Boleslavsky, a Polish émigré actor and theater director. *Queen Kelly* was now to be a part-talkie, with some dialogue synthetically synchronized. This kind of dubbing was (in theory) less expensive than having to reshoot large sections of the picture.

They would capitalize on the leading lady's singing ability this time, too. Right away Boleslavsky shot a scene of the schoolgirl Kelly singing "Ave Maria" in the chapel where she has been sent for punishment. Yet on the third day, filming abruptly ceased; no one quite knows why. Possibly Boleslavsky's inexperience was showing; Erich von Stroheim was a hard act for any director to follow.[5] Swanson remembered that the new scenes "didn't have the same mood or texture" as the earlier footage: "Even the sets clashed."[6] It seems just as likely that the producer was suddenly enthusiastic about a new idea he had to save the picture.

In the last days of 1929, Kennedy contracted with Austrian composer Franz Lehár to furnish "a new waltz": now he wanted to make *Queen Kelly* an operetta.[7] Stroheim had filmed Lehár's *Merry Widow* as a silent picture, and Irving Thalberg reportedly suggested this possibility to Kennedy, saying, "The New York critics loved *The Merry Widow* after I restored the Lehár frosting."[8] Given *Queen Kelly*'s European setting and the leading lady's singing ability, maybe the film could be reworked. Once again, however, nothing came of this plan, and Kennedy began talking about the "gypsy curse" laid on the film.[9]

His prestige picture had gone badly awry—and in full view of everyone in Hollywood. If Kennedy's dilemma elicited little sympathy, however, by now people expected Swanson to land on her feet: "She is still a significant and startling figure in the intricate design of Hollywood," *Photoplay* reported. Gloria is "an amazing woman, who has had everything and lost it and had it again. Over and over. . . . [T]here is still a Swanson future, as there always has been."[10]

Since neither Kennedy nor Swanson was willing to write off the film, efforts to revive *Kelly* kept clicking along. One of the apparently intractable problems with the script was Kelly's suicide attempt. Cast out of the palace and uncertain of her Prince's love, the young girl in Stroheim's picture tries to drown herself by jumping off a bridge. No one liked that idea, and one revision has Kelly pondering a comically exhaustive list of ways to do away with herself: drowning, shooting, razor, gas, rope, and poison.[11] In another version of the story, the orphaned Kelly is of royal birth herself—a secret which has been hidden from the evil queen to keep the child safe. This incarnation makes Kelly into a "little warrior-saint" who fights to save the prince from execution.[12] In the finale, she is restored to her rightful place in society and married to the prince. Queen Kelly sings from the balcony as her loyal, exultant subjects pass by.

For much of 1930, Seena Owen and Walter Byron remained under contract at half-salary so they would be available to work on the picture, should any lightning flash of insight occur to make its completion possible. Yet the more time passed, the less likely this seemed. As sound pictures took over the industry, the last silents in the studios' pipelines had been pushed out, often hastily doctored to make them part-talkies. Soon even these hybrids would be a thing of the past, and *Queen Kelly* would look hopelessly old-fashioned. Even at the risk of losing her entire investment, Swanson could not afford to be seen as out of date herself.

She had taken a shrewd and timely step in making *The Trespasser*, and it made sense for her to keep going in that direction.

Nevertheless, production manager Harry Poppe doggedly prepared yet another new script for *Queen Kelly* late in 1930. (It was never filmed.) Then Swanson's editor Viola Lawrence prepared a cut that resembled Stroheim's original, up to the point of Kelly's suicide leap off the bridge. "Swanson perceived," says Richard Koszarski, "that if Kelly never made it out of the river alive, the film could end right there."[13] Late in 1931, Gregg Toland shot a sequence that ended the film with Kelly dead and the prince in mourning. (Both Swanson and Irving Thalberg were said to have directed the scene.)[14]

Hoping that UA would accept *Queen Kelly* as one of the six pictures she was contractually obligated to make, Swanson finally turned the film in. On a frosty night in February 1932, almost four years after *Queen Kelly* had been conceived, a Stamford, Connecticut, preview audience rejected Swanson's picture. The viewers went from "expectant" to "restless," said UA's observer Al Lichtman. "They laughed at many spots that were intended to be serious." Censors would likely slash the film into incomprehensible bits; the theater owner "could not possibly show a picture of that kind." Martin Quigley, who published several trade journals, was in the audience; he told Lichtman it was "tragic to see Miss Swanson in that kind of a picture."[15] Lichtman recommended that UA decline the film, a verdict Joe Schenck made official. He declared *Queen Kelly* "terrible," "entirely impossible to release . . . We could not even get the price of the prints out of the distribution of the picture."[16]

This judgment finally ended Swanson's ordeal. The picture its star called "poor, dear *Queen Kelly*" was never released in the US and did not even fulfill Gloria's obligation to UA.[17] Rather than making Joe Kennedy's reputation in Hollywood, the film was a total loss. Yet poor, dear *Queen Kelly* refused to die. In 1939, it was exhumed by a producer who purchased the negative for a reported $10,000.[18] Walter Futter intended to plunder the European scenes for stock footage to make a feature on "anti-democratic spy activities in a mythical Balkan kingdom."[19] Swanson's image would be excised entirely.

Queen Kelly was the last of the great eccentric masterpieces of the silent cinema, no less significant because of its truncated state. "We tried to do everything that we could think of to save that picture," Swanson recalled. "[We] got in other directors, we tried to think of it as a dream sequence, as a musical . . . we tried to think of it as everything under the sun."[20] As her affair with the film's producer cooled, the long struggle to bring their offspring to fruition seemed especially poignant. The actress always spoke of Joe Kennedy's "important picture" sadly. For her, *Queen Kelly* "was a child that . . . didn't want to be born."[21]

A far greater sorrow was the collapse of her marriage to Henri. Shortly after Gloria's return to California in late autumn 1929, her husband wrote from Paris to say he would not be joining the family for Christmas. Virginia stayed with her and the children, and Gloria welcomed her friend's support. Young Joseph's slow recovery from a tonsillectomy added to his mother's worries. Remembering her beloved son's tough start in life, she sent Christmas dinner to the LA Orphans' Home. After a big package arrived with presents for the children from the Kennedy family, Swanson sighed and made sure a pile of gifts headed east to them, too. (She saved a thank you note from the future president among her papers.)

The constant gossip about Henri and Constance Bennett was both painful and irritating to Gloria. Throughout 1930 she dodged questions about her husband's affair. "The rumor crop" was "unusually lush and verdant" on the subject of the Swanson love triangle, said one reporter, who thought he heard a "requiem for romance."[22] Once—briefly—it looked as though the separation was "a grand publicity gag" for Swanson's next picture.[23] Reporters trailed Henri and Constance, paparazzi-style, anxious to let the fans know just how often Bennett was seen in the vicinity of the marquis.

Bennett was indifferent to public opinion and looked far sweeter and more innocent than she was; one writer called her "a kitten with platinum claws."[24] (Mary Pickford's nickname for her was Pollyanna Borgia.)[25] She was quick with a comeback: when an overzealous waiter accidentally sprayed Bennett with some of Henri and Gloria's champagne, Henri apologized and Bennett purred, "Think nothing of it, Marquis. I never complain about bathing in champagne."[26]

Bennett enjoyed a contretemps; she was always suing someone or being sued herself. She was happy to stir the pot to heat up her rivalry with Swanson. According to her sister Joan, "The feud between Constance and Gloria was an authentic one, not something contrived by the press." Her sister, said Joan, "created controversy just for the sheer love of battle; it was simply her style."[27]

As angry as she was with Henri, Gloria missed her husband and mourned their lost connection. Her two earlier marriages had been over well before there was a physical separation, but with Henri her hopes and desires had gone deeper. A partner her own age, with whom she had hoped to have children and a sophisticated, international life; a man whom her friends and colleagues liked; someone who did not find her attractive because of her fame but perhaps in spite of it: he had been all this and more.

Yet she had not paid her marriage the attention it needed. Nor had she been honest with Henri about what he was getting into by marrying her: "I'm sure he didn't realize that I was a three-ring circus—that there would be no privacy, that he'd be known as Mr. Swanson, and [that] this would do something to him." Gloria thought the marriage "would never have come to pass if I had told him. Yet it was something deep inside me that I must have known the whole time . . . I wanted my cake and wanted to eat it, too."[28]

At the same time, she acknowledged that her desire for "somebody stronger" than herself kept getting in the way. "A woman," she said, "to be able to love a man, has to be able to look up to him with respect. This is pretty hard to do when you have accomplished more than the other person." Swanson felt she had been "the father" and "the husband" in her household.[29] She wondered what would have happened had she retired from the screen, giving up her career and the demanding, highly public life that went along with it. Yet she had never seriously considered doing so.

Reporters had watched Swanson for more than a decade now, and one harsh assessment hit home: Gloria "is self-conscious and never forgives criticism. . . . She believes she is a keen judge of people, but she isn't. She thinks she is a business man, but she has never proved it. . . . Her one great passion in life is the advancement of Gloria Swanson."[30]

She got the letter she had been dreading from her husband as the New Year began. "Gloria darling," he wrote,

We have come to it . . . that which should never, never have happened . . . has come to be!

. . . .

The fire has burnt the beautiful temple that was our love. We thought it was built of marble, and we wake up to find it has crumbled like the dust of clay. Little can be saved out of the burning ashes. But let's try and preserve our sweet friendship, our regard for each other, our decency!

. . . .

The bridges are broken between us—nothing ever can mend them—we both know it. And though my feelings towards you are sad and very very sweet and loving—I have had to come to the realization that we can never again hope to live together as man and wife.

So, darling, let's face it. I ask you please to make it public that we are separated. Later on in a very quiet way a divorce should come but only when and the way *you* will want it. . . . If you will be sweet enough to do that, darling, it will make things much easier for both of us. . . .

There is lots, lots more I could say to you, Gloria, and would like to say—but what's the use? If you have kept some of my old letters, you may read them. Their only fault is that they did not, could not express half of what I felt for you. That kind of feeling never dies, Gloria, but sometimes it is better to pretend to forget about it.

I am going to seal this letter without rereading it, because if I did I wouldn't send it—and I must.

Good-bye, darling—it's all, all over now.[31]

Gloria read and reread Henri's letter, impressed by his delicacy of feeling and his kindness. He had not mentioned Joe Kennedy. He had not mentioned Constance Bennett. The saddest part of this divorce, she knew, was that she would always love Henri more than the man "on whose account we were separating."[32] Swanson always pretended to believe that her affair rather than Henri's ended their marriage. Stung by her husband's rejection, it was months before she was willing to announce the separation publicly.

Henri had declined to accuse his wife of adultery, but another man was not so circumspect. Since Joe routinely asked Gloria to meet with his business associates, she thought nothing of it when his assistant Ted O'Leary escorted her to a meeting in midtown Manhattan. Only when she was introduced to Cardinal O'Connell of Boston did she realize this might not be a typical business appointment.

An elderly but still powerful man in his seventies, the cardinal did not beat around the bush: he wanted to speak to Gloria about her personal "association" with Joe Kennedy. He knew she was not Catholic and therefore could not grasp the threat to Kennedy's soul that Joe's relation with her posed. The cardinal asked Gloria to stop seeing Kennedy, so that she would no longer be "an occasion of sin" for him.[33] Swanson's response was icy: the cardinal should speak directly to Mr. Kennedy.

Then the cardinal explained that Kennedy had sought permission from the Church to leave his wife and set up housekeeping with

Swanson. This was of course out of the question. Moreover, "as one of the most prominent Catholic laymen in America, Mr. Kennedy was exposing himself to scandal" when he appeared in public with the actress.[34] The cardinal appealed to Swanson's respect for Rose and Joe's family, once again asking her to end the association. Swanson repeated coolly that he needed to speak to Kennedy.

She left the interview angry, humiliated, and perplexed. How had this meeting come about? Had Joe arranged it? If not Joe, then who was responsible? Did Joe even know that she had been summoned to see the cardinal? And had Joe really asked for permission to leave Rose? Ted O'Leary said only that the cardinal had given the order to bring Swanson to him. The Boss knew nothing about it, and Gloria never learned who had orchestrated the meeting.

Most Kennedy scholars find the idea of such a conversation between the actress and the prelate unlikely. Even less likely, most say, is that Kennedy would have asked for a dispensation to end his marriage. Not only was such permission something he could have had no prayer of receiving, but most also find it inconceivable that Kennedy would have seriously considered leaving his family. Others, however, recognize that Swanson did not typically "create events out of whole cloth."[35]

It is impossible to know whether this meeting occurred. If Joe asked for such a dispensation—or even if he told Gloria that he had done so—it may have made her feel more secure about Kennedy's commitment to her, especially as her own marriage unraveled. If Swanson imagined or embroidered her conversation with the cardinal, the most plausible reason is a need to save face. In the same way the actress reshaped the failure of her marriage so it looked like she left Henri, she may have wanted others to believe she controlled her affair with Joe Kennedy. In her story, he becomes a desperate lover who will go to improbable lengths to possess her, not someone whom she could never possess. As Swanson's character Norma Desmond would say twenty years later, "No one leaves a star. That's what makes one a star."

While they were trying to breathe life into *Queen Kelly*, the stock market crashed, heralding the beginning of the Great Depression. Although Hollywood did not feel its ravages for some time, *Queen Kelly*'s failure meant that Swanson had a very rocky ride. Her lover, however, made a great deal of money. Kennedy pulled out of the market early enough not to be harmed and in a good position to pick up for pennies the stocks others discarded. He could afford to be unconcerned about *Queen Kelly*'s financial failure in any event, since his contract with Swanson provided for them to share profits but for her to bear any losses alone. Only his pride was damaged by *Kelly*'s troubles.

Now he wanted to make a picture that assuaged his pride, a hit that originated with him. Swanson thought Joe "had to prove himself to me and to himself." Yet when he commissioned a script for a romantic comedy and presented it to Gloria, she was shocked by how poor it was. There was no getting around it: Kennedy was "a classic example of that person in the arts with lots of brains or drive but little taste or talent."[36]

Swanson gently suggested they ask Allan Dwan to look the script over. Before she could ask Dwan to be diplomatic, however, he told Kennedy it was junk. He suggested they remake *Manhandled* as a talkie.[37] Kennedy was "crestfallen," so Gloria asked Dwan to see if he could find a way to make Joe's story work: "It mean[t] everything to Joe Kennedy to succeed with an idea that started out as his." She reminded Dwan that they had started out with nothing a few times. "Nothing would be preferable" was his reply.[38]

Dwan eventually agreed to take a crack at Kennedy's comedy—but not until he, too, had examined the *Queen Kelly* footage to see if anything could be done with it. He told Kennedy he couldn't understand the plot: "It's either the story of a nun who turned whore, or a whore who turned nun, and I can't figure out which it is. But it's one or the other, and in any case, it stinks."[39] With that, *Queen Kelly* went back on the shelf. Swanson's new picture looked good by comparison. Dwan brought a few writers and actors in, and they improvised situations until they had leavened the heavier-than-usual comedy. Though Kennedy dickered over Dwan's asking price, soon Swanson's old friend was on board to direct.[40]

They needed a title for the picture, a talkie about a wealthy young widow. Dwan suggested that Gloria and Joe solve the problem over dinner: "Why don't you invite all the best writers in town to come over . . . and offer a Cadillac to the fellow who thinks up the best title?" So they did. Hollywood was awash in East Coast writers, and Swanson told the story, reading out bits of dialogue to her guests. "There was a silence," Dwan told Peter Bogdanovich. "They were all rattling their brains when a voice said (not as a suggestion, but just as an exclamation), 'What a widow!' And *that* title was chosen and the guy got a Cadillac. I tell you that just in case you think it's a sane business."[41] Pulitzer Prize-winning playwright Sidney Howard was soon driving around Hollywood in his new car, though Swanson remembered the prize as Joe Kennedy's idea. He had slapped his thigh with delight when he awarded it.

Casting provided another stumbling block, since Kennedy was jealous of any man who even pretended to be in love with his mistress. Joe made a scene when he thought Gloria was getting too chummy with Walter Byron on *Queen Kelly*. (His jealousy may have been warranted: Lois Wilson said Gloria had a "crush" on Byron, who was "no reserved Englishman—not at all!")[42] *What a Widow!* called for Swanson to have "a group of lovesick swells" trailing her as well as two leading men contending for her favors, so Kennedy faced a challenge.[43]

Owen Moore became the society lawyer who woos Swanson. At forty-four, Mary Pickford's ex-husband was a hard-drinking ladies' man. Unfortunately, the producer caught Moore "handling Gloria's right breast during a shot."[44] Kennedy never forgave a wrong: he is said to have thrown a punch at Moore at the film's premiere. Swanson said simply that Moore "was not well" when they made the picture.[45] When Swanson suggested Jack Pickford for one of the two leads, Kennedy accused Gloria of having designs on him. Pickford's drinking and drug use had left only a shadow of the charismatic young man he had been, and Swanson would have been glad to give him a job. "One of [the couple's] few quarrels occurred," according to Lawrence Quirk, "when Joe called Jack 'a hopeless loser.'"[46] Three years later Jack Pickford was dead at thirty-six.

Joe Kennedy wasted no diplomacy. He once refused to hire Mickey Neilan, for good measure calling him a "drunken bum." (On that occasion, Neilan decked Kennedy.) A few years earlier he had rejected Mabel Normand, labeling the actress "a hopeless drug addict" with "no character and no reliability" who was not worth his investment.[47] Normand died of tuberculosis in February 1930, a month before her grieving husband Lew Cody went before the cameras as Gloria Swanson's second leading man in *What a Widow!* Cody had been ill himself and was still angry at Kennedy for denying his beloved wife a chance to work. He had played the other man to Swanson's unhappy young wife more than a decade earlier in *Don't Change Your Husband* and looked his forty-six years. Though Hollywood sentiment ran strongly in his favor, Lew Cody was no one's notion of ideal casting for a bright, lively romantic comedy.

If Kennedy thought he had protected his interest in Swanson by matching her with serviceable but ordinary leading men, he was kidding himself. They needed "six gorgeous young men" to play Swanson's swains, but she only needed one. "Sam Wood sent over one stunner whom we did the favor not to cast in such a trivial part," she said. The young Joel McCrea was "too handsome and too gifted to be wasted."[48] McCrea was a Hollywood native: he had grown up throwing newspapers onto Cecil DeMille's lawn and did stunt work from the time he was a teenager. A boyish twenty-four when he auditioned for Swanson, McCrea lost the part but was welcomed into the actress's bed. She would please herself, with or without Joe Kennedy's approval.

Her fling with Joel McCrea was a wonderful distraction. He was another part-time lover who was often away shooting on location. From Lake Tahoe and Ketchikan, Alaska, McCrea wrote Swanson—whom he called "Mums"—passionately devoted letters: "I don't give a damn about what you have ever been to any one else—I don't even want to hear or know about it—it's what you are *now* to *me* that counts—our lives begin *now*, and the eternal now is all we are sure of."[49] Their eternal now would last through one glorious spring and summer. She also entertained herself with the Argentinian playboy and race car aficionado known as Macoco, who remembered Gloria as "a splendid gal with a sensational body. . . . It was not difficult for me to conquer her heart."[50] She conquered in turn: Miguel Covarrubias pictured Swanson as the muse of Modigliani, Matisse, and Picasso in a wonderful series of caricatures for *Vanity Fair*.

Since the Kennedy-Swanson team was "a little timid," Allan Dwan came up with a plan to streamline the production. "I got the nucleus of the cast together and . . . photographed the entire picture in two days—every scene in master shots, with all the dialogue—but without costumes or makeup or any extras, and none of the action . . . [T]hat way we could see and hear the flow of the story, and were able to correct the parts that were weak."[51] Joe Kennedy had felt so removed from *The Trespasser* that he had not even attached his name to the credits. To compensate, he planned an elaborate, animated title sequence boldly proclaiming just who was responsible for *What a Widow!* This time, everyone would connect the producer to the picture.

With Allan Dwan in charge, *What a Widow!* should have been a pleasure, yet the comic soufflé failed to rise. They did more retakes than anyone expected, the light mood evaporated, and a sense of strain prevailed. Kennedy hired composer Vincent Youmans, whose hit "Tea for Two" had been playing everywhere for months, but the songs he turned in for Swanson were forgettable. A comic production photograph of Youmans playing the piano while Swanson winces and Allan Dwan tries to belt him over the head with a guitar was not, under the circumstances, all that funny.[52]

Then there were the usual production challenges. They wanted to film on the ocean liner *Ile de France* but had to settle for a less glamorous ship. Poor visibility bedeviled their efforts to shoot the New York City skyline from a rented plane for the picture's finale, in which Swanson's character marries Owen Moore just as the Statue of Liberty comes into view (or not). They negotiated with Walt Disney for the animated sequence, but ended up with Dudley Murphy, whose modernist aesthetic was perfect but whose work—as on *The Love of Sunya*—was a long time in coming.

There were successes: architect Paul Nelson contributed chic, ultra-modern sets, and René Hubert fashioned an elegant, streamlined wardrobe for Gloria. With his encouragement, Swanson herself designed a jeweled fan containing a mirror and lipstick. Dwan "opened a scene with a marvelous close-up of me reflected in it," she remembered happily.[53]

Despite the picture's modernist gloss, it was not the critical and commercial success Kennedy sought. Tamarind Brooks's escapades in France fighting off suitors and wearing haute couture were not what audiences wanted as the Depression deepened. The film's comedy felt forced, full of "violent attempts to draw laughter," one reviewer complained.[54] Even the ads seemed miscalculated, playing up the heroine's careless wealth as many looked for their next meal: "With millions and millions she starts on a gay trip to Paris . . . and finds millions and millions, clothes and beaus!"[55]

Selling the picture internationally was complicated by the leading lady's private life, with some markets more problematic than others. UA interoffice communications spelled out the challenge: "Catholic people in Latin-American countries do not look too favorably on third and fourth divorces." As Swanson prepared to do an interview with the Buenos Aires paper *La Nación*, she received advice on what to say (that ideally wives should not work) and how to say it ("in a quietly confidential tone").[56] Under no circumstances, however, should Gloria refer directly to her own marriage or impending divorce.

Although Swanson was dividing her time between Joel McCrea and Joe Kennedy, she dragged her feet about announcing that her marriage to Henri was over. By the summer, however, her husband's patience had run out: when the marquis returned to the US in July 1930, he told a reporter that he had "no knowledge of Miss Swanson's whereabouts."[57] Under the circumstances, Gloria could hardly deny their separation. She finally issued a statement in August acknowledging that she and Henri had lived apart for over a year. She filed for divorce on grounds of abandonment in October.

The fan magazines offered detailed coverage of the dissolution of Swanson's marriage and the love triangle that had apparently precipitated it. Henri's affair with Constance Bennett was "blazing brighter," and the couple was spotted all over Hollywood.[58] Though most writers agreed that working women could not expect to have happy marriages, once in a while a finger was pointed in Henri's direction: "Somehow, he and work never got along," one writer sniffed. It was "inevitable" that when things became less relaxed around the Swanson household, Henri would absent himself: "He had been brought up in an atmosphere of leisure and laughter. It was natural that he should hate the atmosphere of stress and struggle that is artistic creation." Gloria could not have given up working, "since her greatest piece of art is the creation she had made of herself." Nonetheless, she had faced the trials of *Queen Kelly* and the coming of sound alone: "Gloria needed love and encouragement but Henri wasn't there to give it."[59]

Henri "let me go too easily," Swanson reflected sadly. "I went where I could survive."[60] The marquis was quoted as saying only that "everything moves too swiftly in Hollywood for a happy marriage."[61]

Henri did not have an easy time with the impulsive, volatile Constance Bennett, who also carried on an affair with Joel McCrea more or less under the marquis's nose. Bennett handpicked McCrea as her costar and developed "a mad crush" on him, according to one colleague: "The rest of us were just pieces of furniture to her. The minute the director yelled cut, Connie would yank Joel to her portable dressing room, bang the door and not reappear until they were again called to the set."[62] McCrea said only that Bennett was "doggone nice" to him.[63]

By this time, Swanson was already consoling herself with another lover. Dartmouth-educated screenwriter Gene Markey had arrived in California in 1928, slipping easily into the inner circles of movie society, where his debonair manners earned him the nickname "Gentleman Gene." His tall, athletic build and witty, responsive conversation made him attractive to Hollywood's leading ladies: he married Joan Bennett, Myrna Loy, and Hedy Lamarr. Markey was a fun-lover as well, romping at San Simeon with the Hollywood elite. He enjoyed practical jokes as much as Swanson did.

"Gene and I had a gorgeous time," Gloria recalled.[64] Markey, a skilled artist, had already published a book of his caricatures, and he left her love notes with funny little pictures—doodles of himself as a suitor, or images of a closed door with two pairs of shoes cuddled up outside and captioned, "Quiet your nerves this delightful way."[65] Swanson's nerves were often frayed, as she dealt with the endless revisions of *Queen Kelly*, worried about money, and wondered what to do next.

The affair was frequently stormy, and Markey needed his diplomatic skills. He wrote Gloria long, apologetic letters after their quarrels, pledging his eternal love and calling her his "Angel": "Talking to you last night was rather dreadful . . . I felt—and feared so many things . . . and the telephone was so wretchedly inadequate."[66] The pair had public spats. After one argument at the Cocoanut Grove, Swanson left their table, refusing to see Markey or take his calls. When he threatened suicide, Virginia Bowker stepped in, promising to deliver Gloria to Markey's place. Swanson was less gullible: she sent her friend instead, and Virginia found Markey "dressed in a handsome red robe and scarf, a glass of red wine to match in front of the fireplace. It didn't take much persuasion to talk him out of suicide."[67] Like most of her lovers, Markey retained his fondness for Gloria after their affair ended: "Despite what your dark moods counsel," he wrote her, "you are a Child of Fortune . . . and I only hope that I may always be somewhere near."[68]

Another consolation came in the form of a short golden man called Oscar. Once again, Swanson learned that she had been nominated for an Academy Award, this time for *The Trespasser*. She still had mixed feelings about the Academy Awards; now in their third year, they would not become a worldwide preoccupation for a long time. Come November, however, when Oscar went home with Norma Shearer for her performance in *The Divorcee*, Gloria felt a pang.

Then *What a Widow!* fizzled at the box office, and the costly animated sequence announcing Joe Kennedy's name seemed to mock the disheartened producer. No one could miss his flop; he had broadcast it in bold letters. Once again, Swanson found her lover frustrated and dejected. In fact, Joe Kennedy was just about finished with the movie business. He had been extricating himself from his commitments and, now that *What a Widow!* was done, he was ready to move on. He told Gloria he was taking a house in Washington, DC, because he wanted to be "near the real figures of power in the country."[69]

He surprised her with a painting of himself by Geza Kende, who had recently done portraits of Swanson and her children.[70] Kende made Joe look "severe and elegant, very much the chairman of the board, perhaps even a touch of royal family," and Swanson guessed that Kennedy had requested this depiction.[71] "Little by little he grew to be more like the portrait . . . His travels and money gave him a veneer he did not have when I first met him," she said, adding wickedly, "and dear Rose grew with him."[72] That first meeting, when Joe looked like "any average working-class person's uncle" seemed a long time ago.[73]

Swanson chose not to present the end of this relationship directly, in terms of Kennedy's dissatisfaction with the world she lived in and his desire to remain in his own marriage. She did not acknowledge his decision to leave her as the rejection it was. Instead, she recalled being made suddenly and incontrovertibly aware of her partner's financial trickery. Her accountant Irving Wakoff, one of the few employees to survive the Kennedy purge, asked Swanson one day why Sidney Howard's Cadillac had been charged to her personal account: everyone in Hollywood knew that the producer had awarded it to the writer for naming *What a Widow!* Assuming a bookkeeping error, Gloria asked Joe why the Cadillac had not been charged to the picture but rather to her personally. When she questioned him, Kennedy turned white with anger, becoming so agitated that he choked on his dinner.

Swanson knew that Kennedy could be "quick-tempered and unforgiving," although she had only seen him this furious once before.[74] When she overheard him talking on the phone about his mentally disabled daughter Rosemary, she had questioned him about Rosemary's care. Without knowing quite what was wrong with the child, Swanson suggested that Joe bring her to see Dr. Bieler, since diet was such a significant part of any healthy regimen. She described his reaction: "I had seen him angry with other people, but now, for the first time, he directed his anger against me. It was frightening. His blue eyes turned to ice and then to steel. He said they had taken Rosemary to the best specialists in the East. He didn't want to hear about some three-dollar doctor in Pasadena who recommended zucchini and string beans for everything." He "snarled" at her, saying people would think she was "unhinged" if she kept "suggesting that grave illnesses could be treated with squash."[75]

When she tried to reply, Kennedy became enraged: "'I don't want to hear about it!' he roared. 'Do you understand me? *Do you understand me?*'" He regained control of himself quickly, becoming "charming and considerate" once more. "Neither of us mentioned medicine or Rosemary again."[76]

Now Kennedy's unreasoning anger drove a wedge between them. After she questioned his judgment, he left Gloria seated at the dinner table and exited the room without a word: "That was the last I heard from him."[77] She waited for the apology she thought would be forthcoming: "I imagined Joe crushed and ashamed at having behaved so childishly," she said.[78] Instead, he went back to New York and began dismantling their business relations. The affair was over.

In the months ahead, Swanson claimed, she finally discovered the extent of her financial crisis. Even after the Stroheim fiasco, she had remained casual about bookkeeping, uninvolved in the management of her financial affairs. Kennedy's men paid her bills and prepared her taxes, for which her accountant did only the preliminary work. Now she learned that she was responsible for all the bills, not only Sidney Howard's blasted Cadillac. She owed a monumental debt—near a million dollars—on *Queen Kelly* alone.

She had even paid for the gifts Kennedy gave her. The private bungalow she believed was her Christmas present from Joe had been charged to her account: she had paid to build it, and then she had paid Pathé to rent it to her. She had paid for the fur coat Joe bought and put around her shoulders. As she and Irving Wakoff began to disentangle her assets and liabilities, Swanson at long last registered the significance of her money problems. She was not only no better off than she had been when Joe Kennedy came along: her problems were much worse. "I was anything but rich, or even financially independent," she realized. "I had been living a life of royalty, but I had been paying for it out of my own earnings."[79]

This was Kennedy's strategy: the links between his companies meant that (as Cari Beauchamp says) "Kennedy took from one pocket and filled the other, keeping everything on paper aboveboard."[80] Swanson put it another way: "Joe Kennedy operated just like Joe Stalin. Their system was to write a letter to the files and then order the exact reverse on the phone."[81] The studio system was set up to benefit its large and powerful members, with independents forced to pay top dollar for services they needed, yet Kennedy took this to a new level. He treated Gloria Productions as a "sieve" through which he funded his Pathé operations, charging Swanson for loans he made but whose benefits his own company reaped.[82] She paid and paid and paid.

Swanson knew she had had ample opportunity to take charge of her own business earlier, yet the attraction of her affair with Joe Kennedy was that she did not have to trouble herself with such matters. Exhausted and overwhelmed by her fastidious attention to every detail on *The Love of Sunya* and *Sadie Thompson*, Swanson had made a massive course correction, signing away whatever financial security her hard work might have created. Joe Schenck had gotten the profits from *Sadie* and now Joe

Kennedy would reap his share of the benefits from *The Trespasser* and—if there were any profits—from *What a Widow!* Swanson's share of both films would not cover her losses on *Queen Kelly* or pay for her extravagant standard of living. She had foolishly neglected to read the print, much less the fine print, on the agreements made in her name.

It always made Swanson see red that Joe Kennedy claimed to have sorted out her financial mess and left her independent, when their association instead tripled her debt. He realized millions of dollars in profits from his assorted Hollywood enterprises—the sale of his RKO and FBO stock, the fees he claimed from reorganizing companies and arranging mergers, and on and on. He more than recouped whatever he had risked on *Queen Kelly*, while it took Swanson years to climb out of the hole they had dug together.

The lawyers and accountants she hired to make sense of the mess had no access to Kennedy's books, although those records might not have helped much. As one biographer says, "Joe Kennedy spent his life making money—and hiding it. . . . [T]he seemingly straightforward Kennedy was, at best, extremely secretive and, at worst, an incessant liar on all matters involving his financial interests."[83] In fact, Swanson got no help from the Kennedy staff—only a curt announcement from E. B. Derr resigning his power of attorney for Gloria Productions. She felt like she had been fired from her own company.

When asked his impression of Joe Kennedy years later, Allan Dwan said, "I think he was just playing with this business—it was a toy—and he enjoyed it."[84] However, Kennedy was no longer amused by the game. One biographer believes that Joe pretended to be angry with Swanson because he needed a quick and convenient exit: "His instinct told him that Gloria was getting too inquisitive about the money ins and outs . . . [B]y pulling the hurt, high-dudgeon act, Joe rid himself of her."[85] Another claims it was always about the money: Kennedy "saw everything and everyone, from Gloria Swanson to Adolf Hitler, through a lens of dollars and cents."[86]

Gloria had imagined she would be safe with him, just as she had imagined she would be safe with Herbert Somborn, another older man whose business skills she initially admired. In the end, Somborn had also made Gloria pay, for the gifts he gave her and eventually for her freedom. Joe Kennedy was an operator on a far grander scale than anything Herbert Somborn could have imagined, yet this was a familiar story for Swanson: "Once again I had misjudged people and had been deceived by someone I had totally trusted, and I was stunned and in pain. In spite of my reputation for will and stamina and pluck and durability, all I wanted was to call for my mother or to hold my babies in my arms and sob . . . But although I could feel anguish and despair as well as the next woman, I couldn't succumb to them, or wouldn't . . . I just wasn't built that way . . . I was a survivor."[87]

At least one of Swanson's friends thought she was better off without him. Kennedy's shame about his daughter's disability sickened Lois Wilson: "He thought of Rosemary as another of his failures—to be the father of a *retard*—that was humiliating. Gloria should have sensed right at that point what kind of man she had taken up with!"[88] Yet for all his sins, Swanson would retain an equivocal fondness for the wily rogue. She kept one note from the man who wrote in code and left almost no paper trail behind. Scrawled on a bit of stationery from an anti-Communist organization were the words "G I love you. Joe."[89]

Kennedy regaled listeners with stories of his spirited mistress for years. He reportedly enjoyed telling his daughter-in-law Jackie "intimate details" about Swanson's body and her insatiable appetite for sex. Gloria had orgasms not once, Joe said mockingly, but "five times a night."[90] However, his own appetite for the actress had been close to insatiable. According to one friend, Kennedy ruefully claimed that forty was "a dangerous age."[91] He would never again let anyone outside the family get so close.

Gloria eventually came to see that for Joe Kennedy she had represented an ideal combination: both the Marquise de la Falaise and Sadie Thompson, the feisty hooker: "In his mind, I had become the ideal woman . . . the kind of lady who appeals to all ambitious men—the kind who rocks kingdoms and rules international tycoons: the duchess by day, the whore by night. From his pillow talk I got the message: he wanted the real woman in public and the actress in private."[92]

The financial fallout from her association with Joe Kennedy, coming at the same time as the transition to sound and the beginning of the Depression, would remain the biggest setback in Swanson's career. But if she called Joe Kennedy "an adversary who was cruel and strong," she also came to be grateful for the lessons he taught her. Once she had recovered her footing and relinquished her bitterness, Swanson showed a flash of humor at the mention of the Kennedy name: "My two year association with Joe was the best finishing school in the world," she said. "If he couldn't finish me, nobody ever could."[93]

CHAPTER 16

Mad about the Boy

GLORIA SWANSON DID NOT ADMIT DEFEAT EASILY. NOR DID SHE HAVE the luxury of mourning her losses for long: "It was as if the two men— my ex-husband and my ex-paramour—had in some mysterious way, through me, canceled each other out . . . I was completely on my own again, without love and without security."[1]

Swanson's insecurity deepened as the Depression reached Hollywood. The large capital outlays required for the conversion to sound made the studios more reliant on Wall Street financing, and that meant further oversight—some said interference—from money managers intent on protecting their investments. Established stars, even those who had made a successful sound picture or two, could not be certain of their continuing box office power. As Hedda Hopper reported, "The crying need was for some good dialogue writers, and for men with sense enough left to give silent stars a chance to find out if they could speak in this new medium. In our town, though, common sense has no market value. We do everything the hard way."[2]

The drive toward realism that came with sound meant that some silent stars who represented larger-than-life fantasies became passé. Those with strong foreign accents (like Pola Negri and Vilma Banky) or voices that did not match their screen personae (like Charles Farrell) were out as well. Sometimes the fussy and unreliable recording equipment was at fault. Many actresses were hiring vocal coaches, though no one could make Clara Bow's Brooklynese sound like the King's English. That was fine by Bow, who decided she didn't like sound pictures; they were "stiff and limiting," with "no chance for action."[3] Some stars were ready to call it a day. Norma Talmadge took the advice of her sister Constance, who had already retired: "Quit pressing your luck, baby. The critics can't knock those trust funds Mom set up for us."[4] Louise Brooks said Paramount gave her "the salary treatment": "I could stay on without the raise my contract called for, or quit." Brooks figured that the coming of sound was "a splendid opportunity . . . for breaking contracts, cutting salaries, and taming the stars."[5]

Historians disagree about the extent to which the studios guided the transition of the major stars, some arguing that the moguls presided over a wholesale housecleaning: "Throw her out! Mess her up so the competition won't grab her. Use sound—maybe she'll talk funny. Give her the worst director in Hollywood. Make her sing, make her charleston. Throw them all out, that bunch who thought they owned Hollywood! Swanson, Chaplin, Pickford, Fairbanks, Talmadge, the united schmartists. This is the age of studio, producer power. Fit in or get out."[6]

Though it is unlikely that studios sabotaged their proven stars, a move toward prioritizing the producer had been taking place for several years. The established stars were expensive, and they were aging. Why not let new, less pricey talent come to the fore? "Most silent stars were very badly presented in their early talkies," says Richard Koszarski, citing "the inability of Hollywood's best minds to predict a method of pushing silent stars into the age of talkies."[7]

The United Artists were actor/producers, their paychecks directly tied to how much money their films made. Chaplin thumbed his nose at sound, waiting until 1931 to produce *City Lights*, which boasted music and sound effects but kept the beloved Tramp mute: it made $5 million. Mary Pickford lopped her off her golden curls for her first talkie, effectively killing off the young girl who had made her fortune. Her fans were not as loyal to the woman as they had been to Little Mary, but Pickford remained defiant: adding talk to motion pictures was like putting "lip rouge on the Venus de Milo."[8] She made a few more pictures, but her heart was no longer in it. Neither was Doug's: the action/adventure star's energy was flagging, and he was bored with the movies.

With two talkies behind her, Swanson was ready to consider other options. Oscar Hammerstein offered her the lead in his next play, but their schedules conflicted. Negotiations to appear onstage with Basil Rathbone in *A Kiss of Importance* went nowhere. She was offered $50,000 for a 50,000-word autobiography—more than five times what Norma Talmadge got from *The Saturday Evening Post*—but hesitated to deliver what her publicist called "real meat."[9] She was asked to do a singing tour and to make umpteen radio appearances. NBC offered her $4,500 for a radio broadcast in New York, but her travel expenses would eat up half of that amount; unless she could combine the trip with another paying job, it wasn't worth it. Louella Parsons expected actresses to appear

on her Sunkist-sponsored radio show without being compensated at all.
Mary Pickford, Norma Shearer, and Constance Bennett had accepted her
invitation, possibly to forestall Louella's complaints in the Hearst press,
her regular platform. Swanson's staff, however, saw no reason why she
should appear on a commercial program without being paid. Moreover,
film exhibitors disapproved of stars appearing on radio, worried their
own revenues would decrease if people stayed home to listen.

None of these offers was lucrative enough to replace movie work.
When you had heavy debts and an exceptionally high standard of living,
the movies were the only game in town. Swanson owed the taxman. She
owed the lawyers. She owed the people who sold her clothes, jewelry,
furs, and furniture. On the plus side, she owned some investment property, as well as the big house in Beverly Hills, the lease on the New York
apartment, and a beach house in Malibu. *The Trespasser* helped pay down
the monumental debt from *Queen Kelly*, but its success made her other creditors crankier about waiting. Even had she wanted to, Swanson
could not have seriously considered leaving pictures; for years to come,
financial pressures would drive her professional choices.

She had mixed feelings about venturing out alone again, however:
the shelter of a studio affiliation beckoned. Swanson approached Louis
B. Mayer, reasoning that M-G-M's glossy, glamorous approach offered
the closest fit for her own established persona. Mayer seemed amenable
to producing her pictures for release through United Artists, as Swanson
was still required to do. They had nearly hammered out a deal when
Mayer suddenly asked Swanson to see Joe Schenck. "I knew perfectly
well what that meant," she said sourly. "There had been a meeting of the
pinochle club."[10]

Swanson's distaste for Hollywood executives included Schenck, who
had been more preoccupied and less protective of her than Gloria needed on her first UA pictures. As disinclined as she was to negotiate with
Schenck, Swanson had little choice but to offer him first refusal on a
contract. As Bessie Love explained, "If . . . you run into a gentlemen's
agreement among the big boys not to bid against each other while you're
freelancing, you may not realize at first that you are out of work, and
think you are only 'resting' between jobs."[11]

Gloria's meeting with Schenck therefore came as a pleasant surprise.
"He treated me like a long-lost child," she recalled, warming under
Schenck's praise for *The Trespasser* and his pledge to guide Swanson's career with the care she deserved. "At heart Joe Schenck was a very sentimental man."[12] They agreed on a contract for four pictures at a straight

salary of $250,000 each—although her offer from M-G-M was report-edly $1.6 million.[13] The contract offered Gloria both financial stability and freedom from worrying about her box office grosses.

Almost from the beginning there was trouble. Schenck, who wore many hats in the organization, was called away to manage a complex dispute that was shutting UA pictures out of western theaters. He left Sam Goldwyn in charge. Preoccupied with bringing "new faces and fresh personalities" into the UA fold, Goldwyn had little time or inclination to work with Swanson.[14] He was committed to efficiency and thought the UA members should make movies in a more timely and cost-effective manner. In fact, as the 1920s ended, "'The company built by the stars' was beginning to pass out of their hands. It was producer-businessmen-showmen . . . who were to dominate United Artists in the '30s and keep its reputation alive."[15]

For her next picture, Swanson wanted to produce a property she al-ready owned. Though Joe Kennedy had sneered at *Rockabye*, he also advised Gloria to hold on to it: predictions called for "disastrous grosses" through late 1931, with "good material . . . scarcer than ever."[16] A com-plicated melodrama about an actress and adoptive mother who loses her child, it bore similarities to *The Trespasser*. However, *Rockabye* didn't ap-peal to Goldwyn, nor did he want Swanson to produce herself. There were "plenty of explosions in the vicinity of Samuel Goldwyn's confer-ence chambers."[17] The contretemps sent Gloria back to Schenck, who now seemed an ally. "Joe, there are things which have no price," she wrote. "In producing the picture myself I naturally could arrange work-ing conditions which, while they might not fit in with Sam Goldwyn's idea, nevertheless would assure me a much greater degree of comfort."[18] Schenck, however, refused to overrule Goldwyn: Gloria would have to accept his supervision.

Goldwyn did not make this any easier. The producer was intelligent and capable but also brash and undiplomatic. He reportedly made some "uncomplimentary remarks about Gloria's acting [and] her taste in clothes," then offered to purchase *Rockabye* for a laughably low amount.[19] When Swanson refused to sell at a loss, word spread that she was be-ing contentious. One chronicler sympathetic to Swanson scoffed at the idea that "her spirit isn't right. As if without the right spirit and lots of it, Gloria could have survived the last few years!"[20]

The spat with Goldwyn fractured whatever idea Gloria had of an easy, carefree tour of duty. After spending months (and almost $100,000) to develop *Rockabye* for herself, she sold it to RKO in 1932 for Constance

Bennett—who brought her lover Joel McCrea into the picture with her. Swanson took some small satisfaction when Bennett's version, initially deemed unreleasable, struggled through changes of director and cast before limping into theaters. At least Gloria got a paycheck for *Rockabye*.

Goldwyn wanted her to follow *What a Widow!* with another comedy. Though Swanson had reservations about doing two funny pictures in a row, they settled on a story called *Obey That Impulse*. Director Leo McCarey had put Charley Chase and the Our Gang kids through their paces; he had paired Laurel with Hardy. He would direct Mae West, W. C. Fields, and the Marx Brothers. McCarey knew comedy—and he knew right off that *Impulse* was not funny.

Swanson's character, Jerry, is a fashion designer whose inexperienced younger sister falls in love with a cad. Unfortunately, the cad is the same fellow who once betrayed Jerry. When Jerry sets out to rescue her sister, she gets caught up in a series of misunderstandings with her lover, the author of a book called *Obey That Impulse* who takes his own advice seriously. Renamed *Indiscreet*, the picture was planned as a musical comedy, with songs by DeSylva, Brown, and Henderson, a top Tin Pan Alley team whose work was catchy, jazzy, and upbeat.

If McCarey was unimpressed by the comedy, Swanson was underwhelmed by the songs. She thought they were all wrong for her voice, and in short order they were eliminated. The director remembered the whole project as ill-conceived and hurried: "Just before we started, word came out from New York that 'the public was tired of musicals'. . . . So I moved in with Buddy De Sylva and in ten days we wrote another story."[21]

In the rewrite, McCarey exploited an angle that had Jerry pretending to be crazy. The insanity ploy, coupled with the romantic hijinks strung throughout the plot, turned *Indiscreet* into an early screwball comedy, one of the signature genres of the 1930s. Swanson, however, was uncomfortable with the shift and complained to Goldwyn: the script was "radically different" than the synopsis she had approved, which was to have been "elaborated along dramatic lines."[22] She considered "backing out on the whole miserable project."[23] McCarey seemed "sort of wild."[24] Yet Swanson had often thrived in a rambunctious atmosphere of improvisation and makeshift, anarchic energy.

Maybe things would have been different if she had been part of the rewrite team. Swanson's best pictures invariably had a touch of comedy, and she usually helped invent her character's funny business. Now, however, there was a deeper division of labor afoot. McCarey himself complained that he had to keep his involvement in the writing a secret from the producer, since Goldwyn frowned on a director doing a writer's job: he was "a stickler for form . . . If you tried to intrude in someone else's province, he'd step on you right away and say, 'That's not your department. Stay out of it.'"[25]

At least Gloria had a friend in the cast: Ben Lyon, her onetime fiancé and *Wages of Virtue* costar, played the impulse-obeying suitor. However, Swanson adopted a snooty, aloof air with the other players that did the comic enterprise little good. Barbara Kent, who played her younger sister, was disappointed by the woman who had been her screen idol: "She was not exactly unfriendly, but was very, very much the star."[26] McCarey "didn't have much fun" making *Indiscreet*, either, but he was philosophical about it: "It just wasn't a good vehicle; those were hectic days in this business."[27]

What Leo McCarey saw as hectic, Sam Goldwyn saw as efficient. He planned to move Swanson quickly through two more pictures before the year ended. Yet Swanson, smarting from Goldwyn's treatment, was not anxious to oblige. That winter she attended the premiere of Chaplin's new picture, *City Lights*, envying the way Charlie unapologetically occupied a territory all his own. Of course, he was surrounded by all his own people. (Yet even Chaplin confessed that he was "obsessed by a depressing fear of being old-fashioned."[28] There was enough anxiety to go around.)

Swanson worried about losing control of her career, though being in charge of it had been worrisome and thankless in equal measure. Although her new contract did not give her story approval, she knew she would be held accountable—by management and by her fans—if her pictures did not succeed. She was in a ticklish position: recognizably independent but without the organization and the money to make her freedom more than nominal. With Kennedy's abdication, Gloria Swanson Productions had new corporate officers: Swanson, accountant Irving Wakoff, and publicity chief Lance Heath. However, none of them had the uncanny ability of Adolph Zukor or Jesse Lasky to know what audiences wanted even before they wanted it. None of them could guide her through troubled waters. In 1931, Swanson at last hired an experienced attorney specifically to oversee her business interests. Loyd Wright administered the star's affairs conscientiously for fifteen years and was one of the few people who always told her the unvarnished truth.

Over the years some claimed that Swanson made poor decisions because she surrounded herself with sycophants. Others thought she was

simply deaf to opinions that disagreed with her own. In this, as in everything, Swanson was a study in contradictions. She was endlessly curious,
enormously energetic, and preferred the company of the most intelligent
and creative people she could find. She thrived on lively companions who
could teach her new things and offer her new experiences. However, she
did not easily trust others. She preferred to depend on herself, asserting
a fierce, even truculent independence, then complained she had no one
on whom she could absolutely rely. Yet under the forceful pull of her
strong enthusiasms, she sometimes trusted the wrong people too readily.

She was unusually ambitious and, as sole proprietor of the Gloria
Swanson brand, knew she was ultimately responsible for its fate. She
felt keenly her obligation to support her family and staff, yet also spent
recklessly, which lessened her ability to make other choices freely. She
often paid the price in exhaustion and frustration. She had a fair idea of
her abilities and aimed for variety in her projects, both to keep herself
interested and to keep her audiences guessing. Yet her judgment was
sometimes shaky: she could be shrewd but was not always wise. She was
by turns mercurial and mulishly stubborn.

Adolph Zukor, who knew stars and stardom better than almost anyone, claimed there were two qualities on which a durable fame was
built: "The lasting popular star always plays himself or herself, or a part
thereof" and "The star who lasts must have a very strong character—
even if that character is not altogether admirable off the screen."[29] He
might have been describing Gloria Swanson.

She did have good friends who took her down a peg when she became
insufferable. Although Sport Ward teased Gloria about her amorous conquests, he was displeased when her marriage to Henri failed. Swanson
knew it and wired him: "Why in the heck aren't you man enough to acknowledge you don't like it? Love and hisses."[30] Sport replied at length,
enclosing his bitter pill in a gentle dose of sugar. "Since you have opened
the subject," he wrote, "I must admit I am very much disappointed." He
said Gloria had "as much experience as anyone in the movies, and by
this time you should be a better judge than you have shown yourself to
be. I had . . . expected this to be a success, and when I saw it was not, I
was reluctant to criticise."

Sport complained that he had just had Gloria's family portrait made.
Maybe he should set up a bulletin board "whereby new faces can be
added at random against a black ground." He was prepared for a dozen—
"maybe a baker's dozen." If the number went higher, "all that would be
necessary would be to get a new frame and a mat. . . . As soon as you

decide on No. 4, send his photograph at once, and I assure you there will be no delay in getting up the revised family group." He closed by saying, "Although I am a little disappointed, I admire your pluck and 'never say die' spirit. . . . If you don't succeed at first, try, try again. Love and kisses."[31]

Sport had a way of letting Gloria know his feelings without unkindness or derision. He nicknamed her "Della," after de la Falaise, and Swanson answered to it and to him for the rest of his days.

In early 1931, Sport brought the news that Joe Kennedy was escorting a dead ringer for Gloria around Havana and Palm Beach. (He pretended to have confused Paramount actress Nancy Carroll, "all dolled up in your little chiffon dress and big drooping hat," with Gloria, whom Carroll slightly resembled.)[32] Reading between the lines, Swanson understood that Sport felt she was "well rid of Joe."[33] It was embarrassing enough that Kennedy was sharing details of their sex life, but he was also saying he had lost money working with her. That really rankled, and Swanson, better than anyone, knew it wasn't so. The least he could do was stop bragging about a hiding he hadn't even taken.

He had fallen out with everyone in the industry. Eddie Mannix told Gloria that Kennedy threatened to pull M-G-M stock "down to the gutter" if the studio employed his former assistants Sullivan and Derr. He had even reportedly urged Louis B. Mayer not to hire her. This did not surprise Swanson: "If anyone crossed him and his aims, he stopped at nothing to teach them a lesson. He could always go to confession and ease his conscience, if he had one."[34]

Swanson and Kennedy remained in sporadic touch, leading some to conclude that their affair continued well into the 1930s.[35] However, the actress rarely burned bridges. No matter how bitter a falling-out, she did not sever her connections. Despite her fury with Jesse Lasky and Cecil DeMille for tricking her into paying off Herbert Somborn, Swanson resumed friendly contact with both men. She patched things up with Joe Schenck. She held no grudges against her discarded lovers: Mickey Neilan, Joel McCrea, Ben Lyon, Rod LaRocque, and others crossed her path socially over many decades. She shared parental duties with Herbert Somborn and would build a warm friendship with Henri de la Falaise— though she never had a good word to say about Wally Beery. His role in the loss of her sexual innocence and the termination of her first pregnancy remained unforgivable.

Typically, however, Swanson had a pragmatic, even philosophical, sense that life carried on: "For me endings would always be inseparable from . . . beginnings."[36] By the summer of 1931, her affair with Gene Markey had run its course; he soon fell under the spell of Joan Bennett. When Markey married Constance's younger sister in 1932, the score stood at Bennetts 2, Swanson 0.

UA planned a gala London premiere for *Indiscreet* in June, and Gloria looked forward to a reprieve from California and all her cares. She decided to take the children and spend the summer abroad. They stopped in New York, and Gloria and Virginia made the rounds of theater excursions and parties. The Depression was deepening, and plays like *Grand Hotel*, *Green Pastures*, and *Waterloo Bridge* (with Gloria's friend June Walker) offered marvelous escapes. Swanson had become chummy with Clifton Webb, who was on Broadway in the musical revue *Three's a Crowd*. They went clubbing and to see the play Schenck and Goldwyn had acquired for Gloria's next screen venture.

Tonight or Never was an effervescent romance built around the premise that a prima donna cannot be a truly great singer until she falls madly, uncontrollably in love. The mysterious stranger Nella falls for in Venice may be a kept man, but she nonetheless accepts his challenge: to stay with him "tonight or never." The next night in Budapest, Nella gives an impassioned performance and is offered a starring contract with the Metropolitan Opera in New York. Ashamed of giving in to her desire, Nella asks her lover to reform his wild ways; in return, she will give up her performing career. Then he reveals that he is not a gigolo after all, but the Met's contracting agent. All ends happily, with love and employment guaranteed. The play pleased New York audiences with its sharp blend of sass and sex, and Goldwyn snapped up almost the entire Broadway cast. Swanson liked the handsome leading man, Melvyn Douglas in his first movie role.

Goldwyn was particularly pleased by another coup: Coco Chanel would create Swanson's costumes. In fact, he wanted all his actresses to be dressed exclusively by Chanel, onscreen and off. Chanel visited California in April 1931 to observe the movie business. Though she was welcomed by Greta Garbo, Marlene Dietrich, and Claudette Colbert, she was unimpressed, coolly declaring that Hollywood "was like an evening at the Folies Bergères. Once you've said the girls were beautiful and there were a lot of feathers around, you've said it all."[37]

Swanson also balked. She did not feel confident that the French designer knew what it took to make costumes for the screen. Outfitting actresses was different than couturier style: "Actresses are not mannequins displaying gowns. . . . A gown, on the screen, shows off the actress.

And a gown must show off the specific actress who is wearing it," fitting her personality and the action.[38] A fashion leader herself, Gloria did not intend to follow because it suited Sam Goldwyn. She already had a favorite designer, René Hubert, and she preferred his work. Her contract, however, did not give her right of refusal: Chanel was in.

The London premiere of *Indiscreet* was more successful than Swanson expected, with reviews "either enthusiastic or so polite they seemed enthusiastic." At the party at Claridge's, she danced with the exiled King Alfonso of Spain and made friends with Lady Sylvia Ashley. Noel Coward played songs from *Cavalcade*, while Gloria, Doug Fairbanks, and Eddie Goulding sang harmony. Soon she and Virginia were off to Paris with the children; an admirer had lent Gloria his mansion. For the first time in a long while, she said, "I was a free person—no husband, no jealous lover, no secret trysts to keep. I decided to have a good time."[39]

Nowhere was that easier than in Paris. The Depression had not yet reached France, and with Eddie Goulding and Noel Coward around, the City of Lights seemed to sparkle. After the grim determination of Joe Kennedy to make his prestige picture under the withering gaze of American censors, the company of bright, creative people who loved wit and beauty was a blessed relief.

One evening she saw a gorgeous, dark-haired young man sitting alone at a table accompanied by two small dogs, one white and one black. What kind of fellow brings his dogs to a nightclub, she wondered. Her friends explained that Michael Farmer did whatever he pleased, whenever he pleased.[40] Farmer was a fun-loving Irishman who followed the seasons, going wherever the most amusing people gathered. Swanson admired his athletic build: Farmer sailed and hunted, skied and fished. No one knew where his money came from, but he was the protégé of a rich American woman.

Michael Farmer soon made it clear he was prepared to spend all his time amusing Gloria, and she was in the mood to be amused. He took her to his favorite spots for dancing and drinking. They both loved Chez Bricktop, a club run by an African-American woman with flaming red hair and freckles, and "Bricky" loved them both: "Gloria was one of the few American movie stars who were accepted by the Bricktop's crowd," she claimed. "What a lady—and cooool."[41] Bricktop's catered to a small group of wealthy pleasure seekers, artists, and performers. Opera diva Grace Moore sang there for her friends. So did Cole Porter. Michael Farmer had long used the café as his headquarters in Paris, and he was notorious there.

Anything went at Bricktop's, and Farmer often went over the top: "If I had on a dress that he didn't like," Bricktop remembered, "he'd just tear it down the front and say, 'Bricky, go down to Schiaparelli and get a new dress! I'll pay for it.' That always got a laugh, and sometimes I'd deliberately wear something I knew he wouldn't like because when he did it he livened up the whole place. It was hard to get angry at Michael. He was like an overgrown kid. I felt the same way about him as I did about Scott Fitzgerald. . . . There was something light-hearted and elegant about the way those people did everything."[42]

There were always celebrations, and Farmer learned how to drop a bottle of champagne so that it shattered the expensive glass floor panels and made a satisfying pop. "As long as he didn't mind paying, I really didn't mind if he did it," the owner said. "I had a soft spot in my heart for Michael."[43]

It didn't hurt that Farmer was "the best-looking guy in town . . . a real cut-up," and "one of those famous big spenders who are all but extinct now." "There was an *awful* lot of money," Bricktop remembered. "There was an attitude of total abandon that I don't think anyone who wasn't there could really understand."[44]

It didn't take long for Swanson to recover her own spirit of mirth and playfulness in Paris. She enjoyed her fittings with Coco Chanel and attended a fabulous soiree at the designer's home: all-white flowers and white lights adorned a huge tent of gold tissue constructed in the garden. There were wonderful after-hours parties at Gloria's place, too, with music and laughter and always, always champagne. It seemed very far from her California life of incessant worries about money and movies.

Virginia, Eddie, and Gloria spent several weeks cruising the Riviera on Michael Farmer's sailboat. It was a halcyon time, as they glided through the perfect blue waves under Farmer's expert guidance. They went to the fifth-century Cistercian monastery across from Cannes. They drifted down to Monte Carlo, stopping at Antibes and Nice. Sometimes they stayed on the boat; when the mood took them they moved into the Hotel du Cap Eden Roc. They went to Grace Moore's wedding in Cannes, and the bride recalled, "From the way [Swanson and Farmer] caught fire I felt that perhaps we would end up with a double wedding that very day."[45] The Riviera had always been a winter getaway; according to Bricktop, Swanson and Farmer "started Cannes as a summer resort."[46]

Gloria soon felt refreshed and relaxed as she had not in years. Michael's high spirits were infectious; his company reminded her of Mickey Neilan, though "he had a physique like Henri's and the chiseled facial features of a Craney Gartz."[47] He was a good host and always the life of the party. She ignored the fact that when he drank, Michael became jealous and possessive. As long as they were alone, he was divine, but one day after an argument at a garden party, Swanson walked out, leaving Farmer high up in a tree he had climbed. A short time later, Eddie Goulding called, begging Gloria to come help calm Farmer down: he was threatening to commit suicide by sailing out, then scuttling his boat. "Of course I'd promise [Michael] anything if he'd behave," Swanson said, clearly excited by the drama Farmer produced when he was drinking.[48]

Mostly that summer, as they skimmed through the crystal waters, dancing on tiled patios overlooking the sea and drinking champagne, Swanson saw the romantic side of her new lover. She ignored the cables Joe Schenck sent asking when she would return to work: the break was doing her good. Even running into Henri with Connie Bennett on his arm did not distress her.

Gloria had only one worry: she had found a lump on her breast the size of a pigeon's egg. She and Virginia cut their Riviera idyll short to go to Paris, where Gloria saw the physician who saved her life after her 1925 abortion. Swanson trusted Dr. Vodescal, and he put her under ether to do a biopsy in his office. Twenty-four hours later, Gloria nervously went for the results. Smiling, the doctor reassured her that it was only a cyst; they sometimes occurred years after a pregnancy that had not gone full term. "'But this time, my dear Marquise,'" he said, 'you must not interrupt the pregnancy. You may be risking your life if you do. . . . You and the Marquis are going to have your little baby at last.'"[49] The good doctor had no idea his patient was divorced, and Swanson had no idea she was pregnant. She knew immediately, however, that she wanted this baby.

How she would manage it was a puzzle. Swanson's divorce from Henri would not be final for several more months. The irony was devastating: she began her marriage to Henri pregnant with a child she wanted but could not bear because of the month-counting overseers of her fame. Now as her marriage ended, she was pregnant again, and again it would be clear that her child was conceived while she was (more or less) single. She felt it was "an absolute fluke": "For years I desperately wanted a baby with Henri and I couldn't get pregnant. Then for years I was constantly terrified that I would get pregnant with Joe Kennedy—which *he* wanted in the worst way—but I didn't. Now, out of the blue, some black-Irish playboy tips his yachting cap once to me in the moonlight, and bingo!—I'm pregnant."[50]

Though of short duration, the affair had not been a matter of a single evening in the moonlight. Yet Swanson's dilemma was real. She wanted the baby; however, she had no interest in marrying Michael Farmer. They barely knew each other. If gentle, affable Henri had been unable to adapt to life as Mr. Gloria Swanson, Michael Farmer seemed an even less likely candidate. Yet on the few occasions when she tried to break it off, Farmer became so distraught that she couldn't make her decision stick. "What I wanted more than anything were children," Swanson said. "I had only two choices as an unwed woman: having a child and facing the world, especially my world, as an adulteress and my child a bastard. . . . Marriage seemed a solution. But Michael! A father? A husband? This seemed wild, crazy. I was sure he'd agree it was insane, out of the question and that was no kind of life for a playboy."[51]

Swanson asked Virginia and Eddie to help her pull off a big deception. Could they marry—temporarily—and pretend that Gloria's baby was theirs? Later she could adopt her friends' child. She already had one adopted son; no one would care if she adopted again. When Virginia and Eddie just stared at her, Swanson realized how crazy she sounded. Besides, she could not hide for seven months: she was due in California for *Tonight or Never* almost immediately.

At a loss, Swanson finally told Michael she was pregnant—whereupon Farmer surprised her by insisting she marry him. If she refused, he said, he would make a public announcement that she was pregnant. Swanson felt he left her no choice but to accept. Maybe it would all work out; after all, Michael had been claiming since their affair began that Gloria was the only woman he would ever marry. Now it seemed she was stuck with the "handsome devil."[52]

Her friends were surprised and dismayed. Virginia couldn't stand Michael and thought Gloria was making a huge mistake. Yet Swanson could not be dissuaded. With the proud papa by her side, she indulged in dreams of a happy pregnancy and another tiny new member of her family. Little Gloria was almost eleven, Brother almost nine, and Baby would make three. They would have to be discreet about the ceremony, to avoid questions about the timing of the pregnancy. In fact, the best thing Gloria could do now was get back to the States quickly, get married quietly, and begin shooting *Tonight or Never*: soon she would not be able to hide her bump. Virginia loyally packed up the children so Swanson could get on with it.

After the couple arrived in New York in August, the press kept asking Swanson about the new man in her life, with whom she was "apparently on the friendliest terms." Swanson would neither confirm nor deny rumors of her impending nuptials but laughed off suggestions that she and Henri might reconcile: "Anything is possible, but not that."[53] Her coy responses only fueled speculation.

However, she had already secretly married Michael Farmer. Swanson wired ahead from the *Aquitania*, and her friend Dudley Field Malone arranged for a quiet civil ceremony at his estate in Elmsford, New York, a short drive from the city. On August 16, 1931, Gloria Swanson took her fourth husband, with no press releases and no fanfare.

She guarded the news as closely as possible, since she was still legally married to Henri de la Falaise. Swanson was technically committing bigamy when she married Michael Farmer, a calculated risk she hoped would draw neither the wrath of the authorities nor the studio supervisors. She was gambling on no one paying much attention to the difference between a solemnized union and a legal one. Protecting the legitimacy of her child trumped other concerns, yet she also wanted to preserve her career. Now she needed to get back to work quickly before her pregnancy became undeniable. A few hours after the ceremony, the newlyweds boarded a train heading west. Clifton Webb traveled with them, he and Michael behaving "like a couple of kids" along the route.[54]

Yet if Swanson thought she could manage the press, she had an unpleasant surprise in store. Journalists had gotten wind of a good story—especially paired with the likely nuptials of Henri de la Falaise and Constance Bennett—and would not leave Gloria and Michael alone. By the time they got to California, Gloria was issuing outright denials: it was much too soon to be thinking of another marriage, she claimed. For now, Michael Farmer was simply "a marvelous person and a wonderful friend."[55] They dodged reporters, keeping Gloria out of sight as much as possible, as the countdown to November and legality began.

The strain of hiding her belly became pervasive. By the time Gloria started work on *Tonight or Never*, the gowns Coco Chanel created for her no longer fit. A furious Chanel ordered Swanson to lose five pounds around her middle. Instead, Gloria directed a seamstress to make her a long-line rubber girdle that would go from above her knees to her waist. The girdle was so stiff it actually stood up by itself. When it was delivered, Swanson recalled, "We all became hysterical with laughter." It took three assistants to wrangle her into the girdle, and once in, Gloria could not get out by herself. "It did the trick, but it was a pain, and not in the neck."[56] She managed—just barely—to squeeze into the pale orchid velvet gown Chanel had trimmed with diamonds, beads, and mirrors. Now the race was on: "They wanted to shoot [her] scenes before she got too big," a colleague recalled.[57]

Swanson's longtime friend Mervyn LeRoy came from First National to direct. His tough-talking gangster picture *Little Caesar* was a big hit that year; the young man who had played Gloria's brother in 1923's *Prodigal Daughters* was coming into his own. LeRoy was equally adept at comedy, with a well-deserved reputation as a gagman on the set. He had a special fondness for the "goose stick," and LeRoy's friends happily exaggerated their shock and surprise when "goosed." As Douglas Fairbanks Jr. explained, the victims "would jump in the air, scream, run up the nearest ladder or slap the nearest person they saw . . . If they made a sufficiently hilarious scene out of their reaction, it was a near-guarantee of a steady job with [LeRoy] on whatever picture he made next."[58]

Swanson learned to expect a new Jewish joke daily from LeRoy's apparently endless supply, but he fooled her expertly with a special gift. Swanson was "a jigsaw-puzzle nut," LeRoy recalled, so he had the studio carpenters adjust a puzzle for Gloria: "They cut the ends off some of the pieces. Then I rewrapped it and presented it to her. . . . Of course she couldn't do it because of the doctoring. Finally she caught on and wired me a two-word telegram. You can imagine what it said."[59] For all his fooling around, LeRoy was a talented, efficient director who understood that making comedy look easy was a hard job.

After the skullduggery entailed in hiding her marriage and pregnancy from the public, making *Tonight or Never* seemed simple. The script depended on Gloria and Melvyn Douglas having lively sexual chemistry, and their first scene together was a particularly steamy one. "You can't imagine how embarrassing it is to play a love scene with someone you've just said 'how do you do' to," Swanson recalled. "Little did handsome Melvyn Douglas realize when he took me in his arms [that] he was embracing two of us."[60]

However, their acting was suggestive enough to create problems with the Hays Office, which demanded deep cuts to make the love scene between Swanson and Douglas less convincing. A sequence in which Swanson's sexually frustrated character squirms on a chaise longue was deemed too offensive to pass muster. So was another dramatizing her sleeplessness while listening to honeymooners making love in the next room. Even after these changes, *The Hollywood Reporter* called *Tonight or Never* "one of the sexiest pictures of all time," cautioning exhibitors that showing it would be "risky (and risqué) business in the hinterland," where "the hicks will gasp."[61]

Tonight or Never seemed to have everything going for it. Gregg Toland's camera work was beautiful; the sets and costumes were lovely. Yet somehow the mix failed to jell. Most reviewers were kind, if a bit puzzled about just what was off. The *New York Times*' Mordaunt Hall conceded that the picture "stirred up a great deal of merriment" in the theater, but he couldn't get excited about it.[62] Hall, normally a fan of Swanson's, thought Melvyn Douglas overshadowed her. *Variety* thought the picture lacked punch.[63]

Tonight or Never is amusing: there are mistaken identities, fast-paced, witty altercations that disguise the growing attraction between the central couple, and some physical comedy. All of it is managed with a light touch. Yet Swanson is slow where she needs to be dynamic; she languishes when she should fume. She lacks the lithe, girlish grace of other comediennes of the decade—perhaps unsurprisingly, as she was being poured each morning into her tight girdle.

The costumes actually made things worse: Chanel's white satin gown with its rhinestone-encrusted bodice highlighted the actress's thickening waist rather than suggesting the supple energy the role demanded. In fact, one reviewer reported, Swanson's figure "resemble[d] too much a real opera singer . . . a fact which caused the audience to titter audibly."[64]

By then the news was out. The press had learned of Swanson's summer marriage, and the story made headlines throughout the country. Reporters dug up the mayor of sleepy Elmsford, New York, who confirmed that he had married Swanson and Farmer in August, thinking it was "all in a day's work."[65] He could not recall any of the details (such as what Swanson wore to her wedding) but volunteered that he had been pledged to secrecy until November 9 (the day Swanson's interlocutory divorce decree became absolute). Gloria Swanson was a bigamist.

The story remained parked at the front of the Los Angeles papers for two weeks as reporters speculated about what might happen to Gloria—whether she could be prosecuted or even brought to New York to face charges. The case hung on whether Swanson and Farmer had taken up residence together illegally, before her marriage was dissolved. Swanson's attorney declared that the couple had been living separately throughout the autumn, Swanson at her home and Farmer at the Beverly Hills Hotel. This was a victimless crime, but the press had a high old time calling in judicial experts. The couple planned a second wedding ceremony as soon as possible, to remove any doubts about the legality of their union.

In the meantime, Henri de la Falaise was spotted perusing a certified copy of his (now final) divorce decree. "That man has matrimony written all over him," a marriage bureau regular told reporters.[66] A day or two later, Henri and Constance Bennett filed their public notice of intention to wed. After signing the document, Bennett ran from the jostling reporters, her hands covering her face. It seemed literally to be a race to the altar, with Gloria and Michael Farmer beating Henri and Constance Bennett by a hair.

On the ninth of November, Gloria and Michael married a second time in Yuma, Arizona, where they were not required to post banns. Swanson issued a statement saying she had been advised the previous summer that a New York marriage would not interfere with California laws; when she later learned this was untrue, she kept her marriage a secret until she and Farmer could remarry. But now the reporters wanted to see Gloria herself; her continued absence was practically a provocation.

After months of making herself scarce, Swanson was finally spotted in San Francisco ten days after her wedding, where she feigned surprise at the reporters' interest and got away as quickly as possible. She issued a statement through UA: "Mr. Farmer and myself have been on a honeymoon and we are touring points of interest in California . . . I am much surprised to learn that we 'have been in hiding.' We have made no attempts to hide our identities."[67]

The next day, however, she and Farmer were travelling as "Mr. and Mrs. Martin Foster" on a ship leaving for Europe via the Panama Canal. Gloria hurried away when photographers approached. When newsmen knocked on their stateroom door, Farmer opened it "a wee crack," said Gloria was trying to nap, then slammed the door.[68] The front page of the *Los Angeles Times* reported on the "mystery": "Everybody wants to know the reason for the first marriage, solemnized before it could be legal."[69] This was as close as the paper could come to asking the question directly: was Gloria Swanson pregnant?

She was certainly eager to get out of Hollywood. At least she escaped being interviewed about Henri's wedding, which took place the same day she and Michael sailed. Swanson would always have an ache of regret at her failure with Henri and always keep a soft spot for him in her heart. His new wife, however, she simply loathed.

CHAPTER 17

Perfect Misunderstanding

SWANSON HAD MARRIED IN HASTE, AND SHE WOULD REPENT AT leisure—a lot more leisure than she expected. She left the country with her two children and her new husband as soon as her duties on *Tonight or Never* ended, sailing off without a word to Joe Schenck about her plans. No one would pressure her into having another abortion: she had married Michael Farmer so she could have her baby legitimately. When they arrived in France she wrote Schenck saying she needed to rest before making another movie. She wanted a break from worrying about the motion picture business and her place in it and was counting on his "sentimental streak."[1]

The Depression, however, rendered such largesse impossible. The negative publicity over Swanson's union with Husband #4 now made her hefty salary seem like a noose around the corporate neck. Once Schenck realized Gloria was pregnant, he canceled her contract with United Artists. Swanson was now entirely independent, and soon she would believe she had "married a maniac."[2]

Mr. and Mrs. Farmer rebounded into the Parisian social whirl, their months of hiding behind closed doors in California over. The family wintered at the magnificent Suvretta House in St. Moritz, where Michael, an expert climber and skier, put little Gloria and Brother on skis for their first tentative but thrilling runs. Everyone was enchanted with the Alps, and Swanson described life on the "roof of Europe": "Only those who have lived above the clouds can possibly know how uncanny the beauty can be [with] the sounds of bells and laughter coming out of the mist. It can be twenty below zero but the cold is so dry that you uncover your bare shoulders for comfort. It is very intoxicating in more ways than one. It's where lovers should go."[3] Adolphe Menjou and Charlie Chaplin joined them; then Sylvia Ashley and Doug Fairbanks arrived.

Sylvia would soon replace Mary Pickford as Doug's wife. The breakup of the First Couple of Hollywood marked the end of an era.

Swanson's enjoyment of her friends, however, was tempered by her growing fear that she had once again married the wrong man. Michael was "direct from County Cork and the devil. Twenty-four hours couldn't go by without a scene of some kind. It was almost like a child wanting to get attention." Farmer became jealous when he drank too much, and he drank too much routinely. Their fights escalated: "One night coming home . . . he started one of his tirades, and because I wouldn't speak and add to the nonsense, he struck my side with his elbow quite fiercely." Gloria was five months pregnant. She told Michael she was leaving him. She couldn't, Farmer said—he had locked up the family's passports. He offered "all kinds of promises and apologies, even getting down on his knees. It was after a fashion patched up, but never forgotten."[4] Farmer's contrition became less endearing as time passed.

They planned to return to England in the spring for Gloria's confinement, but now she decided to go immediately. Leaving Gloria and Brother in their new Swiss boarding schools, she and Michael headed to London, renting Thelma Lady Furness's spacious house on Farm Street in Mayfair. (Thelma had recently introduced her lover, the Prince of Wales, to Mrs. Wallis Simpson. This turned out to be a tactical error for Lady Furness.) Swanson loved the quiet eighteenth-century neighborhood; she walked "around and around [Berkeley Square] talking to my unborn to hurry up," promising the baby anything "if it would only stop kicking me."[5]

As Gloria paced, her thoughts turned to her financial and professional future. She was unemployed, with no prospects in sight. The cancellation of her UA contract cost her $500,000 in unearned salary; it was "a dreadful financial blow."[6] The last thing she needed was another person leaning on her, but why she thought Michael Farmer would do anything else is a mystery. When they met he was dependent on the kindness of the older American woman he called his adopted "mother." The mysterious Mrs. Hubbard gave Farmer a monthly allowance of $1,000, which kept a bachelor in fine style but would not support his new family. Though Michael could conjure up a steady supply of evening jackets and dinner invitations, he had nothing to call his own. Gloria had no choice but to go back to work as soon as possible.

Elinor Glyn proposed they adapt a classic British novel for the screen: "I do long to see you in a really serious refined sophisticated story full of drama," she wrote, "not about crooks or little 'hotties' who turn into

perfect ladies—overnight!"[7] Glyn recommended *Jane Eyre*, though picturing Swanson as the penniless young governess took some imagination.

More practically, Doug Fairbanks suggested that Gloria make a picture in London. By virtue of her marriage to Michael Farmer, she was a
British citizen and could set up a production company in England. Since
theaters were required by law to devote almost a third of their screen
time to showing British-made films, there was a high demand; it should
be easy to attract financing.[8] The cost of making movies in England was
low; Gloria's international reputation was a considerable asset; and she
needed a job. Why not create one for herself? As she counted down the
weeks to her delivery, Swanson began planning a new picture, not the
classic Elinor Glyn recommended but a bright, modern story.

Michelle Bridgit Farmer was born at home in the early afternoon on
April 5, 1932, with two doctors and the royal family's own midwife in attendance. When Gloria opened her eyes after the delivery, Sylvia Ashley
was at the foot of the bed, the new baby in her arms. Swanson's joy in
her perfect little girl was shot through with a bolt of pure anger at her
friend's boldness: she put out her arms for her child.

Swanson fell blissfully in love with her daughter and was a vocal pro-
ponent of the powerful bond created by breastfeeding: "Why so many
women give up this joy I don't understand."[9] Miss Simonson brought
Joseph and Gloria to London, and the two children were tickled with
their tiny sister. Yet there was no mistaking whose child Michelle was:
her moods went from sunny to stormy in the blink of an eye, just like
her father's. Her family nickname became "April Showers," since she
was either laughing or crying.

Despite Swanson's passionate attraction to her new husband, life with
Michael Farmer was difficult. Almost anything could touch off his jealousy, even the telegrams congratulating them on their daughter's birth.
He questioned Gloria angrily about a note sent by Czech actor Francis
Lederer. How did she know Lederer? When had she last seen him? Had
they been alone? He insisted that Gloria not see her colleagues without him present. Even though the endless details and back-and-forth
negotiations of her film work bored Farmer, he wanted to keep an eye
on Gloria: "Michael was jealous of my shadow," she said. A severe bout
with anemia meant Swanson had to give up nursing ahead of schedule.
With all the tension in the house, she thought, her milk wasn't good for
Michelle anyway: "It was probably curdled."[10]

One day when the new parents were driving their baby daughter
through Hyde Park, Michael reproached Gloria about a dinner meeting

with a UA executive she had failed to mention to him. When she laughed it off, he grabbed her hand and thrust it in his pocket, where she felt a gun. Swanson was torn between her real fear and her sense that this was "so bizarre it couldn't get into a bad movie script: Gloria Swanson riding through lawns of daffodils with one hand holding her new baby and the other pressed by her husband against a gun, with which he was threatening to kill a harmless business associate he claimed to be her lover."[11]

Swanson had to be more and more careful not to trigger her husband's rage. Yet she still also found him enormously exciting and was unwilling to give up her hopes for her new marriage so quickly. To get the children out of the fray, she sent Gloria and Brother with Miss Simonson to Maidenhead outside London.

This time there was no one prodding the new mother to return to work, but Swanson knew she had to get busy. She hoped to make a picture that summer, and shortly before Michelle's birth she set up a new corporation, Gloria Swanson British Productions Ltd. Eddie Goulding and Noel Coward introduced her to a screenwriter who became one of Britain's finest writer-directors. Michael Powell was cutting his teeth in movies when he wrote *Perfect Understanding*; a Gloria Swanson picture was a step up from the low-budget "quota quickies" he had been making.[12]

Perfect Understanding was, of all things, a comedy about marital jealousy. A wealthy modern couple, Judy and Nick, promise to allow each other perfect freedom in their marriage: no restrictions, no matter what. It is only a matter of time before they misunderstand appearances and become mad with jealousy, each convinced the other has been unfaithful. At the last minute, they are saved from a divorce neither really wants and run from the courtroom, anxious to start their life together again.

Swanson wanted to produce, though Loyd Wright and Lance Heath tried to dissuade her. "Beg of you not to prejudice . . . remaining assets by attempting to produce yourself," Wright wired. "Rehabilitation can only come with excellent picture. . . . Good pictures are grossing only 30 and 40 percent of what they have previously grossed."[13] *Tonight or Never*, released three months earlier, had not netted even Swanson's salary.

Swanson, however, stubbornly rejected this advice. She was excited about working in London, "a perfect place to make a talking picture, as Fontainebleau had been perfect for *Madame Sans-Gêne*."[14] British studio facilities were state-of-the-art; Ealing's new studios had been modeled on those at RKO. Talent was qualified, plentiful, and cheap. In fact, British artists would accept one-fifth of what Hollywood actors demanded.

Then, too, the publicity value of Swanson starring in a British production was high: "Even moderate star vehicle here distributed by UA should gross 200,000 UK."[15] Part of the picture would be shot on the Riviera, which would also attract audiences. She had reviewed the figures; there was no way to lose.

Swanson was so certain the picture could be made cheaply and quickly that she was willing to forego a salary: she would wait for the inevitable profits.[16] She knew she could do it all, once again. She wanted to be shooting by June; perhaps an expedited production schedule could net her a new Hollywood contract. If everything went well, she could be back in the States by the end of 1932.

It is hard to see Swanson's optimism as anything other than mulish, yet in the past she had repeatedly defied conventional wisdom, risked everything, and ended up doing her most satisfying and lucrative work. When she moved to New York, when she acquired and produced *Sadie Thompson*, and when she made *The Trespasser*, few would have predicted Gloria Swanson's survival, much less her success. Now she felt confident she could once again prove her critics wrong—her own advisors no less than the UA colleagues who fired her for getting pregnant or the Hollywood know-it-alls who said she was washed up. For good or ill, Swanson trusted her assessment of the opportunities on offer in the British film industry. If her plan sounded like pie in the sky to others, so be it.

Swanson was still a shareholder and still a producing member of United Artists, even though her most recent UA salaried contract had been canceled. She also still owed the company a picture on her original producing contract. Now UA said the company would not offer financing if Gloria acted as her own producer; Schenck and company worried that costs would escalate if no one could rein the star in. Swanson refused to take no for an answer. She lined up financing from private investors and from the London head of UA, guaranteeing these investments with her UA stock. Adding some of her own capital to the mix, she plowed ahead.

Her Mayfair home became the hub of production activity. With the baby sleeping in the nursery down the hall, Swanson and company held story conferences. They discussed sets and costumes, roughed out the shooting schedule, drank endless cups of tea, and decided on the all-British cast members. Almost unbelievably, Swanson planned to use her new husband—who was photogenic but had no acting experience— as the male lead. Part of the company had gone ahead to the Riviera to shoot a speedboat race scene. They swam and basked in the sun at

Eden Roc, relaxing before the most intense period of production began. Swanson cabled Irving Wakoff from the Cannes set: "Worry no more about finding leading man as we have found him and right under our nose. Michael Farmer. Just for fun he and some of his friends helped us out in the regatta and he acted and looked great."[17] She thought she was delivering good news; her stunned advisors thought it was anything but.

Wright and Heath struggled to persuade Swanson she needed a professional actor. They tried flattery: "While we think M[ichael] would be wonderful we are afraid of public reaction."[18] They tried reasoning with her: "Risk in doing this far too great to make whatever box office value he would add worth while. Likely to be too costly gamble under circumstances."[19] The novelty casting might even damage Swanson's ability to get financing on future pictures. When both approaches failed, they told Gloria that even Adelaide (now a corporate officer) agreed with them.[20]

Wright tried to impress upon Gloria how desperate her situation would be if *Perfect Understanding* failed, especially since she was now an investor. He did not want her to be "in the terrible situation of having taken out of the industry a fortune, and throwing it right back into the industry. . . . You are a long way from here, and you undoubtedly are enthused and convinced that your picture will be a success. God help us if it is not a success from a financial standpoint."[21]

Swanson later claimed she had offered Michael a small role in the picture to keep him occupied, "like giving a child a lollipop so he'd leave Mama alone."[22] In fact, she had pondered an even larger role for the unemployed Farmer: early publicity releases claimed he would "present" the film, as Joseph Kennedy had presented their joint ventures. Her fantasies of working closely with a trusted family member were powerful. However, Swanson eventually had to acknowledge that Farmer was erratic and uncontrollable. Once she saw more extensive footage of his performance, she capitulated: his role in the picture would be purely decorative. (In an ironic twist, Henri de la Falaise was producing and directing two films for his wife Connie Bennett's company.)[23]

The lead went to a new screen discovery. Though Gloria had hoped for "a Ronald Colman type," Laurence Olivier was even better: "His good looks were positively blinding. . . . He could almost not make a wrong move, his instincts and technique were so finely coordinated."[24] Even so, she insisted Olivier grow a mustache to look older on screen (he was nearly a decade younger than Gloria). She loved his "wild energy" and enjoyed talking shop with him, later saying that she "could have fallen in love" with Olivier.[25] He was not nearly as sold on the picture—or on film in general. Although he became one of the screen's most unforgettable actors, Olivier did not find his cinematic stride until later in the 1930s; in *Perfect Understanding* he appears overpowered, even intimidated, by his leading lady. He called the film's title "a misnomer if ever there was one."[26]

His assessment turned out to be dead on. By the time Olivier joined the company, Swanson was dissatisfied with director Rowland V. Lee. She paid off his contract and hired *The Trespasser*'s editor, Cyril Gardner, to direct. Yet Gardner brought an unexpectedly morose, worried spirit to the picture: a psychic had warned him that both his parents would soon die—as he would, too, on his return trip to the States. Everyone pooh-poohed the idea, but within a few weeks' time, Gardner's father and then his mother became ill and died. The poor fellow was beside himself and beyond reassurance. (When it was time to go back to the US, a friend got Gardner "totally drunk and . . . practically shoveled him onto the next boat.")[27]

Everything went wrong: "If I thought life in 10 Farm Street was rugged," Swanson recalled, "it was nothing to what making the film would be."[28] Most of the cast and crew came down with the flu. Olivier missed work after he was in a minor car crash. A fire at the film lab destroyed a portion of the negative. (Quick-thinking technicians threw it out the window to save the building from a nitrate explosion; what survived the fire had to be reprocessed more expensively in America.) All these changes and delays meant extra costs, and soon Swanson's inexpensive British picture had overrun its budget.

Even things that could be fixed in-house took time and cost money. The casting change that brought Olivier on board meant that his character—not Michael Farmer's—had to win the boat race that had already been filmed with Farmer triumphant. Rather than reshoot on the Riviera, Olivier's victory was faked in the cutting room. It took all the skill of film editor Thorold Dickinson—one of the masters—to reverse the results. The only break Swanson got came months later, when the British tax department took pity and gave her a clear "no tax" bill.

As her production woes deepened, Swanson reached deeper into her own pocket. Joe Kennedy had called in the middle of the night earlier that summer from Chicago, bubbling with excitement over Franklin Roosevelt's nomination for president. (Swanson claimed she hung up when he wanted to put Roosevelt on the line.) Virginia Bowker told Gloria Joe thought he would get a cabinet post if Roosevelt won the election. More to Swanson's liking, Virginia said Joe would provide financing if she needed help on her picture. Weeks later she remembered that offer, but when she tried to call it in, Kennedy was unresponsive. Swanson saw this as one more of Joe's "unkept promises."[29]

Joe Schenck, too, refused to supplement the budget for *Perfect Understanding*; he had advised Gloria early on to hold its cost under $150,000.[30] However, the man she called an "honorable bandit" was willing to ask UA's major shareholders to consider buying Swanson's stock in the company.[31] They purchased her shares for a paltry $200,000, far less than she would have gotten at any other time, and Gloria sank the money into her unfinished picture. When she at last signed off on the overdue, over-budget film, Swanson's career as an owner-producer of United Artists was officially over.

The perfect disaster called *Perfect Understanding* was released in America during the bank holiday of March 1933. FDR's temporary closure of US banks helped stabilize the country's financial institutions but did not help Swanson's film. Viewers did not want to see a glitzy picture about the misadventures of two socialites whose worst problem was living up to a silly marital contract of their own devising—not when they were worried sick themselves. As the Depression bit down hard, the glamorous settings and costumes and bright, brittle situations which Swanson's audience had long enjoyed no longer did the trick. Rejected by critics and audiences alike, *Perfect Understanding* played to empty houses.

The Roaring Twenties finally ended for Swanson when she found herself unemployed and in a bad marriage to an erratic, alcoholic "Boy" (as Michael Farmer styled himself). For more than a year, she and her husband drifted back and forth across the Atlantic, arguing and making up in London, Paris, New York, and California. Swanson always had offers—to make records, to do radio programs, to endorse products, even to make a personal appearance tour—but never the kind of work that fully engaged her. It certainly never paid the kind of money to which she was accustomed. "It seems as if I will never learn not to let my heart rule my head," she wrote her lawyer despondently. "My career is so jeopardized that all I can see facing me is a stone wall."[32] If there ever was a period when the busy, focused, energetic Swanson was adrift, it was during her marriage to Michael Farmer. It would take her some time to envision and enter her next act.

Her money troubles continued. Swanson was dragged in and out of court as her creditors realized she was less likely than ever to pay her bills. When her furniture was seized, the suit made headlines. Maurice Cleary was making dogged efforts to show he was owed commissions on Swanson's (now defunct) UA contract, and the press documented their battle.[33] Gloria faced these indignities with the chilly hauteur she had perfected long ago. Yet while Swanson's attorneys documented her declining prospects of employment, she was photographed wearing two fabulous new Art Deco bracelets from Cartier's. It was hard to believe Gloria Swanson was broke when she was sporting oversized platinum bangles glittering with diamonds and rock crystal.

The actress was terrified of appearing down on her luck, lest it scare off potential employers, and she had been rich and famous so long she knew no other way to live. She appeared in public often, dressed to the nines. She attended plays and openings, balls and galas, always in smart company: Noel Coward, Clifton Webb, Eddie Goulding, and George Cukor were her companions. "She reveled in these guys," one intimate said; Gloria wanted to "come back as a pansy in her next life."[34] Yet Swanson's position in Hollywood was precarious at best.

With the country down on its knees, Swanson's star persona no longer spoke to audiences enjoying Will Rogers's homespun wisdom or tales of plucky young shop girls. Viewers were happier to see Shirley Temple tap dance her way out of the orphanage than Gloria Swanson take her pick of suitors in fancy dress. The extravagance she personified suddenly seemed indefensible. The expensive, experienced actress—now in her early thirties—was seen as too glamorous for character parts but not young or fresh enough for leads. When she did get a good offer— to replace Claudette Colbert, who had fallen ill on location for DeMille in Hawaii—Gloria demanded such a high salary that Paramount decided to wait for Colbert to recover. She got into (and quickly out of) a contract with a small company which intended only to loan her out and pocket the profits. Then UA remade *Sadie Thompson*: though its star Joan Crawford adored Swanson, Gloria disliked seeing herself replaced onscreen.

A summons from Herbert Somborn surprised Swanson late in 1933. They had managed a polite if frosty relationship for the last decade for their daughter's sake. Now Herbert looked ill and tired. He had cancer, he explained, and hadn't much time to live. He wanted to apologize to Gloria for the way their marriage ended. He had always loved her; there had never been anyone else. Swanson felt years of resentment drain away. "I had called him Daddy fifteen years ago," she reflected. "It didn't seem possible—I hardly knew the man."[35] It would be their final meeting; Herbert Somborn died in January 1934. The legacy he left his daughter—the Brown Derby restaurant, a Hollywood landmark—helped Swanson keep her family afloat.

She had her own cancer scare after finding another lump on her breast. Her friend William Powell had also been seeing a doctor for a lump "in an unmentionable place," and one night they decided to cast their cares to the wind.[36] Though Swanson seldom drank to excess, she got so tipsy she leaped off the high dive fully clothed, while Powell and Carole Lombard looked on. (Gloria's equally intoxicated husband fished her out of the pool.) Swanson's lump was benign, but she felt scarred by her tempestuous marriage, which sapped her energy and left her frustrated.

She frequently vowed to leave her husband, who neither eased her worries nor contributed to their household income. Yet Michael Farmer's wild and passionate nature, revved up by his heavy drinking, still drew her. They often parted in anger, and just as eagerly came together again, sometimes even living apart in their own home: Farmer wrote, begging admission to Gloria's rooms during one quarrel, so that he might kiss her on his way out to dinner. He promised "not to bother [her] again."[37]

Farmer had to return periodically to Ireland to renew his visa, cabling his wife before one solitary voyage, "Loathe thought of ocean without you." (She immediately replied, "Adore worship love you.")[38] He caught Swanson up on all the gossip when he traveled, writing letters that were forty and fifty pages long (he described himself as "an extremist in all things").[39] "You can't imagine what New York is like—parties all the time," Farmer wrote. He went around with Cole Porter and Irving Berlin, and later confessed: "Boy got a little stinking. Boy has hangover today."[40] The Depression had finally reached the City of Lights: "Paris is so dead. The Ritz is empty and the George V Plaza Athenée-Astoria. All those hotels are closing. The Rue de la Paix is like a cemetery—most of the de lux stores are closed. . . . Sad times. . . . The whole world is crazy."[41] He gossiped about Mary Pickford's divorce: "Why can't people divorce nicely? Well, fifty years from now, what does it all matter? Boy loves Girl but God dam it don't you ever divorce me."[42]

Farmer spent Christmas 1933 in Europe with all three children but without Gloria: "Darling you know we are not complete without you so this Christmas does not count." He christened Michelle "Her Highness" for her theatrical personality, reporting that "Gloria is positively beautiful and not at all like photographs[.] Brother looks husky and well. . . . I have kissed them so much for you but nothing seems right with you so far away from all. Lonely Boy."[43] Yet he later complained that he had "one hell of a dull time" on that trip "play[ing] Mother," and intended "to go to parties and have a wild fling" when he got to London. "I used to be very popular in that town once," he reminded his wife.[44]

His correspondence reveals Farmer as loving, insecure, and vindictive by turns. He feared Swanson's friends would turn her away from him and especially wanted her not to see *New Yorker* cartoonist Peter Arno and director Ernst Lubitsch. "*One day* I shall see you pay for this unhappiness I am going through, [if you] continue to be selfish and consider your friends before your husband . . . I have loved you desperately but am realizing that there is such a thing as killing love—you are choking it; and I am unhappy, lonely, and gasping while you continue a normal life."[45] Nonetheless, his habitual closing was "kisses cuddles love taps pets."[46] They often battled over money, once quarreling bitterly about the expense of the conversation itself: Farmer phoned Swanson to ask for $1,000 but ended up spending $800 for the transatlantic call.

In fact, when Farmer was away, he wished Gloria would just stay home: "But I gather you feel you have been married for 2½ years and grant you not much fun either so you are having yourself a wild fling."[47] He suspected Swanson was carrying on behind his back: when she reported a small weight loss, he accused her of taking a new, more athletic lover. He only wondered who among her "friends" it was. At least when Michael traveled she got relief from "the daily hell" of coping with his temper.[48]

Michael Farmer could not provide the domestic stability Gloria craved, yet she felt enervated, unable to act. Finally, Loyd Wright gave her some stern advice: she should end her marriage now. When Swanson protested weakly that her career couldn't stand another divorce, Wright said if she wasn't careful, she would have no career left. He recommended she not sign the paperwork asking for an extension of Michael's visa—without which he could not re-enter the States.

In 1934, while Farmer was away in Europe, things began looking up. Irving Thalberg signed Gloria to a personal contract to make pictures under his guidance at M-G-M. Thalberg was the most prestigious producer in Hollywood; to Swanson it felt like "Christmas in March."[49] Thalberg was looking for the perfect project for her M-G-M debut: what did Gloria think of a remake of Elinor Glyn's *Three Weeks*? Swanson shot to the studio to be photographed lying on a tiger skin rug. However, no one hurried Thalberg. Anita Loos joked about waiting for Irving: "I spent time knitting this scarf. At my salary of $2,500 a week, the studio paid over $20,000 for that scarf."[50] Soon Swanson wondered if a picture would ever materialize.

That spring Swanson wrote to Farmer, who was fishing in Norway, announcing her decision to end their marriage. She had not wanted to rehash the subject of their "inevitable divorce" before he left the States, she said, but now it was time: "I find it impossible to put together all the little pieces that have been so badly torn—and even if I could, for what, to be torn again? Not the things I want, but the things I need to make me happy . . . you cannot possibly give me. You will never know tolerance, understanding nor little kindnesses toward me. . . . The sweetness in our lives is that we have a beautiful baby. . . . Our marriage has served that purpose—why continue it now when it has little else to offer and our lives are so terribly far apart?" No one would be surprised by their divorce, which Gloria intended to get "as quietly as possible on the grounds of incompatibility."[51]

When Farmer returned to Paris from the Norwegian fjords, he instead threatened to sue Swanson: he said he had evidence she was having an affair. Gloria's advisors were worried: "His divorce suit might spoil Swanson's motion picture career. She is just starting a comeback."[52] They hoped Farmer would not noise it about that another Swanson marriage had failed because she was playing around. Her lawyers indicated to Farmer that if he did not wish to have his own unsavory past exposed, he should allow his wife to proceed. The prospect of a divorce was also complicated by British laws; in fact, the Irish Free State did not allow divorce. Farmer threatened to prosecute Swanson—a British subject by her marriage to him—for bigamy if she tried to marry again.

The man who supplanted Michael Farmer was a tall, debonair Englishman, part of the British invasion of Hollywood. "Had you been blindfolded," Swanson recalled, "you would have sworn you were in Mayfair." In fact, Gloria heard Herbert Marshall before she saw him. One evening at a Beverly Hills party, Swanson heard "the most melodious male speaking voice I'd ever heard." It belonged to "a very handsome man with soft brown eyes."[53]

He offered to get her some supper. "That was the beginning," Swanson remembered, "telephone calls, flowers, all kinds of little notes tucked along my personal path, also in my purse or pockets. I was all of 34 and I felt like a school girl again. It was like being alive again to care for someone and have them care for you. Every breath you took seemed to be for them. The foolishness and the laughter that goes with it. When he called me his 'most only,' that did it. I melted!"[54]

Marshall was easy to love, as his former sweethearts Kay Francis and Miriam Hopkins could attest. He also played a witty, refined romantic lead like no one else in the business, partnering Claudette Colbert, Greta Garbo, and Marlene Dietrich. His mellifluous voice and urbane, unflappable manner brought the gentleman thief in Lubitsch's comedy *Trouble in Paradise* to life, but he could play adventurers and scientists with equal aplomb. A stage actor with immense self-possession, Marshall was in great demand when he met Gloria Swanson.

The last few years had been rocky, as Gloria's dreams of a happy marriage and producing her own pictures collapsed. Almost immediately, however, the worried actress forgot her cares, becoming absorbed in the attentions Marshall paid her: "I could no more have prevented it from happening than I could have blown out a klieg light in one small breath or run barefoot up the Matterhorn. Beside him all the other cultivated men I had ever known seemed just a bit coarse."[55]

Once again, Swanson took pleasure and comfort from a new love affair—this time, with a kind, strong man whom she admired. Marshall was a disabled veteran who had lost a leg in France during the 1914–1918 war. He had trained himself to walk on his prosthesis so his limp was barely noticeable. He bore his affliction bravely and seldom complained, though he was often in pain. Marshall was also—like Michael Farmer, like Mickey Neilan, like Craney Gartz, and like Gloria's father—a heavy drinker who used alcohol to hold his demons at bay. If Swanson heard alarm bells ringing when she watched Marshall downing drink after drink, she ignored them. More than anything else, Bart Marshall seemed like a grown-up: a responsible, caring man, unlike the erratic "Boy" whom Swanson had married.

He was an incurable romantic, sending telegrams almost hourly when Swanson traveled. One morning he declared, "A perfectly shocking attack of worshipping is mine today easily recognizable because it happens all the time every day ever." Later the same day he amended his first message: "No I believe it's worse than ever today every love."[56] Marshall sent gardenias to Swanson's train; she sent him her pillow with a red lipstick kiss mark. He was overjoyed: "The pillow has arrived and has had darling every effect on me that even most only could have imagined."[57]

Bart was also married, to British actress Edna Best, and had a baby daughter living in England with her mother. He assured Swanson that his marriage was over; he intended to ask Edna for a divorce. Swanson blithely declared that Marshall's past didn't concern her: "After all, I had one of my own."[58] The accomplished, ladylike Best was popular, however, and Hollywood disapproved—sharply and immediately—of Gloria Swanson and Bart Marshall as a couple.

They were dropped from Hollywood's social register. Left alone together, they became inseparable. It was a quiet time for Swanson: there were trips to the racetrack at Agua Caliente and parties at San Simeon (since Marion Davies and Mr. Hearst understood something about affairs of the heart). Mostly, though, she and Bart holed up at home or escaped to the desert at La Quinta.

In the middle of their social ostracism, Swanson invited Bart to a dressy dinner party at 904. When he arrived, the table was beautifully laid and candles lit. He looked around at the eight guests and let out a roar of laughter: "They were all wax manikins," Swanson explained, "men in black ties and the ladies beautifully coiffed and gowned. It did my heart good to see how much he enjoyed the joke. Of course the two of us got silly and carried on crazy conversations with those on either side of us."[59] Later that night, however, they passed through the dining room again. The chairs were now pulled away from the table, and Swanson realized with dismay that the dummies were legless—a gaffe she hardly knew how to manage, given Bart's injury. Marshall, however, had a wonderful sense of humor, and his reaction—another loud crow of astonished delight at the absurdity of the situation—put Gloria at ease. They laughed until they cried.

It wasn't long before Bart's wife weighed in. Edna arrived in California and asked to meet Swanson, who surprised herself by agreeing. Gloria, however, was adamant: she would not be cast in the role of the other woman. Edna had chosen a separate life when she refused to accompany Bart to Hollywood. The two women discussed what Edna was calling a "trial separation." She wanted to know if Swanson realized that Bart drank too much; the star waved the question aside. Yet Gloria stopped Bart at the door as they left together: "'Please, I beg of you, don't cross this threshold if any part of you must remain here. . . . Please don't follow me if all of you can't.' He took up my hand and together we went out into many more tomorrows—some happy and some sad."[60]

Swanson was in love again—and again refused to let others dictate how she lived her life. She had no intention of giving up Bart Marshall. He made no move to start divorce proceedings but began calling Gloria his "dear wife," writing her that "the heavens opened at La Quinta and married us" (evidently the kind of marriage he preferred).[61]

Swanson's attorney nonetheless advised her to divorce Michael Farmer as efficiently as possible: she was already vulnerable, and in a troubled economy would have even less chance of working if she was perceived as a homewrecker. In European courts, moreover, the father was the legal guardian of any underage children. Two-year-old Michelle was still in Switzerland, and if Michael tried to claim his rights, Swanson would be hard pressed to get custody of her daughter.

In November 1934 Swanson testified in divorce court that her fourth husband, Michael Farmer, was "quarrelsome and abusive."[62] Lois Wilson backed her up, telling the judge that Farmer berated and belittled her friend, often publicly. Farmer "belonged in Europe," Gloria said, just as she belonged in America: "I have my work, and I like to do what I am doing."[63] This time around, the fan magazines were decidedly cooler toward Swanson. *Photoplay* noted that the star observed "one axiom" only: "Career, first, last, and always. Perhaps Gloria feels that only a lone hand, played hard, fast, without quarter or sentiment, can attain the goal she has set herself to conquer. Only she knows."[64]

The children of several celebrities had been threatened after the Lindbergh baby kidnapping in spring 1932, and Swanson feared hers would be targeted. She also wanted to keep her children clear of her volatile marriage. They seemed safe in Switzerland, but reports from their governess now worried her. Michael had moved Michelle and Miss Simonson to Paris to live with his adoptive "mother" while he himself went off cruising. Sammy wrote that the elderly Mrs. Hubbard was in precarious health and had gone "crazy" at the prospect of Michelle going to live with her mother in the States: "Every day she says my son has given me the baby [and] nobody can take her away. She is mine[.] I will go to law about it. I am going to bring her up."[65] Michael had often called Mrs. Hubbard unstable, and Swanson was determined to get Michelle out of the "unhealthy atmosphere" as quickly as possible.[66]

So she hatched a kidnap plan of her own. Her maid Ethel Helmsing retrieved the two older children from school in Gstaad. Then Ethel, Arlette Marchal, and Sammy spirited Michelle, "the only decent and bright spot in the whole awful mistake" of Swanson's marriage to Michael Farmer, back to the US.[67] After several delays—including a stop en route for a polio scare—the children stepped off the train in Pasadena. "I wanted to devour them," Swanson remembered happily.[68]

She reveled in having her children at home. At fourteen, young Gloria was a lovely, calm girl with a peaceful disposition; as her Swiss teacher said, she "live[d] the day, without thinking of the one before, or what comes after."[69] Joseph was a sturdy, intelligent boy of twelve who loved building airplanes and experimenting with his chemistry set. Gloria loved seeing his curious, creative spirit develop, at last in close-up. The children were thrilled to be in public school—all Swanson could afford—and accepted Bart unquestioningly. Time out of the spotlight of their mother's hectic life had seemed to do them no harm.

Michelle was now a busy, energetic toddler, and her carefree, peripatetic father made no effort to challenge Gloria's custody of her. Nor did he help support his child. The divorce became final in November 1935, and Swanson marked "the end of that unfortunate chapter" without regrets.[70] Bart told Gloria he understood why Carole Lombard had nicknamed her "The Hen": "Now that you have your brood under one roof," he asked, "would you like to go up to the roof and sit on it, so you can cackle?"[71]

Bart also aroused Swanson's protective instincts. She accepted his physical limitations, never making, as Marshall wrote, "an unhappy reference to the sort of 'love' that I, with my unspoken lackings, can bring to my angel." He confessed he was often dispirited when he heard others talking about how a man "needs to bring 'size' to his lady," something his war injury apparently made difficult.[72] Swanson declared she "loved him more" for his supposed shortcomings: "Any woman with any maternal instincts would feel even more tenderness."[73]

Bart was also generous and gentle with Gloria's friends. When Lois Wilson found a lump in her breast and was frantic with fear, Gloria and Bart took her out for a drive. Lois was afraid that the man she loved would find her unattractive if she lost her breast. Bart put his arm around Lois, but Swanson took a firmer approach: "I slapped her hand down on Bart's artificial leg and said, if he really loves, it will not change his love for you but enhance it."[74]

Gloria was more relaxed and happy at home, but the mid-1930s were a bleak time for her professionally. While Thalberg mulled over his plans for Swanson, he lent her to Fox for *Music in the Air*, a hit play producer Erich Pommer was transferring to the screen. To warm up her voice and make a little money before shooting began in June 1934, Gloria did a few singing dates in New York and Detroit. Signor Marafioti helped her prepare; his enthusiasm for Swanson's voice, and his offer to train her for a singing career, once again buoyed her spirits.

Music in the Air did not: though it had played in New York and the West End for almost two years, Gloria thought the material seemed dated. She and her one-time discovery John Boles were temperamental opera singers who bickered constantly but were really, deep down, in love. The set, a labored representation of Olde Germany, boasted a Bavarian village and a recreation of the Munich opera house and zoo. There were lavish costumes by René Hubert and music by Oscar Hammerstein II and Jerome Kern; the film even featured Billy Wilder's first-ever writing credit. Nonetheless, it was dead on arrival at the box office—inoffensive but instantly forgettable. Swanson was probably lucky to survive the picture: a heavy iron ring accidentally fell from overhead on the set, knocking her unconscious. (Fox exploited the accident for publicity purposes, extolling Gloria's gameness.)[75]

Pommer thought Swanson, whom he had been pressured to accept, was too old for her part.[76] Her costar Marjorie Main thought Swanson was simply too much: "Busy little bee. Buzzing here, buzzing there, full of suggestions. I'm surprised the director . . . could finish the picture without our star in the driver's seat!"[77] With at least eight writers on the project, however, it is hard to say what constitutes interference and what shows a resolute—if grim—effort to salvage a career.

Worse was to come. Thalberg's planned remake of *Three Weeks* disintegrated when George Hill, who was scheduled to direct, committed suicide in summer 1934. Then Swanson's ally, screenwriter Frances Marion, was badly injured in a car crash, and her long recuperation kept her away from work. For the next several years, projects would be proposed for Swanson, but nothing came to fruition. Some she turned down, like *Riffraff*, a Cannery Row story that became a hit for Jean Harlow and Spencer Tracy; Gloria couldn't see herself as a union organizer's wife. She was fifth in line for *The Merry Widow*, another opera lite role that held little appeal, and even less once she learned Maurice Chevalier had approval of his female costar. (He selected Jeanette MacDonald.)

An original story called "Maizie Kenyon" was written for Gloria, but it was another weepie about maternal sacrifice, and a lukewarm repetition of her *Trespasser* success did not appeal to Swanson. (Frances Marion told her the script stank.) Warners wanted her for a Napoleon story with Edward G. Robinson, Republic for *Manhattan Merry-Go-Round*. There was talk of her doing *Twentieth Century* at Columbia, a role Carole Lombard immortalized. She dropped out of *The Emperor's Candlesticks*, and Luise Rainer did it. She wasn't quite bold (or desperate) enough to say yes to an adaptation of *Lady Chatterley's Lover*.

"I can't afford to make an average picture," she fumed. "It must be a good picture. . . . When one has been a star, the public expects so much more."[78] Swanson had commanded the box office for years; now she seemed to think the right project would restore her former glory. Her pickiness irritated some potential collaborators.

Eddie Goulding wanted to remake *The Trespasser*, and Gloria was happy to sell Warners the rights because she needed the money. Then she discovered she did not control the rights; Joe Kennedy did. The tone of Kennedy's response to her cable left Swanson bemused. He said he was "delighted" to help her out, "as if a whole disastrous partnership had never been formed, as if bountiful were his middle name, as if I were a silly child who would forget to tie her shoes unless he left me specific instructions."[79] *That Certain Woman* was a modest hit for Goulding and Bette Davis in 1937.

Swanson wished she could just make a picture with her real-life leading man. Bart was certainly busy: he made half a dozen films while Swanson waited for one to materialize. She wasn't entirely idle. She did a bit of radio drama, but it was only modestly lucrative and only modestly satisfying. Fans mobbed her, but "it didn't get me back in pictures."[80] More money was going out than coming in. Swanson fretted about meeting her bills but didn't feel she could dismiss her staff: they were family. She also refused to lean on Bart financially. He had his own child to support, and as Swanson now knew, flush times could pass in the blink of an eye. (As Anita Loos said, "Movie money is like Hollywood spangles; it has a tendency to drop off and get lost.")[81] Yet she leaned on him emotionally: "If I hadn't had Bart's loving tender thoughtfulness I wonder what would have happened."[82]

Suddenly, with one invitation from power couple Irving Thalberg and Norma Shearer, she and Bart were again socially acceptable. Swanson, however, was scornful of the false friends who had cut the two of them dead weeks earlier. When people asked her where she had been, she felt like saying, "Home with the plague."[83] If you want to know who your real friends are, she counseled, "Get into some trouble."[84] (Hers were Lois Wilson, Grace Moore, Rod LaRocque and Vilma Banky, Carole Lombard, and Aileen Pringle.)

Swanson's M-G-M contract called for her to make three pictures per year. She had made only one—her Fox loan-out—in almost three years when Irving Thalberg, never a strong man, died suddenly of heart failure in September 1936. The death of the "Boy Genius" was a huge loss for Hollywood. For Swanson, Thalberg's passing also meant the end of her affiliation with M-G-M: head of production Louis B. Mayer resented the performers under personal contract to Thalberg, and "he was a great hater," Colleen Moore remembered.[85] Gloria tried a light touch, writing to Mayer: "Now that you have the bad penny I hope you are half as happy as I am."[86] Yet Mayer's resentment became personal when he learned Swanson was responsible for telling a joke he considered offensive.

Mervyn LeRoy had amused Gloria for years with his inexhaustible supply of Jewish jokes. One day at M-G-M she repeated "a dear little joke" LeRoy had told her about two Jewish men who shared a young mistress to cut costs. The young woman got pregnant and gave birth to twins, whereupon Izzy sent Moe a congratulatory telegram: "Rebecca had twins. Mine died." The joke created chuckles around the studio, until it got to Mayer. Then it stopped dead. Mayer angrily insisted that Swanson was anti-Semitic, and with that, her fate was cemented: "I couldn't get a job. No chance. One after another, members of the Producers Club turned me down. It was the end. I never worked again."[87] As one historian put it, "When Mayer canceled you, everybody canceled you."[88] Yet it took awhile for Swanson to register both the significance and the finality of Mayer's displeasure.

Shortly after Thalberg's death, Swanson accepted an offer from Columbia; there she hit the same brick wall, as one project after another fell through. Everyone got excited about *The Second Mrs. Draper*, and Swanson, visiting London for the coronation of George VI, raced back to Hollywood when studio head Harry Cohn summoned her. Then Cohn suddenly decided that the story of an older woman involved with a younger man would make Swanson unsympathetic; he didn't like it.

The last straw came when Swanson found a play about a young socialite who has only a short time to live. Here, finally, was the property she had been seeking. She staged a dramatic reading of the twenty-five-page treatment for Cohn, giving it her all. He seemed impressed, but when Gloria called him the morning after her private performance, he had decided against purchasing the play: "If David Selznick wants to sell it, that means it can't be any good."[89]

That was all Swanson needed. The cool she had carefully maintained in her dealings with the Hollywood star makers over the last few years evaporated: "In one sentence Harry Cohn had epitomized Hollywood, and deep inside me a dam burst. I flew into the greatest rage of my life. I told him exactly what I thought of him and all the other vulgar boors in the studios who wouldn't know a good story if it bit them." Using her best Sadie Thompson language, "I screamed and swore and called him everything I could think of. I only stopped, exhausted, when I realized I had pulled the thirty-foot telephone cord out of the wall."[90] In 1939, Eddie Goulding guided Bette Davis to an Oscar nomination for Best Actress in *Dark Victory*, but by then Gloria Swanson had left Hollywood for good.

Trouble seldom travels alone, and by 1936 Bart Marshall also worried Swanson. He drank heavily—as he always had—but was not handling his liquor well. He and Gloria began quarreling, and as their perfect understanding evaporated, Bart wrote her letters of apology: "Words are so hollow-sounding. . . . and I am so sick and sorry that I can't think of words now. . . . it is no use to try. . . . I had taken too much to drink—which explains—though it does not excuse—my primitive behavior. . . . I don't ask you to forget it: I only ask you to try not to *remember* it. There was so much—so much—sweetness . . . . I wish you might remember *that*."[91]

The pair had talked about marriage many times, Bart repeatedly promising to divorce Edna. Swanson wanted him to take the initiative, yet she knew by now that avoidance was Marshall's style. He couldn't bear to hurt anyone, and his "trial separation" dragged on. As Bart drank more, becoming morose and withdrawn, Swanson realized he would not act unless pushed.

When Bart went to England to visit his daughter, he left with a letter from Gloria stuffed into his pocket. In it she declared her love but also stated her unwillingness to continue as the other woman. It had become more of a strain than she could bear. Gloria asked Bart to make a final decision about his marriage.

When the phone finally rang from London, Bart told Gloria that everyone thought it was best—for his career and for Edna's—to let the press announce they had reconciled. But it didn't mean anything: he was on his way back to Hollywood and he loved her. Her joy at hearing his voice curdling, Swanson told Bart he should stay in England and make the reunion real. Their romance was over. "Facing what I now knew about Bart was unbearable, but I made myself face it. I might go on loving him, but I would never respect him again or feel happy with him again."[92] If her lover was willing to let her bear the pain and shame of being the other woman indefinitely, she was better off without him.

A few weeks later, Bart tracked Gloria down in New York, begging her to see him. She was shocked by his appearance: he was haggard, bloated, and smelled of drink. Bart apologized to her and began to cry. They both wept. "I was sick at heart," Swanson remembered. "I don't think I ever realized what was meant before by that expression, but I certainly did at that moment. We were both wrecks." Recalling all his kindness to her, she begged Bart to take better care of himself. Then she left before she could change her mind. On a single page in her handwritten memoir, Swanson wrote one line: "I was never so convincingly and thoroughly loved as I was by Herbert Marshall."[93]

CHAPTER 18

Reinventing Herself

AFTER HER OUTBURST AGAINST HARRY COHN, SWANSON WAS FIN-
ished with movies. She had once told Adolph Zukor that every artist
should be compelled to leave California for three months a year. Now
she knew it was time to pull up stakes, to go somewhere she could feed
her imagination and leave behind the same old conversations about the
same old business. So Swanson threw herself a farewell party, packed her
bags, and left the industry—and the industry town—where she found
fame and fortune. Beyond the spotlights, without the guaranteed paychecks and the intense scrutiny of the fans, the executives, the colum-
nists, and her colleagues, she would have a long and vibrant second act.

The self-proclaimed "mental vampire" regretted her abbreviated education; now she determined to use New York City as her classroom.[1]
Settling into the apartment at 920 Fifth Avenue she would call home for
many years, Swanson studied the city's art and architecture, attended
the theater, collected (and read) rare books, and pursued her interests
in fashion and design. None of this produced any income—at least not
at first—but she did nothing by halves. Like her son Joseph, Swanson
loved to tinker with things and observe how they worked: "I just happen to have that kind of a mind. I always figure out card tricks and I can
read a blueprint and understand it."[2] She recalled fooling around with
the idea for a wireless communication device more than a decade earlier. The time had not been right then—someone else had patented the
idea first—but maybe now she could put her endless curiosity to work.
Maybe it could help pay some of the bills.

She kept hearing about the scientists stuck in Nazi Germany and began to hatch a plan: what if she could create a company that would employ both refugee inventors and herself? In no time Swanson convened
a board of directors, all men with industry experience, and Multiprises,
her least likely entrepreneurial adventure, was born. "I had all the

innocence of the brash amateur, so I didn't know enough to put any limits on my catalogue of utopian products-to-be-invented or products-to-be-obtained."[3] She sent an envoy to Berlin in search of scientists who needed employment—and a way out.

Henri de la Falaise, who had split from Constance Bennett and was living in France, came to Gloria's aid, graciously providing a Paris "office" for the new company's "headquarters." He wrote letter after letter assuring the authorities that Multiprises guaranteed jobs for the four Viennese inventors Swanson's envoy located.

In January 1939, Gloria arrived in Paris, and four delighted men met her at the Gare Saint-Lazare, beaming and carrying bunches of violets. Electronics engineer Richard Kobler headed the group and managed its patents office. Leopold Karniol was a chemist and a plastics expert, Anton Kratky a metallurgist, and Leopold Neumann an acoustical engineer. Three were Jews; they had been forced to leave another colleague behind in a German concentration camp. Kobler had twice been detained by the Gestapo as he made his way from Berlin through Zurich to Paris. Their troubles were not yet over: Kobler needed a visa to travel to Brussels before he could leave Europe. Henri wangled Swanson an invitation to a party, where she waylaid the unsuspecting ministry official who could grant Kobler his visa. Soon she had the man under her spell, and Kobler had his travel pass.

It took another six months to get the whole group out of Europe. By the time their temporary US visas expired, the inventors were in New York, Multiprises was up and running, and the US was at war with Germany. Thankfully there was no question of sending Jewish refugees—scientists with steady employment—back to face the Nazis.

Seeing Henri again was a bright spot amid the dark of prewar Paris. Gloria adored his beautiful South American fiancée Emmita and gladly agreed to take legal steps to relinquish the title of marquise so Emmita could carry it. (Connie Bennett had never had official claim to the title, which satisfied Gloria, too.) The war brought Henri and Gloria close again: she helped Emmita raise money for wartime ambulances after the man Gloria called "her marquis" went back into uniform. Henri's memoir, *Through Hell to Dunkirk*, gives a harrowing account of the fight that killed more than half the men in his unit. It says little, however, about the heroism that won him a second Croix de Guerre.

A year or so after his time in Flanders, in a fitting turn of events, Henri and Emmita arrived in New York—only now it was Henri who carried a pledge of employment from Multiprises. Kobler and Neumann, two of the inventors Henri helped escape from Hitler, signed the contract that allowed the marquis's entry to the States: "The lifebelt Henri had helped create for them, they now threw back to him."[4] Swanson's apartment became their home while they recovered and regrouped.

Swanson and company set up an office in Rockefeller Center and acquired a factory in Queens. Multiprises provided financing and marketing for the group's inventions, eventually patenting parts used in manufacturing, recording, appliances, automobiles, and musical instruments. Led by the tiny woman they fondly called "Big Chief," the men worked on inventions with military applications as well. Inspired, Swanson patented several of her own inventions, including a dustless broom and a cigarette holder designed to fit on a finger.[5] Capitalizing on her own instincts and intuitions would help her make a creative living outside the movies.

A domestic crisis brewed while Swanson played with her scientists. Young Gloria, who had remained in California to begin college, was in love. She planned to elope, and Miss Simonson helped the teenager keep her plans secret from her mother. Swanson was taken by surprise, both by her daughter's determination and her employee's treachery. Though the children considered "Sammy" a member of the family, an enraged Swanson tossed her out into the street after sixteen years in the household.

She felt her daughter was too young to get married and wanted Gloria, who had just completed her first year at Stanford, to finish college. Gloria, however, was of age and did not need her mother's consent. Swanson was also hurt that Gloria had confided in Sammy rather than her, yet their lack of intimacy had been years in the making, as the actress flew in and out of her daughter's life. A subdued Swanson stayed in the background for her oldest child's wedding in Los Angeles on June 30, 1939. Gloria and Bob Anderson remained married until his death in 1966, but it took some time for the rift between mother and daughter to mend.

In the furor over the governess's dismissal, Swanson and Joseph, then almost seventeen, also fell out. He protested his mother's decision, and Swanson blew up. Sammy had undermined her parental authority—a concern the teenager was not inclined to take seriously. Weeks of mutinous silence followed, broken by a bitter squabble over Joseph's messy bedroom. Swanson informed her son icily that she had worked since she was younger than he was: "Perhaps it would be good for him to find out about the big, sometimes difficult world out there." She asked him to pack his bags and leave the house. She would give him enough money each week that he wouldn't starve, but from now on he would have to work for anything extra. She expected him to pay his way through college, too: "The boys who did . . . learned more than those who treated college like a country club because their parents paid for it."[6]

Swanson retreated to her room and sobbed into her pillow. An hour later a gentle knock at her door was followed by Joseph's quivering voice: did she mind if he spent the night? "At least fifty times during the night I put my hand on the doorknob to open it," Swanson remembered. "I had such a hurt inside me . . . I wanted to put my arms around him and say forget it, but something stronger than I was would not let me."[7] Her son left home in the morning.

Swanson helped Joseph get a job at an aviation company, and slowly their breach healed. Joseph embraced his independence, working his way through Antioch College, then graduate school, and serving in Germany during World War II. He and his mother shared a love of inventions, and while he trained to become an engineer, Joseph wrote Gloria reports about the piano he was building. He sent her weighty scientific tomes which she read, proud of being able to discuss his work with her son: "We little by little became sweethearts. We loved each other's company [and] had great bull sessions."[8]

Michelle was only seven when Sammy, her beloved governess and the only stable presence in her life, suddenly disappeared; her brother was gone soon afterwards. The night Joseph left home was the first and only time Michelle remembered being permitted into her mother's bed. Swanson hired a succession of replacements for Miss Simonson, but Michelle became nervous and depressed; she particularly struggled at mealtimes. Made to eat detested foods by the detested new nanny her pediatrician had recommended, she began losing weight and soon had trouble keeping anything down. The new governess was harsh and punitive, forcing the child to eat food she had vomited, paddling her, and smearing her with vomit and excrement when she lost control of herself in terror. Michelle remembered her mother looking into her room but turning away from the scene rather than coming to her aid. Swanson did not intervene, believing that the nanny's approach, though strict, had been sanctioned by the doctor and that it would help her daughter overcome her troubles. Michelle instead suffered from eating disorders for years.

Swanson seems to have believed that being tough with her children would prepare them for life's challenges: she loved them but could be remote and unyielding. Michelle recalled trying to apologize to her mother for some childish offense and being completely ignored, just as Adelaide had punished Gloria by locking her in a closet and ignoring her pleas for forgiveness decades earlier. When Michelle ran away from her New Jersey boarding school, appearing at her mother's Manhattan apartment in the middle of the night, Swanson sent her right back. There was no discussion of why Michelle left in the first place.[9] As a parent Swanson was not always wise or kind.

It is hard, too, to imagine sending an adopted child from the only home he has ever known, but Swanson remained convinced she had done the right thing by asking Joseph to leave. She had always been honest with him about his adoption, a practice by no means common then. When her son asked her, just before he went overseas, to help him contact his birth mother, Gloria willingly gave Joseph what little information she had, telling her son she was sure his "real" mother would be proud of him. A few years later, when Gloria dared ask Joseph what he had learned about his parentage, he said he had realized he didn't need to know more: he loved the mother he had.

Multiprises was turning a steady profit, though the invention game was a lot like the motion picture business: you invested a lot before you saw any returns. Swanson often traveled for the company, wooing clients as far afield as South America, and enjoyed combining business with pleasure. Money was always a concern, however, and Swanson earned less from Multiprises once the scientists began doing war work. Concerned about how government policies affected corporate profits, she moved to the right politically. She met Ayn Rand and was impressed by the writer's ideas about the free market. She also began reading everything she could find about Communism, which she believed was a bigger threat than Hitler. Outraged by FDR's effort at a third term ("No other President had thought [he was] indispensable"), Swanson made her first political speech, overcoming her nerves to stump for Wendell Willkie in 1940.[10] She rented a hall in lower Manhattan and let fly, "so feverishly interested in convincing audiences that I forgot to be afraid."[11]

Through her political activism, Swanson reconnected with Adolphe Menjou and received, out of the blue, an offer to star opposite him in an RKO picture. The salary was $35,000, "exactly $35,000 more than any other studio in Hollywood had offered in seven years," Swanson said wryly.[12] *Father Takes a Wife* was a programmer rather than a star vehicle, but the cast and crew treated Swanson with respect, even throwing her a surprise party at her first rehearsal, and she enjoyed being back in front of the cameras after seven years away.

The story was nothing special: Swanson plays an actress who can't quite quit show business. Shipping magnate Menjou—known as "Senior" to his grown son's "Junior"—falls madly in love with her. After they marry, the couple battles over her interest in managing the career of a handsome young singer, played by Desi Arnaz. There is an inter-generational gimmick: Junior becomes jealous of his wife's apparent at-traction to Arnaz, too. The happy ending comes when Swanson and her daughter-in-law both learn they are pregnant.

RKO decided to sell the picture as another of Swanson's glamour roles—only now her costar, not some ingénue, was her sartorial rival. Adolphe Menjou was one of the best dressed men in movies, though he too often felt trapped in clotheshorse parts: "I was stuck with that damned dress suit," he lamented in his aptly named memoir, *It Took Nine Tailors*.[13] Menjou and Swanson each made eighteen costume changes in *Father Takes a Wife*. They even had dueling stylists, Gloria outfitted by René Hubert. The old friends gamely applied themselves to their roles but seized every chance to talk politics, sharing their fears about the spread of Communism.

Swanson also let the press know she had been busy these last years, surprising many with tales of her factory. "We work with an alloy for pre-cision tools so hard we have to drill it with diamonds," she explained.[14] Her industrial efforts might seem unglamorous, but—one way or an-other—diamonds were still this girl's best friend.

Father, however, had little sparkle. Editor-turned-director Jack Hively got "only a minimal performance" from Swanson, said *Time*; the picture earned just "a passing grade."[15] Desi Arnaz put it more bluntly: *Father* was a "lemon."[16] Swanson blamed a lackluster presentation by RKO, which was undergoing a change of management, but the outbreak of World War II also helped defeat the frothy trifle. She returned to New York and to what she herself called "cinematic oblivion."[17]

Swanson's speechifying for Willkie had an unexpected consequence: it helped her confront her stage fright. She had been offered roles in plays for years but always found a reason to refuse. "New York stage producers gave me up as hopeless, because I'd get all excited about a play . . . but when it came to signing on the dotted line . . . I was scared to death at the prospect of facing an audience. I was sure I would forget my lines."[18] Swanson's fear seemed intractable, though she pretended the plays were never quite right.

Then Harold Kennedy came along. The theatrical entrepreneur's ap-proach was unique: he was "clever enough to offer a challenge rather than make an offer."[19] Perhaps Gloria should try summer stock first. "Find out whether you like the stage," he wrote her, "and whether it likes you."[20] Swanson invited Kennedy to her apartment, and he laid out his case. A tour in the provinces would offer an ideal way to get her theatrical bearings. Why go out for the first time under the brightest, harshest lights?

Kennedy, a Yale Drama School and Mercury Theatre alumnus, was a tireless champion of the summer touring circuit. He offered Swanson an opportunity she was shrewd enough to recognize: "Get it over with, he was signaling, and if you're lousy, at least you won't have to go on making feeble, dishonest demurs for the next decade or so; but if you're not, we can both make some money and you can begin a whole new career." With both trepidation and excitement, Swanson accepted his offer. Kennedy, she said, "had called my long-standing bluff, in my own living room."[21]

Tallulah Bankhead brought *Reflected Glory* to Broadway. Gloria Swanson brought it to Poughkeepsie—then Atlantic City, Toronto, Cambridge, and Providence, eight stops in eight weeks before she faced the New York critics from the relative safety of Brooklyn. Kennedy acknowledged that *Reflected Glory*, a lightweight comedy about an actress who wants to retire, wasn't much of a play. However, it was "a good vehicle for Gloria as it allowed her to be flamboyant and to wear a number of dazzling gowns which . . . is exactly what her audience wanted."[22]

As opening night approached Swanson was "beyond terror," and the cast and crew were giving her a wide berth, fearful she would snap.[23] She was still not off the book at the dress rehearsal and begged Kennedy for a postponement: "I was a total wreck. . . . I felt the guillotine was just around the corner."[24] The actress forced her poor director to crouch in a fireplace on the set, script in hand, to prompt her if she stumbled. If Kennedy left his position, she swore she would leave the stage. By then, Swanson said, "I was a tigress to be pitied and Harold was a thin-lipped saint."[25] She looked out on opening night to see Eleanor Roosevelt in the first row. When the curtain went up, Swanson walked onstage to a long and hearty ovation. She opened her mouth, began speaking her lines, and suddenly, miraculously, felt right at home: "In ten days I was a ham."[26]

It wasn't true, Gloria decided, that live performers were more closely scrutinized. "In a theater you can fool everyone past the tenth row if you're good, but on the screen you can't really fool anyone for a second."[27] Yet there was one kind of playgoer she could not fool: the

American women who came out to see Gloria Swanson in the flesh. "Women feel they know [female stars] intimately," Kennedy explained. "They want to see what they look like in person; what they're wearing; what their hairdos are like; and how old they really look." A matinee ticket on the New York City subway circuit cost fifty cents in 1942, and *Reflected Glory* filled the theater day after day, eight performances a week. Kennedy remembered "housewives sitting in the aisles, on the stairways, and standing five deep in the back. Not a man in the house."[28] Audience members discussed Swanson's appearance and her movie career during the performance. (The star finally corrected one woman who kept insisting to her seatmate that Gilbert Roland had been among Gloria's husbands. He hadn't, Gloria said.)

Swanson had gotten lucky. Kennedy was a good collaborator, adept at managing the thousand things that could go wrong on the road. He had even written Gloria's pet pug, Miranda, into the play. Swanson was making decent money: her contract stipulated $1,000 a week, plus 30 percent of the take over $5,000, and they broke house records wherever they went. If the play reflected no glory on anyone (one reviewer said it could have been written by "a mildly talented undergraduate wearing mittens"), Swanson herself got mostly favorable notices and had interested, sympathetic audiences.[29] There were off nights: after one performance in Toronto, Kennedy declared that the only good actor onstage had been Miranda. However, Gloria happily compared herself to "a mongrel with no training" who "learned fast and enjoyed it all."[30]

In November 1942, Swanson and Kennedy took a program of three one-act plays on tour, aiming for a Broadway run. *Three Curtains* was a mixed bag: the section by Arthur Wing Pinero had Gloria take pratfalls and look into trick mirrors; for the G. B. Shaw she was a spy, matching wits with a young Napoleon en route to his military victories. The J. M. Barrie play, however, attracted the most attention. For "The Old Lady Shows Her Medals," Swanson ditched her glamorous outfits and came onstage so fully camouflaged that even her daughter Michelle—now eleven—did not recognize her. By all accounts, Swanson was superb as the elderly woman who pretends to have a son in the military so she, too, can be part of the war effort. When a reviewer called the actress "timid, pathetic and dowdy," he meant it as a compliment.[31] Michelle was puzzled by how her mother managed to cry every night on cue. "I don't cry," Gloria told her, "the old lady does."[32]

From Baltimore to Buffalo, audiences again welcomed Swanson. Yet being on the road in winter meant working harder for less money. A blizzard in upstate New York kept audiences home; so did the new war-time gas rationing policy. *Three Curtains* was a hard show to put on under the best of circumstances. The plays were unconnected, and everyone scrambled to change costumes, sets, and mood during the intermissions, which made the audience restive.

There was no love lost between Swanson and Francis Lederer, the temperamental Prague-trained actor who was her leading man. A decade earlier, Michael Farmer had been jealous of his wife's acquaintance with Lederer, but Swanson couldn't stand the sight of him now. It came to a head in Boston when Lederer disrupted a performance, first accusing Kennedy of trying to upstage him, then mimicking Swanson's voice as she spoke her lines. "The audience was in a state of shock," Kennedy recalled. "They didn't know whether they were at a play or a prize fight."[33] Elliot Norton, the *Boston Post*'s influential critic, came backstage to find the cast members shouting at each other; he ran the story with a banner headline the next day.[34]

Swanson's producer-director friend Jack Wilson reluctantly advised her not to bring the play into New York: "It is a pity, because from your point of view it is a definite tour de force." Wilson expected Swanson's own notices to be "highly complimentary" but worried that the production itself would not be well received.[35] Seven weeks after they set out for Broadway, they conceded defeat and closed the show.

The theatrical bug had bitten Swanson; she spent most of the 1940s onstage. In summer 1943, she and Kennedy toured with a production of *Let Us Be Gay*, which Norma Shearer had done on screen with Rod LaRocque in 1930. This time they ventured as far west as Cleveland and Detroit, in a comedy that allowed Swanson to sparkle in front of another audience of fans. The star's flamboyance and vivacity, combined with her glamour, drew capacity crowds. "Her manner of acting is a little on the operatic side, but when she hits it she rings the bell," said one reviewer. "She has one rare talent for the stage. When she is on you don't much notice anybody else."[36] Others concurred: "Miss Swanson is still a young woman and not, by any manner of means, a miraculous survival of the Viking Age. She seems, to tell the truth, considerably younger than the play she's in."[37]

Like many Hollywood stars, Swanson made personal appearances to lift wartime spirits. She helped open the Cleveland recruiting office of the WAVES and visited manufacturing plants in Michigan and Ohio, surprising workers at an aircraft factory with her knowledge of engineering. (Swanson was always surprising people.) Wherever she went, her glamour attracted attention: hundreds were turned away when she modeled "fashions to welcome the men home" at a department store in Detroit. Gloria Swanson "could give flair to a gunny sack," a fan in Cleveland proclaimed.[38]

Swanson was still looking for that magical, ephemeral experience on stage. "All I live for now is to do a lovely Broadway hit—or just any production where the props all work and the furniture is the same for two weeks running."[39] Then she got an idea: in the past, pictures had been written for her. Why not commission a play? She adored Harold Kennedy and thought his off-the-cuff conversation was better than most theater dialogue. So Gloria went to work on Kennedy, promising to spend every evening out on the town with him if he would lock himself in and write all day. It had worked when they wrote *The Trespasser*. Kennedy agreed, and after three weeks sequestered in his hotel room, he emerged with *A Goose for the Gander*.

Kennedy's first full-length effort was "strictly a comedy, written solely to amuse a nerve-wracked populace."[40] Swanson played a wife returning from a six-week spa vacation to find her husband has installed another woman in their home. Too sophisticated to make a scene, she turns the tables by inviting several male friends to move in as well. Swanson was thrilled to have her own purpose-built property and devoted the spring of 1944 to rehearsals. Kennedy took the part of the wandering husband, and there was once again a role for Miranda, gussied up in a collar of dime-store pearls. With a little luck, they could bring a hit play to Broadway.

As the Allies landed in Normandy on June 6, 1944, a sold-out audience forgot its cares for a few hours at the Cambridge opening of *A Goose for the Gander*. Rose Kennedy came to see Swanson perform and had to fend off congratulations: "Some of those Bostonians who are perennially rooting for a Kennedy," she told her daughter, "thought that Jack had written a play."[41] *Goose* broke house records throughout the northeast for a month. When they moved to Chicago, Gloria got to see her son in uniform. Joseph had invested $5,000 of his own money in the show, and Gloria was touched and happy that he was in the audience, safe for the time being. Soon he would be overseas and in harm's way.

Despite pleasing audiences, however, the play was struggling, its problems deepening the longer they were out. Swanson had a new producer, an attorney with no stage experience. He pushed the company through an unusually grueling season of previews—including a rooftop performance in Philadelphia—that tested whatever lightness of spirit the actors could muster. Then there were constant niggling disagreements about publicity, billing, and box office receipts: more than once, Actors' Equity intervened to enforce Swanson's contract. The relentless pace and constant discord weighed on everyone. Swanson wrote to a backer, "I have never worked harder nor have I ever had such an unhappy association. I'm sure that my health will not stand much more."[42] Even the dogs who replaced Miranda when the pug had puppies were trouble: if they weren't barking at the audience or nipping at the players, they were stealing the show.

Swanson resisted doing personal appearances for the duration of the tour, realizing that once her fans (as Harold Kennedy put it) had "a free look at her they will not pay box office prices for the same privilege."[43] After her character's rival in the play, a well-endowed young actress called Choo Choo Johnson, was voted "the girl most likely to warm my igloo" by soldiers in Alaska, the forty-five-year-old star quietly began applying a little judicious color to her hair.[44]

One advisor urged Gloria to stick it out on the road, arguing that trial and error could only improve the play: "Come [to Broadway] well drilled, with a substantial surplus in cash and then bid New York take a long look at you all. You won't be sorry."[45] When the producer refused to account for the play's revenues, however, Private Joseph Swanson filed suit to force him to do so. By mid-August, Gloria had had enough: she refused to move the current production to New York, and the show closed. For now the goose seemed cooked.

Back at home in New York, Gloria rallied. Within weeks she found new backers and brought a more experienced production team on board, including her Paramount leading man Conrad Nagel. *A Goose for the Gander* opened at the Playhouse Theatre on January 23, 1945. Unfortunately for Swanson, the New York critics were a good deal less forgiving than her summer stock fans. They complained the play was long and old-fashioned, its few laughs insufficient to carry the evening: "Nothing much ever happens, and it is quite a strain helping the play along from scene to scene," said the *Daily News*.[46] The *Daily Mirror* called *Goose* "a candidate for . . . most boring comedy of the year."[47] The critics agreed: Gloria needed better material.

Swanson had been defending *Goose* since its summer premiere: "What if it is superficial and trivial and light as a powder puff?" she argued. "This is war time, and I believe the theater's duty is to offer the people entertainment which will make them forget rather than think; which will offer relaxation instead of reflection."[48] Her protests did no good: three days after the *Times* called *Goose* a "dead duck," closing notices went up.[49] Swanson's Broadway debut had lasted for all of fifteen performances.

Swanson had suffered no shortage of male companions since she and Bart Marshall split. There were younger men: Paul Soskin, a writer-producer from the Crimea with deep dimples, wooed her with sexy letters that insisted he and Gloria had found a "divine spark."[50] He offered her career advice (she should do *The Prisoner of Zenda* with Ronald Colman), fed her muffins with honey, and tried to analyze her past relationships: "In . . . your last two marriages, you've admitted that you were acting on your impulses, it was a case of escape from yourself, you were over-wound, you wanted to change surroundings, other elements such as false pride, whimsy and other instincts so typical of a woman motivated your actions. You were thinking in terms of your personal satisfaction, and just hoping it would work out. . . . Everything was done in haste, in the whirl of glamour, these men were your toys, it was a hysteria." Yet Soskin also acknowledged that "the governing factor" of their relation was their "very strong physical attraction," and that his fits of obsessive jealousy left Swanson "black and unhappy."[51] Since Soskin worked in London most of the time, it was hard work to keep their divine spark lit.

There were reliable, steady fellows who made good escorts and friends but did not awaken any passion in her. Gus Schirmer, heir to the music publishing company, became Gloria's constant companion; they often traveled together and were an on-again, off-again item in the columns for years. An accomplished violinist, Schirmer was fascinated by botany and astronomy and shared these loves with Swanson. He attached himself to her "like a collie," she said. "My smallest wish was a great joy for him to gratify. But . . . there is a limit before one becomes obligated. So I was very honest about my feelings toward him."[52]

Schirmer regaled his friends with tales of the large sums he gave Swanson and the bills he footed for their international holidays. Sport Ward said, "He was inclined to brag somewhat and liked to talk of his many conquests . . . [T]o hear him talk—it was tough on the dames the way they all fell for him."[53] Swanson, who always lived beyond her means, did not complain about Schirmer's largesse; she called him "one of the dearest and most generous men I ever knew."[54]

One night, however, he offered a temptation she had to swallow hard before refusing. Schirmer stayed behind when Gloria's other guests left, looking "like a naughty child" when she discovered him hiding in her bedroom.[55] He had organized a treasure hunt, pronouncing Gloria "hot" or "cold" as she followed his clues through the apartment. At last she discovered the prize: a strong box containing all his shares in the family business. Gus knew she worried about money and wanted to give her the security she craved. Gloria was moved—dumbfounded, really—but knew she could not accept Gus's gift, since she did not love him. Nonetheless, they remained friends for years.

There were also powerful, authoritative, and occasionally ungovernable men. In the mid-1940s, Frederick MacRobert, an attorney and Multiprises board member, became her regular escort, supporting Swanson during her first panicky forays onto the stage. Yet their relation was none too calm: night after night Swanson wrote in her datebook that they had spent an "awful evening!!!!" or a "dreadful day" together.[56]

She never spoke of her brief affair with Aristotle Onassis in the early 1940s, though *Father Takes a Wife*, in which a famous actress marries a shipping magnate, was practically an insider's joke. Onassis, seven years Swanson's junior, described his modus operandi: "I approach every woman as a potential mistress . . . Beautiful women cannot bear moderation: they need an inexhaustible supply of excess."[57] His extravagant, luxurious hospitality was legendary, and Swanson always thrived on passionate excess. Onassis, who was romantically linked with Paulette Goddard, Veronica Lake, and Maria Callas, obviously knew something. Yet he was puzzled by Swanson's affair with Joe Kennedy, reportedly asking his wife Jacqueline Kennedy Onassis whether the attraction was money. Joe had helped Gloria escape the studio system, Jackie explained, a life that "only looked comfortable if you weren't imprisoned in it."[58]

Swanson's love life got a lot more tumultuous with the entrance of William Davey, a wealthy investment broker. They met in October 1944, while Swanson was rehearsing for her Broadway opening. Davey "wasn't a handsome man, but he always looked as if he had just been scrubbed from head to foot," thanks to the ministrations of his full-time valet. He knew his way around society: Davey had been married to silent star Alyce Mills and had squired Peggy Hopkins Joyce and Rhea Gable, Clark's estranged wife. He owned big chunks of Hollywood real estate and promised to build Gloria a yacht with a glass stern. He wanted to take care of her, something Swanson always found seductive. When *Goose for the Gander* faltered on Broadway, Davey urged her to quit working entirely and enjoy life with him. She introduced him to Michelle, then a young teenager in boarding school, and "he charmed her as he had me."[59]

On January 29, 1945, three months after they met, they stood in front of the justice of the peace in Union City, New Jersey. When her

Broadway run ended five days later, Swanson wrote in her datebook, "Play closed. Thank God. Now I can be a real wife." Yet right from the start her fifth husband, who began annotating Gloria's datebook himself, showed signs of dissatisfaction. "Tried vainly to get my bride in the feathers but finally gave up," Davey wrote the day after their wedding: her apartment, which they now shared, was full of Gloria's friends and family.[60]

Soon they were having bitter fights. Swanson's correspondence includes crumpled and torn letters of apology from Davey, begging her pardon for some truly disturbing insults and accusations. Davey was an alcoholic whose personality changed dramatically when he drank: Gloria had again reached not for the bottle but for the man holding one. He began in the morning and continued all day, even coming to the theater "dead drunk."[61] One night she heard Davey stumbling around Michelle's room. She never learned what he was doing there—possibly looking for one of the bottles he had stashed away—but she was shocked and dismayed. She called the valet, who distracted Davey with a drink.

The next day she and Michelle found an Alcoholics Anonymous meeting and slipped in unobtrusively. They picked up all the literature they could carry and went home, Gloria said, "with our arms full of encouragement." She left the material lying around the apartment. Davey got the message, but instead of going to a meeting, he packed up and moved out. "It was obviously the worst thing I could have done . . . It frightened him in some way. . . . There was no way of talking to him or even trying to help him in his despair."[62] They had been married less than two months when Davey departed. He left a note that read, "It was nice as long as it lasted."[63]

Over the next few months, as Davey went on and off the wagon, Swanson felt unsafe and sad. Davey called incessantly; he tried rehab but bounced right back out again. Gloria changed the locks on the doors twice, ashamed that Michelle had to share the "sordidness of it—not a very pretty picture for a young girl."[64] She spent time with friends: Lois, Virginia, Eddie Goulding, Henri and Emmita, ZaSu Pitts. Finally, reluctantly, she filed for a legal separation from Davey, seeking $1,000 a week in support.

All legal hell broke loose. Davey immediately countersued, claiming Swanson had fraudulently misrepresented the state of her finances, her health, and even the comforts of her home. She was in debt, he said, and suffering from a mysterious ailment doctors could not correct. Davey asked that their marriage be annulled, which would free him from alimony payments. With assets valued over ten million dollars, he fought to protect himself from any claims his new wife might make. When the court ordered him to pay Swanson $200 a week until their cases could be settled, Davey sought an injunction against even that amount. (Thirteen-year-old Michelle offered to get a job at a local bakery to ease her mother's money worries.)

All the while, Davey continued to call Gloria, often in the middle of the night, saying he still loved her. She protested that this did not feel like love: Davey had embarrassed her and hurt her ability to find work by saying she was not in good health. He had treated her "like some common woman of the streets," telling lies "just so he would not have to assume the responsibility of support."[65] Swanson agreed to see Davey only if he issued a public statement retracting his "rotten accusations."[66] He promised but failed to do so.

The New York court agreed with Swanson. Judge Eder lashed Davey for claiming Gloria had misrepresented her health when she replied to casual questions like "How are you this evening?" with an equally casual "Fine." These were customary greetings, not efforts to "ascertain . . . her state of health with a view to determining if he should contract marriage with her." Eder dismissed the effort to annul the union, scoffing at Davey's claim that he had moved back to his own place only because Swanson's apartment was "uncomfortable and annoying," with a "noisy refrigerator" and a malfunctioning shower. "The petty annoyances . . . could have been easily corrected . . . even by an oversensitive husband possessed of a prima donna's temperament." Davey had made "a mockery of marriage," seeking wrongly to escape his legal obligation to his wife.[67] The judge ordered Davey to pay.

Instead, he moved back to California and stopped sending Swanson alimony. Gloria's lawyer predicted that Davey would try to wear her down or wait her out. By the end of 1945, her estranged husband owed Swanson more than $12,000 in back payments, and she was spending money she did not have to sniff out where he had hidden his considerable resources.

Davey's deep pockets let him keep fighting. He hired help: after a year's separation from Swanson, he sent detectives to her apartment to search for evidence that she was having an affair. The hired goons broke down her door, rousting Swanson's lover from bed. As he scrambled to lock himself into the bathroom, the detectives rifled through his pants and found his wallet. William Earl Sprackling—known as "Sprack"— was a burly Anaconda Copper executive who had been an All-American football player at Brown. He was also married. The sight of Sprack climbing—naked—out Swanson's bathroom window onto a narrow ledge high over Fifth Avenue must have been memorable. Gloria's son Joseph helped his mother's lover creep across the ledge and into the apartment next door so he could exit the building unmolested.

In the end, Davey spent six weeks in Reno, arguing unsuccessfully for a divorce on grounds of Swanson's mental cruelty. His wife prevailed, winning her decree for desertion in December 1948. Nine months to the day after they were divorced, Davey died suddenly, leaving all his money to charity. Her fifth marriage merited one paragraph in Swanson's autobiography.

Though Michael Farmer had paid no child support for Michelle, he had pledged she would inherit his patron's jewels and money. During the war Swanson learned that Mrs. Hubbard had died, but when she attempted to contact her ex-husband, he had also disappeared. Farmer had last been seen partying on the Riviera as the Germans approached. Until Swanson could locate him, Mrs. Hubbard's estate remained frozen.

Then one day at the end of the war Farmer walked into the Ritz Bar in Paris. He had insulted the wrong soldier in Biarritz a few years earlier and had been placed under house arrest there: he had ridden out the war "interned" in a chateau on the Riviera. When peace came he was free—until he was suspected of collaborating with the occupiers.[68] The promised support for Michelle, money Swanson sorely needed and felt she was owed, would be another long battle.

So back to work Gloria went, spending more time on the road than off for the next few years. She and Harold Kennedy took *Let Us Be Gay* out four separate times. Plays like *Goose* were welcome in the provinces, and she appeared in theaters from Portland, Maine, to Madison, Wisconsin. She still earned good money—$1,000 a week plus a healthy percentage of the gate over $5,000—but now she was the only performer traveling with the play. All the other parts were played by locals. It was exhausting work, made worthwhile only by the legions of fans who came out to see her.

Playwright John Guare ran the light board for Swanson during his apprenticeship in summer stock in New Haven. This meant "bringing up all the stage lights surreptitiously when she came onstage so the audience would subliminally think, gee, isn't everything brighter when she's around? . . . It was called a 'star bump.' Knowing lore like that made me feel there was a secret freemasonry to the theater."[69] (Guare also remembered Swanson yelling at him as he fixed the broken plumbing in her dressing room.)

Swanson did not mind working with amateurs but could not abide people who did not work as hard as she did. Harold Kennedy explained: "Gloria is a perfectionist, which is marvelous for a director but can be a pain in the ass to ordinary mortals who have long since made their peace with mediocrity. . . . She knows exactly what she wants and will settle for nothing less. . . . When she sends the scenic designer explicit instructions that the mantel on the fireplace is to be four feet six and a quarter inches high, that is what she means. And it better not be six and one eighth. She will know in a second and if there is any discussion she'll bring her tape measure out on the stage with her." Gloria's meticulous attention to details of staging, costuming, and lighting came from thirty years' experience in the business, as Kennedy readily conceded. She was "generous and gracious and completely cooperative with fellow actors" and "wonderful" to him.[70]

Hedda Hopper added her two cents' worth: "It takes guts for a girl who's had everything, whose name has been blazoned throughout the world, to play week after week in summer stock with people whose names aren't even known within a radius of five miles."[71] By 1945 most Hollywood actresses of a certain age had disappeared into private life; Mary Pickford, Clara Bow, Colleen Moore, Marion Davies, Pola Negri, Louise Brooks, Greta Garbo, and the Talmadge sisters had all retired. Swanson was the only one of her generation to stay relentlessly in the public eye. She would be on and off the stage for the rest of her life.

There was another place Gloria could get—and give—a star bump: television. She and Robert Balzer, who ran a food and wine emporium in Los Angeles, had been pitching a daily newspaper column they planned to write jointly, "a column sparkling with the highlights of subjects interesting to every member of the reading public: travel, theatre, food and wine, international society, fashion, books, ballet, art, Hollywood movies, philosophy, people, and events. . . . in short, the arts and artists of good living."[72]

Then someone got the brainy idea to star Gloria in a television variety show of her own with the same premise. Television was in its infancy, and Swanson was one of the first movie stars to cross over to the new medium. (The first issue of *TV Guide* pictured her on its cover.) Since most Hollywood actors were contractually forbidden to appear on the small screen, her independence for once proved an asset.

The Gloria Swanson Hour was broadcast live, beginning in June 1948, the same week that New York's WPIX-TV itself debuted on the air. The weekly program featured the actress entertaining famous guests in a set modeled on her own penthouse apartment and decorated with antiques and paintings. Comic shtick with her "butler" Erik Rhodes was a staple, as were segments on fashion, decorating, cooking, and entertaining. Gloria had a big role in crafting the hour, which rested largely on her shoulders. She knew almost everyone in New York, and her real-life friends often appeared: she entertained Edward Steichen, Charles Trenet, Alexander Calder, Madeleine Carroll, Adrian, and Robert Flaherty, as well as prima ballerinas, pilots, chefs, handwriting analysts, and diamond merchants. Swanson's entry into America's living rooms built a new audience for her work, creating an intimacy with viewers unprecedented for a Hollywood star. Forever after, her TV fans felt they knew the real Gloria Swanson.

At first the actress was thrilled by her creative freedom, her high profile, and her steady paycheck (which grew from $200 to $350 a week). She supplied her own costumes and makeup—including the black lipstick that was the only shade visible against the harsh, high-contrast TV lights. However, the lack of experienced professionals in the new medium soon frustrated her. In addition to attracting guests, rehearsing with them, and helping write the program, Swanson found herself moving equipment and instructing technicians how to line up and light shots.

If she thought touring was grueling, early TV work was worse. She was the old show business pro on the set; the inexperienced crew had to be told to oil squeaky doors and dollies, to set the sound levels so everyone was evenly miked, and so on. She needed "three brains" to keep track of it all.[73] Once an electrician forgot to switch on the set lights. He stood mesmerized by the performers—who were madly trying to cue him, ad libbing about how dark it was getting. Finally, an actor walked off and pulled the switch himself.[74] Though the show got positive reviews and helped inaugurate a perennially popular type of daytime TV programming, Swanson called it "the hardest work I have ever known."

New York television in 1948 was hardly apolitical, and Swanson received anonymous letters tipping her off to the Communist affiliations of some coworkers and demanding she inquire more closely into the politics of others. She shared some of these sentiments. Suspicious that the fledgling industry was a haven for Communists, her politics tilted farther to the right, and she signaled her employer about station employees Zero Mostel and Philip Loeb, who were "extremely 'left,' to say the least." She wanted the management to "keep a watchful eye on the personnel [in] key positions. . . . Any professional person would catalogue these men with Paul Robeson and his ilk."[75]

Despite her paranoia, Swanson, too, was a worker. She was agitating for a better contract and conditions when Hollywood once again came knocking at her door.

CHAPTER 19

"You Used to Be Big"

WHEN PARAMOUNT PRODUCER CHARLES BRACKETT CALLED SWANSON in September 1948 about *Sunset Boulevard,* she was already getting tired of TV. She liked the idea of taking a lucrative break in California to do a movie bit for Brackett and Billy Wilder, the hottest producer-director team in Hollywood. Fifteen years earlier, Wilder had been a struggling writer on *Music in the Air;* now he had eight Oscar nominations and two wins—for direction and screenplay—to his credit. Gloria felt certain she could get a week or two off from her show. No, Brackett said, she would be needed for longer: they wanted her for the lead in a major film. What would she think about a salary of $50,000?

Swanson was not their first choice. The early idea—Brackett's, anyway—was to do a comedy about an actress who had lost her hold on the box office. Wilder was lukewarm about the project until someone suggested that the actress had a Midwestern screenwriter as her paid escort. The gigolo would be the central character. When Wilder imagined the actress shooting the younger man, the story suddenly gained traction.[1] With only half the first act down on paper, Brackett and Wilder approached Pola Negri, but Negri was unenthusiastic about portraying a fallen star, and her Polish accent was still disconcertingly thick. Mae West was downright insulted at the suggestion that she was past her prime; she was juggling offers from employers and beaux. The two men went to Pickfair to see if Mary Pickford might come out of retirement to play Norma Desmond. She was intrigued but wanted the script reshaped to focus on her character. Wilder claimed they backed away gently, saving Mary's pride by saying the role was too "vulgar" for her.[2] Pickford maintained she refused the part, suggesting they approach Gloria Swanson instead.[3]

In fact, George Cukor suggested Swanson to Wilder, and the idea quickly acquired the force of inevitability. Gloria had been famous in the silent era; she was still attractive; and she was known for her romantic liaisons. Over lunch on Labor Day, Swanson found Wilder "elfish, witty, confident," and full of energy; like her, he was seldom still. Brackett was the quieter, "more refined" one of the pair.[4] A better diplomat, Brackett claimed they had never seriously considered anyone else for the part. There was only one catch: they wanted Gloria to do a screen test.

"Me? Test? I was revolted," Swanson said. "I said what the hell do you have to test me for? You want to see if I'm alive, do you? Or do you doubt I can act?" She flatly refused. Then her friends went to work on her: one by one, Clifton Webb, Allan Dwan, William Powell—even Mickey Neilan—told Gloria she should test. "Darling George Cukor" was especially persuasive: "That dear man," she said, could "charm the birds out of the trees."[5] Cukor told Swanson she would be remembered for the part of Norma Desmond; that was all the persuasion Gloria needed.

She aced her test, the scene where Joe Gillis first recognizes the aging actress: "You used to be in pictures," he says. "You used to be big." Swanson put on her Gorgon gaze for the first time as Norma Desmond and tried out the line she would make famous: "I *am* big. It's the pictures that got small." Then she went back to New York to wind up her television series.

She was glad to be out of the grind of television work and excited to be preparing for her picture: "Guess it's the old circus horse in me scenting the sawdust again."[6] Yet when she posed for publicity photos with studio head Barney Balaban and Adolph Zukor, who was now chairman of the board at Paramount, the old man took her aside and had a quiet word. Keep your TV show, he advised her, but keep quiet about it: "If anyone hears you say the word television, you will have your mouth washed out." Nonetheless, Zukor said, television was the future. "Everything was small about him but his ideas," Swanson declared.[7]

Though she seldom looked back, she snatched a moment to write to Virginia from a favorite haunt: "I am sitting in a suite at the Beverly Hills Hotel overlooking the old Swanson house. All I have done since I have been here is reminisce. I have seen so many old friends and spots. It has been old home week and a busman's holiday, sandwiched in with tests, interviews and business conferences." Everyone was being "angelic" to her.[8] An enormous sign outside the studio highlighted Paramount's history, with Swanson's picture in first position as the studio's top moneymaker. The casting director told Gloria he was relieved that none of the current stars had finished first: Hope, Crosby, Stanwyck, and Hutton would all have wanted the top spot. "That's when I knew I was home . . . right back in the jungle, up to my ears in the old rat race."[9]

She dined at the Goldwyns' with Cole Porter, Clifton Webb, Ray Milland, and Joan Fontaine and at Errol Flynn's with Mary Pickford, Raoul Walsh, and Billy Haines. Young Gloria was now a mother of three, and Swanson bragged to everyone about her grandchildren, proudly wearing a copper wire bracelet her six-year-old grandson had made to the Oscars in March. Hollywood rolled out its red carpet; because Swanson had a movie coming out, she was once again noteworthy. At the LA opening of the Lunts' play *I Know My Love*, "the show was stolen by a tiny woman with graying hair who needed glasses to read the program. . . . Grandma Swanson was, as always, the queen, and everyone rendered homage by gawking at her and buzzing after the excited fashion of tourists."[10]

With Swanson committed, Wilder and Brackett began fleshing out their story. Inspired by the real-life film history Gloria brought to the project, they hired Cecil DeMille to play himself and Erich von Stroheim as Norma Desmond's mysterious butler and protector, the man who devotes himself to "mending the leaks in her delusions."[11] The resonance with the leading lady's real life got deeper and stranger, and Gloria's role grew. Maurice Zolotow explained, "She exuded such savagery and madness [at her screen test] that Brackett and Wilder shifted the story radically and . . . made Norma Desmond the central role in the film."[12]

Montgomery Clift would play the kept man, pitting the Method actor against the old-style silent star. Two weeks before shooting began, however, Clift pulled out, saying he could not convincingly play the lover of an older woman. In fact, Clift had a complicated personal life he was not eager to have examined, including an on-again, off-again live-in relationship with Libby Holman, the alcoholic singer who had been acquitted of murder after shooting and killing her wealthy husband. Holman was sixteen years older than Clift; the May-December relationship in *Sunset Boulevard* hit close to home.

Losing Clift was a real blow. After a decade in the theater, he had exploded onto the screen in *Red River* and *The Search*; his new film, *The Heiress*, looked like another winner. Wilder and Brackett quickly reconnoitered. Fred MacMurray didn't want to play second banana to Gloria Swanson (though he claimed portraying a gigolo went against his principles). M-G-M would not release Gene Kelly. Marlon Brando was Clift's closest dramatic rival, but he had not yet appeared onscreen.

They eventually picked William Holden from the Paramount talent pool; at least he saved the production money. Some accounts say Holden was eager to sink his teeth into a better part than anything he'd seen since 1943's *Golden Boy*; others, however, suggest that Holden also balked at playing a passive and unheroic character, and that Wilder asked Paramount to enforce the actor's contract.[13] As Joe Gillis, Holden displays a potent blend of ambivalence, self-loathing, and cynicism; *Sunset Boulevard* made him a star.

Little by little the screenplay took shape. First Norma was working on her memoirs; then they became a script by which she would stage her return to stardom. Her mansion, originally planned as an unkempt reflection of Norma's forgotten status, got a facelift, since she was now a woman aggressively planning her return. If Norma Desmond had been a real person, Wilder joked, her oil wells would pay for "four or five gigolos. She would now be living somewhere in Santa Barbara with George Hamilton."[14] The revised script described Norma as a woman with "a curious style, a great sense of high voltage," and "a voice like a ringmaster's whip."[15] It was a bit risky, as Wilder acknowledged, but Swanson "had a period way of acting. Her style was 1920s. You can't learn that. You must grow up with it."[16]

Edith Head tried to strike a balance between making Norma, a wealthy woman, look simultaneously in style and out of it. With Swanson her constant collaborator, Head settled on rendering new designs using old-fashioned materials. Yet she always said it was "impossible" to make the star "look like a has-been."[17] Paramount publicists encouraged an emphasis on Swanson's clotheshorse persona, taking readers on tours of Gloria's own enormous closets and claiming that the actress had (literally) stepped into her old shoes in the studio's costume archives.

Since *Sunset Boulevard* was at best a poisoned valentine to Hollywood, Brackett and Wilder were anxious to keep the story from seeping out. They assigned the film the working title *A Can of Beans* and posted warnings on the scripts: "Due to the peculiar nature of the project, we ask all our co-workers to regard it as top secret."[18] They were divided about how dark to make the story, Wilder leaning toward the ghoulish and macabre, Brackett edging away. The disputes continued even as principal photography began on April 18, 1949.

Erich von Stroheim nudged Wilder toward a darker vision; though he sneered at "the goddamned butler role," he made numerous suggestions about his character.[19] He wanted Max to wear white gloves and have a pronounced limp. More significantly, he suggested that Max had once been Norma's director and that he wrote the fan letters Norma still received. Stroheim also proposed they incorporate a short sequence from *Queen Kelly* into the picture, to show the young Norma/Gloria's breathtaking beauty. Wilder liked this idea, and Swanson gave permission to use the film. Yet when Stroheim wanted to show Max washing out Norma's lingerie, lovingly stroking her silken panties, Wilder drew the line. He remembered hearing that Stroheim had delayed the production of *Greed* for three days back in 1924 "because there wasn't enough horse shit in the streets."[20] Crew members had collected manure to satisfy the director's idea of realism.

Wilder listened respectfully to the older man's suggestions, then went his own way. "The enigma of film-making is that it is at once a dictatorship and a democracy," Wilder explained.[21] Stroheim accepted his director's decisions, seeming satisfied that Wilder knew who he had been. In fact, Wilder delighted in recounting their initial encounter in 1943. He said to Stroheim, "You were ten years ahead of all of us—ten years ahead of the industry!" Stroheim looked at him and said, "Twenty."[22]

If it was "galling" for Stroheim to act the part of Gloria Swanson's manservant, he gave no sign of it.[23] Their young costar Nancy Olson found him "so remote, so proper and polite. [Gloria] was very correct with him, but also very easy. I found her easy with me, too. She had a lovely, graceful demeanor."[24] Swanson claimed she and Stroheim had made their peace long ago.

Gloria compared making the picture to undergoing analysis: "Billy Wilder deliberately left us on our own, made us dig into ourselves, knowing full well that such a script, about Hollywood's excesses and neuroses, was bound to give the Hollywood people acting in it . . . doubts, about the material or about themselves." Since it steered so close to Gloria's personal history in Hollywood, *Sunset Boulevard* demanded she "use all [her] past experience for props."[25] In fact, they culled Gloria's New York apartment for actual props to decorate Norma Desmond's house, a mansion the production rented from J. Paul Getty's ex-wife. Swanson lent the studio dozens of paintings and photographs of herself from her private collection; images from *Sadie Thompson*, *The Trespasser*, and *What a Widow!* are visible throughout *Sunset Boulevard*.

Being surrounded by her younger self at every turn seemed not to bother Swanson. It may have helped that cinematographer John Seitz, an old hand who had shot pictures at Essanay even before Swanson got there, had trouble making her look old enough to play Norma Desmond. Gloria was fifty but looked easily a decade younger; William Holden was supposed to be twenty-five but looked his thirty-one years. They added some gray to Swanson's hair, penciled in some wrinkles, then made some tests. Gloria remembered looking "as if I had been dug up."[26] They soon gave up trying to age Swanson, concentrating instead on making Holden look younger.

Sprack came out to visit right after shooting began, and he reported to Joseph that Gloria was feeling well, looking fine, and enjoying her work: "She is a major sensation on the Paramount lot. As you know, she eats this up."[27] The couple's relationship, however, was on the rocks. Sprack—whom Walter Winchell called Swanson's "Metal Mogul"—was still married.[28] Even so, he had carried on "like a madman" about Gloria's departure for the Coast, and soon after his visit they decided to call it quits.[29] When Hedda Hopper asked Swanson if she was going to marry "a wealthy industrialist," Gloria laughed: "I wish you'd find me such a man."[30] Though Michelle described her mother's romantic life as "busy," Gloria "couldn't seem to keep the men in her life. They would come in big, husky, good-looking fellows . . . and they would wind up being dogs sitting up for pieces of sugar. She had such a dominating personality that she trained them. But then they didn't like it, or she didn't like it, because she was looking for someone who was strong."[31]

Swanson rented a house in Whitley Heights with a courtyard fountain. She and Adelaide, once again a widow, moved in, and Michelle joined them when school ended. Michelle remembered her mother using Norma Desmond's deep, slow voice both on and off the set that summer. "Here comes Norma," Addie would say as Swanson arrived home each evening.[32]

Since Michelle attended boarding school and spent most summers at camp, Gloria had not shared a home with her daughter for years. The teenager had done some modeling after Swanson insisted she get a job, but preening about bored her. She preferred to play tennis or swim and lived in her loafers, which her fashion-conscious mother despised. Gloria worried that her daughter had little drive. "She's had all kinds of offers for television and the stage," she told Louella Parsons. "She is so beautiful and she could have a great success. She has all the poise in the world, a voice like Tallulah Bankhead, and the grace of another Duse. But not Michelle! I have more vitality today than she has."[33] Nonetheless, Gloria began contemplating a screen career for her daughter.

Though her performance in *Sunset Boulevard* was intentionally melodramatic, Swanson's mood was light during the shoot; the dark, brooding film was a happy experience from first to last. It was "a very easy picture to do because it had a something about it from the moment it started," she explained. "It had a spark, and that spark never went out."[34] Wilder agreed, saying, "Everything [I needed] sort of fell into my lap."[35]

Yet he regarded his leading lady as the linchpin: "It didn't quite fall into place until we got Gloria Swanson."[36] She "worked like a dog" and was "an absolute angel," one of the most "pleasant surprises" of his career.[37] Holden told reporters Swanson was usually the first person on set every day, and the last one off.

Her energy surprised others. One long, complicated scene required many takes: "Miss Swanson was waiting on everyone to continue on another take. Finally [Wilder] told her to rest a minute. 'I'm not the least bit tired,' she replied. 'I know,' said Wilder, 'but (pointing to Holden) the kid can't keep up with you.'"[38] Swanson was back in her element: on a film set. She felt challenged and absorbed but scoffed at the idea that it was hard: "I sang every morning on the way to work. Work? What a silly word."[39]

She was glad she was no "waxwork," as the silent-era card players who visit the Desmond household were dubbed. Wilder and Brackett hired former stars H. B. Warner, Anna Q. Nilsson, and Buster Keaton to make up Norma's quartet at bridge. They had known each other for years: Warner played the older man in love with Swanson in *Zaza* back in 1923, when Gloria was twenty-four. Now he was seventy-four and looked "brittle, almost transparent." When Keaton mumbled, "Waxworks is right," they all cracked up. Nonetheless, the short scene they shared "[gave] us all the creeps," Swanson recalled.[40] Wilder biographer Ed Sikov understood why: "By 5:15 Wilder was done with them and they were has-beens again."[41] Swanson's friend Billy Haines, who had been pushed out of the movies for refusing to hide his homosexuality, declined an offer to join the bridge party. His interior design work beat acting: "It's clean," he said, "no mascara on the face."[42] Haines thought *Sunset Boulevard*'s audience was at Forest Lawn cemetery.

Most of the older stars were happy to get the work; as Wilder said, they "weren't exactly busy."[43] Yet the silent era was barely twenty years gone. With the coming of sound, major talent had been swept aside— "given the brush," as Joe Gillis says—and forgotten in a single generation. For every old player with a bit part in *Sunset Boulevard*, there were dozens who simply vanished from the spotlight. Even the name Norma Desmond recalled stars of yesteryear who had not finished well: Norma Talmadge became a cocaine addict, William Desmond Taylor a murder victim.

There were, thankfully, lighter moments in the picture. To entertain Joe, Norma dons oversized shoes, derby, and cane and performs a skillful imitation of Charlie Chaplin, as Swanson had done twenty-five years earlier in *Manhandled*. The day after her performance, the entire cast and crew greeted Swanson wearing derbies. Even Norma's pet chimpanzee had a miniature hat. Swanson thought it "the sweetest tribute."[44] Brackett explained Swanson's power in the role: "Youngsters who never saw her would immediately accept her as an old-time movie queen. Older faces would identify her with the characterization and get a bigger emotional wallop from the story."[45]

This was most evident in the sentimental scene between Swanson and DeMille. When Norma drives onto the Paramount lot—the studio she says she practically built—DeMille welcomes her back with open arms. He treats his protégée gently, making it clear that Norma is not simply or only delusional. He invites her to watch them set up a shot for his current film (*Samson and Delilah*, which DeMille was then filming). The former colleagues talk about the old days in terms that could have been used by the real Swanson and DeMille; he even calls Norma "Young Fellow." *Sunset Boulevard* is full of references to real people and real places, from Tyrone Power and Hedda Hopper to Schwab's drugstore and the Paramount Studios gate. No wonder viewers were confused by the unsettling congruence between Gloria Swanson and Norma Desmond: it was built into the picture. It was, as Swanson said, "as if [I'd] never been away."[46]

Swanson gave Billy Wilder full marks for inspiring others' creativity. He reminded her of Toscanini conducting an orchestra in a "very light, delicate, polite manner—but madly irreverent. I never saw him give a line reading, to me or anyone. And he never showed you how to play a scene. He would discuss a character but he expected you to know how to do the character." The director got her highest praise when she said, "He is like Mr. DeMille."[47]

Wilder offered a slightly different take on his job: "You yourself have to play twenty different parts. You have to be a sycophant, you have to be a sadist, you have to be a nurse, you have to be a cook, you have to be a philosopher, you have to demean yourself, you have to be a screamer. It just depends on the actor. . . . Everybody has his own little weaknesses, and there are different ways of coaxing [a performance] out of them." He concluded wryly, "This is not a profession for a dignified human being."[48]

The picture wrapped in late June, ending with Swanson's final mad scene, in which Norma turns toward her imaginary director and says, "All right, Mr. DeMille, I'm ready for my close-up." It would become one of the most famous lines in movie history.[49] When it was over, Swanson wept: the experience had been "magical."[50] Though the picture's star traditionally gave the cast and crew members gifts, her *Sunset Boulevard* colleagues turned the tables on Gloria, presenting her with an engraved silver cigarette case: "To PROCLAIM THAT GLORIA SWANSON is The Greatest Star of Them All And the Idol of Cast, Staff and Crew of SUNSET BOULEVARD." Their tribute meant more to Swanson than any Academy Award.

She stayed in California, unwilling to break the spell of *Sunset Boulevard*. In August, Swanson's son Joseph married his longtime sweetheart Sue, a happy union that endured until his death. Gloria had recently told Louella Parsons that of her three children, "Joseph and I understand each other the best. He is an electronics genius. He knows all about the inventions of atomic energy, and we have so much to talk about because I have always been interested in inventions."[51] His mother did not attend his wedding.

As Wilder and Brackett edited the film, Paramount publicity expert Max Youngstein made Gloria an unusual proposition. He wanted Swanson to travel across America visiting major Paramount markets to publicize an upcoming release, *The Heiress*. More importantly, she would act as a goodwill ambassador for the studio with American women. Paramount would pay her $1,000 a week for the assignment. *The Heiress* was as prestigious a picture as Hollywood was making in the late 1940s. A moody story of manipulation and betrayal adapted from Henry James's *Washington Square*, it starred Olivia de Havilland, Montgomery Clift, and Ralph Richardson. William Wyler, who had recently released *The Best Years of Our Lives*, had produced and directed.

What Youngstein had in mind was a public relations campaign, an ambitious forerunner of the modern press junket. He believed Gloria Swanson could help Paramount accomplish several different goals by putting a glamorous face on each. In the first place, she could help stave off calls for censorship or cinema boycotts by meeting with the American clubwomen who were opinion makers in their communities. The scandalous romantic liaisons of two married actresses with equally married men—Rita Hayworth's affair with Aly Khan and Ingrid Bergman's with Roberto Rossellini, shortly to be confirmed by both actresses' pregnancies and hasty weddings—created unease in Hollywood. Such stories reminded movie executives uncomfortably of the morals scandals of the 1920s. Then, too, investigations underway by Senator Joseph McCarthy and HUAC into the political affiliations of film workers threatened to swamp the industry in a different but equally unwelcome morals-related dilemma. "Hollywood was trembling," Swanson explained, the studios "spending millions to prove that all Hollywood wasn't bad."[52]

There were other worries as well. Television was cutting into movie grosses, especially in major cities. The change from a wartime to a peacetime economy produced its own strains. Finally, regulations arising from antitrust litigation had disrupted Paramount's traditional releasing schedule, which had "upset the habits of movie goers and seriously affected box office receipts," according to the company president.[53] Paramount wanted Swanson to canvass the attitudes of American women toward contemporary movies, particularly the edgy, adult-oriented pictures being produced in Europe. Last but not least, she was to reach out to Paramount affiliates across the country and offer theater owners and staff a chance to rub elbows with a genuine star.

Paramount wanted to put Swanson's celebrity to use: she could help *The Heiress* (which for all its own star power was pretty gloomy fare) even as she announced her own upcoming release. However, selling either picture mattered less than improving the industry's public image while communicating the appeal and glittery power of a star on parade. Gloria was intrigued and quickly agreed to the trip. Paramount's itinerary specified a whirlwind tour of ten cities in twenty-four days.

Swanson was an inspired choice to represent Hollywood—both familiar and glamorous, reachable and utterly remote. A celebrity whose career American women had followed for decades, she was still graceful and vigorous. She was also a seasoned, media-savvy professional who had been in the public eye since she was a teenager, and who had been on the road doing theater for years. Swanson was adept at talking to strangers yet also conducted herself with the flair and flamboyant style of a diva.

She spent two weeks in New York that fall warming up for the tour. Her suite at The Plaza was command central for a flurry of promotional activities that would have crippled anyone else. On one day she appeared on four television shows on three networks—half live, half prerecorded. At a minimum each program required a walk-through technical rehearsal and a script review. Even casual exchanges on live TV were prepared, and Swanson vetted interview question sets. Doing *The Betty Crocker Show* or *Photoplay Television* meant not just showing up at the appointed time but participating in the preparations as well.

Two days went to rehearsals for *We, the People*, which CBS produced for live TV and radio simultaneously. Swanson enacted a scene from *The Heiress* and discussed modern viewers' tastes with her host, spoofing her own early film career to promote a more realistic cinema aimed at adults. She described a typically implausible silent movie plot: "Gwendolyn

Robin, a poor but honest girl, works behind the necktie counter in a department store. After hours, she is in love with Harold Trueheart, a poor but honest boy who works in a garage. One day Monty Moneybags, a multi-millionaire playboy, comes into the department store and buys a fifty cent necktie from Gwendolyn." The rest of the plot concerns getting Gwendolyn away from Moneybags and back in the arms of Trueheart, who strikes it rich in the meantime. Her host conceded that the story was "a little corny."[54]

Swanson also hosted gatherings for the press at glamorous New York locations, throwing a cocktail party for fan magazine editors at The Plaza one day, presiding over a luncheon at Sardi's the next. She gave a small soiree for William Wyler at Radio City Music Hall (before a performance of *Death of a Salesman* the same evening). She also managed to lunch with Cole Porter, meet Joseph Kennedy for drinks, and give a cocktail party in her suite while packing to leave town. On October 10 she hit the road. At each stop she endured a hectic round of interviews and guest appearances as though she was relaxing at home. Indeed, she kept a schedule very much like the one she had kept in New York.

A tour day began bright and early. In Dallas, the dramatic editor of a major newspaper and his photographer met Swanson at the train at 8:40. They went to her hotel for an interview and pictures. By 10:15 she was taping a radio interview, with a second to tape at 11:15. The local Lions Club gave her lunch at 12:15, during which she made brief remarks. At 1:15 she did another radio interview, this time live. An hour later she was at the Paramount branch office in town to meet employees. At 3:30 Gloria had a leisurely half hour to herself, to change clothes and prepare for the evening's events. At a 4:00 cocktail party across town she met the city's social and business leaders. At 6:00 she did a local television show, and at 7:30 she was guest of honor at a private party hosted by theater executives. After a decent interval she was escorted to the train station, where she boarded a sleeping car and traveled on to her next stop.

She did it all again the next day in another Paramount market. She threw no tantrums, demanded no concessions, and saw everyone Paramount asked her to see. Dozens of tour photographs show Swanson greeting balding salesmen in suits, sitting amid the secretarial pool like she belongs there, shaking hands with theater managers and ushers and ticket sellers across the country. She always looks like she is having a ball. Swanson wrote them all charming, personal thank-you letters.

There were a few concessions to nostalgia, like a visit to Essanay in Chicago and a screening of *Male and Female* at Harvard's Fogg Museum (after which Swanson spoke on "The Early History of the Movies and Their Development"). In every city there were separate interviews for radio, television, newsreels, and newspapers (including local, syndicated, and trade presses). Gloria made copy by attending charitable events and women's luncheons, visiting schools, and sitting in Lions Club and library board meetings. There was always a stop at the Paramount branch office. Each network and syndicate got equal access to the ambassador from Hollywood.

Access was occasionally an issue: some fans angled for more than a handshake or autograph. One Paramount sales rep apologized for not protecting Swanson from his own office vice president, who had been bound and determined to kiss the star on the lips: "The 'Veep' slipped thru your barrage of . . . kiss defenses."[55] The media professionals appreciated her trouper's spirit; one wrote thanking Swanson for her "marvelous cooperation" despite "a heavily scheduled day."[56] Another complimented Gloria's graciousness: "She . . . started chatting as if she had all day, and that all of it was at our disposal. All she had on the calendar for the next half hour were a half a dozen other interviews and a radio program."[57]

Swanson's media blitz in fall 1949 covered every delivery system in a rapidly expanding, competitive marketplace. It was an unusual exercise of star power by a consummate professional interested in proving she could once again be a team player. In San Francisco, Swanson made her pitch for more mature movie subjects and treatments to a carefully chosen group of female leaders that included teachers, librarians, judges, political wives, club presidents, and women involved in motion picture censorship. Yet when she got back to LA, Swanson had to report that the response was not encouraging. Women over 35 wanted more comedies; one drama focusing on alcoholism or race relations per year would suffice.[58] However, American women were unswervingly interested in film star glamour, and whenever Swanson—who had been part of the jet set since its inception—talked about her impromptu shopping trips to Paris, they were riveted.

Wilder and Brackett were tinkering with *Sunset Boulevard*, and in January 1950 they reshot the picture's finale. With musicians playing accompaniment, they filmed Norma Desmond descending the staircase every conceivable way: her arms above her head, then her arms down; with a crazy look on her face, then with a tranquil expression. "I had to do that scene *barefoot*," Swanson explained. "It was hard, because it had to be done in rhythm to the music, with little dance steps. Hedda Hopper

. . . tried it, and almost broke her neck!"[59] After ten takes, they were satisfied. Unsure where to cut, Wilder let the camera run during Gloria's final approach. Later, the out-of-focus effect seemed to capture Norma's cracked perspective as she moves closer to those wonderful people out there in the dark.

Then they took the picture out for previews, to the real people out there in the dark in Evanston, Illinois. The audience began snickering during the opening scene, and Wilder knew the picture was in trouble. He sat, alone and despondent, in the lobby midway through the screening. Head in hands, he looked up as a woman approached. "I never saw such a pile of shit in all my life," she volunteered, mistaking the director for a fellow sufferer.[60] When they previewed the movie in Great Neck, New York, the audience blew raspberries. It fared no better in Poughkeepsie.

The problem was the prologue, in which bodies in a city morgue are heard discussing their deaths. An overweight man says he had a heart attack while making retirement plans; a child describes a bet that he could stay underwater longest. Joe Gillis talks about the swimming pool—Norma Desmond's swimming pool—he entered with a couple of bullet holes in him. With this introduction, the movie proper begins. The scene was long and frankly odd, though Wilder always defended it as one of his best. Yet after three disastrous previews, he knew it had to go. They reedited the picture, and an audience in Detroit in July 1950 was much kinder. *Sunset Boulevard* was still bleak, but the cuts now emphasized the tragedy at the heart of the story.

The Detroit viewers loved Swanson's performance, as their preview cards declared: "Gloria Swanson's acting was wonderful—brought back memories of her early days. *Sunset Boulevard* a fine picture." Many called it her greatest picture: "I enjoyed this more than any picture in years. Gloria still has all it takes for my money." Another viewer commented, "It is a regret not to have had Miss Swanson with us during the past years."[61]

The producers expected *Sunset Boulevard* to be a tough sell at home in Hollywood, since it saw nothing sacred about the movie business. They used a breathtakingly simple strategy to preempt rejection: to see a preview of the film, you had to get your name on a waiting list. By making it a scarce commodity, Paramount raised *Sunset Boulevard*'s profile with industry insiders. Soon everyone was clamoring to be admitted to one of the LA previews. There wasn't an empty seat at the first, most important screening, but Swanson remembered "a dead, dead silence" after the picture ended, "and then they went wild."[62]

Mary Pickford was "shattered" by the film, too overcome to stay and greet Gloria.[63] Not so Barbara Stanwyck: she turned her congratulations into a photo opportunity by kneeling and kissing the hem of Swanson's gown. Louis B. Mayer, however, was irate. He announced that Wilder had profaned the business: he should be "tarred and feathered and run out of Hollywood."[64] "Fuck you," Wilder replied—or, according to a more picturesque account, "Go shit in your hat."[65]

The critics loved *Sunset Boulevard*. The *New York Times* said Swanson had returned to the screen "in a burst of glory," calling her "magnificent in a role that demands subtle shadings of pathos as well as sweeping flourishes and hysteria."[66] "Parts like this come once in a lifetime," said *The Hollywood Reporter*, "personalities like Gloria Swanson come once in a generation."[67] James Agee declared *Sunset Boulevard* "so full of exactness, cleverness, mastery, pleasure, and arguable and unarguable choice and judgment, that [it] can be talked about, almost shot for shot and line for line for hours on end. . . . Miss Swanson, required to play a hundred per cent grotesque, plays it not just to the hilt but right up to the armpit, by which I mean magnificently."[68]

Virginia wrote to Gloria, happily reporting "the crowds, the enthusiasm, the lovely things whispered about you around me, and the applause when the picture was over. I sat there like the silly goose I am, tears running down my cheeks, so happy for you." Like the friend she was, Virginia continued, "It must be a great satisfaction after a few years of heartache, but your courage and determination and pride kept you going. Here's to a bigger (if possible) and long new career. . . . I am sure you will never be able to wear your recent millinery, your head must be so big and rightly so."[69]

Buoyed by such notices—Swanson even got a *Newsweek* cover that summer—the film did exceptionally well in its opening run, breaking records at Radio City Music Hall. Swanson took full-page ads in the trade magazines: "Were I to thank everybody individually for the good will and friendly help on *Sunset Boulevard* I would have to take this entire issue and the next and the next—[ad] infinitum."[70] She also thanked several critics personally. "None of us knew what we had when *Sunset* began," she told Bosley Crowther. "It is all wonderful and exciting and perhaps even still a bit giddy."[71] "It is wonderful to be back in the swim," she wrote the publisher of *The Hollywood Reporter*, "even though it is up to my eyebrows!"[72]

Crowther found *Sunset Boulevard* a "strangely insinuating picture," and kept returning to watch it again. Agee, however, predicted it would take "some miracle of ballyhoo" to make it successful in the heartland.[73] The process by which Norma Desmond became a household name was in fact carefully planned. As Paramount publicist Ted O'Shea reported, the film presented "a great challenge from the standpoint of proper handling."[74] To create word of mouth to match the terrific reviews, they needed a personalized, nationwide campaign. For that they had an ace in the hole: they had Gloria Swanson.

Responses to her recent road trip had been so positive that Paramount's president Barney Balaban wanted Swanson to do another tour, this one explicitly in support of *Sunset Boulevard*. In May 1950, Gloria again headed across country, this time for an even more ambitious promotional trip covering twenty-eight cities in twelve weeks. Swanson first spent four weeks warming up in the New York metro area. "Paramount is trying to get their money's worth out of me," she told Edith Head. "I have no time for anything except interviews, radio and television shows."[75] In fact, her New York schedule was so demanding that she was having second thoughts: "Here I am tired and thoroughly exhausted even before I start this tour."[76] Yet Gloria herself was a perfectionist; she did nothing by halves.

The *Sunset Boulevard* tour was more demanding, with more local and regional events. Swanson rode in a parade celebrating Kansas City's centennial, attended a rodeo in Utah, and visited a veterans' hospital in Oklahoma City. She received the key to the city of Des Moines and in Boston presented the trophy to the "Sunset Boulevard Handicap" winner at Suffolk Downs racetrack. Michelle joined her in New Orleans, where the chef at Antoine's created a special meal in Swanson's honor. (The menu included Salade Sadie Thompson and Cerises Jubilee Madame Sans-Gêne.)

They occasionally previewed *Sunset Boulevard* for small audiences, and Swanson talked about Hollywood everywhere she went. She spoke to mother-daughter groups and high school newspaper editors; she gave prizes for movie-themed contests aimed at teenagers. There were always women's groups on the schedule, and the members often presented their questions in advance. They asked about the movies: who was her favorite leading man? Had anyone ever surpassed Valentino? What kinds of characters did she prefer to play? Did she think silent pictures were better than sound movies? Did her roles reflect her real self? Had she always wanted to be a movie star? They wanted to know how she stayed slim, the secret of her successful career, and what she did to look so young.[77]

Swanson attended exhibitors' conventions and visited Paramount regional offices, recommending that theater owners frequent their lobbies "like they used to do," greeting patrons by name and telling them about coming attractions.[78] There was no substitute for the personal touch. She seems to have won over the most hard-boiled movie promoters. Gloria wrote René Hubert, "If you could see the 'old girl' now! I think I really must be made of steel wire and mule blood."[79] It was a different kind of movie work than her stardom used to require.

At the end of three hectic months, Barney Balaban wrote Swanson a fan letter: *Sunset Boulevard* had "fully justified" the studio's confidence, and everyone was "deeply grateful . . . for the magnificent job you did in the picture and in promoting it." Paramount had received "glowing reports" from all over the country. "Beyond the immediate goal of selling the picture, you succeeded in making an incalculable contribution to the public relations of our industry. Wherever you went, you were an ambassador of good-will for the entire industry. It was a swell job from every viewpoint, and I want you to know that all of us are keenly aware of it."[80]

The glow from *Sunset Boulevard* followed Gloria home to New York, where Sport Ward had planned a treat. That fall he staged a short parody of the film for 200 members of the Society of Illustrators. In it Gloria played "a stylishly overdressed lady" dealing with the body of her drowned lover—Sport, sopping wet, who was painted shades of green and had seaweed coming from his ears and nostrils, from between his toes, and sticking out of his fly.[81] When Swanson saw his getup she laughed so hard she had to be helped offstage.

Gloria took the ribbing in good part: "He was one of my best friends. We were buddies. How our friendship survived, though, I'll never know, because I was usually the butt of his jokes—and he liked nothing better than to embarrass me."[82] For thirty years Sport had also stood by her in need, helped celebrate her triumphs, and made her laugh like no one else. To commemorate the evening, the Illustrators crafted a beautiful souvenir book with caricatures of Swanson by the famous cartoonists in the group. Rube Goldberg, representing the members, declared that Swanson had not "staged a comeback. She has been consistently in our hearts all these years."[83]

Summoned to London that fall for a Royal Command Performance of *Sunset Boulevard*, the star immediately began practicing her deepest curtsey. The days were packed with public appearances and interviews, but the nights were pure fun: Gloria spent one evening dancing the samba with Douglas Fairbanks Jr. and her old beau Gene Markey at the Empress Club, another with Noel Coward, Marlene Dietrich, and Clifton Webb at Tyrone Power's. The papers made a fuss over Swanson's energy, but after Michelle, who was accompanying her mother, skipped a few events, headlines blared: "Swanson, 52, Steps Out. Daughter, 18, Rests."[84] Gloria nevertheless told everyone she was looking for a mother-daughter project to showcase Michelle's talent.

The Command Performance featured a British film, *The Mudlark*, as well as *Sunset Boulevard*, and there were thirty top-tier entertainers in the live stage presentation at Leicester Square's Empire Cinema. Jimmy Stewart, Irene Dunne, Ray Milland, Alec Guinness, and Claudette Colbert all performed. Dietrich sang "Lili Marlene," and the unlikely trio of Tyrone Power, Montgomery Clift, and John Mills performed a musical number. Gloria and her onetime beau, Ben Lyon, acted a scene. Lyon and his wife, Bebe Daniels, had moved to the UK in the 1940s; their popular radio program entertained Londoners during the Blitz, earning the deep affection of the English.

The Empire was packed for the big show: three thousand Londoners paid anywhere from five to twenty-five guineas to see the performance the queen called "the best stage show I've seen in years."[85] Given Britain's postwar austerity, this was a significant outlay. Four thousand more people gathered in the street, where the show was free, and Swanson got the biggest cheer of the evening. When the crowd surged toward her, one paper reported, "She met it without batting a painted eyelid."[86] To greet the king and queen and the two princesses, Gloria wore a simple fitted black dress with black fox fur trimming around her throat, shoulders, and knees. The Queen Mother, however, saved the day, grasping Michelle's hand to prevent her from slipping when she curtsied.

After the show, Gloria and the other stars danced at Londonderry House, which was festooned with red and white carnations, until 3 a.m. Then Swanson went back to her suite at the Savoy, where she broadcast a radio report to the US. She slept for two hours before attending the ceremonial opening of Parliament, then she and Montgomery Clift traveled by train to Cardiff, where they presented a smaller replica of the royal show. The Method actor and the old-time silent star were both mobbed in Wales.

For Gloria, the Command Performance was made sweeter by the letters and calls from old colleagues and friends. Many people remembered her triumph with *The Trespasser* twenty years earlier. A former BBC radio producer wrote, reminding Gloria of their shared excitement before her first big broadcast. They had left the reception and gone into the cramped recording studio, he recalled: "You insisted that I should stand on the other side of the microphone so that you could sing to me and forget the vast audience who were waiting to hear you. . . . Welcome again to this country and to your return to the screen. We have missed you, and now that you have come back, please stay."[87]

Before she left London, Swanson told one reporter gratefully, "When I had my first [success], I didn't know. It was too easy. I had had no education and I was always moving around and not bothering about anything but my fame. . . . But now this second time . . . I know. I'll enjoy it."[88]

CHAPTER 20

Dressing the Part

GLORIA SWANSON'S PERSONAL CREATIVITY HAD LONG BEEN VISIBLE IN the way she chose and wore clothes. The child's large bows and boys' coats gave way to Paramount's furs and feathered headdresses, then the sleek, modern styles of the 1930s and '40s, yet Gloria never lost her fascination with fashion. In September 1950, she received the Neiman-Marcus Award for Distinguished Service in the Field of Fashion, presented since 1938 to the most sophisticated designers and style icons. It was the fashion world's Oscar, and Swanson was the first actress to be chosen. For her trip to Dallas, she designed three gowns, not sure which she would wear to the ceremony: a red and black iridescent silk, a black wool with fox trim, and a white faille tunic and skirt.

To her surprise, when the couturier collection was shown, Gloria heard her own name read out among the world-class designers: Schiaparelli, Balenciaga, Dior, Givenchy, and Gloria Swanson. "Neiman-Marcus had raided my hotel room and was showing my white evening dress!" she recalled. "The whole room burst into applause, and I burst into joyous, uncontrollable tears."[1] It was one of the proudest moments of her life. Swanson told Edith Head how elated she was by this honor, which she shared with "the girls back in the workroom": "I can't tell you how much I love you all and what your help and enthusiasm and generosity and unselfishness have done to make all this possible."[2]

Stanley Marcus told Swanson she should be in the fashion business. In fact, after Marcus admired a three-tiered felt cloche of Gloria's invention, the hat—called "the Tri-traveleur" because its layers could be recombined and reassembled for packing—was rushed into production for Neiman-Marcus. This experience encouraged Swanson to take her interest in clothing design seriously. Back in New York she negotiated a contract with Puritan Fashions for a line of dresses, thus beginning a stable, lucrative, long-term partnership with the company. Swanson made more money as a dress designer than her investment in Multiprises provided, and it was more reliable than her work in the movies, television, and theater.

The "Forever Young by Gloria Swanson" collection was designed not for the chic set but for middle-class, middle-aged women who wanted to look smarter at affordable prices. The well-made silk and rayon dresses had clean lines and were generously sized. Swanson drew on her first-hand knowledge of the tricks women used to make themselves look and feel more attractive. She persuaded Arthur and Carl Rosen—the father-son team who owned Puritan—to leave extra space in the seams and hems so women could buy smaller sizes and let the garments out. She insisted that lower necklines helped aging necks look more swanlike and that sleeves and waistlines be cut to flatter the mature figure: "All the while, the loving image I kept in mind was that of my own dear stout mother."[3]

As a Puritan designer, Swanson traveled twice a year to the shows in Paris and Florence, translating what she saw into cocktail dresses and daily wear. She had "a nose for trends," but this initially got her into trouble: "I wanted to create fashion like my mother had—not follow it. I had to learn the hard way that in the budget dress line this just isn't done. Here you follow trends—you select and edit, you adapt."[4] A stickler for detail, Gloria visited the mills and factories across the US that supplied the fibers and fabrics used in her dresses, shaking union workers' hands and meeting with countless sales representatives. Puritan also marketed dress patterns for women to sew at home, and Gloria tried them out herself, chuckling at Carl Rosen's surprise when he saw the workrooms Swanson had in her Fifth Avenue apartment. Rosen hadn't just acquired a celebrity endorsement: he had gotten himself a committed designer.

Swanson was happiest when she was learning something new, and she talked "Papa" Rosen into going on the road with her to meet the salesgirls who sold his clothes. "We had fun with new ideas. I told the ladies that since Grandmama had torn away the bonnet and shawl, there was no age in style. The body dictated what it could wear. To prove it I had four generations wear the same dress: someone my mother's age, my age, my daughter's age, and then a six-year-old."[5] She did Q&A sessions on her sales tours, and—a lifelong shopper herself—enjoyed absorbing the retail business.

It paid off handsomely. Women lined up to purchase Swanson's creations and to see Gloria herself when she appeared at department stores across the nation. The "5,000 dames" who showed up to greet the star in Columbus, Ohio, may have surprised her manager, but they did not surprise Gloria.[6] From her Paramount expeditions she knew there was a big country out there—only now, instead of movie distributors and journalists, she was finally meeting the fans who had watched her onscreen for years, "those wonderful women out there in the dark who had been responsible for my successful theatrical career."[7]

Swanson's partnership with Puritan lasted twenty years. She spent the 1950s and '60s crisscrossing America in what she came to call her "Death of a Saleswoman" tours, in the process becoming as much a goodwill ambassador for women's health and beauty in midlife as she had been for the motion picture industry.[8] Thanks partly to Swanson's savvy contributions, Puritan's sales surged from $10 million to $100 million a year, providing the actress with a lifelong income. (The company's acquisition of Calvin Klein jeans in the 1970s didn't hurt, either.) Today a staple in vintage markets and online, Swanson's "Forever Young" dresses are a well-preserved remnant of American manufacturing, their styles a snapshot of middle American fashion at mid-century.

As the 1950s began, Gloria was pondering her youngest child's future. Michelle had appeared onstage and on TV with her mother, and Swanson organized a screen test for her at M-G-M. Edith Head helped the slender, dark-haired girl prepare, and David O. Selznick liked what he saw: Michelle showed "extraordinary charm and poise" but would need "proper training before she does anything in pictures. . . . Too many youngsters attempt to start at the top, instead of learning their trade thoroughly from the bottom."[9] Selznick arranged for Michelle to join the La Jolla Players, a small theater company featuring Hollywood actors; at eighteen she understudied *Summer and Smoke* with John Ireland and Dorothy Maguire. But Michelle lacked her mother's fire for performing and was happy to tag along for the Command Performance.

While in London, Michelle fell for a young man and begged to be allowed to abandon her theater contract to return to him. Swanson wanted Michelle to honor her commitment. When she resisted, Gloria took her to a very strange advisor: Joe Kennedy. Michelle remembered being seated in Kennedy's New York office. After Gloria left the room, he asked the young woman if she had slept with her boyfriend. Michelle was shocked by the question and said no. That was all Kennedy had to hear: she should listen to her mother, he said. London would keep. Until that moment Michelle had not realized her mother was afraid she was pregnant. Gloria took her to Kennedy because "she thought he was brilliant," and Swanson had not known how to broach the difficult subject with her daughter.[10]

Her busy pace accelerated in fall 1950 when José Ferrer called the day after Thanksgiving to offer Gloria the lead in a Broadway production of *Twentieth Century*. He would play Oscar Jaffe, a theatrical impresario who desperately needs his former leading lady—on stage and in life—to help him out of his career slump. Swanson would play Lily Garland, the actress who is still spitting mad over Jaffe's infidelities and who would rather shoot him. Stuck together for days as the 20th Century Limited chugs across the country, the two do energetic battle. It was a terrific part, full of piss and vinegar. Was Gloria interested? You bet she was.

There was just one catch: they opened in a month. Gloria was aghast, and Ferrer turned on the charm, insisting they would be ready even sooner: he would produce, direct, and star himself. It was a limited run—only a few weeks—to benefit the American National Theater and Academy. Ignoring Swanson's protests, Ferrer came to her apartment and acted out all the roles for her.

Swanson's charismatic director was a gifted producer and actor equally adept at tragedy (he was Iago to Paul Robeson's Othello) and comedy (he spent part of *Charley's Aunt* in drag). Ferrer had just recreated his hit Broadway performance in *Cyrano de Bergerac* for the screen, and there was talk of an Oscar. He was at the top of his game, though a less likely leading man was hard to imagine. A critic described Ferrer: "His hair is thinning; he has big ears, a large nose, and, although he is not fat, two chins, both of which recede; he has narrow shoulders, a wide chest, a long waist and short legs . . . He is five feet ten inches tall but manages to look smaller by slouching." Whether he was "ugly in a distinguished sort of way" or "distinguished in an ugly sort of way," the writer could not decide.[11]

Swanson found him absolutely captivating. Lured by the prospect of working with the hottest talent on Broadway, Swanson accepted—or, as she said—"I was overwhelmed by his fast talk and before I knew it, it was dress rehearsal."[12] The curtain went up on Christmas Eve.

From start to finish, the experience was charmed. Lily Garland was a wonderful antidote to Norma Desmond, and Swanson loved the crazy comedy, even though it left her bruised: "My osteopath couldn't believe my black and blue marks . . . were coming from a stage performance until he saw our fight." Gloria gave as good as she got. Unlike Carole Lombard, who reportedly had to be encouraged to let rip as Lily Garland, Swanson had no trouble releasing her inner banshee. Ferrer had streamlined the play: "It moved so fast that if there were any old fashioned flaws in it, the audience was not aware of them. The chemistry between us was great. We both had energy plus, and we were small and lithe. The audiences loved it!"[13]

Everyone loved it. Show after show sold out, and Gloria got some of the best notices of her life. The *Times* said she played "with the relish and flavor of a good trouper who is having an uncommonly good time."[14] The other New York papers called her "a capital funmaker" who was "downright wonderful [in] an exacting role."[15] The part showed her off as "a lusty comedienne and a peerless mistress of the art of reaction" in a "mercilessly comic" performance.[16] It was "a demonstration of soaring talent."[17] What's more, the *Daily Mirror* gushed, "She looks like an ingénue."[18] The reviews were an excellent Christmas present—but one line in the *Playbill* credits made her particularly proud: Lily Garland's costumes were "conceived by Gloria Swanson."

It was a wonderful time for the star. All her friends came to see her, and she got flowers and flowery telegrams from up and down Broadway. The play's authors, Ben Hecht and Charles MacArthur, thanked her. Her masseuse, her dentist, her furrier, the mailman at WPIX, and the mayor of New York offered congratulations. Gloria and Ferrer—Joe to his friends—rang in 1951 with an appearance on Tallulah Bankhead's radio variety program *The Big Show*. Their run was extended to June: in all, Swanson performed *Twentieth Century* 233 slaphappy, high-energy times.

There was a brief bump when Swanson, having passed up a movie offer in London to stay in the play, tried to haggle with Ferrer over a percentage of the producer's profits. He turned her down unceremoniously: their identical acting salaries and box office percentages would have to suffice. Gloria met her match in Ferrer. He had even more energy than Swanson, and was already mounting another play: *Stalag 17*, which he directed and produced, opened a few blocks away on Broadway during *Twentieth Century*'s run. Swanson's bid for some of the play's takings did not dampen her camaraderie with Ferrer, and she knew enough to invest in his new effort, a huge success that ran for over a year.

Swanson too had another production going, a daily half-hour radio show featuring interviews with her friends and acting colleagues, plus writers, artists, musicians, and other notables visiting New York. Gloria offered tips on fashion and cosmetics for her female listeners as well. The production schedule for *The Gloria Swanson Show* was grueling; they often recorded two or three programs per day and were always preparing for the next show. At least Gloria could conduct some interviews at home in her apartment. A steady stream of guests came and went: Ginger Rogers, Claudette Colbert, Marlene Dietrich, Ray Milland, William Holden, Tennessee Williams, and of course José Ferrer. A consummate multitasker, Swanson recorded some programs in London during her Command Performance visit and planned to take a sound engineer along on upcoming trips to Paris and Rome. Her six months on the air were a busy, lively, and exhausting time.

Swanson's partner in these efforts was her business manager Brandon Brent, a former society columnist who knew everyone and was adept at keeping Gloria's name in the news. Brandy was ten years Gloria's junior, and their relation provoked references to Norma Desmond and Joe Gillis, especially when Brandy called Swanson "Madam," "the Young Lady," and "the Queen."[19] When reporters heard wedding bells, however, Swanson refused to discuss Brandy's claim that they were engaged. Would she really take a sixth husband? "Who knows?" she said impishly. "I might."[20]

Sunset Boulevard gathered eleven Academy Award nominations in 1951, including Best Picture, Direction, Writing, Art Direction, Cinematography, Editing, Music, and all four acting categories. Swanson had been through the hoopla twice before, but it had been twenty years since her nomination for *The Trespasser*: maybe, just maybe, this time it would be her turn. Though handicappers were calling it "a tight race among the fillies," Charlie Brackett, who was acting president of the Motion Picture Academy, wrote to Gloria "from the stronghold of the enemy," saying he thought her performance "infinitely better" than Bette Davis's in *All About Eve*.[21] At the end of February, both she and Joe Ferrer won Golden Globes for their portrayals of Norma Desmond and Cyrano de Bergerac. Swanson was elated when Billy Wilder took home the prize for direction and *Sunset Boulevard* was named Best Picture. Her Oscar prospects looked good.

If Gloria was jittery onstage the evening of the Oscar ceremony, the audience was unusually responsive and warm. During the play Lily Garland brandishes an Oscar she has won for her movie work. When Swanson held the statuette aloft, the playgoers "sent up a prolonged cheer."[22] Gloria's fans believed they were backing a winner, and she and Joe took five curtain calls that night.

La Zambra's on Fifty-Second Street was the New York headquarters for the ceremony, with a direct radio feed to the coast and photographers galore. Adelaide and Michelle were in Gloria's party, though Addie only agreed to come after José Ferrer—whom she adored and who was nominated for *Cyrano*—invited her himself. Since word was out that he would be called before HUAC as a Communist sympathizer, Ferrer was not expected to win. The nervous Academy voters were not exempt from the fear sweeping the nation; they were, Swanson said, "individuals shaping careers and protecting investments." So Gloria was surprised and delighted when Ferrer's name was read out as Best Actor. "Everyone clapped and cheered" when Joe told reporters he was glad voters had ignored the accusations as "beside the point and . . . untrue."[23]

As she waited for the Best Actress award to be announced, Swanson reminded herself why she disliked such competitions. No two people could play each other's roles: William Holden could not have been Cyrano, and Joe Ferrer would have made a terrible Joe Gillis. Besides, great directors like Griffith and Stroheim and DeMille had never won an Oscar. (In fact, George Sanders bested Stroheim for Best Supporting Actor that night, the only time the latter was ever nominated.) Swanson could honestly say she had never been motivated by prizes. Yet she also knew that the endorsement of the Academy boosted careers, and that too many of the parts she had been offered since *Sunset Boulevard* were clones of Norma Desmond. Maybe an Oscar could change that.

At the reporters' behest, the New York nominees were seated at the same table, with Gloria next to Judy Holliday, who had been nominated for *Born Yesterday*. The two women posed with the fake Oscar from the *Twentieth Century* set, and Swanson was "acutely embarrassed" when a reporter asked them to pretend to fight over it. Then the room fell silent, and the announcement came: Holliday, the dark horse candidate, was proclaimed the Best Actress of 1950. Though Gloria was disappointed, she realized the reporters wanted a high-voltage response: "It slowly dawned on me that they were unconsciously asking for a bigger-than-life scene, or better still, a mad scene."[24] The best they got that night was a photo of Gloria, hands covering her face in a pose that captured her nervous anticipation. Later, the picture was said to portray the star's despair at losing. It made for a better story, Swanson conceded, but it was not true.

"I had a huge specter in the spotlight with me," Swanson mused. "She was just about ten feet tall, and her name was Norma Desmond." It was "that corniest of all theatrical clichés . . . that on very rare artistic occasions the actor actually becomes the part. Barrymore *is* Hamlet. Garbo *is* Camille. Swanson *is* Norma Desmond." At fifty-one, she did not want to become "a shadow of a shadow" by portraying a series of aging eccentrics.[25] If people did not see that Gloria Swanson could profitably play other kinds of parts, "it was time to look around this highly diversified world and find some other things to do before I died."[26]

It took one more Hollywood venture, however, to cure Swanson of the movie bug. Without even the pretense of returning "home" to Paramount as she had for *Sunset Boulevard*, Swanson went to California in August 1951 to shoot her first all-color film, *Three for Bedroom C*. Brenco Pictures, a small independent studio, paid her $20,000 up front for four weeks' filming; she supplied her own wardrobe for another $5,000 and screen credit. Gloria got top billing, a small expense account, first-class travel and accommodations for herself and her maid, and a stand-in to relieve her of the tedious duty of posing for lighting setups. The appeal of this low-budget comedy was not the paycheck, but the chance to play a character different than Norma Desmond—whom she had just played once more for Lux Radio Theater. As Gloria told Fleur and Mike Cowles, "At least I won't be enacting something that combines the worst in Medusa, Salome and Eurydice."[27]

The film nonetheless sought to capitalize on Swanson's reputation and recent roles. She plays an oft-married, aging actress and adoptive mother who was once an enormous star. Ann Haven has just won an Oscar but is ready to leave show business out of frustration with the roles she has been offered lately. The action takes place on a cross-country train and features a manager scheming to lure his greatest asset back to the fold. Director Milton Bren put Swanson relentlessly through her paces: she is seductive, spitting mad, softened by love, maternal, demanding, and businesslike by turns. Although she claimed she enjoyed herself while filming, Swanson seems anything but relaxed on screen.

In fact, *Bedroom C* demonstrates the anxiety about working women that characterizes many postwar films. Ann Haven falls hard for a handsome scientist when they are trapped together on the train. Though he understands theoretical chemistry better than sexual chemistry, he falls for her, too. However, her scientist cannot understand why Ann would even consider a return to the screen, and she reassures him: "I'm primarily a woman. I like to cook, I want security, and I love children." Their marriage will rescue Ann from employment, apparently a fate worse than death.

Swanson gamely participated in an extensive promotional campaign for the picture. She arranged for it to be advertised alongside her Puritan summer 1952 dress collection, the tie-ups creating thousands of dollars' worth of free publicity. She also traveled on the Santa Fe Super Chief— the luxury passenger train on which the film was set—from Chicago to LA, while reporters from eighteen western cities rode the rails with her from one stop to the next. Despite the oppressive heat, Swanson impressed her sales colleagues: she was "as concerned about securing a picture plug as I was," one associate wrote his boss. "It just adds . . . credence to the old maxim, 'The bigger they are, the bigger they are' . . . Swanson is a sweetheart and certainly one of the most interesting ladies I have ever met."[28]

Despite these efforts the film had only modest success, disappointing Swanson's hopes for the deferred compensation she had negotiated.[29] A color picture, it couldn't even be sold for much on television, since 1950s sets were black and white. Once again, Swanson maintained that "the critics seemed disappointed not to find Norma Desmond aboard" the train.[30] The long shadow cast by her monumental performance in *Sunset Boulevard* was hard to escape. Afterwards Gloria summarily rejected scripts calling for her to play an actress, a decision that eliminated most of the film roles she was offered. *Three for Bedroom C* helped derail Swanson's motion picture career: she would not make another movie for more than twenty years.

Michelle, meanwhile, got her first film part in 1951, though *Monte Carlo Baby*, shot in France that summer, was memorable mostly for an early screen appearance by Audrey Hepburn. While they were on the Riviera, Colette spotted Hepburn for *Gigi*, and Robert Amon, a film distributor almost twenty years her senior, spotted Michelle. He proposed marriage in August, and Michelle happily accepted. She had seen enough of stardom to last her a lifetime; she didn't want "that crazy life."[31]

At nineteen Michelle did not need Swanson's consent to marry, but when she arrived in New York to discuss her wedding plans with her mother, the maid whispered that Swanson was not pleased about the match. "She pretended she was happy for us both," Michelle said, but an ugly scene occurred when Gloria realized that the maid had betrayed her confidence: "[Mother] jumped out of bed. She grabbed the girl and put her against the wall. I thought she was going to kill her." The episode no doubt reminded Swanson of how the children's governess had supported young Gloria's plans to elope. She had been wrong then about her oldest child's prospects for happiness, but that did not stop Swanson from warning Michelle about Bob Amon. She had made inquiries: Bob was a gambler and a playboy, just like Michelle's father. He was old enough to be her father, and he was Jewish. Michelle was thunderstruck: "At the time I was so terrified I didn't dare say, 'And my sister's father [Herbert Somborn]? Was he Roman Catholic?'"[32]

Bob had come to New York to meet Swanson, and she asked to see him alone. When he emerged from their three-hour meeting, he told Michelle her mother was right: he was too old for her. Michelle thought it likely that Gloria had upset Bob by suggesting he was a more likely sexual partner for her than her teenaged daughter. Whether Swanson was making a pass or testing her daughter's suitor is unclear. Michelle managed to change Bob's mind, and they told Gloria together that they hoped she would attend the ceremony. The parents of a school friend of Michelle's held a small wedding party for the couple in December 1951. Gloria stayed home with a cold.

The woman Michelle called "Madame Mère" phoned the Fairhurst family home where they were celebrating and asked Michelle to drop by her apartment when the party ended. Mrs. Fairhurst did the unthinkable and chewed Gloria out. "Miss Swanson," she said, "if my daughter were getting married today and I were sick, I would crawl on my hands and knees to be there."[33] Decades later, Michelle remembered her friend's show of solidarity with pleasure, her mother's attitude with regret. Michelle and Bob Amon were married until his death forty-one years later. She never acted again.

Broadway once again beckoned, and in fall 1951 Swanson was deep in rehearsals for *Nina*, a spritely French farce. A husband discovers his wife is having an affair and comes to the lover's apartment to confront the pair and shoot the man. Before he can pull the trigger, however, the husband collapses with a cold. His wife attends him while he recuperates, and the husband and lover make common cause: they will get rid of her instead. At least that is their plan. Nina, however, turns out to be indestructible. The English character actor Alan Webb was Swanson's husband and David Niven, in his Broadway debut, was the lover.

The small cast had only three weeks before they opened in Hartford, and they rehearsed twelve hours a day, six days a week. On the seventh day, Swanson worked on the designs for her costumes. Director Gregory Ratoff was an old friend with both theater and movie experience, and on Halloween night, they faced a friendly audience. Gloria thought *Nina* could be another hit. "However," she wrote her Brenco producers, "only an idiot believes his out of town notices so we shall see . . . There is plenty of polishing to do."[34]

Her optimism dimmed as the cast and script endured more of a scouring than a polish during the five-week out-of-town trial. "By the time we arrived in Boston," Niven recalled, "several scenes had been rewritten and the show was half as good. Two weeks and many rewrites after that, we opened in Philadelphia. . . . headed for big trouble."[35] Swanson was so dissatisfied with the changes, and especially with Ratoff's direction, that she did the unthinkable: she denounced him to a Philadelphia journalist, saying she wanted to leave the play. Her lines were bad, she complained, and there weren't enough of them; *Nina* was no longer a starring role.[36]

After the publicity given Swanson's tirade, *Nina*'s New York opening on December 5 attracted what Niven called "the carrion crows." They got another tasty morsel before the night ended. Niven described his first scene with Swanson:

> She had . . . worn some rather odd garments in Hartford, Boston, and Philadelphia, but now the Pilgrim Company [*sic*] had really excelled itself. Swanson stood there enveloped in a black-taffeta tent. . . . The Bedouin tent with Swanson's head sticking out of the top of it rustled across the stage and flung itself into my arms. Swanson is not tall . . . [W]hen I clasped her to me, the top of her head nestled just to the right of my breastbone. Unfortunately, in my terror of the whole situation, I squeezed too hard in that initial clinch. There was a loud report. This was followed by a twanging noise, and about eight inches of white whalebone shot out of Swanson's chest and straight up my nose.[37]

This was a true costume drama, and entirely too delectable for the reviewers to pass up. It gave them something to snicker about as they dismantled the play. Walter Kerr could not resist: "Miss Swanson has designed her own costumes for the production, and the extent of her misfortunes can be gauged by the fact that one of them came apart on stage. By that time, however, a similar fate had overtaken the whole play."[38] Niven told this story for years, though Swanson maintained that "starfucker talk show hosts like [Dick] Cavett" encouraged him to embroider it.[39]

Her wardrobe malfunction was the least of Swanson's problems. Ratoff had staged the play "with singular maladroitness," said the *Daily News*. John Chapman called Gloria "a pretty good drama critic" for identifying the play's troubles but added, "She'd have been a better critic if she'd stated that she isn't very good in the thing, either."[40] There was general agreement: "Much as all of us would like to see her exciting comeback go right on coming back," Walter Kerr wrote, "it must be said that Miss Swanson is at sea in *Nina*. . . . She falls back on familiar mannerisms, she gives bittersweet readings through clenched teeth, she makes strong and abandoned gestures, she runs her voice up and down the scale in varied cadences, and everything she does is both meaningless and monotonous."[41]

Though the theater was full through the holiday season, *Nina* closed in January after only forty-five performances. Gregory Ratoff departed the scene to have a quiet nervous breakdown, but Swanson—as usual—moved on without looking back. As she packed for a vacation in Florida, she wrote to Joseph: "*Nina* breathed her last with last night's performance. And I can't say that I shed a tear for the old gal's departure. She was a misinterpreted (in translation), misdirected, vastly misunderstood woman . . . far more sinned against than sinning. And now down comes the iron curtain on her, forever."[42]

Before she left town, Swanson thanked several of her critics for vindicating her judgment. She told Brooks Atkinson that she knew it was odd "to write a thank you note to a critic for peeling the hide off a play." Nonetheless, she had long enjoyed his reviews and intended to invite him over "for tea or a more hardy potion" soon.[43] There would be no conflict of interest because, Gloria declared, she was done with Broadway: after *Nina*, she pledged to wait twenty-five years before approaching The Great White Way again. It was a promise she came close to honoring.

Adolph Zukor's prediction that television was the future stayed with Swanson, and she decided to try her hand at developing a TV series. "If I was already a vintage actress in pictures," she reasoned, "I was still a glamorous pioneer as far as television was concerned."[44] In spring 1953, Gloria hired several freelance writers to provide material for a half-hour anthology series shot in Mexico. She wanted "warm, humorous little stories—love stories with happy endings—stories of faith . . . all done with the 'common' approach of a Will Rogers variety."[45] Swanson hosted each episode, bookending the show with mildly amusing commentary of the sort Alfred Hitchcock would make famous. For "Antiques," Gloria railed against husbands who plunked themselves down carelessly in their wives' fragile old chairs. Once she pretended to be stuck on the phone with ZaSu Pitts, gesturing helplessly to her audience while ZaSu chattered on. The dramatic anthology format became a staple of 1950s television programming: Loretta Young, Jane Wyman, June Allyson, and Barbara Stanwyck all followed Swanson from the large to small screen as anthology hosts.

Initially, Gloria was invested—financially and professionally—in every aspect of the production. However, the eighteen months *Crown Theatre with Gloria Swanson* spent in development was too speculative for her taste. Happily, Bing Crosby, who made a bundle investing in recording technology, picked up the show. He moved the production to the old Hal Roach studios in Culver City and provided a generous budget for twenty-six episodes, $5,000 of which went into Swanson's pocket whether she performed or simply introduced the weekly program. Crosby's involvement relieved Gloria of the need to solicit sponsors. It also freed her from assessing her coworkers' politics. She showed little sympathy to one writer worried about the blacklist: "You will have to forgive me if I still think that McCarthy is a great cleaner-upper of a situation that has to be cleaned up in this country," she wrote, expressing her confidence that "these things all come out in the wash."[46] It was more confidence than many felt.

Making a living was a challenge for an actress over fifty, and Swanson always kept feelers out for new opportunities. She augmented her Puritan contract with endorsements for bread, hats, nylons, purses, perfumes, cosmetics, soap, gloves, and lingerie. She filmed ads for Schick, promoting electric razors for ladies who want to be "immaculately clean." Yet she disliked endorsing products she did not use, and the income was erratic at best. She spent a few exhausting weeks reprising *Twentieth Century* in Florida with a hostile producer who wanted a younger actress and did everything he could—in the director's words—"to sabotage the production."[47] She presented a single season's worth of "Gloria Swanson Originals" at Saks. She did guest appearances on shows hosted by Merv Griffin, Arthur Godfrey, Milton Berle, and Edward R. Murrow. Nonetheless, she told Joseph, "It has been pretty tough going."[48] One bright spot was her increasing brood of grandchildren: Joseph now had two daughters, and Michelle, settled in Paris, had a son and daughter as well.

Thankfully the fashion business was good. After Wanamakers in Philadelphia advertised one Swanson style, ten thousand dresses flew out the door within the week. Then Puritan sent Gloria abroad to explore the developing market for ready-to-wear fashions in Europe. Michelle's husband, Bob, advised her on movie possibilities on the continent, and Michelle jokingly offered to fix her mother up with her wealthy landlord: "Two months ago the largest diamond in the world was found in his mine!! He's married but told me that he changes wives every twenty years, so—!!? Better come to Paris!"[49]

Gloria had a more attractive offer in mind: a series of twice-weekly dispatches from Europe for the United Press. She had written the odd article on beauty or fashion over the years, even publishing a few issues of *Gloria Swanson's Diary*, a 1954 newsletter for her fashion customers. She had also recorded many hours of her memories—though she repeatedly denied any interest in producing an autobiography: "I am too busy living my life."[50] Now Swanson turned her hand to writing in a more methodical and consistent fashion.

She wrote about whatever grabbed her: illiteracy rates, bullfighting, benefits for war veterans, modern painting, a camp for Iron Curtain refugees. She described how the Romans welcomed the New Year with fireworks and how the French manufactured perfume in Grasse. She spent a few weeks in a small medieval town in France and wrote about getting to know all seventy-two residents. On a back road she picked up two young British hitchhikers off to see the world, one forty-cent hostel stay at a time, and was tempted to hitch a ride herself. Swanson repeatedly claimed that living abroad made her appreciate America more, and often wrote as though she was just another innocent abroad.

Yet she also told stories of famous friends and glamorous adventures. She went to parties thrown by the Aly Khan and reported on the newest cocktail: "shock rocks" was pink vodka over ice, named for the shade Schiaparelli made fashionable. She wrote about socializing with Anna Magnani, Alec Guinness, Gene Kelly, Frank Sinatra, and Ava Gardner, and about visiting Cary Grant on Stanley Kramer's film set outside Madrid. Seeing Laurence Olivier reminded her of "a crazy weekend on the Thames" while filming *Perfect Understanding*, when Olivier climbed a tall pole and wouldn't come down. She saw Sophia Loren at a celebrity auto rally in San Remo in clothes so tight she may as well have worn "a thick coat of paint." The Moorish bodyguards protecting Francisco Franco and King Faisal II at a parade in Spain rode horses with hooves painted silver and gold. She talked about seeing Luchino Visconti's production of *Uncle Vanya* and about going to the movies: *Night and Fog* and *The Red Balloon* made her pensive for days.[51]

Swanson also reported on Princess Grace's wedding to Prince Rainier in April 1956, and on the Cannes Film Festival, delayed that year by the festivities in Monaco. She remembered her own "royal wedding" and how it felt to turn in her plain American name for a French title. Observing Rainier's appealing shyness, she predicted happiness for the new princess.

Swanson called her 117 articles, which ran in several hundred US newspapers, "the hardest and most disciplined work I ever did."[52] She explained, "They are not just gossip columns thrown together—they are more like essays, and I have to keep them down to 400 words which really means a lot of re-writing."[53] Though the constant deadlines harassed her, Swanson clearly enjoyed writing: "I didn't have time to be a glamor-puss," she recalled proudly. "I was a newshen."[54] If her topics were more often slight than substantial, her approach was fresh and pointed.

She produced her column from a home base of Rome for several months, while she waited—endlessly—to begin an Italian film called *Nero's Mistress*. Swanson was eager to explore movie opportunities abroad, and Nero's scheming, power-mad mother was a fascinating character. Another draw was the chance to play opposite Vittorio De Sica, who had achieved international fame directing unapologetically realistic films like *Bicycle Thieves*. De Sica was also a handsome, suave leading man who took acting jobs indiscriminately to support both his gambling habit and the two families he openly maintained. Swanson expected to work closely with the screenwriters to develop her part, yet as the film's start date approached and passed, no collaborators appeared. They sent lovely flowers to her large, beautiful flat on the via Teodoro every time they postponed, and they arranged a marvelous press party, but no script and no costumes materialized. De Sica was still in production on another film; he joined the cast, which included Brigitte Bardot and Alberto Sordi, two weeks after shooting began.

Swanson found acting with colleagues whose language she did not speak more difficult than she expected. She could not use their speeches as cues; every scene became a monologue. The script was altered everyday, sometimes several times, which made preparations impossible. "It is inconceivable that six writers could have been working six months on . . . a mediocre script full of holes," Gloria complained to Joseph. "Everything in the making of this picture is completely opposite to what I thought it would be." She was on call every morning, though she was seldom summoned to the set before late afternoon. They shot all evening, in a way she found both haphazard and nerve-wracking. By the time the company dined at midnight, Swanson was exhausted. She wrote home with exasperation: "Individually they are wonderful and I love them. But I don't have any real respect for them as craftsmen."[55]

Then winter hit, and Swanson's palatial digs had neither heat nor reliable hot water. Times had certainly changed: now the luscious young Bardot was filmed luxuriating in a milk bath while Swanson stood, drenched and freezing in front of wind machines one long cold night. She finally got the bug the cast and crew had been passing around and faced Christmas 1955 feeling lonelier than she had ever felt. The wolves she saw on the streets of Rome seemed like omens. Gloria confided in her mother, who showed rare compassion: "I am so sorry that the work is so hard. I have never heard you say that before."[56]

Swanson was also worried and angry about another nuisance suit: a former employee claimed he had acted as her agent for *Sunset Boulevard*. If she had to miss Grace Kelly's wedding to return to the States for depositions, she could lose her newspaper column. A similar suit had been dismissed two years earlier—whereupon the plaintiff made headlines by kissing Swanson immediately after the judge ruled against him. In the early 1950s, an obsessed veteran stalked Swanson, threatening to betray US military secrets unless she married him. Defending herself sometimes felt like a full-time job.

As she shivered and sneezed through the Roman winter, a knee Gloria injured in a bicycle spill started acting up; she could only go up and down stairs sideways, like a crab. "Your old Ma is cracking up at last," she wrote Michelle, calling the film "the most rugged experience I ever had."[57] When renovations began in her building, with workmen hammering all morning, Swanson gave up and checked herself into the hospital to rest.

Nero's Mistress did nothing to persuade Swanson she could make a living making films abroad, and she went back home to look for another job. When the picture finally played in the States five years later, some saw it as art-house fare. Others said it should never have seen the light of day.[58]

CHAPTER 21

Not Ready for Her Retrospective

IT WAS ALL GLORIA SWANSON COULD DO TO APPEAR SURPRISED WHEN NBC-TV's Ralph Edwards called her onstage in January 1957 for *This Is Your Life*: the guest of honor had figured out what was in store. One by one, figures from her past—including Jesse Lasky, Rod LaRocque, Lois Wilson, Mack Sennett, Francis X. Bushman, and Allan Dwan—paid tribute to Gloria's long career in the entertainment industry. At fifty-eight, however, Swanson was by no means ready for her retrospective.

During the 1950s and '60s she was more visible than ever, crossing the country for her fashion and theater jobs and appearing in American homes courtesy of the television. Swanson worked constantly and traveled incessantly, but without much ability to direct her own course. She made up for a lack of professional autonomy by spending time on causes that mattered to her. Gloria had long been interested in nutrition and alternative medicine and now began taking those interests seriously, discovering in the process another new identity: health activist.

An unnecessary appendectomy hammered the nail in the coffin of Swanson's faith in traditional medicine. Her New York doctors had insisted on the operation over her objections, but when her abdominal pains returned after the surgery, Gloria claimed she was sure it was an ulcer or an abscess from a twisted intestine: "It's my body, and I know it very well."[1] It was a bitter satisfaction when she was proved right.

In an era when patients were typically compliant, Swanson told her doctors just what she thought. Her body was her business; she called it "the house I live in," believing that her own efforts at healing were more effective than medical intervention.[2] At Dr. Bieler's suggestion, Swanson had experimented with vegetarianism in the 1940s and was convinced she had "starved" a uterine tumor by giving up meat.[3]

Swanson did not allow her limited education to interfere with her enthusiasm for challenges to conventional medicine. Beginning in the early '50s she allied herself with researchers and physicians exploring alternative remedies for cancer, even lending her name to unproved experimental treatments. When others called them quack cures, she hotly defended her right to investigate new holistic theories. She supported the Patients' Aid Society, a consumer protection group that aimed to reduce unnecessary surgeries. She also flirted with Scientology, attracted by its focus on self-healing.

Anything that struck a blow against illness and aging was on her agenda. Enthusiastic about the strength and flexibility yoga offered, Swanson was photographed in the lotus position for her friend Indra Devi's groundbreaking *Yoga for Americans*. (Devi dedicated the 1959 book to Gloria "for her ever-searching, burning, crusading spirit, admirable courage, keen sense of humor and luminous laughter.")[4]

Inventor and aerodynamics pioneer Henri Coanda fascinated Swanson with tales of the elusive fountain of youth. While Gloria stopped short of proclaiming such beliefs, she expressed withering scorn about overweight, visibly unhealthy doctors telling their patients how to live: "Where is the doctor who has lived to be a hundred and then written a book about how he did it?"[5]

She thought briefly that the charismatic Paul Niehans might be such a man and visited his Swiss clinic several times in the late '50s and early '60s, where the doctor offered wealthy private clients his rejuvenating cellular therapy. In this treatment, organ cells taken from sheep embryos were matched with cells from the clients' organs. Neihans injected his personalized mixtures into some very famous buttocks: Winston Churchill, Charlie Chaplin, Charles Lindbergh, Thomas Mann, Pope Pius XII, and Charles de Gaulle all took the treatment. Swanson had "a bad reaction" to it but was also put off by Niehans's attitude: even the best doctors refused to "give credit to Mrs. God"—Gloria's name for Mother Nature.[6]

The primary and best way to take care of oneself, Swanson maintained, was through nutrition. She had followed Dr. Bieler's diet for decades and visited his unpretentious office whenever she was in California. Her interest in eating well drew her to consider the source of her food, and soon she was on a soapbox about crop spraying, especially decrying the highly toxic insecticide Parathion. It might hurt pests, but it would also hurt the pilots who sprayed the fields, the farmers who plowed them, and the people who ate the food grown there. Swanson drank only bottled water and went to enormous lengths to have organic produce shipped wherever she traveled, convinced that when she ate unsafe foods she became sick.

She found an ally in a Democratic congressman from New York. James Delaney was fighting an uphill battle to amend the Food, Drug and Cosmetic Act to ban carcinogenic chemical additives from the food supply. When Swanson offered to help, he asked her to speak to a group of congressmen's wives before a key vote. Gloria gave it everything she had, urging several hundred women to pester their powerful husbands until they approved that "one heavenly clause—nothing that was carcinogenic could be sold to the public."[7]

"I was screaming at the wind until she came along," said Delaney. "Miss Swanson had quite a grasp of the subject herself and . . . she was a spellbinder. . . . I had never been able to arouse any interest in the bill until her speech, but then it gained momentum."[8] Swanson regarded the 1958 passing of the Delaney Clause as the most important work she ever did and her recognition from the fourteen-term congressman her greatest prize. When Congress revisited the issue in 1969, it invoked the Delaney amendment to ban cyclamates, artificial sweeteners that caused cancer in lab animals.

Swanson was making a habit of activism. Invited to talk about nutrition to undergraduates at Fairleigh Dickinson University in 1957, she urged the dining service to commit to providing balanced whole food meals for the students. (The school responded by asking Gloria to commit to funding a research lab.) She talked about health and nutrition in every newspaper and radio interview she did. Even when ostensibly talking about fashion, she worked in comments about beauty's fundamental connection to a healthy diet and lifestyle, ideas not regularly proclaimed at the time.

Most often, though, Gloria volunteered her advice on the television talk shows where she was a frequent guest. From the '50s through the '70s, she harangued, lectured, and sometimes even offered cooking lessons to Jack Paar, Merv Griffin, Johnny Carson, Dave Garroway, David Susskind, Mike Douglas, David Frost, Edward R. Murrow, and Dick Cavett. (Anyone who wanted to make her delectable "Potassium Broth" was welcome to Swanson's own recipe: Cover one cup each of chopped celery, string beans, zucchini, and swiss chard with eight cups of spring water. Cook in a tightly covered pot—preferably a pressure cooker—until the celery is tender. Drain the liquid into a container; cover and refrigerate. Tasty.) Soon her talk show contracts specified "some discussion on the subject of health foods."[9]

Swanson's commitment to her nutritional regime was unwavering. She might be in the business of make believe, she declared, "but I'll be damned if I want my food to be make-believe."[10] When she visited an acquaintance's Ohio home, she foraged for her raw diet in his garden rather than his kitchen: "She picked carrots and radishes and ate like an animal."[11] Gloria became famous for bringing her own food when she dined out. She carried "a hand-hammered tin box packed with her supper of raw almonds, a sardine sandwich on cardboard-like bread, bottled water, and a seaweed salad" even to Sardi's, her granddaughter recalled. "Most everything she ate was brown or shades of green with the exception of goat's milk ice cream."[12]

Nor could Gloria stomach the chemicals used in cosmetics. In the mid-1960s, she began marketing her own line of organic beauty care products. Essence of Nature was made entirely of ingredients you could safely eat: Swanson's strawberry night cream had real strawberries, her cucumber eye cream real cucumbers. She was once again ahead of the curve, as many women now demand good-enough-to-eat beauty products. However, when the chemist formulating her small line started cutting corners and Swanson was unable to guarantee her products' purity, she dissolved the association. She worked intermittently during the '50s and '60s on a book-length manuscript for Prentice-Hall, ruminating in *Beauty Tricks and Truths* on everything from meditation (her most important daily ritual) to exercise, skin care, and aging.

On the television game shows where she became a regular guest, Gloria could not easily hold forth about food. Some producers doubtless regarded this as a good thing: when a sponsor was advertising Swanson TV dinners, no one wanted Gloria Swanson denouncing additives and preservatives. On *I've Got a Secret*, *Password*, *Play Your Hunch*, *The Match Game*, *To Tell the Truth*, *Truth or Consequences*, *Hollywood Squares*, and *Hollywood Talent Scouts*, the star had no chance to proselytize. She stumped panelists on *What's My Line?* but not by talking about diet and nutrition.

Gloria was in demand on shows where lively conversation was prized. She could hold her own with John Lennon and Paul McCartney on *The Tonight Show* or bat away double entendres with Dick Cavett and Janis Joplin without batting an eyelash. Hearing Swanson push back against Mike Wallace's tough questioning recalls a time when a star's television appearance was not always merely a plug for a new movie. Wallace called Gloria "Marilyn Monroe, Grace Kelly, [and] Gina Lollobrigida all in one," then repeatedly asked her whether she considered herself a "commodity" or an actress.[13]

Sometimes the questions were uncomfortably personal. Wallace prodded Swanson—the first guest on his inaugural half-hour live interview

program in 1957—about her failed marriages, quoting Lois Wilson's remark that Gloria was deeply ashamed of the "flaw in her character" revealed by her five divorces. Swanson replied evenly, "I would love to be
supported. I would love it. Nothing would please me more. I would feel
before I die if that could happen, at last I'm a wife and I'm a woman and
I'm fine."[14]

Wallace's questioning hit a nerve with Swanson, who spent the early
1950s as the other woman in retired businessman Lewis Bredin's life.
Gloria counted on Bredin's advice about—though not his contributions
to—her finances, yet five years into their affair Lewis's divorce was still
not final. She was tired of working so hard while he enjoyed his leisure.
Swanson traveled extensively; though Lewis seldom accompanied her,
he griped about her frequent absences and her perfunctory letters.

"You must try to put yourself in my position," she explained during
one Puritan trip. "I'm often awakened at 6:30 after . . . 4 or 5 hours
sleep—from the moment I get off the train I am on a tight schedule—I
have made as many as eight speeches a day—I have gone without meals
and other even more important necessities [and] changed my clothes
four and five times."[15] "I am going to keep trying to slow you down,"
Bredin vowed, but Swanson was not ready—or did not know how—to
slow down.[16]

The last thing Gloria needed was to feel unattractive, yet when Lewis
visited her in Rome, he complained that her eyelids were drooping and
urged her to have cosmetic surgery. She gave in, then spent the next
twenty-five years denying it. With all her talk of natural medicine and
aging gracefully, Swanson was ashamed of having betrayed her principles for her vanity. After awhile, the lie took on a life of its own.

What really rankled, though, was that she was still paying the bills.
Lewis said he had planned for Swanson in his will, but the hereafter was
not the here and now. He did not support the woman he called his "darling half pint," and he stalled on making plans for their shared future.[17]
"You've got to make your own decisions," he wrote. "I'll go along as I can
when I can."[18] He liked his golf, his horseback riding, and his free time.

Things came to a head late in the '50s, when the couple had been
together seven years. They were in Paris, and Swanson had to fly out
for business. Her plane got in trouble and had to make a forced landing.
Back at Orly Airport in the middle of the night, scared and hysterical,
she called Lewis, who mumbled a few comforting words. Then he hung
up and went back to sleep. It was the last straw for Swanson, who felt
abandoned in her hour of need. When she reproached Bredin, they had

a terrible, bitter fight. He accused her of "overweening pride" and "imperious egocentricities," calling Swanson "the great queen of the silent films who is accustomed to having the earth move out of its orbit on her unspoken wish or even slightest indication."[19] Yet he soon wanted to reconcile: "Gloria Darling . . . this prima donna stuff [is] unworthy of us, or at least of me. . . . there has been too much between us, for too long, and with too high hopes for our future to let this mutual display of temperament destroy it."[20]

Yet Bredin's unresponsiveness hurt Gloria and highlighted her longstanding frustration with their relationship. She could not give Lewis "peace and quiet" because she was so harassed by money worries: "May I tell you *again* what I have wanted—I wished to be *supported* like any woman who has proved her *constancy* and love. I have not lost respect because you have been too self-effacing. I've lost something each time you've taken a cheque or money from me." She had paid not only her bills but his: for their travels, their homes, their food, their servants, and more. "That, dear, is what other men do for the women they love or are married to or both. I'm sure if I had these things I would have peace and quiet within my own soul and then could share it."[21]

Swanson found it hard to be criticized for her ambition when she was also expected to be the breadwinner: "I work for [my money] bloody hard and quite frankly I think I should be commended for it." Yet she also felt she was "in a trap," since even this letter had to be written on time snatched from Puritan business: "Eight buyers have just walked into the room. The car is waiting."[22] Lewis returned her letter, annotated with snide comments, and that was that.

Michelle felt it was no loss: "I'm sure you can find a more pleasant companion," she wrote. "I'll bet if you could have all the letters Lewis has ever written it would paint quite a picture!!"[23] All the same, Michelle knew her mother contributed to her own romantic problems: "She wanted to be eternally in love. Ultimately, she was looking for men to dominate her, which never really happened. She was incredibly feminine in appearance, but she had a masculine mind. . . . She made sure what she said was the law."[24]

Swanson's trap, however, was not entirely of her own making. She had the talent and ambition to live a creative, prosperous public life but also her generation's expectation that a loving male partner would support her financially. The high-blown romance she craved drew her to men who were dedicated, imaginative lovers but seldom good providers. When she was expected to foot the bill for any length of time, she struggled with feelings of inadequacy as a woman. The legacy of her alcoholic father was that she was repeatedly drawn to charmingly feckless, hard-drinking, unavailable, or unambitious men for whom she soon lost respect. It was a recipe for instability. Privately, Swanson said, "I feel death is going to grab me if I can't be in love, even if I have to create a fantasy."[25] Yet she eventually withdrew in angry frustration from the men who disappointed her. Her habit of moving quickly ahead without looking back sentenced her to repeating her mistakes. It cost her dearly by deepening her shame at her romantic failures.

Once again, Gloria's answer was to go back to work. One of her two Hollywood Walk of Fame stars is for television, and she earned it—performing for Art Linkletter, Arthur Godfrey, Milton Berle, Pat Boone, Dinah Shore, Gypsy Rose Lee, and Joey Bishop (whom she adored). When Ed Wynn made a game of guessing her identity on his comedy variety program, she said she had "a long association with pictures," whereupon he gleefully announced she must be Grandma Moses! Swanson allowed that hers was "not a new face," and Wynn gallantly said it was "the most beautiful used face I've ever seen."

When Swanson visited with Bob Hope, the talk was strictly scripted patter:

GLORIA: When I started in pictures, stars were dressed lavishly. I remember parties where the swimming pools were filled with champagne.

BOB: Dean Martin was born too late. He might've learned to swim.

GLORIA: Dean Martin doesn't have to swim.

BOB: Steady. No smoking in the studio.[26]

Swanson also acted in dramas and situation comedies, appearing on everything from *The Alfred Hitchcock Hour* and *Kraft Suspense Theatre* to *My Three Sons* and *Burke's Law* (for which she received a Golden Globe nomination). She played herself on *The Beverly Hillbillies*, which was tougher than it looked: "I hadn't the slightest conception of what Gloria Swanson was like."[27]

Despite her aversion to real-life doctors, Swanson starred on both *Ben Casey* and *Dr. Kildare*. "Time is money in television," Richard Chamberlain recalled. "You don't stop for anything." Yet everything stopped each morning when Gloria's maid appeared on set, bearing breakfast on a huge silver tray. As Chamberlain explained, "Nobody had the nerve—because she was a spitfire if she wanted to be—to say let's hurry this up." Swanson acted—and was treated—like a star.

Then Chamberlain saw what the fuss was all about. Swanson was bidding farewell to a dying girl: "She just let loose, and the tears [flowed]. She was wonderful, wonderful, wonderful." Yet when the director announced they had been rehearsing rather than shooting, Gloria struggled to do it again. "She could never get it back," Chamberlain said, "and it kind of broke my heart. She was still good, but she could never get that real, beautiful acting level back."[28] Swanson's demanding schedule often took her from *Good Morning America* to *Midday Live* to *The Tonight Show*: no wonder she found it hard to recapture a no-holds-barred performance.

Audiences could not get enough of Norma Desmond, repeatedly calling for Gloria to reprise or parody her signature role. "When people meet me, they expect me to bite them," she said, scoffing. "I've got nobody floating in my swimming pool."[29] Nor did she live in the past. Yet Swanson took shrewd stock of the demand for *Sunset Boulevard* and her own selling power whenever she channeled the mad movie queen. She had resisted long enough; it was time to capitalize on that success.

A brilliant idea surfaced: to remake *Sunset Boulevard* as a musical play. Swanson relished the challenge of singing in character as Norma Desmond, and in 1955 hired Richard Stapley and Dickson Hughes to rough out *Starring Norma Desmond*. Buoyed by her discussions with Paramount, she began lining up talent, listing suitable directors (Jerome Robbins, Elia Kazan, Josh Logan, George Roy Hill, and José Ferrer made the grade) and producers she considered reliable (David Merrick and Leland Hayward). She wrote Erich von Stroheim in Paris, offering him the part of Max and confiding, "These days not much is required of actors in the way of singing."[30] "I shall just really be marking time," she told a friend, "until my dream can come true."[31] To create a buzz, Gloria recorded demos of the songs and dialogue, playing them for possible investors. She performed "Those Wonderful People" on *The Steve Allen Show* in September 1957, writing Allen at Christmas, "You cannot imagine how much excitement that 'spot' has caused."[32] After several years' effort, it looked like the play—now renamed *Boulevard!*—was headed to Broadway.

She spoke too soon. Paramount was not impressed with Swanson's adaptation, which abandoned the murderous, mad Norma. The musical heroine does not shoot her young lover, but sends him and his age-appropriate girlfriend off with her blessing. Swanson and her writers had given *Boulevard!* a happy ending. In any case, the studio intended to rerelease the film and would not allow any new version to be produced.

Swanson was in shock: how had they encouraged her to go forward, spending years and more than $20,000 to develop the musical if they had no intention of making a deal with her? She wrote to Paramount executive Russell Holman "as one human being to another," pleading with him to help her "salvage this beautiful project."[33] Norma Desmond was *her* role. Holman's reply was polite but unyielding: it would damage Paramount's revenues to allow *Sunset Boulevard* to appear in another form; the studio had never formally authorized Swanson's version.[34] Her collaboration with the writers petered out, according to Hughes, when Swanson developed amorous feelings for Stapley, his sexual partner.[35] Yet Gloria never gave up easily; she worked intermittently on *Boulevard!* for many years.

Between her television appearances, she took several plays on the road, always hoping one would be worth bringing to New York. It was a constant struggle to insure acceptably professional working conditions and accurate accounting. Since her income was tied to her box office receipts, Gloria made fewer personal appearances outside the theater. Ten and twenty years after her first stage performances, audiences were still inspecting Swanson for signs of age: she joked that they wanted to see if she was held together by clothespins. Well, they would have to buy a ticket. Yet she adored her fans, trying to track down a woman in tiny North Belgrade, Maine, who had written her about winning a Gloria Swanson beauty contest twenty-five years earlier. She also often surprised fans with phone calls. (Swanson was addicted to the telephone and had astronomical phone bills: after one high-speed international conversation she told Michelle that being "so bloody economical . . . doesn't become me.")[36]

A young actor who appeared with her in 1959's *Red Letter Day* wrote a perceptive portrait of Swanson during their eleven-week tour of eleven northeastern cities. "All my life I have wanted to see a hurricane," Robert Curtis said. "Now I can say I've spent my summer with one." He marveled at Swanson's legendary energy: she never stopped trying to improve both the play and her performance in it—while also working on her dress business, consulting with her cancer research friends, carrying on a voluminous personal correspondence, and doing countless radio and newspaper interviews. Keyed up after a performance, Gloria often talked Curtis into watching the Late Show on TV with her, then the Late

Late Show, "and if there was an Early Early Show," he said, "we'd watch that." She talked about sleeping but seldom actually slept, as far as Curtis could tell. Yet she looked "utterly divine" in the morning, "as if she'd just been swimming in a lily pond."[37]

Swanson's mania for health impressed Curtis. In the rustic cabin where they once stayed, she swatted mosquitoes all night but refused bug spray (it was unsafe). She warned him off eating beef injected with hormones (also unsafe). She wouldn't use a plastic container for anything edible; glass was the only safe way to store food. In Portland, Swanson griped, "People are so anxious to have everything canned, packaged, bottled, frozen right at their fingertips on the shelf. Every time you preserve a thing, you take something out of it. I'm against preservatives, additives, bleaches and all the rest of it."[38] What then seemed eccentric now seems like common sense.

Traveling with Gloria was like traveling with an army. In addition to her clothes for every occasion, her chauffeur-driven Rolls-Royce was loaded with "toasters, juicers, waffle irons, special meats packed in dry ice, fruits . . . organically grown vegetables, mineral seasoning salts, peanut oil, bread not made with flour, honey and beeswax, vitamins . . . and her own enamel pots and pans because she's certain aluminum does something strange to food cooked in it."[39]

Swanson disliked people using her first name unless invited to do so. She loathed people—even close friends—dropping by unannounced and instructed Curtis to dismiss one would-be visitor: "Tell her I'm having an enema." Swanson could be "a fury" to anyone who didn't share her work ethic, her mania for detail, or her commitment to making the play as perfect as possible. She ripped into prop girls who failed to arrange the set correctly and actors who missed their cues, but she was the first to offer a compliment when things went well. She was unable to delegate responsibility and took charge of the technical rehearsals in each new theater "like the general she must have been in one of her other lives."[40] (Harold Kennedy, who was once again producing, put it differently: "The strong ladies—the Tallulahs, the Swansons, the Ina Claires—are very easy to deal with. They know exactly what they want and it doesn't change from minute to minute or even from year to year.")[41]

What saved Swanson for Curtis was her infectious curiosity and "her pixy sense of humor." She played many a practical joke and laughed uproariously when they were played on her. Although she could be demanding and difficult, Curtis also found Gloria to be an excellent listener, empathic and kind. At sixty she was unpredictable, incongruous, fearless, and "impossible to keep up with." Always looking forward rather than back, "Hurricane Gloria" was "as vital a woman as you'll ever meet, if you live to be two hundred."[42]

Nothing could save *Red Letter Day*. Though it satisfied audiences from Waterville, Maine, to New Jersey, the Boston critics demolished the play. "Gloria's bad luck on the stage is alarming," said Elliot Norton. "Think of the poor plays in which she has foundered!" Yet Norton stated firmly that "there is nothing wrong with Miss Swanson which a good script couldn't fix."[43]

Her 1961 venture, *Between Seasons*, would not make it to New York either. Nor would Kennedy's 1962 play *The Inkwell*, which they reworked as *Just for Tonight* in 1963 and as *Reprise* in 1967. (Swanson loathed its presentation in the round in Chicago: "All illusion gone," she lamented.)[44] Kennedy intended the play as a portrait of "the glamour, the guts, the strength, the possessiveness, and yet deep down that silent inner loneliness" of stars like Swanson. They presented it off and on for ten years, Gloria receiving standing ovations almost everywhere. "We were cowards not to bring it to New York," Kennedy claimed. "It would have been rewarding even for one night."[45]

Swanson finally made her Los Angeles stage debut with *Reprise*. However, she took her latest return to Hollywood lightly, as her resumé in the play's program indicated: "Gloria Swanson insists that too many beautiful trees have already been felled to make pulp on which to print a rehash of her life and career. If anyone in the audience does not know how old she is and how long she's been around, she suggests taking the matter up with someone to the right, or even the left, of you."[46]

The biggest challenge was remembering the names of people who came up and congratulated her. Because Gloria was terrible with names, Kennedy said, she was terrible at gossip: "She invariably has the basic facts but . . . she gets the wrong people into the wrong beds and that creates considerable confusion."[47] When Sennett actress Sally Eilers asked for a signed photograph, Gloria paused, and Eilers helped her out with a laugh: "If you want to sign it Mrs. Wallace Beery, make it out to Mrs. Hoot Gibson."[48]

Swanson never stopped looking for work, typically enjoying the process regardless of the outcome. She tried to acquire *Auntie Mame*, which became a hit for Rosalind Russell. A part she sought in *Thoroughly Modern Millie* went to Beatrice Lillie. She thought about putting on Dorothy Lamour's sarong for a *Road* movie, and was considered for *Pal Joey* with Marlon Brando. Preston Sturges sent her a script, she had a movie possibility in Argentina, and there was talk of a situation comedy series. She tried to corral her dream cast for a film set in Italy: George Cukor (fresh from *My Fair Lady*) would direct; Marlene Dietrich and Swanson would play women married to the same man. There were roles for Vittorio De Sica, Charles Boyer, and maybe Maurice Chevalier. She called this "wonderful, wonderful and gratifying work—creative work."[49]

Sometimes the work was pretty easy. In 1962, Earl Blackwell convened a group of celebrities to promote an Italian cruise line. Joan Fontaine, Charles Addams, Paul Newman, Joanne Woodward, Gore Vidal, and Gloria spent six weeks cruising the Mediterranean. They visited a kibbutz near the Sea of Galilee and rode camels to the Pyramids.

Sometimes the work—or the company—was less congenial. Elaine Stritch remembered the behind-the-scenes cattiness on a 1966 revival of *The Women*. Stritch was struggling with alcohol at the time, and the other women demanded that she leave the show. Stritch skewered the all-star cast years later with hilarious, bitchy precision, but she remembered Swanson as the only one who refused to sign the complaint against her. Gloria recalled the production "wasn't much fun" and believed she herself had been miscast.[50]

She may have been distracted by her new, younger lover. Bill Dufty was a writer who met Swanson at a press conference. As he added a sugar cube to his coffee, "I heard [Gloria's] commanding whisper: 'That stuff is poison,' she hissed. 'I won't have it in my house, let alone my body.'" He accepted a piece of Swanson's "tree-ripened, unsprayed something," and realized he "had never tasted anything better."[51] His brief encounter with Gloria changed his life. A big man, Dufty stopped eating sugar, dropped seventy pounds, and committed himself to natural foods. His health improved, and he taught himself to be a superb organic cook. He became a convert, giving up doctors, shots, pills, and hospitals, even claiming he had burned his Blue Cross card. He wrote Swanson, telling her his story, and she invited him to dinner. Dufty never went home; they spent the next seventeen years together.

He wooed Gloria with two unbeatable skills: he cooked for her, and he made her laugh. Swanson had a soft spot for funny people, and Dufty cracked her up. He also had no interest in her money; Dufty made a satisfying living as a ghostwriter. His biggest seller was Billie Holiday's coauthored memoir *Lady Sings the Blues*; Lady Day was godmother to Bill's son. Dufty had also been a union organizer and a newspaperman. He spoke French, German, and Japanese and was, like Gloria, curious about everything.

Seventeen years younger than Swanson, Dufty was also willing to travel; he cooked and cared for Gloria on the road. Their first outing was to Ohio with *The Women*, where they shared a state-of-the-art mobile home. (Gloria chuckled at the locals' notion that the trailer was "a mobile iron lung" where she was kept on ice until her next scene.)[52] It sweetened the rigors of the road to have her food and her companion close by. She finally shared her passion for organic, simple nutrition and holistic medicine with someone who felt as she did.

Swanson had been in show business for fifty years, and young people were asking more and more often about the silent era. When she and Bill attended a crowded New York screening celebrating the restoration of the Beacon Theatre's mighty Wurlitzer, Swanson marveled at the lustrous movie palace. For years she had been too busy making pictures to see them properly: "I never got to see myself on the screen like others saw me."[53]

When they pulled down the Roxy Theatre, *Life* featured a dramatic full-page photograph of Swanson draped in a red feather boa, her arms raised amid the wreckage. More than 50,000 patrons had seen *The Love of Sunya* at the Roxy during its opening weekend in 1927; now an office building would take its place. Maybe it was time to think about preserving her legacy.

Swanson had deposited her film holdings at the Museum of Modern Art in the 1940s and was dismayed and angry to discover in the 1960s that some reels had decayed beyond recognition. MoMA curators protested that they had no budget to preserve the films; in fact, they had warned Swanson of the dangers to her collection. Like many other film pioneers, however, she had not understood the urgency of protecting her creative work. Reels containing home movies of Swanson's young children were in the worst shape. The only thing left of one film was the eerie sound of Joseph giggling while little Gloria played the harp: the children themselves had completely vanished. When Swanson saw her damaged film, she put her arms around the curator's neck and cried.

As far as Gloria knew, no one had seen the unreleased *Queen Kelly* for years. "The actual footage was gamy enough to stop the picture in 1927. The legends about the film . . . were gamier still." Swanson claimed that retired MoMA curator Richard Griffith told her in the mid-1960s that there had been unexpected interest in her old footage during the 1960 presidential race. Facing tough opposition from Jack Kennedy, Richard Nixon sent some of his campaign strategists—the sort later known as "plumbers," Swanson said—to MoMA to see if anything in the vaults could be used to discredit the Democratic nominee. "Joe Kennedy's checkered career was the soft vulnerable underbelly of Jack's campaign," Gloria remembered.[54] Even Harry Truman had cracked that Jack Kennedy's Catholicism was less an issue than his father's influence: "It's not the Pope [who worries me], it's the pop."[55] Joe had kept a low profile during his son's run for office.

Griffith told Swanson he had hastily moved her collection so no one could rummage around in it. Then Bobby Kennedy got wind of the Nixon campaign's plans, and his people went to the storage facility and had a look around. Swanson knew about Kennedy family loyalty first-hand; she believed "Bobby would destroy [the film] in a minute to keep it out of Nixon's hands."[56] Some of her private footage was missing, and more had turned to dust. She blamed the Kennedys.

The museum steadfastly denied this story, assuring Swanson that her films had neither been moved nor treated improperly. Her home movies had decayed, certainly, but she had been warned. "She promptly put it out of her mind," said MoMA curator Eileen Bowser. When Swanson discovered "that Baby Gloria's baby pictures weren't there[,] she got unjustly furious."[57] Neither Nixon nor the Kennedys had destroyed Swanson's films. If she had wanted to pay for it, Gloria could have saved her own movies.

For Gloria, it was one more bit of *Queen Kelly* bad luck: the film was "my Hope Diamond, my curse." She had kept in sporadic touch with Joe over the years. He had bragged to her about helping Jack win election to the Senate but had also helped Swanson with some tax troubles in the mid-'50s. When she learned of his 1961 stroke, Gloria sent him a telegram signed "Kelly." Yet she harbored no illusions about Joe. She refused Teddy Kennedy's invitation to contribute a few hundred appreciative words to a book the family prepared for Joe after his stroke. When Teddy persisted, Gloria thought he "must be terribly dense not to understand why I couldn't write anything that could be printed."[58]

Swanson moved her film collection to the George Eastman House in Rochester, beginning a warm friendship with curator Jim Card. The retrospective of her films he arranged in May 1966 was as complete as the archive could make it. Swanson's Keystone pictures were there: *The Danger Girl* and *Teddy at the Throttle*, with her adorable Great Dane costar and her first husband Wally Beery. Card showed her DeMille films and her wild, funny romps for Allan Dwan. In the space of a few clips, she went from a comic to a vamp and back again, her skill and versatility putting to rest the idea that Gloria Swanson was just a clotheshorse.

Then came her independent pictures, bits of *Sadie Thompson* and *Queen Kelly*, before a new audience heard her singing in *The Trespasser* and *What a Widow!* There was a young and perfect Michael Farmer with her on the Riviera in *Perfect Understanding*. This time, Gloria's Paramount triumph, *Sunset Boulevard*, took its place within her body of work.

No one at the week-long Eastman House tribute would mix up Gloria Swanson with Norma Desmond. The real actress was too varied, fresh, and funny. She impressed some with her unpretentiousness: "I got fed up looking at that face of mine," she said after the evening gala tribute ended. "First it was a pudding, then it was an old dumpling."[59] (Once when a fan expressed pleasure on meeting her, she said, "I bet you were surprised at the little runt you found." Her "talent for self-deprecation," said Kevin Brownlow, was Swanson's "most unexpected quality.")[60]

Broadcast television was creating opportunities for old films. After Swanson introduced Keaton's comic gem *The General* for TV and appeared in *The World's Greatest Showman*, a program honoring Cecil B. De Mille, she wondered whether her own early work could find a new audience. In 1938, unable to keep paying storage fees on a picture that would likely never see the light of day, she had authorized the destruction of the *Queen Kelly* elements stored in Paris. Yet it was not clear that they had actually been destroyed. Maybe *Kelly*'s moment had finally come.

Swanson deputized her daughter to investigate, and Michelle soon reported that a print of the film had been located, "safe and sound."[61] Organist Lee Erwin composed a new score, and *Queen Kelly* played to a capacity crowd at the Beacon Theatre in May 1967. Then Swanson, clutching her signature carnation, recorded a commentary to accompany *Kelly*'s debut on public TV. The picture was unlikely to shock modern audiences, she said: "*Queen Kelly* was Little Bo Peep compared to what we're seeing today."[62]

Swanson eventually concluded that little money could be made from reissues of her old pictures, predicting instead that "the . . . real future for films is in developing some kind of box to collect money for movies on TV."[63] Others took on the complex restoration of *Queen Kelly*, preserving the unfinished film for future generations.[64]

When the call came that her beloved mother was ill, Gloria was frantic to get to California. Adelaide's physicians diagnosed diverticulitis, and Swanson was convinced her diet was responsible. Since Adelaide hated the "continual rumpus" surrounding her daughter, Gloria and Bill parked their rented mobile home next to Adelaide's rose garden. They tossed out all her processed foods and fed Adelaide a high-fiber menu prepared by Bill. Her white blood count quickly rebounded and her energy returned; soon Adelaide was tending her flowers again. Gloria exulted, reminding her mother that (as Dr. Bieler said) food was the best medicine. Yet as soon as she recovered her strength, Adelaide asked Bill and Gloria to leave. "She couldn't wait to get rid of both of us," Swanson said sadly. "She wanted no part of my life."[65]

Swanson was devoted to her mother, sending Adelaide checks regardless of her own finances and calling her every Sunday without fail from all over the world. Postcards arrived on Addie's doorstep from Port-au-Prince and Venice, Palermo and Barcelona, often signed "Glory" or "Baby." Every year on Gloria's birthday, she sent Adelaide flowers. Swanson treated her mother with uncharacteristic deference and never, ever raised her voice to Addie. There was no one whose respect she sought more avidly nor whose affection she craved as fiercely as she did her mother's. Michelle thought Adelaide was the only person Gloria really loved.

However, her mother was a stern woman who showed little affection to Gloria or her children. Michelle thought her frighteningly severe and knew from an early age that Gloria hid things from Adelaide, fearing her disapproval. When some friends came to visit Gloria at her mother's, Addie demanded to know if they were more of "those people." Yes, the actress grumbled to herself, "those white slavers from the motion picture industry." Despite all she had accomplished—the fame, the accolades, the body of creative work—Swanson felt her mother was disappointed in her. "In my entire life I could only remember one real compliment my mother had ever extended me about my theatrical career: 'My daughter is the hardest working woman I know.' She said it and that was that."[66]

Adelaide turned off her hearing aid when Gloria spoke, nodding her head and pretending to agree with whatever her daughter said. The one word she always heard clearly was goodbye. As Swanson recalled, whenever she said, "'Mother, I have to leave now,' you could hear her sigh and [see] relief spread over her pretty face."[67]

Now Gloria refused to leave LA: she wanted to be near her mother. She swapped houses with George Hamilton and was working on *The Beverly Hillbillies* when Addie became ill again. Against Gloria's wishes, Adelaide went into the hospital, where she rapidly deteriorated. Gloria haunted her mother's room, in her distress riding roughshod over the staff. She hired and fired nurses: "I wanted to kill everybody in sight." Yet once her mother slipped into a coma, Gloria too surrendered, crooning to Addie to let go of her body. Her death was quiet and peaceful.

"At least for three weeks she was my baby and I could take care of her," Gloria told herself.[68]

However, she felt utterly bereft, relying on her daughter Gloria—a recent widow herself—to make the funeral arrangements. A few months earlier, four generations of female Swansons had gathered for a family portrait. Swanson was sixty-seven, but with her mother's passing, she felt unmoored: "I was no longer the frivolous teenager wasting my days hanging around those terrible motion picture people. I was no longer her baby Glory. I was the matriarch of the family now."[69]

Dr. Bieler prescribed a good, long rest (and no sex): Gloria's blood pressure was soaring. Too despondent to do anything but agree, she let Bill pack for Hawaii. Black Point, a rocky promontory overlooking the Pacific, was an idyllic spot with "a natural pool in the rocks, lots of sun, no telephone calls and no visitors." They slept, read, and searched for organic vegetables, eventually finding a small community of Buddhists who grew and cooked their own traditional food. "They were sweet enough to share their good things with us," Gloria recalled.[70] Their new friends taught the couple to chant and meditate, and Swanson's blood pressure soon returned to normal.

In the months after her mother's death, Gloria thought seriously about mortality for the first time. She had, of course, lost friends and lovers. Mickey Neilan died in 1958, right before Cecil De Mille and Eddie Goulding. Erich von Stroheim was gone, too, and Bart Marshall died a few months before Gloria's mother in 1966. Swanson found herself reaching out more to old friends: you never knew when goodbye would be final. When Louella Parsons was hospitalized and doing poorly, Swanson wrote her: "We sort of take it for granted that we will see our friends somewhere in this tiny world. . . . [We go] back to Essanay, Louella, and I have always thought of you as a sweet gentle person."[71] Living each day fully seemed even more important. Her own last act was looming.

Neither the loss of her mother nor her stable partnership with Dufty mellowed Swanson, however, whose work commitments and continual traveling would have wearied a much younger woman. Swanson often lived out of a suitcase; her whirlwind itinerary of November-December 1967 was typical. First she visited her son and his family in San Francisco. Joseph was working on a vehicular guidance system to allow drivers to retrace their routes, and Swanson could not have been more proud of him. It was not entirely a vacation: she also had television programs to tape. Then she and Bill went to New York before continuing on to Paris,

Deauville, and Zurich. They returned to Paris, then visited Lisbon and London before heading back to New York.

They spent the holidays with Michelle's family on the French coast, though Swanson was by no means an easy guest for her daughter. Hurricane Gloria blew in with two carloads of luggage, her lover, and a secretary. Michelle heard screaming upstairs before dinner the evening they arrived: Gloria was berating her secretary for ruining her evening dress. The young woman, distraught, ran out of the house. Michelle brought her back, shivering with the December cold, and confronted her mother. It was a watershed moment: "It was the first time in my whole life that I dared really say something . . . because I never did. I was terrified of her, terrified of her. I knocked, I opened the door, and I said, 'The time of slavery is over. You hired this girl as a private secretary, not to press your evening dress.'"[72] Gloria angrily refused to come down for dinner.

While Swanson sulked in her room, Michelle marveled at her own audacity. "I couldn't stand up to [my mother] even when I was married," she recalled. "I think I put an ocean between her and me because she was impossible. She wasn't dumb. She was a self-made woman. She had read a tremendous amount. She loved to be around smart people and scientific people. She was interested in everything, everything, everything. [But] she was impossible."[73]

Swanson was free with her opinions about her children's—and their children's—lives: "She had opinions on everything," Michelle sighed.[74] When her teenaged grandson Guy visited the States, Gloria praised the young man to his mother: "Everybody who has met him is enchanted with him." Yet—disappointed with her grandson's poor English—she added a barb for Michelle: "It is a damn shame that you did not make it easier for him than yourself [by teaching him English]."[75] When Michelle confided in her mother about some trouble with her own daughter, Gloria wrote: "I am sorry to hear about your child problems. God knows what I went through with mine and a 'nanny.' Thank goodness they did not have psychiatrists in those days, as you and Joseph and Gloria would have gone." She also complained that her other daughter—whom she called "Gloria Anderson"—made excuses not to visit her.[76]

Michael Farmer was back in Michelle's life, and Gloria disapproved of her seeing the father she had never really known. Swanson did not want to talk about her fourth husband—ever—or to hear about the money Michelle and Bob occasionally gave him. She herself refused to give Farmer anything, relenting only once when she learned he was thinking of publishing his memoirs. The small amount Swanson offered came with a warning: "Be sure [you] toe the line of truthfulness, because there are too many people who can check on things."[77] It was no accident that a society column published soon after said, "The high spot in [Farmer's] present life occurs when he opens a letter and a check from Gloria Swanson drops out."[78]

For a few years after Addie's death, Gloria felt drained. "To say that I am pooped is putting it mildly," she wrote Michelle. "I feel just like a dray horse that has been beaten up a hill."[79] A doctor told Swanson she was suffering from arthritis and might end up in a wheelchair; being sedentary was anathema to Gloria. In 1969, she bought a small farm with a pine grove—but without electricity—in Colares, Portugal, where she could live cheaply, grow vegetables, and relax. She was more or less hiding out, once again determined to heal herself the natural way.

Michelle thought Gloria was still grieving Adelaide's death. She encouraged her mother, who was struggling to keep 100 pounds on her tiny frame, to take it easy and eat more. Yet when Michelle did not rush to Portugal to take care of her, Gloria blamed Bob Amon, writing him angrily: "Must I be on my deathbed to have some time with [Michelle] alone?" Something Bob had said about Swanson being a millionaire rankled: "If I neglected my children and didn't have much of their childhood, it was because I was working to become your millionaire mother-in-law."[80] Michelle tried to explain her feelings: "Although I get nervous when you are with me, it's only because I want everything to be perfect for you, and it never is, and that I love you so very dearly."[81]

Her Eastman tribute piqued Swanson's desire to find her lost films, especially *Beyond the Rocks* and *Madame Sans-Gêne*. Though they were conspicuously missing from her retrospective, Gloria was confident that prints of both her Valentino collaboration and her French picture would surface. The search deepened her interest in film preservation and gave her a new crusade.

A lead about the missing pictures took Swanson to an unlikely place for an American tourist in December 1968: the Soviet Union. During the Third Reich, Hermann Goering, commander-in-chief of the Luftwaffe, had amassed a personal fortune, plundering public and private art collections across the continent. A cinema fan, he had also stolen whatever films appealed to him. The postwar division of Germany left some of Goering's collection behind the Iron Curtain. The Soviet film archive was rumored to be the largest in the world, but no one had been able to gain access to the vaults. Official requests yielded nothing, so Swanson decided to do some sleuthing on her own. She and Bill arranged a trip to Moscow, bringing a few of Swanson's movies along to show to students at the State Institute of Cinematography.

Bill, whom Gloria affectionately called "my Irish cruise director," organized a stopover in Warsaw on the way, where Swanson saw "thousands of Polish noses" just like hers.[82] They celebrated their arrival in Moscow on a cold, dark day with caviar and champagne courtesy of the black market: fresh vegetables and fruit were much harder to find. Gloria had been warned to expect suspicion and hostility in Russia, since she had often spoken out against Communism. Yet hers was a goodwill mission, and she and Dufty encountered friendly hospitality wherever they went.

The students at the film school loved *His New Job*, the Chaplin short featuring a teenaged Swanson, and Gloria agreed: the Tramp never got old. (Chaplin had welcomed Gloria warmly when she visited the London set of *A Countess from Hong Kong* in 1966. Impressed anew by Chaplin's vigor and artistry, she told her companion, "I suppose he is the most creative man it is possible to meet.")[83] However, the Russian students' response to *Sunset Boulevard* surprised Swanson: they "took it for a validation of the [Soviet] policy against the star system." Gloria apparently failed to see why. Though she talked about her missing pictures everywhere they went, she turned up no new clues at all. If "Hitler's fat friend"—as Swanson called Goering—had taken her films, the Russians weren't saying.[84]

An unexpected delight of the trip was Gloria's meeting with the state minister for nutrition. Approaching seventy, Swanson was again healthy, and the official complimented her appearance and her stamina. Obesity and alcoholism, however, were big problems in the USSR: might he ask about her diet? Gloria told him about being stuck with caviar when she longed for fresh fruit and vegetables. They had several long, wonderful conversations. Swanson concluded, "As far as peace and freedom were concerned, what goes on in our kitchens is much more basic than what goes on in our parliaments and our Politburos."[85]

She and Dufty headed north to Leningrad by train, marveling at the long nights and the windswept stations almost engulfed by snow. A month was not long enough to see this magnificent country. During a short stay in Sweden, their hotel fielded calls from "all the Swansons and Svensens south of the Arctic Circle." After a newspaper "had the bright idea of flying some of these self-styled relatives to meet with me at a gala family reunion," Gloria knew it was time to go home.[86] She had always wanted a big family, but enough was enough.

CHAPTER 22

Last Act

THOUGH GLORIA SWANSON WOULD NEVER HAVE TRADED PLACES WITH anyone, Coco Chanel's life might have tempted her. So when word came that Katharine Hepburn was leaving the Broadway musical *Coco*, Gloria threw her beret in the ring: "Here I was, seventy years old, being offered a chance to do something I'd never done. What did I have to lose?"[1] She faced down the footlights, singing Mickey Neilan's "Wonderful One" and a patter song from *The King and I* for the producers.

As negotiations got underway, Swanson headed west to Palm Springs, where she trained "like a prize fighter" for the part. She practiced with an accompanist daily, then drove around town singing aloud to audiocassettes to drill the music into her head. Back in New York, she hired jazz great Mabel Mercer as her voice coach; together they gave Gloria's green baby grand piano a workout. Kay Thompson, the ultimate musical comedy professional, started Gloria on a walking program to limber her up, and Swanson soon felt fit and strong. Bill cheered her on; so did her daughter Gloria, who had remarried and relocated to New York.

Plans stalled, however, when the producers decided to allow Swanson only three preview performances: "What's the infernal hurry?" she wondered.[2] Hepburn, who had done forty previews, warned her that the show was terribly hard work. Another sticking point: Hepburn was reportedly earning $10,000 a week, while Swanson had been offered only $1,500.[3] Then Gloria heard that the management wanted to get *Coco* reviewed quickly so they could let some of the expensive musicians and supporting cast members go: "In a rush to get back their huge investment, they wanted to strip the show."[4] She decided to bow out, then confronted stories that she had made unreasonable demands. "I only wanted what Katie had received," she pointed out, protesting the image of herself as a "temperamental, nutty actress."[5] Danielle Darrieux replaced Hepburn, and the play soon closed.

Swanson felt like "a race horse, all revved up, with nowhere to go . . . then the divine design began to appear." Out of the blue, she was invited to replace Eileen Heckart in the hit comedy *Butterflies Are Free*. It was a good part for an actress of a certain age: a strong-willed mother who comes to Greenwich Village to break up the affair between her blind son and his hippie girlfriend. It was simpler than *Coco*, with "not one change of costume in the entire show," the former clotheshorse explained. Swanson had walked out on *Lenny* shortly after it began, shocked and troubled by that play's sordid vulgarity. The "wonderful, healthy laughter" of *Butterflies* was an antidote to such tastelessness.[6] Swanson felt hesitant about going right on to Broadway and asked to tour with the play first; unlike many old-timers, she was not afraid of the rigors of the road. The producers agreed quickly. She went off to Portugal, resting and running her lines, and by the time she joined the cast in Chicago in October 1970, she was letter-perfect.

Gloria's only grounds for complaint was her costume: "[It] looked as if my blind son had ordered it from a mail order catalogue. . . . It made me look seventy going on ninety when I ought to look forty-five."[7] An ugly brown wig added insult to injury. Two hairdresser friends came backstage in Chicago and tore into Swanson for her dowdy look. She promptly tossed the costume, changing her hair color and putting on a smart French pantsuit. To give the interfering mother character some depth, Swanson imagined that Mrs. Baker blamed herself for her son's blindness. "Had Mama foolishly taken experimental drugs during her pregnancy? Did something happen in the delivery room?" she asked herself. "The mother had to feel responsible in some way for her son's infirmity."[8]

They took the play to nineteen cities over the next seven months, a grueling tour that nonetheless steadied and readied Swanson for their New York engagement. She wrote Michelle from Cincinnati, "This is my fourth performance here and at last my heart has settled to a normal speed."[9] Swanson's longtime secretary Gladys Griffith came out of retirement to help Gloria start her tour. After she went home, Swanson realized anew how lucky she had been: "After 28 years with Miss Griffith, I was truly spoiled. Her kind of people had gone out of style."[10]

Yet after Gloria was hospitalized in Wilmington for an uncontrollable nosebleed—something she attributed to her poor diet on the road—Bill Dufty once again came to the rescue. The Swanson army traveled on its stomach, and he finished the tour as Gloria's cook, moving his hot plate into her hotel room. "Nobody yet has had the nerve to ask me if I'm your lover," he announced one day in St. Louis. "Don't you find that some-what insulting?"[11]

After a week of previews, *Butterflies* opened in New York in September 1971. Swanson was treated as a returning celebrity and greeted with standing ovations. Her producer, Arthur Whitelaw, roped Shubert Alley off for an opening night party, projecting Gloria's silent movie images on the walls. The reviews were good, the box office strong: twenty years after *Twentieth Century*, she finally had her Broadway hit.

Interviewers reached for fresh angles on yet another Swanson return to the limelight. One reporter wrote, "I had come to [her] apartment at 10 p.m., warned to expect a dragon in furs. I stayed until 4 a.m., munching cucumber sandwiches with organic mayonnaise, sipping herb tea, charmed and fascinated. . . . I watched that face for hours, the arched eyebrows, high cheekbones, blazing blue eyes, bright red mouth, *the* face of the '20s and the '40s, almost a caricature of those decades, but now as-tonishingly coming back into fashion. Gloria Swanson had won again."[12] If people wanted to scrutinize Swanson with binoculars in the theater—and they did—she acknowledged their interest candidly. This time her *Playbill* biography read, "Name, nose, teeth, bosom, hair, kidneys—ev-erything but the eyelashes—is real."[13]

Gloria's nonconformist attitudes made good copy. Asked her opinion of modern youth, she readily endorsed some of the "new values," es-pecially natural childbirth: "Those girls who have their babies after two hours of squatting are wonderful. That's the way Mrs. God intended it," she told one paper. She was less enthusiastic about women's liberation: "I want a man to know more, and I want him to pick up something when I can't. Physically, I want him stronger. Mentally, I want him stronger." If Swanson seemed not to register the facts of her own case, the inter-viewer did: "As five ex-husbands could testify, there are few men . . . who can match wits and skills with Gloria Swanson."[14]

Butterflies' limited run was extended, and a new leading man came on in January. The producer thought Dirk Benedict looked too physically fit to be believable as a blind man, but Gloria championed his cause. "Fortunately for me," Benedict wrote, "Miss Swanson saw no reason why a blind person couldn't come in any size, shape or form."[15] Gloria put it this way: without good actors supporting her onstage, she said, "I can stink to high heavens."[16]

Benedict was interested in Swanson's "magical, mystical, foreign" food. He joined her and Bill for dinner at her apartment and left with his first bag of brown rice. Swanson—whom Benedict came to call "my meatless, sugarless mom"—started him on the macrobiotic diet that restored his health.[17] Backstage at the Booth Theatre became a Swanson clinic, with Japanese diagnosticians and shiatsu masseurs dropping by and vegetable broth steaming in the dressing rooms.

For the first time in Swanson's adult life, she was "a one-woman show: I was my own makeup man, my own hairdresser, my own secretary, my own cleaning woman, and my own chauffeur."[18] Taxi drivers and traffic cops called out to Gloria each night as she drove through Times Square to the theater, regular as clockwork, in her little yellow Toyota. When the show closed in July 1972, she had played Mrs. Baker 666 times.

After Bette Davis, fearful of being stung, refused a role in the television movie *Killer Bees*, Swanson leaped at the chance. She was eager to take the part of the German matriarch who controls her adult children—and a swarm of dangerous bees. It "appealed to something primeval in me," she claimed.[19] Her character was a horrific version of Mrs. Baker, another willful mother threatened by her grown son's hippie fiancée. To suggest the woman's steely inflexibility, Gloria had a corset with strong stays built. She added a squint, starting speaking with a German accent, figured out which way was up on the antiquated undergarment, and was ready to go.

The picture shot for ten days in the Napa Valley on the old Niebaum estate that became Francis Coppola's winery. She liked the director, Curtis Harrington, who knew and loved early movies, and her young colleagues Kate Jackson and Edward Albert were skillful and agreeable. Swanson secured a small part for the wine expert Robert Balzer, then got a kick out of seeing her longtime friend deliver her eulogy in the film.

The only problem were her 700,000 tiny costars. Advertisements for the film promised: "She controls the bees. They'll kill for her—and die for her. She's their queen and she'll live forever." Yet Swanson knew she did not control the bees and sincerely hoped their handlers did. Since it was too late in the season for drones, they refrigerated fully equipped bees, then sliced off their stingers while the bees were drowsy. For Gloria's big scene, the sleepy bees were placed all over her body. When the arc lights warmed up, the bees gradually revived and began crawling over her. It was important that she remain calm, and the cast and crew applauded Gloria when the scene ended without a hitch. (Swanson admitted stuffing her ears with cotton to keep any wandering bees out.)

She said the bees did "little ballets, buzzing beautifully for the cameras," and her director thought Gloria's organic sensibility helped her performance.[20] In fact, the cameraman had more trouble making Swanson look her age under the lights than they had getting the bees to behave. *Killer Bees* did well in the ratings and was shown in reruns for years.

In 1957, Mike Wallace had asked Gloria if she was done with the movies. She answered his question with one of her own: "Are they through with me?"[21] Now all of a sudden her phone was ringing again. *Airport 1975*, a sequel to the phenomenally successful *Airport*, was crowd-pleasing, popcorn-selling escapist fare. Pictures like *The Poseidon Adventure* and *The Towering Inferno* had audiences lined up around the block. Disaster was in.

Gloria, however, did not like the character proposed for her: an aging movie star with a drinking problem. It was "another nut" part: "Why did all actresses have to be tiresomely temperamental and crazy? I'm an actress, and I'm not temperamental."[22] When she made this speech to producer William Frye, he laughed and said in that case she could just play herself. That was all Swanson needed to hear. She worked out her dialogue with the writers, incorporating cutting remarks about airline food. "Gloria Swanson" would carry her own meal on the plane; the bourbon in the script became carrot juice. Edith Head's costumes provided the necessary movie star glamour. As she signed the contract, Gloria marveled at her cinematic voyages: she had gone from being tied to the railroad tracks to being endangered on a jumbo jet. *Airport 1975* would be her final film.

The plot was ludicrous. An incapacitated 747 is flying on autopilot after colliding with another plane. Only capable stewardess Karen Black and her lover, a flight instructor on the ground, can save the day. At last—the clock ticking on a leaking fuel supply—heroic Charlton Heston parachutes into the open cockpit and lands the plane. While this is happening, the plane's passengers behave the way humans behave in crisis at high altitudes: unpredictably. On board are a singing nun and several Hare Krishnas, a child on her way to an organ transplant, a man who can't stop talking, and a woman who can't stop drinking. "Gloria Swanson" is mainly concerned with saving audiocassettes of her memoirs. She dumps her jewelry and stashes the story of her life in the crash-proof safe with which she travels. Eventually they all ride the inflatable slides to the ground and safety, "Gloria" clutching her memoirs to her tightly.

It had been more than twenty years since Swanson made a Hollywood film, but not much had changed. The only thing she found disconcerting was being gawked at by visitors on the Universal Studios tour. She felt like "a sideshow . . . tourists would be brought past my bungalow. I could have been the snake lady."[23] The crew members collected the white cards on which Swanson wrote out her lines as souvenirs. It was enough to make anyone feel old.

Asked endlessly about her age, Gloria derided "the impotent old goats" who cast Hollywood movies for thinking that an actress was washed up at thirty-five. She scoffed at producers who left their wives for girls who could be their granddaughters, claiming that "European men don't even like younger women."[24] She also blasted most American films: female characters were "weak and willing," she said, because "producers are afraid of women. . . . They're terrified of women who have firm opinions."[25] She made it clear she preferred a man who was not threatened by her intelligence, "someone with whom I can have mental intercourse on any subject."[26] Swanson also held forth about fashion. The actress who had once worn a $100,000 gown embroidered with 100,000 pearls expressed astonishment that blue jeans were now permissible in Paris. Though she hated to compromise, she said, she wanted to be à la mode and so had begun wearing jeans—with sables.

Airport 1975 earned its $4 million budget back many times over and spawned several more sequels. It was relentlessly parodied, even prompting a feature-length spoof, *Airplane!* Gloria and her colleagues laughed all the way to the bank.

Swanson particularly enjoyed laughing at herself. A devoted fan of *The Carol Burnett Show*, she roared with delight whenever Carol played the delusional movie star "Nora Desmond." One night she wrote Burnett a fan letter and was promptly invited to appear on the show. It was one of Swanson's happiest television experiences.

Burnett and company kidded Gloria as a voracious consumer of younger men. For "A New-Fangled Tango," Gloria wore a blood-red Bob Mackie gown. Six faux Valentinos in bolero jackets and brillantined hair twirled her around, hoisted her aloft, and passed her overhead as she sang about preferring tangos with "not much movement but lots of action." (Gloria called it "the beanbag number.")[27]

Another sequence featured one of Carol's recurring characters, the cleaning lady, who sets a film reel in motion while dusting, then magically goes behind the screen to become part of a silent movie. She meets Swanson dressed as the Little Tramp, and they have charming adventures—drinking champagne from the Tramp's holey boot, being chased by a huge Keystone-style cop, exchanging a flower. Then the cleaning lady is back in the dusty projection room, reality sadly restored, until she reaches into her pocket and finds the flower. She sits down on a bucket and sings a wistful song about silent movies: "They were inspired—insane—absurd, and they said it all without a sound, without a word."

Gloria was feted on a milestone birthday—her seventy-fifth—with a retrospective in Paris at the Cinematheque Française. Legendary French film curator Henri Langlois had been in Swanson's sights for some time: he was her last, best hope for finding *Madame Sans-Gêne*. Langlois had apparently located a print in 1939, but with the outbreak of World War II it disappeared. Though representatives of the Motion Picture Association of America had made "a Scotland Yard-like search" for the picture in France in the '50s, the consensus was that "Langlois knows where to find motion pictures where nobody else would look for them."[28]

Gloria spoke passionately about the subject to a British journalist: "Do you know if Paris had been bombed during the last war, this film would have been an invaluable record? We shot [inside] Fontainebleau, Malmaison, Compiegne . . . [I]t's a crime that it is lost." Langlois was known to be crafty and secretive about his archive's holdings, and Swanson simply refused to believe he did not have her film stashed away: "Is Henri Langlois an old man? Is he older than I am? Because if he is, I'll outlive him and I'll see it yet. I would go down on my KNEES to this man . . . Just let me look at it, I'd say, I'll keep your secret."[29]

Despite her tough talk, Swanson, like many before her, was charmed by Langlois. When French minister of culture André Malraux cut government subsidies to the Cinematheque in May 1968 in an effort to force Langlois out, she stood up for him publicly. She cabled demanding his reinstatement, saying the rest of the world was decades behind France because of Langlois's "vision, dedication, and courage."[30] Images of the locked and shuttered Cinematheque went viral, and Malraux was forced to reinstate the beloved curator. The irony is that many rare films disappeared because of Langlois's carelessness; Gloria's suspicion that he might be hiding *Madame Sans-Gêne* was not out of the realm of possibility. The film is still considered lost.

There were other losses: no one Swanson's age was immune to them. The passing of Henri de la Falaise in October 1972 left Gloria pensive. "When [my mother] was quite old," Michelle said, "I asked her, 'Who was the man you loved the most of all your husbands and friends?' She said Henri."[31] In 1950, Swanson herself said as much in an account of their courtship she prepared for *Photoplay*. Yet she left these private thoughts out of the essay's published version: "My marriage to Henry gave me the only real peace and happiness I had ever known—or have ever known since. Of my five marriages this one . . . came the nearest to being what I, in my haus-frau heart, have always wanted a marriage to be. You can take the others and lump them all together and they would not make a marriage . . . He was then and he remains in memory a more delightful companion than any I have known."[32] Swanson's desire to see her lost film once more—the one she made while young and in love with her handsome, brave marquis—was surely heightened by the loss of Henri.

She was devastated when her son Joseph died suddenly in July 1975. At fifty-two his death was "much too soon, much too young."[33] Years earlier, Gloria had written to his wife Sue about the unusual understanding she felt with her adopted son: "It is inexplainable [*sic*] the close bond there is spiritually and mentally between us." She considered the fact that she and Joseph were not biologically related "a mishap along the line somewhere."[34] There was no one whose intellect Swanson valued or delighted in more, and their all-night conversations were legendary in the family. As Michelle recalled, when Brother came to New York, Gloria and he "would talk until 4:00 in the morning."[35] Gloria admired Joseph's inventive spirit and his ability to puzzle through a problem. His early death was one of the great sorrows of her life.

Swanson was a proud great-grandmother when she decided to marry again. She had resisted making her longtime companion Bill Dufty seem like "just a number—number six."[36] (By some accounts, that number was too low: as one gossip columnist cracked, "She had other husbands than her own.")[37] Bill didn't care what anyone said: he would think of himself as Gloria Swanson's first organic husband. His joke settled the issue, and they were married quietly in 1976, on his sixtieth birthday. Gloria told reporters that she and Dufty "totally understand each other. Besides, my life is one surprise after another."[38]

Her candor about marital relations surprised some. "My sex life is very healthy," she proclaimed on one talk show, saying that menopause awakened women sexually. "It's really the beginning of everything because there's no worry about [pregnancy]. Women find a sense of freedom and abandonment." (In private, however, she said she had not been bold enough to experiment sexually with other women.) Gloria explained her frankness to her astounded listeners: "I'm a matriarch now, and I can say anything I want to!"[39] She might be a grandmother of seven, but she refused to be ashamed of what was natural.

Swanson had finally found a companion who wanted to take care of her. Nonetheless, she regularly told Bill off, insisting, "We can not live under the same roof *ever*."[40] She now believed marriages should be revaluated periodically—at one, five, and ten years—before they became permanent. Dufty just laughed, calling himself the holder of "the world's endurance record in three categories: cook, lover and . . . husband."[41] Bill Dufty was there until the end.

In lieu of a honeymoon, the couple went on an extended tour to publicize Dufty's new book, an account of how refined sugar acts like an addictive drug in the human body. He dedicated *Sugar Blues* to the woman who had introduced him to natural foods twenty years earlier: "Gloria Swanson, whose life changed my death." On speaking engagements and at book signings, Swanson lent her star power to their shared crusade for better nutrition. She talked about how Bill looked "like a Buddha, all blubber," when they met.[42] She also confessed her own weakness for chocolate ice cream sodas: she and Muhammad Ali had contemplated starting an ice cream business a few years back, using natural date sugar as their sweetener. The food's purity mattered more to her than the individual ingredients: "I eat *anything* as long as it hasn't been tampered with."[43] However, Swanson hated seeing people "destroying themselves with knives and forks."[44]

She and Bill volunteered with New York City's Department of Education. Convinced that poor nutrition was related to learning disabilities, they began doing cooking demos in city schools. (Bill prepared a lunch he called "Whole Food is Soul Food.") Being recognized by children surprised Swanson, until she realized that they knew her not as the slave girl with the lion on her back but as the old lady with bees in her bonnet.

Though she never steered clear of controversy, Swanson was asking for it when she filed a lawsuit in August 1977 against avant garde filmmaker and author Kenneth Anger for libel and defamation. *Hollywood Babylon*, Anger's salacious history of Hollywood, told unflattering, unexpurgated, and unsubstantiated stories of stars from the silent era to the '60s. What Anger did not say outright about the stars' sexual perversity and luxuriant self-indulgence he insinuated. Swanson claimed the book damaged her reputation "through false innuendo, imputations and suggestions," particularly in passages portraying her as "a woman of loose morals" who acted as a "courtesan and concubine." Anger had intimated that "to further her artistic career in pictures, she took drugs and engaged in many sexual contacts with motion picture producers and directors."[45] She sought $8 million in damages.

In fact, Anger's treatment of Swanson was relatively mild: one had to read carefully between the lines to conclude that she had spent time on

Mack Sennett's casting couch or been part of the orgies shown in Erich von Stroheim's pictures. There was the barest mention of Joe Kennedy, and it was no secret that Gloria and Joe had had business—if not private—relations.[46] Anger was not always so circumspect: his claim that Clara Bow had sexually serviced the entire USC football team had Bow's sons contemplating legal action.

Swanson's suit enraged Anger, a devotee of black magic who favored putting spells on people who crossed him. In the months before Swanson's suit was heard, she began receiving threatening mail from Anger: cards addressed to "Faded Glory" advised her to "'Know Thy Enemy'—which you obviously *don't*." At Christmas he sent "Season's Curses." She received a photograph of herself with pins and nails stuck in it and a note saying, "Wishing You a Speedy Termination of Existence."[47] The pièce de resistance was a doll-sized painted wooden coffin with the funereal inscription "Hic Jacet Gloria Swanson." It was filled with packets of sugar.

Swanson was terrified and angry. Everyone in her building—and a team of New York's Finest—was on the alert, but Anger's missives kept mysteriously arriving. She had of course been stalked before. During the 1920s, one fan wanted desperately to become king of the League of Nations, with Gloria as his queen. "We had a great deal of trouble with him," Swanson remembered.[48] In the 1950s, the FBI had taken the obsessed veteran who offered Gloria military secrets off her hands. Twenty years later, Kenneth Anger's sugar-filled coffin and hate mail were frightening reminders of the price of celebrity.

After the court upheld his constitutional rights, Anger cooled. In *Hollywood Babylon II*, published after Swanson's death, he crowed, "[Tinseltown's] real, bona fide, black-magical witch was none other than that flower of Chicago's stockyards, the *late* Gloria Swanson. DING, DONG, THE WITCH IS DEAD! And not her maid, not her secretary, not her effete sixth husband can bring Old Gloria back to life again. Gloria's gone. *Sic Transit Gloria Mundi*!"[49]

Most of her New York neighbors were friendlier than Kenneth Anger. Gloria and Bill became close to John Lennon and Yoko Ono when the couple was fighting John's deportation from America. Lennon was a fan of Dufty's books and gave stacks of them to friends. Along with Norman Mailer, Isamu Noguchi, Dick Cavett, and Geraldo Rivera, Swanson testified on John's behalf at the highly publicized 1976 immigration hearing that granted him permanent residency in the US. Lennon, alas, paid a high price for his celebrity a few years later. Shortly before his death by a fan's bullet, he talked about the kind of star power he admired: "Making Sid Vicious a hero, Jim Morrison—it's garbage to me. I worship the people who survive—Gloria Swanson, Greta Garbo. . . . No, thank you. I'll take the living and the healthy."[50]

Garbo was in fact a close neighbor of Swanson's in Manhattan. The reclusive actress told William Frye, Swanson's *Airport 1975* producer, that she had received a nice letter from Gloria: "We both live in New York, near each other," Swanson had written. "We are both alone, we have similar lives. Why don't we have dinner sometime? Please come over and have dinner with me."[51] They had been friends years ago in Hollywood, but Garbo did not reply to Gloria's letter; she was too used to her solitude. She pressed Frye, however, for details of Swanson's relationship with Bill Dufty: Garbo wanted to know if they had sex.

Swanson spent some of her energy honoring the past, reaching out to Allan Dwan, Raoul Walsh, and René Hubert "from one survivor to another."[52] She accepted honors at the Telluride Film Festival for her contributions to the history of cinema, wrote the forward to her friend Frances Marion's book on early Hollywood, and participated in the re-opening of the Astoria Studios.

Yet most of her energy went to considering the future and living in the present. Swanson still considered herself a working woman, though she threw most of the scripts she received across the room. There was talk of a sequel to *Sunset Boulevard* (Gloria said she was keeping a body in the swimming pool just in case) and talk of a movie with her long-ago rival Pola Negri. Instead, Swanson performed *Look Back in Laughter*, a one-woman show based on her career, for one night only on each coast. "Many people are old because they don't want to change," she proclaimed.[53]

She loved New York's vibrancy and became a fixture in the city, even taking up jogging. As she entered her eighth decade Swanson could be seen doing her two miles around Central Park. It improved her stamina for the late nights she spent partying with Truman Capote in the club of the moment, Studio 54.

It also fueled her energy for another political campaign. Before her marriage Swanson had been angry about the unequal tax burden on single people: she thought Uncle Sam unfairly penalized unmarried citizens. With her friend, industrialist and tax resister Vivien Kellems, she held a one-night "tax rebellion rally" after a performance of *Butterflies Are Free*. "After ten minutes, the audience was ready to march on Washington," Swanson crowed.[54] Both Swanson and Kellems testified before the

House Ways and Means Committee about taxation, whereupon Gloria was promptly audited.[55] The women got support from an unexpected quarter: the gay press, which spoke for taxpayers who could not legally marry. In 1980, Swanson chaired the New York chapter of Seniors for Reagan-Bush, convinced the new administration would reform the tax code she abhorred.

From Central Park to Studio 54 to the campaign trail did not seem a stretch: Swanson had always used her prodigious energy to do as she pleased and did not mind contradictions. She might jog, for instance, but she did not take public transport. The one rainy day she hopped a bus, she had no idea where to put the fare and expected the driver to drop her at her corner. "I made an ass of myself," she said cheerfully.[56]

Swanson was by no means ready to concede her place in the public eye or her reputation for glamour and collaborated for over a decade with photographer Jack Mitchell, who shot hundreds of images of the actress in New York. Swanson loved being photographed: when Mitchell approached her, she didn't ask why. "Her response was, 'When?'"[57] He shot Gloria riding in her Rolls, clowning around at home, putting on her false eyelashes, even taking a bath, her leg up on the tub, Dietrich-style—though Swanson wanted her new maid to know that she was wearing a swimsuit under the bubbles.

In the 1970s and '80s she spent time with Andy Warhol—posing for him, being photographed with him, and being interviewed for his magazine, *Interview*. When Warhol's Factory colleague Paul Morrissey filmed his *Sunset Boulevard* parody *Heat* in 1972, Swanson treated the imitation as flattery, though she declined to appear in one of Warhol's films herself.[58] When Warhol actress Candy Darling died at twenty-nine of lymphoma, Swanson saluted the coffin from the back seat of her Rolls-Royce, wearing a white veil, white fur, and white gloves.

Swathed in elaborate outfits, her hair now in a platinum bob, her huge eyes dominating a thinner, older face, the elderly Swanson sometimes seemed like a caricature of the gorgeous young movie star. She came in for her fair share of (mostly appreciative) caricature by a newly visible group of female impersonators who practiced getting the look and low voice of Norma Desmond just right. By highlighting the campy side of classic Hollywood stars, these entertainers made Bette Davis, Mae West, Joan Crawford, Tallulah Bankhead, and Gloria Swanson relevant to new audiences. Homage didn't come any sweeter than Charles Pierce's portrayal of Swanson as Norma Desmond swanning around at Alcatraz several years after her arrest for murder: her prison sun suit was by Edith

Head, her ball and chain by Cartier. Swanson was the first to applaud. If—as Bill Dufty said—his wife wanted to "come back as a pansy in her next life," she would find a new audience ready and waiting.[59]

For a charity auction to benefit the Actors Fund retirement home, Swanson offered to sculpt the head of the highest bidder, displaying a life-size bust of herself and another of Bill Dufty as samples of her work. "On the night of the auction, I was all a-twitter," she remembered, "like an old maid at a box social or a youngster selling kisses in a booth at the fair." She badly wanted someone to like her work. In the end, "a Greek god" of a stockbroker, encouraged by his wife, had the winning bid. The New York papers carried photos, and soon Swanson received a startling offer: a young TV writer-producer knew a London gallery that wanted to show Swanson's sculptures. Brian Degas was "a real ball of fire . . . not your typical art dealer at all," Gloria said. Before she knew it, she had committed to exhibiting several pieces and making half a dozen new ones. Degas also wanted to display her oil paintings. Swanson had never had a solo show of her work and was nervous: "Practically the last private part of my life was suddenly public."[60]

Her deadline fast approaching, Swanson turned her library into a studio, ordered fifty pounds of clay, and sent out an SOS for models. She hired a nursing mother and child for a piece called "And There Shall Be Life." Dancers Geoffrey Holder and Carmen de Lavallade found a young ballerina to pose for her. She did nothing but sculpt for several months and loved every minute. In December 1978, Swanson's one-woman show opened at the posh Hamiltons Gallery in Mayfair. Painter Sara Leighton remembered the evening: "Everyone, in capital letters, had turned up to honour the 'Grand Dame' of the silver screen who looked frankly incredible." For Leighton, Swanson's "undoubted talent as a sculptor" was eclipsed by her beauty. Though she walked with a slight stoop, she had "the clearest, most lustrous pair of enormous blue eyes."[61] Degas had also arranged for Gloria to appear at the National Film Theatre, and the South Bank was crammed with film fans.

High from her successful exhibit, Swanson and Dufty headed to Japan, and the trip offered Gloria unexpected healing. They made a pilgrimage to Mount Koya, where they stayed in the Buddhist temple. After they slipped into heavy brown kimonos and warmed themselves with green tea, the high priest greeted them. He "seemed to be giving us some kind of blessing as he thumbed his round beads," Swanson recalled. Then a young monk translated: "His holiness wants you to know that his mother saw all your movies."[62] Gloria Swanson was a stranger nowhere in the world.

They feasted on a traditional meal: miso soup, tiny watermelon slices, jellied sesame seeds with kudzu—and slept on sturdy futons. Then, rested and refreshed, Bill and Gloria made the trip to the summit. "If there is anything like that mountaintop in the western world, I do not know its name," Swanson said. The most important temple to the Shingon Buddhist tradition stood in a natural cathedral of enormous trees. There were ancient graves all around, and Swanson felt "the community of millions of spirits." Then she noticed a tiny, doll-sized stone figure at the base of a giant cedar. Peering around, she saw dozens, then hundreds of the small figures. Her guide told her they were children's memorials, adding that the one at their feet asked "forgiveness for a child who was aborted."[63] The grave was 400 years old.

Swanson thought of the child she had sacrificed to her career. She always imagined that it was a boy, a son to inherit the childless Henri de la Falaise's title. That choice was "the greatest regret of my life," she said. "Nothing in the whole world is worth a baby."[64] The monks showed her how to pay her respects. "I burned my incense wishing there were a tiny stone figure somewhere for my little one."[65] She wept, and one of the monks consoled her. She recalled his words: "'We all choose our parents. We choose everything. No blame.' I believed him. The message came to me too directly for me to disbelieve it."[66]

The consolation Swanson felt helped heal her old sorrow. It would also help when her granddaughter Bridget, Michelle's child, took her own life soon after. Gloria reflected on the "unimaginable" loss: "I now had to learn to count death as a blessing too." It was not an easy lesson. During the first few awful days, she and her daughter seldom hung up the phone between France and New York, what Swanson called their "umbilical cord." Finally, Michelle asked Gloria to make her a bronze head of Bridget. Feeling it would be impossible, she hesitated. Then she thought, "What does a grandmother hen do after she counts her chickens? When one doesn't come home to roost, she scratches away in the clay." Suddenly, sculpting her beloved granddaughter, the child with the "French velvet voice," was the only thing to do.[67] Sharing this loss brought Gloria and Michelle closer. "We never cuddled until [my mother] was quite old," Michelle recalled.[68] Now, finally, Gloria began to offer her daughter embraces instead of air kisses.

Her family gathered in California to celebrate Swanson's birthday in 1979. Gloria waited until everyone arrived to make her entrance, then hobbled down the steps in an old-fashioned bonnet and white lace gloves. Leaning on a cane, she greeted her guests in a trembling voice:

it was a perfect impersonation of a lady of eighty. Then she ripped off her disguise and the revelry began. It took more than a number on the calendar to slow Swanson down.

Brian Degas, buoyed by the success of the London exhibit, wanted Gloria to tackle her long-delayed autobiography right away. For years she had pretended disinterest. Anyone can write a memoir, she said: "I want to become famous as the one and only who hasn't."[69] After hemming and hawing for decades, on her eightieth birthday Swanson signed a contract with Random House for the story of her life. "There are going to be a lot of bodies twirling in the ground," she pledged.[70] Gloria never threw a piece of paper away: she had seven decades of correspondence, contracts, photographs, clippings, audio recordings, and memorabilia to sort, as well as several incomplete drafts filed away. Working with Bill and two assistants, she settled in for a long look backward. "We are in a bottomless pit," she wrote Phyllis Diller. "The entire apartment looks like a file drawer."[71] They eventually had to rent another living space because the apartment was buried in paper.

Dufty was an experienced ghostwriter, and his organizational help was invaluable, but *Swanson on Swanson* was written in the actress's own voice and in her own words, as the archival holdings make clear. She turned in the manuscript a year to the day after she signed the contract, joking with reporters that it had been "a natural delivery."[72] After the book's eighty-year gestation, she said, "Nobody can claim that it was premature."[73]

Even before it appeared, there was speculation about the book's contents. The Kennedy family reportedly tried to get Swanson to omit her affair with Joe; Random House said only that her account of their relation was "unashamedly direct," which fanned speculation.[74] Gloria told Barbara Walters she wanted to make it clear once and for all that her adopted son Joseph was not Kennedy's child. Besides, "if you don't write your own book, someone who has never been within a hundred miles of you will do it from old newspaper clips."[75] The Kennedy affair was the lead story of most of the book's advance press. *Ladies' Home Journal* published a long, racy excerpt, calling the affair "the unspoken scandal of its time."[76]

Swanson on Swanson appeared to strong notices in November 1980. Calling it "a peppery account of a clever and headstrong individual," the *New York Times* declared, "Movie stars' memoirs don't get any better."[77] The book had "the push of a tidal wave," said the *Los Angeles Times*.[78] Reviewers recognized the author's zest for life and approved her lack of bitterness: "While she dismisses husbands and lovers like a parade ground sergeant[,] she gives us their virtues and the good times without meanness or self-justification. She allows each his moment, however brief, in the sunlight of her approval."[79] The volume begins cleverly, with Swanson's triumphal 1925 return to Hollywood as the Marquise de la Falaise de la Coudraye, certain despite the celebrations that she has already hit the pinnacle of her success. As one reviewer noted, Swanson had answered her own question—where do I go from here?—compellingly: "She went everywhere." This was no mean feat for a woman who was, by her eighteenth birthday, a divorcee with a ninth grade education.[80]

Swanson explained, "I've given my memoirs far more thought than any of my marriages. You can't divorce a book."[81] She embarked on an eight-week, twenty-two-city publicity tour but was soon saying, "I'm fed up with me. I'd rather be getting on with doing something."[82] Looking back was especially challenging for someone so temperamentally attuned to looking ahead.

Most of the icons of the silent era—Pickford, Fairbanks, Chaplin, DeMille, Valentino, Sennett, Stroheim—were gone. Since Gish and Garbo seemed unlikely to publish revealing memoirs, Swanson's book stood alone. Since she herself looked and acted younger than her years, she attracted even more attention. At eighty-one, she barely needed glasses. Her reflexes were so good she could catch something she dropped before it hit the floor. She got a second wind at 11:00 p.m. and typically stayed up until 2:00 or 3:00 a.m. She loathed being assisted, treated as though she was incapable of getting around on her own. She was so flexible—"like rubber," she said—she claimed that she expected to fit in a hatbox rather than a coffin when the time came.[83]

She was "glowing, energetic, impossibly stylish," said Molly Haskell in *Vogue*. "No one—not even someone who's been drinking purée of green beans and zucchini and celery all her life—has a right to look this good at eighty-one."[84] Swanson always conceded she had good genes but confessed she could not have published her book while her mother was alive: Adelaide "would have had a fit."[85] She also volunteered another beauty secret: "A bore never crosses over my threshold twice."[86]

Brian Degas took quite a bit of credit for himself, shouldering aside Bill Dufty. Degas said he had shaped Swanson's book: "I structured it dramatically. I wanted it to read like a novel." He told the *Times* he had possession of the original manuscript, which "will be worth a lot of money after Gloria dies," a distasteful remark under the best of circumstances.[87]

Degas acted as Swanson's handler, and he had her on a short leash. He interrupted one interview repeatedly, telling the reporter not to tire her—while Swanson protested she was anything but fatigued. "Call me if the questions are impossible," Degas instructed Gloria, who replied brusquely: "He hasn't asked any impossible questions. And I'm *not* tired."[88] The peevish exchange was not pretty.

Haskell's encounter with Degas left a sour taste in her mouth: "The only touch of the pampered and overprotected movie goddess [comes] when [Degas] calls to make sure I am going to get a 'fresh' angle and lures me into his office with mention of the 'one thousand pages that didn't get into the book.'" He wanted to force feed Haskell ideas for her interview: "'The theme, Molly, is survival, courage, compassion!'" As the author of *From Reverence to Rape*, the first book on women in film, Haskell did not need Degas's instructions. "The effect of all this is to make me think I'm walking on eggshells," she wrote, "when in fact the woman who greets me at the door seems quite capable of handling anything on two legs." Haskell concluded that Swanson, who expressed "no resentment or sentiment" about the men in her past, generally had the upper hand in her relationships: "I think those men were lucky to get out alive."[89]

Swanson credited Degas with helping her "see things that I was unwilling to see," but her friends thought she did not see Degas clearly.[90] Gloria and Bill became estranged; they separated but did not divorce. Worried that her infatuation with the younger man would harm Gloria, her friend and archivist Raymond Daum warned Michelle that Degas (whom he called "that monster") was manipulating her mother. Daum claimed that Degas "capered around" the apartment when Gloria was ill, excited by the prospect of the money he could make from her death.[91] It was a troubling episode in what otherwise seemed a triumphant chapter.

Plans Gloria had sketched out for a rest in Portugal with Bill and then another book on her favorite topic—health—came to nothing. There were a few more appearances and accolades. She received a lifetime achievement award from the National Board of Review and was honored at the Deauville American Film Festival. She appeared on French TV wearing the honors she had received from the government while making *Madame Sans-Gêne*. At a charity roast in Washington, DC, the audience roared when she said, "All right, Mr. Pulitzer, I'm ready for my prize."[92] She named her Desert Island Discs for the BBC (Gershwin's *Rhapsody in Blue*, a Puccini aria, a Strauss waltz, and Mel Tormé's version of "Wonderful One") and talked with Stephen Sondheim and Hal Prince about a new musical version of *Sunset Boulevard*.

Always, Swanson was a vision of glamour. Richard Avedon shot a fabulous big close-up of Gloria laughing for *Vogue*, her gray hair curly and wild. She wore a gorgeous fur coat and held a single carnation for Blackglama's iconic "What Becomes a Legend Most" series—though Swanson preferred to be considered a survivor rather than a legend.[93]

Ever the enterprising businesswoman, she sold more than 100,000 items detailing her personal and professional enterprises to the Harry Ransom Humanities Research Center in December 1982. The Gloria Swanson Collection—620 boxes of papers, plus art, audio recordings, books, films, scrapbooks, posters, and memorabilia—found a home in Austin, Texas.

Swanson never stopped trying to find *Madame Sans-Gêne*. Shortly before her death she called the Library of Congress to inquire about the picture and was disappointed to learn it was not in Washington, though the library had several other silent films of hers. When she asked if she could borrow them, Paul Spehr, the assistant chief of the motion picture division, had to tell Swanson that they only loaned films to institutions. He remembered, "There was hardly an instant before the response came: 'But, my dear, I AM an institution.'"[94]

Swanson's last creative project combined art, motherhood, and a feeling for the future: she was commissioned to do a painting for a first-day cover of a stamp commemorating the United Nations' Decade for Women. At the UN reception she told her audience that most of her life's work had been collaborative, done as part of a team. As a painter, however, she had to take full responsibility for what she produced, and she was grateful for the opportunity. "It was a gentle speech," she said, "not at all a fighting one," like many she had made in the past.[95] Gloria's painting showed the earth in a comet of light, the continents and oceans arranged to suggest an embryo. Its caption read: "Woman, Like Mother Earth, Has an Eternal Rendezvous with Spring."

Even at the end, Gloria was looking ahead. Less than a month before her death, she told the *Wall Street Journal*, "The future is going to be wonderful . . . I flew the Concorde to Europe and it was terrific. Psst—you're there! All those computers are going to make people smarter. I'm going to get one and learn to use it." She also spoke fearlessly of her own future: "There is so much more to us than just our physical bodies. . . . There has to be another dimension of life. I'm sure of it."[96]

Following a visit to her beloved Paris, Swanson had a mild heart attack at home in New York on March 20, a week before her eighty-fourth birthday. After a brief hospital stay, she died in her sleep on April 4, 1983. At her request she was cremated, with no public funeral or display. The *New York Times* eulogized her on its editorial page in a headline taken from *Sunset Boulevard*: Gloria Swanson was "The Greatest Star of Them All."

ACKNOWLEDGMENTS

THOUGH GLORIA SWANSON REPEATEDLY DENIED HER INTEREST IN writing an autobiography, she produced several drafts and recorded many, many hours of reminiscences over the years. The version in *Swanson on Swanson*—for my money, the best Hollywood memoir ever written—is therefore only one story of her life, the one that satisfied her in 1980.

Three decades later, my own understanding of Swanson has been deepened, strengthened, and often challenged by the thousands of documents and artifacts held in the Gloria Swanson Collection at the Harry Ransom Humanities Research Center at the University of Texas at Austin. In fact, Swanson had me at the researcher's version of "hello"—the first day I spent examining her papers in Austin.

As a favor, Cates Baldridge had done a brief reconnoiter of the Swanson archive while he was in Texas conducting his own research. "You aren't going to believe this place," he said when he returned home. He was right. I owe a huge debt of gratitude to Cates, my first "research assistant," for his loving encouragement and his willingness to read my early drafts.

I have worked in archives all over, and the Ransom Center is—hands down—the best. During the months I spent in Texas, the professionalism of the staff members was equaled only by their personal warmth. Many people went out of their way to make me feel at home in Austin: Debbie Smith, Kurt Heinzelman, and Ginger Edwards, I am talking about you. Pat Fox conjured up endless boxes of documents for me during the day. Then after the archives closed, she took me to all the special places the locals usually keep to themselves. Pat's friendship made my long research trips feel like vacations. Albert Palacios did yeoman's work preparing the photographs for this book and was gracious and cheerful throughout. For Steve Wilson, curator extraordinaire, I reserve my highest compliments. With good humor and good sense, he paved every part of this long road for me. Endlessly excited about the treasures he protects, Steve is happiest sharing them with others. He has my thanks and lasting affection. I also acknowledge with gratitude the generous support of the Andrew W. Mellon Foundation.

I have also had first-rate assistance from Anthony L'Abbate and Jared Case at the George Eastman House in Rochester. My "insider" at the Margaret Herrick Library, Becky Fenning, helped me start this project. I thank Charles Silver at the Museum of Modern Art for his many years of devoted service to film scholars. Madeline Matz made my time at the Library of Congress deeply pleasurable: imagine a curator so devoted to her work that she volunteers after retirement to identify films no one has yet recognized. I also owe thanks to Luke McKernan at the British Film Institute and to Julie Le Perdriel at the Cinémathèque Française. Heather Flynn at Kent State University's Special Collections and Archives was most helpful, as was Harry Miller at the Wisconsin Center for Film and Theater Research. Of course, my "home" archive is in nearby Bucksport, Maine: thanks always to Karan Sheldon and David Weiss at Northeast Historic Film for their support of scholars.

Gloria Swanson's daughter, Michelle Farmer Amon, welcomed me into her Normandy home and answered my questions about her mother and her family life without hesitation. She treated me as an honored guest, putting me at ease even when we talked about sensitive subjects. I am grateful for Mrs. Amon's trust and will always remember the sunshine and strawberries in her French garden. Thanks go to Edmund Rosenkrantz for organizing my contact with the Swanson family and assisting with the necessary permissions.

A surprising number of people shared their Swanson pictures, memorabilia, and memories with me. I particularly thank Barb Nicolls, Eileen Kleinkopf, Al and Phyllis Fuchs, Clif Olds, Sandy Marple at Neiman Marcus, Stephen Sondheim, Michael Maslin, Vance Muse, John-Paul DeRosa, Jerry Murbach, and Richard Berenson, past president of the Society of Illustrators (which should really be called the Society of Fun Lovers). I regret not spending more time with Tim Rooks, who was enthusiastic about this project early on.

I also owe thanks to the film scholars who contributed their expertise generously, especially Graham Petrie, Matthew Bernstein, Molly Haskell, Frank Tomasulo and Erica Fox, Peter Lehman, Gabrielle Kelly, and Paul Spehr. The Oscar-winning Kevin Brownlow managed to make me feel like my questions were intriguing rather than bothersome. Dennis Doros at Milestone Films preserves films, finds them new audiences, and shares his knowledge freely. He is an inexhaustible resource (and a Jersey boy).

I have also found Swanson aficionados and experts among the scholars and film lovers gathered at festivals and collectors' screenings from Pordenone and Bologna to Syracuse, Rochester, Stockholm, and Cannes. The biennial Women and the Silent Screen meetings have been nourishing, rewarding, and fun. I owe special thanks to those who programmed rare Swanson films because they knew I was coming (thank you, Graham) and to those who provided hospitality while I was on the road: Rob Edelman and Audrey Kupferberg, Charlie Hunt and Nancy Cole. Craig Bradley and Elizabeth Webb made it clear that their Paris home was my Paris home: merci beaucoup!

In Maine, the superb resources of Bowdoin College can hold their own against anything a big university can offer. Thanks to Sherrie Bergman, Guy Saldanha, and the ILL staff at Hawthorne-Longfellow Library for putting the world—and many hard-to-find resources—at my fingertips. Marianne Jordan and Cara Martin-Tetreault helped me polish my proposal till it shone. Gustavo Faverón Patriau assisted with translation, and Ann Ostwald extended my research funds more than once. Kevin Johnson, Nate Miller, Chelsea Shaffer, and Laurie Holland went beyond the call of duty repeatedly. And then there is Emily Briley: I got really, really lucky the day she walked in the door (even though I still cannot persuade her to watch a movie in black and white). I could not be happier to have Aviva Briefel, Shu-chin Tsui, Elena Cueto Asin, Birgit Tautz, and Sarah Childress as partners in Film Studies.

I have had countless conversations about this biography with my extraordinary extended family of Bowdoin colleagues. Every one of these dear friends now knows more about Gloria Swanson than he/she ever expected to. The game of "One Degree of Gloria Swanson" is now officially over, folks. My thanks to Susan Tananbaum, Sarah Conly, Kathleen O'Connor, Madeleine Msall, Frank Mauceri, Bill VanderWolk, Michele Lettiere, Rachel and Michael Connelly, Steve Cerf, Penny Martin, Helen Cafferty, Janice Jaffe, Barbara Weiden Boyd, Ann Kibbie, Sara Dickey, David Page, Mike Kolster, Christy Shake, Susan Wegner, John Fischer, Jill Pearlman, Daniel Hope, Mary Pat McMahon, Howie Vandersea, Henry D'Alessandris, Jack Flynn, Bill York, Anne Clifford, Jane Paterson, Mary Pols, Barbara Harvey, Oceanna Miller, Jim Mullen, and "Magic Bob" Vilas.

I am always challenged and rewarded by my students; many are now valued friends. Brandon Doyle, Sharon Baldwin, Andrea McCarty, Jim Flanagan, Audrey Amidon, Heidi Holmstrom, Ivano Pulito, Jim Bittl, Jon Knapp, David Shuck, and Parker Towle all contributed to this book. I am proud of them and grateful to them. Krystle Allen Leveille and Rebecca Genauer—both brilliant film historians—were early readers who stayed through the long haul. Thank you for making me smarter.

Bowdoin College provided generous support for my work in the form of release time and travel funds. Thanks to Dean Cristle Collins Judd for prizing faculty research.

My path to publication became easier and more enjoyable through others' acts of kindness. Bowdoin President Barry Mills sent me to his friend Glenn Kaplan, creative director at Barnes & Noble, who advised me about the world of publishing. Jay Parini—biographer, novelist, poet, and beloved friend—generously shared his expertise and nudged me along.

Since Swanson was photographed by every major portraitist of the twentieth century, I had a ball sifting through hundreds of images of her. Ellen Graham graciously shared both the wonderful portrait included here and stories of photographing Gloria. As a longtime admirer of Nickolas Muray, I was delighted to find that his daughter Mimi Muray Levitt was part of the Bowdoin family. Thank you, Mimi, for sharing your father's work. I also received generous and expert help from Jana Hill at the Amon Carter Museum, Nancy Kauffman at the George Eastman House, Leigh Montville and Shawn Waldron at Condé Nast, and the marvelous Eugenia Bell at the Richard Avedon Foundation.

It's a small world after all: one of the greatest pleasures of this whole process has been reconnecting with Jeff Kleinman. Many years ago in Charlottesville we learned to project films together. Now he is my agent and head of Folio Literary Management. Who would have guessed? Jeff's patience, insight, acuity, and good humor are boundless, and boy, do I owe him.

For my friends at the University Press of Mississippi, I have nothing but praise and thanks. From the beginning Leila Salisbury made it clear that the press intended to give Gloria the regal treatment—and they have extended it to me, too. The deft guidance provided by Leila and by Valerie Jones and their enthusiasm for this volume has made every bit of the work easier and more rewarding. Film scholar Peter Tonguette was the best copyediting partner I could have hoped for. I am a fan of his work on Orson Welles and eagerly await his new book on Peter Bogdanovich. Anne Stascavage, Courtney McCreary, and Shane Gong Stewart supported the project diligently, and Pete Halverson provided the book's gorgeous design. I could not have landed at a better press or had a happier collaboration.

My nearest and dearest put up with inattention, excuses, and postponed visits, yet never stopped cheering me on. My oldest friends Laureen Fredella and Roberta Albright let me slide. The Dube family sent meals and good wishes while I holed up to write. The extended Welsch clan—including the Hayes family, the Gouldmans, the Rowans, the DeLeos and the Hunts—got used to hearing too much about Gloria Swanson and very little about anything else. My niece Ariel Hayes did lots of heavy lifting during her year in Maine. But my nonagenarian mother Marion Kokoska took the cake: when her daughter finally wrote a book, she finally became a reader. I am so grateful for all their love and support.

My partner Michael Dube listened to every page of this book—often repeatedly. He made too many dinners, saw too many movies alone, and loved me anyway. Thanks, Bub. It means everything to me.

People always ask me how I came to choose Gloria Swanson as a subject, and I have never had a good answer. Sometimes I say I wanted to write about a performer who made the transition to sound, or that Swanson interested me because of her long, varied career in media. Sometimes I say it was because there was such a large archive of her papers to dig through. This is all true, and she has certainly been lively company—peppery, intelligent, restless, demanding, and never, ever dull. Now, however, I believe that somehow—mysteriously—Gloria Swanson chose me. For that, I will always be thankful.

NOTES

Swanson produced many draft versions of her autobiography over many years. There are holographs as well as typescripts, notes, and lists, many annotated in her hand. I have referred to these in the notes as "GS manuscript," indicating when relevant her efforts at revision or deletion. If the manuscripts are named, I have given their names. Swanson also recorded her memories on wire reels in the 1950s; these I have called "wire recordings." In these manuscripts and recordings, Swanson often spoke more candidly and in greater detail than in her published autobiography. These materials are held in the Gloria Swanson Papers at the Harry Ransom Humanities Research Center, University of Texas at Austin (GSP). This collection also has Swanson's correspondence, business records, and thousands of photographs.

References to unpublished manuscripts on specific topics, such as *Beauty Tricks and Truths*, are also from the Gloria Swanson Papers.

The Gloria Swanson Papers includes a massive clippings collection. I have given the fullest citation possible for all clippings found there. The designation "GSP" after a citation to a periodical indicates that it was found in this collection.

Kevin Brownlow's interview with Swanson was done in preparation for the Thames Television 1980 series *Hollywood*.

Material from the author's interviews with Michelle Farmer Amon is indicated.

I consulted the following additional institutions for research material:

British Film Institute Special Collections
Cinémathèque Française
George Eastman House
Kent State University Special Collections
Library of Congress
Margaret Herrick Library, Academy of Motion Picture Arts and Sciences
Museum of American Illustration, New York
Museum of Modern Art
University of California at Los Angeles
Wisconsin Center for Film and Theater Research

ABBREVIATIONS

GSP: Gloria Swanson Papers
SOS: *Swanson on Swanson* (New York: Random House, 1980).
NYT: *New York Times*

CHAPTER 1. GLORY

1. *SOS*, 12.
2. Ibid., 16.
3. Wire recordings.
4. "Memory Snapshots," undated manuscript, GSP.
5. Ibid.
6. Ibid.
7. *Chicago American*, undated, GSP.
8. *Beauty Tricks and Truths*, 5.1, GSP.
9. Ibid.
10. Wire recordings.
11. *Beauty Tricks and Truths*, 5.3, GSP.
12. *SOS*, 19.
13. *Beauty Tricks and Truths*, 5.2, GSP.
14. Wire recordings.
15. Mrs. H. Crampton Jones to GS, January 4, 1983, GSP.
16. Wire recordings.
17. Ibid.
18. *Beauty Tricks and Truths*, 3.2, GSP.
19. Wire recordings.
20. *Beauty Tricks and Truths*, 15.2, GSP.
21. Lincoln School notebook, GSP.
22. Kiehn, *Broncho Billy and the Essanay Film Company*, 150.
23. Card, *Seductive Cinema*, 141. Bushman also claimed he had repeatedly shooed Swanson from the studio gates. Davis, *King of the Movies*, 65.
24. Wire recordings.
25. *SOS*, 28.
26. Ibid., 33.
27. GS manuscript, GSP.
28. Louella Parsons, "In and Out of Focus," *New York Morning Telegraph*, April 16, 1922.
29. Lahue, *World of Laughter*, 30.
30. Wire recordings.
31. George C. Pratt to GS, January 20, 1956, GSP; see also her reply, February 28, 1956.
32. Maturi, *Beverly Bayne, Queen of the Movies*, 7.
33. Wire recordings.
34. Helen Dunbar played in four of Swanson's starring vehicles: *The Great Moment, Beyond the Rocks, The Impossible Mrs. Bellew*, and *Fine Manners*.
35. Bowser, *The Transformation of Cinema 1907–1915*, 179.
36. Lahue, *World of Laughter*, 26.
37. Wagenknecht, *Stars of the Silents*, 95.

38. Arnold, *Lorenzo Goes to Hollywood*, 167.
39. Joyce Milton says Chaplin tested Swanson to please Leona Anderson, his Chicago hostess and the studio founder's wife. Gloria's Aunt Inga was the Andersons' nanny. Milton, *Tramp*, 85.
40. Chaplin, *My Autobiography*, 166.
41. *SOS*, 40–41.
42. Huff, *Charlie Chaplin*, 55.
43. Kobal, *People Will Talk*, 7. Swanson thought she looked less like Chaplin in *Sunset Boulevard* because her face had thinned.
44. Brownlow, *The Parade's Gone By*, 505.
45. Chaplin, *My Autobiography*, 165–66.
46. Louvish, *Keystone*, 100.
47. Wire recordings.
48. Ibid.
49. Kiehn, *Broncho Billy and the Essanay Film Company*, 223.
50. LeRoy, *Mervyn LeRoy: Take One*, 120.
51. Kennedy, *Edmund Goulding's Dark Victory*, 118.
52. Brooks, *Lulu in Hollywood*, 28.
53. GS manuscript, GSP.
54. Wire recordings.
55. Ibid. She also claimed she left Essanay as a result of these remarks.
56. Morley, *Tales from the Hollywood Raj*, 35.
57. *SOS*, 38.

CHAPTER 2. FUNNY GIRL

1. *SOS*, 46.
2. Clarence G. Badger, "Reminiscences of the Early Days of Movie Comedies," *Image* 6 (May 1957), 110. Accounts differ: Beery may already have had a contract with Keystone, possibly contingent on Swanson's being offered one as well.
3. *SOS*, 47.
4. Sennett, *King of Comedy*, 89, 91, 99.
5. Louvish, *Keystone*, 58.
6. *SOS*, 48.
7. Louvish, *Keystone*, 305.
8. *SOS*, 49.
9. Ibid., 54.
10. Paris, *Louise Brooks*, 219.
11. *SOS*, 56–57.
12. Clarence G. Badger, "Reminiscences of the Early Days of Movie Comedies," *Image* 6 (May 1957), 109–10.
13. Watson, *The Keystone Kid*, 107–8.
14. Brownlow interview.
15. Cooper, *Dark Lady of the Silents*, 181.
16. Dale, *Comedy Is a Man in Trouble*, 101–2.
17. Keaton, *My Wonderful World of Slapstick*, 130.
18. *SOS*, 52.

19. Ibid., 53.
20. Ibid.
21. Ibid., 57.
22. Ibid., 59.
23. Ibid., 61.
24. Ibid.
25. Ibid., 62.
26. Sennett remembered paying Beery $50.00 to Swanson's $65.00. Goodman, *The Fifty Year Decline and Fall of Hollywood*, 440.
27. Judy Klemesrud, "Name, Nose, Teeth, Bosom, Hair, Kidneys—Everything But Eyelashes—Is Real," *NYT*, October 10, 1971, 14.
28. *SOS*, 71.
29. Ibid., 74.
30. Harry C. Carr, "An Interview in Great Danish," *Photoplay*, July 1917, 29.
31. *SOS*, 76.
32. Ibid., 77.
33. "Ingenue Peeved Because She is Not a Vampire," February 1917, scrapbook 61, GSP.
34. "Mack Sennett Weekly," March 19, 1917, GSP.
35. Louvish, *Keystone*, 140–41.
36. Swanson made a single short, *Baseball Madness*, at Universal-Victor in 1917.
37. Brownlow interview.
38. GS manuscript.
39. Brownlow interview.
40. Mack Sennett, "The Psychology of Film Comedy," *Motion Picture Classic*, November 1918, 70.
41. *SOS*, 79. Elsewhere she said Sennett "got angry and tore up my contract." GS to George C. Pratt, February 28, 1956, GSP.
42. Sennett, *King of Comedy*, 134.

CHAPTER 3. TRIANGLE

1. GS manuscript.
2. Triangle was founded to capitalize on the talents of D. W. Griffith, Thomas Ince, and Mack Sennett. Sennett operated Keystone as an independent venture during Swanson's tenure there.
3. *SOS*, 87.
4. Ibid., 86.
5. Mann, *Wisecracker*, 92.
6. *SOS*, 85–86.
7. Ibid., 85.
8. *Motion Picture Classic*, March 1918.
9. Scrapbook 79, GSP.
10. Triangle press sheet, GSP.
11. Triangle Collection, Cinémathèque Française.
12. *Station Content* publicity report, Triangle Collection, Cinémathèque Française.
13. *SOS*, 96.
14. Ankerich, *The Sound of Silence*, 63.

15. *SOS*, 93.

16. Ibid.

17. Ibid.

18. Brownlow interview.

19. Pickford, *Sunshine and Shadow*, 104.

20. *SOS*, 92.

21. Brownlow, *The War, the West, and the Wilderness*, 131.

22. Triangle press sheet, GSP.

23. Ibid.

24. *SOS*, 97.

25. Wire recordings.

26. *SOS*, 90.

27. Wire recordings.

28. *SOS*, 52–53.

29. Ibid., 98.

30. Ibid.

31. Studio synopsis, Triangle Collection, Cinémathèque Française.

32. Reviewing Board report, June 21, 1918, Triangle Collection, Cinémathèque Française.

33. GS manuscript. She recalls her Triangle stay as a bit longer than it was.

CHAPTER 4. THE LIONS' DEN

1. Swanson's first day of work at FPL was November 7, 1918, the day the "false armistice" was declared. Four days later the war was officially over.

2. Koury, *Yes, Mr. DeMille*, 204.

3. Wire recordings.

4. DeMille, *Autobiography*, 212.

5. "Don't Change Your Husband," *Motion Picture Magazine*, May 1919.

6. *SOS*, 101.

7. Ibid., 102.

8. Ibid.

9. Birchard, *Cecil B. DeMille's Hollywood*, 138.

10. "Why Gloria Swanson is Always Broke," *Theatre Magazine* 219 (May 1919), 304.

11. MacCann, *Films of the 1920s*, 24.

12. Kobal, *People Will Talk*, 31.

13. *SOS*, 104–5.

14. Fritzi Remont, "Diving Into Drama," *Motion Picture Magazine*, December 1918, 103.

15. *SOS*, 111.

16. Dick Hyland, "Won By a Nose," *Photoplay*, November 1928, 59.

17. DeMille, *Autobiography*, 222.

18. McCandless, *New York to Hollywood*, 48.

19. Essoe, *DeMille: The Man and His Pictures*, 66.

20. Brownlow interview.

21. Koury, *Yes, Mr. DeMille*, 201.

22. *SOS*, 117.

23. Marsh, *Screen Acting*, 105.

24. Higham, *Cecil B. DeMille*, 73.

25. Brownlow interview.
26. It was the first effort of Mitchell Leisen, who designed costumes, then assisted DeMille before becoming a director himself.
27. Wire recordings.
28. Ibid. Wilson joined Swanson on some of the recordings.
29. Ibid.
30. Kobal, *The Art of the Great Hollywood Portrait Photographers*, 76.
31. Wire recordings.
32. Brownlow interview.
33. Wire recordings.
34. *SOS*, 122.
35. Brownlow interview.
36. *SOS*, 124.
37. Ibid., 135.
38. GS manuscript.
39. *SOS*, 140.
40. Ibid., 137.
41. Ibid.
42. Ibid., 139.
43. Wire recordings.
44. *SOS*, 139–40.

CHAPTER 5. IN THE FAMILY WAY

1. Julian Johnson, *"Male and Female,"* Photoplay, December 1919, 72.
2. Hampton, *History of the American Film Industry From Its Beginnings to 1931*, 220–22.
3. GS manuscript.
4. Elizabeth Peltret, "Gloria Swanson Talks on Divorce," *Motion Picture Magazine*, December 1919, 74.
5. GS manuscript.
6. *Cincinnati Tribune*, November 9, 1919, GSP.
7. *New York Journal American*, November 21, 1919, GSP.
8. *Los Angeles Times*, November 1, 1919, GSP.
9. GS manuscript.
10. Moore, *Silent Star*, 109.
11. *Los Angeles Leader*, October 10, 1920; scrapbook 61, GSP. See also "Gloria Swanson Tries the Simple Life," *Motion Picture Classic*, September 1918, 51.
12. Clipping, scrapbook 61, GSP.
13. "Miss Swanson to Wed," *Los Angeles Times*, November 1, 1919.
14. Delight Evans, "Don't Change Your Coiffure," *Photoplay*, August 1919, 74.
15. Wire recordings.
16. Delson, *Dudley Murphy*, 11.
17. Hazel Simpson Naylor, "Piloting a Dream Craft," *Motion Picture Magazine*, April 1921, 87.
18. "Miss Swanson to Wed," *Los Angeles Times*, November 1, 1919.
19. GS to Herbert Somborn, undated, GSP.
20. Wire recordings.

21. GS to Herbert Somborn, undated, GSP.

22. Herbert Somborn to Equity management, December 31, 1919, GSP.

23. Wire recordings.

24. Drew, *Speaking of Silents*, 120.

25. *SOS*, 145.

26. DeMille, *Autobiography*, 220.

27. Birchard, *Cecil B. DeMille's Hollywood*, 150.

28. Ibid.

29. "Why Change Your Wife?" *Motion Picture Magazine*, July 1920.

30. Adela Rogers St. Johns, "What Does Marriage Mean?" *Photoplay*, December 1920, 28–31.

31. Koury, *Yes, Mr. DeMille*, 79–80.

32. Wire recordings.

33. Graham, *Hollywood Revisited*, 84.

34. Bickford, *Bulls, Balls, Bicycles and Actors*, 169.

35. Agnes de Mille, *Portrait Gallery*, 181.

36. Wire recordings.

37. Edwards, *The DeMilles*, 86.

38. Mandelbaum, *Screen Deco*, 37.

39. Birchard, *Cecil B. DeMille's Hollywood*, 157.

40. "The Screen," *NYT*, October 18, 1920, 21.

41. Wire recordings.

42. Ibid.

43. *Parkinson* television program, December 2, 1978, videocassette at British Film Institute.

44. Ankerich, *The Sound of Silence*, 86.

45. Windeler, *Sweetheart*, x.

46. *Parkinson* television program, December 2, 1978, videocassette at British Film Institute.

47. *SOS*, 149–50.

48. Ibid., 147.

49. Ibid., 148.

50. Ibid., 153.

51. Ibid., 154.

52. Scrapbook 60C, GSP.

53. Higham, *Cecil B. DeMille*, 84.

54. "Abolish Film Star System," *NYT*, October 31, 1920, 22.

55. "The Screen," *NYT*, September 21, 1921, 20.

56. *Parkinson* television program, December 2, 1978, videocassette at British Film Institute.

57. Wire recordings.

CHAPTER 6. THE GREAT MOMENT

1. Card, *Seductive Cinema*, 202.

2. Glyn, *Three Weeks*, 165–66.

3. Lasky, *Whatever Happened to Hollywood?* 56.

4. Scott, *Hollywood When Silents Were Golden*, 57.

5. Cecil Beaton, "The World of Elinor Glyn," *Times (London)*, October 26, 1974, 8.

6. *SOS*, 159.

7. Slide, *They Also Wrote for the Fan Magazines*, 72. Glyn conceded, "The public adore her. She has a 'sex charm' which attracts the men." Etherington-Smith, *The 'It' Girls*, 223.

8. Etherington-Smith, *The 'It' Girls*, 218.

9. "Filmdom with Elinor Glyn," GSP.

10. Kobal, *People Will Talk*, 611.

11. Mortimer Raymond, "A Review," *New Statesman* 21 (May 1923), 144.

12. Chaplin, *Autobiography*, 203.

13. Cal York, *Photoplay*, May 1921, GSP.

14. *SOS*, 162.

15. Windeler, *Sweetheart*, 102.

16. *SOS*, 165.

17. Ibid., 164.

18. Wire recordings.

19. *Movieland* (c. 1949), GSP.

20. Brownlow, *The Parade's Gone By*, 422.

21. Moore, *Silent Star*, 100.

22. Ibid., 101.

23. Wire recordings.

24. Adele Whitely Fletcher, "Instead of the Silken Gloria," *Motion Picture Magazine*, December 1921, 29.

25. *St. Louis Star*, October 5, 1921, GSP.

26. Cal York, "Plays and Players," *Photoplay*, October 1922, 65.

27. *SOS*, 155.

28. Butters, *Banned in Kansas*, 141–42.

29. Hays, *Memoirs*, 357–58.

30. Statement of Mary Miles Minter to District Attorney, February 7, 1922, 16.

31. Minter statement, 8–9, 11, 33. Even the news reports did not take Neilan seriously as a beau. See Long, *William Desmond Taylor*, 431.

32. *SOS*, 168.

33. Higham, *In and Out of Hollywood*, 133.

34. *Parkinson* television program, December 2, 1978, videocassette at British Film Institute.

35. Wire recordings.

CHAPTER 7. HER GILDED CAGE

1. *SOS*, 192.

2. Zukor, *The Public Is Never Wrong*, 207.

3. Wire recordings.

4. Glyn, *Romantic Adventure*, 300.

5. *SOS*, 174.

6. Louella Parsons, "In and Out of Focus," *New York Morning Telegraph*, April 16, 1922.

7. Wire recordings.

8. Ibid.

9. Loos, *The Talmadge Girls*, 84–86.

10. Wire recordings.

11. Ibid.

12. *SOS*, 176–77.

13. Ibid., 179–80.

14. Wire recordings.

15. Ibid.

16. Ibid.

17. Moore, *Silent Star*, 103.

18. Wire recordings.

19. *Philadelphia Public Ledger*, December 3, 1922, GSP.

20. *Motion Picture Chronicle*, December 6, 1922, GSP.

21. Rosenberg, *The Real Tinsel*, 179.

22. *Richmond (VA) News Leader*, October 11, 1922, GSP.

23. "Movies Classified in Brutal Fashion," *New York Sun*, December 28, 1922, GSP.

24. *SOS*, 182.

25. GS manuscript.

26. *SOS*, 182.

27. Wire recordings.

28. Ibid.

29. "GS Adopts Boy," *Los Angeles Times*, October 9, 1922, GSP.

30. "GS Tells of Greatest Thrill in Career," unnamed clipping, December 6, 1922, GSP.

31. Wanamaker, *Early Beverly Hills*, 65.

32. Wire recordings.

33. Blesh, *Keaton*, 239.

34. Ibid., 183.

35. Menjou, *It Took Nine Tailors*, 85.

36. Moore, *Silent Star*, 155.

37. Unnamed clipping, December 14, 1922, GSP.

38. *Baltimore Morning Herald*, July 7, 1923, 5, GSP.

39. *Mercury (Hobart, Tasmania)*, September 3, 1923, 8, GSP.

40. GS, forward to movie edition of *Prodigal Daughters*, January 1923.

41. Kanfer, *Groucho*, 195.

42. *San Fernando (CA) Democrat*, December 24, 1922, GSP.

43. Brownlow interview.

44. *Marion (IN) Leader-Tribune*, October 1, 1922, GSP.

45. Unnamed clipping, January 1, 1922, GSP.

46. Alan Dale, "My American Wife," *New York American*, January 1, 1923, GSP.

47. *Wausau (WI) Record-Herald*, October 27, 1922, GSP.

48. L. L. Clement, "Under the Lash," *Tacoma (WA) Ledger*, May 8, 1922, GSP.

49. GS holograph manuscript.

50. Wire recordings.

51. Ibid.

52. Ibid.

53. Ibid.

54. Ibid.

55. *SOS*, 188.

56. Ibid., 189.
57. Wire recordings.
58. *SOS*, 189.
59. Ibid., 190.
60. Ibid.
61. Wire recordings.
62. GS manuscript.
63. Ibid., GSP.
64. *SOS*, 191.
65. Lasky, *I Blow My Own Horn*, 166.

CHAPTER 8. EAST COASTER

1. Swanson claimed she approached Wanger, but he was working in Britain at the time. Wanger returned to Astoria in June 1924.
2. *Zaza* was a Belasco-adapted French play which Paramount had already made in 1915 with Pauline Frederick. It had also been a Leoncavallo opera, sung by Geraldine Farrar at the Met the same year.
3. Adela Rogers St. Johns, "Artistic Efficiency—That's Dwan," *Photoplay*, August 1920, 57, 109.
4. Bogdanovich, *Allan Dwan*, 70.
5. Brownlow interview.
6. Wire recordings.
7. "Tear Fatigue Newest Movie Ailment," *Oakland (CA) Tribune*, October 1, 1922, GSP.
8. *Record*, September 27, 1923, GSP.
9. *SOS*, 199.
10. The house was so cold that the family moved out early. She sued Schenck to recover her rent payment. "Gloria Swanson Sues," *NYT*, September 4, 1924, 40.
11. *SOS*, 198.
12. Ibid., 199.
13. Ibid., 198.
14. Ibid., 196.
15. Koszarski, *Hollywood on the Hudson*, 40.
16. *SOS*, 196.
17. Brownlow, *The Parade's Gone By*, 104.
18. Fritzi Remont, "The Delightful Contradictions of Gloria," *Motion Picture Classic*, July 1919, 74.
19. Marjory L. Adams, "Something Besides Clothes to Gloria Swanson," *Boston Daily Globe*, July 15, 1923, 24.
20. Wire recordings.
21. *SOS*, 200.
22. Wire recordings.
23. *SOS*, 201–2.
24. Ibid., 201.
25. When Swanson moved to the Park Chambers Hotel at Sixth Avenue and Fifty-Eighth Street, so did the salon.
26. Steichen, *A Life in Photography*, unpaged.

27. *SOS*, 201.

28. Wire recordings.

29. Ibid.

30. Ethel Barrymore originated the role on Broadway as *The Laughing Lady*; the *Times* declared Swanson's version "an evening of delight." "The Screen," *NYT*, March 10, 1924, 18.

31. GS manuscript.

32. *SOS*, 212.

33. Wire recordings.

34. *SOS*, 213.

35. Adela Rogers St. Johns, "Gloria! An Impression," *Photoplay*, September 1923, 105.

36. Wire recordings.

37. *SOS*, 204.

38. Ibid., 205.

39. Wire recordings.

40. *SOS*, 209.

41. Bogdanovich, *Allan Dwan*, 70.

42. Ibid., 71.

43. Ibid., 75. Dwan could be tough on actors: for a scene in *A Society Scandal*, he made Ricardo Cortez drink real brandy. Cortez kept making mistakes, requiring take after take, finally becoming so inebriated that Dwan put him to bed on set. Cortez awoke at four in the morning, trapped among the equipment and props in the pitch black. "After that," said Dwan, "he . . . did everything right the first time." Ibid., 70.

44. "A Shopgirl's Romance," *NYT*, July 29, 1924, 9.

45. "Manhandled," *Movie Weekly*, August 23, 1924.

46. Nonetheless, Paramount stuck to a safe line of advertising, claiming the reasons to see "Gloria's Greatest" were "More drama! More gowns! More zip! More fun! More pep!" *Manhandled* movie herald, author's collection.

47. *SOS*, 196.

48. Wire recordings.

49. Mordaunt Hall, "The Screen: Princess Swanson," *NYT*, October 7, 1924, 26.

50. *SOS*, 277.

51. He was more likely a tinsmith or a furrier. Negri was raised in poverty in the Warsaw ghetto after her father was arrested for anti-Czarist activities.

52. Joseph Jefferson O'Neill, "Charlie and Pola Will Have World's Best Wishes When Knot is Tied," *Boston Daily Globe*, February 4, 1923, A1.

53. Carr, *Four Fabulous Faces*, 50.

54. *SOS*, 186.

55. Negri, *Memoirs of a Star*, 214.

56. Ibid., 228.

57. Chaplin, *Autobiography*, 300. Negri was also suffering from the (almost immediate) backlash against foreign talent. The fight with Swanson disguised the hostility some felt for Pola as part of the "foreign legion" invading Hollywood.

58. Cooper, *Dark Lady of the Silents*, 212.

59. Zukor, *The Public Is Never Wrong*, 6, 221.

60. In truth, Negri was disgusted pretty quickly with the way films were made in Hollywood and, like Swanson, agitated for better collaborators and better projects.

61. Zukor, *The Public Is Never Wrong*, 226.
62. Christopher Dodd, "Mother's Boy and Children's Friend," *Independent Rowing News*, May 23, 1988, 8.
63. Wire recordings.
64. *SOS*, 218.

CHAPTER 9. FRENCH IDYLL

1. Terry Ramsaye called this "a scheme of star transplantation." Ramsaye, *A Million and One Nights*, 824.
2. Zukor, *The Public Is Always Right*, 226.
3. Wire recordings.
4. Mordaunt Hall, "Fine Opportunity Missed in Foreign Legion Film," *NYT*, November 30, 1924, X5; Mordaunt Hall, "The Screen," *NYT*, November 24, 1924, 15.
5. GS manuscript.
6. By 1925 *Madame Sans-Gêne* had already had a long life. The 1893 Sardou play toured France, the US, and England to acclaim, then appeared as a novel in 1898. Toscanini conducted Geraldine Farrar in a 1915 opera version. Two French films had already been made (in 1900 and 1911), both starring Réjane, who had originated the role. After Swanson's version, the film was remade another three times in the US, Argentina, and France.
7. Abel, *The Ciné Goes to Town*, 419.
8. Ramsaye claimed Allan Dwan was slated to direct, but the French demanded "a native director." *A Million and One Nights*, 825.
9. Wire recordings.
10. Ibid.
11. Ibid.
12. Abel, *French Cinema*, 30.
13. André Daven to GS, undated, GSP.
14. Wire recordings.
15. Ibid. There was considerable resistance to allowing American companies to produce and distribute uniquely French stories, even with French casts and crews. See Abel, *French Cinema*, 28.
16. *SOS*, 223.
17. Wire recordings.
18. Ibid.
19. Ibid.
20. *SOS*, 227.
21. The Belgian government thanked Swanson by naming a ward in the hospital at Woluwe-Saint-Pierre for her. "Belgians Honor Swanson," *Moving Picture World*, November 22, 1924, 310.
22. *SOS*, 229–30.
23. Wire recordings.
24. André Daven to GS, undated, GSP.
25. Wire recordings.
26. André Daven to GS, undated, GSP.
27. Wire recordings.

28. *SOS*, 230.

29. Ibid., 238.

30. Ibid.

31. Wire recordings.

32. *SOS*, 230.

33. Clement Douglas, "Gloria Swanson, America's Own Marquise," *Motion Picture Classic*, May 1925, 94.

34. *SOS*, 233.

35. Ibid., 233–34.

36. Wire recordings.

37. *SOS*, 242.

38. Wire recordings.

39. Ibid.

40. André Daven to GS, undated, GSP.

41. Wire recordings.

42. Ibid.

43. *SOS*, 519.

CHAPTER 10. AMERICAN ROYALTY

1. *SOS*, 243.

2. Fan mail, GSP.

3. See "Gloria Swanson Under Knife in Paris Hospital," *Chicago Tribune*, February 19, 1925; "Gloria Swanson Recovering," *Moving Picture World*, March 7, 1925, 38; "2 Liners Due Today; 2 Going to Europe," *NYT*, March 24, 1925, 30.

4. Wire recordings.

5. Brownlow interview.

6. A. Chester Keel, "What Next Gloria?" *Photoplay*, April 1925, 32.

7. James R. Quirk, "Everybody Calls Him 'Henry,'" *Photoplay*, June 1925, 35.

8. Ibid., 34.

9. "The Talk of the Town," *New Yorker*, April 11, 1925, 4.

10. Lasky, *I Blow My Own Horn*, 191.

11. *SOS*, 7.

12. Ibid., 5.

13. GS, "My Most Wonderful Experience," annotated manuscript for 1950 *Photoplay* essay, GSP.

14. Wire recordings.

15. Ibid.

16. Carr, *Four Fabulous Faces*, 54.

17. Wire recordings.

18. Lasky, *I Blow My Own Horn*, 192.

19. *SOS*, 7.

20. Adela Rogers St. Johns, "Hollywood's First Nights," *Photoplay*, July 1925, 29.

21. Zukor, *The Public Is Never Wrong*, 229.

22. "The Talk of the Town," *New Yorker*, April 11, 1925, 4.

23. "The Talk of the Town," *New Yorker*, March 3, 1934, 14.

24. Kobal, *People Will Talk*, 3.

25. This was already a Hollywood chestnut when it appeared in *Time* magazine in 1941. "The New Pictures," September 29, 1941, 85.

26. Wire recordings.

27. *SOS*, 245.

28. Zukor, 230.

29. Adela Rogers St. Johns, "Hollywood's First Nights," *Photoplay*, July 1925, 28.

30. *SOS*, 8.

31. Steen, *Hollywood Speaks*, 249.

32. GS, "My Most Wonderful Experience," annotated manuscript for 1950 *Photoplay* essay, GSP.

33. *SOS*, 10.

34. GS, "My Most Wonderful Experience," annotated manuscript for 1950 *Photoplay* essay, GSP

35. Moore, *Silent Star*, 106.

36. Adela Rogers St. Johns, "Mack Sennett's Glamour Girls," *American Weekly*, November 21, 1948, unpaged.

37. Swanson repeatedly invoked these figures to describe the emotions provoked by her return.

38. *SOS*, 11.

39. Wire recordings.

40. Griffith, *The Movie Stars*, 68.

41. Wire recordings.

42. Kobal, *People Will Talk*, 20.

43. Bogdanovich, *Allan Dwan*, 77–78.

44. Balio, *United Artists*, 14.

45. "Gloria Plans Her Future," *Movie Magazine*, October 1925, 42. The French release contained more historical episodes; American audiences were perceived as "restless" during these parts. *SOS*, 269.

46. *Movie Weekly* published the name of Joseph's biological mother as Mrs. Mary Smith. June 6, 1925, 36.

47. Mordaunt Hall, "Charming View of France in 'Madame Sans Gene,'" *NYT*, April 26, 1925, X5.

48. *SOS*, 265.

49. Ibid., 269–71.

50. Lasky, *I Blow My Own Horn*, 191–92.

51. *SOS*, 273.

52. Lasky, *I Blow My Own Horn*, 191–92.

53. *SOS*, 273.

54. "Gloria Swanson and the Filming of 'Stage Struck,'" *Wetzel (WV) Democrat*, August 21, 1925. Web.

55. *Stage Struck* was the first commercial film produced in West Virginia.

56. *SOS*, 274.

57. Bogdanovich, *Allan Dwan*, 78.

58. *SOS*, 275.

59. "Gloria Swanson and the Filming of 'Stage Struck,'" *Wetzel (WV) Democrat*, August 21, 1925. Web.

60. Edmonds, *Hot Toddy*, 70–73.

61. Both matters dragged on. After a jury deadlocked on the process server's suit, Swanson settled with him.

62. *SOS*, 277.

63. André Daven to GS, undated, GSP.

64. "Marquis Defends Right to a Title," *NYT*, October 7, 1925, 8.

65. *SOS*, 279.

66. Ibid., 280.

67. Mann, *Kate*, 82.

68. *Photoplay* said the film had three directors. Cal York, "Studio News and Gossip East and West," *Photoplay*, September 1926, 102, 106.

69. *SOS*, 281.

CHAPTER 11. DECLARATION OF INDEPENDENCE

1. "The Talk of the Town," *New Yorker*, March 20, 1926, 13.

2. GS manuscript.

3. "As We Go to Press," *Photoplay*, July 1926, 76. The masked ball sequence was slyly said to have been "four months in the making." Cal York, "Studio News and Gossip East and West," *Photoplay*, September 1926, 106.

4. *SOS*, 281.

5. Ibid., 282.

6. GS manuscript.

7. Joe Schenck to GS, June 22, 1926, GSP.

8. GS to Hiram Abrams, June 24, 1926, GSP.

9. GS to C. B. DeMille, June 9, 1926, GSP.

10. GS to C. B. DeMille, June 22, 1926, GSP.

11. Joe Schenck to Bertram Nayfack, July 13, 1926, GSP. Schenck wanted to avoid "high production costs" on "a sans gene or something similar."

12. GS to C. B. DeMille, July 9, 1926, GSP.

13. *SOS*, 283.

14. GS manuscript.

15. Cal York, "Studio News & Gossip—East and West," *Photoplay*, October 1926, 94.

16. Henri de la Falaise to GS, undated (c. 1925), GSP.

17. Gloria Swanson, "What My Experiences Have Taught Me: The Star Talks Frankly," *Motion Picture Classic*, July 1926, 87.

18. Cal York, "Studio News & Gossip—East and West," *Photoplay*, November 1926, 119.

19. *SOS*, 286.

20. Though Roxy paid $50,000 to show *Sunya* on opening night, he lacked the purchasing power of the major studios and might have preferred Fritz Lang's *Metropolis*. Melnick, *American Showman*, 273.

21. *Potemkin* officially premiered at the Biltmore Theater on December 5, 1926, after censors examined it for several weeks.

22. According to Murphy's biographer, "If Murphy needed confirmation that Hollywood had no idea what to make of *Ballet mécanique*, he got it [in *The Love of Sunya*]." Delson, *Dudley Murphy*, 11.

23. *Sunya* was not Boles's first picture. He had two small parts for M-G-M before returning to New York and the stage.

24. GS manuscript.

25. Ibid.

26. *SOS*, 293.

27. Seabury, *The Public and the Motion Picture Industry*, 60.

28. *SOS*, 287.

29. Contract between Gloria Swanson Productions and Harold Flammer, Inc., December 22, 1926, GSP.

30. Citing this sequence, Brownlow observes that images of the poor "were shown less and less during the twenties." *Behind the Mask of Innocence*, 290.

31. *SOS*, 287.

32. GS manuscript.

33. "The Skyline," *New Yorker*, March 19, 1927, 75–76.

34. "A Trip Through the New Roxy Theatre," *NYT*, February 27, 1927, X7.

35. "The Love of Sunya," *Picture Play Magazine*, June 1927, unpaged.

36. Mordaunt Hall, "Gloria Swanson's Picture," *NYT*, March 20, 1927, X7.

37. "The Love of Sunya," *Picture Play Magazine*, June 1927, unpaged.

38. Harriette Underhill, *New York Herald Tribune*, GSP.

39. Griffith, *The Movie Stars*, 177.

CHAPTER 12. LET IT RAIN

1. I. S. Horne (Horne's Zoological Arena) to GS, March 18, 1927, GSP.

2. Josef von Sternberg directed Marlene Dietrich in a version called *The Devil is a Woman* (1935).

3. Lance Heath to Bruce Gallup, May 5, 1927, GSP.

4. "The Don'ts and Be Carefuls," in Vieira, *Sin in Soft Focus*, 214.

5. *SOS*, 298.

6. Ibid., 302.

7. "The Talk of the Town," *New Yorker*, March 17, 1928, 17.

8. The owners wanted $100,000, but Revnes convinced them that "there was not a chance on earth of one of the big producers making [the picture]." Maurice Revnes to GS, May 16, 1927, GSP.

9. Tom Moore to William Weaver, June 4, 1927, GSP.

10. Lance Heath to Bruce Gallup, May 26, 1927, GSP.

11. The Swanson Producing Corporation became Gloria Swanson Productions in February 1927.

12. *SOS*, 298.

13. Letter to Joe Schenck, June 10, 1927, GSP.

14. *SOS*, 307.

15. Will Hays to Joe Schenck, June 11, 1927, GSP.

16. GS letter, June 13, 1927, GSP. Copies went to William Fox, Winfield Sheehan, Abe Warner, J. J. Murdock, Marcus Loew, J. Robert Rubin, Robert Cochrane, Joe Kennedy, Sam Katz, Sidney Kent, Adolph Zukor, Jesse Lasky, John McGuirk, Sam Spring, and Richard Rowland.

17. Somerset Maugham to GS, July 30, 1927, GSP.

18. *SOS*, 318.

19. Tom Moore to Pierre Bedard, June 30, 1927, GSP.

20. Tom Moore to Pierre Bedard, August 24, 1927, GSP.

21. Pierre Bedard to Claude Parker, August 10, 1927, GSP.

22. Pierre Bedard to Tom Moore, July 26, 1927, GSP.

23. See Pierre Bedard to Grace Crossman, May 12, 1927, GSP.

24. Maurice Revnes to GS, June 16, 1927, GSP.

25. Pierre Bedard to Tom Moore, July 5, 1927, GSP. Bedard asked Louella Parsons for a retraction, saying Revnes had been hired "temporarily without title or authority." Pierre Bedard to Louella Parsons, July 1, 1927, GSP.

26. Charles Durning, "The Gate Women Don't Crash," *Liberty*, May 14, 1927, 31, 33.

27. *SOS*, 314.

28. Ibid., 316.

29. Ibid., 317.

30. Ibid.

31. Barrymore, *We Barrymores*, 182–83.

32. GS to Tom Moore, July 7, 1927, GSP.

33. Stevens, *Conversations*, 24.

34. GS to Tom Moore, July 7, 1927, GSP.

35. Pierre Bedard to Tom Moore, July 5, 1927, GSP.

36. Pierre Bedard to Tom Moore, July 26, 1927, GSP.

37. Stevens, *Actorviews*, 67. Swanson compared playing opposite Barrymore and Walsh to playing tennis: "The better your opponent or your partner is, the better you will play." *SOS*, 318.

38. *SOS*, 321.

39. *Sadie Thompson* script, GSP.

40. Walsh, *Each Man in His Time*, 206–7.

41. Ibid., 178, 202.

42. Cooper, *Dark Lady of the Silents*, 228.

43. F. Vance de Revere, "How Will Gloria's Marriage End?" *Motion Picture Classic*, November 1925, 25, 84–85.

44. *SOS*, 319–20.

45. Walsh, *Each Man in His Time*, 202, 205, 208.

46. Allan Dwan appraised one of Henri's stories as "very amusing but too short." Dwan, March 29, 1927, GSP.

47. "Sees Her Husband Off," *NYT*, August 15, 1927, 21.

48. "Ile de France Sails; Visitors Delay Her," *NYT*, August 21, 1927, 14.

49. Henri de la Falaise to GS, August 15, 1927, GSP.

50. Henri de la Falaise to GS, August 16, 1927, GSP.

51. GS manuscript.

52. Pierre Bedard to Tom Moore, August 27, 1927, GSP.

53. GS manuscript.

54. Three cameramen received credit on the picture: Barnes, Marsh, and Robert Kurrle. Swanson sent effusive personal thanks to both Kurrle and Marsh, adding a personal check for $500 to Marsh.

55. *SOS*, 322.

56. GS to Al Lichtman, UA sales director, September 10, 1927, GSP.

57. GS to Tom Moore, September 10, 1927, GSP.

58. Arthur Kelly, executive in charge of foreign distribution for UA, to Pierre Bedard, September 13, 1927, GSP.

59. Joe Schenck to GS, September 14, 1927, GSP.

60. Tom Moore to Pierre Bedard, September 17, 1927, GSP.

61. Tom Moore to GS, September 15, 1927, GSP.

62. Tom Moore to GS, August 31, 1927, GSP.

63. Decision of the Board of Censors of the Irish Free State, August 1927, GSP.

64. Arthur Kelly to Pierre Bedard, September 9, 1927, GSP.

65. Arthur Kelly to Pierre Bedard, September 12, 1927, GSP.

66. Dorothy Herzog, "Swanson Now Producer as Well as Star," *New York Daily Mirror*, GSP.

67. Joe Schenck to GS, September 15, 1927, GSP.

68. Pierre Bedard to André Daven, April 8, 1927, GSP.

69. Sennett, *King of Comedy*, 58.

70. Pickford, *Sunshine and Shadow*, 152.

71. Joe Schenck to GS, September 15, 1927, GSP.

72. GS to Joe Schenck, September 15, 1927, GSP.

73. Pickford, *Sunshine and Shadow*, 152.

74. Windeler, *Sweetheart*, 151–52.

75. Eyman, *Mary Pickford, America's Sweetheart*, 147.

76. Windeler, *Sweetheart*, 111. Windeler acknowledged "some personal friction with Mary" when Swanson joined UA. Windeler, 151.

77. Elinor Glyn to GS, October 1, 1927, GSP.

78. "As We Go to Press," *Photoplay*, March 1927, 6.

79. Mann, *Wisecracker*, 135.

80. GS to Joe Schenck, October 11, 1927, GSP.

81. Joe Schenck to GS, September 16, 1927, GSP.

82. Joe Schenck to GS, October 12, 1927, GSP.

83. Preview cards for *Sadie Thompson*, GSP.

84. GS to Pierre Bedard, November 13, 1927; November 17, 1927, GSP.

85. Pierre Bedard to GS, November 16, 1927, GSP.

86. Grace Crossman to Tom Moore, November 22, 1927; Grace Crossman to Pierre Bedard, November 22, 1927, GSP.

87. Henri de la Falaise to GS, September 12, 1927, GSP.

88. Tom Moore to Milton Cohen, December 29, 1927, GSP.

89. Ibid.

90. Grace Crossman to GS, December 30, 1927, GSP.

CHAPTER 13. THE SWAMP

1. *SOS*, 327.

2. Ibid., 330.

3. Ibid., 331.

4. Robert Kane to Joseph P. Kennedy, November 7, 1927, Smith, *Hostage to Fortune*, 61.

5. Joseph P. Kennedy to Robert Kane, November 15, 1927, Smith, *Hostage to Fortune*, 68.

6. *SOS*, 333.

7. Kennedy, *The Story of the Films*, 16.

8. GS Kennedy holograph.

9. Ibid.

10. *SOS*, 340.

11. Ibid., 341.

12. Joseph Kennedy to Milton Cohen, December 20, 1927, Smith, *Hostage to Fortune*, 69.

13. *SOS*, 341.

14. GS Kennedy holograph.

15. *SOS*, 342.

16. GS Kennedy holograph.

17. Lasky, *RKO*, 15.

18. GS Kennedy holograph. Others say Moore procured women for Joe and later for Jack Kennedy. See Hamilton, *JFK: Reckless Youth*, 116, 166.

19. E. B. Derr to Pat Sullivan, January 25, 1928, GSP.

20. Pat Sullivan to E. B. Derr, January 25, 1928, GSP. They also called Kennedy "Big Boy."

21. Milton Cohen to GS, January 25, 1928, GSP.

22. *SOS*, 350.

23. Pierre Bedard to GS, February 28, 1928, Goodwin, *The Fitzgeralds and the Kennedys*, 388.

24. Gilbert, *American Vaudeville*, 394. Gilbert claims Kennedy "double-crossed" Albee in his purchase of the company.

25. Interview with Ken Murray in Wagner, *You Must Remember This*, 177–78.

26. *SOS*, 355.

27. GS Kennedy holograph.

28. *SOS*, 351.

29. Ibid., 353.

30. Ibid., 356–57.

31. GS Kennedy holograph.

32. "Liner Paris Docks Half a Day Early," *NYT*, April 18, 1928, 25.

33. Marx, *Mayer and Thalberg*, 74.

34. Bazin, *What is Cinema?* 27.

35. Harry Carr, "Hollywood's One Real Genius—'Von,'" *Photoplay*, May 1928, 138.

36. *SOS*, 345.

37. Harry Carr, "Hollywood's One Real Genius—'Von,'" *Photoplay*, May 1928, 39.

38. *SOS*, 347.

39. Kennedy was also talking with Cecil DeMille while they negotiated with Stroheim.

40. GS Kennedy holograph.

41. Mordaunt Hall, "Miss Thompson's Shadow," *NYT*, February 12, 1928, 115.

42. Nelson B. Bell, "Columbia," *Washington Post*, January 9, 1928, 16.

43. *Screenland*, May 1928, GSP.

44. Brentano's receipt dated May 17, 1928, in Goodwin, *The Fitzgeralds and the Kennedys*, 393.

45. *SOS*, 367.

46. Goodwin, *The Fitzgeralds and the Kennedys*, 393; Leamer, *The Kennedy Women*, 175.

47. Goodwin, *The Fitzgeralds and the Kennedys*, 393.

48. Ibid., 395.

49. Joseph P. Kennedy to Henri de la Falaise, March 3, 1928, in Smith, *Hostage to Fortune*, 70.

50. *SOS*, 362–63.

51. GS Kennedy holograph.

52. "Miss Swanson's New Role," *NYT*, January 27, 1929, X8.

53. Louis B. Mayer to Joseph P. Kennedy, May 25, 1928, Smith, *Hostage to Fortune*, 62.

54. Irving Wakoff to Grace Crossman, June 9, 1928, GSP.

55. GS Kennedy holograph.

56. Windeler, *Sweetheart*, 144, 147.

57. Adelaide Woodruff to GS, August 4, 1928, GSP.

58. GS manuscript.

59. Stroheim's biographer claims this was intended as "a parody of Hollywood 'style.'" Curtiss, *Von Stroheim*, 246.

60. *SOS*, 358.

61. Robert E. Sherwood, "The Silent Drama," *Life*, January 1, 1925, 24.

62. GS Kennedy holograph.

63. "Sound and Garments," *NYT*, September 9, 1928, 115.

64. E. B. Derr to Lance Heath, August 22, 1928, GSP.

65. Noble, *Hollywood Scapegoat*, 79.

66. The contract, dated October 20, 1928, is held at the Cinémathèque Française.

67. *SOS*, 366.

68. Ibid., 368. Rose Kennedy remembered that Gloria was their houseguest. See Kennedy, *Times to Remember*, 117; Madsen, *Gloria and Joe*, 212–13.

69. *SOS*, 366. Madsen reports without attribution the rumor that Kennedy did impregnate Swanson and that she had an abortion at his insistence. That abortion delayed the start of *Queen Kelly*. Madsen, *Gloria and Joe*, 209–10.

70. Joseph P. Kennedy to Henri de la Falaise, October 31, 1928, Smith, *Hostage to Fortune*, 78.

71. Frederick James Smith, "Photoplay Reviews the Film Year," *Photoplay*, January 1929, 65.

72. *SOS*, 368.

73. Ibid., 369.

74. Koszarski, *The Man You Loved to Hate*, 215–16.

75. Thomas, *Thalberg*, 80.

76. Koszarski, *The Man You Loved to Hate*, 205.

77. Hays, *Memoirs*, 344.

78. Koszarski, *The Man You Loved to Hate*, 215. According to Ivano, Stroheim filmed the real brothel staff for the scene where the prince returns from his all-night revels.

79. Erich von Stroheim to Harold Miles and Louis Sarecky, November 13, 1928, GSP.

80. Glazer said his sole contribution to *The Merry Widow* was to leave Stroheim alone. Koszarski, *The Man You Loved to Hate*, 203, 153.

81. *SOS*, 369.

82. E. B. Derr to Joseph P. Kennedy, December 7, 1928, Goodwin, *The Fitzgeralds and the Kennedys*, 405.

83. Benjamin Glazer to E. B. Derr, December 10, 1928, GSP.

84. *SOS*, 370.

85. Ibid.

86. GS to Al Lichtman, December 13, 1928, GSP.

87. Erich von Stroheim to Al Lichtman, December 13, 1928, GSP.

88. *SOS*, 371.

89. GS Kennedy holograph.

90. "As We Go to Press," *Photoplay*, May 1929, 10.

91. Russell Birdwell, publicity director on *Gone With the Wind*, discovered the device during the 1930s. Lasky, *RKO*, 57.

92. *SOS*, 372.

93. Noble, *Hollywood Scapegoat*, 74. Wood says Stroheim may have invented the European segment "as a means of enticing Swanson and Kennedy" into the production. Wood, *Queen Kelly*, 18–19. On December 18, 1928, Stroheim signed a new contract, retaining the rights to his original African story. This contract is held at the Cinémathèque Française. For Stroheim's later use of the material, see Koszarski, *The Man You Loved to Hate*, 213, 267.

94. "Half an Hour with Von Stroheim," *NYT*, May 28, 1928, 108.

95. GS to Joseph P. Kennedy, January 21, 1929, Goodwin, *The Fitzgeralds and the Kennedys*, 407.

96. *SOS*, 373.

CHAPTER 14. PEOPLE WILL TALK

1. Eugene Walter report, UA 1929, GSP.

2. Ibid.

3. Ibid.

4. GS, "I Am 'Not' Going to Write My Memoirs," *Sight and Sound* 38.2 (Spring 1969), 62.

5. Koszarski, *The Man You Loved to Hate*, 201. Stroheim's "well-documented excesses, both financial and directorial . . . brought the picture down on top of him." Koszarski, 230.

6. GS Kennedy holograph, GSP.

7. E. B. Derr to Edward Moore, January 25, 1929, Smith, *Hostage to Fortune*, 81. Crafton believes Stroheim's reluctance to make a talkie led to his firing. Crafton, *The Talkies*, 304.

8. Cedric Belfrage, "Hollywood, Suburb of Heaven," *Film Weekly*, February 25, 1929, 8.

9. Ruth Biery, "The Troubles of Gloria," *Photoplay*, June 1931, 45.

10. Wood, *Queen Kelly*, 22.

11. GS Kennedy holograph.

12. Joseph P. Kennedy to Henri de la Falaise, March 13, 1929, Smith, *Hostage to Fortune*, 82.

13. GS Kennedy holograph.

14. *SOS*, 376.

15. Goodwin, *The Fitzgeralds and the Kennedys*, 409.

16. Joseph P. Kennedy to Henri de la Falaise, March 13, 1929, Smith, *Hostage to Fortune*, 82.

17. Katherine Albert, "They Must Suffer to Be Beautiful," *Photoplay*, October 1929, 33.

18. Sylvia [Ulbeck], *Hollywood Undressed*, 115.

19. Joseph P. Kennedy to Henri de la Falaise, March 13, 1929, Smith, *Hostage to Fortune*, 82.

20. GS Kennedy holograph.

21. Smith, *Hostage to Fortune*, 62.
22. UA wanted to prevent its independent producers from aligning themselves with studios (and thus starving UA of product).
23. Joseph P. Kennedy to Henri de la Falaise, March 13, 1929, Smith, *Hostage to Fortune*, 82.
24. Goulding "Salvage Association" document, GSP.
25. Lance Heath to Bruce Gallup, March 6, 1929, GSP.
26. Joseph P. Kennedy to Henri de la Falaise, April 15, 1929, Smith, *Hostage to Fortune*, 83.
27. By mid-April, Kennedy estimated the loss as between $800,000 and $1,000,000.
28. Amanda Smith, "Family History," *New Yorker*, October 16 and 23, 2000: 114–15.
29. GS Kennedy holograph.
30. Ibid.
31. Edmund Goulding to GS, March 27, 1929, GSP.
32. Edmund Goulding, "The Talkers in Close-Up," *National Board of Review Magazine* 3 (July 1928), 4.
33. "There's gold in them thar tonsils," *Photoplay* observed. "Reeling Around with Leonard Hall," *Photoplay*, June 1929, 70.
34. *Photoplay*, April 1929, 21.
35. "Crashing the Lambs," *Motion Picture News*, May 9, 1925, 2042.
36. Bogdanovich, *Allan Dwan*, 84.
37. GS Kennedy holograph.
38. Paris, *Louise Brooks*, 70.
39. Lasky, Jr., *Whatever Happened to Hollywood?* 55.
40. Schulberg, *Moving Pictures*, 298–300.
41. GS Kennedy holograph.
42. Ibid.
43. Ibid.
44. GS *Trespasser* holograph.
45. Ibid.
46. *SOS*, 381.
47. Gaynor won for *Sunrise*, *Street Angel*, and *7th Heaven*. The policy allowing recognition for different performances within the same category was soon discontinued.
48. GS Kennedy holograph.
49. GS manuscript.
50. Quirk, *The Kennedys in Hollywood*, 295.
51. "Prolific": Brownlow interview; "having a ball": GS *Trespasser* holograph.
52. GS manuscript.
53. Such trouble more likely occurred on the *Queen Kelly* sound tests run by Stein in April, with a script Swanson disliked and a director she barely knew.
54. GS *Trespasser* holograph.
55. Bill Dufty quoted in Kennedy, *Edmund Goulding's Dark Victory*, 80.
56. Goulding remade *The Trespasser* as *That Certain Woman* with Bette Davis in 1937.
57. *SOS*, 386.
58. Leamer, *The Kennedy Women*, 175.
59. Ibid., 185.
60. Quirk, *The Kennedys in Hollywood*, 3–4.
61. Gala premieres were originally planned for Paris, Berlin, and Brussels, as Kennedy thought public appearances would revive Swanson's name in Europe. These plans were dropped after sound prints of *The Trespasser* were delayed.

62. GS Kennedy holograph.

63. Ibid.

64. *SOS*, 389.

65. Rose Kennedy, *Times to Remember*, 186–87.

66. "London Women Fight to See Miss Swanson," *NYT*, September 10, 1929, 15.

67. Swanson carried disfigurement insurance against such a possibility. Rose Kennedy, *Times to Remember*, 190.

68. "London Women Fight to See Miss Swanson," *NYT*, September 10, 1929, 15.

69. *SOS*, 389.

70. Ernest Marshall, "Cinema Notes from London Town," *NYT*, September 29, 1929, X9.

71. Rose Kennedy, *Times to Remember*, 189.

72. Ibid.

73. Goodwin, *The Fitzgeralds and the Kennedys*, 415.

74. Ibid., 416.

75. Rose Kennedy, *Times to Remember*, 186.

76. *SOS*, 387.

77. Ibid., 401. Quirk says Kennedy had a brief affair with Constance Bennett, which Swanson eventually learned from Eddie Goulding. Kennedy had less luck seducing Greta Garbo and Joan Crawford, though Crawford found Kennedy's "take-charge vitality" appealing. Quirk, *The Kennedys in Hollywood*, 69, 73.

78. Correspondence between Joe and Henri makes it clear that the marquis and Bennett were acquainted as early as April 1929.

79. Bill Dufty claimed that Rose's patronizing attitude toward Swanson in her 1975 memoirs spurred Gloria to write her own book. Beauchamp, *Joseph Kennedy Presents*, 276.

80. Joseph P. Kennedy to Henri de la Falaise, October 2, 1929, Smith, *Hostage to Fortune*, 86.

81. "La Marquise Chez Elle," *NYT*, September 29, 1929, X8.

82. Helena Huntington Smith, "Ugly Duckling," *New Yorker*, January 18, 1930, 27.

83. "Shadows That Pass in the Night," *NYT*, November 17, 1929, X6.

84. Mordaunt Hall, "Miss Swanson's First Talker," *NYT*, November 2, 1929, 11. Hall attended a second screening to satisfy himself about Swanson's voice.

CHAPTER 15. THE CRASH

1. Barney (probably Ben) Glazer to GS, November 2, 1929, GSP.

2. Kennedy, *Edmund Goulding's Dark Victory*, 85.

3. Swanson gave Eddie's sister rights to the song in 1972 "as a gesture of friendly relations." By this time both Joe Kennedy and Eddie Goulding were gone. Kennedy, *Edmund Goulding's Dark Victory*, 282.

4. Kennedy, *Edmund Goulding's Dark Victory*, 85.

5. Boleslavsky was to receive a "Technical Interpretation" credit rather than one for direction. *Queen Kelly* script, GSP.

6. *SOS*, 396.

7. Franz Lehár contract, December 27, 1929, GSP.

8. Lasky, *RKO*, 50.

9. Joseph P. Kennedy to Henri de la Falaise, December 14, 1929, Goodwin, *The Fitzgeralds and the Kennedys*, 413.

10. Katherine Albert, "What Next for Gloria?" *Photoplay*, July 1929, 124.

11. This script is held at the Cinémathèque Française.

12. *Queen Kelly*, Wood/Daves script, GSP. Joan of Arc's canonization in 1920 created a vogue for the female warrior.

13. Koszarski, *The Man You Loved to Hate*, 225.

14. Curtiss calls this one of Thalberg's "few directorial chores." Curtiss, *Von Stroheim*, 251. Stroheim said Swanson directed this ending; see Noble, 74. See also Swanson's remarks in Kobal, *People Will Talk*, 12. Inevitably, this version pleased no one.

15. Al Lichtman to Loyd Wright, February 10, 1932, UA Collection, Wisconsin Center for Film and Theater Research.

16. Joe Schenck to Dennis O'Brien, February 29, 1932, UA Collection, Wisconsin Center for Film and Theater Research. By 1932, the silent picture could no longer be considered a "Special Feature Photoplay," which Swanson was contracted to produce.

17. Koszarski, *The Man You Loved to Hate*, 217. It was shown at a single art house in Paris and played briefly in South America. See Herb Golden, "Swanson's 1929 Fiasco is Finally Reviewed as a Museum Piece," *Variety*, July 26, 1950, 119. A synchronized score recorded on discs is lost. See Eric Myers, "Stroheim and *Queen Kelly*," *Sight and Sound*, 15.2 (Spring 1976).

18. Swanson stored the negative in Paris at her own expense for years. Though the US government had a lien on her film holdings, the 1938 book value of *Queen Kelly*'s negative was zero. Charles E. Millikan to Gloria Swanson, September 7, 1938, GSP.

19. See Herman G. Weinberg, "Celluloid Trumpet Blasts," *Sight and Sound*, 8.30 (Summer 1939), 58. Koszarski says Futter never used the material. Two hundred reels were eventually destroyed by a flood in filmmaker Dudley Murphy's basement. Koszarski, *The Man You Loved to Hate*, 225.

20. Brownlow interview.

21. Wood, *Queen Kelly*, 22.

22. "Let's Drop In and Gossip with Old Cal York," *Photoplay*, September 1930, 48; *Photoplay*, October 1930, 46.

23. "Reeling Around with Leonard Hall," *Photoplay*, November 1930, 80.

24. Bruno, *Venus in Hollywood*, 49.

25. Bennett, *The Bennett Playbill*, 201.

26. *SOS*, 390.

27. Bennett, *The Bennett Playbill*, 220–21.

28. Wire recordings.

29. Ibid.

30. Harry Lang, "So This is Gloria," *Photoplay*, September 1930, 84.

31. Henri de la Falaise to GS, undated, GSP.

32. *SOS*, 400.

33. Ibid., 394.

34. Ibid.

35. Beauchamp, *Joseph Kennedy Presents*, 277.

36. *SOS*, 392, 397.

37. Allan Dwan to GS, February 5, 1930, GSP.

38. *SOS*, 398.

39. Koszarski, *Von*, 256.

40. Dwan received $41,000 for the picture. *What a Widow!* file, GSP.

41. Bogdanovich, *Allan Dwan*, 89–90.

42. Quirk, *The Kennedys in Hollywood*, 300.

43. *SOS*, 400.

44. Quirk, *The Kennedys in Hollywood*, 299.

45. *SOS*, 401.

46. Quirk, *The Kennedys in Hollywood*, 302.

47. Ibid., 294, 296.

48. *SOS*, 400.

49. Joel McCrea to GS, undated, GSP.

50. Alifano, *Tirando Manteca al Techo* (*Hurling Lard at the Ceiling*), 21. This translation by Gustavo Faverón Patriau.

51. Bogdanovich, *Allan Dwan*, 90.

52. *Photoplay*, June 1939, 126.

53. *SOS*, 401.

54. Mordaunt Hall, "The Screen," *NYT*, October 4, 1930, 15.

55. Publicity material for *What a Widow!* GSP.

56. Warren Nolan to Lance Heath, November 13, 1930, GSP.

57. "Hays, Back, Tells of Film Agreement," *NYT*, July 30, 1920, 30.

58. "Last Minute News," *Photoplay*, November 1930, 6.

59. Ruth Waterbury, "Gloria, Connie and the Marquis," *Photoplay*, August 1930, 118-19, 33.

60. GS Kennedy holograph, GSP.

61. "Gloria Swanson Sues for Divorce," *NYT*, October 22, 1930, 26.

62. Marion Shilling interview in Ankerich, *The Sound of Silence*, 208.

63. Kobal, *People Will Talk*, 309.

64. GS manuscript.

65. Gene Markey to GS, undated, GSP.

66. Ibid.

67. GS manuscript.

68. Gene Markey to GS, undated, GSP.

69. *SOS*, 402.

70. The full-length portrait of Swanson is seen in *Sunset Boulevard*.

71. *SOS*, 401–2.

72. GS Kennedy holograph.

73. *SOS*, 327.

74. GS Kennedy holograph.

75. *SOS*, 380.

76. Ibid.

77. GS Kennedy holograph.

78. *SOS*, 403.

79. Ibid., 405.

80. Beauchamp, *Joseph P. Kennedy Presents*, 215.

81. Ibid., 307.

82. Ibid.

83. Hersh, *The Dark Side of Camelot*, 44–46.

84. Bogdanovich, *Allan Dwan*, 91.

85. Quirk, *The Kennedys in Hollywood*, 43.

86. Beauchamp, *Joseph P. Kennedy Presents*, xvi.

87. *SOS*, 406.

88. Quirk, *The Kennedys in Hollywood*, 57.

89. Note on Constitutional Educational League paper, GSP.

90. Hamilton, *JFK: Reckless Youth*, 67–68. Joe also reportedly bragged to Jackie about his "conquest" of Marion Davies. See Heymann, *A Woman Named Jackie*, 142.

91. Leamer, *The Kennedy Men*, 60. Kennedy reportedly said, "When I was forty, I went overboard for a certain lady in Hollywood . . . It ruined my business. It ruined my health, and it damn near ruined my marriage."

92. GS Kennedy holograph.

93. Ibid.

CHAPTER 16. MAD ABOUT THE BOY

1. *SOS*, 404.

2. Hopper, *From Under My Hat*, 186.

3. Elisabeth Goldbeck, "The Real Clara Bow," *Motion Picture Classic*, September 1930.

4. Loos, *The Talmadge Girls*, 2.

5. Louise Brooks, "Mr. Pabst," *Image* 5, (September 1956), 152–53.

6. Mordden, *Movie Star*, 54.

7. Koszarski, *An Evening's Entertainment*, 312.

8. "Mary Pickford See Talkies as Lipstick on Milo," *Los Angeles Times*, March 18, 1934, 1.

9. Warren Nolan to GS, December 20, 1929, GSP.

10. *SOS*, 406.

11. Love, *From Hollywood With Love*, 105.

12. *SOS*, 406–7.

13. This amount was probably exaggerated. Ruth Biery, "The Troubles of Gloria," *Photoplay*, June 1931, 140.

14. "Mr. Goldwyn's New Job," *NYT*, November 30, 1930, X5.

15. Bergan, *The United Artists Story*, 9. Warner Bros. sought to take over UA in 1929; Jack Warner planned to impose production quotas on the company's star-producers. See Walker, *The Shattered Silents*, 176.

16. Joseph P. Kennedy to Virginia Bowker, undated, GSP.

17. Muriel Babcock, "Deceptive Quiet Falls on 'Rock-a-Bye' Rumpus," *Los Angeles Times*, May 17, 1931, B9.

18. GS to Joe Schenck, March 26, 1931, GSP.

19. Muriel Babcock, "Deceptive Quiet Falls on 'Rock-a-Bye' Rumpus," *Los Angeles Times*, May 17, 1931, B9.

20. Ruth Biery, "The Troubles of Gloria," *Photoplay*, June 1931, 140.

21. Bogdanovich, *Who the Devil Made It*, 403.

22. GS to Sam Goldwyn, April 9, 1931, GSP.

23. *SOS*, 408.

24. GS manuscript.

25. Bogdanovich, *Who the Devil Made It*, 403.

26. Ankerich, *The Sound of Silence*, 160.

27. Bogdanovich, *Who the Devil Made It*, 402–3.

28. Robinson, *Chaplin*, 420.

29. Zukor, *The Public Is Never Wrong*, 183.

30. GS to Sport Ward, October 7, 1930, GSP.

31. Sport Ward to GS, October 23, 1920, GSP.

32. Sport Ward to GS, February 9, 1931, GSP.

33. *SOS*, 407.

34. GS Kennedy holograph.

35. Swanson spottings continued at the family compound; some witnesses claimed they occurred only when Rose was not home.

36. *SOS*, 406.

37. Charles-Roux, *Chanel*, 269.

38. Lois Shirley, "How to Adapt Screen Modes," *Photoplay*, July 1931, 33.

39. *SOS*, 409–10.

40. The two dogs signaled Farmer's availability to both men and women. Kennedy, *Edmund Goulding's Dark Victory*, 98.

41. *Bricktop*, 161.

42. Ibid., 152.

43. Ibid., 149.

44. Ibid., 123, 148–49.

45. Moore, *You're Only Human Once*, 185.

46. *Bricktop*, 172.

47. *SOS*, 411.

48. GS manuscript.

49. *SOS*, 413.

50. Ibid., 414.

51. GS manuscript.

52. Ibid.

53. "Gloria May Wed Again, She Admits," *Los Angeles Times*, August 15, 1931, 1.

54. GS manuscript.

55. "Gloria Swanson Home; Michael Comes Along," *Los Angeles Times*, August 21, 1931, 1.

56. GS manuscript.

57. Sheridan Gibney in McGilligan, *Film Crazy*, 137.

58. Fairbanks, *The Salad Days*, 164.

59. LeRoy, *Take One*, 100.

60. GS manuscript.

61. "'Tonight or Never' Swell Production; LeRoy Triumph," *Hollywood Reporter*, November 5, 1931, 3.

62. Mordaunt Hall, "The Screen," *NYT*, December 18, 1931, 29.

63. "Tonight or Never," *Variety*, December 22, 1931, 15.

64. "'Tonight or Never' Swell Production; LeRoy Triumph," *Hollywood Reporter*, November 5, 1931, 3.

65. "Star's Ties Revealed: Gloria Swanson Wed in August," *Los Angeles Times*, November 7, 1931, 1.

66. "Marquis Looks Doomed to Early Trip to Altar," *Los Angeles Times*, November 11, 1931, A1.

67. "Dame Rumor Amazes Gloria: Bride Denies She and Mate in Hiding," *Los Angeles Times*, November 20, 1931, A10.

68. "Bennett-de la Falaise Wedding Set for Today; Gloria Swanson and New Spouse on Cruise," *Los Angeles Times*, November 22, 1931, 14.

69. "Miss Swanson Arrives; Pair to Sail for Europe," *Los Angeles Times*, November 21, 1931, A1.

CHAPTER 17. PERFECT MISUNDERSTANDING

1. *SOS*, 419.

2. GS working chronologies, GSP.

3. GS manuscript.

4. Ibid.

5. Ibid.

6. Ibid.

7. Elinor Glyn to GS, June 22, [1932?], GSP.

8. The Cinematograph Act of 1927 sought to prevent the British film industry from being overwhelmed by pictures from abroad. For each film imported, exhibitors had to show a certain number of British productions.

9. GS manuscript.

10. Ibid.

11. *SOS*, 425.

12. Powell worked on Hitchcock's *Blackmail*, the UK's first sound picture. Since then he had been learning his craft on cheap pictures unlikely to be exhibited outside Britain.

13. Loyd Wright to GS, March 12, 1932, GSP.

14. GS manuscript.

15. GS to Loyd Wright, 1932, GSP.

16. Swanson eventually waived her percentage of the profits; she received a salary of $150,000.

17. GS to Irving Wakoff, June 9, 1932, GSP.

18. Loyd Wright to GS, March 12, 1932, GSP.

19. Lance Heath to GS, March 15, 1932, GSP.

20. Loyd Wright to GS, July 14, 1932, GSP.

21. Ibid.

22. GS manuscript. Swanson planned to cast Farmer as the lead at least as early as March 1932.

23. He made *Legong: Dance of the Virgins* (1935) and *Kliou the Killer* (1936) in Bali and Indonesia, as well as several pictures in French and English versions for RKO.

24. *SOS*, 427.

25. GS manuscript; *Parkinson* television program, December 2, 1978, videocassette at British Film Institute.

26. Olivier, *Confessions of an Actor*, 92.

27. *SOS*, 497. Gardner lived another ten years.

28. GS manuscript.

29. GS working chronologies, GSP.

30. Joe Schenck to GS, June 7, 1932, GSP.

31. *SOS*, 501.

32. GS to Loyd Wright, September 2, 1932, GSP.

33. Cleary was awarded a judgment of $37,500.

34. Bill Dufty intimated that Goulding and Coward "put Farmer up to the Swanson romance." Kennedy, *Edmund Goulding's Dark Victory*, 99–100.

35. *SOS*, 431.

36. Ibid., 429. Powell endured an experimental treatment before defeating his colorectal cancer.

37. Michael Farmer to GS, undated letter (c. 1932), GSP.

38. Michael Farmer to GS, December 15, 1933, GSP; GS to Michael Farmer, December 15, 1933, GSP.

39. Michael Farmer to GS, January 18, 1934, GSP.

40. Michael Farmer to GS, December 16, 1933, GSP.

41. Michael Farmer to GS, January 22, 1934, GSP.

42. Michael Farmer to GS, December 16, 1933, GSP.

43. Michael Farmer to GS, December 24, 1933, GSP.

44. Michael Farmer to GS, January 10, 1934, GSP.

45. Michael Farmer to GS, October 5, 1931, GSP.

46. Michael Farmer to GS, December 16, 1933, GSP.

47. Michael Farmer to GS, January 18, 1934, GSP.

48. GS manuscript.

49. *SOS*, 435.

50. Loos, *Cast of Thousands*, 112.

51. GS to Michael Farmer, March 10, 1934, GSP.

52. Unsigned letter to Seymour Berkson, April 4, 1934, GSP.

53. GS manuscript.

54. Ibid.

55. *SOS*, 437.

56. Herbert Marshall to GS, May 10, 1934, GSP.

57. Ibid., May 11, 1934, GSP.

58. *SOS*, 438.

59. GS manuscript.

60. Ibid.

61. Herbert Marshall to GS, April 28, 1934, GSP.

62. "Politics Blamed by Lois Wilson as Gloria Swanson Gets Divorce," *Portland (Maine) Press Herald*, November 8, 1934, 1–2.

63. "Gloria Swanson Seeks a Divorce," *NYT*, April 24, 1934, 27.

64. Mildred Mastin, "The Husbands in Gloria's Career," *Photoplay*, July 1934, 40.

65. Edith Simonson to GS, May 8, 1934, GSP.

66. GS to Edith Simonson, undated letter (c. 1934), GSP.

67. GS to Loyd Wright, November 17, 1934, GSP.

68. GS manuscript.

69. J. M. Racine, Chalet Marie-José, Gstaad, to GS, April 9, 1934, GSP.

70. Loyd Wright to GS, November 26, 1935, GSP.

71. GS manuscript.

72. Herbert Marshall to GS, September 8, 1935, GSP.

73. GS manuscript.

74. Ibid. The lump proved benign.

75. Press release, *Music in the Air*, GSP.

76. Pommer's son claimed Thalberg "had a commitment he wanted to shove off on somebody else." Hardt, *From Caligari to California*, 146.

77. Hadleigh, *Hollywood Lesbians*, 42.
78. Sheilah Graham, "Gloria Swanson Tries Comeback," *Spokesman-Review (Spokane, WA)*, February 18, 1937, 5.
79. *SOS*, 446.
80. Ibid., 449.
81. Loos, *Cast of Thousands*, 86.
82. GS manuscript.
83. *SOS*, 443.
84. GS manuscript.
85. Moore, *Silent Star*, 208.
86. GS to Louis B. Mayer, January 28, 1937, GSP.
87. GS manuscript.
88. Mordden, *Movie Star*, 16.
89. *SOS*, 450.
90. Ibid.
91. Herbert Marshall to GS, undated, GSP.
92. *SOS*, 448.
93. GS manuscript.

CHAPTER 18. REINVENTING HERSELF

1. "Elsa Maxwell's Party Line," *New York Post*, August 18, 1943.
2. "Gloria's Career," *Motion Picture Herald*, August 24, 1940.
3. *SOS*, 453.
4. Ibid., 465.
5. Swanson carries it in *Sunset Boulevard*.
6. GS manuscript.
7. Ibid.
8. Ibid.
9. Author's interview with Michelle Farmer Amon.
10. GS manuscript.
11. "Elsa Maxwell's Party Line," *New York Post*, August 18, 1943.
12. *SOS*, 466.
13. Menjou, *It Took Nine Tailors*, 202.
14. Jerry Breitigam, "Gloria Glorious as Camera Greets Her Again," undated clipping, GSP
15. "The New Pictures," *Time*, September 29, 1941, 83.
16. Arnaz, *A Book*, 127.
17. *SOS*, 467.
18. GS manuscript.
19. *SOS*, 467.
20. Kennedy, *No Pickle, No Performance*, 37.
21. *SOS*, 468.
22. Kennedy, *No Pickle, No Performance*, 37.
23. *SOS*, 468.
24. GS manuscript.
25. *SOS*, 468.
26. GS manuscript.

27. *SOS*, 469.

28. Kennedy, *No Pickle, No Performance*, 39.

29. *Providence (RI) Journal*, August 11, 1942, GSP.

30. GS manuscript.

31. *Springfield (MA) Sunday Union and Republican*, December 20, 1942, GSP.

32. GS manuscript.

33. Kennedy, *No Pickle, No Performance*, 45.

34. Elliot Norton, "Backstage Row Ends Play's Run," *Boston Post*, January 9, 1943, 1.

35. John C. Wilson to GS, January 4, 1943, GSP.

36. William F. McDermott, *Cleveland Plain Dealer*, July 14, 1943, GSP.

37. Russell McLauchlin, *Detroit News*, October 10, 1943, GSP.

38. Peter Bellamy, *Cleveland News*, July 14, 1943, GSP.

39. "Elsa Maxwell's Party Line," *New York Post*, August 18, 1943, GSP.

40. Program for *A Goose for the Gander*, GSP.

41. Rose Kennedy to Kathleen Kennedy Hartington, June 30, 1944, Smith, *Hostage to Fortune*, 596.

42. GS to J. W. Reish, July 29, 1944, GSP.

43. Harold Kennedy to Rod Waggoner, June 28, 1944, GSP.

44. *A Goose for the Gander* program, GSP.

45. John Huntington to GS, July 20, 1944, GSP.

46. John Chapman, *New York Daily News*, January 24, 1945, GSP.

47. Robert Coleman, *New York Daily Mirror*, January 24, 1945, GSP.

48. Ann Marsters, "Excursions in Stageland," *Chicago American*, July 23, 1944, GSP.

49. Lewis Nichols, "Dead Duck," *NYT*, January 24, 1945, 16.

50. Paul Soskin to GS, January–February 1939, GSP.

51. Paul Soskin to GS, January 29, 1937, GSP.

52. GS manuscript.

53. Sport Ward to GS, July 7, 1937, GSP.

54. GS manuscript.

55. Ibid.

56. 1943 datebook, GSP.

57. Evans, *Nemesis*, 183.

58. Ibid., 101.

59. GS manuscript.

60. 1945 datebook, GSP.

61. GS manuscript.

62. Ibid.

63. Quoted in petition for separation, January 26, 1946, GSP.

64. GS manuscript.

65. GS to William Davey, October 15, 1945, GSP.

66. 1945 datebook, GSP.

67. Justice Morris Eder, *New York Law Journal*, January 26, 1946, GSP.

68. Farmer was eventually cleared of all charges.

69. John Guare, "The Art of Theater IX," *Paris Review* 125 (Winter 1992), 72.

70. Kennedy, *No Pickle, No Performance*, 34–35.

71. Hopper, *From Under My Hat*, 168.

72. "Going Places with Gloria Swanson and Robert Balzer," prospectus for newspaper column, GSP.

73. Wayne Oliver, *Louisville Courier-Journal*, August 15, 1948, GSP.

74. "Birth of a Telefilm," *TV Guide*, May 22–28, 1953, GSP.

75. Swanson composed multiple drafts of this letter, inserting and then omitting Charlie Chaplin from the list of those she named. GS to Robert Coe, WPIX station manager, January 4, 1949, GSP.

CHAPTER 19. YOU USED TO BE BIG

1. Wilder reportedly scribbled the film's premise on a scrap of paper a decade earlier: "Silent picture star commits murder. When they arrest her she sees the newsreel cameras and thinks she is back in the movies." Deutsch, *Me and Bogie*, 156–57.

2. James Linville, "Billy Wilder: The Art of Screenwriting," *Paris Review* 138 (Spring 1996), 55.

3. Whitfield, *Pickford*, 338.

4. *SOS*, 479.

5. Zolotow, *Billy Wilder in Hollywood*, 161.

6. Jack Hirshberg, "Hollywood Hearsay," March 1949, GSP.

7. GS manuscript.

8. GS to Virginia Bowker Stubbs, February 25, 1949, GSP.

9. Stanley Frank, "Grandma Gloria Swanson Comes Back," Part Two, *Saturday Evening Post*, July 29, 1950, 56.

10. Stanley Frank, "Grandma Gloria Swanson Comes Back," Part One, *The Saturday Evening Post*, July 22, 1950, 30–31.

11. James Agee, "Films of the Month: *Sunset Boulevard*," *Sight and Sound* 19.7 (November 1950), 283.

12. Zolotow, *Billy Wilder in Hollywood*, 162–63. Swanson worried that the story was too close to her life: "I didn't want anyone to confuse the part with me. So they changed it. That's all gone now. It has nothing to do with my own life." Undated clipping, GSP.

13. Zolotow, *Billy Wilder in Hollywood*, 163.

14. Stevens, *Conversations*, 308.

15. *Sunset Boulevard* script, December 21, 1948, GSP.

16. *Billy Wilder Speaks*, directed by Volker Schlondorff (2006).

17. Steen, *Hollywood Speaks!* 249.

18. *Sunset Boulevard* script, December 21, 1948, GSP.

19. Koszarski, *The Man You Loved to Hate*, 288.

20. Stevens, *Conversations*, 310.

21. Billy Wilder, "One Head Is Better Than Two," *Films and Filming* February 1957, 7.

22. Crowe, *Conversations with Wilder*, 267.

23. Lennig, *Stroheim*, 445.

24. Lally, *Wilder Times*, 200.

25. *SOS*, 481–82.

26. GS manuscript.

27. W. E. Sprackling to Joseph Swanson, April 28, 1949, GSP.

28. Walter Winchell, undated clipping, GSP.

29. GS to Virginia Bowker Stubbs, February 25, 1949, GSP.

30. Hedda Hopper column, March 31, 1949, GSP.

31. Author's interview with Michelle Farmer Amon.

32. Andrew Wilson, "Living with Norma Desmond," *Observer (UK)*, March 8, 2003, 9.

33. Louella Parsons column, *Baltimore American*, April 3, 1949, GSP.

34. Gloria Swanson, "I Am 'Not' Going to Write My Memoirs," *Sight and Sound* 38 (Spring 1969), 62.

35. Stevens, *Conversations*, 307.

36. Linville, "Billy Wilder," 55.

37. "Worked like a dog" and "pleasant surprise": "Interview with Billy Wilder," *Playboy*, June 1963, 65; "absolute angel": Linville, "Billy Wilder," 56.

38. Armand Archerd column, April 26, 1949, GSP.

39. GS manuscript.

40. *SOS*, 483.

41. Sikov, *On Sunset Boulevard*, 295.

42. Ezra Goodman, "Ringing Up the Curtain on William Haines," *NYT*, June 5, 1949, X5.

43. Linville, "Billy Wilder," 56.

44. Zolotow, *Billy Wilder in Hollywood*, 166. Wilder teased Swanson that the chimpanzee had been her character's last lover.

45. Stanley Frank, "Grandma Gloria Swanson Comes Back," Part Two, *Saturday Evening Post* July 29, 1950, 56.

46. Jack Hirshberg, "Hollywood Hearsay," March 1949, GSP.

47. Zolotow, *Billy Wilder in Hollywood*, 248.

48. Stevens, *Conversations*, 311, 333.

49. The American Film Institute ranks this line at #7 (ahead of "May the Force be with you") on its list of top movie quotes.

50. Zolotow, *Billy Wilder in Hollywood*, 249.

51. Louella Parsons column, *Baltimore American*, April 3, 1949, GSP.

52. *SOS*, 485.

53. Summary report of the annual stockholders meeting of Paramount Pictures Corporation, June 5, 1951, GSP.

54. *We, the People* script, GSP. Swanson is describing the plot of *Manhandled*.

55. John Tassos (Paramount, Washington, DC) to GS, undated, GSP.

56. Jim Castle (Paramount, Kansas City) to GS, October 31, 1949, GSP.

57. W. Harley Rudkin, *Springfield (MA) Daily News*, October 15, 1949, GSP.

58. GS to Max Youngstein, December 11, 1949, GSP.

59. Judy Klemesrud, "Name, Nose, Teeth, Bosom, Hair, Kidneys—Everything But Eyelashes—Is Real," *NYT*, October 10, 1971, 14.

60. Zolotow, *Billy Wilder in Hollywood*, 167.

61. *Sunset Boulevard* preview cards, GSP.

62. GS interviewed by John Russell Taylor at the National Film Theatre, London, September 10, 1981, held at the British Film Institute.

63. Whitfield, *Pickford*, 337.

64. Zolotow, *Billy Wilder in Hollywood*, 168.

65. "Fuck you": Zolotow, *Billy Wilder in Hollywood*, 168; "Go shit": David Freeman, "Annals of Hollywood: *Sunset Boulevard* Revisited," *New Yorker*, June 21, 1993, 76.

66. Thomas M. Pryor, "Hollywood Story: Candid Views of Filmdom in 'Sunset Boulevard,'" *NYT*, August 13, 1950, X81.

67. *Hollywood Reporter*, April 17, 1950, quoted in Sikov, *On Sunset Boulevard*, 304.

68. James Agee, "Films of the Month: *Sunset Boulevard*," *Sight and Sound* 19.7 (November 1950), 284.

69. Virginia Bowker Stubbs to GS, undated, GSP.

70. *Variety*, August 24, 1950; *Hollywood Reporter*, August 25, 1950, GSP.

71. GS to Bosley Crowther, September 19, 1950, GSP.

72. GS to Billy Wilkerson, September 21, 1950, GSP.

73. "Strangely insinuating": Bosley Crowther, "Hollywood Scandal: Some Further Observations on the Nature of 'Sunset Boulevard,'" *NYT*, August 27, 1950, X1; "Ballyhoo": James Agee, "Films of the Month," *Sight and Sound* 19 (November 1950), 283.

74. Ted O'Shea to Paramount publicity department, August 23, 1950, GSP.

75. GS to Edith Head, April 20, 1950, GSP.

76. GS to Max Youngstein, April 24, 1950, GSP.

77. Question cards, *Sunset Boulevard*, GSP.

78. GS to G. Lightstone (Paramount, Toronto), July 22, 1950, GSP.

79. GS to René Hubert, May 30, 1950, GSP.

80. Barney Balaban to GS, August 14, 1950, GSP.

81. Society of Illustrators, "An Enchanted Evening with Gloria Swanson," October 13, 1950, Museum of American Illustration, New York.

82. GS manuscript.

83. Society of Illustrators, "An Enchanted Evening."

84. *(London) Evening Standard*, October 26, 1950, GSP.

85. *Daily Mail (UK)*, November 2, 1950, GSP.

86. *Manchester (UK) Weekly News*, November 1, 1950, GSP.

87. Theo. V. Norman to GS, October 29, 1950, GSP. Swanson replied on November 21, 1950: "How I should have liked to at least talk with you on the telephone! For I remember all of the things that you set forth . . . almost as clearly as you do. Those were happy days . . . youthful days."

88. Paul Holt, "Queen Gloria Gets Second Chance," *(London) Daily Herald*, October 25, 1950, GSP.

CHAPTER 20. DRESSING THE PART

1. *SOS*, 509.

2. GS to Edith Head, September 2, 1950, GSP.

3. *SOS*, 51.

4. *Beauty Tricks and Truths*, 5.13b, GSP.

5. GS manuscript.

6. Brandon Brent to Edward Alperson, October 2, 1951, GSP.

7. GS manuscript.

8. *Providence Evening Bulletin*, August 21, 1959, GSP.

9. David O. Selznick to GS, February 15, 1950, GSP. Swanson was also discussing a contract for Michelle with producer A. L. Rockett.

10. Author's interview with Michelle Farmer Amon.

11. Gilbert Millstein, "All the Stage is His World," *NYT*, March 25, 1951, 151.

12. GS manuscript.

13. Ibid.

14. Brooks Atkinson, "At the Theatre," *NYT*, December 25, 1950, 23.

15. John Chapman, *New York Daily News*, December 25, 1950; Richard Watts, *New York Post*, December 26, 1950.

16. William Hawkins, *New York World Telegram*, December 26, 1950.

17. Howard Barnes, *New York Herald Tribune*, December 25, 1951.

18. Robert Coleman, *New York Daily Mirror*, December 25, 1950.

19. Brandon Brent to Edward Alperson, October 2, 1951; October 5, 1952, GSP.

20. "That Old Feeling," *Time*, March 3, 1952, 42.

21. Bob Thomas, quoted in *SOS*, 250; Charles Brackett to GS, December 9, 1950, GSP.

22. *SOS*, 254.

23. Ibid., 257.

24. Ibid., 257, 259.

25. Ibid., 259–60.

26. Ibid., 489.

27. GS to Mike and Fleur Cowles, undated, GSP.

28. Gary Stevens to Albert Lee Lesser and Phil Solomon, June 27, 1952, GSP.

29. She would get $50,000 if the picture made more than $550,00.

30. *SOS*, 501.

31. Andrew Wilson, "Living with Norma Desmond," *Observer (UK)*, March 8, 2003, 9.

32. Author's interview with Michelle Farmer Amon.

33. Ibid.

34. GS to "Brenco," probably Milton Bren and Claire Trevor, November 5, 1951, GSP.

35. Niven, *The Moon's a Balloon*, 264.

36. "New Play in Manhattan," *Time*, December 17, 1951, 78.

37. Niven, *The Moon's a Balloon*, 264–65.

38. Walter F. Kerr, *New York Herald Tribune*, December 6, 1951.

39. GS manuscript.

40. John Chapman, *New York Daily News*, December 6, 1951.

41. Walter F. Kerr, *New York Herald Tribune*, December 6, 1951.

42. GS to Joseph Swanson, January 13, 1952, GSP.

43. GS to Brooks Atkinson, December 12, 1951, GSP.

44. *SOS*, 504.

45. GS to Julian (Bud) Lesser, July 5, 1952, GSP.

46. GS to Bud Lesser, December 28, 1953, GSP.

47. Tom King to GS, January 22, 1953, GSP.

48. GS to Joseph Swanson, October 28, 1953, GSP.

49. Michelle Farmer Amon to GS, June 17, 1955, GSP.

50. "Miss Gloria Swanson is Induced to Talk About Her Legend," *Times* (London), October 16, 1961, 16.

51. United Press columns, GSP.

52. Nelle Penley, "Gloria Swanson in Superb Performance at Lakewood," *Bangor (Maine) Daily News*, August 5, 1959, 4.

53. GS to R. Lawrence Siegel, March 22, 1956, GSP.

54. L. Pierce Carson, "Gloria Swanson Doesn't Like World Trend Today," *Napa Valley Register*, December 17, 1973, 2.

55. GS to Joseph Swanson, January 9, 1956, GSP.

56. Adelaide Woodruff to GS, January 3, 1956, GSP.

57. GS to Michelle Farmer Amon, January 7, 1956, GSP.

58. Bardot next made *And God Created Woman*; cinematographer Mario Bava's next project inaugurated the golden age of Italian horror.

CHAPTER 21. NOT READY FOR HER RETROSPECTIVE

1. *SOS*, 476.
2. Gloria Swanson, health manuscript (1972), GSP.
3. *SOS*, 474.
4. Devi, *Yoga for Americans*, unpaged.
5. "Think Young," *Saturday Evening Post*, March 1977, 66.
6. GS to Wolfgang Goetze-Claren, October 19, 1971, GSP.
7. GS manuscript.
8. *Nashua (New Hampshire) Telegraph*, October 29, 1969, 20.
9. Contract for appearance on *What Every Woman Wants to Know* with Bess Myerson, 1971, GSP.
10. Kathleen Hendrix, "Gloria Swanson: Birthday Girl at 80," *Los Angeles Times*, April 2, 1979, F1.
11. David Rollins, quoted in Ankerich, *Broken Silence*, 289.
12. Brooke Anderson, "Thoughts on Gloria Swanson," press book for Milestone Films' restoration of *Beyond the Rocks*, 2005.
13. *The Mike Wallace Interview*, April 28, 1957, GSP.
14. Ibid.
15. GS to Lewis Bredin, undated, GSP.
16. Lewis Bredin to GS, May 5, 1952, GSP.
17. Lewis Bredin to GS, undated, GSP.
18. Lewis Bredin to GS, May 16, 1952, GSP.
19. Lewis Bredin to GS, August 22, 1958, GSP.
20. Lewis Bredin to GS, August 30, 1958, GSP.
21. GS to Lewis Bredin, undated, GSP.
22. Ibid.
23. Michelle Amon to GS, September 2, 1958, GSP.
24. Andrew Wilson, "Living with Norma Desmond," *Observer (UK)*, March 8, 2003, 9.
25. GS manuscript.
26. Script from *The Bob Hope Show*, October 12, 1958, GSP.
27. Gloria Swanson, "I Am 'Not' Going to Write My Memoirs," *Sight and Sound*, 38 (Spring 1969), 62.
28. Richard Chamberlain interview, Archive of American Television. Web.
29. Kobal, *People Will Talk*, 4.
30. GS to Erich von Stroheim, March 14, 1955, GSP.
31. GS to "D.A.," May 5, 1955, GSP.
32. GS to Steve Allen, December 22, 1957, GSP.
33. GS to Russell Holman, February 16, 1959, GSP.
34. Russell Holman to GS, February 20, 1959, GSP.
35. In 1994 Hughes workshopped a three-character musical play, *Swanson on Sunset*, chronicling the unsuccessful effort to bring *Boulevard!* to the stage.
36. GS to Michelle Amon, April 7, 1965, GSP.
37. Robert Curtis, "I Live With Gloria Swanson," 1959 typescript, GSP.

38. Harold L. Cail, "Gloria Swanson Is Far From Ready, Mister, To Be Taken Out and Shot," *Portland (Maine) Evening Express*, August 5, 1959, 17.

39. Curtis, "I Live With Gloria Swanson," GSP.

40. Ibid.

41. Kennedy, *No Pickle, No Performance*, 114.

42. Curtis, "I Live With Gloria Swanson," GSP.

43. Elliot Norton, *Boston Daily Record*, August 31, 1959, GSP.

44. Philip K. Scheuer, "Gloria Swanson, 68, Going Strong on Youth Stuff," *Los Angeles Times*, October 1, 1967, 24.

45. Kennedy, *No Pickle, No Performance*, 51–52.

46. *Red Letter Day* program, Margaret Herrick Library.

47. Kennedy, *No Pickle, No Performance*, 91.

48. GS manuscript.

49. GS to Michelle Amon, May 5, 1965, GSP.

50. GS manuscript.

51. Dufty, *Sugar Blues*, 1.

52. GS manuscript.

53. Ibid.

54. Ibid.

55. Drew Pearson, "The Washington Merry-Go-Round," *Washington Post*, May 5, 1960, D15.

56. GS manuscript.

57. Ronald S. Magliozzi, "Film Archiving as a Profession: An Interview with Eileen Bowser," *Moving Image* 3 (Spring 2003), 137.

58. GS manuscript.

59. "Sic Transit Gloria," *Newsweek*, May 30, 1966.

60. Brownlow, *The Parade's Gone By*, 372.

61. Michelle Amon to GS, January 15, 1963, GSP.

62. Judy Klemesrud, "Name, Nose, Teeth, Bosom, Hair, Kidneys—Everything But Eyelashes—Is Real," *NYT*, October 10, 1971, 13. Swanson hoped to sell the picture; however, the public television screenings depleted the market.

63. "Flash in the Pan?" *Time*, March 2, 1953, 90.

64. Dennis Doros did a state-of-the-art restoration for Kino International in 1985. Curtiss says Swanson also showed the film in Paris in 1957. Swanson and Stroheim apparently discussed reworking the film together. Curtiss, *Von Stroheim*, 321.

65. GS manuscript.

66. Ibid.

67. Ibid.

68. Ibid.

69. Ibid.

70. Ibid.

71. GS to Louella Parsons, March 22, 1963, GSP. Parsons lived almost ten more years.

72. Author's interview with Michelle Amon.

73. Ibid.

74. Ibid.

75. GS to Michelle Amon, July 6, 1969, GSP.

76. GS to Michelle Amon, October 10, 1967, GSP.

77. GS to Michael Farmer, January 9, 1959, GSP.

78. Aileen Mehle writing as Suzy Knickerbocker, "Mike Farmer Wails in Wales," *New York Mirror*, October 5, 1959, GSP.

79. GS to Michelle Amon, October 10, 1967, GSP.

80. GS to Bob Amon, undated, GSP.

81. Michelle Amon to GS, August 9, 1969, GSP.

82. GS manuscript.

83. Brownlow, *The Parade's Gone By*, 507.

84. GS manuscript.

85. Ibid.

86. Ibid.

CHAPTER 22. LAST ACT

1. GS manuscript.

2. *Coco* manuscript.

3. J. A. Engels, "Swanson: Still Star at 72," *Los Angeles Herald-Examiner*, September 12, 1971, F1.

4. GS manuscript.

5. Bob Thomas, "Gloria Swanson Upset over False 'Coco' Reports," *Nevada Daily Mail*, July 19, 1970, 8, GSP.

6. GS manuscript.

7. Ibid.

8. Ibid.

9. GS to Michelle Amon, October 29, 1970, GSP.

10. GS manuscript.

11. Ibid.

12. Maggie Paley, "Gloria Swanson is Back, Full of Organic Beans," *Life*, September 17, 1971, 77.

13. Judy Klemesrud, "Name, Nose, Teeth, Bosom, Hair, Kidneys—Everything But Eyelashes—Is Real," *NYT*, October 10, 1971, D13.

14. J. A. Engels, "Swanson: Still Star at 72," *Los Angeles Herald-Examiner*, September 12, 1971, F4.

15. Benedict, *Confessions*, 60.

16. Judy Klemesrud, "Name, Nose, Teeth, Bosom, Hair, Kidneys—Everything But Eyelashes—Is Real," *NYT*, October 10, 1971, D13.

17. Benedict, *Confessions*, 60, 141.

18. GS manuscript.

19. Ibid.

20. Ibid.

21. *The Mike Wallace Interview*, April 28, 1957, GSP.

22. GS manuscript.

23. Ibid.

24. Mary Murphy, "Swanson: A Star is Reborn," *Los Angeles Times*, May 24, 1974, 21.

25. Richard Cuskelly, "Gloria Swanson: A Legend Denies It," *Los Angeles Herald-Examiner*, November 17, 1974, 5.

26. Gloria Greer, "Gloria Swanson at 75: On the Move," *(Riverside, CA) Press-Enterprise*, June 28, 1974.

27. GS manuscript.

28. "Scotland Yard": B. Bernard Kreisler to GS, August 22, 1959, GSP; "Langlois knows": Robert Crevenne to B. Bernard Kreisler, April 27, 1951, GSP.

29. GS, "I Am 'Not' Going to Write My Memoirs," *Sight and Sound*, 38 (Spring 1969), 60.

30. GS to M. Nogures, February 15, 1968, GSP.

31. Author's interview with Michelle Amon.

32. GS, "My Most Wonderful Experience," annotated manuscript for 1950 *Photoplay* essay, GSP.

33. *SOS*, 518.

34. GS to Joseph and Sue Swanson, November 27, 1955, GSP.

35. Author's interview with Michelle Amon.

36. *SOS*, 515.

37. Joyce Haber, "Gloria Swanson Living Her Legend," *Los Angeles Times*, July 28, 1974, 23.

38. Christopher P. Andersen, "At 76, Gloria Swanson Has a New Crusade—and a New Mate to Go With It," *People*, February 16, 1976, 35.

39. "Swanson Discusses Sex After 70," *Time*, October 18, 1976.

40. GS to William Dufty, February 28, 1974, GSP.

41. Dufty, "Introduction," in Benedict, *Confessions*, xi.

42. *Time*, February 17, 1976.

43. Judy Klemesrud, "Name, Nose, Teeth, Bosom, Hair, Kidneys—Everything But Eyelashes—Is Real," *NYT*, October 10, 1971, D13.

44. GS manuscript.

45. "'Babylon' Suit," *Los Angeles Herald-Examiner*, December 15, 1977.

46. Anger included a letter (wrongly) attributed to Swanson that viciously condemned Lana Turner for her involvement in the 1958 death of Johnny Stompanato, although Walter Winchell (the source) had already printed a correction. This letter did not appear when Anger's book was reprinted.

47. Anger mailings to GS, GSP.

48. Wire recordings.

49. Anger, *Hollywood Babylon II*, 13.

50. John Lennon, *Playboy* interview, January 1981, 101.

51. William Frye, "The Garbo Next Door," *Vanity Fair*, August 2000.

52. GS to Allan Dwan, April 24, 1981, GSP.

53. Susan Taylor, "Gloria: Quit Eating Poison," *Los Angeles Herald-Examiner*, August 9, 1971.

54. GS manuscript.

55. She was denied a jury trial to fight the IRS' demands. Swanson eventually settled her debt for thirty-five cents on the dollar, calling it a victory.

56. Maggie Paley, "Gloria Swanson is Back, Full of Organic Beans," *Life*, September 17, 1971, 77.

57. Mitchell, *Icons and Idols*, 18.

58. Swanson told John Russell Taylor she would have preferred to direct. Interview at the National Film Theatre, London, September 10, 1981, footage held at the British Film Institute.

59. Kennedy, *Edmund Goulding's Dark Victory*, 100.

60. GS manuscript.

61. Leighton, *Of Savages and Kings*, 214–16.

62. GS manuscript.

63. Ibid.

64. *SOS*, 519.

65. GS manuscript.

66. *SOS*, 519.

67. GS manuscript.

68. Author's interview with Michelle Amon.

69. Gloria Swanson, "I Am 'Not' Going to Write My Memoirs," *Sight and Sound* 38 (Spring 1969), 58.

70. Lee Graham, *Canyon Crier* (Toluca Lake, CA), February 21, 1977, 6.

71. Gloria Swanson to Phyllis Diller, undated, private collection.

72. *Publishers Weekly*, April 11, 1980.

73. *Hollywood Studio Magazine*, June 1980.

74. Dick Lochte, "Swanson Delivers Autobiography," *Los Angeles Times*, October 19, 1980.

75. *Time*, October 13, 1980.

76. "Gloria Swanson: The Movie Star and the Magnate," *Ladies' Home Journal*, November 1980, 66.

77. Janet Maslin, "A Star Remembers," *NYT*, November 9, 1980, 12.

78. Malcolm Boyd, "Inside View of Swanson's 'Glamorous Ghetto,'" *Los Angeles Times*, November 16, 1980, 10.

79. Brigitte Weeks and Armistead Maupin, "Woman With a Past," *New West*, November 3, 1980, 34.

80. Sally Struthers, "The Book Page," *Hollywood Reporter*, December 19, 1980, 24.

81. Clyde Haberman and Albin Krebs, "Notes on People," *NYT*, March 10, 1979, 12.

82. Michael J. Bandler, "Swanson on Swanson," *Modern Maturity*, October-November 1980, 73.

83. Steven M. L. Aronson, "Gloria Swanson," *Interview*, February, 1981.

84. Molly Haskell, "The Other Side of the Legend," *Vogue*, December 1980, 265.

85. Michael J. Bandler, "Swanson on Swanson," *Modern Maturity*, October-November 1980, 72.

86. Kevin Thomas, "Gloria Swanson: Between Glamor Puss, Old Shoe," *Los Angeles Times*, February 24, 1974.

87. Carol Lawson, "Behind the Best Sellers," *NYT*, January 25, 1981, BR8.

88. Steven M. L. Aronson, "Gloria Swanson," *Interview* February, 1981.

89. Molly Haskell, "The Other Side of the Legend," *Vogue*, December 1980, 325.

90. *SOS* Foreword, unpaged.

91. Raymond Daum to Michelle Amon, April 19, 1982, GSP.

92. "Gloria Swanson, Beyond the Singe," *Washington Post*, December 12, 1980.

93. Michael J. Bandler, "Swanson on Swanson," *Modern Maturity*, October-November 1980, 70.

94. Paul Spehr to the author, September 21, 2010.

95. *SOS*, 498.

96. Frederick C. Klein, "Actress and Ex-Senator Believe in Conquering Age by Staying Active," *Wall Street Journal*, March 10, 1983, 10.

GLORIA SWANSON
FILMOGRAPHY

The Ambition of the Baron (1915)
Essanay Film Manufacturing Company. 2 reels. Released January 1915.
Cast: Francis X. Bushman, Beverly Bayne, Thomas Commerford, Lester Cuneo, Joseph
   B. Totten, Betty Browne, Helen Dunbar, Richard Travers, Gerda Holmes.

Sweedie Goes to College (1915)
Essanay Film Manufacturing Company. Directed by Richard Foster Baker and/or E.
   Mason Hopper. 1–2 reels. Released February 1915.
Cast: Wallace Beery, Ben Turpin, Charlotte Mineau, Virginia Bowker.

His New Job (1915)
Essanay Film Manufacturing Company. Produced by Jess Robbins. Scenario by Charles
   Chaplin. Directed by Charles Chaplin. Also known as *Charlie's New Job*. 2 reels.
   Released February 1915.
Cast: Charles Chaplin, Ben Turpin, Leo White, Charlotte Mineau, Charles J. Stine, Robert
   Bolder, Arthur W. Bates, Jess Robbins, Charles Hitchcock, Frank J. Coleman, Charles
   Insley, Bud Jamison, Billy Armstrong, Agnes Ayres.

The Fable of Elvira, Farina and the Meal Ticket (1915)
Essanay Film Manufacturing Company. Directed by R. E. Baker. From the screen story
   by George Ade. 3 reels. Released Spring 1915.
Cast: Gerda Holmes.

The Broken Pledge (1915)
Essanay Film Manufacturing Company. Scenario by Louella Parsons and Edmund Lowe.
   1–2 reels. Released June 1915.
Cast: Wallace Beery, Harry Dunkinson, Virginia Bowker.

The Romance of an American Duchess (1915)
Essanay Film Manufacturing Company. 2 reels. Released Fall 1915.
Cast: Richard C. Travers, Sydney Ainsworth, Estelle Scott, Ruth Stonehouse.

A Dash of Courage (1916)

Keystone Film Company. Distributed by Triangle. Directed by Charles Parrott. Photographed by Paul Garnett. 2 reels. Released May 1916.

Cast: Harry Gribbon, Guy Woodward, Bobby Vernon, Frank Opperman, Wallace Beery, William Mason, Raymond Griffith.

Hearts and Sparks (1916)

Keystone Film Company. Distributed by Triangle. Directed by Charles Parrott. Assistant director: Daniel Albert. Supervised by Mack Sennett. Scenario by Hampton Del Ruth. Photographed by Paul Garnett. 2 reels. Released July 1916.

Cast: Hank Mann, Bobby Vernon, Nick Cogley, Billie Bennett, Tom Kennedy, Joe Lee, "Slim" Summerville, Wallace Beery.

A Social Cub (1916)

Keystone Film Company. Distributed by Triangle. Directed by Clarence Badger. Assistant director: Don O'Brien. Supervised by Mack Sennett. Scenario by Harry Wulze. Photographed by J. C. Bitzer. Also known as *A Social Club*. 2 reels. Released August 1916.

Cast: Bobby Vernon, Elizabeth De Witt, Reggie Morris, Harry Gribbon, Josef Swickard, Della Pringle.

The Danger Girl (1916)

Keystone Film Company. Distributed by Triangle. Directed by Clarence Badger. Supervised by Mack Sennett. Working title: *Love on Skates*. 2 reels. Released October 1916.

Cast: Bobby Vernon, Helen Bray, Myrtle Lind, Reggie Morris, Eddie Sutherland, Bert Gillespie, Josef Swickard.

Haystacks and Steeples (1916)

Keystone Film Company. Distributed by Triangle. Directed by Clarence Badger. Assistant director: Burt Lund. Supervised by Mack Sennett. Photographed by J. C. Bitzer. Working title: *Farm Story*. 2 reels. Released November 1916.

Cast: Bobby Vernon, Reggie Morris, Della Pringle, George Felix, Eva Thatcher, Helen Bray, Josef Swickard.

The Nick-of-Time Baby (1917)

Keystone Film Company. Distributed by Triangle. Directed by Clarence Badger. 2 reels. Released February 1917.

Cast: Bobby Vernon, Earle Rodney, Sylvia Ashton, Clarence Lyndon, Helen Bray, Teddy the dog.

Teddy at the Throttle (1917)

Keystone Film Company. Distributed by Triangle. Directed by Clarence Badger. Photographed by J. C. Bitzer. 2 reels. Released April 1917.

Cast: Bobby Vernon, Wallace Beery, May Emory, Blanche Phillips, Teddy the dog, Charles Bennett, Bert Gillespie.

Baseball Madness (1917)

Victor Film Company. Distributed by Universal. Directed by Billy Mason. Written by Billy
    Mason and Albert Russell. 3 reels. Released May 1917.

Cast: Billy Mason, Orin Jackson, Countess Du Cello, Marc Fenton, Victor Potel.

Whose Baby? (1917)

Keystone Film Company. Distributed by Triangle. Directed by Clarence Badger. Electrical
    effects: Paul Guerin. Working title: *A Mock Bigamist*. 2 reels. Released July 1917.

Cast: Bobby Vernon, William Irving, Clarence Lyndon, Ethel Teare, Charles Bennett, Tom
    Kennedy, Edgar Kennedy, Vera Steadman, Edith Valk, Phyllis Haver, Florence Clark,
    Myrtle Lind, Roxana McGowan, Virginia Nightengale, Marvel Rea, Charles Force,
    Sylvia Ashton, Guy Woodward.

The Sultan's Wife (1917)

Keystone Film Company. Distributed by Triangle. Directed by Clarence Badger. Also
    known as *Caught in a Harem*. 2 reels. Released September 1917.

Cast: Bobby Vernon, Joseph Callahan, Frank Bond, Blanche Payson, Gonda Durand,
    Roxana McGowan, Vera Steadman, Edith Valk, Teddy the dog.

The Pullman Bride (1917)

Paramount-Mack Sennett Comedies. Distributed by Famous Players-Lasky. Directed
    by Clarence Badger, with Hampton Del Ruth. Assistant director: Harry Kerr.
    Photographed by J. R. Lockwood. 2 reels. Released November 1917.

Cast: Mack Swain, Chester Conklin, Laura La Varnie, Tom Kennedy, Polly Moran, James
    Donnelly, Gene Rogers, Frank B. "Jack" Cooper, Vera Steadman, "Abdul the Turk"
    Maljan, Glen Cavender, Bert Gillespie, Tony O'Sullivan, Phyllis Haver, Clarence
    Lyndon, Elinor Field, Marvel Rea.

FEATURE FILMS

Society for Sale (1918)

Triangle Film Corporation. Directed by Frank Borzage. Scenario by Charles J. Wilson.
    Story by Ruby Mildred Ayres. Photographed by Pliny Horne. 5 reels. Released April
    1918.

Cast: William Desmond, Herbert Prior, Charles Dorian, Lillian West, Lillian Langdon.

Her Decision (1918)

Triangle Film Corporation. Directed by Jack Conway. Scenario by Charles J. Wilson Jr.
    Based on a story by Lotta Gannet. Photographed by Elgin Lessley. 5 reels. Released
    May 1918.

Cast: J. Barney Sherry, Darrell Foss, Ann Kroman.

Station Content (1918)

Triangle Film Corporation. Directed by Arthur Hoyt. Scenario by Charles J. Wilson. Story
    by Catherine Carr. Photographed by Elgin Lessley. 5 reels. Released June 1918.

Cast: Lee Hill, Arthur Millett, Nellie Allen, Ward Caulfield, May Walters, Diana Carrillo.

You Can't Believe Everything (1918)

Triangle Film Corporation. Directed by Jack Conway. Scenario by Charles Mortimer Peck. Based on "Smoke," by Norman Sherbrook. Photographed by Elgin Lessley. 5 reels. Released June 1918.

Cast: Darrell Foss, Jack Richardson, Edward Peil, George Hernandez, Iris Ashton, Grover Franke, Kitty Bradbury, Bliss Chevalier.

Everywoman's Husband (1918)

Triangle Film Corporation. Directed by Gilbert P. Hamilton. Scenario by Charles J. Wilson Jr. Story by John Clymer and G. Logue. Photographed by Tom Buckingham. 5 reels. Released July 1918.

Cast: Joe King, Lillian Langdon, George Pearce, Lillian West, Jack Livingston, Walt Whitman, Ed Brady.

Shifting Sands (1918)

Triangle Film Corporation. Directed by Albert Parker. Assistant director: Amy E. Sacker. Scenario by Catherine Carr. Story by Charles Turner Dazey. Photographed by Pliny Horne. 5 reels. Released August 1918.

Cast: Joe King, Harvey Clark, Leone Carton, Lillian Langdon, Arthur Millett.

The Secret Code (1918)

Triangle Film Corporation. Directed by Albert Parker. Scenario by Catherine Carr. Story by Adela Rogers St. Johns. Photographed by Pliny Horne. 5 reels. Released September 1918.

Cast: J. Barney Sherry, Rhy Alexander, Leslie Stewart, Joe King, Dorothy Wallace, Lee Phelps.

Wife or Country (1918)

Triangle Film Corporation. Directed by E. Mason Hopper. Scenario by Charles J. Wilson. Story by Harry Mestayer. Photographed by Clyde R. Cook. 5 reels. Released December 1918.

Cast: Harry Mestayer, Gretchen Lederer, Jack Richardson, Charles West.

Don't Change Your Husband (1919)

Famous Players-Lasky. Distributed by Paramount-Artcraft. Presented by Jesse L. Lasky. Directed by Cecil B. DeMille. Assistant director: Sam Wood. Story and scenario by Jeanie Macpherson. Based on a novel by David Graham Phillips. Photographed by Alvin Wyckoff. Edited by Anne Bauchens. Art director: Wilfred Buckland. 5 reels. Released January 1919.

Cast: Elliott Dexter, Lew Cody, Sylvia Ashton, Theodore Roberts, Julia Faye, James Neill.

For Better, For Worse (1919)

Famous Players-Lasky. Distributed by Paramount-Artcraft. Presented by Jesse L. Lasky. Produced and directed by Cecil B. DeMille. Assistant director: Sam Wood. Scenario by Jeanie Macpherson and William C. de Mille. Story by Edgar Selwyn. Photographed by Alvin Wyckoff. Art director: Wilfred Buckland. Edited by Anne Bauchens. 7 reels. Released April 1919.

Cast: Elliott Dexter, Tom Forman, Sylvia Ashton, Raymond Hatton, Theodore Roberts, Wanda Hawley, Winter Hall, Jack Holt, Fred Huntley.

Male and Female (1919)
Famous Players-Lasky. Distributed by Paramount-Artcraft. Presented by Jesse L. Lasky. Directed by Cecil B. DeMille. Scenario by Jeanie Macpherson. Based on *The Admirable Crichton*, by Sir James M. Barrie. Photographed by Alvin Wyckoff. Art director: Wilfred Buckland. Costumes by Mitchell Leisen. 9 reels. Released November 1919.
Cast: Thomas Meighan, Theodore Roberts, Raymond Hatton, Robert Cain, Lila Lee, Bebe Daniels, Julia Faye, Rhy Darby, Mildred Reardon, Maym Kelso, Edward Burns, Henry Woodward, Sydney Dean, Wesley Barry, Edna Mae Cooper, Lillian Leighton, Guy Oliver, Clarence Burton.

Why Change Your Wife? (1920)
Famous Players-Lasky. Distributed by Paramount-Artcraft. Presented by Jesse L. Lasky. Production manager: Howard Higgins. Directed by Cecil B. DeMille. Assistant director: Sam Wood. Scenario by Olga Printzlau and Sada Cowan. Story by William C. de Mille. Photographed by Alvin Wyckoff. Costumes by Clare West and Mitchell Leisen. Edited by Anne Bauchens. 7 reels. Released May 1920.
Cast: Thomas Meighan, Bebe Daniels, Theodore Kosloff, Clarence Geldart, Sylvia Ashton, Maym Kelso, Lucien Littlefield, Edna Mae Cooper, Jane Wolfe.

Something to Think About (1920)
Famous Players-Lasky. Distributed by Paramount. Presented by Jesse L. Lasky. Directed by Cecil B. DeMille. Story by Jeanie Macpherson. Photographed by Alvin Wyckoff and Karl Struss. Edited by Anne Bauchens. 7 reels. Released October 1920.
Cast: Elliott Dexter, Theodore Roberts, Julia Faye, Monte Blue, Mickey Moore, James Mason, Togo Yammamoto, Theodore Kosloff.

The Great Moment (1921)
Famous Players-Lasky. Distributed by Paramount. Presented by Jesse L. Lasky. Directed by Sam Wood. Scenario by Monte M. Katterjohn. Story by Elinor Glyn. Photographed by Alfred Gilks. 7 reels. Released September 1921.
Cast: Alec B. Francis, Milton Sills, F. R. Butler, Arthur Hull, Raymond Blathwayt, Helen Dunbar, Clarence Geldart, Julia Faye, Ann Grigg.

The Affairs of Anatol (1921)
Famous Players-Lasky. Distributed by Paramount. Presented by Jesse L. Lasky. Directed by Cecil B. DeMille. Scenario by Jeanie Macpherson. Photographed by Alvin Wyckoff and Karl Struss. Working title: *Five Kisses*. 9 reels. Released September 1921.
Cast: Wallace Reid, Elliott Dexter, Bebe Daniels, Monte Blue, Wanda Hawley, Theodore Roberts, Agnes Ayres, Theodore Kosloff, Polly Moran, Raymond Hatton, Julia Faye, Charles Ogle, Winter Hall.

Under the Lash (1921)
Famous Players-Lasky. Distributed by Paramount. Presented by Jesse L. Lasky. Directed by Sam Wood. Scenario by J. E. Nash. Based on *The Shulamite*, by Alice Askew and

Claude Askew. Photographed by Al Gilks. Assistant director: A. R. Hamm. 6 reels. Released October 1921.

Cast: Mahlon Hamilton, Russell Simpson, Lillian Leighton, Lincoln Stedman, Thena Jasper, Clarence Ford.

Don't Tell Everything (1921)

Famous Players-Lasky. Distributed by Paramount. Presented by Jesse L. Lasky. Supervised by Thompson Buchanan. Directed by Sam Wood. Scenario by Albert Shelby Le Vino. Story by Lorna Moon. Photographed by Al Gilks. Assistant director: A. R. Hamm. 5 reels. Released November 1921.

Cast: Wallace Reid, Elliott Dexter, Dorothy Cumming, Genevieve Blinn, Baby Gloria Wood, De Briac Twins.

Her Husband's Trademark (1922)

Famous Players-Lasky. Distributed by Paramount. Presented by Jesse L. Lasky. Directed by Sam Wood. Adaptation by Lorna Moon. Story by Clara Beranger. Photographed by Al Gilks. 5 reels. Released February 1922.

Cast: Richard Wayne, Stuart Holmes, Lucien Littlefield, Charles Ogle, Edythe Chapman, Clarence Burton, James Neill.

Beyond the Rocks (1922)

Famous Players-Lasky. Distributed by Paramount. Presented by Jesse L. Lasky. Directed by Sam Wood. Adaptation by Jack Cunningham. Based on the novel by Elinor Glyn. Photographed by Alfred Gilks. 7 reels. Released May 1922.

Cast: Rudolph Valentino, Edythe Chapman, Alec B. Francis, Robert Bolder, Gertrude Astor, Mabel Van Buren, Helen Dunbar, Raymond Blathwayt, F. R. Butler, June Elvidge.

Her Gilded Cage (1922)

Famous Players-Lasky. Distributed by Paramount. Presented by Jesse L. Lasky. Directed by Sam Wood. Adaptation by Elmer Harris and Percy Heath. Based on the play by Anne Nichols. Photographed by Alfred Gilks. 6 reels. Released August 1922.

Cast: David Powell, Harrison Ford, Anne Cornwall, Walter Hiers, Charles A. Stevenson.

The Impossible Mrs. Bellew (1922)

Famous Players-Lasky. Distributed by Paramount. Presented by Jesse L. Lasky. Directed by Sam Wood. Scenario and adaptation by Percy Heath and Monte M. Katterjohn. Based on the novel by David Lisle. Photographed by Alfred Gilks. 8 reels. Released October 1922.

Cast: Robert Cain, Conrad Nagel, Richard Wayne, Frank Elliott, Gertrude Astor, June Elvidge, Herbert Standing, Mickey Moore, Pat Moore, Helen Dunbar, Arthur Hull, Clarence Burton.

My American Wife (1922)

Famous Players-Lasky. Distributed by Paramount. Presented by Jesse L. Lasky. Directed by Sam Wood. Scenario by Monte M. Katterjohn. Based on the story by Hector Turnbull. Photographed by Alfred Gilks. 6 reels. Released December 1922.

Cast: Antonio Moreno, Josef Swickard, Eric Mayne, Gino Corrado, Edythe Chapman, Aileen Pringle, Walter Long, F. R. Butler, Jacques D'Auray, Loyal Underwood, Mary Land.

Prodigal Daughters (1923)

Famous Players-Lasky. Distributed by Paramount. Presented by Jesse L. Lasky. Directed by Sam Wood. Scenario by Monte M. Katterjohn. Based on the novel by Joseph Hocking. Photographed by Alfred Gilks. 6 reels. Released April 1923.

Cast: Ralph Graves, Vera Reynolds, Theodore Roberts, Louise Dresser, Charles Clary, Robert Agnew, Maude Wayne, Jiquel Lanoe, Eric Mayne, Antonio Corso.

Bluebeard's 8th Wife (1923)

Famous Players-Lasky. Distributed by Paramount. Presented by Jesse L. Lasky. Directed by Sam Wood. Scenario by Sada Cowan. Based on the play by Alfred Savoir. Photographed by Alfred Gilks. Hair dressed by Hattie Tabourne. 6 reels. Released August 1923.

Cast: Huntley Gordon, Charles Green, Lianne Salvor, Paul Weigel, Frank Butler, Robert Agnew, Irene Dalton, Majel Coleman, Thais Valdemar.

Zaza (1923)

Famous Players-Lasky. Distributed by Paramount. Presented by Adolph Zukor. Directed by Allan Dwan. Scenario by Albert Shelby Le Vino. Based on the play by Pierre François Samuel Berton and Charles Simon. Photographed by Hal Rosson. 7 reels. Released September 1923.

Cast: H. B. Warner, Ferdinand Gottschalk, Lucille La Verne, Mary Thurman, Yvonne Hughes, Riley Hatch, Roger Lytton, Ivan Linow.

The Humming Bird (1924)

Famous Players-Lasky. Distributed by Paramount. Presented by Adolph Zukor and Jesse L. Lasky. Directed by Sidney Olcott. Adaptation by Forrest Halsey. Based on the play by Maude Fulton. Photographed by Harry Fischbeck. Edited by Patricia Rooney. Technical advisor: Jacques d'Auray. 8 reels. Released January 1924.

Cast: Edward Burns, William Ricciardi, Cesare Gravina, Mario Majeroni, Adrienne D'Ambricourt, Helen Lindroth, Rafael Bongini, Regina Quinn, Aurelio Coccia, Jacques D'Auray.

A Society Scandal (1924)

Famous Players-Lasky. Distributed by Paramount. Presented by Adolph Zukor and Jesse L. Lasky. Produced and directed by Allan Dwan. Scenario by Forrest Halsey. Based on the play by Alfred Sutro. Photographed by Hal Rosson. 7 reels. Released March 1924.

Cast: Rod LaRocque, Ricardo Cortez, Allan Simpson, Ida Waterman, Thelma Converse, Fraser Coalter, Catherine Proctor, Wilfred Donovan, Yvonne Hughes, Catherine Coleburn, Marie Shelton, Dorothy Stokes, Cornelius Keefe.

Manhandled (1924)

Famous Players-Lasky. Distributed by Paramount. Presented by Adolph Zukor and Jesse L. Lasky. Directed by Allan Dwan. Supervising editor: William Le Baron. Scenario by

Frank W. Tuttle. Based on the story by Arthur Stringer. Edited and titles by Julian Johnson. Photographed by Hal Rosson. 7 reels. Released August 1924.

Cast: Tom Moore, Lilyan Tashman, Ian Keith, Arthur Housman, Paul McAllister, Frank Morgan, M. Collosse, Marie Shelton, Carrie Scott, Ann Pennington, Brooke Johns, Frank Allworth.

Her Love Story (1924)

Famous Players-Lasky. Distributed by Paramount. Presented by Adolph Zukor and Jesse L. Lasky. Directed by Allan Dwan. Scenario by Frank Tuttle. Based on the story by Mary Roberts Rinehart. Photographed by George Webber. 7 reels. Released October 1924.

Cast: Ian Keith, George Fawcett, Echlin Gayer, Mario Majeroni, Sidney Herbert, Donald Hall, Baroness de Hedemann, Jane Auburn, Bert Wales, General Lodijensky.

Wages of Virtue (1924)

Famous Players-Lasky. Distributed by Paramount. Presented by Adolph Zukor and Jesse L. Lasky. Produced and directed by Allan Dwan. Scenario by Forrest Halsey. Based on the novel by P. C. Wren. Photographed by George Webber. 7 reels. Released November 1924.

Cast: Ben Lyon, Norman Trevor, Ivan Linow, Armand Cortez, Adrienne D'Ambricourt, Paul Panzer, Joe Moore.

Madame Sans-Gêne (1925)

Famous Players-Lasky. Distributed by Paramount. Presented by Adolph Zukor and Jesse L. Lasky. Directed by Léonce Perret. Screenplay by Forrest Halsey. Based on the play by Victorien Sardou and Emile Moreau. Photographed by George Webber. 10 reels. Released April 1925.

Cast: Emile Drain, Charles De Roche, Madelaine Guitty, Warwick Ward, Henry Favieres, Renée Heribelle, Suzanne Bianchetti, Denise Lorys, Jacques Marney.

The Coast of Folly (1925)

Famous Players-Lasky. Distributed by Paramount. Presented by Adolph Zukor and Jesse L. Lasky. Directed by Allan Dwan. Screenplay by Forrest Halsey. Adaptation by James Ashmore Creelman. Based on the novel by Conigsby William Dawson. Photographed by George F. Webber. 7 reels. Released September 1925.

Cast: Anthony Jowitt, Alec Francis, Dorothy Cumming, Jed Prouty, Eugenie Besserer, Arthur Housman, Lawrence Gray.

Stage Struck (1925)

Famous Players-Lasky. Distributed by Paramount. Directed by Allan Dwan. Screenplay by Forrest Halsey. Adaptation by Sylvia La Varre. Story by Frank R. Adams. Photographed by George Webber. Art director: Van Nest Polglase. 7 reels. Released November 1925.

Cast: Lawrence Gray, Gertrude Astor, Marguerite Evans, Ford Sterling, Carrie Scott, Emil Hoch, Margery Whittington.

The Untamed Lady (1926)

Famous Players-Lasky. Distributed by Paramount. Presented by Adolph Zukor and Jesse L. Lasky. Directed by Frank Tuttle. Scenario by James Ashmore Creelman. Photographed by George Webber. Based on the story by Fannie Hurst. 7 reels. Released March 1926.

Cast: Lawrence Gray, Joseph Smiley, Charles Graham.

Fine Manners (1926)

Famous Players-Lasky. Distributed by Paramount. Presented by Adolph Zukor and Jesse L. Lasky. Directed by Richard Rosson. Screenplay by James Ashmore Creelman. Story by James Ashmore Creelman and Frank Vreeland. Photographed by George Webber. 7 reels. Released August 1926.

Cast: Eugene O'Brien, Helen Dunbar, Walter Goss, John Miltern.

The Love of Sunya (1927)

Swanson Producing Corporation. Distributed by United Artists. Directed by Albert Parker. Screen story by Earle Browne. Based on *Eyes of Youth*, by Charles Guernon and Max Marcin. Photographed by Robert Martin. Art director: Hugo Ballin. Assistant director: Paul Madeux. Production manager: Robert Schable. Consultant: Dudley Murphy. 8 reels. Released March 1927.

Cast: John Boles, Anders Randolf, Andres De Segurola, Hugh Miller, Ian Keith, Pauline Garon, Flobelle Fairbanks, Raymond Hackett, Ivan Lebedeff, Robert Schable, John Miltern, Forrest Huff.

Sadie Thompson (1928)

Gloria Swanson Productions. Distributed by United Artists. Directed and written by Raoul Walsh. Based on "Rain," by Somerset Maugham, and *Rain*, by John Colton and Clemence Randolph. Titles by C. Gardner Sullivan. Photographed by Oliver Marsh, George Barnes, and Robert Kurrle. Art director: William Cameron Menzies. Edited by C. Gardner Sullivan. Assistant director: William Tummel. Production manager: Pierre Bedard. 9 reels. Released January 1928.

Cast: Lionel Barrymore, Raoul Walsh, Blanche Frederici, Charles Lane, Florence Midgley, James A. Marcus, Sophia Artega, Will Stanton.

Queen Kelly (1928)

Produced by Joseph P. Kennedy. Distributed by United Artists. Direction, story, and scenario by Erich von Stroheim. Photographed by Ben Reynolds, Gordon Pollock, and Paul Ivano. Art directors: Harold Miles and Richard Day. Edited by Viola Lawrence. Music by Adolf Tandler. Assistant directors: Eddy Sowders and Louis Germonprez. Costumes by Max Ree. 11[?] reels. Not released in the US.

Cast: Walter Byron, Seena Owen, Sidney Bracey, William von Brinken, Sylvia Ashton, Tully Marshall.

The Trespasser (1929)

Gloria Productions. Distributed by United Artists. Presented by Joseph P. Kennedy. Story, dialogue, and direction by Edmund Goulding. Photographed by George Barnes and Gregg Toland. Art director: Stephen Goosson. Edited by Cyril Gardner. Music by

Josiah Zuro. Sound technician: Earl A. Wolcott. Wardrobe by Ann Morgan and Judge Johnson. Song "Love, Your Magic Spell Is Everywhere," by Edmund Goulding and Elsie Janis. 10 reels. Released October 1929.

Cast: Robert Ames, Purnell Pratt, Henry B. Walthall, Wally Albright Jr., William Holden, Blanche Frederici, Kay Hammond, Mary Forbes, Marcelle Corday.

What a Widow! (1930)

Gloria Productions. Distributed by United Artists. Presented by Joseph P. Kennedy. Directed by Allan Dwan. Adaptation and dialogue by James Gleason and James Seymour. Story by Josephine Lovett. Photographed by George Barnes. Art director: Paul Nelson. Edited by Viola Lawrence. Music director: Josiah Zuro. Songs by Vincent Youmans. Orchestrations by Hugo Felix. Recording engineers: Earl A. Wolcott and D. A. Cutler. 10 reels. Released September 1930.

Cast: Owen Moore, Lew Cody, Margaret Livingston, William Holden, Herbert Braggiotti, Gregory Gaye, Adrienne D'Ambricourt, Nella Walker, Daphne Pollard.

Indiscreet (1931)

Feature Productions, Inc. A DeSylva, Brown & Henderson Production. Distributed by United Artists. Presented by Joseph M. Schenck. Directed by Leo McCarey. Assistant director: Harry Scott. Written by B. G. DeSylva, Lew Brown, Ray Henderson, and Leo McCarey. Photographed by Ray June and Gregg Toland. Art director: Richard Day. Edited by Hal C. Kern. Costumes by René Hubert. Music director: Alfred Newman. Sound recording by Oscar Lagerstrom. Production manager: James Dent. Songs by B. G. DeSylva, Lew Brown, and Ray Henderson. 92–94 minutes. Released April 1931.

Cast: Ben Lyon, Arthur Lake, Barbara Kent, Monroe Owsley, Maude Eburne, Henry Kolker, Nella Walker.

Tonight or Never (1931)

Feature Productions, Inc. Distributed by United Artists. Presented and produced by Samuel Goldwyn. Directed by Mervyn Le Roy. Assistant director: Gordon Hollingshead. Written by Ernest Vajda. Based on the play by Lili Havatny. Photographed by Gregg Toland. Sets by Willy Pogány. Edited by Grant Whytock. Gowns by Chanel of Paris. Musical director: Alfred Newman. Sound technician: Vinton Vernon. 82 minutes. Released December 1931.

Cast: Melvyn Douglas, Alison Skipworth, Ferdinand Gottschalk, Robert Greig, Warburton Gamble, Greta Meyer, Boris Karloff.

Perfect Understanding (1933)

Gloria Swanson British Productions, Ltd. Distributed by United Artists. Directed by Cyril Gardner. Story by Miles Malleson. Adaptation by Michael Powell. Dialogue by Miles Malleson and Garrett Graham. Photographed by Curt Courant. Art director: Oscar Werndorff. Edited by Thorold Dickinson. Gowns by Ann Morgan. Musical director: Philip Braham. Orchestration by Leonard Hornsey. Sound recording: A. D. Valentine. Production manager: Sergei Nolbandov. Titles by E. McKnight Kauffer. 81–84 minutes. Released March 1933.

Cast: Laurence Olivier, John Halliday, Nigel Playfair, Michael Farmer, Genevieve Tobin, Charles Cullum, Nora Swinburne, O. B. Clarence, Mary Jerrold, Peter Gawthorne,

Rosalinde Fuller, Miles Malleson, Ben Webster, Herbert Lomas, Charles Childerstone, Evalyn Bostock.

Music in the Air (1934)

Fox Film Corporation. An Erich Pommer Production. Directed by Joe May. Screenplay by Howard I. Young and Billie Wilder. Based on the operetta by Jerome Kern and Oscar Hammerstein II. Continuity by Robert Liebmann. Photographed by Ernest Palmer. Art director: William Darling. Costumes by René Hubert. Music director: Louis de Francesco. Musical adaptation by Franz Waxman. Dances by Jack Donohue. Sound by A. L. Von Kirbach. Songs by Jerome Kern and Oscar Hammerstein II. 81–85 minutes. Released December 1934.

Cast: John Boles, Douglass Montgomery, June Lang, Al Shean, Reginald Owen, Joseph Cawthorn, Hobart Bosworth, Sara Haden, Roger Imhof, Jed Prouty, Christian Rub, Fuzzy Knight, Marjorie Main.

Father Takes a Wife (1941)

RKO Radio Pictures, Inc. Produced by Lee Marcus. Directed by Jack Hively. Assistant director: William Dorfman. Dialogue director: Peter Godfrey. Screenplay by Dorothy Fields and Herbert Fields. Photographed by Robert de Grasse. Art director: Van Nest Polglase. Art director associate: Albert D'Agostino. Edited by George Hively. Set decorator: Darrell Silvera. Gowns by René Hubert. Other wardrobe by Edward Stevenson. Jewelry by Laykin and Co. Musical director: Roy Webb. Recorded by Hugh McDowell Jr. 79 minutes. Released October 1941.

Cast: Adolphe Menjou, John Howard, Desi Arnaz, Helen Broderick, Florence Rice, Neil Hamilton, Grady Sutton, George Meader, Mary Treen, Ruth Dietrich, Grant Withers.

Sunset Boulevard (1950)

Paramount Pictures, Inc. Produced by Charles Brackett. Directed by Billy Wilder. Assistant director: C. C. Coleman Jr. Written by Charles Brackett, Billy Wilder, and D. M. Marshman Jr. Photographed by John F. Seitz. Special photographic effects by Gordon Jennings. Process photography by Farciot Edouart. Art directors: Hans Dreier and John Meehan. Edited by Arthur Schmidt. Editing supervisor: Doane Harrison. Art decorators: Sam Comer and Ray Moyer. Costumes by Edith Head. Musical score by Franz Waxman. Sound recording by Harry Lindgren and John Cope. Makeup supervised by Wally Westmore. 115 minutes. Released August 1950.

Cast: William Holden, Erich von Stroheim, Nancy Olson, Fred Clark, Lloyd Gough, Jack Webb, Franklyn Farnum, Larry Blake, Charles Dayton, Cecil B. DeMille, Hedda Hopper, Buster Keaton, Anna Q. Nilsson, H. B. Warner, Ray Evans, Jay Livingston.

3 for Bedroom C (1952)

Brenco Pictures Corporation. Distributed by Warner Bros. Produced by Milton H. Bren and Edward L. Alperson Jr. Written and directed by Milton H. Bren. Based on the novel by Goddard Lieberson. Photographed by Ernest Laszlo. Art director: Boris Leven. Edited by Arthur Hilton. Wardrobe creations by Gloria Swanson. Wardrobe by Norma, Olive Konitz, and Gene Martin. Music by Heinz Roemhild. Sound by Earl Crain Sr. 74 minutes. Released June 1952.

Cast: James Warren, Fred Clark, Hans Conried, Janine Perreau, Ernest Anderson, Steve Brodie, Margaret Dumont, Richard "Skeets" Gallagher.

Nero's Mistress (produced 1956; released 1962)

Les Films Marceau and Titanus. Distributed by Manhattan Films International. Produced by Franco Cristaldi. Directed by Steno. Written by Rodolfo Longo, Sandro Continenza, Diego Fabbri, Ugo Guerra, and Steno. Photographed by Mario Bava. Art director: Piero Filippone. 90–100 minutes. Released June 1962.

Cast: Alberto Sordi, Brigitte Bardot, Vittorio De Sica, Giorgia Moll, Ciccio Barbi, Mario Carotenuto, Mino Doro, Furlanetto, Carlo Tamberlani, Arturo Bragaglia.

Airport 1975 (1974)

Universal Pictures. Produced by Jennings Lang and William Frye. Directed by Jack Smight. Written by Don Ingalls. Photographed by Philip Lathrop. Art direction by George C. Webb. Edited by J. Terry Williams. Set decorator: Mickey S. Michaels. Costumes by Edith Head. Music by John Cacavas. Sound by Melvin M. Metcalf Sr. and Robert L. Hoyt. 106 minutes. Released October 1974.

Cast: Charlton Heston, Karen Black, George Kennedy, Efrem Zimbalist Jr., Susan Clark, Helen Reddy, Linda Blair, Dana Andrews, Roy Thinnes, Sid Caesar, Myrna Loy, Ed Nelson, Nancy Olson, Larry Storch, Martha Scott, Jerry Stiller, Norman Fell.

WORKS CITED

Abel, Richard. *The Ciné Goes to Town: French Cinema 1896–1914*. Berkeley: University of California Press, 1994.

———. *French Cinema: The First Wave, 1915–1929*. Princeton, NJ: Princeton University Press, 1984.

Affron, Charles. *Lillian Gish: Her Legend, Her Life*. New York: Scribners, 2001.

Alifano, Roberto. *Tirando Manteca al Techo (Hurling Lard at the Ceiling)*. Buenos Aires: Proa Amerian, 2011.

Altman, Rick. *Silent Film Sound*. New York: Columbia University Press, 2007.

Anger, Kenneth. *Hollywood Babylon*. San Francisco: Straight Arrow Books, 1975.

———. *Hollywood Babylon II*. New York: E. P. Dutton, 1984.

Ankerich, Michael G. *Broken Silence: Conversations with 23 Silent Film Stars*. Jefferson, NC: McFarland, 1993.

———. *The Sound of Silence: Conversations with 16 Film and Stage Personalities Who Bridged the Gap Between Silents and Talkies*. Jefferson, NC: McFarland, 1998.

Arnaz, Desi. *A Book*. New York: William Morrow and Company, 1976.

Arnold, Edward. *Lorenzo Goes to Hollywood: The Autobiography of Edward Arnold*. New York: Liveright Publishing Corporation, 1940.

Balio, Tino. *Grand Design: Hollywood as a Modern Business Enterprise, 1930–1939*. New York: Scribners, 1993.

———, ed. *Hollywood in the Age of Television*. Boston: Unwin Hyman, 1990.

———. *United Artists: The Company Built by the Stars*. Madison, WI: University of Wisconsin Press, 1976.

Barbas, Samantha. *The First Lady of Hollywood: A Biography of Louella Parsons*. Berkeley: University of California Press, 2005.

Barrymore, Lionel, and Cameron Shipp. *We Barrymores*. London: Peter Davies, 1951.

Bazin, André. *What is Cinema?* Translated by Hugh Gray. Berkeley: University of California Press, 1967.

Beauchamp, Cari. *Joseph P. Kennedy Presents: His Hollywood Years*. New York: Alfred A. Knopf, 2009.

———. *Without Lying Down: Frances Marion and the Powerful Women of Early Hollywood*. New York: Scribners, 1997.

Benedict, Dirk. *Confessions of a Kamikaze Cowboy*. North Hollywood, CA: Newcastle Publishing, 1987.

Bennett, Joan, and Lois Kibbee. *The Bennett Playbill*. New York: Holt, Rinehart and Winston, 1970.

Bergan, Ronald. *The United Artists Story*. New York: Crown, 1986.

Bernstein, Matthew. *Walter Wanger, Hollywood Independent*. Minneapolis: University of Minnesota Press, 1994.

Bickford, Charles. *Bulls, Balls, Bicycles and Actors*. New York: Paul S. Eriksson, Inc., 1965.

Birchard, Robert S. *Cecil B. DeMille's Hollywood*. Lexington, KY: University Press of Kentucky, 2004.

Blesh, Rudi. *Keaton*. New York: Collier Books, 1966.

Bogdanovich, Peter. *Allan Dwan: The Last Pioneer*. New York: Praeger, 1971.

———. *Who the Devil Made It*. New York: Alfred A. Knopf, 1997.

Bowser, Eileen. *The Transformation of Cinema 1907–1915*. New York: Scribners, 1990.

Brady, Frank. *Onassis: An Extravagant Life*. Englewood Cliffs, NJ: Prentice-Hall, 1977.

Bricktop, and James Haskins. *Bricktop*. New York: Atheneum, 1983.

Brooks, Louise. *Lulu in Hollywood*. New York: Alfred A. Knopf, 1983.

Brownlow, Kevin. *Behind the Mask of Innocence*. New York: Alfred A. Knopf, 1990.

———. *The Parade's Gone By*. New York: Bonanza Books, 1968.

———. *The War, the West, and the Wilderness*. New York: Alfred A. Knopf, 1979.

Bruno, Michael. *Venus in Hollywood: The Continental Enchantress from Garbo to Loren*. New York: Lyle Stuart, 1970.

Butters Jr., Gerald R. *Banned in Kansas: Motion Picture Censorship, 1915–1966*. Columbia, MO: University of Missouri Press, 2007.

Card, James. *Seductive Cinema: The Art of Silent Film*. New York: Alfred A. Knopf, 1994.

Carr, Larry. *Four Fabulous Faces: The Evolution and Metamorphosis of Garbo, Swanson, Crawford, and Dietrich*. New York: Arlington House, 1970.

Chaplin, Charles. *My Autobiography*. New York: Simon and Schuster, 1964.

Charles-Roux, Edmond. *Chanel: Her Life, Her World, and the Woman Behind the Legend She Herself Created*. New York: Alfred A. Knopf, 1975.

Cohen, Paula Marantz. *Silent Film and the Triumph of the American Myth*. New York: Oxford University Press, 2001.

Cooper, Miriam. *Dark Lady of the Silents: My Life in Early Hollywood*. Indianapolis: Bobbs-Merrill, 1973.

Crafton, Donald. *The Talkies: America's Transition to Sound 1926–1931*. New York: Scribners, 1997.

Crowe, Cameron. *Conversations with Wilder*. New York: Alfred A. Knopf, 1999.

Crowther, Bosley. *Hollywood Rajah: The Life and Times of Louis B. Mayer*. New York: Holt, Rinehart and Winston, 1960.

Curtiss, Thomas Quinn. *Von Stroheim*. New York: Farrar, Straus and Giroux, 1971.

Dale, Alan S. *Comedy is a Man in Trouble: Slapstick in American Movies*. Minneapolis: University of Minnesota Press, 2000.

Davis, Lon, and Debra Davis. *King of the Movies: Francis X. Bushman*. Albany, GA: BearManor Media, 2009.

DeCordova, Richard. *Picture Personalities: The Emergence of the Star System in America*. Urbana: University of Illinois Press, 1990.

Delson, Susan. *Dudley Murphy, Hollywood Wild Card*. Minneapolis: University of Minnesota Press, 2006.

de Mille, Agnes. *Portrait Gallery*. Boston: Houghton Mifflin, 1990.

DeMille. Cecil B. *The Autobiography of Cecil B. DeMille*. Englewood Cliffs, NJ: Prentice-Hall, 1959.

Deutsch, Armand. *Me and Bogie*. New York: G. P. Putnam's Sons, 1991.

Devi, Indra. *Yoga for Americans*. Englewood Cliffs, NJ: Prentice-Hall, 1959.

Drew, William. *Speaking of Silents: First Ladies of the Screen*. Vestal, NY: The Vestal Press, 1989.

Dufty, William. *Sugar Blues*. Radnor, PA: Chilton Book Company, 1975.

Edgerton, Gary. *The Columbia History of Television*. New York: Columbia University Press, 2007.

Edmonds, Andy. *Hot Toddy: The True Story of Hollywood's Most Sensational Murder*. New York: William Morrow, 1989.

Edwards, Anne. *The DeMilles: An American Family*. New York: Harry N. Abrams, 1988.

Essoe, Gabe, and Raymond Lee. *DeMille: The Man and His Pictures*. South Brunswick and New York: A. S. Barnes and Company, 1970.

Etherington-Smith, Meredith, and Jeremy Pilcher. *The 'It' Girls: Lucy, Lady Duff Gordon, the Couturiere 'Lucile,' and Elinor Glyn, Romantic Novelist*. New York: Harcourt Brace Jovanovich, 1986.

Evans, Peter. *Nemesis*. New York: HarperCollins, 2004.

Everson, William K. *American Silent Film*. New York: Oxford University Press, 1978.

Eyman, Scott. *Empire of Dreams: The Epic Life of Cecil B. DeMille*. New York: Simon and Schuster, 2010.

———. *Lion of Hollywood: The Life and Legend of Louis B. Mayer*. New York: Simon and Schuster, 2005.

———. *Mary Pickford: America's Sweetheart*. Toronto: Harper Collins, 1990.

Fairbanks Jr., Douglas. *The Salad Days*. New York: Doubleday, 1988.

Falaise, Henry de la. *Through Hell to Dunkirk*. Harrisburg, PA: Military Service Publishing, 1943.

Fischer, Lucy, ed. *American Cinema of the 1920s: Themes and Variations*. New Brunswick, NJ: Rutgers University Press, 2009.

Gabler, Neal. *An Empire of Their Own: How the Jews Invented Hollywood*. New York: Crown Publishers, 1988.

Gilbert, Douglas. *American Vaudeville: Its Life and Times*. New York: McGraw-Hill, 1940.

Gish, Lillian. *The Movies, Mr. Griffith and Me*. New York: Avon, 1969.

Glyn, Elinor. *Romantic Adventure*. New York: E. P. Dutton, 1937.

———. *Three Weeks*. New York: Duffield and Company, 1907.

Golden, Eve. *Golden Images: 41 Essays on Silent Film Stars*. Jefferson, NC: McFarland, 2001.

Goldwyn, Samuel. *Behind the Screen*. New York: George H. Doran Company, 1923.

Goodman, Ezra. *The Fifty Year Decline and Fall of Hollywood*. New York: Simon and Schuster, 1961.

Goodwin, Doris Kearns. *The Fitzgeralds and the Kennedys: An American Saga*. New York: Simon and Schuster, 1987.

Graham, Sheilah. *The Garden of Allah*. New York: Crown Publishers, 1970.

———. *Hollywood Revisited: A Fiftieth Anniversary Celebration*. New York: St. Martin's Press, 1985.

Grieveson, Lee, and Peter Kramer, eds. *The Silent Cinema Reader*. New York: Routledge, 2003.

Griffith, Richard. *The Movie Stars*. Garden City, NY: Doubleday, 1970.

Guiles, Fred Laurence. *Marion Davies: A Biography*. New York: McGraw-Hill, 1972.

Hadleigh, Boze. *Hollywood Lesbians*. New York: Barricade Books, 1994.

Hamilton, Nigel. *JFK: Reckless Youth*. New York: Random House, 1992.

Hampton, Benjamin. *History of the American Film Industry From Its Beginnings to 1931*. Reprint, New York: Dover, 1970.

Hansen, Miriam. *Babel and Babylon: Spectatorship in American Silent Film*. Cambridge: Harvard University Press, 1991.

Hardt, Ursula. *From Caligari to California: Erich Pommer's Life in the International Film Wars*. Providence, RI: Berghahn Books, 1996.

Hays, Will H. *The Memoirs of Will H. Hays*. Garden City, NY: Doubleday, 1955.

Hersh, Seymour M. *The Dark Side of Camelot*. New York: Little, Brown and Company, 1997.

Heymann, C. David. *A Woman Named Jackie*. New York: Lyle Stuart, 1989.

Higashi, Sumiko. *Cecil B. DeMille and American Culture*. Berkeley: University of California Press, 1994.

Higham, Charles. *Cecil B. DeMille*. New York: Charles Scribner's Sons, 1973.

———. *In and Out of Hollywood: A Biographer's Memoir*. Madison, WI: Terrace Books, 2009.

———. *Merchant of Dreams: Louis B. Mayer, M.G.M. and the Secret Hollywood*. New York: Donald I. Fine, 1993.

Hilmes, Michele. *Radio Voices: American Broadcasting, 1922–1952*. Minneapolis: University of Minnesota Press, 1997.

———, and Jason Loviglio, eds. *Radio Reader: Essays in the Cultural History of Radio*. New York: Routledge, 2002.

Hocking, Joseph. *Prodigal Daughters*. New York: Fleming H. Revell, 1921.

Hopper, Hedda. *From Under My Hat*. Garden City, NY: Doubleday, 1952.

———, and James Brough. *The Whole Truth and Nothing But*. Garden City, NY: Doubleday, 1962.

Hudson, Richard, and Raymond Lee. *Gloria Swanson*. New York: Castle Books, 1973.

Huff, Theodore. *Charlie Chaplin*. New York: Henry Schuman, 1951.

Hunter, Tab, with Eddie Muller. *Tab Hunter Confidential: The Making of a Movie Star*. Chapel Hill, NC: Algonquin Books, 2005.

Jacobs, Lea. *The Wages of Sin: Censorship and the Fallen Woman Film, 1928–1942*. Berkeley: University of California Press, 1995.

Jenkins, Henry. *What Made Pistachio Nuts? Early Sound Comedy and the Vaudeville Aesthetic*. New York: Columbia University Press, 1992.

Kanfer, Stefan. *Groucho: The Life and Times of Julius Henry Marx*. New York: Knopf, 2000.

Keaton, Buster, and Charles Samuels. *My Wonderful World of Slapstick*. Garden City, NY: Doubleday, 1960.

Kellow, Brian. *The Bennetts: An Acting Family*. Lexington, KY: University Press of Kentucky, 2004.

Kennedy, Harold J. *No Pickle, No Performance: An Irreverent Theatrical Excursion from Tallulah to Travolta*. Garden City, NY: Doubleday, 1978.

Kennedy, Joseph P. *The Story of the Films*. New York: A. W. Shaw, 1927.

Kennedy, Matthew. *Edmund Goulding's Dark Victory: Hollywood's Genius Bad Boy*. Madison: University of Wisconsin Press, 2004.

Kennedy, Rose Fitzgerald. *Times to Remember*. New York: Bantam Books, 1975.

Kiehn, David. *Broncho Billy and the Essanay Film Company*. Berkeley: Farwell Books, 2003.

King, Rob. *The Fun Factory: The Keystone Film Company and the Emergence of Mass Culture*. Berkeley: University of California Press, 2009.

Kirkpatrick, Sidney D. *A Cast of Killers*. New York: E. P. Dutton, 1986.

Kobal, John. *The Art of the Great Hollywood Portrait Photographers 1925–1940*. New York: Knopf, 1980.

———. *People Will Talk*. New York: Alfred A. Knopf, 1985.

Koszarski, Richard. *An Evening's Entertainment: The Age of the Silent Feature Picture, 1915–1928*. New York: Scribners, 1990.

———. *Hollywood on the Hudson: Film and Television in New York from Griffith to Sarnoff*. New Brunswick, NJ: Rutgers University Press, 2008.

———. *The Man You Loved to Hate: Erich von Stroheim and Hollywood*. New York: Oxford University Press, 1983.

———. *Von: The Life and Times of Erich von Stroheim*. New York: Limelight, 2001.

Koury, Phil. *Yes, Mr. DeMille*. New York: G. P. Putnam's Sons, 1959.

Lahue, Kalton C. *World of Laughter: The Motion Picture Comedy Short, 1910–1930*. Norman, OK: University of Oklahoma Press, 1966.

Lally, Kevin. *Wilder Times: A Life of Billy Wilder*. New York: Henry Holt, 1996.

Lasky, Betty. *RKO: The Biggest Little Major of Them All*. Englewood Cliffs, NJ: Prentice-Hall, 1984.

Lasky, Jesse L. *I Blow My Own Horn*. New York: Doubleday, 1957.

Lasky Jr., Jesse L. *Whatever Happened to Hollywood?* New York: Funk & Wagnalls, 1975.

Leamer, Laurence. *The Kennedy Men 1901–1963*. New York: William Morrow, 2001.

———. *The Kennedy Women: The Saga of an American Family*. New York: Ballantine, 1994.

Leider, Emily Wortis. *Dark Lover: The Life and Death of Rudolph Valentino*. New York: Farrar, Straus and Giroux, 2003.

Leighton, Sara. *Of Savages and Kings*. Maidstone, Kent: Bachman & Turner, 1980.

Lennig, Arthur. *Stroheim*. Lexington, KY: University Press of Kentucky, 2000.

LeRoy, Mervyn. *Mervyn LeRoy: Take One*. New York: Hawthorn Books, 1974.

Long, Bruce. *William Desmond Taylor: A Dossier*. Metuchen, NJ: The Scarecrow Press, 1991.

Loos, Anita. *Cast of Thousands*. New York: Grosset & Dunlop, 1977.

———. *A Girl Like I*. New York: The Viking Press, 1966.

———. *Kiss Hollywood Good-By*. New York: The Viking Press, 1974.

———. *The Talmadge Girls*. New York: The Viking Press, 1978.

Louvish, Simon. *Cecil B. DeMille: A Life in Art*. New York: St. Martin's Press, 2007.

———. *Keystone: The Life and Clowns of Mack Sennett*. New York: Faber, 2003.

Love, Bessie. *From Hollywood With Love*. London: Elm Tree Books, 1977.

Lynn, Kenneth. *Charlie Chaplin and His Times*. New York: Simon and Schuster, 1997.

Maas, Frederica Sagor. *The Shocking Miss Pilgrim: A Writer in Early Hollywood*. Lexington, KY: University Press of Kentucky, 1999.

MacCann, Richard Dyer, ed. *Films of the 1920s*. Lanham, MD: The Scarecrow Press, 1996.

———, ed. *The First Film Makers*. Metuchen, NJ: The Scarecrow Press, 1989.

———, ed. *The Silent Screen*. Lanham, MD: The Scarecrow Press, 1997.

———, ed. *The Stars Appear*. Metuchen, NJ: The Scarecrow Press, 1992.

Madsen, Axel. *Gloria and Joe: The Star-Crossed Love Affair of Gloria Swanson and Joe Kennedy*. New York: William Morrow, 1988.

Mandelbaum, Howard, and Eric Myers. *Screen Deco: A Celebration of High Style in Hollywood*. Santa Monica, CA: Hennessey and Ingalls, 1985.

Mann, William J. *Kate: The Woman Who Was Hepburn*. New York: Henry Holt, 2006.

————. *Wisecracker: The Life and Times of William Haines, Hollywood's First Openly Gay Star.* New York: Viking, 1998.

Marion, Frances. *Off With Their Heads! A Serio-Comic Tale of Hollywood.* New York: Macmillan, 1972.

Marsh, Mae. *Screen Acting.* Los Angeles: Photo-Star Publishing, 1921.

Marx, Samuel. *Mayer and Thalberg: The Make-Believe Saints.* New York: Random House, 1975.

Maturi, Richard J., and Mary Buckingham Maturi. *Beverly Bayne, Queen of the Movies.* Jefferson, NC: McFarland, 2001.

McCandless, Barbara, Bonnie Yochelson, and Richard Koszarski. *New York to Hollywood: The Photography of Karl Struss.* Fort Worth, TX: Amon Carter Museum, 1995.

McGilligan, Patrick. *Backstory: Interviews with Screenwriters of Hollywood's Golden Age.* Berkeley: University of California Press, 1986.

————. *Film Crazy: Interviews with Hollywood Legends.* New York: St. Martin's, 2000.

McLean, Adrienne L., and David Cook, eds. *Headline Hollywood: A Century of Film Scandal.* New Brunswick, NJ: Rutgers University Press, 2001.

Melnick, Ross. *American Showman: Samuel "Roxy" Rothafel and the Birth of the Entertainment Industry, 1908–1915.* New York: Columbia University Press, 2012.

Menjou, Adolphe, and M. M. Musselman. *It Took Nine Tailors.* New York: McGraw-Hill, 1948.

Milton, Joyce. *Tramp: The Life of Charlie Chaplin.* New York: HarperCollins, 1996.

Mitchell, Jack. *Icons and Idols.* New York: Amphoto Art, 1998.

Moore, Colleen. *Silent Star.* New York: Doubleday, 1968.

Moore, Grace. *You're Only Human Once.* Garden City, NY: Doubleday, 1944.

Mordden, Ethan. *Movie Star: A Look at the Women Who Made Hollywood.* New York: St. Martin's, 1983.

Morley, Sheridan. *Tales from the Hollywood Raj: The British, the Movies, and Tinseltown.* New York: The Viking Press, 1983.

Nasaw, David. *The Chief: The Life of William Randolph Hearst.* New York: Houghton Mifflin, 2000.

Negri, Pola. *Memoirs of a Star.* Garden City, NY: Doubleday, 1970.

Nichols, Beverley. *The Sweet and Twenties.* New York: British Book Centre, 1958.

Niven, David. *The Moon's a Balloon.* London: Hamish Hamilton, 1971.

Noble, Peter. *Hollywood Scapegoat: The Biography of Erich von Stroheim.* New York: Arno Press and The New York Times, 1972.

Olivier, Laurence. *Confessions of an Actor.* New York: Simon and Schuster, 1982.

Paris, Barry. *Garbo.* New York: Alfred A. Knopf, 1995.

————. *Louise Brooks.* New York: Alfred A. Knopf, 1989.

Pickford, Mary. *Sunshine and Shadow.* Garden City, NY: Doubleday, 1955.

Pizzitola, Louis. *Hearst Over Hollywood: Power, Passion, and Propaganda in the Movies.* New York: Columbia University Press, 2002.

Quirk, Lawrence J. *The Films of Gloria Swanson.* Secaucus, NJ: The Citadel Press, 1984.

————. *The Kennedys in Hollywood.* New York: Cooper Square Press, 2004.

Ramsaye, Terry. *A Million and One Nights: A History of the Motion Picture Through 1925.* New York: Simon and Schuster, 1926.

Robinson, David. *Chaplin: His Life and Art.* New York: McGraw-Hill, 1985.

Rosenberg, Bernard, and Harry Silverstein. *The Real Tinsel*. New York: Macmillan, 1970.

Sardou, Victorien. *Madame Sans-Gêne*. Paris: Albin Michel, 1912.

Schatz, Thomas. *The Genius of the System: Hollywood Filmmaking in the Studio Era*. New York: Pantheon Books, 1988.

Schulberg, Budd. *Moving Pictures: Memories of a Hollywood Prince*. New York: Stein and Day, 1981.

Scott, Evelyn. *Hollywood When Silents Were Golden*. New York: McGraw-Hill, 1972.

Seabury, William Marston. *The Public and the Motion Picture Industry*. New York: Macmillan, 1926.

Selznick, Irene Mayer. *A Private View*. New York: Alfred A. Knopf, 1983.

Sennett, Mack, with Cameron Shipp. *King of Comedy*. Garden City, NY: Doubleday, 1954.

Sikov, Ed. *On Sunset Boulevard: The Life and Times of Billy Wilder*. New York: Hyperion, 1998.

Slide, Anthony. *Silent Players*. Lexington, KY: University Press of Kentucky, 2002.

———, ed. *They Also Wrote for the Fan Magazines*. Jefferson, NC: McFarland, 1992.

Smith, Amanda, ed. *Hostage to Fortune: The Letters of Joseph P. Kennedy*. New York: Viking, 2001.

Sragow, Michael. *Victor Fleming: An American Movie Master*. New York: Pantheon, 2008.

Staggs, Sam. *Close-Up on Sunset Boulevard: Billy Wilder, Norma Desmond, and the Dark Hollywood Dream*. New York: St. Martin's Press, 2003.

Steen, Mike. *Hollywood Speaks! An Oral History*. New York: G. P. Putnam's Sons, 1974.

Steichen, Edward. *A Life in Photography*. Garden City, NY: Doubleday and Company, 1963.

Stevens, Ashton. *Actorviews: Intimate Portraits*. Chicago: Covici-McGee, 1923.

Stevens Jr., George, ed. *Conversations with the Great Moviemakers of Hollywood's Golden Age*. New York: Alfred A. Knopf, 2006.

Stringer, Arthur, and Russell Holman. *Manhandled*. New York: Grosset and Dunlap, 1924.

Swanson, Gloria. *Swanson on Swanson*. New York: Random House, 1980.

Thomas, Bob. *Golden Boy: The Untold Story of William Holden*. New York: St. Martin's Press, 1983.

———. *Thalberg: Life and Legend*. Garden City, NY: Doubleday, 1969.

Ulbeck, Sylvia. *Hollywood Undressed: Observations of Sylvia as Noted by Her Secretary*. New York: Brentano's, 1931.

Ulman, S. George. *Valentino as I Knew Him*. New York: Macy-Masius, 1926.

Vance, Jeffrey. *Douglas Fairbanks*. Berkeley: University of California Press, 2008.

Vasey, Ruth E. *The World According to Hollywood, 1918–1939*. Madison: University of Wisconsin Press, 1997.

Vazzana, Eugene Michael. *Silent Film Necrology*. 2nd ed. Jefferson, NC: McFarland, 2001.

Vieira, Mark A. *Irving Thalberg: Boy Wonder to Producer Prince*. Berkeley: University of California Press, 2010.

———. *Sin in Soft Focus: Pre-Code Hollywood*. New York: Harry N. Abrams, 1999.

Villecco, Tony. *Silent Stars Speak: Interviews with Twelve Cinema Pioneers*. Jefferson, NC: McFarland, 2001.

Wagenknecht, Edward. *Stars of the Silents*. Metuchen, NJ: The Scarecrow Press, 1987.

Wagner, Walter. *You Must Remember This*. New York: G. P. Putnam's Sons, 1975.

Waldman, Harry. *Paramount in Paris*. Lanham, MD: The Scarecrow Press, 1998.

Walker, Alexander. *The Shattered Silents: How the Talkies Came to Stay*. New York: William Morrow, 1979.

Walker, Brent E. *Mack Sennett's Fun Factory.* Jefferson, NC: McFarland, 2010.

Walsh, Raoul. *Each Man in His Time: The Life Story of a Director.* New York: Farrar, Straus and Giroux, 1974.

Wanamaker, Marc. *Early Beverly Hills.* Charleston, SC: Arcadia Publishing, 2005.

———, and Robert L. Nudelman. *Early Hollywood.* Charleston, SC: Arcadia Publishing, 2007.

Watson, Coy. *Keystone Kid: Tales of Early Hollywood.* Santa Monica, CA: Santa Monica Press, 2001.

Whalen, Richard J. *The Founding Father.* New York: New American Library, 1964.

Whitfield, Eileen. *Pickford: The Woman Who Made Hollywood.* Lexington, KY: University Press of Kentucky, 1997.

Windeler, Robert. *Sweetheart: The Story of Mary Pickford.* New York: Praeger, 1973.

Wood, Bret. *Queen Kelly: The Complete Screenplay by Erich von Stroheim.* Lanham, MD: The Scarecrow Press, 2002.

Zolotow, Maurice. *Billy Wilder in Hollywood.* New York: Putnam, 1977.

Zukor, Adolph, and Dale Kramer. *The Public Is Never Wrong.* New York: G. P. Putnam's Sons, 1953.

PHOTOGRAPH CREDITS

Ingénue. Author's collection.

Swanson at eight. Courtesy of Gloria Swanson Inc./Harry Ransom Center, The University of Texas at Austin.

Bathing Beauty. Courtesy of Gloria Swanson Inc./Harry Ransom Center, The University of Texas at Austin.

The Sultan's Wife. Author's collection.

Teddy at the Throttle. Courtesy of Gloria Swanson Inc./Harry Ransom Center, The University of Texas at Austin.

With Wallace Beery. Courtesy of Gloria Swanson Inc./Harry Ransom Center, The University of Texas at Austin.

Beery as "Sweedie." Courtesy George Eastman House Motion Picture Department Collection.

As a Christian slave in *Male and Female*. Karl Struss (1886–1981). Courtesy Amon Carter Museum of American Art, Fort Worth, Texas.

Gloria Swanson in the Lion's Den-Fantasy Sequence from *Male and Female*. Karl Struss (1886–1981). Gelatin silver print, 1919. © Amon Carter Museum of American Art, Fort Worth, Texas, P1983.23.171.

With Thomas Meighan in *Male and Female*. Courtesy of Gloria Swanson Inc./Harry Ransom Center, The University of Texas at Austin.

Captain Joseph Swanson. Courtesy of Gloria Swanson Inc./Harry Ransom Center, The University of Texas at Austin.

Don't Change Your Husband. Author's collection.

Undraped by Alfred Cheney Johnston. Author's collection.

Herbert Somborn. Courtesy of Gloria Swanson Inc./Harry Ransom Center, The University of Texas at Austin.

Baby Gloria. Courtesy of Gloria Swanson Inc./Harry Ransom Center, The University of Texas at Austin.

Mickey Neilan. Author's collection.

Under the Lash. Author's collection.

Vamping. Photograph by Nickolas Muray, © Nickolas Muray Photo Archives. Courtesy George Eastman House Motion Picture Department Collection.

On the set of *Beyond the Rocks.* Courtesy of Gloria Swanson Inc./Harry Ransom Center, The University of Texas at Austin.

Kissing the open palm. Courtesy of Gloria Swanson Inc./Harry Ransom Center, The University of Texas at Austin.

The Humming Bird. Courtesy of Gloria Swanson Inc./Harry Ransom Center, The University of Texas at Austin.

Zaza. Courtesy of Gloria Swanson Inc./Harry Ransom Center, The University of Texas at Austin.

Seen by Edward Steichen. Courtesy of Steichen/*Vanity Fair;* © Condé Nast.

Caricatured by Miguel Covarrubias. Courtesy of Covarrubias/*Vanity Fair;* © Condé Nast.

Manhandled. Courtesy of Gloria Swanson Inc./Harry Ransom Center, The University of Texas at Austin.

As Peter Pan. Courtesy of Gloria Swanson Inc./Harry Ransom Center, The University of Texas at Austin.

With Henri de la Falaise on the set. Courtesy of Gloria Swanson Inc./Harry Ransom Center, The University of Texas at Austin.

With Gloria and Brother. Courtesy of Gloria Swanson Inc./Harry Ransom Center, The University of Texas at Austin.

As a laundress in *Madame Sans-Gêne.* Author's collection.

As a duchess in *Madame Sans-Gêne.* Courtesy of Gloria Swanson Inc./Harry Ransom Center, The University of Texas at Austin.

Returning to America as the Marquise. Author's collection.

Incognito in *The Coast of Folly.* Author's collection.

As the daughter in *The Coast of Folly*. Courtesy of Gloria Swanson Inc./Harry Ransom Center, The University of Texas at Austin.

As the waitress in *Stage Struck*. Author's collection.

As Salome in *Stage Struck*. Courtesy of Gloria Swanson Inc./Harry Ransom Center, The University of Texas at Austin.

With Raoul Walsh. Courtesy of Gloria Swanson Inc./Harry Ransom Center, The University of Texas at Austin.

The Love of Sunya. Courtesy of Gloria Swanson Inc./Harry Ransom Center, The University of Texas at Austin.

Sadie Thompson. Author's collection.

With Lionel Barrymore. Author's collection.

At home in Beverly Hills. Courtesy of Gloria Swanson Inc./Harry Ransom Center, The University of Texas at Austin.

At the microphone. Author's collection.

Joseph P. Kennedy and Henri de la Falaise. Courtesy of Gloria Swanson Inc./Harry Ransom Center, The University of Texas at Austin.

With Seena Owen in *Queen Kelly*. Author's collection.

With Erich von Stroheim. Courtesy of Gloria Swanson Inc./Harry Ransom Center, The University of Texas at Austin.

Contemplating her rosy future. Photo by Ernest Bachrach. Courtesy of Gloria Swanson Inc./Harry Ransom Center, The University of Texas at Austin.

With Eddie Goulding, Noel Coward, and Laura Hope Crews. Courtesy of Gloria Swanson Inc./Harry Ransom Center, The University of Texas at Austin.

Streamlined in *The Trespasser*. Photo by Ernest Bachrach. Author's collection.

With Melvyn Douglas in *Tonight or Never*. Author's collection.

With Michael Farmer. Author's collection.

With Laurence Olivier in *Perfect Understanding*. Author's collection.

On a tiger skin for *Three Weeks*. Author's collection.

With Herbert Marshall. Courtesy of Gloria Swanson Inc./Harry Ransom Center, The University of Texas at Austin.

Family portrait by Clarence Sinclair Bull. Courtesy of Gloria Swanson Inc./Harry Ransom Center, The University of Texas at Austin.

With Adolph Menjou in *Father Takes a Wife*. Courtesy of Gloria Swanson Inc./Harry Ransom Center, The University of Texas at Austin.

With Billy Wilder. Author's collection.

With William Davey. Courtesy of Gloria Swanson Inc./Harry Ransom Center, The University of Texas at Austin.

On the set of *Sunset Boulevard*. Author's collection.

As Norma Desmond in *Sunset Boulevard*. Courtesy of Gloria Swanson Inc./Harry Ransom Center, The University of Texas at Austin.

On tour for *Sunset Boulevard*. Courtesy of Gloria Swanson Inc./Harry Ransom Center, The University of Texas at Austin.

In London for the Command Performance. Courtesy of Gloria Swanson Inc./Harry Ransom Center, The University of Texas at Austin.

With Michelle. Courtesy of Gloria Swanson Inc./Harry Ransom Center, The University of Texas at Austin.

Oscar night, 1951. Author's collection.

With David Niven. Author's collection.

With her mother. Courtesy of Gloria Swanson Inc./Harry Ransom Center, The University of Texas at Austin.

In the ruins of the Roxy Theatre. Photo by Eliot Elisofon/Time Life Pictures/Getty Images.

As Charlie Chaplin with Carol Burnett. Courtesy of Gloria Swanson Inc./Harry Ransom Center, The University of Texas at Austin.

Killer Bees. Author's collection.

Her sculpted self-portrait. Courtesy of Gloria Swanson Inc./Harry Ransom Center, The University of Texas at Austin.

With William Dufty. © Ellen Graham. Courtesy of Gloria Swanson Inc./Harry Ransom Center, The University of Texas at Austin.

Blackglama fur ad. Courtesy of Gloria Swanson Inc./Harry Ransom Center, The University of Texas at Austin.

Gloria Swanson, New York, September 4, 1980. Photograph by Richard Avedon.

Cover photo by Ernest Bachrach from *The Trespasser*. Courtesy of Gloria Swanson Inc./ Harry Ransom Center, The University of Texas at Austin.

Inside cover image from *Don't Change Your Husband*. Author's collection.

INDEX